BOTTOM LINE YEAR BOOK

1996

BY THE EDITORS OF

Bottom Line

PERSONAL

Copyright © 1995 by Boardroom®, Inc.

10   9   8   7   6   5   4   3   2   1

Boardroom® Classics publishes the advice of expert authorities in
many fields. The use of a book is not a substitute for legal,
accounting or other professional services. Consult a competent
professional for answers to your specific questions.

Library of Congress Cataloging in Publication Data
Main entry under title:

Bottom Line Yearbook 1996.

   1. Life skills—United States.   I. Bottom line personal.
ISBN 0-88723-111-X

Boardroom® Classics is a registered trademark of
Boardroom®, Inc.
55 Railroad Avenue, Greenwich, CT 06830

Printed in the United States of America

Contents

4 • THE SKILLED TRAVELER

5 • SHREWD MONEY MANAGEMENT

6 • INVESTING TO WIN

7 • EFFECTIVE MANAGEMENT TECHNIQUES IN THE OFFICE

8 • FINANCIAL ANALYSIS AND CONTROL IN THE OFFICE

9 • WHAT ALL BUSINESSPEOPLE NEED TO KNOW

1

A Healthier You

What Deepak Chopra, MD, Does to Live Much Longer... And Much, Much Better

Having watched many friends and loved ones grow old, fall ill and die, most of us operate under the assumption that the same lies in store for us.

In fact, while there's no way to stop the aging process, we can dramatically reduce the toll the years take on us. We can lead active, vital lives well into our 80s, 90s—and beyond.

Believe it or not, all it takes is a change in the way we see ourselves and the world.

If that claim sounds too strong to you, consider this dramatic but little-known study, conducted by Harvard researchers in 1979...

Two groups of healthy men age 75 and older spent a week at a country resort. Members of the first group were simply told to enjoy themselves.

The second group was told to "make believe" they were living in 1959. For this group, all ref-

erences to the modern world were eliminated. On the reading table were issues of *Life* and *The Saturday Evening Post* from 1959. The only music played was at least 20 years old. And all talk had to refer to events and people of 1959.

The results of this play-acting were remarkable. Compared with the first group, the make-believe group showed significant improvements in memory and manual dexterity.

They became more active and self-sufficient. Stiff joints became flexible, and muscle strength, hearing and vision improved. Their faces even looked younger.

What did this study demonstrate? That through psychological intervention, virtually all the so-called "irreversible" signs of aging can be reversed.

That study and several others conducted since then have convinced me that each of us has the power to influence—to a remarkable degree—how quickly we age. I've decided to make the most of this awareness by eating lots of fresh fruits and vegetables, by performing yoga and running for an hour a day, by taking

1

vitamin supplements—and by following several anti-aging strategies…

•*I try to be flexible.* Psychological studies on people who have made it to 100 suggest that one reason for their extreme longevity is that they are extremely adaptable in the face of stress. They respond creatively to change, are largely free of anxiety and have a capacity to integrate new things into their lives. To ensure that you'll be adaptable in old age, you must work on being that way well before you get there. That's why I'm always on the lookout for ways to reduce conflict, anxiety and worry in my life.

I also try not to have impossibly high expectations. I'm convinced that by making my life easier, I'm making myself less vulnerable to disease and the other common aspects of aging.

•*I try to be aware of my body.* To gain some control of the aging process, we must first have some awareness of it. Sadly, most of us are blind and deaf to the subtle cues our bodies keep giving us.

No matter what I'm doing, I try to be aware of what's going on with my body. Each time I experience a minor ache or pain or even a feeling that something's not right, I take a few moments to focus my attention on the painful part of my body. Doing this helps initiate the healing process.

Here's an awareness-promoting technique I've found useful…

Sit quietly and relax your body. Envision a goal that's very important to you—greater energy and alertness or more youthful enthusiasm, for example. Expect and believe that you will achieve that goal. Try not to give in to doubt or worry—they only interfere with success. Just know that the message was delivered and that your result is on its way.

•*I acknowledge psychological pain.* Too many of us are victims of our own emotions. We fail to confront and "work through" the inevitable hurts we all suffer…and the pain gets locked up inside.

I used to be like that. Not any more. *What I do now:*

•*I pay attention to my pain—and the sensations it causes in my body.*

•*I keep a diary.* Each day, I record arguments, disappointments, failures and other causes of emotional pain—as well as my responses to these painful stimuli.

I might write down something like, "I felt angry or irritated because of X." Then I consider whether anger or irritation really was an appropriate response.

•*I release my pain through ritual.* I might go so far as to jot down the source of my pain on a piece of paper—and then bury the paper or flush it down a toilet. Or I might simply go for a long run.

•*I share my painful experiences with a loved one.* I try not to blame anyone. I just let my loved one know how I feel. The simple act of describing my emotions to someone else helps me get rid of the bad feelings…and it trains me to choose my emotions, rather than simply let them happen to me.

•*I live a balanced life.* Living in harmony with the body's rhythms means not going to extremes. If we push the cycle of rest and activity in the wrong direction, we hasten the aging process.

The most striking example of how our bodies reflect an unbalanced lifestyle is heart disease. It's a major affliction of the elderly. And it's the cause of more deaths than all other diseases combined. As we all know by now, heart problems usually stem from too much fatty food and too little exercise.

I believe that to be truly balanced, a life must be split into thirds…

•One third should be spent sleeping.

•One third should be spent working. I believe our life's work should not only be pleasurable, but also should give us some spiritual fulfillment and serve humanity in some way.

•One third should be spent in recreation—reading, seeing a movie, making love, going swimming, watching a sunset, etc.

This morning, I got up at 4:30, meditated until 5:30 and wrote until 6:30. Between 6:30 and 8:00, I went running. Right now it's only 8:30 AM, and already I've had a lot of fun. In a few minutes I have a meeting, and then I'll go see a few patients in the afternoon. This evening, I'll meditate again and then have a nice dinner. By 10:00 PM I'll be in bed.

•*I try not to overreact to problems or annoyances.* If I miss a plane, I say to myself, "This moment is as it should be." I accept things as they are. You may not be able to change this moment and you certainly can't change the past, but you can influence the future. The best way to do that is to live totally in the present. After all, certainty would be so boring.

•*I don't take myself too seriously.* Seriousness arises from fear, or from an impulse to impress or manipulate people. I prefer to be carefree and lighthearted.

That doesn't mean that I am irresponsible. "Responsibility" means having the ability to respond. The measure of our responsibility is how creatively we respond to the challenges we're given. You don't have to be serious to do that.

•*I meditate.* Each day, I spend two hours meditating. I'm convinced that this is the real key to slowing down the aging process. Not everyone needs to meditate as long as I do—15 to 20 minutes is probably enough.

The connection between aging and the body's release of stress hormones such as cortisol and adrenaline has been strongly demonstrated. Daily meditation is perhaps the best way to reduce the levels of stress hormones.

Recent studies have shown that people who've been meditating for several years have remarkably low levels of cortisol and adrenaline in their bloodstream...and their abilities to cope with difficult situations are very strong.

There is simply no substitute for the creative inspiration, knowledge and stability that come from knowing how to contact your core of inner silence.

Source: Deepak Chopra, MD, director of the Institute for Mind/Body Medicine and Human Potential at Sharp Health Care in San Diego. Dr. Chopra is former chief of staff at New England Memorial Hospital in Boston. He is the author of several books, including *Ageless Body, Timeless Mind*, Random House, New York.

Seven Quick Stress Busters

1. Stick colored dots on all your clocks. Whenever you check the time, use them as a reminder to take a deep, relaxing breath.

2. Instead of hitting the shower the moment your alarm goes off, lie quietly in bed for a few minutes, listening to sounds from inside the house or outdoors.

3. Let the phone ring two or three times before answering. Use the time to pause and become aware of your breathing.

4. Try driving with your radio turned off. Concentrate on the act of driving—the feel of your hands on the wheel, the sound of the road, the images in your visual field.

5. At least once or twice a week, eat lunch by yourself, in quiet contemplation.

6. Pay attention to the walk to your car after work.

7. To ease the transition from office to home, change clothes when you get home.

Source: Saki F. Santorelli, EdD, associate director, Stress Reduction Clinic, University of Massachusetts Medical Center, Worcester.

Inside Psychotherapy

Psychotherapy is the general name for a variety of psychological approaches to help people resolve emotional, behavioral or interpersonal problems. The goal isn't to advise, direct or tell people what to do but to assist them in taking more active and effective charge of their lives.

There are three broad areas of living where therapy can help:

•*Personal growth.* You needn't be in the throes of great distress to consider therapy. You may have reached a point at which you're dissatisfied and want more out of life. Or you may simply wish to fulfill your potential—to grow through self-exploration.

•*Problems of everyday living.* You may be experiencing distress over something specific—relationship trouble, parent-child conflict, serious illness or a major life transition such as having a baby, changing jobs, entering middle age or losing a parent.

•*Emotional and behavioral disorders.* More severe mental or behavioral disturbances can produce symptoms of a psychiatric disorder.

Examples: Symptoms of depression like feeling so hopeless that you can't get out of bed …being unable to stop after you've had your first drink…inexplicable panic attacks…or repetitive nightmares and flashbacks reliving a traumatic event.

For what kinds of problems is psychotherapy most helpful? In deciding whether you might benefit from psychotherapy, ask yourself…

• Am I distressed enough that I want to do something about it?

• Am I able to handle my problems on my own or do I need more support?

• How much is my distress affecting my personal and business lives?

• Are my problems getting in the way of my daily functioning?

Which therapy approach is best for my problem? There are five basic categories of psychotherapy.

The *psychodynamic* approach focuses on the psychological issues and conflicts that underlie emotional problems. This type of therapy requires an ability to put your thoughts and feelings into words, a genuine interest in understanding yourself better and a desire to use your relationship with your therapist as a vehicle for understanding and working through your problems. It's best suited for issues arising from long-standing internal or interpersonal conflicts.

The *behavioral* approach involves modifying specific behaviors and self-defeating habits. *Underlying assumption:* Emotional problems are learned responses to the environment that can be modified or unlearned. You must be willing to carry out "homework" between sessions and to accept focused and limited goals. The behavioral approach is best for treating phobias, obsessions, shyness, faulty social skills, hostility, anxiety or loneliness and other problems with clear, definable symptoms.

The *cognitive* approach focuses on self-defeating or negative thoughts. If you're comfortable thinking things through rationally and reflectively, cognitive therapy may be appropriate for you. It's particularly helpful with panic attacks and agoraphobia. It's also effective for depression, anxiety, obsessive-compulsive disorder, psychosomatic illness, paranoia, eating disorders and chronic pain problems.

The *family systems* approach focuses on the couple or family rather than the individual. *Aim:* To change dysfunctional patterns of communication and interaction within the couple or family. It's the right approach whenever a couple or family agrees it has mutual problems.

The *supportive* approach aims to provide support rather than facilitate change. It's designed to help individuals through acute turmoil that undermines their ability to function —the loss of a job, death of a loved one, a divorce or a serious illness or disability.

How do I find the right therapist? Follow these six steps:

1. Acknowledge your need for help.

2. Have a working idea of what you want help with.

3. Know what to look for. Although no license is required to practice psychotherapy, it's best to find someone who is a licensed professional—a licensed psychologist, psychiatrist, social worker, psychiatric nurse or marriage and family therapist, etc. Such a practitioner is held accountable to a state regulatory agency as well as professional and ethical standards of conduct.

Get the names of potential therapists from other therapists or mental health professionals, community mental-health centers or local professional associations for psychiatry, psychology, social work and nursing.

Caution: Be wary of recommendations from current or former clients. They're often too close to their therapists to have an objective view.

4. Check the therapist's credentials. Call your state licensing board or professional associations. Phone the therapist and say you'd like to ask some questions about his/her areas of specialization and professional qualifications before making an appointment.

Psychiatrists should have completed a residency in psychiatry, including training in psychotherapy…be board-certified…have full membership in the American Psychiatric Association…and have graduated from a psychotherapy institute.

Psychologists should have a doctorate in psychology or a related field…be licensed or certified in your state…have full membership in the American Psychological Association… and be registered in the National Register of Health Service Providers.

Social workers should have a master's in social work with a clinical concentration…be licensed or certified in your state…have full membership in the National Association of Social Workers.

5. Make an appointment for a consultation. Make it clear that you're not starting therapy but discussing starting therapy. If a therapist resists the idea of an initial consultation, thank him/her, then say good-bye.

A consultation is a mutual interview. The therapist wants to know about you and what you're looking for. You want to know how the therapist works, what kind of therapy he/she will recommend—and why. Expect to pay for this consultation.

6. Assess the consultation. Was it favorable, questionable—or unacceptable? Your impressions of the therapist and how he interacted with you are just as important as his credentials and what kind of therapy he does. Whatever your initial impression of the therapist, defer any final decision until after the consultation. Don't let the therapist pressure you into making an on-the-spot decision.

What questions should I ask during the first meeting? While a good match is critical, therapy is also a professional relationship. Since you're contracting for a service, it's important to work out an explicit set of agreements.

Agree on…

• The goals that you want to work toward.

• The format (individual, group, couple or family therapy).

• The therapeutic approach.

• The setting (usually the therapist's office).

• How frequently you'll meet.

• Session length. The standard is 50 minutes for individual and couples therapy, 75 to 90 minutes for group and family therapy.

• Roughly how long it should take you to reach the goals you've set.

• The therapist's stance on medication to help you psychologically.

How can I afford therapy? The standard fee is based upon an hourly rate, but many thera-pists use sliding-fee scales or reduced fees for clients who can't afford their regular fee.

If you like the therapist and feel the fee is more than you can afford, don't be afraid to ask if you can be seen for less.

Major health insurers, including health-maintenance organizations and managed-care programs, generally include both inpatient and outpatient mental-health benefits. Most policies that allow you to choose your own therapist offer a certain dollar amount of coverage per year, irrespective of the therapist's fee. Other policies pay a portion of the fee per session, generally from 50% to 80%. There is often an annual deductible.

• *How can I tell if therapy is really working?*

Periodically evaluate—with your therapist—how your therapy is going. Review your focus and goals, your progress and your working relationship with your therapist.

Ask yourself how safe the therapeutic relationship feels, whether your therapist has your best interests at heart, whether you feel appreciated and believed in and whether you have a sense of increased competence and self-mastery.

If you're in doubt about how therapy is going or if you and your therapist disagree after talking it over, ask for a second opinion from another therapist. If your therapist tries to dissuade you, that should raise serious ethical questions about your therapist's relationship with you.

Important: Bear in mind that as you work on your problems, you may have to feel a little worse before you can feel better.

How will I know when to end treatment? Ending therapy is often the most important phase of treatment. That's when the work you've done either comes together—or doesn't.

You'll know it's time to end therapy when you feel you've developed the ability to manage on your own and you're confident that you can tackle this next period of your life with your own resources.

Talking about ending therapy can be uncomfortable for you and your therapist. But if you put off this discussion until you're 100% certain that you're ready to leave, there will never be a right moment.

Instead, discuss the issue over time. Set a date so that your remaining work can be done with a definite end in sight.

Review your therapy. Acknowledge what you accomplished and what you didn't, and allow yourself to mourn.

Important: Recognize the anxiety caused by ending therapy for what it is. You always have the option of going back to therapy if you find you can't make it on your own.

Source: Jack Engler, PhD, an instructor in psychology at Harvard Medical School, Boston. He is co-author, with Daniel Goleman, PhD, of *The Consumer's Guide to Psychotherapy*, Simon & Schuster, 1230 Avenue of the Americas, New York 10020.

Mind/Body Connection

People who keep secrets about painful or embarrassing experiences have more aches, pains, colds, fatigue, depression and anxiety than those who express their feelings openly. In one study, 90% of approximately 300 people surveyed who expressed their deepest, darkest secrets said they were glad they did.

Source: Dale Larson, PhD, associate professor, counseling psychology, Santa Clara University, California.

How to Decode Your Body's Secret Language

When a person experiences pain…or has an itch…or develops an annoying "tickle" in the throat…or even gets very sick, it's usually because that person's body is trying to tell him/her something.

That notion may sound farfetched, given modern medicine's penchant for blaming ailments on germs or other physical causes. Yet after seeing patients for more than 30 years—first as a family doctor and now as a psychiatrist—I've found it to be true in a surprisingly large number of cases.

By "acting up" in some way, the body is signaling the presence of repressed emotions—

typically anger, sadness, jealousy or fear. Unless immediate steps are taken to express these emotions in an honest, straightforward way, they continue to plague our minds and our bodies.

Are emotions themselves to blame? Not at all. Simply experiencing powerful emotions—positive or negative—poses no threat to health.

It's when you try to stifle these emotions, or fail to express them—verbally—that your body rebels. Refusing to acknowledge negative emotions is like having a toxic waste dump in your house. Sooner or later, there's sure to be a leak.

Misconception: Holding in your emotions will reduce their intensity. In fact, holding emotions in doesn't stifle their physical effects—it intensifies them.

Emotional origins of common ailments:

• *Common cold.* Colds are caused by viruses, but viruses rarely establish a foothold in your body unless you're experiencing fatigue or psychological stress.

Typical scenario: Stress resulting from a disappointment, rejection or another unhappy event or situation lowers the immunity…a virus invades the nose and throat…and a cold develops. I've seen that pattern countless times in my medical practice.

• *Cough.* Coughing often goes hand-in-hand with a cold. But sometimes you cough when you'd like to express a strong emotion or opinion…but feel uncomfortable doing so. When you open your mouth to speak, anxiety forces your epiglottis shut, triggering a cough as you "swallow" your words.

• *Headache.* Bottling up intense emotions changes patterns of blood flow in the brain, causing dilation of blood vessels. This, coupled with muscular tension, can cause a severe headache.

One patient of mine had terrible migraines. She also had a husband who loved to fill the house with friends and family. Having company over made her nervous, but she kept this "character flaw" to herself. I urged her to let her husband know her feelings. When she did, her headaches stopped.

• *Lower back pain.* That part of the back between the upper and lower body (the lumbosacral joint) must bear considerable weight. If strenuous exertion forces it to carry too much, supporting muscles tighten up and go into spasm. The pain can be intense, even disabling.

The "burden" that sends the lumbosacral joint into spasm can be emotional as well as physical. If you're carrying more responsibility, stress or guilt than you can bear, your back muscles tighten up just as if you were saddled with a literal load. Unless you share the burden with others and ask for needed help, the relentless strain on your back will eventually force you to lay the burden down.

• *Nausea and vomiting.* The human digestive system has evolved to vomit back up overly rich foods. In a similar way, our minds become familiar with a certain lifestyle—and a certain level of success. Too much success is like a too-rich dessert. Both can cause us to throw up.

Example: A patient of mine called up one night, vomiting uncontrollably. When I asked what might have triggered the problem, she said she had just gotten a long-awaited promotion. The new job meant added privileges and status—wonderful, but also terrifying. Her body was telling her, "Maybe it's all too much."

• *Skin disorders.* Amply supplied with nerves, the skin is exquisitely sensitive to emotions. Blood vessels lying just under the surface open or close, making you blush when you're embarrassed…or blanch when you're frightened.

Problem: Strong emotions that persist for a long period of time can cause eczema or other skin disorders.

Think of your skin as a silent organ of communication. A sudden itch may be your skin's way of saying, "I want you to like me, I want to be touched." The message of adolescent acne is often, "I'm in conflict, I'm afraid."

Listening to your body:

To avoid psychologically based ailments, it's essential to stay in touch with your feelings.

Problem: Negative feelings are often so well hidden that it's impossible to know what's wrong until your body starts telling you. Or we try to squelch negative feelings altogether. With a little practice, however, you should have no trouble picking out the source of trouble—and

taking steps to remedy the problem before it gets out of hand.

• *Review recent aggravations.* Did the IRS notify you of an impending audit? Are your in-laws coming for a visit? Did your spouse criticize you in front of friends?

Ask yourself: Did something happen to cause my symptoms—something that I didn't notice? It's like replaying a videotape to catch something you didn't understand the first time around—whether that was 30 minutes ago, yesterday or last week.

• *Share your feelings with others.* As long as you can communicate what you feel, emotions are unlikely to build up and cause you bodily harm.

If you discover you're about to be audited, for example, tell a coworker, taxi driver, waiter, etc. Voice your worst fears. The more people you share your emotional burden with, the less it will weigh upon you.

Example: Once I was sued for negligence after an accident occurred on my property. Just before the trial started, I attended a professional conference. When a colleague I saw there asked how things were going, I told him, "Things are awful." "I'm being sued." He was very sympathetic—as were several other people I told that day.

I discovered that each time I told my story, it seemed to hurt a little less. When the trial started a few days later, I felt relaxed and confident in court. I came on like a tiger…and won the case.

If you live alone or lack close friends, a therapist can provide an essential ear to unburden toxic events…and help you improve your ability to build a network of supportive people.

If you are too ashamed to talk about your problems, talk into a tape recorder…or write about them in a journal.

If you're religious, share what's troubling you with your clergyman…or directly in prayer.

Source: Martin Rush, MD, a psychiatrist in private practice in Middletown, Ohio. He is the author of *Decoding the Secret Language of Your Body: The Many Ways Our Bodies Send Us Messages,* Simon & Schuster, 1230 Avenue of the Americas, New York 10020.

What is a Physiatrist? Who Needs One? When?

If you have no idea what a physiatrist is, you're not alone. In a recent survey, only about 10% of people did.

But if you're experiencing chronic pain or a disability from multiple sclerosis, arthritis, a neurological condition or an old sports injury, you should know that a physiatrist is an MD or DO who specializes in rehabilitation.

Typically, a physiatrist works with other doctors who treat the underlying medical problem.

Example: A rheumatologist finds it difficult to control a patient's arthritis with drugs, so a physiatrist takes over to try to find other approaches that will reduce pain and increase mobility.

The physiatrist's first goal is to pinpoint the cause of the impairment. That might involve anything from a simple physical exam to high-tech tests like magnetic resonance imaging (MRI) and electromyography, which checks nervous system function.

In some cases, the physiatrist prescribes pain-killing drugs…or, if necessary, refers the patient to a surgeon. But physiatrists rely mostly on conservative treatments, such as lifestyle changes, adaptive equipment and special exercises to strengthen muscles.

Most people see a physiatrist only after being referred by another doctor. If you're recovering from an accident or battling a chronic illness, it certainly makes sense to ask your doctor if you should see one.

You can also arrange to see a physiatrist on your own, if you feel his/her skills can help you live better.

To find a good physiatrist, ask friends and/or your family doctor for a referral. *Also:* Request a list of physiatrists in your area from the American Academy of Physical Medicine and Rehabilitation, 1 IBM Plaza, Suite 2500, Chicago 60611. 312-464-9700.

Important: Many physiatrists specialize—in musculoskeletal disorders for example, or brain injuries. Make sure the physiatrist you choose is experienced at treating your problem.

Source: Robert Biedermann, DO, resident in physical medicine and rehabilitation, University of Missouri, Columbia.

Chronobiology— How to Organize Your Day For Maximum Productivity and Health

The Biblical idea that there's "a time for every purpose under heaven" is gaining scientific support. Recent research tells us that like all living things, the human body follows an internal rhythm that mirrors the cosmic cycle, creating a day and night in every single cell.

Directed by a master clock in our brains, hundreds of bodily functions wax and wane every 24 hours, helping us live efficiently on our 24-hour planet.

There's a time when our reflexes are fastest…a time when we're most creative…a time to nap…a time to hold important meetings…a time to eat…and a time to refrain from eating.

The study of these daily rhythms* is called *chronobiology.* Here's how to put this science to work for you…

The right time:

Over the course of a day, physiological functions—alertness, physical capabilities, etc. —change in response to signals from a region of the brain called the hypothalamus.

Time of day makes an enormous difference. According to one researcher, the decline in cognitive ability that occurs from peak to trough is roughly equivalent to the effect of three or four alcoholic drinks—or the loss of a half night of sleep.

By taking these cyclical fluctuations into account, you can plan your day for peak performance…

*These rhythms are unrelated to biorhythms, a pseudoscientific system that claims to identify critical days on the basis of one's birth date.

•7 AM to 8 AM. As soon as possible after you wake up, expose yourself to bright light—preferably sunlight—even if it's overcast. That will help you become alert faster.

•9 AM to noon. During this three-hour span, we reason most clearly, concentrate best and are most creative. It is an ideal time for tackling the day's most intellectually demanding tasks.

•11 AM. Most people are sharp, attentive and cooperative at this time. Short-term memory is at its peak, fostering intelligent dialogue. It is a good time to schedule important meetings.

•Noon. Complex decision-making skills are in high gear.

•1 PM to 2 PM. People tend to be particularly cheerful at this time of day, so it's a good time for a harmonious lunch. Food eaten now is burned more efficiently than food eaten later in the day. That's why it's best for dieters to make lunch a bigger meal than dinner.

•2 PM. Daydreaming peaks. Not a good time for adding numbers, monitoring dials, performing high-vigilance tasks…but poets and novelists may find this a particularly creative hour. If you must perform high-vigilance tasks at this time, schedule frequent breaks.

•2 PM to 3 PM. Alertness ebbs during this "after-lunch" period—whether you eat lunch or not. Because drowsiness is such a problem now, it's a poor time for meetings, driving and focused thinking.

•3 PM. Early-afternoon blahs are starting to lift. This is an ideal time for sorting the mail, typing and other mundane physical tasks…and for dental appointments. *Reason:* Your sensitivity to pain is at its lowest point, and your dentist's hand steadiest.

•3 PM to 5 PM. Long-term memory is at its peak. A good time to take classes or commit things to memory.

•4 PM. Use this time to proofread letters, review contracts, check details. Your ability to detect errors peaks from now through early evening. *Also:* Plan tomorrow's schedule.

•5 PM. This is the best time of day to work out. Your coordination is peaking, as are your strength and reflexes. Workouts are more enjoyable, too.

•5 PM to 7 PM. Taste and smell are especially acute. A good time for your evening meal.

•8 PM to 10 PM. Alertness is still high enough to do bills, read, socialize.

Fortunately, the body's timetable can be overridden—at least to some extent. Being physically active, socializing with friends or simply being under psychological stress can fill you with energy during the early-afternoon slump.

A surge of nervous adrenaline can keep you on your toes while delivering a 3 PM presentation. (Just don't count on an alert, attentive audience.) Your body is most sensitive to the energizing effects of caffeine in the afternoon—when you're likely to need it most.

Sleep rhythms:

Your body clock doesn't shut down while you sleep. Every 90 minutes or so, your brain cycles between dream sleep and deeper, non-dream stages. However, the most restorative portion of your slumber takes place in the first four hours after you retire.

If for some reason it's impossible to get a full night's sleep, go to bed at your normal time and get up early.

To fall asleep fast and stay asleep through the night, it's important to keep regular hours. That means going to bed and waking up at roughly the same time—on weekends as well as on weekdays.

If you get up in the middle of the night to use the bathroom, do not turn on bright lights. *Reason:* Your body is especially sensitive to light at around 4 AM. If you turn on a bright light at this time, you're programming your body to awaken at the same time the next morning.

Better: Use a night-light to find your way around at night.

Afternoon naps are also programmed into our internal clocks. If you take a daily nap, schedule it for approximately 12 hours after the midpoint of your previous night's sleep (3 PM, if you slept from 11 PM to 7 AM). A nap taken at that time will be more restful and restorative than a nap taken at any other time of the day.

Surprisingly, sexual pleasure and fertility do not seem to be linked to time of day. However, many men find that their erections are strongest immediately after wakening.

Natural variations:

Not all adults live on exactly the same timetable. "Larks" become alert early in the morning. "Owls" don't feel fully functional until late in the day.

Understanding these natural variations can be important—especially in families with adolescent children.

From puberty through the early 20s, the body clock runs on a late schedule. A teenager who stays up until 2 AM or 3 AM and sleeps until mid-morning is only doing what comes naturally. To reflect this reality, at least one state's medical society has adopted a resolution urging a change in the high-school schedule.

Sickness and health:

Blood pressure, blood sugar, heart and respiration rate and other physiological functions vary throughout the day. Fluctuations in metabolism can render the same medication considerably more potent at 9 AM than at 9 PM (or vice versa). For this reason, timing is often crucial in the case of chemotherapy drugs and other powerful, potentially toxic medications.

Some diseases are clearly worse at certain times. Asthma attacks tend to strike in the morning, for example, and osteoarthritis is most severe in late afternoon. Your doctor should take biological rhythms into account when prescribing medication.

Few doctors have much knowledge of or interest in biological rhythms—but it may be worth trying to find one who does. Ask your doctor if biological rhythms are important in your illness. If he/she doesn't know, ask your local librarian to help you do an on-line computer search on your illness and on "biological rhythms." Then make a printout for your doctor.

Pharmaceutical manufacturers are certainly taking an interest in chronobiology. One drug company is now testing a heart drug that releases its active ingredient at different rates over the course of a day—in sync with the body's ever-changing metabolism.

What you can do now: If you're concerned about your blood pressure, have it checked at several different times of the day. An individual whose blood pressure is always normal in the morning may have high blood pressure at other times of the day.

If you have arthritis or another chronic disease, become aware of the daily cycle of your symptoms. Discuss adjusting your medication schedule with your doctor. Pay attention to your body. See if your symptoms vary during the day and if the hour you take medicine makes any difference.

Source: Lynne Lamberg, a science writer and the author of *Bodyrhythms:Biological Clocks and Peak Performance*, William Morrow, New York.

Exercise for the Elderly

Tai chi improves balance and may help reduce the risk of falls in elderly people. The ancient Chinese exercise—which involves gentle turning and pivoting—teaches participants to focus on how their weight is distributed. Older women who did tai chi three times a week for six months, along with leg presses and brisk walking, experienced a 17% improvement in their ability to balance on one leg. Those who only stretched and practiced tai chi once a week had no significant improvement.

Source: James Judge, MD, assistant professor of medicine, University of Connecticut School of Medicine, Farmington. His study of 21 women was reported in *Physical Therapy,* American Physical Therapy Association, 1111 N. Fairfax St., Alexandria, Virginia 22314.

The Aging Process

Many of our assumptions about aging and its effects on health and well-being aren't true. Muscle weakness, loss of energy, greater susceptibility to illness, difficulty in getting around—much of this decline is due not to aging itself, but to inactivity and poor nutrition.

Study after study shows that regular exercise and a healthy diet can slow—or even reverse — the deterioration in fitness, vitality and independence that we associate with aging. Even if you haven't been health-conscious in the past, you can still reap benefits by changing your lifestyle now...whether you're 50, 60—or 90. Biomarkers...

In our laboratory research, we've singled out ten biomarkers—biological signs of aging—that are highly responsive to changes in exercise and/or diet.

The first four are closely related—and they affect the remaining six.

The four key biomarkers:
- Muscle mass.
- Strength.
- Basal metabolic rate.
- Percentage of body fat.

As muscle is lost with age and inactivity, there's a corresponding loss of strength. The body's metabolic rate also decreases, so that it takes fewer calories to maintain the same weight. The likely result is an increase in body fat. These changes can, in turn, lead to problems ranging from diabetes to heart attack. All four key biomarkers can be controlled with exercise. *The other six biomarkers...*

- *Aerobic fitness.* Aerobic capacity is the ability of the heart, lungs and circulatory system to absorb and distribute oxygen. This capacity is greater among regular exercisers.

- *Blood-sugar tolerance.* Ten percent to 15% of people age 50 and older have Type II diabetes, and another 15% are considered to be at high risk for developing the disease. It has serious complications if left untreated. A low-fat diet and regular exercise can control symptoms —and even prevent the disease.

- *Cholesterol/HDL ratio.* Even more important than a low total cholesterol count (which should be under 200) is the ratio of total cholesterol to "good" cholesterol, or HDL. That ratio should be 4.5 or lower to help protect against heart disease. Diet and exercise can help keep it there.

- *Blood pressure.* If it's high, you're at greater risk of heart attack and stroke. Exercise and a low-fat diet can help to keep it under control.

- *Bone density.* A decline in bone mineral content can lead to osteoporosis—the condition in which bones become porous, brittle and vulnerable to breaking. Increasing the intake of calcium may play a role in strengthening bones. Weight-bearing exercise (running, cycling, weight training) may be even more effective.

- *Internal temperature.* As an aging body loses its ability to regulate temperature and fluids, heat stroke becomes a serious danger. Older people in good physical shape adjust better to heat. Their bodies hold more water, and they sweat more—the body's natural cooling mechanism.

Because the sense of thirst decreases with age, older people need to make a point of drinking plenty of fluids in order to prevent dehydration.

Exercise and aging...

Our thinking about exercise has changed in the years since the fitness boom began. We now know that significant benefits can be gained from even small amounts of exercise, if done regularly and consistently.

Of course, it's even better if you have the motivation and commitment to work out vigorously at least four times a week. But anything you do to move your body is better than no exercise at all. The key is to keep it up—or you'll lose the gains you've made. For many people, the simplest way to work more activity into the day is by walking.

Examples: Parking at the far end of the grocery-store parking lot instead of hunting for a parking space near the entrance...walking around the golf course instead of riding in the cart...walking up one or two flights of stairs instead of using the elevator...going for at least a five-minute walk around the block every morning and evening.

Once mild exercise has become a habit, you may be inspired to begin a more formal fitness program. Of course, you should check with your doctor first. *The ideal exercise program will include:*

- *Strength training*—to build muscle mass and increase your metabolic rate. This will make aerobic exercise easier.

Strength conditioning works the muscles against resistance—either with weights or by using the body's own weight against gravity, as with push-ups or pull-ups. For cheap hand weights, fill empty gallon containers of milk with water or sand.

Weight training is not just for muscle-bound kids. People in their 90s have successfully started working with weights…and increased their muscle mass as a result.

Workouts should be about 20 minutes each, two to three times a week. The weight should be heavy enough to tire your muscles in ten repetitions. Rest when you've reached your limit and then do another ten. Increase the weight as you grow stronger.

You can learn an all-around series of resistance exercises from books (the instructions are in my book, among others) or classes. Be sure to use correct form—both to avoid injury and to work the muscles as efficiently as possible. Your local Y or health club should have instructors who can help you learn correct technique.

• *Aerobic exercise.* This is the kind of workout that leaves you slightly out of breath for a sustained period of time—and keeps your circulatory system in shape.

Examples: Running, swimming, cycling, brisk walking.

The American College of Sports Medicine recommends a minimum of 30 minutes of aerobic exercise, three times a week. That's a good guideline…but I don't want to discourage people from doing less if this schedule seems too difficult.

Major studies conducted by Steven Blair at the Cooper Institute in Dallas indicate that even shorter exercise sessions may slightly increase life expectancy. If you take a 15-minute walk every day, that's terrific—keep up the good work.

• *Stretching*—to increase flexibility and prevent injury. Begin and end every exercise session with five to ten minutes of gentle stretching. This warm-up and cool-down time will help prevent injuries, and increase flexibility in muscles. For people with arthritis, stretching can greatly increase range of motion.

Reversing aging through diet…

If we continue our usual eating habits while calorie needs decline, the muscle-to-fat ratio will continue to shift in favor of fat.

Eat nutrient-dense foods—foods that supply more nutrients with fewer calories. This means shifting away from the traditional American high-fat diet to one that emphasizes carbohydrates and is low in fat.

Learn which kinds of food are higher in fat calories and then make simple, logical choices until it becomes routine.

Example: Substitute a low-fat muffin for your morning croissant or doughnut.

You don't have to calculate the fat percentage of everything you eat, but you should read labels to find out what proportion of a food's calories are from fat, carbohydrate and protein.

Formula: One gram of fat equals nine calories…one gram of protein or carbohydrate equals four calories.

Supplements…

The one vitamin supplement I recommend —under a doctor's supervision—is vitamin E, 200 to 400 International Units per day. There's evidence that this vitamin can strengthen immune function—which may become compromised with age—and protect against heart disease. It's also an antioxidant—it acts against the oxidation of fats in the body that may contribute to aging.

Source: William Evans, PhD, director of the Noll Physiological Research Center, Pennsylvania State University, University Park, PA. He is co-author of *Biomarkers: The Ten Keys to Prolonging Vitality*, Fireside Books, 1230 Avenue of the Americas, New York 10020.

How to Beat Family Illness Genes

• *Research your relatives* to discover what diseases run in your family.

• *Research any family illnesses.* It may now be possible to treat or prevent such diseases.

• *Assess your lifestyle* to determine if changes made will decrease your risk.

• *Listen to your "inner self"* to determine if you're telling yourself that you're fated to be ill and die young.

• *Don't be unduly impressed* by medical advances. Remarkable treatments for rare diseases are fascinating and can overwhelm your own sense of responsibility for your health.

Source: Joan C. Barth, PhD, family therapist in Doylestown, Pennsylvania, and author of *It Runs in My Family: Overcoming the Legacy of Family Illness,* Brunner/Mazel Publishers, 19 Union Square W., New York 10003.

The Antioxidant Revolution

Antioxidants are invisible allies in our drive to improve health. They are good scavenging molecules that ride the bloodstream, gobbling up molecules of unstable oxygen called free radicals. The oxygen is called free because each molecule is seeking another molecule to cling to.

Free radicals are good in that they kill bacteria, help fight inflammation and control the tone of the smooth muscles, which regulate the blood vessels and internal organs. The problem starts when hordes of them run wild. *Unchecked free radicals…*

• Injure the lenses of the eyes, causing cataracts.

• Harm skin tissue, fostering premature signs of aging.

• Change, through oxidation, the particles of low-density lipoprotein (LDL) into bad cholesterol in the walls of blood vessels so that white blood cells can't destroy them. The result is a gradual buildup of plaque inside the artery walls that can lead to heart disease, strokes and heart attacks.

• Enter individual cells, damaging the nucleus and the genetic code (DNA) it contains. The damaged cell can become part of a cancerous lesion or tumor.

Internal antioxidants cling to free radicals, stopping their forays into tissue. But aspects of modern life tend to create too many free radicals for endogenous antioxidants to defuse. You can counter that overload by reducing your exposure to free radicals and adding more external (exogenous) antioxidants to your defenses. *Amplify your antioxidant power with three simple steps…*

• Consume the right amounts of certain vitamins in a combination of food and daily supplements.

• Engage in frequent moderate exercise.

• Make your home, work and recreational environments as healthy as possible.

Daily antioxidant diet:

My dietary recommendations start with the standard ones.

• Eat as little fat as possible, especially animal fat.

• Include plenty of grains and fresh fruits.

• Avoid fried foods.

• Steam, don't boil, vegetables, and eat lots of them, especially broccoli, brussels sprouts, cabbage, cauliflower, spinach and collard greens.

• In addition, take a daily "antioxidant cocktail" (in pill form) of vitamin C, vitamin E and beta carotene (a precursor—provitamin—of vitamin A). Vitamin A itself can be toxic in large amounts. And the foods that contain it—liver, butter, eggs—are loaded with fat and cholesterol.

Health professionals often claim that you can get all the nutrients you need from a balanced diet. For some nutrients, that's true, although it would require you to eat, say, 15 oranges a day to consume enough vitamin C…or three cups of butternut squash for beta carotene.

A sufficient quantity of vitamin E would be loaded with fat and calories—a cup of sunflower seeds or almost seven cups of peanuts.

For about six dollars a month, the "cocktail" will:

• Protect you against many forms of cancer.

• Build stronger defenses against cardiovascular disease (hardened arteries, heart attack, stroke).

• Help prevent cataracts and macular degeneration (a major cause of blindness for people older than 65 years of age).

• Delay the onset of premature aging.

• Boost your immune system.

• Decrease your risk of developing early Parkinson's disease.

All this is true even if your cholesterol profile doesn't improve.

What to buy: Choose the cheapest generic brand that otherwise pleases you. No additives …small enough to swallow. The expiration date should be at least a year away.

Buy natural vitamin E, made from vegetable oil. Synthetic vitamin E is made from turpentine or petroleum.

Warning: Don't be deceived by the word "natural" on the label. Keep reading until you see d-alpha (not dl-alpha) tocopherol or tocopheryl. The word acetate or succinate after that designation means the vitamin is more biologically active. That's good—but not crucial.

Take your vitamins with meals... and not all at once. More than 500 mg (milligrams) of vitamin C taken at the same time, for example, may wash out of the body with urine or bowel movements.

To pursue fitness for health and longevity—or if you don't exercise, daily supplements should total...

• *Vitamin E:* 400 IU (International Units—approximately equal to 400 mg)

• *Vitamin C:* 1,000 mg twice a day, split into two doses

• *Beta carotene:* 25,000 IU (approximately equal to 15 mg)

To pursue athletic fitness, regularly achieving more than 80% of predicted maximum heart rate during exercise...or if you weigh more than 200 pounds, daily supplements should total...

• *Vitamin E:* 1,200 IU

• *Vitamin C:* 2,000 mg (women), 3,000 mg (men), split into two or three doses

• *Beta carotene:* 50,000 IU

Optional: 50 to 100 micrograms of selenium, a mineral most people can get from food—seafood, kidney, liver.

I don't recommend taking coenzyme Q-10, sometimes mentioned as a helpful antioxidant. It may enhance the body's absorption of vitamin E, as vitamin C does, but research is scanty. Adjust your "cocktail" as necessary.

All women start to need more vitamin E and beta carotene when they reach age 50.

All men need more vitamin C than women.

Smokers (including passive smokers) need more vitamin C than nonsmokers.

People who exercise heavily need more vitamin C than those who are sedentary, to combat the extra free radicals they create.

My own daily supplement intake: Increased if I'm scheduled for a heavy physical workout—is

400 IU of natural vitamin E, 1,000 mg of vitamin C and 25,000 IU of beta carotene.

Taking the full amount indicated here beyond what's contained in your food is perfectly safe for most people. It's a good idea, though, to check with your doctor.

Possible side effects:

If you take blood thinners (anticoagulants such as aspirin and Coumadin) for heart problems, have your blood tested once or twice a year for cholesterol and other lipids (fatty elements in the blood). Supplemental vitamin E could raise your lipid levels.

Vitamin C tablets can dissolve tooth enamel if chewed. Swallow them. And don't take more than 4,000 mg a day...too much can cause diarrhea and increase the risk of kidney stones.

Beta carotene supplements may be unwise for people who smoke more than a pack of cigarettes a day. They may also cause liver damage if combined with an ounce or more of pure alcohol daily (two four-ounce glasses of wine or one mixed drink).

Anyone who has recently had surgery...who is extremely overweight...or who has a chronic condition such as diabetes or heart disease must obtain a doctor's approval before making a radical change in diet or exercise.

Since publishing *The Antioxidant Revolution,* I'm constantly asked if I make money from vitamin companies. The answer is *no.*

What I do want to promote is the fight against free radicals. It can be won—once we all understand how to muster all the defenses available.

Freedom from free radicals:

While fighting free radicals created by oxidating foods, your body must also combat free radicals caused by the environment. Even non-athletes encounter atmospheric problems that pummel them with free radicals...which seem to encourage inflammation of the muscles, ligaments and joints due to injuries from sports or accidents, arthritis and other long-term conditions.

Take steps to minimize or eliminate your exposure to...

• Your own and others' cigarette smoke. It promotes lung cancer and early signs of aging, such as wrinkled skin.

•*Air pollutants:* Smog, ozone, vehicle exhaust, chemicals in factories. These have direct links to diseases of the heart and lungs, including lung cancer.

•Ultraviolet rays from sunlight or sunlamps that emit those rays (not all do).

•Total radiation from electromagnetic fields, emitted by high-voltage wires...televisions...electric blankets...computers...microwave ovens.

Short-term strategy: Don't try to change your life all at once. Start with your biggest problem. If you smoke, or someone in your home smokes, that's your greatest danger and the best place to start.

Long-term strategy: Describe in writing the environments associated with all your regular activities for one week. Deliberately reduce your exposure to free radicals in each case.

Examples: Wear sunblock and a hat in the sun...commute or jog before or after rush hour ...don't jog within 30 feet of a busy highway... avoid smoky bars and lounges or lunchrooms at work...fly airlines with smoke-free flights.

Source: Kenneth H. Cooper, MD, MPH, president and founder of the Cooper Aerobics Center, Dallas, which includes the Cooper Clinic and the Institute for Aerobics Research. He has written *Dr. Kenneth H. Cooper's Antioxidant Revolution,* Thomas Nelson Publishers, Nashville.

How Well Can You Smell?

Although the sense of smell is usually viewed as a source of pleasure, it also plays a key role in protecting us from environmental hazards. *An inability to smell (anosmia) makes you vulnerable to...*

•*Fires and gas leaks.* People who cannot smell lack the ability to detect gas leaks and smoke. Equipping your home with smoke detectors will protect you against fire. Natural gas monitors are available from Lab Safety Supply, 800-356-0783.

Self-defense: If your home has gas ranges or gas heat, keep it well ventilated—especially during the winter. Periodically open an outside door or crack a window. If you're moving,

consider buying a home that has electric cooking and heating rather than gas.

•*Food poisoning.* Because they cannot smell rancid, moldy food, people with anosmia must use extreme caution when eating leftovers.

Self-defense: Eyeball everything you eat before you eat it. If there's any doubt about a food's freshness, have a friend check it—or throw it out.

•*Workplace hazards.* For most occupations, a poor sense of smell is of little consequence. But it is often a dangerous liability for firefighters, chemists, certain factory workers, etc.

Self-defense: Talk to your boss about making arrangements with a colleague to alert you to any dangers—including fires. If it's impossible to use a "buddy system," you may have to find other work.

Anosmia can also hinder your ability to taste and enjoy food. *Reason:* What we think of as taste is actually a combination of taste and smell.

Coping strategy: Select foods that are strongly sweet, sour, bitter or salty. Those four flavors alone can be detected by the taste buds on your tongue. You can taste them even if you cannot smell.

If you notice a decline in your ability to smell, consult a specialist in sensory disorders. Usually, the best choice is an ear, nose and throat specialist certified by the American Academy of Otolaryngology. Ask your primary doctor to refer you to one.

The otolaryngologist will use a variety of tests to determine the cause of your anosmia. Frequently, anosmia is simply the result of sinus congestion caused by an allergy or a severe cold.

Congestion prevents odor molecules from reaching the delicate odor-sensitive cells lining the roof or top of the sinuses (the olfactory epithelium). Fortunately, congestion-related anosmia usually goes away on its own in a few days or weeks.

But colds aren't the only cause of anosmia. *Other causes include...*

•Advancing age. Men typically start to lose their ability to smell around age 65, women about 70. Most age-related anosmia is irreversible.

•Chronic sinusitis. Even a small amount of sinus inflammation can prevent odor molecules from reaching the olfactory bulb.

Fortunately, oral and topical steroids, along with antibiotics in case of infection, usually resolve the problem. If drugs fail, minor outpatient surgery may be necessary to widen narrowed nasal passages.

•Head trauma. About 5% of people who sustain a severe head injury (typically in a car accident) develop anosmia. Even without treatment, one-third of these people gradually regain their sense of smell. But about two-thirds of the time, scar tissue or damage to the olfactory bulb renders the anosmia permanent. There is no effective treatment for such cases of anosmia.

Source: Heather J. Duncan, PhD, research assistant professor of otolaryngology, University of Cincinnati College of Medicine, Cincinnati, Ohio.

Chronic Pain and How to Overcome It

Our brains are programmed to interpret pain as a sign of acute injury. Almost instinctively, we stop what we're doing…we limit our movement…and we get help. When pain is chronic, however, these instincts are counterproductive. Inactivity won't heal a bad back, constant headaches or arthritis—it just creates more problems.

People come to our pain center seeking total relief. But that isn't always possible. What they must really learn is to manage their pain, to focus on quality of life. That way, they can learn to live happily, even with pain.

Overreacting to pain:

One of the first things I ask new patients to do is to describe their pain. More often than not, they describe not the sensation of pain, but what the pain means to them.

Typical responses: "Pain makes my life miserable…pain drives away my friends…it means that something is terribly wrong…it consumes my whole life…it makes me irritable and angry."

Such negative thoughts can be more devastating than the pain itself. This "pain-button thinking" turns every twinge into a catastrophe. Do any of these "catastrophizing" thoughts sound familiar?

•Things are bad and getting worse.
•This pain will destroy me.
•My body is falling apart.
•Poor me.

Thinking that severe pain must mean some dreadful disease adds mental anguish to physical discomfort. Many people experience pain as a form of punishment—like being spanked as a child. That only makes it worse.

None of these negative thoughts makes sense. Becoming aware of your pain-button thinking is the first step to getting rid of it.

Enduring discomfort:

One of the most important strategies for coping with chronic pain is to develop a capacity to endure discomfort.

Modern Americans are so accustomed to comfort and convenience that we expect it. As a result, we're less able to withstand pain than people were a century ago. A minor ache that our ancestors might not have given a second thought to can debilitate us.

To have a full life, you must be willing to tolerate some discomfort.

The real cause of chronic pain:

Although few pain sufferers are aware of it, chronic pain usually goes hand in hand with tense, weak muscles.

Example I: Most chronic headaches are the result of muscular tension. You may feel the pain in the front of your head, but it's really coming from tight muscles in your neck and shoulders.

Example II: Pain blamed on osteoarthritis sometimes comes not from the joints themselves but from stiff muscles around the joints. Exercising to strengthen those muscles and make them more limber will diminish your pain—even if your joints remain stiff.

Example III: Weakened or tense muscles are responsible for at least 80% of chronic back pain. Even when a high-tech test like magnetic resonance imaging (MRI) shows evidence of herniated disks, there's no proof that these are causing the pain. In fact, 40% of people who display spinal abnormalities on an MRI (including herniated disks) have no pain.

Perhaps the most effective way to tame chronic pain is to relax, stretch and strengthen your muscles.

Pain-relief strategies:

• *Breathe from your belly.* Most people move their chests in and out when they breathe. *Problem:* This type of breathing places constant strain on the muscles of your neck and shoulders, exacerbating headaches and back pain.

Better way: Place your hands on your belly or over your head and relax your shoulders. Breathe so that your abdomen goes in and out while your chest remains still. Once you get the hang of it, practice belly breathing without using your hands—and try to breathe that way all the time.

• *Get regular exercise.* If your pain is too severe to permit aerobics classes, jogging or weight-lifting, try walking or swimming. They will increase the flow of blood and oxygen to muscle cells without causing more pain.

Pacing is essential. Plan to finish your walk or swim before you become tired. If necessary, start off by going only a very short distance. Increase the distance gradually. Concentrate on gentle, stress-free motions.

• *Reduce psychological stress.* Stress intensifies pain by restricting blood flow and tightening muscles. And negative feelings speed the transmission of pain impulses from the body to the brain. Pleasant emotions help block the transmission of pain signals.

Learn to recognize the links between tension and pain. Notice the situations that cause back pain or headache to flare up. Consider what role might be played by your thoughts and emotions. Once you've tuned in to the triggers, look for better ways to solve problems and eliminate hassles.

Helpful: Keep a "pain diary" that details what you're doing and thinking when pain strikes.

If you notice that you can sit for 45 minutes before your back starts to hurt, for example, you can then make it a point to get up before that time is up.

Once you break the association between a specific activity and pain, you'll avoid the anticipation that makes pain a self-fulfilling prophecy. This way, you'll gradually increase your endurance.

• *Be more assertive.* If chronic pain limits your energy, you must learn how to set limits—to say "no" in a reasonable way, without anger or guilt.

Also important: Good planning skills. Each morning, make a list of what needs to be done that day. Recognize that focusing wisely on the top 20% of your list will fulfill 80% of your needs. Intelligent management of your time prevents the fall behind/catch-up spiral that exacerbates chronic pain.

• *Get enough sleep.* Go to bed and get up at the same time every day…and avoid caffeine, alcohol, sleeping pills and naps. Use your bed for sleeping and sex only.

If you're not sleepy—or if you wake up in the middle of the night—get out of bed. Read or listen to music until you're drowsy.

Essential: A firm mattress. If your body "gels" into position on a soft mattress, you'll wake up in more pain than if you had moved around throughout the night.

• *Steer clear of painkillers.* While they're helpful for acute pain, long-term use often causes severe side effects. Regular use of painkillers can actually cause some forms of chronic pain.

As your ability to tolerate discomfort grows, cut back gradually—under your doctor's supervision, of course.

Source: Norman J. Marcus, MD, president, International Foundation for Pain Relief, and medical director of the New York Pain Treatment Program at Lenox Hill Hospital, both in New York City. He is the author of *Freedom from Chronic Pain,* Simon & Schuster, New York.

Simple Stress Relief

Rank "stress triggers" by order of importance, then learn to ignore those on the low end of the scale. Ask yourself: How important is this in my life? Will I remember this in three months or even three days? Do I have control over what's happening? Each day, set aside time to introduce some form of relaxation into your life. Example: Take a few deep breaths each time you hang up the phone…or take a five-minute walk if you feel especially anxious. Friendships and hobbies also act as stress buffers. Eating low-fat, high-carbohydrate snacks (such as pretzels) releases the calming brain chemical serotonin into your system. Also helpful: Getting more sleep.

Source: Allen Elkin, MD, psychologist and director, Stress Management and Counseling Center, New York.

How to Manage Pain

A number of technologically advanced methods, from electrical stimulation to potent drugs, have been developed to help people deal with chronic pain. Some of these can be quite effective. Yet to a surprising degree, pain can be managed at the level of the mind—sometimes as effectively as through medical means.

Unlike many other cultures, where pain is seen as part of life, the typical American attitude to pain is, "Turn it off—as soon as possible." Television ads for analgesics carry the message, "You don't deserve pain, and our product will get rid of it in only 20 seconds—our rival's product will take 30 seconds."

I don't mean to say that pain-relieving medications should be abandoned—for they can be very valuable.

The danger occurs when people think first of getting rid of the pain—and are no longer impelled by it to address the issues it raises.

If we run to the medicine cabinet every time we feel a twinge, we deprive ourselves of valuable advice from our bodies…and may fail to take the avoiding actions that would prevent the problem from recurring.

After many years of working with leprosy patients and diabetics, for whom lack of pain sensitivity can lead to loss of limbs and other tragic consequences, I have come to believe that pain is actually a great gift. It compels us to notice when some part of the body is in danger. People who don't have the ability to feel pain envy it. They don't know when to snatch their hands from a cooking pot that they don't know is hot, avoid walking on an injured foot or seek treatment for a minor infection before it becomes advanced.

Instead of seeing pain as an enemy to be attacked and destroyed, we can benefit by listening to what our aches and pains have to say —and in doing so, we'll often find that they are friendly.

Example: If I get a headache, instead of thinking, "What a nuisance—I haven't got time for this," I take an hour or so to think through what might be causing the pain. Am I accepting too much stress? Have I stopped living in accordance with my priorities? Have I been pushing myself beyond endurance?

I believe that if people would take the time to resolve major conflicts in their lives—instead of dulling the pain so they can rush back to their destructive routines—they would suffer far less from headaches, stomachaches, back pain and other chronic problems.

We can deal with pain more constructively by understanding and appreciating how the system works.

Pain has three stages:

Pain begins with a signal (stage one) sent by nerve endings at the point that is damaged or in danger.

This signal travels along the spinal cord as a message to the brain (stage two). Often, reflexes will cause us to take avoiding action before the next stage is reached—and we're never even aware of a pain sensation.

In addition, distractions—such as the excitement of an athletic event or family reunion, the tension of a political debate, the thrill of an amusement-park ride or the stress of battle—can temporarily prevent transmission of the pain message. Think of the base of the brain as a gateway through which pain signals must pass before they're recognized and interpreted by the brain. When the body is sending many kinds of nerve signals at once, a kind of bottleneck forms—not all the signals can get through.

One intervention that works at this stage is called Transcutaneous Electrical Nerve Stimulator (TENS). This device is placed on the skin and produces a mild electrical current, stimulating thousands of nerve endings in the affected area—and overwhelming the spinal "gate." The patient feels a slight prickling sensation. Within seconds, intense pain can become much more tolerable—or even disappear.

Patients can use these machines in a medical office or rent them for use at home. For chronic pain, a device can even be surgically implanted in tissues beside the affected nerve, with the patient able to switch the current on and off by pressing a spot on the skin.

But the principle is hardly new. For many years before TENS came along, I used to give patients a stiff-bristled hairbrush and show them how to run it along the hand, leg or foot that was hurting. Just as with TENS, thousands of nerve endings would fire, creating a bottleneck at the spinal "gate" and quickly relieving the pain.

Epidural anesthesia also acts at stage two. A long-lasting local anesthetic is injected just outside the covering of the spinal cord. Nerves that pass through this sheath are temporarily knocked out—before the pain message gets to the brain.

Stage three:

The conscious perception of pain only occurs after the message reaches the brain (stage three)—and the brain chooses a response. Many kinds of narcotics work at this level—but while these drugs can relieve pain, many are highly addictive. Fortunately, it's at this third stage that pain has the greatest potential to be affected, for better or worse, by what we think about it.

Using the mind to manage pain:

Even at the signal and message stages of pain, over which we have little conscious control, we can still make a profound difference by listening to the pain and looking for a pattern.

Under what conditions does discomfort occur? Can we experiment with healthy changes —in movement, diet, posture, sleeping habits or other practices—to lessen it?

Pain and the mind:

But when our attempts at avoiding stressful conditions fail to relieve chronic pain, we can draw on the power of the mind to affect our perception of it.

We can learn about those factors that magnify the awareness of pain...find ways to control those factors and begin to manage the pain, instead of feeling that pain is controlling us.

Factors that can exacerbate pain include...

• *Fear.* If I feel a twinge and wonder if it's arthritis or cancer, I will become obsessed with the pain, and my worry will make me less able to tolerate it.

Antidote: Get the facts. Control. If I believe I have some influence over the source of pain, I will handle it more comfortably.

Example: In a series of experiments, subjects had a fold of skin placed in a small vise. Either the experimenter or the subject then turned a screw to tighten the vise, while the subject described the amount of pain felt and an instrument measured the actual amount of pressure. When subjects tightened the vise on themselves, they happily turned the screw much further than they would allow the experimenters to do—and reported much less discomfort than when the experimenters were in charge.

Obviously, we can't always control the diseases or injuries that give rise to chronic pain. But we can develop a sense of control over our responses by...

• Seeing pain as a friend rather than an enemy.

• Recognizing that pain is a protective system.

• Gathering good information about the source of the pain.

• Respecting what it tells us about our limits.

• Appreciating the fact that the system works.

• *Inactivity.* When we can't get rid of pain, a common response is to stop all activity— which can lead us to focus on the pain to the exclusion of everything else. That is one reason pain at night almost always feels worse than during the day—we don't have our normal routines to distract us.

It's true that you should take advantage of pain's protective function by limiting activities that hurt the affected area. But that doesn't mean eliminating every other stimulus from your life.

Antidote: Healthy distraction. Acknowledge your limits and use those parts of your body that do function normally. If your hand hurts, go for a walk. If you're recovering from foot surgery, write a letter to a friend.

One of the most effective forms of distraction is helping others, whether by growing flowers and delivering them to someone who's ill or volunteering to spend time with children in a hospital or day-care center.

Example: During World War II, I was a surgeon at a London hospital. When the nurses on our ward were called up for military service, we realized we would either have to close the ward—or turn the patients into nurses. We gave all the patients who could move—even those in wheelchairs—jobs to do, from making beds and carrying meals to watching another patient's intravenous drip and reporting when it needed to be changed. A wonderful sense of fellowship and mutual responsibility overtook the ward—and the patients needed half as much pain medication as before they'd been called on to help.

Voluntary service also helps to combat loneliness—another important way of managing pain.

• *Anger and bitterness.* As a hand surgeon, I'm sometimes called upon to operate on someone who has filed suit against a motorist or other person responsible for his/her injury.

I'm not against fair compensation, but today's awards are often so high that it pays a person to be deformed...and I've noticed that many of the patients involved in bitter lawsuits take much longer to heal. I don't believe they're faking or imagining the pain—but their anger at and desire to punish the person who hurt them seems to enhance the pain...and may even interfere with the body's healing mechanism.

Antidote: Forgiveness. Whether our anger is recent or has lasted for years, the act of forgiveness can release us from emotional as well as physical misery. Sometimes, this requires the assistance of a compassionate counselor who can help us to unearth buried resentments...or remind us that the person who wronged us was wrestling with his/her own pain.

Most of us have had the experience of being forgiven by someone we have wronged. Extending that same balm to others can be profoundly soothing.

Forgiveness makes room for the healing power of gratitude, awe at the miraculous efficiency of all our body's mechanisms, including sight and hearing as well as pain, and the powerful recognition that a life without pain would be miserable indeed.

Source: Paul Brand, MD, world-renowned hand surgeon and leprosy specialist. His years of pioneering work among leprosy patients earned him numerous prestigious awards. He is co-author of several books, including *Pain: The Gift Nobody Wants,* HarperCollins, New York.

Women Continue to Get Shockingly Substandard Medical Care

For the past several decades, American women have been systematically excluded from most research on new drugs, medical treatments and surgical techniques. As a result of this neglect, women are often denied the life-saving and life-extending treatments routinely offered to men.

Example I: Women are less likely than men to be referred for angioplasty, a surgical technique proven to clear blocked coronary arteries.

Example II: Women with AIDS are less likely than men to be prescribed the drug AZT.

Example III: Among sufferers of kidney failure, women are 30% less likely than men to receive kidney transplants.

This sex bias pervades medicine, directly undermining the treatment women receive in clinics, hospitals and doctors' offices across the country.

Common problems women face when seeking medical care:

• *Having your symptoms dismissed as being "all in your head."* Medical mythology has it that women are "complainers" whose symptoms often stem from emotional stress. This insidious attitude among doctors keeps women from getting the diagnostic tests they need.

In a recent study, only 4% of women with abnormal stress tests received follow-up tests necessary for pinpointing arterial blockages.

But these important tests were ordered for 40% of men with abnormal stress tests.

Similarly, because women's physical complaints are often viewed as evidence of psychological problems, women are more likely than men to receive prescriptions for psychiatric drugs.

Women make up 66% of those diagnosed with depression, yet they receive 73% of prescriptions for psychiatric medication—and 90% when the prescribing doctor is not a psychiatrist.

Self-defense: Communicate your problem to your doctor as clearly and concisely as possible.

Before your office visit, make a list of the questions you want to ask—in order of importance. If you get interrupted before you're through, at least you'll have covered the most crucial information.

If you feel your doctor is being dismissive, say so. If he/she still refuses to take your problem seriously, find another doctor.

• *Having your symptoms of heart disease go unrecognized.* Unlike men, women experiencing a heart attack often do not experience the classic symptoms—pain radiating down the arm or the elephant-sitting-on-your-chest type of pain.

Self-defense: Women should realize that vague abdominal discomfort, nausea, vomiting and shortness of breath can all be signs of heart attack. Take these symptoms very seriously. Make sure your doctor does, too.

• *Not being told to have routine mammograms and Pap smears.* Women over 65 account for almost half of the deaths from cervical cancer and are at greater risk of breast cancer than women of other age groups. But these older women are less likely than younger women to get the appropriate screening tests, often because their doctors fail to refer them for testing.

Self-defense: Annual mammograms, clinical breast exams and pelvic exams are recommended for all women 50 to 64 years of age.

The National Cancer Society recommends mammograms every one to two years for women 40 to 49 years of age.

A panel convened by the National Cancer Institute and the National Institute on Aging urges women 65 to 74 to have a clinical breast exam annually and a mammogram every two years, and women 75 and older to have both tests every two years. After three consecutive Pap smears with normal results, older women should have a Pap smear at least every three years. Younger women also need routine Pap smears.

• *Not being told that lumpectomy is a safe alternative to mastectomy.* Ninety percent of women with breast cancer are eligible for lumpectomy (removal of the tumor and a small margin of tissue), yet more than half undergo mastectomy (removal of the entire breast). The type of surgery a woman receives depends on such nonmedical factors as where she lives, her age, income and race.

Most likely to have a mastectomy: Black women, Medicare recipients, older women and women who live in the Midwest or South.

Self-defense: If your doctor says you need a mastectomy, get a second opinion—from a surgeon unaffiliated with your doctor's institution. Ask your doctor if he/she is aware of studies showing that lumpectomy followed by radiation is just as effective as mastectomy in treating early-stage breast tumors.

For more information on lumpectomy, call the National Cancer Institute at 800-4-CANCER.

• *Not having your early warning signs of AIDS recognized in time for effective treatment.* AIDS is now the fifth-leading killer of reproductive-age women. Yet many doctors continue to operate under the mistaken belief that "women don't get AIDS." As a result, women with clear signs of AIDS often fail to get tested for the disease.

Self-defense: If you're involved in a new sexual relationship or if you're in a relationship with a man who may be unfaithful, insist that he wear a condom.

If you have recurrent vaginal yeast infections, genital herpes or cervical dysplasia, get tested for the AIDS virus. These conditions may be an early sign of infection.

• *Being subjected to a needless hysterectomy.* More than half of the 500,000 hysterectomies performed annually in the US are medically unjustified.

Self-defense: Women should know about the proven alternatives to hysterectomy. *Example:*

Uterine fibroid tumors, which are usually benign, can often be shrunk with medication, then removed in a comparatively minor surgical procedure called *myomectomy.*

Women should also ask about *subtotal hysterectomy*—a procedure in which only the top of the uterus is removed and the cervix is left intact. This method, which is common in Europe, helps women maintain sexual responsiveness.

• *Being prescribed drugs that were never properly tested in women.* Women may suffer more or different side effects than men who take the same medication. *Example:* Doctors are often unaware that some drugs cause adverse reactions when combined with estrogen-replacement therapy and oral contraceptives.

Self-defense: If you're experiencing troublesome side effects, ask your doctor if you can switch to another medication. Realize that antianxiety drugs and postmenopausal estrogen taken together increase the risk of seizures and reduce the effectiveness of estrogen in treating hot flashes and other symptoms of menopause.

Hormone-replacement therapy (HRT) and oral contraceptives decrease the liver's metabolism of tricyclic antidepressants, leading to a greater risk of toxicity in women. For some women, doses of antidepressants may also need to be increased premenstrually.

• *Being urged to go on hormone-replacement therapy despite the continuing debate over its long-term safety.* Estrogen must be used continuously to maintain its benefits on the bones and heart. But most women—fearful of the link between estrogen and breast cancer—take HRT for a few years to relieve hot flashes and other menopausal symptoms and then stop.

Self-defense: Women may get almost as much protection if they take HRT to relieve short-term symptoms, discontinue it and start up again in their 70s. It's something to discuss with your doctor.

• *Being overmedicated.* Many common medical complaints of older women—including confusion and incontinence—may be caused by overmedication. Older women take drugs at twice the rate of older men, and are more apt to take multiple medications, increasing their risk of toxic side effects.

Self-defense: Older women should be aware that they metabolize many drugs differently than men. In women older than 65, for example, psychotropic drugs have a longer half-life, meaning that they remain in the body longer. To reduce the risk of side effects, physicians may need to reduce the doses of these drugs by one-third.

Elderly women also need to know that high doses of antipsychotic medication may increase their risk for chronic side effects such as tardive dyskinesia, a neurological disorder that results in abnormal movement of the mouth and tongue. Dextroamphetamine—a drug that tends to induce euphoria and increased alertness in men—sedates post-menopausal women.

• *Receiving medical care that is haphazard or fragmented.* While men may see one doctor for all their health-care needs, women must see a gynecologist for a Pap smear and pelvic exam, an internist for a general physical exam and a radiologist for a mammogram.

Typically, one doctor doesn't know what the other is doing. Services often overlap, wasting time and money—and leading to inadequate care.

Self-defense: Find an internist with training in gynecology, qualifying him/her to perform pelvic exams and Pap smears. Find out whether there's a comprehensive women's health center in your community. These centers, generally affiliated with a major teaching hospital, offer one-stop medical care. Practitioners with training in gynecology, general medicine, cardiology, menopause care, oncology, infectious diseases, endocrinology and bone metabolism make themselves available to you during a single appointment.

With this trend toward women-centered care, women may finally be seen by the medical establishment not as a collection of reproductive organs but as human beings with hearts and lungs and colons and kidneys—just like men.

Source: Leslie Laurence, author of the nationally syndicated newspaper column "Her Health" and co-author of *Outrageous Practices: The Alarming Truth about How Medicine Mistreats Women,* Fawcett Columbine, New York.

2

Your Doctor— Your Medication

Key Questions to Ask Your Doctor

If you grew up believing in the notion of the kindly, authoritative family doctor, it might seem inappropriate or disrespectful to sit your doctor down for a job interview. But in today's health-care world, it really is a good idea to do just that.

Some doctors stress prevention. Some rely on drugs to treat their patients while others are quick to recommend surgery.

Some read medical journals and take classes to keep up with advances in treatment. Others haven't learned much since medical school.

What approach does your current doctor— or a prospective new doctor—bring to your treatment? Ask him/her the following ten questions, and you should get a pretty good idea.

These questions can be used to screen a new doctor…to evaluate one you've been going to for years…or simply to make sure a particular drug, surgical procedure or diagnostic test is really appropriate.

The time to ask them isn't during a regular examination, but during a specially scheduled visit. *Make the interview situation clear:* "Before I ask you to take care of my family and me, I want to find out about you." Some doctors object to being interviewed. Others are happy to oblige you. The best bet is to ask for 30 minutes of the doctor's time at lunch hour.

• *How many patients do you see?* Beware of any doctor who tries to squeeze in more than 40 patients a day. He may be struggling to come out of debt, or trying to spend as much time in the office as possible to escape a poor home life. An overextended doctor may be addicted to work—and dysfunctional in a way that impairs his judgment.

• *How do you keep up-to-date?* A good doctor sets aside one to four hours a week to read medical journals and three to five days a year for continuing medical education (CME) classes, depending on his specialty. The average doctor falls short of these goals. Unfortunately, hospitals aren't good at making sure their doctors stay current.

23

To get a better idea of a doctor's competence, ask a few of his colleagues. Nurses are often particularly good sources of information.

•*Do you follow a healthy lifestyle?* There's a clear link between a doctor's lifestyle and his interest in helping patients maintain good health habits. A fat, workaholic MD who smokes a pack a day probably won't be very effective at promoting wellness among his patients.

If you're at all interested in using diet, exercise, stress reduction and other techniques to prevent illness, seek out a doctor who lives his own life accordingly.

•*Do you keep your appointments?* Excessive time in the waiting room is the top complaint patients have against doctors. On average, doctors see their patients 38 minutes after the scheduled time.

Some extremely competent doctors have poorly organized practices. Your doctor may not even know how long his patients are waiting.

To minimize waiting time: Let the doctor know you'd prefer to be seen on time. Complain if you feel you're being mistreated in scheduling. *Helpful:* Ask for the first appointment of the day, or the first one after lunch.

Always call ahead to make sure the doctor is running on time.

•*Will you let me see my medical records?* Although the doctor owns his patients' records, you do have a right to see yours. A doctor who is sincere about wanting to work with patients will encourage that. Some have copying machines and assistants who can help patients review their records—just to encourage their patients to do so.

•*Do you encourage patients to be partners in their own care?* The more a patient understands his illness and what he must do to get well, the better the outcome and the lower the cost of care. A good doctor understands this.

If you're facing a major operation (like hip replacement or open-heart surgery), or if you have diabetes or another chronic disease, being a participant in health-care decisions is especially important. It can spell the difference between an uneventful recovery and serious complications.

Conscientious doctors provide their patients with highly detailed, written descriptions of the course of treatment they intend to follow. They might also have a nurse contact patients periodically, to make sure treatment is going as planned…or schedule regular consultations for patients suffering from chronic illnesses.

•*Do you have a financial interest in a hospital or medical lab?* Doctors' referral patterns can be influenced by financial considerations. In Florida, for example, studies have shown that doctors who own labs or surgical centers tend to refer their insurance-carrying patients to these facilities.

It's not necessarily inappropriate for a doctor to own part of a medical facility, but it should be a "red flag." In some states, it's illegal for doctors to have a financial stake in the facilities to which they refer patients.

•*How experienced are you at performing this particular procedure?* Many doctors perform certain operations—even though they have little training in the procedure. But experience can make a big difference, especially for major or particularly delicate operations, such as open spine-surgery. For any major operation, make sure your doctor performs the procedure at least 50 times a year.

Your insurer probably keeps records of which doctors perform which procedures in your area. You can also contact a local hospital and get the names of doctors who do the procedure regularly.

•*Why are you prescribing this particular drug?* With the drug industry pumping out dozens of new medications a year, it's impossible for doctors to stay absolutely up-to-date on medications. But your doctor should be able to explain why you need drug therapy and why a specific drug is best for you.

Perhaps the drug is less likely to cause side effects than alternatives…or it's less likely to interfere with the action of other drugs you're taking. Maybe it's simply been around longer and is therefore a known quantity.

•*Why do I need this diagnostic test?* Some doctors are so afraid of being sued for malpractice that they offer all sorts of diagnostic tests—even when there's little legitimate medical reason for doing so.

Problem: Such "defensive" testing is costly and time-consuming…and it can expose you to needless risk.

Instead: Ask your doctor to give a clear explanation of why the test is absolutely necessary. He should be able to say, "This is what I'm looking for—and here's how I'll use the test results."

Source: Paul Keckley, PhD, founder and president of the health-care market research and planning firm, The Keckley Group, Two Maryland Farms, Suite 128, Brentwood, Tennessee 37027. Dr. Keckley is the author of *99 Questions You Should Ask Your Doctor and Why,* Rutledge Hill Press, 211 Seventh Ave. N., Nashville 37219.

How to Check Your Doctor's Credentials

Check a doctor's credentials by calling the American Board of Medical Specialties (ABMS) at 800-776-2378, Monday through Friday, 9 AM to 6 PM, Eastern Time. *Trap:* As competition increases, some doctors are advertising themselves as specialists in areas in which they haven't received training. The ABMS hotline tells whether a physician is certified by a recognized board and in what specialty.

Source: Melvin Schrier, OD, optometrist in private practice in New York.

The Art and the Politics Of Getting the Best Second Opinion

A second opinion offers you a different—and invaluable—perspective on a medical problem…but it can also be confusing.

How do you know when you need a second opinion?

Whom should you consult for that second opinion?

And what should you do with the information—especially if it is vastly different from the first opinion?

To obtain optimal care today, it's vital that you not be intimidated by physicians. Patients are often too respectful of doctors and thus reluctant to ask questions or voice concerns for fear of offending them or sounding ignorant.

Reality: You have a right—and an obligation—to be assertive when gathering information about your condition. It's the only way you can make an informed, intelligent decision about your treatment.

Actually, the first step when a doctor makes a diagnosis or recommends a treatment isn't to seek a second opinion. The first step is to thoroughly question your primary doctor about his/her reasons for suggesting the course of action.

If you're not sure what to ask, try saying, "This is a bit overwhelming. If you were in my position, Doctor, what questions would you ask to understand the situation better?"

Push for specifics—for example, statistics on the exact percentage of sufferers who respond to the proposed treatment. *Also ask about…*

•The risks and side effects of the treatment…and the odds that you'll experience a bad outcome.

•The benefits and how much you are likely to gain from the treatment.

•Any alternative treatments that you should consider—and the reasons why they are—or are not—recommended for you by the doctor.

•The costs and how fully they are reimbursed typically by health insurance.

When to get a second opinion:

There are several appropriate reasons why you may want a second opinion…

•If, after talking things through with your doctor, you're unsure about a treatment.

•If the treatment is so major that it will irrevocably change your life.

•If you have a condition about which experts disagree on the best treatment.

Example: Some doctors believe one third to one half of all cardiac surgeries are unnecessary and that drug therapy may offer equal benefit. If your case falls into an area where medical opinions differ, your personal judgments about the risks and benefits various therapies may hold for you should ultimately decide your course of action.

•If your insurer requires a second opinion before it will pay for treatment.

In all scenarios, be up front with your primary physician about seeking a second opinion. You may need him to talk with the other doctor, and you'll want copies of your records. Appropriate phrasing…

"I respect your opinion, but I'm obligated to myself to get a second opinion and gather all the information I can. This doesn't mean I don't have confidence in you."

The doctor shouldn't be offended by this approach.

Finding a second-opinion doctor:

When you seek your second opinion, it is critical that you obtain one that is independent of your first doctor's opinion. *Suggestions…*

•Don't see a doctor who practices in the same office—or even the same hospital—as your first consulting specialist. Colleagues tend to agree with the first opinion rather than risk offending one another or jeopardizing a lucrative referral source. Make sure your first- and second-opinion doctors are financially and socially independent of each other.

•Take with a "grain of salt" the first doctor's recommendation of a physician. Inquire about his relationship with that physician and exactly why he's recommending him/her. If the second-opinion doctor is a buddy of your first doctor, he will likely agree with the first opinion, and it won't be worth your time to see him.

•Go to a hospital across town—or even to a hospital in another town. That's often the best way to find someone who doesn't know the first doctor you saw and has no financial or personal ties to him.

•Go to a physician who practices in a different type of institution than the first doctor you consulted.

Reason: Because of their diverse practice settings and exposures, they're most likely to give you different perspectives on your problem.

Example: If, for your first opinion, you saw a physician affiliated with a community hospital, find a physician who has privileges at a medical-school hospital for the second.

•Ask your family doctor—your general doctor, not the specialist whose opinion you are trying to verify—for a recommendation. He may know the top specialists in town.

•Contact the American Board of Specialists (800-776-2378) for names of board-certified physicians in your area. Call each doctor's office and ask for his credentials, training, affiliations and track record with the treatment you're considering. Call the hospital each is affiliated with or the Board of Specialists to verify information. An academic affiliation is usually a good sign.

Information to bring with you:

Advise the second doctor that you've seen another physician already and that you're seeking a second opinion on a proposed course of action.

Be sure to bring all medical records and originals or copies of X rays and lab reports with you. That way, the second physician will quickly be brought up to speed on your case and won't need to repeat a lot of tests. By moral obligation—and law, in many states—these materials are available to you, although the physician may charge a nominal fee for reproducing them.

What to make of the second opinion:

•Be on the alert for any subtle signals that indicate the second doctor disagrees with the first doctor—and be sure to follow up these signals with pointed questions.

Example: While reviewing your chart, the doctor says, "I wonder"…or "That's unusual."

Don't let such seemingly innocuous comments slide. Press the doctor for details. What exactly does he wonder about? What is unusual? Would he have a different approach to your problem?

•Encourage the first- and second-opinion doctors to discuss your case. There is nothing wrong with the two doctors you've consulted discussing your case—provided their assessments are not clouded by professional or personal friendships or other nonrelated biases. Together, they may arrive at a joint decision about the best treatment for you.

Example: For early breast cancer, one surgeon may recommend mastectomy (removal of the whole breast)…whereas another may suggest a lumpectomy (removal of just the malignant tissue) followed by radiation therapy. The treatments are equally effective for many—but not for all—women. The two surgeons may find a common ground for a recommendation on whether a lumpectomy or mastectomy will be better for you. Or if they continue to disagree, they should isolate the basis of their disagreement so you and perhaps another consultant can decide what to do.

Third opinion:

If the two doctors can't reach a consensus, seek a third opinion. Then—armed with the information you've gathered—go with your gut feelings and personal preferences about which treatment will bring you the most benefit and the least harm.

Source: Richard N. Podell, MD, clinical professor of family medicine, University of Medicine and Dentistry of New Jersey–Robert Wood Johnson Medical School in New Brunswick, New Jersey. He is the author of *When Your Doctor Doesn't Know Best,* Simon & Schuster, New York.

What You Don't Know Can Hurt You

Doctors often don't inform patients about the side effects of prescribed drugs because they fear patients will imagine they suffer the side effects they are told of. A patient who does suffer a side effect may mistakenly attribute it to the illness rather than the drug—a potentially dangerous mistake.

Source: Sidney Wolfe is director of the Health Research and Advocacy Group, a branch of Public Citizen, 2000 P St. NW, Washington, DC 20036.

Cutting Doctors' Fees

Nearly all doctors are cutting their fees for patients…*but you have to ask. Important:* Negotiate directly with the doctor. *Also:* Think of your visit as a business transaction—*you are paying for a service.* Doctors can't afford to lose customers. *Helpful:* Call around to find out what other doctors charge. *Negotiating examples:* A flat price to remove several moles instead of paying "per mole"…a lower cost for a flu shot…*removing* stitches at no extra charge …quantity discounts for regular treatment of a chronic condition, such as allergies.

Source: Charles B. Inlander is president of People's Medical Society, 462 Walnut St., Allentown, Pennsylvania 18102, and co-author of more than a dozen books on health.

Your Medical Records Aren't as Private as You May Think

Nothing is more sensitive than your medical records. They detail everything from what illnesses you've been treated for…to what drugs you've been prescribed…to whether you've ever seen a psychiatrist.

For the past decade or so, medical records, along with credit-card and bank-account records, have been stored in vast computer databases. Not surprisingly, this sensitive information often falls into the hands of people who really have no business knowing the details of your private life.

Example: A doctor at a Chicago hospital recently counted the people who had access to patient records. He stopped when he reached 75…and that number included only individuals able to obtain the records without breaking hospital rules. Many of those counted were secretaries, file clerks, auditors and others with no meaningful role in patient treatment.

Your private medical information is also routinely made available to direct marketing firms, health-insurance companies and other organizations. Yet the information contained in these records is often irrelevant—or inaccurate.

Self-defense strategies:

• *Check your medical records for accuracy.* Many doctors prefer not to show patients their records, because they feel that the medical jargon contained in the records might be misleading or upsetting.

If your doctor is hesitant about showing you your medical records, ask that they be sent to another doctor of your choice who can interpret them for you.

A comprehensive set of your medical records is probably on file at the Medical Information Bureau (MIB), an insurance-industry association that collects and disseminates data relating to the insurance policies of more than 12 million people.

The MIB not only allows individuals access to their records but also has a procedure for correcting these records.

If you've been rejected by an insurer or just want to see if the MIB has a report on you, request a report from MIB at Box 105, Essex Station, Boston 02112 (617-426-3660). If a report exists, it should arrive about a month after you mail in your request. There is no fee.

• *Never volunteer information to an employer, insurer, etc.* You gain nothing by giving more. It can only come back to haunt you. When filling out forms, give as little information as is acceptable.

• *Ask your doctor not to disclose information about you.* Insist that he/she get your written permission before disclosing information to anyone else. If your doctor asks to forward information about you, ask what exactly is being disclosed, and for what purpose. Insist that he follow the same rule you do—give out only relevant information.

• *Check your employer's policy regarding medical records.* Companies that manufacture or distribute dangerous substances (such as toxic chemicals) must maintain such records. Other companies that administer their own medical programs may also maintain such records.

Ask your company's personnel director whether your medical records are included in your personnel file. If so, ask to see them. If you notice any mistakes, ask that they be corrected.

If there's a written policy regarding medical records, ask to see it. Don't worry about appearing paranoid. Companies now expect employees (and prospective employees) to ask. It's not an uncommon request.

Special problem: Company-sponsored employee-assistance programs. Such programs —designed to help employees deal with depression and other personal or financial problems—may pledge to keep whatever you disclose confidential. However, no federal law requires them to do so.

If you're thinking of participating in such a program, find out the circumstances under which information about you might be released to your employer—and be sure to get it in writing.

• *Consider paying medical bills in cash.* This approach is taken by many executives, politicians, military personnel and others who want to protect their careers from the stigma of psychotherapy or other potentially embarrassing treatment. You'll have to forgo reimbursement by your health insurance company, but your medical information will have less exposure.

• *Think twice before signing insurance releases.* When you apply for health or life insurance or submit an insurance claim, you may be asked to sign a release granting the insurer access to your medical records.

If the release seems too broad, strike out portions that permit unlimited access to information not directly relevant to the service. Check to make sure the insurer permits such deletions.

• *Be wary of magazine or TV ads offering free medical information.* When you respond to such offers by filling out a form or placing a phone call, a marketer somewhere links your name with at least the possibility of a certain health problem.

And since marketers buy mailing lists from one other, the data may be joined with other personal information you disclose to another marketer down the line.

Source: David F. Linowes, professor of political economy and public policy at the University of Illinois, Urbana-Champaign. A former chairman of both the Presidential Commission on Privatization and the US Privacy Protection Commission, he is the author of *Privacy in America,* University of Illinois Press, University Press Building, 1325 S. Oak, Champaign, Illinois 61820.

Avoiding Medication Errors

•Inform your doctor of all drugs you take—prescription and over-the-counter. That way, he/she can make sure you're not being over-medicated.

•Ask your doctor or pharmacist to explain all possible side effects of all drugs you take. Any new symptoms that appear after you start a new drug are probably caused by that drug. Tell your doctor about any such symptoms right away.

•Make sure drug therapy is appropriate for your condition. If you're unsure, ask your doctor.

•Before starting a new drug, ask if it's possible to discontinue another drug you're already taking. Also ask if it's possible to start the new drug at a lower-than-normal dose.

•Do not take any drug for longer or shorter than necessary. Again, tell your doctor if your symptoms change.

•Make sure you understand all instructions regarding dosage.

•Discard old drugs to make sure they're not taken by mistake.

•Ask your primary-care physician to coordinate your drug use. Never feel uncomfortable about asking questions.

Source: Bruce Yaffe, MD, an internist and gastroenterologist in private practice in New York City.

How to Cut Your Medication Costs

Drug costs are soaring. Last year, prices of the top 20 prescription medications climbed more than 4% over 1993 levels. That's 50% faster than the rate of inflation.

Fortunately, there are practical ways to keep drug costs down…

• *Avoid drugs altogether unless you really need them.* Medications should be used only when their potential benefits outweigh the potential risks. *Problem:* Some doctors prescribe drugs just to make patients feel "taken care of." And many patients use prescription or over-the-counter (OTC) medications for conditions that could be treated safely and effectively—and more cheaply—without drugs.

Example: People often take prescription muscle relaxants for minor aches and pains. Or they take antibiotics for colds and other viral infections that do not respond to antibiotics. (If your doctor prescribes an antibiotic for a cold, ask him/her to explain why. You might be better off treating your cold with bed rest and fluids.)

• *Get the best medication you can.* There are now more than 3,000 drugs on the market. But because most doctors aren't familiar with all of them, they tend to prescribe the same few ones over and over again.

Example: Nearly 100 prescription blood-pressure medications are now available. Yet most doctors prescribe only one medication from each of several chemically different groups—such as calcium channel blockers, beta blockers and diuretics.

Self-defense: Before filling a prescription, ask your doctor and your pharmacist if there are similar drugs that cost less.

Your pharmacist may know more about medications than your doctor and may be able to suggest an alternative medication even if your doctor is unable to. If you suspect that's the case, ask your pharmacist to speak with your doctor about the appropriateness of prescribing it.

• *Request generics.* Generics can cost up to 70% less than their brand-name counterparts. Yet doctors are often hesitant to prescribe generics. *Reason:* Like many of their patients, they assume medications that cost more must be better.

That's simply not so. By law, generics and brand names have the same active ingredients.

But some generics are absorbed up to 20% faster or 20% slower than their brand-name counterparts. For some conditions, such as epilepsy, switching between the generic and the brand-name medication can cause problems.

Self-defense: Whenever starting a new medication, ask your doctor to prescribe the generic.

• *Opt for over-the-counter drugs.* Some prescription drugs—Motrin, for example—are available in lower doses as OTC medications.

In some cases, you'll save at least 20% by purchasing the OTC version. The difference in dosage can be made up by taking several non-prescription pills instead of one prescription-strength pill. Ask your doctor if a prescribed medication is available without a prescription—and compare prices.

• *Pick a pharmacy carefully.* People often shop for drugs at the most convenient pharmacy—a costly mistake. A prescription that runs $60 at your neighborhood drugstore might cost half that elsewhere. Big discount-chain pharmacies are usually cheapest.

• *Check out mail-order pharmacies.* If you need antidepressants, birth-control pills or other medications for chronic conditions, mail order can save you a bundle. Again, call around. Prices also vary significantly among mail-order pharmacies.

Mail-order possibilities:

• *Action Mail-Order Drug Company.* For prescription and OTC medications. 800-452-1976.

• *Medi-Mail.* For prescription and OTC medications. 800-331-1458.

• *American Association of Retired Persons (AARP).* For prescription and OTC medications. 800-456-2226.

• *Cystic Fibrosis Foundation Pharmacy Services.* Specializes in antibiotics, enzyme supplements, vitamins and other medications that meet the needs of cystic fibrosis sufferers. Many drugs are offered at below-wholesale cost. 800-541-4959.

Mail-order pharmacies aren't suitable for acute infections and other conditions that can change quickly and unpredictably. *Reason:* By the time the prescription arrives, your condition could be worse.

Source: Val Ulene, MD, a Los Angeles–based physician and author. She and her father, Dr. Art Ulene, a health reporter for the NBC *Today Show,* are the authors of *How to Cut Your Medical Bills,* Ulysses Press, Box 3440, Berkeley, California 94703.

Common HMO Traps— And How to Escape Them

As more than 11 million Americans are already aware, joining an HMO can be an excellent way to save money on medical bills.

But HMOs can end up costing you money and providing less than optimum health care. *Here's how to avoid the most common HMO traps...*

Trap: Feeling uncared for. Today's HMO doctors are sometimes so strapped for time that they often leave the simple tasks such as taking blood pressure for nurses and assistants. They pop in for a brief evaluation, then rush off to the next patient.

While nurses and assistants generally are capable of performing these tasks without problem, this division of services causes some patients to feel neglected by their doctor.

If you feel that way, don't hesitate to speak up. Tell your doctor that you would prefer that he/she take your blood pressure and perform other similar tasks. Surprisingly, most doctors are willing to oblige—if you ask nicely.

Trap: Getting "stuck" with a doctor you don't like. Most HMOs let you pick a doctor from a list of practitioners affiliated with the HMO. To make sure you select a doctor with whom you can develop a good rapport, schedule a preliminary appointment.

Ask about his medical training...his approach to illness prevention...and his general philosophy regarding medical care. If the doctor's responses don't reassure you, schedule an appointment with another doctor. Even if the doctor you select turns out to be a dud, however, you're far from "stuck." Contact the HMO administrator and ask to find a new doctor.

In an effort to minimize administrative work, most HMOs are reluctant to talk about switching doctors...but they will generally let you switch if you insist.

Trap: Assuming an HMO will cover you while traveling. Most HMOs refuse to pay for care rendered out of town or by doctors outside the organization. *Exception:* Genuine emergencies, such as a heart attack, automobile accident, etc.

If you spend a considerable amount of time away from home, find out in advance exactly what medical expenses your HMO will cover. It may be necessary to purchase conventional fee-for-service health insurance instead of your HMO coverage.

Trap: Getting a second opinion that's biased. When getting a second opinion, it's important to find a doctor who has no significant relationship with the doctor who provided the first opinion. A doctor who is a friend or close colleague of the first doctor is not a good bet.

Problem: In an HMO, the doctor who provides the second opinion belongs to the same HMO as your primary doctor. He may be hesitant to give you an honest, unbiased opinion—simply because he fears offending his colleague.

Solution: Check whether the HMO permits you to get a second opinion from a doctor outside the HMO. If not, consider going outside the HMO network for the second opinion anyway—even if it means you must pay for it.

How to Get Your HMO to Pay Up

People often assume that once they join a health-maintenance organization (HMO), filing medical claims will be streamlined and trouble-free.

In fact, when it comes to delayed payment of benefits and denial of legitimate claims, HMOs are no different from conventional fee-for-service health insurers.

HMO subscribers usually pay a flat monthly fee for medical care, regardless of how much or how little care they need. HMO doctors are usually paid a fixed monthly fee per patient, regardless of how much care they deliver.

This arrangement usually works well for simple diagnostic and preventive services. But in cases involving costly or experimental treatment, HMOs may be less likely than conventional insurers to make prompt reimbursement or authorize needed treatment.

Here's how to protect your interests—and what to do if your HMO refuses to pay your claims or provide necessary treatment.

Before you sign up:

• *Check out the HMO's reputation.* If your employer has contracted with an HMO, you may have little choice regarding your health insurance. *If you do have a choice:* Contact the agency that oversees HMOs in your state (typically the department of insurance or the department of corporations). Inquire about the HMO's track record.

If the HMO you're considering has a long history of complaints from consumers, find another insurer.

• *Examine the list of doctors who participate in the HMO.* The more doctors in the HMO's network, the less likely you'll be saddled with a doctor you don't like. *Also:* The more cardiologists, oncologists and other medical specialists on the roster, the better.

• *Find out if the HMO is willing to pay for "unusual" care.* Some HMOs are unwilling to pay for bone-marrow transplants and other costly—but lifesaving—treatments. Some are reluctant to pay for emergency care rendered to members when they're out of town. To get a sense of how strict the HMO you're considering will be in evaluating your claims, ask how it would handle these two situations.

• *Find out who is responsible for making difficult medical decisions.* The best HMOs let their doctors decide which tests are necessary, how long a patient must be hospitalized, whether a specialist must be called in, etc. Steer clear of HMOs that hire managed-care companies to perform this task.

After signing up:

• *Take an active role in the claims-filing process.* Like all insurers, HMOs insist that claims be filed in a certain way. If anything is wrong —a missing or improperly filled-out form, for example—an HMO is liable to deny the claim …or at least delay payment until the matter is cleared up.

With conventional fee-for-service health insurance, patients are responsible for filing their own claims. HMOs handle these claims for their patients, sending their members a monthly statement of benefits paid.

While this arrangement works well for routine care, it can work against you in the event of a complex claim.

Self-defense: Ask the HMO to send you copies of all claims filed on your behalf. Review them, and see that any missing information is promptly provided to the HMO's home office. Keep copies of all documentation submitted with your claim.

• *Create a paper trail.* If your HMO doctor is reluctant to order a costly or experimental test or procedure that you're convinced you need, get a second opinion. If this doctor agrees with you, ask him/her to write to the HMO on your behalf. (Some HMOs pay for second opinions, others do not.)

If you feel that your HMO doctor isn't doing all that he can do to ensure that the procedure is covered, write to your HMO yourself.

Your aim: To establish a written record that supports your case. This will come in handy should you need to appeal the denial of a claim…or take the HMO to court.

If your claim is denied:

• *File an immediate appeal.* Be sure to follow the instructions outlined in your HMO handbook very carefully. Communicate with the HMO by registered mail—even if you're not required to do so. Keep copies of your letters and return receipts. Mark the dates of response in your calendar.

The HMO's first response to your appeal will probably be to reiterate the denial of your claim. Don't let that discourage you. Go on to the next step in the appeals process…and keep pursuing the matter until you've exhausted all the remedies outlined in the booklet. If the dispute is not settled, it will probably be referred to a third party for mediation.

Types of claims most commonly denied: Claims involving long-term rehabilitative care …bone-marrow transplants for metastatic breast cancer or other treatments the HMO deems "experimental" or "not medically necessary."

• *Let the HMO know that you mean business.* The HMO's "administrative remedy" is not your only remedy—and it's very important that the HMO knows you know that.

In each letter you write regarding your appeal, explain why you feel your benefits were wrongfully denied. Include the following sentence: "This appeal relates only to the denial of the benefits in question, but does not constitute, and shall in no way be deemed, an admission that I am limited in my right to pursue a 'bad faith' remedy in state court."

• *File a complaint with the state.* If the appeals process proves futile, contact the appropriate state agency (the department of insurance or the department of corporations) and ask about the procedure for filing a formal complaint against the HMO.

Expect your claim to take anywhere from a month to a year to process. Most states receive a large number of complaints and lack the staff to deal with them in a timely fashion. But filing this complaint will extend the paper trail—a good strategy if it ultimately becomes necessary to file a lawsuit.

• *Hire a lawyer.* If the HMO has acted in bad faith, it may be liable for punitive or emotional-distress damages as well as the benefits owed.

Exception: If you joined the HMO through an employer, you're probably entitled to sue only for unpaid benefits and attorney's fees.

Be sure that the lawyer you hire specializes in "bad faith" claims or insurance matters. If you need a referral, contact your state bar association.

Problems specific to medicare claims:

When Medicare recipients join an HMO, they're essentially assigning their Medicare benefits to that HMO. Of course, these individuals are also entitled to disenroll if they are dissatisfied with the HMO's services—something that should be kept in mind.

Medicare benefits are determined by one's state of residence. In California, for example, Medicare pays $520 per person per month, the highest rate in the country. When the government contracts with an HMO to be a provider of Medicare benefits, it agrees to send 95% of that amount per subscriber to the HMO each month.

HMOs sometimes deny claims that Medicare would normally pay. Instead of getting complete rehabilitative care, for example, elderly persons belonging to HMOs are often sent to skilled nursing facilities (SNFs), where the level of service is often poorer than at an acute rehabilitation hospital.

In some cases, HMOs encourage patients to disenroll when they need expensive treatment. This way, the HMO gets to use your Medicare allotment while you're well…and transfer costs back to the taxpayers when your care gets expensive.

In a recent case, a 75-year-old man was denied a bone marrow transplant on the grounds that it was "experimental." His appeal was also denied. He disenrolled from the HMO —and Medicare paid.

Self-defense: Compare the benefits you believe you'll get from an HMO very carefully with what you would receive from Medicare and a Medicare supplemental policy.

If you need a costly procedure and your HMO has denied your claim or request for treatment, check with Medicare. If Medicare covers the procedure, it may be better to disenroll from the HMO immediately than to delay lifesaving treatment while you wrestle with the HMO appeals process. In some cases, legal action may be necessary.

Source: William M. Shernoff, founding partner of Shernoff, Bidart & Darras, a Claremont, California, law firm that specializes in consumer claims against insurance companies. He is the author of *How to Make Insurance Companies Pay Your Claims,* Hastings House, Mamaroneck, NY.

Smart Ways to Cut Your Medical Bills

In the ten years between 1980 and 1990, US expenditures on health care more than doubled.

In 1990, each citizen's share of the bill was $2,566. By the year 2000, just four years from now, the Health Care Financing Administration predicts that each share will soar to $5,712. That's $22,848 for a family of four.

Here's how to stretch your health-care dollar right now—without sacrificing top-quality care…

1. Stay well. The cheapest illness to treat is the one you never get. Adjust your lifestyle to reduce your risk of serious (and expensive) ailments—particularly cancer and heart disease.

What to do: Exercise for at least 30 minutes three times a week (see a doctor first if you're older than 35 or have a medical condition)… eat a low-fat, high-fiber diet…have no more than two drinks a day…and don't smoke.

2. Take advantage of free health care. In many parts of the country, shopping malls and drugstores offer everything from eye exams and flu shots to screenings for high blood pressure, diabetes and cancer.

These services are not scams. Yes, they publicize the store or hospital offering them. But they also provide valuable free care. The same tests can cost upward of $200 in a doctor's office.

3. Pick the highest deductible you can afford. Health-insurance policies with high deductibles charge lower premiums. If you're young and in good health, for instance, pushing your deductible to $5,000 saves you up to 40% on premiums.

4. Read your insurance policy very carefully. Find out exactly what's covered, and be sure to submit claims for everything for which you can expect reimbursement.

People often assume they can't get reimbursed for incidental items—the small lancets diabetics use to obtain blood samples, for instance. Many policies do cover such items. But you have to submit a claim for them before you can be reimbursed.

5. Ask your doctor if he/she "accepts assignment." That means he accepts the portion that the health-insurance company pays as full payment for your bill. More doctors take assignment than you might think, because collecting from nonpaying patients is such a hassle.

6. Avoid emergency rooms. In a true emergency, of course, a visit to the ER can save your life. But using the ER for nonemergency care is very expensive. You'll pay up to ten times more than if you got the same treatment in your doctor's office.

If your child has an earache Saturday night, phone your doctor. He should be able to give you an idea of how serious the problem is— and may be able to treat the illness swiftly and cheaply by writing a prescription…or by recommending simple at-home care.

7. Scrutinize your hospital bills. Hospital bills are notoriously inaccurate, and in cases where inaccuracies occur, they favor the hospital 80% of the time.

Before surgery, many items are placed in the operating room just in case the doctor needs them. Patients are mistakenly billed for them even if the doctor never uses them.

Check with the surgeon after surgery. Did he use all the equipment and supplies you were billed for? Was medication ordered that you never needed? If you find discrepancies, call the hospital billing department. Ask that your bill be reduced.

8. Ask your pharmacist about cost-cutting measures. Pharmacists are often knowledgeable about simple but effective ways to cut prescription costs.

Example I: Buying a 90-day supply of drugs rather than three 30-day supplies. That way, you pay only one co-payment instead of three.

Example II: Buying generic drugs. They cost significantly less than brand names.

Some insurance companies have special arrangements with mail-order pharmacies. Making use of such an arrangement can lower your drug bills even more.

If your insurance company does not offer such an arrangement, a discount pharmacy in your community is likely to have lower prices than most mail-order pharmacies.

Source: Rich Gulling, RPh, MBA, a registered pharmacist and adjunct professor of finance at Wright State University, Dayton, Ohio. He is the co-author of *Stay Well Without Going Broke: Winning the War Over Medical Bills*, Starburst Publishers, Lancaster, PA.

Avoid Over-the-Counter Overdose

Don't mix aspirin or acetaminophen (Tylenol) with cold medications. *Trap:* If the cold medication also contains aspirin or a similar analgesic, you could overdose—suffering stomach irritation, ringing in the ears or liver

damage. *Also:* Avoid decongestants and nasal sprays while taking diet pills. Both can contain similar or identical ingredients that can result in overdose. Always read labels carefully before taking any over-the-counter medication.

Source: Lisa Tuomi, PharmD, drug-information coordinator, Stanford University Medical Center, Stanford, California.

When Good Medicine Can Be Bad for You

Racial and ethnic heritages affect how well some medicines work and whether they result in any side effects. *Reason:* The ability to metabolize drugs is controlled by enzymes, and enzymes may work differently in different groups. *Examples:* Asians tend to metabolize some drugs more slowly and so are more at risk for side effects…African-Americans don't respond as well to beta blockers for high blood pressure as they do to diuretics or calcium channel blockers. *Bottom line:* Prescriptions must be tailored to the individual.

Source: Richard A. Levy, PhD, vice president, National Pharmaceutical Council, Reston, Virginia.

Aspirin Bonus

Regular users of aspirin as a heart attack preventive may be deriving some protection against colorectal cancer, according to a recent Harvard University study. But further studies need to be done before doctors can recommend taking either aspirin or anti-inflammatory pills—both of which seem to ward off cancer. The known self-defenses against colorectal cancer are maintaining a healthy and varied diet (low in fat and rich in fruits, vegetables, whole grains and fiber), exercise and taking diagnostic sigmoid or colonoscopy tests as ordered by your doctor.

Source: Moshe Shike, MD, gastroenterologist and nutritionist at Memorial Sloan-Kettering Cancer Center, New York City.

Acetaminophen Danger

Mixed with alcohol, large doses of this over-the-counter painkiller can cause acute liver failure—even in people with no previously diagnosed liver problems. *Major brands:* Ny-Quil, Panadol, Tylenol.

At greatest risk: Problem drinkers who take acetaminophen throughout the day to relieve pains such as from a headache or toothache.

Source: William M. Lee, MD, professor of internal medicine, University of Texas Southwestern Medical Center, Dallas.

Certain Drugs and Your Senses

Certain drugs can disturb your sense of taste and smell. *Taste:* Metronidazole, clofibrate, ampicillin, tetracycline, nifedipine, captopril, nitroglycerine patch, glipizide. *Smell:* Diltiazem, codeine, streptomycin, amitriptyline.

Helpful: If you suspect a drug of altering your sense of taste or smell, ask your doctor about switching to another drug. *Also:* Drink plenty of fluids. That helps reduce taste/smell side effects.

Source: Susan Schiffman, PhD, professor of medical psychology, Duke University, Durham, North Carolina.

 # Headache Pills Can Cause Headaches

Taking up to the maximum dosage twice a week of over-the-counter pain relievers is usually safe. Taking them more often can worsen symptoms and cause a rebound effect after you decrease or stop medication—so the headache comes back even stronger.

Self-defense: Be especially careful with products containing caffeine and medications with decongestants. They are most likely to cause headache rebound when medication is stopped. If headaches persist, see your doctor.

Source: Robert G. Ford, MD, neurologist and medical director, Ford Headache Clinic, Birmingham, and the author of *Conquer Your Headaches,* International Headache Management, 3918 Montclair Rd., Suite 102, Birmingham, Alabama 35213.

Painkiller Danger

Taken in high doses and for long periods of time, Advil, Nuprin, Motrin, Aleve, Naprosyn, Indocin and other non-steroidal anti-inflammatory drugs (NSAIDs) may cause elevated blood pressure. Often used to treat arthritis, gout and other painful conditions, NSAIDs have long been known to cause small increases in blood pressure. *Now:* A recent study links these drugs to an increased need for antihypertensive therapy, particularly among the elderly. Although the link was found with prescription NSAIDs, users of over-the-counter versions of these drugs often take more—sometimes much more —than the label recommends.

Self-defense: Take only as much of any NSAID as is prescribed or indicated on the label, or switch to Tylenol or another pain reliever containing acetaminophen. Aspirin in low doses has not been linked to increases in blood pressure.

Source: Jerry H. Gurwitz, MD, assistant professor of medicine, Harvard Medical School, Boston. His study of NSAID use among 9,411 Medicaid patients was published in *The Journal of the American Medical Association,* 515 N. State St., Chicago 60610.

Which Painkiller Is Best for You?

With so many brightly colored boxes crowding drugstore shelves these days, choosing an over-the-counter painkiller can be a difficult and frustrating experience.

Just a few years ago, aspirin and acetaminophen (sold primarily under the Tylenol name) were the only choices. Ibuprofen (Advil, Motrin and Nuprin) came next. And now the painkiller naproxen (Aleve) is available over the counter, too.

Which painkiller is right for you? People differ in their response to these drugs, and a medication that works for one problem might not work for another.* It's a good idea to try several ones and see which works best for which conditions.

A look at what's available...

Aspirin:

Bayer aspirin, Bufferin, Excedrin, etc., are very effective for treating headache, fever and muscle pain resulting from overuse, sprains or mild cramps.

Problem: Aspirin can irritate the stomach—even cause it to bleed. It generally should be avoided by people with ulcers or inflammation of the stomach or esophagus.

Special danger: Aspirin can cause a potentially fatal inflammation of the brain called Reye's Syndrome when taken by children with a viral infection like chicken pox. Feverish children under age 16 should never be given aspirin—even baby aspirin. They should be given acetaminophen instead.

Acetaminophen:

It's good for headache and fever—but not so good for muscle or joint pain. It's less irritating to the stomach than any other nonprescription painkiller.

Caution: In higher-than-recommended daily doses, acetaminophen can damage or even destroy the liver. You should take no more than eight extra-strength (500 mg) or 12 regular (325 mg) tablets a day.

Ibuprofen:

Ibuprofen is highly effective against menstrual cramps and other forms of inflammation. It's less irritating to the stomach than aspirin—but more irritating than acetaminophen.

For maximum benefit, take ibuprofen before you start to feel pain. Obviously, you can't predict a headache. But if you always get cramps around the same time of the month, for in-

*Over-the-counter painkillers are appropriate only for minor aches, pains, fever and inflammation. If you're experiencing severe pain, see a doctor.

stance, or if you're preparing for a tough tennis match, consider taking a precautionary dose.

Naproxen:

There's been a lot of hype about naproxen recently. Naproxen is a very effective painkiller. Like ibuprofen, it's much better at controlling toothache pain than aspirin or acetaminophen. And—it lasts for up to 12 hours, as compared with four hours for other nonprescription painkillers.

Naproxen may be a little more expensive than other painkillers. But when you take into account how long it lasts, it's not out of line.

Like aspirin and ibuprofen, naproxen belongs to a family of drugs called nonsteroidal anti-inflammatory drugs (NSAIDs). These drugs are very similar, so if you've had an allergic reaction to aspirin or ibuprofen, you should probably steer clear of naproxen, too.

More about painkillers:

• *Never take more than one type of painkiller at a time.* Doing so can cause severe reactions, including increased stomach irritation, ulcers and bleeding. If the first drug you try doesn't bring relief, wait four hours—or, in the case of naproxen, 12 hours—before trying something else.

• *Avoid alcohol when taking painkillers.* Combining aspirin, ibuprofen or naproxen with alcohol can irritate the stomach—or, in extreme cases, cause bleeding or ulcers. If you typically have more than three drinks a day, talk to your doctor before taking any over-the-counter painkiller.

• *Beware of painkillers labeled "extra-strength."* Such preparations can contain large amounts of caffeine, which can cause sleeplessness and other problems. Read labels carefully before buying.

• *Don't be fooled by "buffered" products.* Consumers often assume that these products—which contain an antacid—are easier on the stomach. Not so. Buffered aspirin is absorbed faster than regular or "enteric-coated" aspirin, but it's no easier on the stomach.

Enteric tablets do protect your stomach against irritation, because they're not absorbed until they reach the intestine. But they take longer to act. So, if you want quick relief for a headache, sprain or fever, nonenteric formulations are probably better.

• *Buy generic.* Generic forms of aspirin, acetaminophen and ibuprofen are just as effective—and much cheaper—than their brand-name counterparts. Naproxen isn't yet available in generic form.

• *Watch out for marketing gimmicks.* Some drug makers attempt to pass off a general-purpose painkiller as a remedy for a specific problem—back pain, for instance. Others claim that their remedy has been endorsed by an independent consumer's group, even though the remedy is identical to remedies that haven't been endorsed. Pain "powders," popular in the South, are nothing more than powdered aspirin or acetaminophen.

Source: Timothy Fagan, MD, associate professor of medicine and pharmacology, University of Arizona College of Medicine, Tucson. He works extensively with painkillers in clinical studies and in his private practice.

Antacid Danger

Orange juice should not be mixed with antacids like Maalox or Amphojel. *Reason:* Orange juice increases the body's absorption of the aluminum in these antacids by as much as tenfold. Consumed on a regular basis, even tiny amounts of aluminum can accumulate in the body and cause health problems. *Rule of thumb:* Wait at least three hours after taking aluminum-containing antacids before drinking orange juice.

Source: *Environmental Nutrition,* 52 Riverside Dr., New York 10024.

Old-Fashioned Remedies Are Still Effective

Leeches and maggots are two icky but effective medical therapies now making a comeback. Leeches are helping reattach severed fingers, toes and limbs. Their saliva has anticoagulant, antibiotic and anesthetic properties. Maggots, applied to wounds, consume dead

tissue while leaving healthy tissue alone. They also excrete an infection-fighting antibacterial substance.

Source: Jane Petro, MD, professor of surgery, New York Medical College, Valhalla.

Extend Your Hospital Stay

Hospital stays can be extended—even when your insurance coverage runs out. *Common route:* Filing an appeal. In some cases, appeals may be too stressful. *Better:* Have a family member speak with the hospital's patient representative, who will contact your insurer and is often successful when your doctor thinks extra days are necessary.

Source: Alexandra Gekas is executive director of the National Society for Patient Representation and Consumer Affairs, One N. Franklin St., Chicago 60606.

Healthier Hearing

A free hearing test can identify hearing problems in your own home. *How it works:* Call 800-222-3277 from 9 AM to 5 PM, EST, Monday through Friday. Request your local Dial-A-Hearing Screening-Test number. Call that number from a quiet room using a corded telephone (not a cordless or cellular phone). A recording will play four tones for each ear. If you don't hear all eight, see a doctor or audiologist.

Source: Occupational Hearing Services, Box 1880, Media, Pennsylvania 19063.

Eye-Exam Danger

Eye dilation may carry some risk for certain people. Dilating the pupils allows your eye doctor to perform a more thorough eye exam and is often recommended, especially for older adults.

Risk: The drugs used for dilation can interact with other medications or impact other health problems.

Important: Discuss any medical conditions with your eye doctor before allowing your eyes to be dilated—especially if you have heart disease or hypertension…take antidepressants… have allergies…or have a history of—or are suspected of having—glaucoma.

Source: Stephen Miller, OD, director, Clinical Care Center, American Optometric Association, St. Louis.

What Everyone Should Know About Medical Consent Forms

For minor ailments, doctors usually presume that their patients consent to treatment. When serious illness is involved, however, your doctor may ask you to sign a "consent form" before proceeding with treatment.

A consent form is a legal document that limits the doctor's liability should something go wrong with your care. It should be a red flag that what the doctor is proposing is risky or experimental.

Examples: Having an invasive test or surgery …or taking a new, unproven drug.

In signing a typical consent form, you limit your ability to sue for malpractice. *Exception:* If your doctor or any other medical personnel are negligent in caring for you, you can sue.

Before signing a consent form…

• *Ask the doctor to explain the risks and benefits of the recommended treatment—and any alternatives to treatment.* Signing the form should merely put in writing what you and the doctor have already discussed and decided.

• *Read the form carefully.* Have the doctor clarify anything you don't understand. *Important:* You have the right to amend the form as you see fit—by jotting in the margins. Indeed, you don't have to sign the form at all. But if you don't—or if the doctor disagrees with your changes—he/she may decline to provide treatment.

• *Request a copy of the form to take home and show to others.* That includes family members, friends or other doctors—even your lawyer, if it should become necessary. Scrutinize the form carefully before signing. If you are too ill to sign the form, a family member can usually sign it on your behalf.

Source: Norman Fost, MD, MPH, director of the medical ethics program and professor of pediatrics at the University of Wisconsin Medical School, Madison. He is the author of an article on medical consent published in the *Journal of the American Medical Association*, 515 N. State St., Chicago 60610.

3

Health Problems—
Health Solutions

The Flesh-Eating Disease...
Protect Yourself and
Your Family

The spate of deaths caused by the "flesh-eating disease" has led some Americans to speculate that we are facing a new epidemic.

In fact, no one knows just how many people are hit by the flesh-eating disease (necrotizing fasciitis). Estimates range from 10,000 to 30,000 cases a year, although no firm statistics are available.

Necrotizing fasciitis is a gruesome ailment. Death can occur within a day or two following the onset of symptoms. So it's essential to know the warning signs—and to seek medical help at the first sign of trouble.

Necrotizing fasciitis is caused by a virulent strain of Streptococcus Group A, a microbe that's responsible for strep throat, rheumatic fever and more.

Here's how to protect yourself from this potentially deadly bacterium.

Necrotizing fasciitis:

In this form of strep A infection, strep bacteria penetrate the skin and produce toxins that rapidly destroy muscle and fat tissue. In many cases, the entry point is a minor wound—a small cut or scrape, a chicken-pox lesion, even a bruise. In other cases, it's not clear how the bacteria get in.

Key symptom: Redness at the injury site, often spreading in streaks up the arm or leg. The area may turn purple or blue. Blisters may appear—a sure sign of advanced infection.

Diagnosis may require surgically opening the skin to examine the underlying tissue. Diseased tissue must be removed.

Toxic shock:

Streptococcal toxic-shock syndrome (strep TSS) is a form of Group A strep infection that causes a precipitous decline in blood pressure—and organ failure. It is most common in individuals between the ages of 20 and 50.

Key symptom: Sudden, severe pain, especially in the extremities. This is often accompanied by chills, fever and/or other flulike symptoms.

Some patients become confused or aggressive or lapse into a coma.

Strep TSS is not the same as toxic-shock syndrome, the disease that received so much media attention 15 years ago. That syndrome is caused by staphylococcus, another common bacterium. It is associated with tampon and intrauterine-device (IUD) use.

Staph TSS kills about one percent of its sufferers. Unlike strep, staph rarely invades the bloodstream or causes tissue destruction.

Mortality from strep TSS can be as high as 70%.

Strep throat:

The most familiar manifestation of strep A infection is strep throat. This superficial infection of the mucous membranes lining the mouth and throat is easily treated with antibiotics.

Danger: If left untreated—or if antibiotic treatment is interrupted—strep throat can lead to serious complications, including...

• *Pneumonia.* This occurs when strep bacteria migrate from the throat to the lungs. Strep-related pneumonia complicated by strep TSS killed puppeteer Jim Henson several years ago.

• *Rheumatic fever.* This strep infection of the heart valves can cause heart failure—and death. Early symptoms, which typically appear several weeks after a sore throat, include muscular aches and pains or swelling of the knees, ankles or wrists. In some cases, the condition goes unnoticed for years—until the heart valves are severely damaged.

• *Impetigo.* This strep infection begins with "crusty skin." Impetigo may spread on the skin but does not invade the skin, so scarring is rare. Without proper treatment, it can progress to kidney failure within several weeks.

Many diseases, one treatment:

The standard treatment for all forms of Group A strep is a course of penicillin or, if the patient is allergic to penicillin, erythromycin or cephalosporin...intravenous antibiotics accompanied by fluid replacement for life-threatening infections...and supplemental oxygen, if necessary. Necrotizing fasciitis typically requires immediate (inpatient) surgery to remove dead tissue. In extreme cases, amputation may be necessary.

Danger: Antibiotics are often ineffective against advanced cases of strep A infection.

How to protect yourself:

Given the low incidence of virulent strep A infection, there's certainly no need to panic every time you get a sore throat.

But since these diseases progress so rapidly, early detection is essential. Notify your doctor if you experience fever and severe deep pain that persists for more than two days. Although such symptoms generally are not cause for alarm, your doctor may decide to monitor you by phone.

Seek medical care immediately if you have...

...streaking or increasing redness at the site of a cut, scratch or sore.

...fever in combination with increasing pain —especially if the pain is in an extremity or at the site of an injury.

Important: If you take antibiotics for any kind of bacterial infection, be sure to finish the entire course of the prescription—even if symptoms disappear. If you fail to take all the pills your doctor prescribed, the antibiotics may fail to eradicate the infection.

Source: Dennis L. Stevens, MD, PhD, professor of medicine at the University of Washington Medical Center in Seattle, and chief of infectious diseases at the Veterans Affairs Medical Center in Boise, Idaho.

Headache Relief

Rub hands together to create heat. Then gently press your palms onto your eyelids.

Source: Joseph Primavera III, PhD, codirector, Comprehensive Headache Center at the Germantown Hospital and Medical Center, Philadelphia.

Headache Danger

Everyone gets a headache occasionally, but sudden changes in frequency, severity or pattern are cause for concern. *Examples:* Morning headaches may be caused by intracrania tumors. Similarly, headaches accompanied by other symptoms such as limb weakness or numbness, vomiting or dizziness could signal a tumor that is interfering with brain function. The sudden onset of an excruciatingly severe headache could be caused by a ruptured brain aneurysm. See a doctor about any unusual symptoms.

Source: Seymour Solomon, MD, director, Montefiore Medical Center Headache Unit, Bronx, New York.

Varicose Veins... Questions and Answers

Just a decade ago, anyone who consulted a doctor about unsightly varicose veins would often have been advised to "live with it."

The only available treatment—surgery—involved large incisions, potentially risky anesthesia and a hospital stay. It was used only in extreme cases—leg ulcers, phlebitis, etc.

Today, 90% of unsightly blue, bulging varicose veins—as well as the tiny "spider veins" that pop up from toe to groin—can be easily removed without surgery.

Varicose veins and spider veins are extremely common, affecting 10% of men and 50% of women in the US. Often, they run in families. If one or both of your parents had varicose veins, the odds are you will, too.

Causes:

What causes varicose veins? Researchers now believe they develop in individuals whose leg veins have weak walls, weak valves or fewer than the normal number of valves. Fewer valves forces the existing valves to work harder, causing them to fail, resulting in visible veins.

Your leg veins help transport blood against the pull of gravity back to the heart—a long haul. When valves located along the saphenous vein—the main vein running along the inside of the calf—fail to open and close properly, blood pools in the legs. The veins bulge under the pressure of the pooled blood and become permanently dilated (varicosed).

Preventing varicose veins:

Although little can be done to prevent varicose veins, certain tactics aimed at improving circulation in the legs can forestall their appearance...

- Get plenty of exercise.
- Don't cross your legs.
- Don't sit or stand for long periods of time. Vary your position.
- Maintain an ideal weight.
- Elevate your legs when you sit or sleep.

Treatment options:

The first step in treating varicose veins is to determine how many veins are affected, exactly where they're located and how big they are. To do this, doctors use ultrasound imaging, much like that used to view developing fetuses.

No single treatment is right for everyone. In fact, most people need several different forms of treatment, including...

- *Sclerotherapy.* A chemical solution injected into the vein closes it off, causing the vein to collapse and slowly disintegrate.

Each sclerotherapy session lasts 15 to 30 minutes—time for up to 50 separate injections. All you feel is a slight pinprick.

Following treatment, your leg will be wrapped in an elastic bandage. It must be left in place for several hours. As with the other two forms of therapy, it's important to walk as much as possible in the days following treatment. This helps get your blood circulation going again.

Occasionally, blood leaks into surrounding tissue, causing brown stains that may take several months to fade.

A sclerotherapy solution called polydeconal —now widely used in Europe—should be approved for use in this country in the near future. Especially mild, it seems less likely to cause complications or pigmentation problems.

- *Laser therapy.* Spider veins are eliminated by short, intense bursts of laser light beamed onto the skin. Each 15- to 30-minute laser session—virtually painless—permits "zapping" of multiple spider veins.

Freckle-like dark spots appear around the treated area, but these disappear within two weeks.

On the horizon: A laserlike tool called the *photoderm* uses a broader light spectrum and emits light in longer pulses than a conventional laser. It permits treatment of larger blood vessels and is less likely to damage surrounding tissue.

• *Surgery.* Reserved only for the saphenous vein. Two incisions are required—a one-inch cut just under the pubic hair and a half-inch cut in the lower part of the ankle. Through these incisions the surgeon removes the entire vein.

The surgery takes 30 to 60 minutes. The entire hospital stay is about four hours. The surgery is performed under local, spinal or general anesthesia.

Other than having to change the dressings, little aftercare is involved. Though tiny, the incisions may hurt for a while. Leg bruises and swelling sometimes occur. These last from a few days to a few weeks.

Mini-phlebectomy, a modified surgical technique, can be performed right in the doctor's office. It involves local anesthesia, smaller incisions...and allows you to walk home two hours later. It's an "in-between" treatment—used when sclerotherapy is difficult to perform and surgery is inappropriate.

Source: Luis Navarro, MD, senior clinical instructor of surgery at Mount Sinai Medical Center and director of the Vein Treatment Center, both in New York City. He is the author of *No More Varicose Veins,* Bantam Books, New York.

When to Avoid Chiropractic Treatments

Chiropractic treatments carry a small—but significant—risk of stroke. In a recent survey of 177 neurologists, 21% reported seeing patients who had suffered a stroke following manipulation of the neck. *To avoid trouble:* Ask your chiropractor to avoid rapid, twisting movements of your neck. Avoid chiropractic treatments altogether if you have osteoporosis...a neck injury...a tumor in your neck...a history of stroke or transient ischemic attack (ministroke). *Also:* Avoid neck manipulation if you

experience dizziness when you look up. That suggests impaired blood flow to your brain.

Source: Walter Carlini, MD, PhD, a neurologist in private practice in Medford, Oregon.

How to Heal Back Pain Quickly and Easily

Most back pain stems not from herniated disks or other structural problems, but from an inappropriate response to anger and other negative emotions.

As Snoopy once said, "There's nothing like a little physical pain to keep your mind off your emotional problems."

This kind of back pain is called tension myositis syndrome (TMS). It starts when unpleasant, repressed emotions—anger in particular—threaten to bubble up.

Oxygen deprivation:

If you are unable to deal with anger on a conscious level, your mind will respond by creating a distraction. It instructs the autonomic nervous system to restrict blood flow to the postural muscles and underlying nerves.

Result: A state of mild oxygen deprivation called ischemia. It leads to a host of symptoms, including pain, numbness, tingling and sometimes weakness—in the neck, shoulders, back and limbs. Although the pain is often severe, it doesn't actually damage the body. That's very important to remember.

It's not that people with stress-induced back pain can't cope with their emotions. It's quite the opposite—TMS occurs because they cope too well. They keep a lid on emotions that threaten to interfere with their daily lives.

Many people suffering from back pain are perfectionists. These individuals generate a lot of subconscious anger and anxiety in response to the pressures of everyday life. Intensely competitive, they are accustomed to putting a great deal of pressure on themselves. They often feel as if they have not done enough.

In the 21 years I've been treating back pain, I have found that the key to a speedy recovery is a willingness to accept the idea that the pain is caused by emotional factors—both conscious and unconscious. That's something many patients are unwilling or unable to do.

Caution: Don't simply assume you have TMS. See a doctor for a thorough exam to rule out legitimate physical causes of back pain. *Examples:* Tumors, cancer, certain bone diseases.

If the doctor can find no physical explanation for your pain, you probably have TMS. Even in many cases where there is a structural abnormality, TMS may be responsible for your pain.

The good news for TMS sufferers is that they need not change their personalities, solve all their problems or stop repressing their feelings. Most patients get better—often in as little as four weeks—simply by learning about TMS… and changing their perceptions about their backs.

Pain-relief strategies:

Here's the advice I give my patients with back pain…

• *Disregard familiar back-pain warnings.* Most of us have been warned about "incorrect" ways to bend, lift, sit, stand and lie in bed. Believe it or not, these are all giant myths.

Reality: The back is not a fragile, delicate structure that must be pampered. It is immensely strong. And in most cases—including those involving severe pain—the back is anatomically normal. Yes, you may have pain. But it's not necessarily a back abnormality.

• *Think psychological—not physical.* Any time you experience pain, shift your attention away from the physical—and onto the psychological. *Questions:* Are you worried about a family or financial problem? Is there a recurrent source of irritation in your life? Are you putting yourself under too much pressure? Are you a perfectionist? Do you feel the need to please everyone around you?

If you answer "yes" to any of these questions, you're filling yourself with resentment and possibly rage—two hallmarks of the TMS personality.

When you accept that the pain is simply your mind's attempt to mask these emotional factors, the pain usually stops.

• *Avoid perfectionism.* Since I wrote *Healing Back Pain*, I've become increasingly aware of the role that high expectations—of ourselves and of others—play in back pain.

Also, when we try too hard to be "people-pleasers," to help others, to do things for others, we create severe psychological pressure in ourselves. The internal self resents this enormously. And—that is where the anger comes from.

• *"Talk" to your brain.* This sounds silly, but it works. Let your brain know you are not going to put up with this state of affairs, and you'll find that your back pain quickly dissipates. Many of my patients tell me that by doing this, they can abort an episode of back pain almost immediately.

• *Discontinue all physical treatment.* Anti-inflammatory drugs, heat, massage, specific exercise, acupuncture, physical therapy, learning to relax—all these presuppose a physical disorder. They may offer temporary relief, but unless you get to the root cause—psychological problems—the pain will keep coming back.

• *Don't assume the worst.* Individuals often panic during an acute attack, assuming they will be laid up for days or even weeks. But this attitude only prolongs the pain.

Better: If necessary, remain in bed and take a strong painkiller. But even if temporarily bedridden, keep testing your ability to move around. Resume physical activity as soon as possible—not only walking and other gentle activities, but also bending, lifting, jogging, playing tennis, etc.

One success story:

One patient whom I had successfully treated for low back pain two years previously called recently to say she had developed pain in her neck, shoulder and arms. She blamed this pain on an emotional problem involving her husband and teenage stepdaughter…but she was unwilling to address the matter directly. *Result:* Her pain gradually worsened until it was difficult to move her arms.

One day she decided to face the problem squarely and confront her husband. When she did, they found a quick and surprisingly easy solution. *Result:* The situation was defused and her pain disappeared.

Most of my back-pain patients are able to sort through their emotional problems on their own. Others need the help of a psychologist. In general, I recommend counseling for back-pain sufferers whose symptoms fail to improve after six weeks.

To stay focused:

I remind my patients that staying focused on their goal of eliminating back pain is crucial to their ultimate success. *A few reminders:*

•The pain is due to TMS, not to a structural abnormality.

•The direct reason for the pain is mild oxygen deprivation (ischemia).

•TMS is a harmless condition, caused by my repressed emotions.

•The principal emotion is repressed anger.

•TMS exists only to distract my attention from the emotions.

•Since my back is basically normal there is nothing to fear.

•Physical activity is not dangerous.

•I must resume all normal physical activity.

•I will not be concerned or intimidated by the pain.

•I will shift my attention from the pain to emotional issues.

•I intend to be in control—and not let my subconscious mind control me.

•I must think psychological at all times, not physical.

Source: John Sarno, MD, professor of clinical rehabilitative medicine, New York University School of Medicine, New York. He is the author of *Healing Back Pain*, Warner Books, New York.

Beware of Tap Water And Contact Lenses

Tap water may contain organisms that contaminate contact lenses and cause severe infections to lens wearers. *Self-defense:* Use prepared contact-lens solutions. Be sure to clean and disinfect your lenses every time you remove them for storage.

Source: Melvin Schrier, OD, optometrist in private practice in New York.

Latest Tap Water Risk

Cryptosporidium is a microscopic organism that can cause serious intestinal disease in people with kidney problems, those who are HIV-positive and others with weak immune systems. New regulations require water companies to filter particles more thoroughly than before—since cryptosporidium can "hide" in particles. If your water company issues an alert, boil all water that you ingest for at least one minute (for drinking, cooking, brushing teeth, washing produce, etc.)…or use bottled water.

Dilemma: What do you do when there is no known cryptosporidium problem? A company's filtration system may not always be working optimally…and current cryptosporidium tests are not as accurate as they could be. It seems extreme to advise that everyone take precautions all the time—especially since in healthy individuals ingesting cryptosporidium is not that severe—causing a bout of diarrhea, nausea and abdominal pain that is resolved completely within one to two weeks.

Bottom line: Unless you're in a high-risk group, taking defensive measures all the time is a personal choice.

Source: Richard P. Maas, PhD, is director of the Environmental Quality Institute, one of the largest research centers on tap-water purity in the US, and associate professor of environmental studies, University of North Carolina, Asheville.

Five-Day Plan for Overcoming Insomnia

One in every three adults has trouble falling or staying asleep. If you're one of them, you're probably all too familiar with the anti-insomnia basics…

•Avoid alcohol for two hours before bedtime.

•Avoid caffeine and tobacco for six hours before bedtime.

•Use your bed only for sleeping and sex, not for reading, eating, etc.

•Don't exercise, have heated discussions or engage in other stimulating activities close to bedtime.

If you've tried those steps to no avail, a shift in how you think about sleep—plus a few specific techniques—should pave the way to more restful slumber. Apply them faithfully, and you're likely to see a difference in just five nights.

•Don't try to sleep. The more you pursue a good night's rest, the more elusive that rest becomes. So stop trying so hard. Be more passive. *Think of sleep as…*

…a gentle force that will overcome you if you let it.

…an ocean wave. You're a surfer. Get into position and wait.

…a friend who will soon visit. If you make the proper preparations, she's sure to drop in—perhaps unexpectedly.

•Eliminate muscle tension. When you climb into bed, your muscles should be totally relaxed, your breathing slow, rhythmic and deep. If not, use deep breathing to promote relaxation. *What to do:*

1. Inhale slowly through your nose. Count to five as you feel the air inflate first your abdomen, then your chest. Breathe out just as slowly.

2. As you inhale, become aware of tension in your upper chest, arms, neck and head. As you exhale, feel the tension go.

3. As you breathe in again, feel the tension in your abdomen and lower chest. Breathe out and let it go.

4. Feel the tension in your legs and lower body, and release it.

Practice relaxation on a daily basis—outside of bxed. If you make the mistake of trying it out when you're anxious about sleep, you're likely to stay tense…and to associate the technique itself with muscular tension.

•Relax your mind. If racing thoughts or intrusive worries keep you awake, a calming mental image will help drive them away.

Image I: You're lying on an air mattress in a tropical sea. The waves are lapping softly all around you, and you can feel the light, warm breeze on your skin.

Image II: You're walking down a curving staircase or riding down an escalator. As you descend, you sink deeper and deeper into relaxation. When you reach the bottom, doors open and you walk into a beautiful, sunlit garden.

•Rethink your attitude toward noise. It's not so much blaring sirens, loud music and other sounds that disrupt your sleep—it's your own sense of anger and irritation at being exposed to these sounds when you're trying to sleep. If your bedroom is noisy, you must contend with two enemies—the noise itself, and the emotional turmoil it can cause.

Self-defense: Substitute calming thoughts for the negative ones you usually experience.

Example I: Instead of "The traffic here is so noisy. I hate it!"…think "It's a loud, lively neighborhood all right. But I can get used to a little noise."

Example II: Instead of "Why do the neighbors—those inconsiderate fools—play music so late?"…think "This is just one night. I'll switch on a fan to cover up the noise."

Earplugs not only block out noise, they give you a sense of control that lowers your anxiety level—whether you choose to use them or not.

•Buy a bigger bed. The average person shifts position a dozen times during the course of a night. Your bed partner may disturb your sleep without your being aware of it. A double bed is too small for two adults. *Better:* Two twin beds, pushed together…or two twin mattresses on one box spring. If all else fails, get separate beds.

•Get regular exercise. Try to work out for at least 30 minutes, four times a week. *Best time:* Late afternoon or early evening, five to six hours before bedtime.

Payoff: A workout that boosts your heart rate also raises your body temperature. Five or six hours later, your temperature will rebound to a level below normal. This slight reduction in body temperature is very conducive to sleep.

A hot bath produces the same temperature-lowering effect. However, it works best two to three hours before bedtime.

Caution: If you go to bed within two hours of exercising, your body temperature will still be above normal when you close your eyes. That makes falling asleep more difficult.

•Consider sleep restriction. Paradoxically, one of the best ways to get good sleep is to restrict the amount of time you spend in bed. Spend fewer hours in bed, and you will fall asleep faster and awaken less during the night. You'll spend more time in the deep, restorative stages of sleep and less in the lighter stages.

•Keep a "sleep log" to figure out how long you actually sleep. Note when you fall asleep, how long you're awake during the night, and when you awaken in the morning.

If you're getting about six hours of sleep right now, count back six hours from when you plan to get up, and don't go to bed before then. If you have to get up at 6 AM, for example, go to bed at midnight.

Gradually extend your time in bed. Go to bed at 11:30, and see if your sleep remains sound. Then go to bed earlier, if you want. Experiment to learn what bedtime works best for you.

•Use your new-found time. Use the hour or more that you formerly spent tossing and turning to clean out a drawer, read a book, watch a video, etc. Doing so puts a positive spin on sleep restriction. Instead of lying there wishing you could sleep, you make productive use of the time.

Caution: Avoid activities that are physically or emotionally arousing. Tackling a career project just before bedtime usually isn't a good idea.

•Relax about sleeping less. Many people assume that if they don't get a full night's sleep, they'll make themselves vulnerable to illness or unable to do their job.

In fact, losing an hour or two of sleep has virtually no negative consequences. If you're alert during the day, you're getting enough sleep at night.

But if you feel chronically sleepy in the daytime, then ask your doctor to refer you to a sleep disorders center at a good hospital. Daytime drowsiness may be caused by a potentially serious sleep disorder such as sleep apnea, a form of disturbed breathing.

As long as you keep from becoming anxious or depressed over your sleep loss, it will harm neither your job performance nor your health.

•Every day, get out of bed at the same time. Other than avoiding caffeine, alcohol and nicotine before bedtime, waking up at the same time each day will do more to improve the quality of sleep than any other step you can take. Establishing a regular daily pattern strengthens your sleep-wake rhythms.

Common mistake: Sleeping late on weekends. Appealing as this may be, it can perpetuate problems by disrupting your sleep rhythm. If you get up late Saturday and Sunday mornings, you won't be sleepy at your usual bedtime on Sunday night. Even people who usually sleep easily are often plagued by "Sunday night insomnia."

If you really want to sleep in on Sunday morning, stay up Sunday night until you're sleepy. If you sleep less than usual, it won't hurt you.

If you find it hard to get up and stay up at the appointed hour, lighten up—literally. Exposing your retinas to bright light cues your body to make the transition from sleep to waking. Interior lights generally aren't bright enough to do the trick. Instead, go outside into daylight…or spend 20 to 30 minutes next to a sunny window.

What about naps? Some people find that daytime napping disrupts the sleep-wake rhythm, exacerbating their nighttime problems. But for about 20% of people, knowing that they can count on an extra 30 minutes of sleep helps reduce their anxiety about insomnia.

If you nap now, try skipping it for a day or two. If you've been avoiding naps, try one.

Source: James Perl, PhD, a psychologist in private practice in Boulder, Colorado. Dr. Perl is the author of *Sleep Right in Five Nights: A Clear and Effective Guide for Conquering Insomnia,* William Morrow & Company, Inc., New York.

How to Beat Insomnia

Do you take too long to fall asleep…toss and turn all night…wake up often or much too early?

More than 100 million Americans have trouble sleeping. During the day, they feel tired and irritable, doze off at inappropriate times or can't concentrate. Their problem is insomnia—nonsleep.

Lack of sleep qualifies as insomnia only if a person wants to sleep more but is unable to fall asleep or stay asleep...and if lack of sleep regularly disturbs a person's daytime mood and energy level.

For some people, three hours of sleep a night is enough, while others need ten. *Average sleep per night:* Seven and a half hours.

Like pain, insomnia is a symptom—not a disease. *Possible causes:*

• *Psychological problems.* Anxiety and depression top the list. Psychological stress causes more than half of the cases of chronic insomnia.

• *Medical problems.* Arthritis, back pain, indigestion, etc., can keep you awake. So can breathing difficulties, from allergies and asthma to a nonstop cough. *Other health considerations...*

• *Drugs.* Prescription or nonprescription medications containing caffeine, ephedrine, aminophylline, norepinephrine or amphetamine frequently disturb sleep.

Examples: Some antidepressants...high blood pressure medications...muscle relaxants ....diet pills...bronchodilators (for asthma)...diuretics (to increase urination)...painkillers (Excedrin, Anacin, Midol, others)...steroids...thyroid preparations...cancer chemotherapy drugs.

Some medications that don't cause insomnia by themselves may do so when taken in combination with others. Make sure all your doctors —and your pharmacist—know all the drugs you're taking.

Important: Don't stop taking any prescription drug without first discussing your insomnia with your doctor.

• *Apnea.* During sleep, some people stop breathing for ten to 90 seconds at a time, then jerk awake—many times a night. This potentially dangerous condition is called apnea. If you think this may be happening to you, get an evaluation at a sleep-disorders center. Snoring is often associated with apnea. *Ways to relieve snoring:* Lose weight...sleep with your head elevated on pillows...never sleep on your back. More than 300 patented antisnoring devices are on the market, but these suggested steps are usually enough to alleviate snoring.

• *Restless-legs syndrome.* This is a powerful urge to move the legs all night. You may suffer from this if you notice that your sheets and blankets are all over the place in the morning or if your partner complains that you're kicking all night.

Often helpful: Avoid caffeine...exercise... with your doctor's approval, take iron, calcium, folic acid and vitamin E supplements—but usually prescription drugs are necessary to suppress restless legs.

• *Lifestyle factors.* Any of these can disturb your sleep...

• Drinking more than two cocktails, beers or glasses of wine a day.

• Abusing narcotics.

• Drinking coffee, tea or cola in the afternoon or evening.

• Smoking cigarettes.

• Severe stress at home or at work.

• Taking life too seriously.

• Not exercising.

• *Poor sleep habits.* It's easy to get in a rut and perpetuate habits that fight sleep. Bed can become a sexual battlefield—or a symbol of the frustrating failure to sleep. Some people sleep well only on weekends or anywhere except in their own beds.

Curing your own insomnia:

More than 80% of insomniacs can overcome their problems by identifying the causes and taking steps to eliminate them.

• *Keep a daily sleep log and day log.* In the sleep log, write the length of any naps you take, sleeping medications taken, what time you turned out the lights, how long you think it took you to fall asleep, total minutes awake all night, how often you woke, when you got up, total hours slept and how refreshing your sleep was.

In the day log, indicate the amount and type of exercise you did, any incidents—or thought of those incidents—that have upset you. Also record what and when you ate and drank—particularly high-sugar foods and caffeine—as well as medications taken.

After a week or two, choose your two best and two worst nights. Think about why you identified them that way. Can you make any changes to repair the situation?

• *Reduce caffeine.* Drinking a can of cola or cup of coffee in the late afternoon may keep you awake at midnight. Sensitivity to caffeine can increase with age. Anyone's sleep can be disturbed by having more than three cups of coffee or cola or several pain pills containing caffeine a day. Those amounts can be addictive, too.

• *Limit alcohol.* Late-night drinking will cause your sleep to be troubled and fragmented. Reliance on alcohol could also lead to dependency. And never mix alcohol with sleeping pills.

• *Don't smoke.* Nicotine is a stimulant. Insomnia is among smokers' greatest complaints. Cigarettes raise blood pressure, speed up heart rate and stimulate brain-wave activity, making it hard to relax. Smokers tend to wake up in the middle of the night, possibly experiencing nicotine withdrawal.

Sleeping hints:

• *Avoid sleeping pills.* They can be habit-forming. When you stop taking them, withdrawal may worsen your problem.

• *Spend less time in bed.* You'll end up with more hours of satisfactory sleep. Try the Bootzin technique for a few weeks: Whenever you are in the bed worrying about sleeping, get out of bed and do something else until you feel sleepy again. You'll be conditioning yourself to associate your bed with sleep rather than with nonsleep.

• *Find interesting things to do.* It's necessary to have at least a moderately exciting day in order to sleep soundly. Join a social group, do volunteer work or get involved in a community project.

• *Allow time to wind down.* Trade massages with a family member. Work on a crossword puzzle. Make love.

• *Keep a regular schedule.* Try to go to bed at roughly the same time each night. Then no matter how long you slept, get up at your usual time in the morning.

• *Exercise.* Aim for 20 minutes of exercise that increases your heart rate at least three times a week. Late afternoon is best.

• *Try napping.* Short naps (up to 30 minutes in the afternoon) help about one in five insomniacs. At night, they are less anxious since they've already slept some.

Caution: For four out of five insomniacs, naps are a mistake. Experiment. You'll know in about a week whether naps help or hinder your sleep at night.

• *Set yourself up for sleep.* Success may be as simple as buying a new mattress, installing room-darkening shades, creating "white noise" (by turning the radio dial between two FM stations), taking a warm bath before bedtime or having a light snack before bed.

Sleep-disorders centers:

Although sleep disorders are among the most common problems that doctors encounter, few know how to treat them—most have spent only about two hours on the subject in medical school. Insomnia is often misinterpreted as anemia, a thyroid disorder or laziness. For many people, a sleep-disorders center is the answer.

Sleep-disorders centers can provide the competent staff, advanced testing equipment and helpful counseling techniques needed to find the root of your problem. Such centers help four out of five people with sleeping problems in general and three out of four with insomnia.

Anyone can open a sleep lab. Some are run by quacks, but many are excellent. The American Sleep-Disorders Association (1610 14 St. NW, Rochester, Minnesota 55901, 507-287-6006) has accredited hundreds of centers nationwide. Ask the association to recommend a center near you.

Source: Peter Hauri, PhD, director of the insomnia program and codirector of the Sleep-Disorders Center, both at the Mayo Clinic, Rochester, Minnesota. Dr. Hauri established one of the first clinical sleep-disorders centers in the US and was a cofounder of the American Sleep-Disorders Association. He is the co-author of *No More Sleepless Nights*, John Wiley & Sons, Inc., New York.

How to Beat Chronic Fatigue

Of all the ailments that bring patients to my office these days, fatigue is the most common. Many people suffering from exhaustion are convinced that they have chronic fatigue syndrome (CFS). This still-mysterious ailment is a real disease. But most cases of fatigue aren't even close to CFS.

Recently, a young woman dragged herself into my office—depressed and too tired to work. She was convinced that she had a terrible disease. Initially, she insisted that sleep was no problem. But when I questioned her closely, she admitted that she was having trouble falling asleep. And she was waking up several times a night to go to the bathroom—the result of a four-cup-a-day tea habit. She also complained of nighttime neck pain.

This woman had expected the tea's caffeine to boost her energy. But as a mild diuretic, all it did was disrupt her sleep, leaving her even more tired the following day. I urged her to avoid tea after 4 PM and prescribed a mild painkiller. And—she's improving.

This is a typical story. People start feeling tired for a variety of simple reasons. Then, in an attempt to overcome their fatigue, they make lifestyle choices that start them on a downward spiral.

They gulp down caffeinated beverages. They eat whatever's "easy," giving up on healthful meals that might be harder to prepare. They stop exercising, not realizing that exercise boosts energy levels. Eventually fatigue gives way to depression—itself a leading cause of fatigue.

If you did have CFS, you'd find it hard to work for even two hours a day, much less slog through a 40-hour workweek. See your doctor for a complete physical just in case—especially if six or more of the following symptoms show up abruptly...

- Persistent mild fever.
- Sore throat.
- Swollen glands.
- Muscle weakness.
- Muscle pain.
- Prolonged fatigue after exercise.
- Frequent headaches.
- Migrating joint pain.
- Memory problems or confusion.
- Sleep problems.

If your doctor determines that you do have CFS, he/she may recommend low-dose antidepressants and a minimal exercise program. *Also:* Contact the National Chronic Fatigue Syndrome Association, 3521 Broadway, Suite 222, Kansas City, Missouri 64111 (816-931-4777). Ask about CFS support groups in your area. Read *The Doctor's Guide to Chronic Fatigue Syndrome* by Harvard physician Dr. David Bell (Addison-Wesley, One Jacob Way, Reading, Massachusetts 01867).

If you don't meet the criteria for CFS, consider what else might be causing your fatigue. *Examples:* Too little sleep...misuse of coffee, nicotine or other stimulants...lack of exercise ...allergies...chronic congestion...indoor air pollution...ongoing psychological stress. Your doctor should test you for anemia, thyroid disease, Lyme disease, lupus, diabetes and other illnesses that can cause fatigue.

Avoid caffeine and alcohol for at least four hours before bedtime. A drink at dinner time is OK, but after that it's best to avoid alcohol. It disrupts the dream cycle and dries out your mouth.

Make sure your pillow, sheets and especially your mattress are comfortable. If you have a restless bedmate, consider investing in a king-size bed. Keep the room at a comfortable temperature. If necessary, use ear plugs and an eye mask.

If you snore, tell your doctor. Snoring is often associated with sleep apnea, a condition in which the sleeper awakens briefly countless times a night—without ever realizing it.

There are several ways to control apnea—from weight loss or surgery to the use of special respirator-like machines at night. In some cases, all it takes is a tennis ball sewn into the back of your pajamas. That keeps you from sleeping on your back—the position associated with snoring.

Source: Bruce H. Yaffe, MD, is an internist and gastroenterologist in private practice, 121 E. 84 St., New York 10028.

Heart Attack/Salt Connection

Cutting back on salt reduces the chance of a heart attack. High sodium intake is associated with enlargement of the heart muscle, which increases the risk of heart attack. When patients with enlarged hearts cut their sodium consumption to 1,600 milligrams a day, their blood pressure declined and so did the size of their heart muscles.

Source: Richard Devereux, MD, is professor of medicine at Cornell University Medical College, New York City.

Heart-Attack Death Risk Reduced

Cholesterol-reducing drugs do reduce risk of dying of heart disease in patients who've suffered a heart attack. In the first study of its kind, patients given the drug simvastatin (Zocor) had a 30% lower risk of dying prematurely from any cause, and a 42% lower risk of dying from coronary heart disease than those given a placebo. *Also:* The simvastatin group had 37% and 34% fewer bypass operations and major coronary problems, respectively.

Source: Terje R. Pedersen, MD, head, critical-care unit, Aker Hospital, Oslo, Norway. His study of 4,444 heart-attack and angina patients, age 35 to 70, was published in *The Lancet,* 42 Bedford Square, London WC1B 3SL, England.

One in Ten Heart Attacks Is Painless

These attacks can be just as deadly as conventional attacks, which cause severe chest pain. *Symptoms:* Arm numbness or shoulder pain that is unrelated to injury or exertion…nausea…weakness…breathlessness…drenching sweat…dizziness…rapid heartbeat. If several of these symptoms occur simultaneously to someone at high risk, seek immediate medical help. *At high risk:* Smokers, men over 60, people with high cholesterol.

Source: Mark Perlroth, MD, professor of medicine, Stanford University Medical Center, Stanford, California.

Post–Heart-Attack Treatment

For many patients, especially those with no further symptoms after their attacks, there is frequently no added survival benefit—but very high expense—to procedures that open blocked blood vessels. Many doctors, however, perform cardiac catheterization, balloon angioplasty or bypass surgery increasingly often on heart-attack patients.

Self-defense: Always ask whether any further treatment is really needed. *If you're over age 65:* Experts had been concerned about the use of thrombolytic drugs to break down blood clots in older heart-attack patients. *New findings:* They are beneficial…and often eliminate the need for operations.

Source: Mark McClellan, MD, PhD, is faculty research associate in the department of health-care policy, Harvard University School of Medicine, Boston.

Bypass Surgery— Who Really Needs It?

The number of heart bypass operations performed in the US is soaring—from 20,000 in 1971…to 200,000 in 1987…to an estimated 400,000 this year.

For individuals whose heart vessels are so blocked that they feel chest pain (angina) even while resting, bypass surgery can be a lifesaver. But estimates are that up to half of bypass operations may be unnecessary—exposing patients to needless expense and risk of death.

Self-defense: If a doctor recommends bypass surgery for you, be sure to get a second opinion if…

…you feel no chest pain while resting.

…you feel slight chest pain only when you exert yourself—when running to catch a bus or taking a hike up a hill, for instance.

In these instances, medications and lifestyle changes—quitting smoking, exercising more and eating less fat—are better.

Why? Because although generally safe, bypass surgery is not without risk. Two percent of patients younger than 70 who undergo bypass die from the surgery, and 3% to 4% of people older than 70 die.

And bypass surgery is only a quick fix. Heart vessels can clog up again—especially if lifestyle changes aren't made.

Don't get a second opinion from another doctor in your own doctor's practice or HMO. *Better:* A doctor who practices at a local hospital —especially one that's affiliated with the cardiology department of a university.

If bypass surgery is necessary, shop around. Surgeons and hospitals that do the most bypass surgery procedures have the best survival rates.

Helpful: US News & World Report's annual guide to the best hospitals in America, published in the magazine each July. For a reprint of the most recent guide, send a $2 check or money order to *US News & World Report* Reprints, 2400 N St. NW, Washington, DC 20037, 202-955-2398.

Source: Thomas B. Graboys, MD, associate professor of medicine at Harvard Medical School and director of the Lown Cardiovascular Center at Brigham and Women's Hospital, both in Boston.

Silent Heart Disease

"Silent" heart disease is now the leading cause of sudden death in the US. Fortunately, there are ways to defend yourself against this insidious and often lethal illness.

Heart disease occurs when there is a reduction in blood flow to the heart—which, in turn, is usually caused by the accumulation of fatty material in one or more coronary arteries. This process of oxygen starvation is known as myocardial ischemia.

At one time, doctors believed that a coronary artery had to be almost completely occluded before the heart sustained any damage. Now it's clear that significant damage can occur even with partial blockage.

A blockage in the coronary arteries can cause a variety of symptoms—from simple angina (chest pain) and palpitations to a full-blown heart attack. But up to 80% of these episodes of ischemia are silent—that is, they produce no pain or any other symptoms. For every chest pain a person experiences, he/she may have four periods of silent myocardial ischemia (SMI).

SMI can occur at any time. It can last just a few seconds, or go on for several hours.
Who gets silent ischemia?

There are four key risk factors…

1. Cigarette smoking. Smokers are ten times more likely than nonsmokers to suffer a heart attack.

2. High blood pressure. Sixty million Americans have it.

3. Elevated blood cholesterol.

4. Family history of premature heart disease.

Other, less significant risk factors for SMI include being over 40…being male…being obese…having diabetes…being under severe psychological stress…not getting regular exercise. The more risk factors you have, the greater your risk.

Although he loved to exercise, the well-known runner and author Jim Fixx was at very high risk for silent ischemia. He was a 52-year-old former smoker with high cholesterol and a family history of heart disease.

Self-defense strategies:

•If you smoke, stop.

•Keep blood pressure and cholesterol in check. If they're elevated, make an effort to lose weight, get regular exercise, avoid excessive intake of alcohol and use meditation or another form of stress relief.

In some cases, cutting back on your intake of salt lowers blood pressure. Cutting out fatty, cholesterol-rich foods is good for your cholesterol levels, too. In fact, many scientists strongly recommend becoming a vegetarian to prevent or even reverse coronary-artery disease. Your total cholesterol level should be below 200.

Your LDL (bad) cholesterol should be no higher than 130.

If these measures fail, you'll probably need to take antihypertensive and/or cholesterol-lowering medication.

• *Reduce psychological stress.* Try to maintain your sense of humor. Learn to delegate responsibility, and take comfort from friends and family.

Helpful exercise: Close your door, disconnect the phone and sit quietly. Visualize a color...or repeat a mantra. Do this once or twice a day for five or 10 minutes each time.

• *If you're diabetic, keep your blood sugar under strict control.* Use diet, follow a weight-reduction plan and take medication.

Screening for silent ischemia:

If you're 40 or older and have one or more risk factors for SMI, see your doctor for a complete physical examination. *Also:* Request a treadmill stress test.

This test—in which an electrocardiogram is taken as the patient runs at increasing speeds on a treadmill—is the single most reliable nonsurgical screening procedure for diagnosing coronary artery disease.

If the stress test reveals heart disease, your doctor will probably prescribe nitrates, beta blockers or calcium-channel blockers. Depending on how many risk factors you have, you may want to get tested every few years.

Stress tests are offered by most cardiologists and many primary-care doctors. Unless you're already experiencing symptoms of heart disease, they are usually not covered by health-insurance plans.

Source: Harold L. Karpman, MD, clinical professor of medicine and a cardiologist at the University of California, Los Angeles School of Medicine. He is the author of *Preventing Silent Heart Disease: How to Protect Yourself from America's #1 Killer*, Henry Holt, New York.

Benefit for Rheumatoid-Arthritis Sufferers

Rheumatoid-arthritis sufferers may benefit from gammalinolenic acid (GLA), a fatty sub-stance found in the seeds of evening primrose and borage plants. It reduced joint tenderness by 40% and joint pain by 15%. Side effects—uncommon—included mild constipation, flatulence and diarrhea.

GLA has not yet been officially recognized as a therapy for any ailment, but it is available in many health-food and drug stores. *Important:* Consult a doctor before taking GLA.

Source: L.J. Leventhal, MD, clinical assistant professor of medicine and associate chief of rheumatology, The Graduate Hospital, University of Pennsylvania, Philadelphia.

Most Common Cause of Gum Recession

Brushing too hard is the most common cause of gum recession. The front six top and bottom teeth are most vulnerable.

Self-defense: Use a soft-bristled brush. Hold it gently with your thumb and index finger as if gripping a pencil. Ask your dentist to show you how hard to brush.

Source: Robert Pick, DDS, MS, associate clinical professor of periodontics, Northwestern University Dental School, Chicago, speaking at a meeting of the American Academy of General Dentistry, 211 E. Chicago Ave., Suite 1200, Chicago 60611.

Much Better Dental X-Ray Method

Computed Dental Radiography (CDR) cuts radiation exposure by between 40% and 90% (exposure varies with the type of X-ray unit the dentist uses). The images can appear immediately on a computer screen. The dentist can enlarge—up to six times—and sharpen the picture...then print out the image. This is especially important for patients who need frequent X rays during complex procedures, such as root canal...or pregnant women who have dental emergencies. *Cost:* About 35% more than conventional X rays. It is covered by insurance to the extent that X rays are covered by each respective policy.

Source: Alan Winter, DDS, is associate clinical professor of dentistry, New York University School of Dentistry, and partner, Park Avenue Periodontal Associates, 30 E. 60 St., Suite 302, New York 10022.

Alzheimer's Disease Predictor

Dementia—including that caused by Alzheimer's disease—can now be predicted up to four years in advance. Subjects are asked to memorize and then recall a series of words and objects. Each subject must rapidly name objects within a category, such as vegetables, and quickly find and copy a series of symbols. Given to those in their 70s and 80s, these neurological tests are better at predicting who will not develop dementia, rather than identifying those who will.

Source: David Masur, PhD, associate clinical professor of neurology, Albert Einstein College of Medicine and Montefiore Medical Center, New York City.

Life-Saving News About Strokes

Each year, 500,000 Americans suffer a stroke. Roughly one third of these individuals die. For many of the two thirds who survive, the process of rehabilitation is long, frustrating—and often unsuccessful.

Until quite recently, there was little doctors could do to help stroke victims. Strokes seemed to strike out of the blue, and a patient's chances of full recovery seemed to depend almost as much upon luck as upon medical intervention.

Now: There are real strategies for preventing and treating strokes. And as long as the patient gets immediate medical attention, many strokes that would have been debilitating or even fatal just a few years ago can be stopped before they cause permanent brain damage. Tremen-

dous progress is also being made in stroke rehabilitation.

John R. Marler, MD, a clinical research administrator in the division of stroke and trauma at the National Institute of Neurological Disorders and Stroke answers questions to explain the latest breakthroughs.

• *What causes a stroke?* Strokes occur when blood circulation is cut off to a section of the brain, causing brain cells in the affected area to die. *This happens in one of two ways...*

•A blood clot lodges in a blood vessel in the brain. A stroke of this type is called an ischemic stroke.

•A blood vessel in the brain bursts. This is called a hemorrhagic stroke. Ischemic stokes are five times more common than hemorrhagic strokes.

Either way, the part of your mind or body controlled by the affected brain cells—your ability to move, feel, talk or think—is temporarily or permanently impaired.

• *What can I do to prevent a stroke?* There is now incontrovertible evidence linking stroke to high blood pressure and to smoking. You can protect yourself by not smoking...and by keeping your blood pressure under control.

Blood pressure can be reduced via weight loss, diet, exercise or medication—or some combination of these. If you don't know what your blood pressure is, ask your doctor to check it.

If you're still smoking, stop. *Good news:* Many people who've had trouble quitting in the past are finding success with nicotine patches.

• *Is it true that aspirin helps prevent stroke?* Recent studies suggest that taking aspirin on a daily basis cuts the risk of stroke by 10% to 60%, depending upon the other risk factors you have.

Self-defense: If you're 50 or older and you're not already taking aspirin as a way to prevent stroke and/or heart disease, ask your doctor if you could benefit from aspirin.

• *What role does cholesterol play?* Keeping your cholesterol and triglyceride levels within normal limits—via diet and/or cholesterol-lowering drugs—helps prevent stroke by keeping fatty plaques from building up in your arteries.

This plaque-buildup process, called atherosclerosis, is similar to the one that leads to blockage of coronary arteries. In fact, because the disease process leading to ischemic stroke is similar to that leading to heart attack, such strokes are essentially heart attacks of the brain.

Finally, diabetics are two to four times more likely than non-diabetics to suffer a stroke. *Reason:* They tend to get atherosclerosis and its attendant problems. If you have diabetes, you can lower your risk of stroke by following your doctor's advice on weight loss, diet, exercise and medication.

• *What other conditions indicate an increased risk of stroke?* One common condition is a bruit (pronounced BROO-ee). This is a whooshing sound made by blood as it flows through an artery—typically the carotid artery in the neck—that's been partially clogged by fatty plaque.

You cannot always hear a bruit yourself, but a doctor can—by placing a stethoscope over your carotid artery. The presence of a bruit suggests that the artery may be dangerously narrowed. Unless steps are taken to remove the blockage, you're more likely to have a stroke.

Another common warning condition: An irregular heartbeat. This condition, atrial fibrillation, can cause formation of blood clots that can cause stroke.

• *What if I have one of these conditions?* If you have atrial fibrillation, ask your doctor about thinning your blood by taking either aspirin or the prescription anticoagulant warfarin (Coumadin).

If your doctor discovers that you have a bruit—or if you have other risk factors for stroke—consider having Doppler ultrasound. This exam—similar to that used by obstetricians to examine fetuses—enables doctors to determine just how badly blocked the artery really is.

If the carotid artery is blocked by 60% or more, your doctor may recommend an endarterectomy. In this procedure, a surgeon slices open your artery, removes the plaque and then sews it shut again.

Before you agree to an endarterectomy, be sure to get a second, or even a third, opinion.

Trap: Not all medical centers are adept at performing Doppler ultrasound. As a result, many patients are told that they need surgery even when they don't.

You want to avoid endarterectomy if at all possible. *Reason:* Even with a highly skilled and experienced surgeon, up to 6% of people who undergo the operation have a stroke and/or die on the operating table.

• *How can I tell if I'm having a stroke?* You probably won't feel any pain, but all of a sudden you will feel one or more of the following...

•Severe weakness in an arm or leg.

•Unexplained numbness in an arm or leg.

•Inability to speak, read or understand what people are saying.

•Partial or complete loss of vision—in one or both eyes.

•Severe clumsiness—an inability to hold a fork, walk, type, etc.

If the symptoms clear up in a few minutes, you've probably had a "mini-stroke," also known as a transient ischemic attack (TIA). Mini-strokes occur when a blood clot forms in the brain but then quickly breaks up on its own...or when an artery in the brain goes into spasm.

Never ignore a mini-stroke. Although it's not necessarily dangerous in its own right, it means that you're at very high risk of having a major stroke. If you've had a TIA, ask your doctor about steps to take to reduce your risk of having "the big one." Typically, this involves taking aspirin or warfarin or having an endarterectomy.

• *What should I do if I think I'm having a stroke?* Call 911 immediately! Even if the symptoms disappear in a few minutes, you'll still need to have a complete and immediate medical evaluation.

Trap: Waiting for your spouse to get home—or for your doctor to return a call—only delays proper treatment. That can mean the difference between life and death.

Although no drugs have been approved specifically for the immediate treatment of stroke, many hospitals are now trying out drugs that thin the blood...dissolve clots...or preserve brain cells from damage.

Some of these drugs have shown great promise. So, if you are at risk of stroke, make it a point to become informed about what is available at hospitals in your area. But to derive any benefit from these drugs, you must get to the hospital right away. Even an hour's delay may be too long.

•*If I have a stroke, how can I improve my odds of recovering?* How quickly—and to what extent—you recover depends in large part on the size and location of the brain damage. However, there are important steps you can take to boost your chances of a speedy—and complete—recovery…

•Seek support from your family and from a good rehabilitation center.

•Use all the resources at your disposal—doctors who specialize in stroke rehabilitation, physical therapists, occupational therapists, speech therapists, etc.

•Join a support group. For information on groups in your area, call the American Heart Association's Stroke Connection at 800-553-6321…or the National Stroke Association at 800-787-6537.

Remember that stroke affects the entire family. Psychological stress is a big problem for stroke patients and their caretakers alike. That's why support groups are so important.

Source: John R. Marler, MD, clinical research administrator, stroke and trauma division, National Institute of Neurological Disorders and Stroke, Bethesda, Maryland.

 Lyme Disease Season

Self-defense: Look very carefully for tiny (two millimeters by three millimeters) black ticks on your body—and on household animals—immediately after coming inside. The ticks are most active from April through June. The primary sign is a large pink-red bull's-eye rash on the skin—at least three inches in diameter—usually around the tick bite. It is often accompanied by fever or flulike symptoms. What seems like a summer flu even without a rash may be a sign. If you see a tick, remove it carefully by grabbing it with fine-pointed tweezers and lifting it straight away from the skin. Be careful not to break it. Look for ticks in the groin area or under the upper line of underwear, under the bra or at the back of the knee.

Parents should check behind children's ears. If Lyme disease develops, early antibiotic treatment is usually effective.

Source: Michael F. Finkel, MD, medical director, Western Wisconsin Lyme Disease Center, Eau Claire.

Annette Funicello Tells How She Copes with Multiple Sclerosis

Seven years ago, I was diagnosed with multiple sclerosis—an often debilitating neurological disorder that causes vision problems, muscle weakness and poor coordination.

At the time, I knew nothing about the illness—and I decided to keep it that way. For several years, I avoided thinking and talking about MS—and kept my diagnosis a secret from everyone but my mother, husband and children. I didn't even tell my father. I thought I could beat MS on my own and no one would ever have to know.

Looking back, I can see that my refusal to learn about my illness and my need to hide it were attempts to fend off fear. Unfortunately, the ignorance and secrecy only fueled my anxiety.

Since then, I've found far more effective ways of coping with MS…and with chronic illness in general. Here's what I wish I'd known earlier…

•*Educate yourself.* Learn as much about your illness as you can—whether it's MS or another chronic ailment.

There are still many unanswered questions about MS—including what causes it, how best to treat it and what any individual's prognosis will be. Yet the more I've learned about MS, the more I realize that there is plenty of good news…

•*MS is not fatal, contagious or hereditary.* That's why I always use the term illness rather than the more frightening word disease when speaking about MS.

•*MS is not always progressive.* The damaged nerve cells that are characteristic of MS sometimes heal on their own, although we're still not sure under what conditions. Roughly three quarters of people with MS experience spontaneous remissions during the course of their illness—and, in some cases, complete relief of symptoms. And researchers are getting close to finding a cure.

Sources of information: Your doctor, your local library and nonprofit organizations such as the National MS Society, 733 Third Ave., Sixth Floor, New York 10017, 800-344-4867. These organizations can put you in touch with support groups and other local resources.

• *Admit you have a problem—and ask for the help and understanding you need.* To convince family and friends that nothing was seriously wrong with me, I became a good liar. When I started having trouble with my balance, for example, I blamed it on tendinitis and a bad knee. Being dishonest with people I cared about sapped my self-esteem.

When you lie, you have to work hard to keep your stories straight. That takes a great deal of energy. It also creates a lot of psychological stress. As someone coping with the symptoms of MS, I certainly didn't need more of that.

I kept my illness secret partly because I didn't want to hurt anyone. But by avoiding people, making excuses and hiding the truth, I suspect I caused them—and myself—even more pain.

I "went public" with my diagnosis in 1992. I wasn't trying to be noble. Reporters from the tabloids had started knocking on neighbors' doors, trying to confirm rumors that my unsteady balance stemmed from a drinking problem. I realized I had to tell the truth—in public—before someone created an ugly story.

Once I did, a huge weight was lifted off my shoulders. There was an outpouring of support from friends and strangers alike. The calls, cards and letters made me realize how much I'd been cheating myself by trying to bear this burden alone.

My family has been wonderful, too. On bad days, when my symptoms flare up, they understand and aren't frightened—and I don't need to hide it.

Having MS has changed the way I view other people's disabilities. I used to feel sorry for wheelchair-bound people and those with other disabilities. Not anymore. I know that I don't want pity…and that people who cope with disability every day are tough. We learn to live with our challenges. We do our best with what we have.

• *Keep busy—but know your limits.* The busier I am, the less time I have to think about my illness. That helps me avoid the temptation of self-pity.

Since my diagnosis, I've launched several business ventures. More important, I started the Annette Funicello Research Fund for Neurological Diseases, which will help finance research into MS and related illnesses.

As busy as I am, I'm careful not to get overtired. In the beginning, I pushed myself too hard. I thought that by refusing to slow down, I could prove that my illness didn't really exist.

Now I rest when I need to. I hold most of my business meetings at home. When I travel, I keep my schedule as light as possible.

What's important is balance. Resting doesn't mean retiring from life.

• *Find ways to cope that work for you.* While I would not presume to tell anyone else how to deal with a chronic illness, I think that sharing information is important. So here are three things I've discovered that help me. Maybe they'll help you or someone close to you, too.

1. *Stay cool.* Because heat exacerbates MS symptoms, it's important to keep body temperature down—especially in summer. My favorite way to keep cool is to suck on crushed ice.

2. *Elevate the legs.* I've found that ten minutes of lying down with a pillow under my knees and lower legs seems to make walking easier. I might do this several times a day.

3. *Follow a healthy lifestyle.* I firmly believe that anything that reduces stress helps fight illness. I feel much better now that I've given up smoking and drinking alcohol. I've also noticed that my symptoms are less bothersome when I eat a low-fat diet.

• *Stay optimistic.* I've tried more than two dozen treatments for MS, from acupuncture to vitamins to various prescription drugs. I discuss everything with my doctor and make sure I understand the risks and side effects of each treatment I try.

I must say that I'm very skeptical of "fad" treatments such as hyperbaric chambers...removing fillings from the teeth...chelation therapy. I keep my spirits up by making the most of my good days, and by remembering how many people are working to solve the puzzle of MS. I take one day at a time, and if one treatment doesn't work, I go on to the next.

So far, nothing has led to a remission. Although that's a little discouraging, I haven't stopped fighting—far from it.

I've always been religious, and my faith has been a great help. I know that my illness has a purpose, even though I don't yet know what that purpose might be.

I take comfort in knowing that the prayers of many loved ones are behind me. I keep a smile on my face—and I never give up hope.

Source: Annette Funicello was a star of the popular 1950s television series, *The Mickey Mouse Club.* She also starred in the motion pictures, *Babes in Toyland* and *The Shaggy Dog,* as well as several beach-party movies with Frankie Avalon.

Ms. Funicello is the recipient of numerous awards, including the Helen Hayes Award, given by Saint Clare's Hospital and Health Center in New York City, in recognition of her professional accomplishments and her efforts to raise public awareness about MS. Her autobiography, *A Dream Is a Wish Your Heart Makes,* was published by Hyperion, 114 Fifth Ave., New York 10011.

Allergy Enemy

Most vacuum cleaners stir up more allergens than they capture, thus helping to trigger allergy attacks. *Helpful:* Microfiltration vacuum cleaner bags, which have a two-ply design to trap even the smallest allergens. Look into a new machine if yours leaks out air (and allergens) through poor gasket seals and fittings. *Look for:* A model with a double-layer dust bag.

Best: An upright model with a heavy outer cloth that has an impermeable covering. *Also consider:* A cleaner with a High-Efficiency Particulate Arresting (HEPA) filter. They're expensive—between $500 and $1,000—but extremely effective at removing allergens.

Source: University of California, *Berkeley Wellness Letter,* Box 412, New York 10012.

Don't Learn to Live with Urinary Incontinence

Whether it involves an occasional drip or daily puddles, urinary incontinence is messy, uncomfortable, embarrassing—and more common than one might expect. Half of all women and one of every five men experience incontinence at some time.

Sadly, the prospect of a public accident leads many people to limit their activities outside the home. So what starts out as an occasional embarrassment turns into a debilitating condition.

Good news: Incontinence can usually be corrected or significantly improved—via special exercises, behavioral training, drugs or surgery. Behavior treatments alone are beneficial for most adults.

Types of urinary incontinence:

•*Urge incontinence.* This type makes it hard to get to the bathroom in time.

Usual causes: Infection of the bladder or urethra...prostate enlargement (common in men older than 50)...thinning of urethral tissues (common in postmenopausal women).

•*Stress incontinence.* Urine is accidentally released when you cough, sneeze, lift something heavy, exercise or do anything else that applies a sudden force to the lower body. Stress incontinence is far more common among women than among men.

Usual causes: Weakness in the tissues that surround and support the bladder and urethra. The urinary sphincter can be weakened by pregnancy—the fetus presses down on the pelvis, causing stretching and sagging...or by childbirth, when tissues are stretched or torn as the baby passes through the vagina. In men, stress incontinence often stems from damage to pelvic tissues caused by prostate surgery.

In a misguided attempt to solve their problem, incontinence sufferers make many mistakes. *Examples:*

•Turning to sanitary napkins or adult diapers prematurely, when the problem could be treatable.

•Reducing intake of water and other fluids. Cutting back on fluids can cause dehydration.

And doing so is pointless anyway, because there's always enough urine in the body for an accident—even if you've avoided drinking for hours.

Reducing your intake of caffeine and alcohol might help, since these beverages act as diuretics. But many antihypertensive medications are diuretics as well. Individuals taking these drugs should not stop taking them without first consulting their physician.

To help determine what triggers your accidents, keep a detailed bladder diary for at least a week. For every accident, describe the time and place, the extent of the urine leakage and the situation in which it occurred. List any possible triggers—coughing, lifting, running water, arriving home. Once you've pinpointed your triggers, the following techniques often prove helpful with both kinds of incontinence...

•*Kegel exercises.* They strengthen the urinary sphincter and other pelvic muscles, boosting your ability to "hold it in."

What to do: Squeeze your pelvic muscles. Go to the toilet and start to void. Once the stream of urine has started, try to stop it. If you can slow the stream of urine even slightly, you are using the right muscle. You should feel a "pulling" sensation in your anus, but your buttocks and abdomen shouldn't move. Hold the tension for three counts, then release and rest for three counts.

This squeeze-release pair counts as a single Kegel exercise. Do 15 exercises a day while lying down, 15 while sitting (at your desk, in your car, on the bus, etc.) and 15 while standing (brushing your teeth, waiting in line at the bank or supermarket). Improvement usually begins in two weeks.

•*Behavioral training for urge incontinence.* When you feel the urge to urinate, don't rush to the bathroom. The jiggling motion of your bladder increases the likelihood that urine will be released accidentally. Instead, sit or stand quietly for a few moments until the urgency subsides. Squeeze your pelvic muscles quickly several times, pausing briefly in between. Breathe deeply. Concentrate on suppressing the urge to urinate.

When the urge has diminished, walk to the bathroom at a normal pace, repeatedly squeezing those muscles. This technique is particularly helpful in case the urge to urinate strikes while you're on the highway or another place without ready access to a bathroom.

•*Behavioral training for stress incontinence.* Refer frequently to your bladder diary. If you find that your incontinence occurs with coughing, sneezing or other physical activity, squeeze your muscles just before and during these activities. This helps to keep the urethra closed holding the urine in.

Whether or not you consider your urine loss a problem and whether or not you want treatment, you should see your doctor for an evaluation. Incontinence is a sign that something isn't right. Don't ignore it. A visit to your doctor will reveal any easily reversible cause of incontinence as well as any type that requires immediate treatment. Consult an internist, urologist, gynecologist or geriatrician. Or ask a local hospital or medical school for the name of an incontinence clinic. Wherever you get help for your problem, be sure to take along your bladder diary.

In some cases, individuals seeking medical help for incontinence must undergo urodynamic testing. *Procedure:* Special equipment measures physical conditions such as pelvic muscle tone and how much urine your bladder can hold.

Health-care providers use a variety of techniques to control incontinence, including...

•*Biofeedback.* A type of behavioral training, biofeedback uses special equipment to help you learn how to control your pelvic muscles and bladder. It is especially useful in helping people to identify the proper muscles and contract them correctly. Some people can learn to control pelvic muscles without biofeedback. However, many exercise the wrong muscles and could benefit from biofeedback.

With this training, a probe is usually inserted into the vagina or rectum. Measurements taken from the probe are displayed so that you can watch what your muscles are doing.

With this immediate feedback, you can learn quickly and be assured that you are exercising properly.

•*Bladder training.* Another type of behavioral training, this therapy alters your voiding habits. You go to the bathroom on a regular schedule and the time between voids is gradually increased. Bladder training helps both stress and urge incontinence.

•*Drug therapy.* Prescription drugs are available both to prevent bladder spasms (urge incontinence) and to strengthen the urethral sphincter (stress incontinence).

Some who take these drugs have side effects. Dry mouth is the most common side effect of the drugs that prevent bladder spasms. Older women, especially prone to incontinence, should ask a doctor about taking estrogen to reduce irritation of and thicken the tissues of the urethra.

•*Collagen injections.* This therapy is useful only for patients with a type of stress incontinence called urethral insufficiency. Bovine collagen, a viscous substance derived from cattle bones, is injected into tissue surrounding the urethra. This helps keep it closed except for urination.

•*Electrical stimulation.* In this therapy, an electrical probe inserted into the vagina or rectum emits a low-intensity current that stimulates the muscles supporting the bladder and urethra.

•*Surgery.* For some types of incontinence, surgery is the best and only appropriate treatment. Certain physical conditions, such as a urethral obstruction or a hole in the bladder (fistula), can be corrected only via surgery.

Source: Kathryn L. Burgio, PhD, director of the continence program at the University of Alabama at Birmingham, and associate professor of medicine at the university's medical school. She is the co-author of *Staying Dry: A Practical Guide to Bladder Control,* Johns Hopkins University Press, 701 W. 40 St., Baltimore 21211.

Beware of Halogen Lights

Recent studies on mice suggest that light from halogen lamps can cause skin cancer. In one study, tumors developed in all of the mice exposed to unfiltered halogen light—even when exposure was limited to 90 minutes a day. No mice developed cancer when the light was covered by a glass filter. *Self-defense:* Make sure all halogen bulbs—especially those in desk lamps—are covered with glass filters. The glass filters out cancer-causing ultraviolet rays.

Source: Sylvio de Flora, MD, director, Institute of Hygiene and Preventive Medicine, Genoa, Italy.

Adult Acne Is on the Rise

Dermatologists have reported an increase in cases of acne in women in their 30s and 40s. *Suspected culprit:* Psychological stress from our increasingly fast-paced society. Acne sufferers should ask a doctor about topical antibiotics and other acne drugs. Stress-reduction techniques, such as meditation, yoga and biofeedback, can be helpful when signs of stress in the sufferer are readily apparent.

Source: Alan Shalita, MD, professor and chairman, department of dermatology, State University of New York Health Sciences Center, Brooklyn.

How to Avoid Colds and Flu

If you're looking for a surefire way to avoid a runny nose and sore throat...sorry, I can't give you one. But there are ways to cut your risk of cold and influenza—and there are ways to hasten your recovery should you fall ill.

One thing that doesn't work is avoiding cold, wet weather. Colds and flu are caused by viruses. You catch them by coming into contact with them—not by going outside with wet hair. These strategies will work...

•*Consider an annual flu shot.* The vaccine prevents influenza only—its high fever and the feeling of having been "hit by a truck." It does not protect you against the score of viruses that cause the common cold. Flu shots are essential for people older than 65, smokers, people with chronic diseases like diabetes or asthma...and those who tend to get lots of colds.

• *Don't smoke*. Colds and flu are not only more common among smokers, but also are more severe and longer lasting. *Also:* Smokers are more likely than nonsmokers to develop secondary bacterial infections like pneumonia, sinusitis or ear infections.

• *Practice good hygiene*. Wash your hands frequently. If you touch someone or something that might harbor a cold or flu virus (a telephone, for example), try not to touch your face. *Reason:* Cold and flu viruses enter the body via the mucous membranes of your mouth, eyes and nose. If no virus makes contact with these membranes, infection won't occur.

• *Drink lots of fluids*. That helps moisturize your mucous membranes—which, in turn, boosts their resistance to viruses. Drink at least four 8-ounce glasses of water a day.

• *Eat crackers, soups and other salty foods*. These foods aren't usually considered healthful, but during cold and flu season they can help your body retain water. That helps keep your mucous membranes moist.

• *Use a hot-steam vaporizer*. That's another way to keep your mucous membranes moist. *Caution:* Cool-mist units can become contaminated with fungus.

• *Take vitamin C*. I recommend 1,000 milligrams a day for my patients.

If you do get sick…

• *Gargle with salt water or mouthwash*. That relieves sore-throat pain and kills the virus.

• *Use over-the-counter remedies*. Aspirin, ibuprofenen provide temporary relief of fever and other symptoms.

At night, take a nighttime cold remedy like NyQuil. During the day, use an antihistamine like Sudafed.

Nose drops work better than nasal sprays for relieving nasal congestion. *Caution:* Nose drops can be habit-forming. Don't use them for more than five days at a time.

For coughs, I tell my patients to take Robitussin DM.

If your symptoms are severe enough that you suspect influenza, ask your doctor about amantadine or rimantadine. These drugs sig-

nificantly shorten the duration of influenza, although they're not effective against colds.

• *Use antibiotics with extreme caution*. They're great for treating bacterial infections—but ineffective against viral infections like colds or flu. Even worse, taking antibiotics for a cold or flu can make a secondary bacterial infection harder to treat. Reason: By killing off relatively benign throat bacteria, you encourage the growth of virulent strains. If your doctor doesn't prescribe antibiotics, don't encourage him/her to do so.

Cold and flu symptoms usually disappear within a week or two in nonsmokers but can last up to a month in smokers.

If your symptoms persist, or if you have an unusually high fever or white spots at the back of your throat (a symptom of strep throat), see a doctor.

Source: Bruce H. Yaffe, MD, is an internist and gastroenterologist in private practice, 121 E. 84 St., New York 10028.

The Best Way to Remove a Splinter

Coat the splinter with a nontoxic glue (such as Elmer's). When the glue dries, gently peel it off, pulling out the splinter in the process. To loosen stubborn splinters, soak the affected part of the body in water before applying the glue. If there are no signs of infection, most small splinters can safely be left alone. The body will either push them out or break them down.

Source: Richard J. Sagall, MD, editor, *Pediatrics for Parents*, 358 Broadway, Suite 105, Bangor, Maine 04401.

 **High Blood Pressure Treatment Alert**

Overly aggressive treatment of high blood pressure may raise risk of sudden heart attack.

Among patients receiving drug therapy for high blood pressure, those with a diastolic (lower) reading of 80 or less were 20% more likely to suffer a heart attack than those whose diastolic reading was 85 or higher.

It gets worse: Reducing blood pressure to 75 increased risk by 60% ...to 70, by more than 200%. If you're taking antihypertensive medication, make sure your diastolic blood pressure doesn't fall below 80. Ask your doctor about taking the smallest dose necessary.

Source: David Siscovick, MD, associate professor of medicine and epidemiology, University of Washington Medical School, Seattle.

What Deodorant Ads Don't Tell You About Body Odor

Body odor is caused not by perspiration alone—which is odorless—but by skin bacteria that thrive on perspiration and on sweat-soaked skin. To keep body odor in check, you must get rid of these bacteria.

For most people, all that's needed is a morning shower with an antibacterial soap like Lever 2000...followed up with antiperspirant.

Antiperspirants contain aluminum salts, which stop wetness by temporarily plugging sweat glands.* Because they're a more efficient means of applying this salt, roll-ons are more effective than sticks or aerosol sprays.

Deodorant crystals, sold at many natural foods stores, can irritate the skin, and are of uncertain effectiveness.

If these measures prove inadequate, consider trying...

•*Absorbent powder.* After your morning shower, sprinkle Bromi-Talc Plus or a similar product on your underarms and genitals. For feet, I recommend baked bromhidrosis (severe perspiration odor) powder, available without a prescription.

•*Damp-mopping.* If you develop a "5 o'clock odor" and can't get home to shower again, simply use a washcloth on the offending areas—typically your underarms and/or genitals. Even without soap, damp-mopping is usually effective. Damp-mopping with soap can be as effective as showering.

•*Prescription antiperspirant.* If your odor problem persists, you may be suffering from a pathological form of perspiration called hyperhidrosis. It's best treated by a dermatologist, who will probably recommend a prescription antiperspirant.

Prescription antiperspirants are up to ten times more effective than antiperspirants sold over the counter. *Strongest:* Drysol (about 20% aluminum salt). Next is Certain-Dri (12%), followed by Xerac AC (7%). Nonprescription antiperspirants contain 1% to 2% aluminum salt.

Oddly enough, antiperspirants are most effective when applied at bedtime, following a shower, rather than after a morning shower. *Reason:* It takes up to eight hours for the aluminum salt to form effective plugs. People sweat very little while sleeping, so don't worry about building up odor overnight.

To keep the antiperspirant from rubbing off, cover your underarms in plastic wrap before going to sleep. A second application of antiperspirant in the morning adds even more protection.

Problem: One should not do this without consulting a physician. These antiperspirants stop perspiration so effectively, they can dry out and irritate surrounding areas of skin—which don't sweat as much. In such cases, treat these areas with a fragrance-free, hypo-allergenic moisturizer such as Curel moisturizing lotion. If necessary, I prescribe Lac-Hydrin, a concentrated moisturizing lotion.

•*Electric current.* A final option—appropriate only for the most severe cases of problem perspiration—is a device called Drionic. Applied to the underarms, feet, hands, etc., this electronic device sets up a mild electric current —too mild to shock you, but strong enough to plug the pores completely. Its benefits may last several days. *More information:* General Medical Co., 1935 Armacost Ave., Los Angeles 90025, 800-432-5362.

Source: Nelson Lee Novick, MD, associate clinical professor of dermatology, Mount Sinai School of Medicine, New York City. He is the author of *Super Skin: A Leading Dermatologist's Guide to the Latest Breakthroughs in Skin Care*, Random House, New York.

Herbal Tea and Pregnancy Danger

Many so-called natural ingredients found in herbal teas can be dangerous to a pregnant woman's unborn baby. *Examples:* Slippery elm, cohosh, pennyroyal, mugwort, tansy and other ingredients found in some herbal teas have been linked to miscarriage.

Bottom line: Stay away from all nonprescribed herbs or herbal teas that contain ingredients not ordinarily found in your diet…or check with your doctor about the herbal teas you want to drink.

Source: *What to Eat When You're Expecting* by Sandee Eisenberg Hatthaway, RN, Sante Fe. Workman Publishing, New York.

Feeling Sad After Baby Comes

Believe it or not, it's not at all unusual to feel sad after giving birth to a baby. In fact, 80% of new mothers experience a mild form of depression called "baby blues."

Usual cause: Dramatic hormonal changes, coupled with the disorientation of being released from the hospital and the odd sensation of having the breasts engorged with milk.

Baby blues typically start three to five days after childbirth. They usually go away without treatment in a matter of hours or days. All that's needed is an occasional nap and supportive care from friends and family.

But up to 30% of new mothers develop postpartum depression (PPD), a far more severe and long-lasting psychological disturbance. It involves not only sadness but also anxiety, low self-esteem, crying spells and insomnia.

PPD typically occurs three to eight weeks following childbirth. It can be successfully controlled with antidepressants or psychotherapy.

Problem: PPD often goes undiagnosed and untreated. And without treatment, it can persist for months or even years. In especially severe cases, PPD can lead to a form of psychosis that causes women to harm their babies.

Self-defense: New mothers should know how to distinguish simple baby blues from PPD. At the first sign of PPD, consult a doctor.

Source: Valerie D. Raskin, MD, assistant professor of psychiatry, University of Illinois College of Medicine, Chicago, and the co-author of *This Isn't What I Expected: Recognizing and Recovering from Depression and Anxiety after Childbirth*, Bantam Books, New York. For more information on postpartum depression, call Depression After Delivery (800-944-4773) or Postpartum Support International (805-967-7636).

Natural Claustrophobia Relief

Apples may relieve claustrophobia. The smell of green apples changed subjects' perceptions of space, making rooms seem bigger. Barbecue smoke made rooms seem smaller. Odors such as vanilla, popcorn, the seashore, cucumber and coconut had no effect.

Source: Alan Hirsch, MD, director, Smell and Taste Treatment and Research Foundation, 845 N. Michigan Ave., Chicago 60611.

Which State is Healthiest?

If you guessed California, with its gleaming health clubs and laid-back lifestyle, guess again. It comes in 28th, tied with Delaware.*

*This ranking takes into account disease rates, lifestyle, access to health care, occupational safety and disability and mortality.

Rank	State
1	New Hampshire
2	Minnesota
3	Utah
3	Connecticut
5	Hawaii
6	Vermont
7	Massachusetts
8	Iowa
9	Virginia
10	Kansas
10	Colorado
10	Nebraska
13	Wisconsin
14	Maine
15	New Jersey
16	North Dakota
16	Washington
16	Maryland
19	Rhode Island
19	Ohio
21	Pennsylvania
22	Indiana
22	Oregon
24	Michigan
25	Idaho
25	Montana
25	Arizona
28	Delaware
28	California
30	North Carolina
30	Illinois
32	Texas
33	Missouri
33	Oklahoma
33	South Dakota
36	Georgia
36	Wyoming
38	New York
38	Florida
38	Kentucky
38	Alaska
42	Tennessee
43	New Mexico
43	Nevada
45	Alabama
46	South Carolina
46	Arkansas
48	West Virginia
49	Mississippi
50	Louisiana

Source: Northwestern Life Insurance Co., Box 20, Minneapolis 55440.

Hepatitis Warning

Travelers to developing countries should be vaccinated for hepatitis A. If the vaccine is unavailable, they should receive a shot of immune globulin. *Reason:* Each month, as many as three in 1,000 travelers staying in a developing country are infected with the disease, making it the most frequent vaccine-preventable infection in travelers. *Added danger:* People born after 1945 have limited natural immunity—and so are even more susceptible to infection.

Source: Robert Steffen, MD, division of epidemiology and prevention of communicable diseases, Institute of Social and Preventive Medicine, University of Zurich, Switzerland.

Chronic Congestion

Most people who suffer from chronic nasal congestion eventually give up on over-the-counter antihistamines and decongestants.

Problem: These remedies aren't particularly effective at relieving symptoms...and they can leave you feeling anxious—or very drowsy.

When my patients complain about nasal congestion, I often recommend Claritin. This prescription antihistamine is far more effective than over-the-counter antihistamines and works without affecting your mind.

If a patient taking Claritin needs a decongestant as well as an antihistamine, I usually prescribe Claritin-D. For extreme cases, I often prescribe *beclomethasone* (Vancenase) nasal spray along with Claritin.

Also helpful: Neo-Synephrine nose drops or Afrin nasal spray. *Caution:* These medications can be habit-forming. Use for no more than three days at a time.

In some cases, I also recommend rinsing out the nostrils each morning with a spritz of warm water or a saline solution. *Best for nasal douching:* Birmingham Nasal Douche. It's available without a prescription at drugstores.

Allergy culprits:

If your congestion persists despite these measures, odds are you're suffering from an allergy.

In warm months, pollen is the usual culprit. One of the best ways to limit your exposure is to use your air conditioner as much as possible.

Air conditioners are very effective at trapping pollen. In fact, pollen levels inside a car with windows rolled up and air conditioner turned on can be one-fiftieth as high as levels outside.

Pet allergens—saliva, urine and dander (particles of dead skin)—can also play a role in chronic congestion. If you own a dog or cat, keep it out of your bedroom—at least while you're asleep. Doing so will cut your exposure to these allergens by a factor of 1,000.

Cockroach droppings are another common cause of congestion. If you've got roaches, call in an exterminator...and call him/her back at the first sign of the roaches' return. Even if the insecticides used by the exterminator prove irritating, they're unlikely to cause congestion.

Dust mites are another common culprit. They live in bedding, upholstery, curtains, etc. To limit their numbers, get rid of throw rugs and needless pillows. Choose wood furniture over upholstered pieces and wooden or tile floors over rugs.

If you insist on carpeting, opt for a short-nap, 100%-synthetic instead of wool. All-cotton rugs are okay, too, *if they're washed regularly.* Use synthetic padding underneath the carpet—or no padding at all.

Use curtains made of washable cotton or synthetic fabric. Wash them weekly. Leave curtains either open—or closed. Moving them back and forth stirs up a lot of dust.

Clean mattresses and box springs—then encase them in zippered vinyl slipcovers. Replace down or feather pillows and comforters with hypoallergenic versions.

Keeping dust under control:

Each time you clean, you stir up dust that can cause congestion. I tell my patients to clean house no more than once a week. If possible, call in a professional cleaning service...or have a friend or family member who does not suffer from allergies do the cleaning for you. *When cleaning...*

• *Avoid vacuuming.* Use a damp mop on floors and ceilings, a damp cloth on walls and furniture. Wipe down books, picture frames, wallpaper, venetian blinds and other "dust magnets" very carefully. It's best to clean these items *outdoors.*

• *Treat carpets with an anti-allergen solution* —Allergy Control, Acarosan or Rid. These products are available at allergy supply centers.

• *Get rid of mold.* Never leave damp or dirty clothing lying around. It breeds mold. *Also:* Attics, crawl spaces, basements, laundry rooms and other areas prone to mold should be scoured with Lysol or Clorox.

To prevent mold from returning, keep household humidity at 40%. Humidity meters are available at hardware stores or allergy supply centers.

If your home is very humid, consider installing a room air conditioner, an exhaust fan or a dehumidifier.

If your house is too dry, vaporizers and steam inhalators are usually a bad idea. *Reason:* They can spew mold and/or bacteria into the air, making you even more congested.

Safer: Ultrasonic vaporizers. As long as you fill them with distilled water—and as long as they're cleaned on a daily basis—they will not spread mold or bacteria.

Allergy shots:

If your symptoms persist, your doctor may suggest allergy shots. Shots have several drawbacks. They can cause severe allergic reactions ...they're inconvenient and costly...they require a painstaking skin-testing process...and they take several years to become completely effective. But for cases in which drug therapy is little help—or in which drugs cause adverse reactions—allergy shots may be best.

Source: Nelson Lee Novick, MD, associate clinical professor of dermatology, Mount Sinai School of Medicine, New York City. Dr. Novick, who is board certified in both dermatology and internal medicine, is the author of 12 books, including *You Can Do Something about Your Allergies: A Leading Doctor's Guide to the Prevention and Treatment of Common Allergies,* Bantam Books, 1540 Broadway, New York 10036.

4

The Savvy Traveler

Simple Secrets of Happier Traveling

More than ever, business travelers who are either inexperienced or insufficiently vigilant can end up with outrageously high travel costs, as well as discomfort or physical exhaustion.

The good news is that it doesn't have to be that way. *Ten ways to save the company valuable dollars, time and energy—and enhance your safety and comfort on the road...*

Air-travel secrets:

• *Always challenge quoted prices.* Today, when you call an airline to make reservations, the agent will not voluntarily quote the cheapest price. He/she will invariably begin with the most expensive—the first price that comes up on the computer. Many travel agents will also initially quote that price because it saves them time.

To get the best deal, keep challenging the price you are quoted until you get what the agent convincingly says is really the cheapest alternative.

Helpful: If your company has a regular travel agent, enter into a contract that guarantees the agent will always give you the best available price.

• *Pay attention to your flight number.* Flights on major, scheduled airlines always have two- or three-digit flight-number codes. A four-digit number may mean you are booked on a commuter airline that flies smaller planes.

Unless you have no alternative, opt for a safer, more comfortable flight on a larger aircraft.

Hint: If you are flying abroad...or your domestic trip involves connecting flights...even though your main carrier is a major airline, a part of your trip may be with a smaller, partner company. When you make your reservations, find out exactly what airline and aircraft you will be flying on. If commuter airlines are involved, ask for alternatives.

• *When you reserve a flight in economy class, ask for a seat in an exit row.* That will give you more leg-room during the flight...and provide the best chance of a quick escape, if necessary.

Condition: The airline will meet such requests, but will often require the passenger to show up in person to collect his/her boarding pass. *Reason:* It wants to make sure the individual can move quickly and is physically able to open the exit hatch in case of emergency.

• *Preorder airline meals.* If you have strong dietary preferences, ask the airline or travel agent about the menu when you make your reservation. Avoid unpleasant surprises by specifying your choice from among 12 or more menus, including different foods and alternative diets.

Car-rental secrets:

• *Consider fill-up costs.* Many car-rental companies now offer the option of buying a full tank of gas from them up front at a reasonable per-gallon price and not having to worry about returning the car with a full tank or being stuck with their exorbitant fill-up prices at return time.

Trap: This is not necessarily a bargain, since renters usually have a few gallons left in the tank when they return the car, even if they don't have time to fill it up. Before buying a full tank of gas at the outset, calculate how many gallons at the rental company's reduced price it will take to cancel out the savings on the fill-up price.

Example: Acme Car Rental charges $1 per gallon for a full tank of 15 gallons at the beginning of the trip, but $1.50 per gallon to fill it when you return the car. It does not pay for you to shell out $15 up front for a tankful unless you expect to return the car with less than five gallons in the tank.

Of course, if you will be returning with, say, eight gallons, the cheapest way to go would be to fill up on your own just before returning the car, at perhaps $1.20/gallon.

• *Avoid unnecessary rental-car insurance.* Business travelers should forgo the Collision (or Loss) Damage Waiver (CDW or LDW) or Personal Accident Insurance (PAI) offered by a rental company if their personal auto insurance policies already have it. Most cover accidents to rental cars.

Also, many credit cards provide secondary insurance coverage for auto rentals that pays for the deductible and other costs covered by the CDW.

Hotel secrets:

• *Maximize safety and security.* Avoid rooms above the sixth floor—the maximum height that fire-department ladders can reach.

For security in motels, avoid ground floor rooms off the parking lot. If you can't get a room on a higher level, take one facing the interior courtyard.

• *Get a nonsmoking room.* Ask for a room reserved for nonsmokers—most US hotels now have them.

• *Choose the location of your room.* To improve the chance of a good night's sleep, make sure your room is far away from elevators and vending machines.

• *Know what you're paying for.* Ask about charges for any services you want to use, such as a fitness center, when making reservations. You may get a better deal up front.

Source: Harold Seligman, president, Management Alternatives, business travel consultants, Stamford, Connecticut, and a frequent business traveler.

How to Stay Healthy During Your Travels... And After

No matter what your destination or reason for traveling, staying healthy is a prime concern whenever you are far from home.

Fatigue, stress, an upset stomach or worse can spell disaster for your vacation—or sap your business productivity. Fortunately, the wear and tear of travel can be kept to a minimum with some simple advance planning.

Here are easy ways to make your travel more comfortable—and healthful.

Self-care checklist:

Your chief consideration when packing for a trip will be where you're going, how long you'll be away and what the climate is like at your destination. But no matter what sort of trip you are planning, bring along a well-stocked self-care kit. It should be easily accessible in your carry-on luggage and should contain...

• *Antacid.* Familiar store-bought remedies such as Maalox, Mylanta, Gelusil, Tums or

Rolaids combat stomach upset, heartburn and abdominal cramping sometimes caused by unfamiliar food or drink—or overindulgence in either.

• *Diarrhea remedy.* Over-the-counter preparations like Imodium A-D, Kaopectate or Pepto-Bismol are all effective at stopping diarrhea. Tablets are easier to take along on a trip, although the liquid forms of these medications usually offer faster relief.

• *Laxative.* On the road, constipation is often more of a problem than diarrhea.

Reason: Your diet while traveling is apt to lack high-fiber foods. Also, it may be difficult while traveling to maintain a regular exercise routine. Take along some Metamucil or Senokot just in case.

• *Antihistamine.* The over-the-counter medication Benadryl is effective against a host of potential allergens and irritants and is well-tolerated by most people. If you have to stay alert, ask your doctor to prescribe Seldane. It causes little or no drowsiness.

• *Antibiotic.* For tooth abscesses, severe bronchitis, festering skin wounds or other stubborn bacterial infections, ask your doctor to prescribe an antibiotic in advance.

Caution: Antibiotics should be used only under a doctor's supervision. Call your doctor at home for instructions.

• *Motion-sickness remedy.* Dramamine or Bonine tablets and scopolamine skin patches (Transderm Scop) are effective. The patches are especially useful if you'll be spending long periods of time at sea, although they can cause dry mouth and, in the elderly, confusion.

Caution: Dramamine and Bonine can cause drowsiness. Avoid them if you have to stay alert.

• *Athlete's foot remedy.* Include antifungal foot powder or solutions like Lotrimin, Micatin or Tinactin in your travel kit since showers in hotel rooms and fitness centers are not always fungus-free.

• *Sunscreen, sunglasses and hat.* These are a must for travel to sunny places or if you intend to be outdoors for extended periods of time. Your sunscreen should have an SPF of at least 15 and should guard against both UVB and UVA rays.

• *Insect repellent.* Look for one that contains 20% to 30% DEET.

• *Aspirin, acetaminophen or ibuprofen.*

• *Decongestant and facial tissues.*

You might also want to bring along a basic first-aid kit containing an antibacterial cream or ointment, bandages, gauze, thermometer, scissors, tweezers and a pocketknife.

If you wear corrective lenses, pack a spare pair of contacts or eyeglasses—plus your prescription.

If you intend to swim in unchlorinated water, take along a remedy for swimmer's ear—an infection marked by redness, itching and pain of the outer ear canal. I recommend an over-the-counter preparation called Vosol.

Fighting jet lag:

Anytime you fly across several time zones, you disrupt the body's circadian rhythms. The resulting jet lag should be thought of not as a special problem, but as another form of manageable stress. To control it:

• *Avoid alcohol during your flight.* Alcohol, a depressant, can aggravate lethargy and fatigue, two classic symptoms of jet lag. It can also cause restlessness, which can disturb your sleep or keep you from sleeping altogether. And because it acts as a diuretic, alcohol can leave you feeling dehydrated.

• *Limit your consumption of caffeine.* Like alcohol, caffeine is a diuretic that can leave you feeling dehydrated and out of sorts. Too much caffeine can also cause nervousness, anxiety, tremors and insomnia.

• *Drink plenty of water.* Recent studies have shown that even slight dehydration can cause listlessness and fatigue and can even make you more prone to mental errors—symptoms similar to those of jet lag.

Bear in mind that you may be dehydrated even before departure. *Reason:* Your eating and drinking patterns may be erratic in the hours before your flight. Breathing dry cabin air only increases this dehydration and all its enervating effects.

Drink plenty of water or other nonalcoholic beverages before and during your flight—one 8 ounce glass every two to three hours.

• *Adapt to local time as quickly as possible.*

Example: If you land in Paris the morning after an all-night flight, have no more than a brief, 90-minute nap—then stay awake until it's 9 PM or 10 PM in Paris.

Schedule nonstressful activities and eat light, refreshing meals on your arrival day. Pack a swimsuit and use the hotel's pool or hot tub to help you relax.

Safe food and drink:

Regions of the world fall into three "tiers":

• Europe, North America, Australia.

• Israel and the Caribbean.

• The rest of the Middle East, most of Africa, the Far East and other developing regions.

When you travel to the second or third tier, you must be especially vigilant about what you eat and drink. *Self-defense:*

• *Eat cooked food while it is still hot.* Make sure meats are well-done. Throughout developing countries, undercooked beef and pork are major sources of tapeworms and other parasites. Likewise, all poultry, seafood and vegetables should be fresh and thoroughly cooked.

• *Avoid peeled fruits (and those with broken skin).* Watch out for raw vegetable salads, too. They can be contaminated with bacteria from food preparer's hands or from the water used to rinse the vegetables.

• *Avoid custards, pastries and other baked desserts.* These foods are often contaminated with microbes that trigger gastric distress, especially if improperly refrigerated. *Exception:* Served still hot from the oven, they are generally safe. If you want dessert, stick to wrapped candy or fruit you can peel yourself.

• *Stick to bottled or canned beverages.* And watch out for ice cubes. Avoid milk, milk products and foods prepared with milk unless you're sure they have been properly pasteurized.

• *Avoid bread left lying in open baskets.* It may have been exposed to flies and other disease-bearing insects. If you're not certain whether bread has been properly stored, remove the crust and eat only the interior of the loaf.

Avoiding infectious diseases:

If you are planning a trip to the tropics, ask your doctor about protecting yourself against malaria, yellow fever, schistosomiasis and other potential threats. If you need immunizations, get them at least a month before your departure.

Malaria—probably the most serious of all the infectious diseases found in the tropics—used to be easily controlled with medication. *Now:* In many parts of the world there are drug-resistant strains of malaria. Chloroquine and other anti-malarial drugs are virtually useless against them.

A new drug called mefloquine (Lariam) is often effective against drug-resistant malaria. Doxycycline can combat stubborn strains but should not be taken by children or pregnant women.

To avoid malaria, ask your doctor about taking prophylactic drugs. These must be taken one week before you travel.

Source: Karl Neumann, MD, editor and publisher of *Traveling Healthy,* 108-48 70 Rd., Forest Hills, New York 11375. He is also the co-editor of *The Business Traveler's Guide to Good Health While Traveling,* Chronimed Publishing, 13911 Ridgedale Dr., Minnetonka, Minnesota 55305.

Safer Flying

Avoid wearing clothing made of synthetic blends when traveling by plane. *Reason:* In the event of a crash and fire, the material can increase your risk of burns. *Better:* More fire-resistant *natural* fibers, especially wool and wool blends…a leather jacket…clothing that covers as much of your body as possible. *Also:* Wear shoes that won't limit your mobility should you need to evacuate the plane…if losing your glasses will incapacitate you, wear a safety strap to help keep them in place.

Source: *Collision Course: The Truth About Airline Safety* by Ralph Nader, founder of Public Citizen, a consumer advocacy group in Washington, DC, Tab Books, 13311 Monterey Lane, Blue Ridge Summit, Pennsylvania 17214.

Secrets of Much, Much Safer Travel

Among popular destinations, what are the most dangerous places to visit now? The riskiest country for American tourists at the moment is probably Egypt, where fundamentalist forces, in their fight with the government, have targeted foreign travelers.

Despite security at major hotels in the big Egyptian cities, bomb blasts are a constant threat. Especially dangerous are trips to the pyramids and ruins, where high-quality security is difficult to provide and tourists are prime targets.

In major areas of several other countries, travelers also run the risk of getting caught in the crossfire of civil uprisings. *Examples:*

• *Chiapas, Mexico,* where a civil war is simmering. The recent currency devaluations and financial crisis in Mexico have resulted in more panhandlers and street crime in major cities.

• *Caracas, Venezuela,* where students are protesting.

• *Quito, Ecuador,* where tension over the soaring cost of living and a recent gas price hike could lead to antigovernment riots.

• *Rio de Janeiro, Brazil,* which probably has the world's worst street-crime problem due to the police's inability to control gangs of youths and beach thieves. Now several private hotels employ their own security forces on the beaches.

Safer Brazilian beach alternatives: Recife, about 1,000 miles northeast of Rio de Janiero ...Santos, which is 150 miles south.

How can I find out more about crime in places I plan to visit? The best on-site source for specific travel advisories about crime is the Regional Security Officer (RSO) at the US Embassy in the country that you are thinking of visiting.

To obtain an RSO's name and phone number abroad, call the State Department (202-647-4000) and ask for the desk officer in charge of your destination. Expect delays in getting the information, and plan to make follow-up calls since desk officers are not trained or equipped to handle the public.

For travel advisories: Call the Office of American Citizens Services (202-647-5225)...or for faxed information on up to ten countries, call 202-647-3000.

Pinkerton Risk Assessment Services' PET-Fax (703-525-6111) provides the latest information on crime and terrorist activities in a country. It also lists embassy and consulate locations and their phone numbers...entry requirements... weather and currency data...holiday schedules, etc. *Pinkerton's World Status Map* newsletter identifies danger areas around the globe.

How can I make sure that I'll get good medical care if I get sick while I'm abroad? Don't leave without a travel insurance policy. Costs range from $3.50 and up per person, per day, and according to your age. *Your policy should:*

• Provide $100,000 major medical coverage, including evacuation costs.

• Assist you in locating the nearest, most appropriate medical care.

• Direct you to English-speaking doctors and translators.

• Make guaranteed payments, if required, to the physicians, hospitals and the organization providing evacuation transportation.

Response time depends on your location, but with such insurance you'll get the quickest attention possible. Top resources...

• *AEA International–Individual Traveller Programme* is particularly strong in the Far East. 800-468-5232.

• *Trav-Med-MEDEX Assistance.* 800-732-5309.

• *USAssist.* Ask for the individual policy, which will provide you with medical and evacuation coverage in case of emergency. 800-756-5900.

• *Wallach & Company* is a broker for such insurance and can discuss the advantages of various policies. 800-237-6615.

How can I be sure that the regional airline I'm flying on within another country is safe? In March of 1995, a *Frequent Flyer* article rated foreign airlines based on the number of fatal accidents per million departures, as compared with the same statistic for US airlines.

Most dangerous: Flights within Africa, Latin America and the Middle East. Also, flights inside China, Colombia, Eastern Europe, Indonesia, Nigeria and Russia. Flights in the former Soviet Union are notoriously unsafe, and several Chinese airlines have had crashes and been subject to hijackings.

For information about credible threats to an airline, airport or flight or to find out if a foreign airline conforms to FAA safety standards, call the FAA Consumer Hotline (800-322-7873).

How can I be sure my hotel is safe? As always, steer clear of hotels located in rough neighborhoods. The US Embassy's RSO in that country can alert you.

To guarantee your safety once you're inside your hotel room, make sure windows are not accessible from the street and both windows and balcony doors are locked.

For added security: Pack an attachable door lock, which is available from Magellan's Essentials for the Traveler (800-962-4943). It will come in handy when your hotel door lacks a door chain.

Cheap alternative: A common, rubber doorstop or wedge, which will prevent the door from being opened.

What types of clothing attract trouble? Anything that marks you as a tourist is an open invitation to street criminals. Avoid white or pink leisure clothes, jogging suits and stretch pants… Hawaiian shirts…and bright shorts. Also avoid garments that you assume will be native to the country, such as bush jackets in Brazil or Africa. Such outfits tend to be the stuff of adventure movies, not everyday apparel. In addition, they are often so new they stick out.

Safer: When you arrive, spend an hour looking at people on the street. Observe what those in your age group are wearing. Try to blend in —even if it means wearing coats and ties on your vacation. Buy some local shirts and pants …or an inexpensive overcoat that's popular in that country.

What are the most common street scams now —and how do I avoid them? The most common street crime is still the bump-and-run. A thief— or one member of a crime team—jostles you, then grabs your briefcase, suitcase or wallet while you're distracted. Aggressive criminals may use a knife or razor to cut a bag's strap or snatch a bag or parcel while passing on a bicycle or rollerblades. *Prevention…*

• Travel with old, nylon luggage, rather than fancy, leather bags, which invite theft.

• Keep your purse and fanny pack under your sweater or coat, where they can't be seen by thieves and pickpockets.

• Hide your wallet and passport in a concealed, shoulder-strap pouch.

Strategy: I carry about $50 worth of cash and a canceled credit card in my front pants pocket. If I'm held up, this will satisfy almost any thief.

Important: Avoid getting loaded down with suitcases or bulky packages. Use luggage with rollers and exterior hooks to hang smaller bags on larger ones.

Reason: You always need to have one free hand to push through a crowd or to protect yourself.

How can I keep from getting ripped off by taxi drivers? The best way to avoid an expensive "scenic" route is to establish a fair price before you get in the cab.

A policeman at the airport or the personnel at your hotel can provide you with estimates. You can also ask your hotel doorman to pay the driver, then reimburse the doorman.

What if I lose my passport? As soon as you arrive in a foreign country, go to the American Consulate and ask to register as a US citizen. It will let them know that you are in the country and eliminates a lot of paperwork and trouble if your passport is stolen. If you can't register, then keep a photocopy of your passport and a picture of yourself separate from your luggage.

Source: Peter Savage, a consultant with The Parvus Company, an international security firm, 8403 Colesville Rd., Suite 610, Silver Spring, Maryland 20910. A former foreign-service officer with the State Department in Latin America, he is the author of *The Safe Travel Book,* Lexington Books, New York.

How to Choose the Travel Guidebook for You

There are at least three guidebooks on any one location in the travel section of your local bookstore. Here are the questions to ask in order to choose the one that will best serve your needs…

• *When was the book published?* Travel guidebooks fall into two categories—those that provide essays describing the mood and ambience of locations…and those that provide specific information. If you need price ranges, phone numbers and data on hotels, restaurants and sites, be sure the book you choose was published within the current year.

• *Are places and events that suit your lifestyle explored adequately?* The author's tastes or interests may be quite different from your own.

Example: Luxury hotels may receive more attention than mid-range–priced ones…or native culture may be ignored in favor of lengthy descriptions of what you would consider to be tourist traps. Flip through the book to see what's covered.

• *Does the book adequately include details?* The better guidebooks provide a great deal of information about the hotels, restaurants and locations they cover.

• *Are the maps clear and detailed?* You'll probably carry the guidebook around with you and refer to it often. Therefore, maps should show side streets, not just main thoroughfares. The names of long streets should appear several times along the routes if necessary…and major landmarks should be precisely identified.

• *Was the book right?* While you're on vacation —or after you return from your trip—look up a few entries to see if the descriptions match your experiences.

Examples: Is the pool in your hotel accurately described? Are the restaurants as good as the book says they are? How are other hotels described?

This test not only will tell you whether the book is truly up-to-date, it will also say a great deal about the quality and standards of other travel books by the same author.

Source: A travel expert who has visited more than 100 countries and has written about the travel industry for more than 25 years.

Check for Hidden Deals Before Buying Airline Tickets

Carriers often cut fares in extremely competitive markets—to the point where they are actually below nationally advertised "discount" rates. *Bottom line:* Have your travel agent

search for the lowest fare, not the latest "bargain" advertised in your local newspaper.

Source: Tom Nulty, president, Associated Travel Management, Santa Ana, California.

Saving on Airfares

Save big on airfares by studying a map before you purchase tickets. Make a list of cities within driving distance of your destination and ask about the fares to those cities. *Example:* A recent round-trip fare from Chicago to Cincinnati for a family of four was $1,028. By flying to Louisville, a route with a "friends fly free" program to a city that is one hour's drive from Cincinnati, the round-trip fare was $196.

Source: Tom Parsons, editor of *Best Fares Discount Travel,* 1111 W. Arkansas Lane, Arlington, Texas 76013.

Getting the Lowest Airfare

To be sure of the lowest airfare, ask your travel agent if it would be cheaper to fly on a different day…at a different time of day…during a different week of the month…on an earlier departure date…or at designated off-peak times. Also ask your travel agent if there are any special seasonal or promotional fares available. Be sure to ask about other airlines. Travel agents may promote particular airlines unless you specifically ask for quotes on others. Before finally agreeing to a flight, ask directly if the agent knows any way you could get a lower fare.

Source: *Retirement Angles: 1,001 Ways to Make Your Life Better Today and Tomorrow* by Donald Korn, financial writer in New York, Shot Tower Books, 150 E. Palmetto Park Rd., Suite 320, Boca Raton, Florida 33432.

How to Fly for Much, Much Less

You're flying the Miami-Tokyo route, sipping coffee, happily reading the newspaper and looking forward to a great vacation. Suddenly, you overhear a conversation between fellow travelers sharing seats in your section. What a great deal they got on their tickets—only $698 for a round-trip ticket. You put your newspaper down. You can't believe what you heard. You paid $1,325 for the exact same ticket…and you thought that you had gotten a good deal!

Did the ticketing agent make a mistake?

No. On any given flight any number of different people could be paying any number of different fares for the exact same flight.

People who aggressively pursue inexpensive fares, rather than passively accept an airline reservationist's or a travel agent's first suggestion, get the best fares.

These are the travelers who make it their business to understand the air-travel marketplace, have a certain amount of flexibility in their travel plans, carefully select the airline, know where the best place is to buy their tickets and take the time to be savvy shoppers.

To help you get rock-bottom prices on airfares…

• *No-frills travel agencies.* If you know where you are going, when you want to get there, what airline you want to fly and what your flight number is, you will be able to get an additional discount off an already discounted ticket price because no-frills agents rebate you their commission and charge a flat fee instead.

Example: Travel Avenue (800-333-3335) will issue you a ticket at the lowest possible price the airline allows, mail you the ticket and include the rebate in the envelope as well! The profit for the agent? They charge a $15 fee for domestic tickets—and $25 for international tickets.

• *Air taxis.* If you are traveling as a group of three or more, consider hiring a small, private plane. There are 3,000 independent, federally licensed operators with 6,500 planes ready to take off at any hour you like. Add up the total cost of the group's tickets on a scheduled airline and see if the approximately $1 per mile round-trip an independent would charge you makes sense. Look in the *Yellow Pages* under "Aircraft Charter" or "Aircraft Rental" and call them all to compare costs not only with the major airline, but with each private operator.

• *Status fares.* You can get up to 75% off your ticket price if you are a student under age 26, an active-duty member of the military (or a dependent), a child traveling with an adult, part of a family or a senior citizen. To get a status fare, you've got to let the booking agent know you're eligible.

• *Consolidators.* During the course of the year, about one third of the available seats on planes are empty. In anticipation of this, airlines sell batches of deeply discounted seats to consolidators, who in turn sell the tickets at great discounts to the public. There are no advance-registration requirements. You'll realize savings of up to 65% on national as well as international flights. The airlines do not want these discounted prices to be common knowledge, so consolidators play the game by not letting you know exactly what airline you'll be on until you receive your ticket a day or two before departure. However—if you tell the consolidator your preferences for major versus lesser-known airlines, whether you want a non- or minimum-stop flight with direct routing versus indirect multiple-stop routing and the lowest possible price versus higher price with frills, you'll get what you want. Call Travel Bargains (800-872-8385) or watch the advertisements in your Sunday newspaper for "discount" brokers.

• *Banks.* Many banks offer travel rebates as a way to build customer loyalty and encourage the use of their credit cards. Even if you think you've zeroed in on the lowest possible price for your ticket, check with your bank to see if you can shave off an additional 5% to 10%.

• *Gimmicks.* Cereal boxes, detergent products, statement stuffers in credit-card bills and coupons in the back of travel guides have all been known to offer discount certificates for up to 25% off fares.

Some stores (Radio Shack, for example) have teamed up with airline marketing departments to offer merchandise that comes complete with an airfare-discount ticket.

Some mail-order catalogs will sell you a discount certificate—good for 25% off your airfare for just $25!

Supermarkets like Stop & Shop, Shop Rite, Super Value, Acme and Great Scott occasionally sell—at rock-bottom prices—a redeemable certificate to customers who spend $50 to $100 a week on groceries. These gimmicks can be a source of extraordinary bargains! Watch for them, and take advantage.

• *Personal computers.* If you've got a modem-equipped personal computer, you've got immediate access (for an hourly usage fee) to the latest airfares as they are updated.

The Official Airline Guides (OAG) Electronic Edition, Eaasy Sabre and *Travelshopper* publish airfares. These databases are available through CompuServe (800-848-8199) and Delphi (800-544-4005) networks.

• *Last-minute travel clubs.* These clubs get fabulous bargains when an airline sells its last-minute inventory directly to the club at discounted prices.

Make sure, however, when you join a club that its gateway city (a major city with a national or international airport) is near you so that you don't have to spend more money traveling to a distant city to get on the discounted flight.

Last-minute clubs: Last Minute Travel, Boston (800-527-8646)…One Travel Place, Illinois (800-621-5505)…Vacations to Go, Texas (800-338-4962).

• *Airline ads.* When major airlines announce extraordinarily low fares, reach for your telephone fast. Virgin Atlantic Airways once offered a $99 New York–London round-trip ticket. Within nine minutes all $99 seats were booked. Continental once offered a New York–Honolulu $99 fare!

• *International low-fare airlines.* Foreign-owned airlines like Air Jamaica (800-523-5585), Cathay Pacific (800-233-2742), Icelandair (800-223-5500), Malaysia Airlines (800-421-8641), Thai Airways (800-426-5204) and Virgin Atlantic (800-862-8621) fly international routes that include stops in major US cities and sometimes offer extraordinary bargains compared with better-known, better-advertised airlines.

Dialing to save dollars:

There are more than 250,000 airfare changes daily. These changes happen so quickly that you can talk with an airline reservationist, get a price, hang up the phone, call the same airline back and be given yet another price.

Persistence pays:

You must be a persistent caller. When you call, always ask questions like "Could I get a lower fare if I buy my ticket further in advance?" and "Would it be less expensive to fly off-peak or on a different day?"

Keep calling around—Sunday mornings are a slow time for the airline reservationists—making and canceling courtesy reservations that will hold a seat for you for 24 hours. (Ask specifically for a "courtesy" reservation. The airline will hold your seat for 24 hours.) It's the folks who look for a better deal right up to the day of departure who swap the best "deal of the century" stories.

Source: Bob Martin, a travel authority and the author of numerous travel books including *Fly There for Less*, Teak-Wood Press, Kissimmee, Florida.

More Airfare Opportunities

Besides the 10% discounts almost all airlines routinely offer anyone over 60 or 62, there are two major ways to save on airfares…

• *Coupon booklets.* American Airlines, America West, Continental, Delta, Northwest, United and USAir sell booklets containing four or eight coupons. Each coupon is good for a flight on any of that airline's domestic routes. A booklet of four coupons costs from $495 and a booklet of eight coupons costs from $920, depending on which airline you use. So you can fly up to eight times a year for $115 to $129 each way.

• *Senior pass.* Continental Airlines sells a Freedom Passport to travelers age 62 and older. You can fly routes in the US, Canada and the Caribbean (140 destinations) as often as once a week for four months…or once a week for one year.

You can buy inexpensive add-ons to Mexico, Central America, Hawaii, Europe and the South Pacific. You can renew for a second year up to 90 days after the expiration of the one-year pass for a discounted price.

Airlines also sometimes offer seniors spur-of-the-moment, additional discounts when new routes open or during slow periods. But these deals are top secret until the last minute. Then, once you break through the busy signal to a reservation clerk, the seats are taken.

Better way: Combine the 10% discount with discounts from coupons and Continental's Passport. Despite some restrictions, including advance bookings and refunds, these discount fares will get you where you want to go, inexpensively.

Source: Lynne Scanlon, a travel writer and the author of *Overcoming Jet Lag,* Berkley Publishing, New York.

Chances of Being Bumped from a Flight

Southwest: 3.48 passengers per 10,000 bookings in early 1994...*Continental:* 3.42...*TWA:* 2.71...*America West:* 2.19. Best performers— *United:* 0.59... *American:* 0.64...*Delta:* 0.94.
Source: US Department of Transportation.

Missed Connecting Flight... What to Do

If you miss a connecting flight, because of bad weather or other schedule disruptions, you may not have to wait for the designated carrier's next flight out. *Key:* A little-known Domestic General Rules Tariff (Rule 240). Under this regulation, some airlines may put you on a competitor's flight—even first class—if it could get you to your destination earlier than their next flight.
Source: Kelli Wayt, American Express Travel, Colorado Springs.

Latest Airport Scam

Thieves are stealing valuables as they emerge from weapon-detection machines. *How it works:* Crooks walk through metal-detection check-

points ahead of intended victims. If victims are delayed—or are asked to walk through again— the crooks take cameras, carry-on bags, etc., after the items clear electronic inspection. *Solution:* Don't let your guard down at the airport— even in seemingly safe and well-protected areas.
Source: Paul Grimes, editor-at-large at *Condé Nast Traveler,* 360 Madison Ave., New York 10017.

Airplane Air Is Best Up Front

There is less carbon dioxide toward the front of the plane. Cabin air, which is partly fresh and partly recirculated, has been blamed for headaches, congestion, dizziness and drowsiness on long flights.
Source: John D. Spengler, PhD, professor of environmental health, Harvard School of Public Health, Boston.

How to Sleep in the Air

Getting to sleep on airline seats that never seem to recline far enough requires preparation and savvy. *You'll need...*

• Ear plugs.

• Inflatable neck pillow.

• Sweater.

• Eye mask on which you have taped the words, "Do Not Disturb."

Your aim is to fall asleep while the plane is taking off and climbing. *Reason:* From departure gate to takeoff, no fresh air is circulated in the cabin. You're likely to feel drowsy anyway.

Before takeoff:

• During the seating process, secure a blanket and airline pillow.

• Place the pillow behind your head, the blown-up inflatable pillow behind your neck and the mini-blanket over you. Fasten the seatbelt over the blanket.

• Insert earplugs.

•Put on the eye mask.
After takeoff:
•Recline.

•Remove the top part of your seat-back. This foam rubber headrest piece is attached to the frame by easily-removable Velcro fasteners. Place this piece behind the small of your back (this gives you a few more inches of recline and a flatter sleeping surface).

•Replace the airline pillow behind your head. (It will cover part of the exposed seat frame.)

•Sleep through the meal served shortly after takeoff…you've ensured your privacy by wearing the "Do Not Disturb" mask, and by keeping your fastened seatbelt visible outside the blanket.

Send a message to your unconscious to wake you up when the plane reaches the beginning of its descent. This is the point from which the plane starts its descent. You'll hear the engines whine at a higher pitch…and if you've programmed yourself, you'll be awakened. Passengers won't prepare for landing for 15 minutes —enough time to use the restroom.

Source: Diana Fairechild, author of *Jet Smart*, which offers 200 ways to beat jet lag, *Jet Smart*, Box 300, Makawao, Maui, Hawaii 96768.

Get the Best Deal When Using Your Credit Card Abroad

When traveling abroad and using a credit card, watch out for the conversion fee that many banks charge to convert charges in foreign currencies to dollars. As with traveler's checks—some banks do and some banks don't charge a fee, generally 1% of the purchase amount. So if you have several cards, it's worth checking with the issuers to see which one offers the best deal on foreign-currency conversion. Then weigh this against other factors. *Note:* The conversion fee is not included in the legally required disclosure box that appears in credit-card promotional material.

Source: Gerri Detweiler, a consumer-credit consultant in Woodbridge, Virginia. She is the author of *The Ultimate Credit Handbook*, Good Advice Press, Elizaville, NY.

Overseas Telephone Charges… How to Save More

Save big on overseas telephone charges by using *International-Plus*—a calling service that uses the combined call volume of its members to get the best discount rates from carriers. Customers don't need to change their long-distance carrier and can call at any hour. *Also:* There is no minimum usage level to get the low rates. *Example:* A call to Great Britain will cost only 35¢ a minute, compared with typical charges of $1 to $1.50 through a regular carrier. *Other rates:* France and Germany, 41¢…Japan, 45¢. For more information, call SMS of Malibu, California, at 310-457-6296.

Source: Daria Hoffman, managing editor, *Update*, 20 Railroad Ave., Hackensack, New Jersey 07601.

Smart Reservation Tactics

Assure hotel reservations by charging room deposits on a major credit card. MasterCard, Visa, American Express and Diners Club all have contractual agreements with hotels that require them to honor reservations of card users or find comparable accommodations nearby, with free transportation to the alternate lodging.

Source: Tom Wall, editor, *Condé Nast Traveler*, 360 Madison Ave., New York 10017.

Smarter Hotel Phone Use

Many hotel phone-call accounting systems do not bill calls that last less than 55 seconds. If a call is completed that quickly—perhaps requesting a call back—there may be no charge.

Source: Harry Newton, publisher, *Teleconnect*, 12 W. 21 St., New York 10010.

Free Cars for Long-Distance Travel

Free cars for long-distance trips are available through drive-away companies. People who want their cars driven somewhere can contact the companies and pay a fee. Potential drivers call the companies to find out if a car is available to be transported where and when they want to go. *Requirements for drivers:* A good driving record...a deposit of about $200...at some firms, references. The driver pays for food, fuel and lodging on the road. *More information:* Check the *Yellow Pages* under "Automobile Transporters."

Source: Jinx Smith, owner, A-1 Automovers, Phoenix, quoted in *The Tightwad Gazette,* RR1, Box 3570, Leeds, Maine 04263.

Weather Report for the '90s

The winter's strange weather for 1995—both warmer and wetter than normal in most of the US—is part of an evolving pattern that could persist for three to four more years. *Cause:* Ultra-fine debris thrown into the atmosphere—by the massive 1991 eruption of Mount Pinatubo in the Philippines...and by volcanic eruptions in the New Guinea area. *Short-term outlook:* February weather will continue mild over most of the US with above-average precipitation from the West Coast through Texas to the Southeast. *Longer-range forecast:* Rains will taper off this spring with mild temperatures. If no further eruptions occur, our weather could return to normal by the end of the century.

Source: Paul Handler, PhD, editor of *Atlas Forecasts,* a newsletter for businesses that depend on weather trends, 706 W. Oregon St., Urbana, Illinois 61801.

How to Get Paid To See the World

If you enjoy traveling and making extra money, there is an opportunity that nearly all travelers overlook—starting a small import business. If you do it right, you travel as much as you want, take a tax deduction for your expenses and earn a second income. For those at or near retirement, the venture can especially make sense.

Reason: Once people leave their first career, they usually have the time and desire to travel plus the experience that it takes to become a successful importer.

Getting started:

How many times have you been overseas and spotted a item that you wished you could buy back home? Chances are, if you want the item, other consumers would, too.

So the next time you visit another country, bring back a few samples.

Best bets: Textiles, folk art, specialty clothing, decorative items and unusual kitchen appliances.

Many countries, for instance, have cooking utensils that American consumers would have difficulty finding.

Example: Manual food mills from France.

Others have clothing that isn't normally found in this country.

Example: Heavy wool socks from Afghanistan.

Stick with items that you know something about. If you don't, there's a risk that you'll buy something that catches your eye overseas, only to discover later that it's either of low quality or already marketed in the US.

Best places to look for importable goods: Developing countries, especially China, India, Africa, Indonesia and South America are excellent for finding folk art, hand-made products and low-priced manufactured goods. Europe is still a resource for household items not normally seen in the US, and the former Eastern Bloc is turning out inexpensive manufactured items, including clothing.

Added advantage: Most developing countries have been granted preferential tariff treatment, meaning that goods can be imported at a low rate or even duty-free in some cases. These countries include Indonesia, India and China. A few more highly developed countries, such as Hungary and Thailand, enjoy this tariff treatment as well.

When you bring back the samples, show them to different types of retailers you think might be interested in selling them. Don't overlook outlets where your product could be an attractive sideline instead.

Examples: Small, decorative items that a florist might want for filling out the overall line, or artwork that an interior decorator could sell.

If a retailer is unsure, offer to put a few items on consignment.

Don't be afraid to go to the buying offices of major department stores. It's usually easier than you think to get an appointment because buyers are always on the lookout for small items that catch customers' attention.

It pays to tell as many people as you think appropriate that you're in the importing business. Word will spread.

Example: One successful importer holds a holiday reception to show off merchandise.
Bringing home the goods:

Once you have an overseas supplier and a domestic buyer, it's time to put in an order and arrange to ship the goods to the US.

It's essential to line up a representative in the foreign country who can make sure that your supplier is complying with the volume and specifications of your order. If you order 10,000 brass bells to be shipped December 15, for example, a representative can make sure the manufacturer doesn't ship 5,000 iron bells on February 1.

To find a reliable representative, ask for recommendations from the American consulate, a local bank or law firm with which you're now doing business or members of the business community, especially Americans who do business in the country from which you are importing.

Safest move: Test the reliability of a supplier and a representative by first placing a small order. Then increase the volume as your confidence grows.

As business increases, it also makes sense to tie shipments to some monetary assurance, such as letters of credit. Essentially, it means your supplier doesn't get paid until he/she provides documentation that your order has been filled and shipped to your specifications.

Representatives are usually paid a percentage of the total order, so it's in their interest to handle the shipment well—in order to get larger jobs in the future.

Also helpful: A freight forwarder who can oversee the actual shipment—from the time your foreign supplier puts it on a ship or plane to the time it arrives at your home or warehouse.

Since many forwarders don't like handling small shipments, it's smart to learn the process yourself.

How it works: Your supplier is responsible for packaging and putting your goods on a ship or plane. You receive a bill of lading when the shipment is made. This tells you what is being sent, how it's sent, and when and where it's scheduled to arrive.

If the goods are coming by ship, for instance, you go to the pier named on the bill of lading, locate a customs agent and open the shipment for inspection.

If duty is owed, you pay it at the pier and then claim possession of your goods.
The payoff:

Even though your initial imports may be small in number, the profit may be impressive. In many cases, you may sell the goods you import for twice your total outlay. Moreover, once you begin importing as a business, your outlays—or a portion of them—can qualify as expenses for tax purposes. This includes the cost of travel as well as meals and lodging.

It doesn't take many shipments before the profits and the tax breaks will actually pay for as much worldwide travel as you want. In many cases, you can even bring along a companion whose travel costs may also be expensed, depending on the amount of work the companion does on the trip.

Source: Stanley Gillmar, president, Inversiones Metropolitanas, Inc., importers, 105 Alta St., San Francisco 94133. Mr. Gillmar is also the coauthor of *How to Be an Importer and Pay for Your World Travel,* Ten Speed Press, Box 7123, Berkeley, California 94707.

Cruise-Ship Safety

Before your next trip, contact the US Public Health Service to see how your cruise ship stacked up under government inspections of quality of water, storage, handling/preparation of food and cleanliness. *Contact:* Vessel Sanitation Program, Centers for Disease Control, 1015 N. American Way, Room 107, Miami 33132, 305-536-4307. The program's Green Sheet compares scores for all inspected ships—or you can get a full report on the ship you will be sailing on.

Volunteer Vacations

Being a volunteer on vacation is not only rewarding and relaxing, but fun, too. *My favorite volunteer vacations...*

United States:

• *Smithsonian Research Expeditions* allow volunteers to work with leading scientists and researchers on a wide range of field projects. Recent ones include studying turtles in the Caribbean and an archaeological dig in Saltville, Virginia. No training is needed. Volunteers must be 18 years or older and in good health.

Details: Trips last one to two weeks. Food and lodging may be included.

Smithsonian Research Expeditions, The Smithsonian Associates, 1100 Jefferson Dr. SW, Washington, DC 20560. 202-357-4800.

• *Student Conservation Association* uses volunteers in national parks throughout the US to forge trails and build footbridges, restore ecologically damaged areas, stabilize stream banks and improve habitats for wildlife and fish. Other projects involve working with tourists at campsites and information centers.

Details: Trips last 12 weeks. Food and lodging or camping equipment are provided.

Student Conservation Association, Box 550, Charlestown, New Hampshire 03603. 603-543-1700.

• *Volunteers for Outdoor Colorado* needs help improving public lands throughout the state—from major cities to remote wilderness areas. Projects include trail building, tree planting, revegetation and even carpentry. Volunteer programs are run on weekends during the spring, summer and fall.

Details: Weekends only. Food, lodging and airfare are not provided. Volunteers stay in camps. *Cost:* Transportation to the site.

Volunteers for Outdoor Colorado, 1410 Grant St., B-105, Denver 80203. 303-830-7792.

International:

• *Ffestiniog Railway Co. in Porthmadog, Wales,* gives steam-engine train buffs the chance to get hands-on experience. Volunteers work on one of the oldest commercial railways in the world. It runs about 13½ miles in the Snowdonia Mountains. Work includes helping to operate the locomotive, repairing track and assisting passengers. No experience is required, and volunteers can choose the aspect of the railroad they would like to work on.

Details: Trips are for varying lengths of time throughout the year. Food and lodging are not included but are available at low cost. *Cost:* Transportation to site.

Volunteer Resource Manager, Harbour Station, Porthmadog, Gwynedd, Wales LL49 9NF. 011-44-1766-512340.

• *Bardou Restoration Project* accepts volunteers to help restore a medieval village in France's Cévennes Mountains, about 500 miles south of Paris. Work includes painting, plastering and more elaborate structural work on houses and public structures. Other tasks include clearing forests and mountain paths and even sheepherding. Volunteers are accepted in spring and fall.

Details: Minimum stay is one month. Food is not included but food is available at low cost.

Bardou Restoration Project, Bardou, 34390 Olargues, France. 011-33-67-97-7243.

• *World Teach* brings volunteers to Shanghai to teach English to Chinese high-school students. Participants are immersed in an intense exchange with students, living and eating with them while getting a chance to study the Chinese language and customs. No teaching credentials or special language skills are required although volunteers are expected to be college students or graduates.

Details: Trips last eight to ten weeks. Food and lodging are included.

Harvard Institute for International Development, One Eliot St., Cambridge 02138. 617-495-5527.

Source: Bill McMillon, who has taken many volunteer vacations during the past ten years. He is the author of *Volunteer Vacations: Short-Term Adventures that Will Benefit You and Others,* Chicago Review Press, 814 N. Franklin St., Chicago 60610.

5

Shrewd
Money Management

Financial Strategies for Working Couples

Few two-income couples take full advantage of their financial power. And they don't concentrate on making their money work for them.

Think about it. If you both were living separately, you would each have rent or mortgage payments…phone and utility bills…and it wouldn't be as much fun to dine at home. So don't spend all of your double income…use it to your advantage.

Attitudes about money:

There are two types of people—*savers* and *spenders*. For better or worse, they tend to marry each other. The result is often conflicting views of money and how it should be spent and invested. To make matters more stressful, both adults in dual-income households usually are aggressive about having their way.

Result: It's easy to find yourself trying to control each other's financial behavior in ways that generate conflict.

Solution: Sit down with your partner and confront your money attitudes. Then discuss how best to handle your finances. Take a close look at your overall financial picture. *Ask yourselves:*

•How much of your respective incomes do you want to save?

•What are your savings goals (vacation, new car, down payment on a house, college for the kids, retirement)?

•Should you be accountable to each other for *all* of your spending…or should you each have a private account?

•How many credit cards will you use? Or will you cut up all but one of your cards and take a weekly cash allowance?

Another way to limit the amount of damage done by reckless spending habits is to set up separate accounts for a portion of your earnings. Pay your household expenses out of one joint account.

Remember: Depending on your state of residence, you may be responsible for your spouse's debts…and your spouse's bill-paying habits could affect your credit report.

Share the financial chores:

In many households, the financial chores are divided. One person pays the bills and balances the checkbook, while the other invests and organizes the taxes. However, it is far better if both of you understand and are responsible for all aspects of your finances. After all, you never know when you'll have to take over the entire job of financial management.

Added benefits: If the *spender* had to balance the checkbook and pay the bills, he/she might not be so willing to buy impulsively. If the person who handles the checkbook understood more about investing, he would probably better understand why it is so important to make out that monthly check to the mutual fund to save for college or retirement.

Reconcile tax strategies:

Spouses often have different views about how to handle their income taxes and organize their records, especially if they prepare their own tax returns.

Example: You may be an aggressive filer who claims every deduction, while your spouse may be more conservative for fear of triggering an audit.

Important: If both of you sign the return, both of you are liable for any mistakes, disallowances (when the IRS disallows a deduction) or penalties.

Strategy: Seek professional tax-filing help. Find a CPA who makes both of you comfortable. It may be worth the extra expense to give you peace of mind about your taxes.

Retirement accounts:

IRAs offer a tremendous opportunity to save for your future. You may each deduct a $2,000 contribution to an IRA if neither you nor your spouse is covered by an employer-sponsored retirement plan, such as a 401(k). Even if you do participate in such a plan, you still might be eligible to deduct some IRA contributions, depending on your income level. Check with your tax adviser. Even better than an IRA is a company-sponsored 401(k) plan. Try to contribute the maximum amount allowed, especially if your company matches your contributions.

Important: Some couples leave retirement planning to the highest earner. *That causes two problems...*

•The couple doesn't save enough to meet their retirement needs.

•One of them may be at a big disadvantage if they ever divorce.

Strategy: If you *can't* afford to contribute the maximum amounts to two company savings plans, concentrate all your savings in the plan that offers the best deal.

Example: If your spouse's employer matches employees' retirement contributions but your employer does not, you might consider having your spouse contribute more. But each of you should have savings in your own name.

Life insurance needs:

If both of you are working, you might need additional life insurance to replace some of the income that would be lost if one spouse died.

That means you must figure out how much supplemental income you would need, especially to cover long-term expenses such as mortgage payments or college costs. *Helpful:* Comparison shop for the least expensive term life insurance from a highly rated company.

Helpful: Get term insurance quotes from *SelectQuote* (800-343-1985)...and *TermQuote* (800-444-TERM).

Alternative: If you don't have a policy, consider buying a first-to-die whole-life policy. It will insure the life of the person who dies first and might be as much as 40% cheaper than buying separate policies for each of you.

Important: Make sure that the policy can be converted to cover a surviving spouse without a new physical exam.

Health insurance:

Be careful about tampering with your health insurance. Since both of you have jobs, you may be able to save some money on your coverage. For example, you might opt out of one partner's plan and let the other plan cover you both.

Warning: Such a move could leave you vulnerable if the covered spouse loses his job.

Compare the two plans, and figure out how much you could save by dropping one of them. If the savings are considerable, find out if you can temporarily drop one and then get back into it later—without being subject to restrictions for preexisting conditions.

If not, consider keeping both plans, despite the extra cost.

One income:

Just because both of you are working now doesn't mean your family will always have two incomes.

Examples: One of you may decide to take time off to change careers, raise children or go back to school. There is also the real risk that one of you will lose your job at some point.

Bottom line: Being a two-income family gives you power, leverage and maneuverability right now. Change your attitudes about spending and saving. Think of spending less now not as a penalty, but as a form of deferred consumption with a real bonus—the interest or gains you can earn on the money you save.

Remember: If you don't see the money, you won't spend it. Start automatic monthly deductions from your paycheck or checking account into a stock or money market mutual fund. Let your money work as hard for you as you work for it.

Source: Terry Savage, the well-known personal financial expert and registered investment adviser for stocks and commodities. She is a syndicated columnist for *The Chicago Sun-Times* and the author of *Terry Savage's New Money Strategies for the '90s*, HarperBusiness.

Financial-Planning Reminder

Update financial documents regularly to account for family changes, such as marriages, divorces, births and deaths. Make sure all intended beneficiaries are listed properly on trusts, wills, life insurance policies, pension forms, mutual funds, etc.

Source: Jeff Saccacio, partner, Coopers & Lybrand, Los Angeles.

Financial-Planning Mistakes Can Be Avoided

It's one thing to make a New Year's resolution to—at last—get your financial plans in shape. It's another thing to get those plans right.

Here are the most common financial-planning mistakes people make and how you can avoid them…

• *Mistake:* Not setting specific planning goals. Financial planners always want you to start by thinking about and stating your goals…clearly. *Most people do have goals:* Retiring early, building a college fund for their children and so on. The trouble is most of the time those goals are too vague.

Worse: Most people don't quantify those goals or put priorities on them. What they really have is sort of a wish list. They have five goals, all of equal importance—and there's no way on earth they can achieve all of them.

Be very specific about each goal. If it's college for the kids—what kind of college, private or state? What kind of private college? And what about graduate school? Do you anticipate having to help support your children after undergraduate school?

If the goal is to retire at age 60—where? Will you need a place less expensive than where you are now? Will you need to spend the same amount each year after you retire than you do now?

• *Mistake:* Not calculating what your plans will actually cost. Talk about what each goal means in actual dollars and cents. Translate that into what you have to accumulate…projecting out for inflation, too.

You are then likely to find that you have to choose among goals—not Harvard but a $15,000-a-year college for your son if you want to be able to retire at 60. And you'll have to consider a move to Arizona or North Carolina, rather than keep your house in Connecticut or move to Palm Beach.

You don't have a financial plan if you haven't quantified, prioritized and integrated your goals…and figured out what they will cost. And, remember, if you want to reach your goals, they must be realistic.

• *Mistake:* Not looking before taking financial leaps. Do your research. If you are planning a move that you think will cut your expenses, be very sure of your facts.

I have clients who quit high-paying jobs in the Northeast to retire early to some southwestern state, counting on being able to buy a house there for less than they got for the house they sold. And they wouldn't have to pay state taxes either.

Both things were true. But within a year they found that property taxes where they moved were far higher than they had been paying. And living costs weren't that much less either. The move didn't cut their spending at all, but they couldn't move back home because they couldn't afford to buy another house where they had been living.

• *Mistake:* Basing your plans on faulty assumptions. Many people now in their 50s and 60s remember having to pay huge estate taxes on what they inherited from their parents because no proper planning was done. They won't make the same mistake, they think, so they start giving assets to their children to remove them from their estates.

But some of them are giving away now what they will need for themselves later. This is especially true for single women. They look at assets of $1 million and want to give away $400,000 so their remaining estate ($600,000) will not be taxed.

Younger people sometimes think they don't have to plan for retirement or college for their children because they stand to inherit a valuable house and other assets from their parents. First, their parents may live a very long time and spend it all. And second, those young people will need a lot more than they think they do now.

If you want your plan to work, it must be realistic.

• *Mistake:* Not reviewing your plans once they're made. You can't just make financial plans and assume they will stand unchanged for the rest of your life. You change. Economic conditions change. Investment opportunities change. And the tax law changes.

Your plan may assume you will make 8% to 10% a year on your investments. But along comes a year like 1994, when you have to be lucky to make anything. You will always have years like that…and when they come they will force you to adjust your thinking and your plans.

Get the papers out at least once a year and look them over carefully. Make sure your plans say what you now want them to say.

• *Mistake:* Trying to do it all yourself. Of course it's self-serving for me to say this, but I truly feel that people will be better off if they have an expert look over what they do themselves—especially their projections of how much they will need in the future.

I feel people should consult with a qualified attorney on their estate plans…and have a tax person look over their taxes. You may not be able to keep up with all the changes in tax laws and other factors that can affect your plans.

My suggestion: Bring your plans and projections at least once a year to someone skilled enough to ask the right questions.

• *Mistake:* Underestimating the high cost of raising kids. Don't assume that expenses for your children will end when they graduate from college. There is nothing automatic about that. You must decide how much to spend on your children and for how long.

For many people there comes a time when it's a choice between your own comfortable retirement for 25 or 30 years and giving money to your children…hard as it is to say "no" to them. It's especially hard for many middle-class parents who fear that their own children may be headed for a future that may not be very financially rewarding.

• *Mistake:* Assuming you will live forever. Most people just can't face estate planning. They procrastinate and procrastinate because of some underlying fear that if they plan for their death, they will die.

Once you reach your 40s, you must have the main elements of your estate plan in place. You can't wait until you retire to think seriously about it.

You need a will, a power of attorney, a health power of attorney to make decisions relating to your care if you cannot and a living will.

Get these basics done. You can then change whatever needs to be changed in the future as events change, your own judgment changes about trustees, guardians and attorneys.

Overcome that fear and think about how

much easier you will make it for those you leave behind.

• *Mistake:* Mishandling an inheritance. People often fail to integrate an inheritance into their financial plans. They are tempted to treat the money as a windfall—to be spent now for luxuries they otherwise couldn't afford. That inheritance could be a lifesaver in the years ahead—given all the talk about cutting Social Security benefits and the continuing escalation of health-care and long-term–care costs.

• *Mistake:* Underestimating how long you are likely to live in retirement. Many people still fail to put all they can into tax-deferred retirement accounts at work or into Keoghs for the self-employed. Or they borrow all too casually from these accounts to meet current expenses.

Not so long ago people could get away without serious retirement planning because there was Social Security and Medicare and company pension plans to rely on...and because they were likely to die only a few years after retirement. None of the above is the case today.

Work out how long you are likely to live in retirement and how much you will need to carry you through those years. Making realistic plans for retirement will increase your chances of being secure when you're older.

Source: Alexandra Armstrong, chairperson, Armstrong, Welch & MacIntyre, Inc., financial consultants, 1155 Connecticut Ave. NW, Washington, DC 20036.

New Bank—New Policies

If your bank changes hands, be sure to find out the new owner's policies. Banks pay different interest rates...provide services such as checking accounts at different costs...have different fees, such as overdraft charges...and have different policies, such as check-hold periods. If you do not like the policies of the new bank, look elsewhere.

Source: Edward F. Mrkvicka, Jr., president, Reliance Enterprises, a financial-consulting firm in Marengo, Illinois, and the author of *The Bank Book,* HarperCollins, Ten E. 53 St., New York 10022.

When Not to Use Your Safe-Deposit Box

Do not keep cash, savings bonds or securities in safe-deposit boxes. Theft is on the rise as robbers distract guards, make wax impressions of master keys and return with copies to loot boxes. Because it's impossible to prove that currency was in the box, your loss may not be covered by the bank. *Better:* Keep cash in a fireproof home safe. Also keep savings bonds and securities at home—but keep copies at the bank for proof of ownership.

Source: Edward Mrkvicka, Jr., is a bank consultant in Marengo, Illinois, and the author of *The Bank Book,* HarperCollins, New York.

The Secrets of Borrowing Smarter

Interest rates have been climbing for nearly a year...and that trend should continue at least until mid-1995. Higher rates, in turn, keep raising the risk of recession.

Yet Americans continue borrowing "as if there's no tomorrow," taking on debt that will burden them for years to come.

Important: You don't have to fall into the debt trap that hurt so many people in the 1980s. Here are my rules for borrowing smart today... and recognizing when you owe more than you can handle...

Credit-card borrowing:

• *Demand a better deal.* Credit-card issuers are fiercely competing for your business. If you have a balance outstanding and a good record of making payment, they won't risk losing you to a competitor.

In the past month, we've seen people lower the rate on their card debt from 15% to 9%... 8%...or even 7% for the next six months...*just by asking.*

Helpful: Take advantage of card solicitations you get in the mail if the rates are low...but make sure the seductively low rate applies for at least six months. It's not worthwhile to transfer a balance for a rate that is good for only a few months.

Warning: If you plan to apply soon for a mortgage, don't keep your old credit card after transferring the balance to a new one. Mortgage lenders consider your *potential* debt as well as *actual* debt. The more credit cards you own, they calculate, the more debt you conceivably could pile up.

• *Scrutinize the fine print.* Your card statement may announce in bold letters that you don't have to pay anything this month. Keep looking. Somewhere on that page is the tiny-print caveat that if you don't pay anything this month, interest charges will accrue.

Example: Many merchants today offer great-sounding deals: "Buy now, and owe nothing for six months." But in six months, you'll owe the entire balance on all you've charged. *If you can't pay:* You'll be charged interest retroactively...and typically at a super-high rate of 20% or more.

"No-payment-until-whenever" deals are great only if you know you can afford to pay the balance when the "free" period is over.

Home mortgages:

• *Go with an adjustable-rate mortgage.* You don't want to lock in today's high rates with a fixed mortgage. As rates rise and fall over the years, your average cost is likely to come out lower with a variable-rate mortgage than with a fixed rate.

Make sure your adjustable-rate mortgage can't increase by more than two percentage points in one year or by more than six percentage points over the life of the loan.

Exception: With a 15-year mortgage, you probably have no choice but a fixed-rate loan. A 15-year loan can make sense if you're nearing retirement and want the mortgage paid off by the time you stop working.

Home-improvement loans:

• *Borrow only as much as you need.* It's safer to borrow a specific amount for a specific purpose than to take as much as your bank will lend you. If you need $5,000, don't borrow $15,000.

Problem: The rate on home-equity loans keeps rising as interest rates generally rise. A lot of people who took such loans to finance home improvements in the past couple of years may find it difficult to make their payments now that rates are up.

Car loans:

• *Don't talk financing until you've negotiated the price of the car.* Dealers often quote a higher price if they know how you'll finance the purchase with them...or that you plan to lease rather than buy. When that happens, you wind up paying more...even if you get a low rate on the loan.

College financing:

• *Borrow cheap by taking a home-equity loan—or tapping your 401(k) plan at work.*

The advantages: Interest on a home-equity loan of up to $100,000 is tax-deductible.

Interest on a 401(k) loan typically is one or two percentage points above the prime rate. Since you are borrowing from your own 401(k) account, you're paying off the loan—including interest—to yourself.

Important: You must repay a 401(k) loan within five years. Otherwise the Internal Revenue Service will consider it a distribution from your retirement account. The IRS will then demand income taxes on the full amount...plus a 10% early-withdrawal penalty if you're under age 59½.

Warning: Don't borrow from your 401(k) plan if your job is in danger. If you leave for any reason, you'll have only up to six months to repay any outstanding 401(k) loan before it's deemed a taxable distribution.

Overdoing it:

How can you tell if you're getting too deeply in debt? *Two danger signals:*

• Letting installment debt get over 20% of take-home pay...

• Letting debt, including mortgage debt, exceed 40% of take-home pay.

You're in trouble if you...

...use credit cards to borrow cash as well as to make purchases.

...can't afford to set aside an emergency account equal to at least three months of living expenses.

...switch an unpaid balance to a new credit card for a lower rate...and promptly run up a new balance on the old card.

...make only minimum required payments on all credit cards and credit lines because that's all you can afford.

...borrow on one card to pay another.

...routinely get past-due notices on your bills.

...mail checks to creditors unsigned, in the hope that will delay their processing and buy you a little more time.

...have soaring monthly bank fees because you are being charged for so many bounced checks.

...can't afford to save anything in your 401(k) or Individual Retirement Account, because all your money is going to pay down debt.

...aren't filing income-tax returns because you're afraid you'll owe more than you can pay.

...get calls from collection agencies so often you're on a first-name basis with the agency's staff.

Undoing what you've overdone:

If you are in debt over your head, here's what I suggest you do...

• *Acknowledge the problem.* The worst thing you can do is bury your head in the sand.

Example: The longer you delay filing a tax return, the more interest and penalties you'll owe in addition to the tax.

If you file a return and candidly acknowledge you don't have the money to pay the tax you owe, the IRS is much more willing to work things out with you then, rather than later when they catch up with you.

• *Talk to your creditors.* Banks, credit-card companies and department stores usually are very willing to work out a payment schedule that's easier for you to meet...if you level with them about your difficulties.

• *Consider a debt-consolidation loan.* Using a home-equity loan to pay off other debts makes sense only if it won't put your home in jeopardy. Never borrow more than 25% of the equity you have in your home.

Important: As a rule, debt-consolidation loans are dangerous. By paying off your other debts, you open up all your existing credit lines, making it way too easy to get buried in debt anew. But if you must borrow to pay off pressing debt and a home-equity loan would put your home at risk, then a debt-consolidation loan may be your only choice.

Source: Scott Kahan, certified financial planner and president of Financial Asset Management Corp., 220 Fifth Ave., New York 10001.

Former Bank President Tells How Not to Be Outsmarted by Your Bank

I'm always amazed at how people go out of their way to get an extra eighth of one percent on a CD...and then pay their banks much more than that in fees they have been told are unavoidable.

Reality: Banks don't want you to know their fees and interest rates are negotiable. Often all you have to do is ask.

Example: Most banks will give senior citizens, the disabled and students free checking accounts. But you have to ask.

Strategy: Learn the chain of command at your bank. If you encounter a bank employee who won't negotiate fees, ask to speak with his/her boss. Most senior personnel would prefer you to be happy with the bank, especially if you are a good customer.

Here is how to minimize your ATM fees, your overdraft charges and the penalties for falling below minimum-balance requirements...

• *Use a small bank.* Your bank should be one of the smallest in your area. A big bank won't go the extra mile for you because it doesn't feel it needs your business. A small bank will be flexible because it needs satisfied customers in order to attract new customers and to grow.

• *Don't use ATMs—except in emergencies.* Not only can they be costly, they prevent you from establishing important personal relationships with bank officers. Those cordial relationships can help you get better rates and terms on bank loans and services.

• *Avoid overdraft charges.* Ask your bank to electronically monitor and "red flag" your checking account…and telephone you if it is overdrawn. Most community banks will give you until 3 PM the same day to come in with a deposit before they bounce a check—saving you a $15 to $25 overdraft charge and the embarrassment of a returned check.

• *Ask for minimum-balance requirements to be waived.* Many banks will waive these requirements if you insist. If your bank won't, consider a credit union, which usually is cheaper and offers better service. For more information, call the Credit Union National Association at 800-358-5710.

• *Plan before you borrow.* Go into the bank and update your personal financial statement every six months or so—even if you don't need a loan. Strike up conversations with the people who help you.

Reason: You want at least one teller, one loan officer and one bookkeeper to know your face. Anyone can borrow if they have good collateral. But if you need a loan based only on collateral, you're much more likely to get it if you—and your credit history—are familiar to the bank's employees.

• *Refuse unnecessary products.* Banks are intimidating to average consumers, who are afraid to question what is put in front of them.

Example: Most people are so happy to get a car loan, they're afraid to refuse the hugely overpriced credit–life- and -disability insurance the bank often adds to the loan. Even worse—they don't realize that because the insurance cost has been added to the loan, the premium is subject to a finance charge.

Source: Edward F. Mrkvicka, Jr., president of Reliance Enterprises, Inc., a national financial-consulting firm. A former CEO of an Illinois bank, he is the editor of *Money Insider* newsletter and the author of *The Bank Book: How to Revoke Your Bank's "License to Steal"—and Save Up to $100,000,* Harper Perennial, New York.

Secret Bank Accounts

The government of the Bahamas committed itself to continuing bank confidentiality and secrecy laws. The Bahamas does not share tax or financial information with other countries. Banking information can be revealed only on the order of the Supreme Court in a criminal case—and tax rules of foreign countries are not considered criminal. Banks also are financially sound—foreign parents of local banks are required to guarantee the liabilities of their subsidiaries, and such banks include Citicorp and Royal Bank of Canada. *Also:* There is no Bahamian income tax. But, of course, American taxpayers are required to report their worldwide income.

Source: James Smith, governor of the Bahamas Central Bank, the government of the Bahamas, Nassau, the Bahamas.

Credit-Card Companies' Dirty Little Secrets

Never have so many companies issued so many different credit cards with so many different features. There are now more than 20,000 MasterCard and Visa programs—in addition to the credit cards offered by American Express. Here's how to cut through the advertising claims and get the best deal.

• *Determine which type of credit card is best for you.* This depends on your spending habits. If you pay your bill in full, shop around for the lowest annual fee. If you carry a credit balance from month to month, look for a card with the lowest interest rate.

Important: Get a new credit card or negotiate a new rate if you are paying more than 13% to 14% in interest.

Strategy: To negotiate a rate, call your credit-card issuer and ask for a rate that is competitive with offers you've received in the mail or seen in ads. If you pay on time and charge regularly, chances are your issuer will match the rate—at least for one year.

• *Compare competing credit-card solicitations.* If you have a good credit rating, you'll probably receive many offers in the mail. Save them, and clip ads for one month. By going through them all at once, you won't get confused trying to remember different interest rates and fees.

When you start going through the material you have collected, look for a box of fine print at the end of each credit solicitation and ad. *By law, the issuer must...*

•Disclose the credit card's interest rate and annual fee.

•State whether the rate will increase after a set period, such as 90 days, and by how much.

•State whether the card carries any additional fees.

• *Watch out for ads boasting rates that are less than 10%.* In most cases, these are known as teasers—rates that are designed to grab your attention and attract your business. These bargain-basement teaser rates usually are good for only 90 days—and they then jump to much higher levels.

Another seemingly attractive advertising claim is a low rate if you agree to transfer your debt from other cards to the new one. This can be a good deal, but check to see if you will be charged for the service. When you agree to consolidate debts, a credit-card company uses cash to pay off your outstanding balances and may charge you for the cash advance.

Check the disclosure box—or call the company—for a clear explanation. If you like the credit card, politely insist that the company lower the fee.

• *Ask your old credit-card company to report to credit bureaus that your account has been closed*—after you have received your new credit card. Creditors won't do this unless you ask because they hope you will resume using the credit card in an emergency.

Trap: If you leave all of these accounts open, you may have difficulty getting a loan or a mortgage.

Reason: When a bank looks at a credit report and sees that you have eight or more credit cards, it worries that you may default on its loan—since you could easily become overextended.

• *When you travel and use your credit card overseas, the issuer may charge you a conver-*

sion fee. The fee to convert charges in foreign currencies is usually 1% of the charge.

Important: This fee is not included in the disclosure box. Before traveling, call the issuer to see if it charges for conversions. If it does, determine if the card offers enough benefits in other areas to make up for this drawback. Otherwise, shop around for another card to use for foreign travel.

• *An affinity card may not be all it says it is.* Affinity cards pledge to donate a portion of what you've charged to a charitable organization. *Drawbacks:*

•They can have high interest rates and/or fees.

•Some card issuers prohibit charities from revealing exactly how much money they receive in donations from the issuer. This secrecy makes it impossible to know whether your goodwill is really helping.

Strategy: Apply for an affinity card only if you can get as good a deal as you could on another card. Otherwise, find the right card for you and make your donations directly to the charity.

• *In order to receive a substantial amount of money back from rebate cards, you have to charge more than you think.* These issuers offer rebates based on the amounts you charge. In many cases, you must charge thousands of dollars each year to get back or be credited just $100. Rebate cards also typically charge higher interest rates than other cards do.

• *Specialty cards, such as frequent-flier cards, are only good deals if you use them correctly.* For instance, I have one airline's frequent-flier charge card. I put all of my charges on it and pay my balance in full each month. Though the $65 annual fee is relatively high, I travel frequently, and my charges entitle me to receive a free plane ticket each year.

For most people, the card would not be worthwhile. You usually have to charge $25,000 a year to earn the ticket. Most people charge only about $3,000.

Still, if you own a small business or charge a lot, frequent-flier cards—and automobile-rebate cards—can be good deals for you.

• *Read everything your credit-card issuer sends you.* Most people simply toss out additional mail from issuers or inserts placed inside bills. They just assume these are solicitations that they do not want or need.

Caution: In some cases, these mailings may be important notices.

Example: If you have a fixed rate, your issuer can raise it, but by law must give you 15 days' notice. Most issuers inform you of increases through an insert with your bill.

Source: Gerri Detweiler, a consumer-credit consultant in Woodbridge, Virginia. She is the author of *The Ultimate Credit Handbook*, Good Advice Press, Elizaville, NY.

Easy Way to Cut Credit-Card Costs—Significantly

If you carry a balance, call your bank and ask for its low introductory rate. Competition among bank cards and American Express has forced many banks to make special deals to hold on to customers. *Example:* A New York bank recently cut a customer's 16.8% rate to 8.9% for 12 months, provided he transferred at least $1,000 of debt from another card. The bank also waived the transfer fee.

Source: Gerri Detweiler is a consumer advocate and author of *The Ultimate Credit Handbook*, Good Advice Press, Elizaville, NY.

Best Credit Reference You Didn't Know You Had

Major credit cards that you've paid on time over time can be your best credit reference—

even better than a mortgage or car loan. That's because home and car loans are secured, while your credit-card payment record demonstrates your reliability when paying off unsecured debts. Don't overdo it. Banks will view a timely payment record on two or three credit cards in your favor, but they may hold it against you if you have too many cards...your cards are always charged up close to your credit limit... you take out a new card and immediately run it up to its limit.

Source: Gerri Detweiler, consumer-credit expert, 6076 Trident Lane, Woodbridge, Virginia 22193.

Beware of Saving For a Rainy Day

Do not put too much money aside for a rainy day. The common recommendation—to keep enough cash for six months' worth of living expenses—forces you to hold significant amounts of money in very-low-interest locations like savings accounts.

Better: Keep enough cash to handle small-scale disasters such as the need for a new refrigerator or major car repairs. Put the rest of the rainy-day money into a good stock fund.

Reason: The fund should provide good returns, eventually being worth far more than you need to live for six months. In case of personal disaster when stocks are down, tap home equity or get a credit card cash advance—then repay the loan by selling shares of the fund after the market recovers.

Source: Jonathan Clements, financial writer for *The Wall Street Journal* and author of *Funding Your Future: The Only Guide to Mutual Funds You'll Ever Need,* Warner Books.

6

Investing to Win

Golden Rules for Achieving Financial Independence

The biggest long-term financial risk that investors face is the shrinking value of a dollar. If every dollar you have today is worth only 50 cents 10 years from now, you're in trouble.

The solution is to have as little of your money tied to a dollar as possible. How can you afford to invest your long-term money in money market accounts, bonds, cash-value life insurance or certificates of deposit? These are money savers, not money makers.

Stay ahead of the shrinking dollar:

Your money's value lies in what it can buy. To compensate for the decline in the value of the dollar, put your money where it has a chance to grow significantly. The only two investments that are likely to do that over time are real estate and stocks.

While real estate has its benefits, especially if you own your home, there are big drawbacks to its growth potential...

• Real estate requires a substantial investment —even if you get a large mortgage.

• Real estate is mostly illiquid—you may not be able to sell the property when you want to.

• Real estate that you own and rent out must be managed. You can delegate responsibilities to a managing agent, but you must always make the important decisions.

The case for stocks:

People who fear stocks fear losing money. But if they are investing for the long-term value, that fear is unfounded. The value of the market historically goes up and down—but in the long term, it goes on to new highs.

When you buy stocks or stock mutual funds, your investment is not tied to the shrinking value of a dollar. It's tied to the value of growing companies. Therefore, you have an opportunity to more than compensate for the loss in a dollar's value.

Important: Investing in the stock market is not the only road to riches. It is wise to also examine your spending habits and saving patterns.

Six keys to success:

• *Live within your means.* In order to save money, you must fight to keep from spending what you have earned. Recognizing that there is a limit to the amount of money you can spend is the first step to long-term financial planning. Everyone enjoys spending money, but your taste in restaurants, clothes, home furnishings and cars must be weighed against your financial priorities.

Example: When my wife and I were married in 1954, we were determined to become financially independent. We kept a daily record of every cent we spent. A*t the end of every month, we analyzed where our money went and asked ourselves two questions:* Were we getting our money's worth and were we satisfied with the way we were spending our money? If the answer to either question was no, we changed our spending the next month and found money to invest.

This may seem boring and unproductive, but we found it can be very helpful.

Once you have saved money, you place a different set of priorities on what you want. Eventually, you will end up being able to do everything you truly want to do rather than just satisfying your impulses. Remember, your purpose in life is not to save—it is to be able to do what you want to do when you want to do it.

• *Build up an emergency fund.* The classic advice is to have six months' living expenses in investments that can be easily liquidated. But six months of living costs is a lot of money for most people, and setting this much aside may leave you with nothing to invest for the long term.

Solution: My wife and I never kept much more than one month's expenses in the bank. We wanted our money to work for us, so we used our long-term investments as part of our reserve. When we needed extra money temporarily, we used our investments as collateral for short-term bank loans—at low rates. We paid off these loans later, out of our income.

Important: Before we borrowed, we were always sure we had the means to pay the money back at any time.

• *Start saving early.* It takes much less money to reach your goal than you think, thanks to the extraordinary power of compounding.

Example: If from age 20 to age 65 you save $50 a month and get an average annual return of 8%, at age 65 you can take out $1,658 every month until you reach age 100. While you would have put in a total of $27,000, you will be withdrawing a total of $693,300. By comparison, to reach the same goal if you started saving at age 30, you would have to save $112 a month—more than twice as much.

It is never too late to start saving. You have more time remaining today than you will ever have again. Time also allows us to make up for errors in judgment we may make along the way.

• *Pay yourself first.* Think of investing as your number-one financial obligation each month. It comes down to your personal priorities. How can you become financially independent if you don't pay yourself first?

A simple rule of thumb is to save at least 10% of your gross income. As you earn more, increase this percentage. You can always find the money to meet this goal if you are absolutely determined to do so. Don't overlook small—but constant—saving opportunities.

Example: Several years ago, I decided I was spending too much for razor blades. I switched from using a blade a day to using one every four days. Each blade costs about $1 now, so I have reduced my daily cost to 25 cents a day—an annual savings of $274. I invest the money I've saved.

• *Reach for higher returns—even at some risk.* Smart people don't try to avoid risks but simply hold them within reasonable limits. In fact, those who stick to so-called safe investments face the greatest risk of all—the shrinking value of a dollar.

The higher the rate of return, the less money you have to save and the more you can eventually take out.

Example: At a 10% return instead of 8%, the 20-year-old saving $50 per month in the previous example would be able to withdraw $3,729 a month instead of $1,658, from age 65 to age 100.

Surprising: The extra benefit of two more percentage points comes to a total of $869,702.

• *Know the limits of your knowledge.* Before you invest, ask yourself whether you truly have the expertise to buy and sell individual stocks. Do you really know what stocks to buy and when to buy them? Do you have enough time to keep an eye on them throughout the week?

I have never owned a marketable individual stock in my life. Years ago, I decided a professionally managed investment such as a mutual fund could make a lot more money for me over time than I could make for myself…and I used to be a portfolio manager.

The added value of professional management can be substantial.

Example: Consider a hypothetical investment of $100 a month in the Dow Jones Industrial Average (DJIA) for 20 years and the same amount invested in a top mutual fund that invests in a wide range of growth stocks for the same amount of time and returns about 20%.

The average annual return from the unmanaged DJIA for any 20-year period from July 1, 1971, through March 31, 1994, was less than 15%—about five percentage points less than the growth mutual fund.

There are short-term risks, but the longer you stay invested, the better your chances are of doing well.

Source: James E. Stowers, founder and chairman of Twentieth Century Mutual Funds, a family of more than two dozen no-load funds with total assets of more than $25 billion. He is the author of *Yes You Can…Achieve Financial Independence,* Andrews and McMeel, Kansas City, MO.

When Buying Stocks that Investors Shun is Smart…

Richard S. Huson keeps the Crabbe Huson Equity Fund consistently outstripping the *S&P 500* by buying stocks suffering from what he calls "low investor esteem."

What contrarian-investor Huson looks for is a company with what he sees as good fundamentals that has performed well in the past… but that investors have abandoned.

So far, that strategy has paid off. Crabbe Huson Equity Fund has returned investors 14½% a year annually over the past five years. *Huson illustrates his approach by offering three situations he likes today…*

• *Apple Computer.* Less than two years ago, AAPL stock traded in the mid-60s. It goes for barely half that now. Yet it still has a solid balance sheet and a very loyal customer base. *Problem:* Investors want to be certain that the company will score with its new line of high-powered, versatile Power PC models.

• *The Limited.* It was once an investor favorite …with such powerful retailing names as Lerners, Limited, Express, Victoria's Secret, Abercrombie & Fitch. More recently it has fallen out of favor…and its shares currently sell for about half of what they once did.

Source: Richard S. Huson, principal and portfolio manager, Crabbe Huson Equity Fund, One Financial Center, 121 SW Morrison, Suite 1415, Portland, Oregon 97204. Crabbe Huson Equity Fund is a no-load fund with a 0.19% 12b-1 fee.

How to Pick Winning Stocks

Over the long term, stock market surges tend to occur in short, unpredictable bursts. You won't benefit if most of your assets are in cash.

The key is smart stock picking. If you choose well, you won't need to own dozens of different companies to maximize your portfolio's potential for profits. In my typical client's portfolio, for example, there are only about 12 stocks.

Here are my stock-picking secrets that anyone can use…

• Only buy stock in companies whose businesses you understand—and whose products either you or people you know use. Put another way, if you like the company's product, you'll probably like its stock.

Of course, a preference for a company's product is not the only reason to buy a stock…but it is an essential first step. If I understand what the company makes and I use its products at work or at home, I will have a pretty good idea of whether the company is on the right track.

Example: A few years ago, we purchased Dell Computer equipment for the office and were very pleased with it. I knew that if Dell products met our needs, they probably were meeting the needs of many other companies. So I bought Dell stock in May 1991 at an average price of $16. I sold it in February 1993 at $37—more than doubling my clients' money in less than two years.

•Buy stock in companies that are not followed closely by analysts. Wall Street analysts tend to move in packs, praising or panning the same companies at the same time. As a result, some of the market's best values are overlooked, mostly because these companies are too small for big analysts to cover.

Many of the stocks in our clients' portfolios fall into this category. They are tracked by only three or four analysts. Just because these companies are small, however, doesn't mean they don't have great upside potential.

Investors must keep their eyes and ears open to find good stocks that analysts don't follow closely. Even if you don't personally own or use a product, your friends and relatives may. Their reactions can steer you toward some good companies.

Examples: You can ride in their new cars… or listen to them talk about their new sports equipment.

Another way to discover top-quality products is to read *Consumer Reports.** It is an excellent source of information on a wide variety of high-quality products.

Once you've decided on some good companies, call their public relations departments for a list of analysts who follow their stocks. If a company has a long list of analysts from big-name investment firms, such as Merrill Lynch, Paine Webber and Smith Barney, forget about it. A much better sign is if only a handful of regional firms follow the company.

•Consider buying into companies that are controversial—at least from the viewpoint of Wall Street analysts. Sometimes I'll buy stock in an undervalued company that is shunned by

Consumer Reports, 101 Truman Ave., Yonkers, New York 10703.

Wall Street. Many times analysts ignore a company's stock because they have a fundamental misconception about the company's product or future potential.

Example: Callaway Golf is a small maker of expensive golf clubs. Its share price declined by 30% in October 1993, when it was reported that much of its action came from investors who were short-sellers—investors who borrow money to buy a stock that they expect will decline.

In the case of Callaway, the short-sellers were wrong. Sales continued at their torrid pace. The short-sellers didn't realize that Callaway's patented golf club design was a breakthrough and that avid golfers will pay almost any price for equipment that delivers improved performance.

I first bought Callaway (NSE:ELY) at $7½ in October 1992. Today, the stock is at $39⅛—up more than five times what I paid for it.

Strategy: One of the best ways for individual investors to find stocks that Wall Street believes are controversial is to follow the financial print and TV media. They often focus on which companies are unpopular with the professional investment community.

Example: I like to follow Dan Dorfman, a CNBC-TV commentator, not because I agree with him but because his opinions can be highly influential in driving a company's stock price.

•Buy stocks in companies that have relatively low price/earnings ratios. I'm all for purchasing growth stocks, which sell at high prices and are expected to move even higher as the company grows.

But I don't want the stock's price to be so high that the downside risk is perilous. A portfolio could be hurt badly if the stock drops dramatically.

The average price/earnings ratio of the stocks in my clients' portfolios is 12. That is below the market average of 18. However, the average growth rate of my clients' stocks is 25%, vs. 14% for the *S&P 500 Index.*

•Buy stocks in companies that have positive technical momentum. This means keeping an eye on a company's volume—the number of shares it trades in a single day. The volume is listed in the stock tables next to the stock price.

It's best to buy when a company's price and volume rise…or when its price declines along with its volume.

Example: You've been following a stock and notice its daily volume is around 50,000 shares. After a few weeks, the price begins to climb—and its daily volume is up around 150,000 shares. This would be a very positive sign indicating a buying opportunity.

•It is just as important to know when to sell as it is to know when to buy. My company has a rule for selling most stocks. Generally, once a stock's price drops 20% from its high during the time we own it, we sell.

The 20% figure is arbitrary, but if the stock price drops by that much, it could be a sign of trouble. This automatic sell strategy limits losses—and removes the emotion from a difficult decision.

It's also important to sell when your stock produces a solid profit. On the upside, I sell when I've reached a target price. This target price is established by multiplying the company's expected growth rate by its earnings-per-share estimate for the following year. These numbers can be found in any company's analyst's report, which you can get through your broker.

Source: Douglas K. Raborn, chairman of Raborn & Co., an investment advisory firm with $145 million under management, 777 E. Atlantic Ave., Atlantic Plaza, Delray Beach, Florida 33483.

Growth Stock Warning Signal

Consider selling a growth stock when its *relative strength* declines steadily over a period of months. Relative strength is the stock's price performance compared to that of the *S&P 500* or another broad market index. *Key:* A high price/earnings (p/e) ratio by itself is not a warning sign concerning a growth stock. *Reason:* A growth stock has a high p/e. But the high p/e must be justified by above-average performance. A slippage in performance as measured by relative strength is a warning sign that there may be earnings problems ahead and also warns that

growth-oriented investors may soon be bailing out of the stock, depressing its price.

Source: Arnold Kaufman, editor, *The Outlook*, 25 Broadway, New York 10004.

Rules of Stock Picking

The key rules for making profitable stock investments:

•*Buy a stock* only if it is priced at less than you think it is worth now…and only if you believe it will be worth more tomorrow. Buying at a low price is absolutely fundamental to making profits.

•*Buy on bad news* that temporarily depresses a stock's price.

Example: The Bhopal disaster sent Union Carbide's stock price plummeting from $50 to $33. This created a buying opportunity, since Union Carbide remained a well-run company that makes valuable products. It's stock ultimately rebounded to $69.

•*When a stock seems like a bargain*, investigate further to be sure it actually is. Understand why the rest of the market has priced it low and why you think its price will go up nonetheless.

•*Quantify the bargain you see.* Don't buy a stock because it "seems" like a good deal. Figure out the stock's value in dollar terms considering factors such as cash flow and future earnings.

•*Investing is hard work.* If you take shortcuts you can expect to get second-rate results.

Source: *Global Investing the Templeton Way*, as told by John Templeton to Norman Berryessa, money manager, and Eric Kirnzer, associate professor of finance, University of Toronto, Irwin Professional Publishing, 1333 Burr Ridge Pkwy., Burr Ridge, Illinois 60521.

The Virtues of Investing In "Wallflowers"

It's hard for the average investor to hold an out-of-favor stock for any period of time in the hope it will recover enough to be sold at a profit.

Glamour stocks always have the sexiest stories to tell...get the most publicity...and are covered by most analysts.

Out-of-favor "value" stocks attract fewer analysts. What publicity they get tends to be mostly unfavorable.

This is especially true in today's uncertain investment climate...and is likely to remain so until the new GOP legislative agenda and the economic outlook become clear. Right now, the conventional wisdom is that it only pays to gamble on red-hot growth.

My suggestion: Gird yourself against popular opinion, and favor stocks that don't seem to be going anywhere.

Reason: The record is all in favor of long-term investing in value stocks—out-of-favor issues whose market prices don't reflect their true value.

Bottom line: Our own studies track the performance of all companies on the New York Stock Exchange for almost 50 years. In the long run, value stocks have outperformed not only the overall market by a wide margin...but glamour stocks by as much as 40% to 50%.

The long wait:

Value investing is a strategy for virtually all seasons. Only when the market is wildly overpriced do you have to be cautious. Even when the market is *relatively* high, there are sectors that are underpriced.

To find value stocks, first you must find out-of-favor industry groups with good prospects. If you don't have the time or expertise to look for these groups, you're better off in a value mutual fund. A fund also gives you the diversification you need if you have limited capital.

Forbes runs an annual mutual fund guide that lists value funds. Also check out the fund ratings in *Money, Kiplinger's Personal Finance* and *Morningstar Mutual Funds*. They show whether a fund favors growth or value investing.

Do-it-yourself: If you want to make your own stock choices, buy a diversified portfolio of *financially strong* companies that are selling at *10 or 11 times earnings*. That's well below the current market multiple of 16—meaning the average stock today is selling at 16 times earnings. The daily stock tables in major publications will show the price to earnings (p/e) for each listed stock.

How we do it: We look at how cheap an industry group is relative to the overall market using a number of measures.

We look to see how the average figures for an industry compare with average figures for the overall market in such key areas as...

- Ratio of stock prices to earnings.
- Ratio of stock prices to company book values (assets less liabilities).
- How much the stocks in the group yield ...based on average stock price and average dividend.

We also look at the financial strength of companies within the group. When we establish that a group is cheap relative to the overall market, we begin looking at individual companies and their growth prospects.

You can collect the same data on industry groups in either the *Value Line Investment Survey* or Standard & Poor's *Industry Survey*, available at most major libraries.

Long haul: Probably the hardest part of value investing is waiting for the payoff. Some value managers can wait as long as six years for a stock to pay off.

I personally think three to four years is a good rule of thumb. Ninety percent of the time, we hold a stock at least that long. We've owned Philip Morris for a decade and it has gone up six or seven times. If you like a stock, keep it.

You shouldn't just hold blindly though. There are times when companies decay and the future is no longer promising. If the fundamentals deteriorate, make a change, but that should be a rare happening.

When to get out:

For most people, knowing when to sell a stock is even harder than knowing when to buy.

But in value investing, the rule is pretty clearcut: Other things being equal...consider selling a stock when its price to earnings ratio gets up to the average price to earnings ratio for the overall market.

When that happens, the stock in question is no longer an out-of-favor value stock…which was your reason for buying it in the first place.

Source: David Dreman, chairman, Dreman Value Management, LP. Dreman Funds, 10 Exchange Pl., Jersey City, New Jersey 07302.

When to Switch Stockbrokers

Brokers pitch stocks harder toward the end of the month. *Reason:* Every month, major brokerage firms add up each broker's production for the previous 12 months. That figure determines how much the broker will make for the next month. A broker who is having a slow month will make more pitches—or more trades in discretionary accounts—toward the end of the month. But none of this necessarily benefits the investor. If a pattern of end-of-the-month calls or trades develops, find another broker.

Source: John Markese, president, American Association of Individual Investors, 625 N. Michigan Ave., Chicago 60611.

Investment Planning Made Easy

During the many speeches that I give around the country each year, I'm asked hundreds of questions about money and investing. *Here are the answers to the questions that I'm asked most frequently…*

Should I take my retirement money as a lump sum? Annuity? Many pensions offer retirees two forms of payment—a little at a time through an annuity or as a lump sum. This decision could be the most important financial decision of your life—but it is very hard to get an objective opinion.

Reason: The annuity is an insurance-industry product, so people in the insurance business are likely to tell you to take your pension as an annuity. People in the investment management business will tell you to take it as a lump sum and roll the money over into an investment account.

The answer to this question draws attention to an important lesson. There are few all-or-nothing decisions in personal finance. People who are willing to sacrifice some potential income for the assurance that they will receive steady payments are best served by taking part of the money as a lump sum and part as an annuity.

Strategy: If you retire at or before the normal retirement age, you generally should take the lump sum. Then when you are older, there is nothing to prevent you from investing in an annuity.

There are some very innovative annuity products being developed, such as immediate payment variable annuities. Your money is invested in mutual funds, and you begin receiving investment payments immediately.

In a few years, you probably will have a better choice of annuity products. If you can't wait, shop around. Don't just take the annuity your employer or broker offers. This is a competitive business, and once you buy, it's difficult to change your mind.

Important: If you or your spouse go into a nursing home, your lump sum distribution would have to be used to help pay nursing home costs. A lot of people in that situation wish they had chosen an annuity for part of their savings because nursing-home care has wiped out their long-term savings. An annuity at least assures a continuing income—for your spouse and for you if you leave the nursing home.

If you made just one investment today, what would it be? *There are two candidates…*

• *A 20-year zero-coupon Treasury bond.* These bonds sell at discounts to their face values, so you receive the full amount when they reach maturity. If you buy a 20-year zero-coupon bond now, your money will grow at an annual rate of around 8%. In 20 years, it will almost quintuple with no risk. But you should buy zero-coupon bonds only for your tax-deferred retirement account. Otherwise, you will have to pay income taxes on "imputed interest"—interest you don't receive in cash until the bond matures but that the IRS requires you to pay each year you own the bond.

•*A fund that invests exclusively in science and technology stocks.* Our economy is in a fundamental period of transition. The old blue chip manufacturers have had their day. A new generation of blue chip stocks is emerging—and, of course, many of them will be science and technology companies. *How much should I invest in stocks vs. bonds? Rule of thumb:* Multiply your age times 80% (0.8). The result will give you the maximum percentage that you should invest in bonds for the long term.

Example: At age 50, you should have at most 40% of your portfolio in bonds (0.8 times 50). I would put 50% of that money in highly rated municipal bonds, 25% in corporate bonds and 25% in Treasury bonds of different maturities—or in mutual funds that invest in those bonds.

Right now, municipal bonds—particularly those in your home state—are providing a significant yield advantage over Treasuries for investors in the 28% tax bracket and higher.

Example: A 10-year Treasury bond currently yields 8%, while a 10-year municipal bond yields about 6.6%. But once you take federal income tax out of the Treasury bond interest, its yield drops to 5.52%. If you're in the 31% or higher federal tax bracket, the municipal advantage is even greater.

The rest of a sound long-term portfolio would go into growth investments—particularly stocks. That strategy may strike some investors as dangerous. But you can reduce your risk by spreading your equity holdings among different sectors of the stock market. When one or more sectors decline temporarily, your other sectors will rise.

Right now, I advise my clients to put 40% of their portfolios into income-producing stocks or funds that hold these stocks.

I also advise my clients to divide the rest of their portfolios evenly among three other types of funds—specifically growth, foreign stock funds and small-cap funds.

What kind of estate planning do I need? At the very least, you should have three documents…

•*Will.* Make sure that it is valid and up-to-date.

•*Living will.* This tells doctors that you don't want to be kept on a life-support system if you're terminally ill.

•*Durable power of attorney.* This appoints someone to run your finances if you become incapacitated. If you neglect to draw up one, the court will decide who will look after your finances…and the court's choice is not always best.

Important: If you or your spouse have an estate that is valued at more than $600,000, you will need a credit shelter trust. It allows each spouse to take advantage of the $600,000 exemption from estate taxes. By creating such a credit shelter trust, an estate of $1.2 million or more will avoid paying more than $200,000 in taxes when the surviving spouse dies.

Should I pay-down my mortgage early? Many people argue against doing this. They believe that the money you use to pay-down your mortgage at a faster rate could be invested elsewhere at a higher return.

They also point out that mortgage payments are tax deductible. Even so, I am strongly in favor of reducing the time it takes to pay off a home loan.

Reasons: Your return on other investments will rarely be much higher than the interest payments you'll save by paying down the mortgage. Also, one of the most important things for investors is the ability to sleep well at night. I think there is a major psychological benefit to knowing that you are paying down your mortgage at a rapid rate.

It is great to enter your retirement mortgage-free. Even an extra $100 a month can make a big difference.

How much life insurance do I need? Start out by considering two numbers…

•*Minimum amount of coverage:* Five times your annual spending, including taxes.

Example: If you earn $50,000 and save $5,000 annually, you should have five times $45,000 in coverage. That amount will provide your family with time to get on firmer financial footing if something happens to you.

•*Maximum amount:* Ask an insurance agent to provide an estimate. Believe me, he/she won't leave much out.

For most people, the best amount lies between the minimum and the maximum.

Example: If you have children who are not in college yet, you might insure your life for five times your annual spending—plus a sufficient amount to pay off your mortgage and fund the children's college educations.

When should I sell a mutual fund? Let's assume that you bought a mutual fund because it had a solid long-term record, and nothing has changed about the management of the fund.

A fund has to perform below the average for funds in its category for two consecutive years before I will consider selling it. For instance, a growth fund must trail other growth funds...a small-company fund must trail other small-company funds, etc.

You can find category averages in *Barron's* every week under "Lipper Mutual Fund Performance Reports."

My approach means you have to be patient —but it will probably be rewarding. When a good fund underperforms for a year, it often snaps back and does very well afterward.

Source: Jonathan Pond, president of Financial Planning Information, Inc., 9 Galen St., Watertown, Massachusetts 02172, and the author of *The New Century Family Money Book*, Dell, New York. He appears regularly as a commentator on PBS-TV's *Nightly Business Report.*

Three Reasons to Fire Your Money Manager

Fire a money manager when 1) He strays from his stated goals. *Example:* A manager who promises to invest in growth stocks begins to invest in value stocks. He has either misrepresented himself or lost his confidence. 2) There is high turnover in the manager's key support staff. The manager's performance record reflects his team's past efforts. New employees shouldn't get their education at your expense. 3) Your own objectives change. You may have an excellent manager, but if his expertise doesn't meet your current needs you should still replace him. *Key:* It's hard to fire a friend, so keep your relationship with your money manager strictly business.

Source: *The Lump Sum Handbook, Investment and Tax Strategies for a Secure Retirement*, by Anthony Gallea, senior vice president, Smith Barney, Prentice Hall, Englewood Cliffs, NJ.

Economic Indicators That You Can Trust

Question: The government reports a huge gain in consumer spending in retail stores. *Should you...*

A. Buy stocks because the economy is certain to boom?

B. Sell stocks because the strong report will lead to tight money and higher interest rates from the Federal Reserve?

C. Neither of the above?

Answer: C—neither of the above.

Reason: To compile this report, the Commerce Department samples retailing establishments. But it doesn't sample enough to do the job right.

You can't be sure any month's retail sales report accurately measures consumer spending. You can be sure one month's report will be revised significantly the next month.

Verdict: The retail sales report gets my top award as the worst economic report Uncle Sam puts out. Don't use it to make decisions about investing...or anything else.

Background:

Overall, the quality of our economic reports is good...especially compared with other countries. They allow government policymakers to make reasonable judgments in diagnosing the economy...individuals to make reasonably good business and investment judgments.

Problem: While many key government reports are accurate and worth noting...some are badly flawed.

Solution: You must know which reports to pay attention to and which to never use as the basis for serious decisions.

Here's how I rate key reports...the worst first, then the best. It's easy to follow these reports, because each is reported by newspapers...magazines...radio and television. *These reports contain serious flaws...*

The awful eight:

1. *Retail sales.* For all the reasons noted above.

2. *The unemployment rate.* The Labor Department does a good job counting people who have jobs, but a terrible job counting people seeking jobs.

Result: You have wild swings in the unemployment rate from month to month for reasons that are difficult to understand. It is mind-boggling trying to figure out what this report means.

3. *Producer prices.* This report, which covers wholesale prices, isn't bad in itself. But economic change has reduced its usefulness as a predictor of future inflation.

It used to be that if you saw raw material prices in this report going up, you could bet your bottom dollar that ultimately consumers would pay those higher prices. Now, with business focused on cutting costs instead of raising prices, higher raw material prices get damped down before they reach consumers.

4. *Consumer prices.* As widely followed as this report is, it is fundamentally flawed. It measures price changes for a basket of goods and services that the average consumer is assumed to buy. But the contents of that basket aren't changed often enough to keep up with changing tastes.

Also, there's no adjustment for improvements in quality. The report considers it inflationary if your new TV costs more than last year's model …with no recognition that this year's model may be better made…with more advanced features.

Verdict: The report overstates consumer price inflation by one to one-and-a-half percentage points each month.

5. *Personal income.* This isn't really a bad number. But month-to-month changes can be distorted by such things as an increase in Social Security payments or a big farm subsidy payment. That makes it hard to track how much consumers have available for spending each month.

Better: The companion report on personal consumption expenditures, which does better than retail sales in measuring what consumers spend.

6. *Consumer savings.* The government takes personal income, subtracts personal spending and assumes we've saved the rest. That makes us sound like the least thrifty people on earth.

What it misses is that we use our savings to buy stocks, bonds and houses, which then appreciate in value. Your home's appreciation is an important component of net worth that this report ignores.

7. *The money supply.* This used to be widely followed for its supposed ability to predict inflation. But how can you separate out the US money supply when the financial markets are as globally integrated as they are today?

Also, look at the huge shift by individuals in how they hold their money balances…from bank accounts, which count in the money supply, to mutual funds, which don't. Money supply alone doesn't tell you anything about where inflation is headed.

8. *Gross domestic product.* This measures the whole economy. And it does give you an overall sense of how the economy is doing. *But I am cautious about the numbers for several reasons…*

•There often are significant revisions once the report is out. Growth in the fourth quarter of 1993 was first reported as 7½%. That was revised to 7% and then to 6.3%. Those are big revisions.

•Anything produced in the economy adds to growth, even if it isn't sold and winds up in inventory, rusting on a shelf. But most of the time, a buildup in inventories of unsold stuff… far from being a growth item…will cut into future growth.

Better: Final sales…published with this report …count only what is actually sold. That makes it your best guide to underlying momentum in the economy.

The sacred seven:

The seven reports to best help you keep up with the economy…

1. *Durable goods orders.* Most of the government's orders figures are excellent…particularly new orders for durable goods (things made to last for at least three years). The numbers are accurate…not subject to major revision…and very good for forecasting the economy.

2. *Supply delivery times.* One sign of a strengthening economy is that it keeps taking longer for new orders to get filled. Then you must hire more people. That makes this a good leading indicator of both production and employment.

Important: This indicator doesn't come from the government but is found in the monthly report of the National Association of Purchasing Management.

3. *Industrial production.* This report, from the Federal Reserve, has a hard time measuring production in high-tech industries. And it measures manufacturing, a declining share of our economy. But if you understand these limitations, it's a very solid report on what is still an important part of the economy.

4. *Nonfarm payrolls.* At the same time the Labor Department is doing a bad job measuring unemployment, it does a good job counting the number of people actually at work. This report is published as part of the unemployment report.

5. *Monthly motor vehicle sales.* These come from the automakers and are timely and accurate.

6. *Housing starts.* Most reports on housing activity are very good. This counts the number of new homes started each month...and the number of permits to build new homes in the future. It's accurate and seldom revised.

7. *Commodity prices.* You can read *The Journal of Commerce* for prices of 18 industrial commodities. More widely published are the Commodity Research Bureau figures on prices for both industrial and agricultural commodities. Commodity prices are very sensitive to demand pressures. Generally they give you a clue, very early, as to when there might be a pickup in inflation.

Source: David M. Jones, executive vice president and chief economist for Aubrey G. Lanston & Co., a securities firm at One Chase Manhattan Plaza, New York 10005. He is the author of *The Buck Starts Here*, Simon & Schuster, New York.

Before You Use On-Line Investment Advice... Read This

On-line investment advice varies greatly in quality. A lot of excellent information is available—but scam artists also operate in this unregulated environment. *Best:* Use computer networks to collect data that help you form your own opinion. Beware of hype and promises delivered over a network. Don't assume that bulletin boards police those who make

claims through them. Don't rely on advice received from any person who hides his/her identity. Don't believe any claims about "inside information" or "pending news releases." Don't overlook the conflict of interest that exists when a person who touts an investment also sells it.

Source: North American Securities Administrators Association, One Massachusetts Ave. NW, Suite 310, Washington, DC 20001.

Never Invest with Phone Marketers

It is alright to deal with a broker or mutual fund by phone, but never deal with a stranger who calls you. Some calls may be legitimate—but few are. Just hang up. *Also:* Never invest when a seller tries to rush you or impose a time limit. Any legitimate investment should give you plenty of printed information to read—and adequate time to digest it and ask questions.

Source: Robert Carlson, editor, *Bob Carlson's Retirement Watch,* 1420 Spring Hill Rd., McLean, Virginia 22102.

Diversification Lessons

A well-diversified portfolio is of great importance. Investors could narrow their losses through proper diversification and enhance their gains when there is market recovery. Here are four lessons about diversification.

Lesson #1: The past is rarely prologue. The people with the biggest losses were those who invested in last quarter's or last month's or last year's high flyers. People who do that are almost always assured of disappointing themselves.

Does that mean people shouldn't invest in those areas? Absolutely not. It does mean not to spend too much of your assets chasing one year's hot sector...whether it's gold...natural resources...or anything else.

Lesson #2: Stick with stocks.

Cash is okay as one part of a diversified investment strategy. If you're totally into cash... you'll win occasionally...but lose most of the time.

Lesson #3: Play the field. The essence of diversification is not putting all your money into one type of stock...or stock fund. Far better to be in all four major stock market sectors: Growth, growth and income, small-cap and international.

Better: Growth and income and international funds held up reasonably well during the correction. If you had hedged your bets and also invested in such funds...that would have partially offset losses in the aggressive-growth category.

Lesson #4: Ladder bond maturities. Diversification covers a lot of ground. Diversify among kinds of stocks. Diversify between stocks and bonds. Diversify among types of bonds. And then ladder your bond portfolio by diversifying among bond funds of differing maturities.

A well-diversified bond portfolio includes not only Treasury, tax-exempt and corporate bonds, but also laddered maturities within each of those categories.

Example: Bond investors who were really hurt in the first half were those who reached for yield, by weighting their portfolios very heavily with long-term bonds and funds. Over the first six months, the average long bond lost 6%, the average intermediate bond lost 4% and the average short-term bond lost 2%.

That was proof, once again, that the higher the yield, the higher the risk. Bondholders whose losses were most acceptable were those who abided by the old rule: *Don't place a heavy bet on any one maturity.*

What to do now:

For optimum diversification you'd need at least 10 different funds...four stock funds and six bond funds. If that sounds like too much, at least diversify among an array of stock and bond funds.

A reasonable allocation of your money would be 60% in stock funds...40% in bond funds. Invest equal amounts of each of the funds you pick.

•On the stock side, you need aggressive growth, growth and income, small-cap and international funds.

As for the number of individual stocks you need to be well-diversified, I'll defer to the the-

oreticians who suggest stock in 10 to 12 different companies—100 shares each—could provide adequate diversification. That is assuming they are in varying categories.

International is another sector where the easiest way to diversify is through funds. I'm a strong believer in international funds free to invest in many countries. Buying a fund that just invests in a single region or an individual country isn't getting you enough diversification.

•On the bond side, we're talking three categories: Municipals, corporates and Treasuries. But you really need funds of differing maturities in each of those categories.

Example: Instead of a long municipal bond fund for maximum yield, consider an intermediate muni fund or short-term muni fund. Either way, you reduce your yield a little and your risk a lot.

Consider the same approach in corporate and Treasury bonds.

Better: It's easiest to ladder maturities with bond funds. You'd have to pay a fortune to get that same diversity with individual issues.

Source: Jonathan D. Pond, president, Financial Planning Information, Inc., 9 Galen St., Watertown, Massachusetts 02172. He is the developer of *Jonathan Pond's Personal Financial Planner,* an interactive software program, Vertigo Software, 58 Charles St., Cambridge, Massachusetts 02141.

How to Become a Millionaire—Investing Only $50 a Month

Mutual funds are giving individual stocks a good name. During the past few years, a growing number of investors have become less fearful of the stock market as they grew more comfortable with stock mutual funds.

Now many fund investors are thinking about taking the next step—*investing in individual stocks.* While this strategy may seem more risky than investing in funds—whose portfolios are managed by pros—it is not as complicated as it appears. You also don't need a lot of money to get started. You can invest as little as $50 a month—and can become a millionaire in about 40 years.

The big secret:

I came up with the figure of $50 after recently polling high school juniors and seniors. They told me that they waste at least $15 to $20 a week on things they don't really need—snacks, candy, video games, etc. That totals $60 to $80 a month—or $720 to $960 a year.

If that's how much passes through kids' hands each month, think about how much you must waste. Many adults tell me they waste much more.

If you could harness all that money—or even just $50 a month—and use it to start a regular investing program, you would be well on your way to becoming a millionaire...maybe even a *multi*millionaire.

Strategy: If you invested $50 each month in the finest companies and reinvested your dividends—and your money grew at 13% to 15% annually, which is the rate at which these companies have appreciated since World War II—your portfolio would be worth a great deal over the long term. *Earnings potential:*

- After 10 years—$12,500 to $14,000.
- After 20 years—$54,900 to $70,700.
- After 30 years—$198,800 to $300,000.
- After 40 years—$817,700 to $1,570,000.

The easy way to invest:

The key is to select the stocks of a few major companies that have had long histories of rising earnings and dividends. I call these *America's finest companies.*

These make up my superior universe of stocks, which has consistently outperformed such broad market averages as the Dow Jones Industrial Average (DJIA) and the S&P 500 Index.

Important: Forget about market timing—a strategy that is followed by some experts who try to buy stocks when they are just about to rise and sell stocks just before they go into a slump. It's impossible to predict the future, and nobody can consistently time individual stocks or the market.

Better: Invest whenever you have some extra money, regardless of whether the market is up or down. Investing doesn't have to be difficult if you follow my five-point program.

1. Invest in proven winners—companies that have paid higher dividends per share annually for at least 10 consecutive years.

These companies consistently out-distance the stock market. You can pick proven winners from my book—or by using *Value Line* or *Standard & Poor's,* which are available in most libraries.

Make sure each company has a *Dividend Reinvestment Plan (DRP)* that does not charge a commission. A DRP uses stockholder's quarterly dividends to buy additional shares rather than sending the dividends to the stockholder in the form of cash payments.

Also, make sure each company has an optional cash payment plan, which allows stockholders to buy additional shares directly through the company without paying brokers.

Call the investment relations departments of your target companies to determine if they have such plans.

Try to own between five and eight stocks—*each in a different industry.* This range will help your portfolio deliver outstanding results, and the diversity will cushion you during a downturn in different sectors of the economy.

2. Open a brokerage account to purchase your initial stocks in these companies. To enroll in a company's DRP, you must first own a single share of its stock.

Don't be intimidated by the thought of opening a brokerage account. It usually takes just a few minutes on the phone with a broker who will ask you for some basic information. Then you'll need to complete some documents—and that's all.

Consider using a discount broker. Their commissions are typically 50% below those charged by full-service brokers. Though most don't provide investment advice or analysts' reports, you won't need their advice if you follow my five-point program.

On the other hand, don't worry too much about commissions—since you're only buying your first share of each company through the broker. You will make future purchases directly through the companies.

3. Sign up for each company's DRP. After you've enrolled in a DRP, your next quarterly dividend will be used to buy a fractional share of stock.

Newly purchased shares must be registered in your name and sent directly to you—they are not kept by your broker. Each quarter, the company will mail you a statement showing exactly how much stock you own.

4. Buy more shares commission-free. The company's optional cash-payment plan allows you to buy additional shares of stock by mailing the purchase price directly to the company, without paying a commission for the new shares.

Typically, the minimum purchase price is $25 and the maximum ranges from $3,000 to $5,000.

I suggest investing in a different company each quarter—rotating among all of the companies you have chosen. At the end of the year, rebalance to concentrate future purchases in the underinvested companies.

5. Don't sell your stock unless you must. I don't advocate unloading your purchases unless you need the money—or unless a company is no longer paying higher dividends per share over 10 consecutive years. If you need to sell stock, it can be done through the company.

Source: Bill Staton, CFA, president of The Financial Training Group, which holds personal finance seminars nationwide, 300 East Blvd., Unit B-4, Charlotte, North Carolina 28203. He is the editor of *Bill Staton's Money Advisory,* a monthly newsletter, and the author of *How to Become a Multimillionaire on Just $50 a Month* (cassette and guidebook).

Municipal Bond Trap

Avoid investing in states that have approved —or intend to approve—tax cuts. Lower taxes mean lower revenue, which over the long term could result in a lower bond rating and could mean reduced spending on programs to attract new business. *Strategy:* Before buying municipal bonds, ask your broker to send you his/her firm's outlook report on the state. *States to avoid now:* California, New Jersey and New York.

Source: James Lynch, the editor of *Lynch Municipal Bond Advisory,* a newsletter that tracks the performance of municipal bonds, Box 20476, New York 10025.

How to Reduce Mutual Fund Risk

Mutual funds are terrific investments, but many people are confused by the growing number of choices and are troubled by the stock market's volatility.

Strategies for reducing mutual fund risk:

•*Avoid smaller funds.* Funds that have assets of less than $200 million tend either to perform extremely well—or to be major disappointments. That's because their managers take big chances, hoping that a heroic performance will attract new investors. In some cases, this strategy works. But it also can backfire, making this type of fund extremely risky.

Self-defense: Stick with larger funds. Their managers are more conservative because they don't want to scare away shareholders who have entrusted them with billions of dollars.

•*Avoid funds with high expense ratios.* High expenses—greater than 1% for a stock fund and 1.5% for a bond fund—reduce your profits. In some cases, they also mean more risk. Managers of funds that charge shareholders high expenses are more likely to invest in higher-risk securities to produce higher returns and justify expenses. This is especially true for bond funds. Call your fund to find out your expense rates.

•*Pay close attention to bond-fund maturities.* Bond-fund investors can cut risk by buying funds with shorter maturities. Long-term bonds are hit much harder than short-term bonds when interest rates rise.

When rates rise from, say, 6% to 8%, investors no longer want the old 6% bonds. They would rather buy new 8% ones. Since fewer people would want to hold on to the 6% bonds over many years, given this interest rate climate, the longer bonds drop further in price.

Solution: Seek a risk/reward balance by buying a bond fund with a variety of maturities.

•*Diversify intelligently.* Don't simply seek safety by investing in more funds. Six funds can be as risky as one if they all have the same investment style.

Common mistake: Buying six of last year's top-performing mutual funds. The odds are good that their high rankings were due to similar investment styles and objectives.

Solution: When diversifying, buy stock funds that have different investment philosophies—such as value, growth, equity income, etc.

Also, buy funds that invest in different sized companies, such as small-, mid- and large-cap stocks. A phone representative from each fund should be able to tell you in which types it invests.

• *Buy at least one fund with significant international exposure.* The world's stock markets do not always move in the same direction at the same time. By being invested in a fund that invests abroad, you are limiting your risk if the US market falls.

Though there are many excellent mutual funds that invest abroad, many domestic funds have sizable international holdings. Some have as much as 20% in foreign stocks. Call the fund, and ask for the percentage.

Source: Don Phillips, publisher of *Morningstar Mutual Funds,* an independent consumer newsletter that evaluates funds, 225 W. Wacker Dr., Chicago 60606.

What Mutual Fund Managers Don't Want You to Know

When markets perform poorly and business drops off at mutual funds, some fund *managers* take bigger risks …while fund *marketers* look for ways to polish their funds' images. There's nothing illegal about either strategy, but the results can confuse the average investor.

Here's how some funds bend the rules and how you can stay informed and protect your money…

• *A fund's name doesn't always reflect its investment strategy.* In an effort to offset lackluster performance, some funds have gone beyond their original mandates, expanding into other types of investments.

Unfortunately, a fund can legally call itself almost anything it wants. The Securities and Exchange Commission (SEC) requires only that 65% of a fund's assets be invested according to the strategy outlined in its prospectus. As a result, a fund's name can mislead average investors who may not understand this subtlety or know the rules.

Example I: Last year, one growth and income fund didn't provide much income—yielding only 0.5%—which is about the lowest yield of any mutual fund with the word *income* in its name.

Example II: At times, one insured municipal bond fund had 30% of its assets in municipal bonds that were *not* insured. In 1994, it suffered a 10.24% loss on a total-return basis.

Important: Before you invest, call the fund and ask about its holdings. Are they the kinds of securities you want to own? Do they accurately represent the impression you had from the fund's name? If you already own the fund, is it still investing the way you want it to?

• *You probably have more exposure to foreign securities than you think.* Though many funds state in their prospectuses that their stakes in foreign securities are limited to 10% of their portfolios, this self-imposed cap is often circumvented by buying American Depositary Receipts (ADRs).

ADRs are listings by foreign companies on US stock exchanges, and they are purchased through brokers just as you would purchase stocks.

While ADRs can be great investments, having them in your portfolio means you have more foreign risk.

Example: One growth fund whose prospectus states that it has a 10% cap on foreign securities has nearly 25% of its assets in foreign stocks and ADRs.

Helpful: Give your mutual fund portfolio a checkup. Analyze all the holdings in your fund to determine the real percentage of your investments tied to foreign markets. While the fund will provide you with the percentage over the phone, make sure that any ADRs are part of the total percentage.

• *You may owe taxes on funds—even if they don't do well.* In their struggle to outpace a gloomy market, many mutual fund managers buy and sell stocks more frequently. When these buy and sell transactions occur, there frequently are capital gains—which means that there are taxes to pay on those gains.

In many cases, the funds take those gains for legitimate strategic reasons. But the effect is that shareholders owe taxes on those gains—even though other holdings may have lost more money and overall the fund may have performed poorly for the year.

Example I: One growth stock fund—with a return of negative 6.7% last year—paid out $1.08 per share in capital gains at the end of the year. That was 10.2% of its price per share.

Example II: A growth fund that lost 12.8% paid out $1.57—or 9.7% of its price per share.

Funds that do a lot of trading—such as growth or aggressive growth funds—are best bought for your Individual Retirement Account (IRA), since the capital gains are tax-deferred. Funds that do a lot of trading have annual turnover ratios that are greater than 100%. This information can be obtained through the fund.

Index funds are better for taxable holdings, since they buy and sell stocks much less frequently.

• *Who is managing your fund?* More and more funds are using teams to manage the assets. From the fund's perspective, a team keeps one manager from making too much of a name for himself/herself. It also deters investors from pulling out their money when a star manager leaves for another fund—either within the fund family or at another company.

Problem: With a team, you never know who is the brains of the operation—or whether you should pull out your money because the person behind the fund's success has left.

Self-defense: Call the fund annually, and ask for the names of the managers. Then ask who is responsible for investing the money. If the response is the entire team, ask for the name of the team leader and about his experience. Also ask how long each team member has been with the fund.

• *Performance numbers are becoming clearer.* Ads that promote funds often cast them in the best light by comparing their performances with benchmarks that make them look good... or by ignoring benchmarks that made them look bad.

Example: In the 1980s, one group of funds regularly compared itself with the S&P 500 Index in a prominent box in the shareholders' report. In 1989, when they didn't do well, the box disappeared.

This trend is changing. Starting this year, the SEC requires that returns be calculated uniformly on shareholders' reports. Now that funds must be consistent, be vigilant in monitoring the comparison. Take a look at last year's performance. It will show how the fund did in a terrible market. And compare the three- and five-year returns.

Source: Don Phillips, publisher of *Morningstar Mutual Funds,* an independent research company that tracks and rates open-end mutual funds, 225 W. Wacker Dr., Chicago 60606.

The Best No-Load Mutual Funds For People Older Than 50

The smartest investors are *assertive* investors. I mean people who expect to get higher returns at lower risk.

Is such a thing possible? Absolutely. The key is to concentrate your mutual fund investing where it will do you the most good.

The real secret of mutual fund investing is that there are funds that are true *superstars*—and funds that are quantifiably *dogs.* (I call them *supperstars* because they're so bad that they'll eat your supper at your expense.)

Most funds, of course, are somewhere in the middle. *Two keys to assertive investing...*

• Learning to tell the difference between the big winners and the also-rans.

• Being in the right types of funds at the right time.

Strategies:

If you are under age 85, you're a long-term investor. *Seriously.* The biggest mistake you can make is playing it too safe. You don't want to run out of money before you run out of life.

Solution: Don't invest for income. Invest for long-term gains and sell portions of your holdings when necessary to meet living expenses.

Trap: Don't unload your top-performing funds simply because you've reached a certain age. That makes no sense. There's no age at which you should have to settle for mediocrity.

Don't listen to your broker: Brokers are the least likely people to lead you to the best-performing mutual funds. First, they're trained to sell high-commission, heavy-load funds, which may turn you into a loser before you even start. Second, they're trained to sell bond funds. Bond funds are not where long-term investors want to be.

This is especially true in an environment of rising interest rates. Through the first nine months of 1994, bond mutual fund investors lost $22 billion more in asset value than they collected in dividends.

Strategy: When rates are rising, you're better off investing fixed-income money in bonds rather than bond funds. Bonds guarantee that your principal will be returned with interest. No bond fund can guarantee that.

Types of Funds to Own:

Most of the money that people make in mutual funds comes from being in the right type of fund rather than selecting a particular fund.

Example: In 1993, the *best-performing* growth funds returned 20% to 30%, which is certainly nothing to sneeze at. At the same time, however, the *average* emerging market fund was up 67%! Many did much better.

Despite this spectacular move, international funds should still account for an enormous portion of your portfolio, somewhere between 30% and 50%. *Why?* Because that's where the real economic growth will be in coming years and decades.

Besides, the US bull market is tired. Many of the bull markets around the world, however, are just getting started. Some of these markets can double in the next two years.

Many economies abroad are experiencing phenomenal growth. China's economy is now *slowing down* to a *14% growth rate!*

Strategy: When you buy international funds, either dollar cost average or wait until there is a correction before making your commitment. Emerging markets, in particular, are so volatile

that it's a virtual certainty that you'll encounter a correction in six months.

Source: William E. Donoghue, editor of the Seattle-based *Donoghue On-Line,* a mutual fund performance and charting service and the author of *William E. Donoghue's Mutual Fund SuperStars: Invest in the Best, Forget About the Rest,* Elliott & James, 2212 15 Ave. W., Seattle 98119.

Where to Invest Now To Take Advantage of The Major Trends Coming In the Next Five Years

Investors who want to do well over the next five years will have to change the way they think about the US economy and the forces that have driven its growth since the early 1980s.

Consumer spending will continue to represent two-thirds of the economy. But as consumers face high taxes, less job security and greater rent or mortgage expenses, they will be much less willing to spend their money aggressively.

Result: Consumers are going to be much more price and value conscious than ever before. Therefore, the economy of the near future will not be led by consumer goods industries, the way it was in the 1980s. *Instead, the 1990s will be dominated by the following investment trends...*

• Companies that specialize in capital goods and technology will thrive. By capital goods, I mean companies in the machinery and machine-tool, electrical equipment, construction and railroad industries. A strong capital goods cycle will enable leading companies to show sustained earnings growth. Low-cost producers in the specialty steel and construction engineering areas look attractive.

In the technology area, telephone equipment, cellular and cable, and computer software companies should also be in the forefront. These will be the leadership stocks of the 1990s, just the way Merck and Philip Morris were in the 1980s.

• Small companies, in general, will have a great deal of growth potential. The boom cycles of small-cap companies typically last six or seven years.

We are currently about halfway through a cycle that began in the early 1990s, so we still have a ways to go before they reach overvaluation. Look for niche companies with innovative services and technologies.

•Outsourcing services will benefit from the trend of producers to cut costs. Increasing productivity is the name of the game these days, and the most successful companies will be those that do this by whatever means they can.

More and more companies will shed their noncore businesses that face stiff competition from companies that dominate specific fields and have successfully cut costs.

The outsourcing industry—which contracts to perform services that were formerly done by companies in-house—will expand rapidly.

This field includes companies that provide computer services, temporary office help, legal and accounting assistance and building security and maintenance services.

•Companies that reorganize their management structures will do best. The rest of the 1990s will be a period of redefining the large, bulky company, which has become obsolete. Big, inefficient companies are slimming down.

Some of the most exciting companies will be those in the middle or just on the brink of financial turnarounds. Look for large companies that have had problems and are undergoing radical downsizing.

•International investing will also be critical to the success of an investor's portfolio. As the economies of the less-developed nations begin to take off, there will be increased exporting of capital to these emerging markets. This trend is already well recognized, so it is important to go slowly in identifying attractive areas.

Strategy: Over the long term, invest 10% to 20% of your portfolio in international funds.

Invest by dollar-cost-averaging in mutual funds that have major stakes in Southeast Asia and South America.

•Companies that cater to older Americans will remain strong. Even though it's no longer news, America is graying. By the year 2000, 20% of the population will be age 65 or older. Companies that prosper will cater to this generation by providing such things as security services and long-term-care facilities.

•Food providers will grow as the world's standard of living improves. As less-developed nations improve their economies, eating well will no longer be a luxury—or even a problem —for their citizens.

This trend will lead to increased demand for foodstuffs, thereby boosting the fortunes of companies specializing in agribusiness. Fertilizer companies, machinery makers and bioscience companies all will benefit.

Inflation outlook:

It's still not clear whether the rest of the 1990s will be dominated by low or rising inflationary pressure. Although the consensus among most economists and other experts is that inflation may remain low, I expect periodic reflation scares that will upset the markets.

This means investors will have to do some significant inflation hedging. Inflation hedges are natural resource and energy companies and positions in gold and gold stocks.

It also means a greater turnover of your investments rather than sticking mainly to the buy-and-hold philosophy that was so successful in the 1980s. The stocks recommended are for the next few years. Of course, it is always important to review and update stocks relative to price.

Source: Robert J. Farrell, senior vice president and senior investment adviser of Merrill Lynch, North Tower, World Financial Center, New York 10281-1319. He is one of Wall Street's most respected stock market analysts.

7

Effective Managing Techniques in the Office

Little Things Mean a Lot... Lessons in Managing

People who go far in their careers have a lot in common. They know what they want, are highly motivated and work hard to reach their goals.

But these characteristics alone do not guarantee success. Successful people also must be superb managers, recognize opportunities and take advantage of them elegantly.

The basics:

•*Support others when they are down.* This is the most overlooked way to improve your chances of success.

For reasons that psychologists have yet to fully understand, most of us back away from colleagues who are facing personal or professional problems. Perhaps we fear that their bad luck will rub off on us.

Actually, when a colleague is facing a stressful period, it is the best time to step in and lend a hand. If you respect the person you're offering to help, your emotional or professional assistance will not only help him/her regain his balance, but he will also never forget that you were there when he needed you.

Example I: If the quality of the work from one of your staff members has declined and you know he is having a problem at home, try to relieve the pressure. One way is to say "I understand that you've been having difficulty balancing your work with everything you have going on at home." I appreciate that you are doing as well as you are during this period. Then suggest ways in which you might help, including staying late or handling some of his work.

Example II: If a colleague at another company is having serious problems with his manager—or has been fired—offer to help him find a job ...or suggest his name at your company for possible freelance work.

When you stand by someone who is down on his luck, you'll gain respect as a leader and become a tower of strength...win the person's friendship, probably for life...and enjoy higher levels of teamwork and respect from your own colleagues.

• *Applaud other people's work.* Recognizing the accomplishments of coworkers—your peers and those on your staff—is a powerful force and a relatively easy one to use. Applaud the good work of your superiors, too.

By telling a coworker that he has done a great job, you are creating a motivating environment. You're also setting yourself up as someone who is worthy of respect.

Strategy: Internal memos or notes work well. Stopping by to tell people about their work—even if they aren't in your department—is good, too. Recognition is inspiring, and you never know where you—or they—will be down the road.

When you recognize your colleagues' day-to-day victories, they'll begin to reciprocate. In fact, they'll respond to your needs far more quickly than they would if you tried to motivate them by scolding or threatening them.

Important: Your praise and thanks must be sincere. If not, your motives will be questioned and you will develop a negative reputation for being phony.

• *Remind others of what you've done for them—very gently.* I know of a box company in Chicago that doesn't just send bills to its customers. It also prints on the invoices the number of times that orders have been delivered on time.

You can use the same principle to boost your own career. When you help a colleague on a project, for example, congratulate him when it succeeds and tell him how much you enjoyed helping. You're delivering praise, but you're also subtly reminding the person that you pitched in on his behalf.

An even more effective strategy is to have a friend carry your message. You might, for example, mention to one coworker how much you liked assisting another coworker. It will get back to him eventually.

• *Give credit to all who deserve it.* In many companies, there's such fierce competition among workers that people try to hog the limelight or claim sole credit for themselves. That attitude always backfires. Colleagues eventually become resentful and hostile.

By sharing credit with as many people as possible, however, you elevate your stature in the eyes of coworkers and create a network of people who owe you favors.

Important: Like recognition, credit must be sincere. And don't just tell a colleague that he deserves credit for a good idea—be sure to tell that person's boss at the appropriate time as well.

Take special care to give credit to a rival. It makes you appear even more important. It might also disarm him.

• *Become a stickler for details.* Many people in managerial positions are so busy or have such large staffs that they believe they shouldn't have to bother with the day-to-day details of their jobs or departments.

But being constructively detail-oriented is actually one of the most important ways to achieve success today.

Someone who is known for being aware of everything that is going on in his department—and who makes sure that the work is getting done accurately and according to his standards—is highly respected by those below and above him.

Those people who work for you will be forced to raise their standards and not let mistakes happen. Those above you will trust you with more responsibility since you will have a reputation for making sure nothing slips through the cracks.

By leaving the details to others, you are inviting problems that will only cause you to take the heat or put blame on others—both of which are not signs of leadership or strength.

Example: When I first got a job in Washington, DC, back in the 1970s, I was responsible for sorting and going through files. It turned out that I could learn more about the business from these files than from just about any other source. So each day I stayed two or three hours after work to read through the files.

After two months, I had a firm grasp of what the business was all about, and I knew the names and places that the company felt were most important.

By sweating all the details, you will increase the odds of knowing more than anyone else every time you walk into a meeting...and you will have a reputation for being committed to excellence.

Source: Tom Peters, one of the country's best-known management consultants and president of the Tom Peters Group, 555 Hamilton Ave., Palo Alto, California 94301. He is the author of six books, including *The Pursuit of WOW!*, Vintage Books, New York.

Performance Review Etiquette

During a performance review, do not discuss pay raises or promotion prospects. These topics have such an emotional impact on employees that they will overwhelm the point of the review—which is how the employee is performing the job.

Source: Don Schackne, employee relations consultant, Delaware, Ohio, quoted in *Office Systems '94*, 941 Danbury Rd., Box 150, Georgetown, Connecticut 06829.

How to Hire the Right People... Regularly

Irving Shapiro is one of the unique success stories in American business. Not merely because he rose to the top of the world's largest chemical company, but also because he did it without having an MBA...without being a member of the DuPont clan...and without any formal training in engineering or chemistry.

He was also the first lawyer to head the Wilmington, Delaware-based giant.

Since his retirement from DuPont, Mr. Shapiro has spent 13 years in the Wilmington office of Skadden, Arps, Slate, Meagher & Flom, where he advises clients on a wide variety of matters, including better hiring.

Looking back over his career, Mr. Shapiro thinks he might have benefited from getting an MBA, which he says provides useful skills—especially for those in financial jobs. However, he attributes much of his own business success

to his ability to hire good people. *He shares his secrets of successful hiring...*

Basically, I take a commonsense approach, looking first at the individual's educational qualifications and work experience. But that's just the beginning. The key ingredient I look for is wisdom.

Important: There are millions of highly educated people who aren't wise. And there are some uneducated people who have a quality of wisdom that I think may reflect something from the genes. *To assess a candidate's wisdom, you must answer two key questions...*

• Does the person have the capacity to see things other people don't see?

• Does the person have the capacity to choose between a variety of alternatives and make the right choice?

The other trait I look for is enthusiasm. *I ask myself...*

• Is this person turned-on?

• Does the person enjoy what he/she is doing—and will work be a pleasant experience for him/her, or is it just a means toward a livelihood?

When you get a combination of wisdom, ability and enthusiasm, you usually have someone who works out quite satisfactorily.

Key ingredient: Good chemistry...

• Will this person fit into the organization and work well with other people?

• Or, is this person a loner who is going to go off by himself/herself?

Sometimes there's nothing wrong with a lone wolf—a person who is a researcher, for example. But if you are trying to hire someone who is going to be dealing with customers, you want a person who is outgoing and who knows how to communicate with different kinds of people. Snapshot of the brain:

Having said all this, however, I don't think an intense interview is an adequate way to determine a person's qualities. It is a process we go through, but I don't base my judgment about an individual solely on an hour's interview. Many people become tense in the interview setting and others are simply inarticulate. *Helpful:*

• Have candidates talk to several people their age who are doing the same type of work at the company. Then they can gain some perspective on what it's like to work for the company and decide whether they think they would enjoy working there, too.

• Expose management candidates to two or three top executives—to test the comfort factor on both sides.

• Read something a candidate has written. Studying written material is the best way to test whether someone who may be very glib in an interview really has any quality of intellect. Whether it is one page or ten, I find that writing gives you a quick snapshot of how a person's mind works—whether it's on the ball or just floating around in midair. A person's writing reveals whether he/she has judgment and whether he/she possesses good thinking ability —the ability to develop the facts about an issue and then come to a proper conclusion.

Also, the nonsense about which college a person went to was pretty much overcome as a result of the GI bill after World War II. A lot of people who came from colleges no one ever heard of turned out to be quite able in business. A person's alma mater matters only to others who came from that college. To hire on that basis is usually a mistake.

Gut judgment:

In the final analysis, a hiring decision boils down to making a gut judgment about whether a candidate possesses the key traits—enthusiasm, ability and wisdom—and good chemistry. But it's still a roll of the dice. And—sometimes you get fooled.

More than once, however, when I've had worries about hiring someone, he/she has turned out to be a real star. When that happens, it makes you realize there must have been something exciting about the quality of the person's intellect that made you decide to take a chance on him/her.

I believe some people have a natural flair for relating to other people and dealing with customers. I'm always interested in knowing whether a candidate has ever worked along "Main Street" in a retail store. That's the best way to gain experience in dealing with customers.

The loyalty factor:

At DuPont, where I had my greatest experience, we thought anyone who was at the company for five years would be there for the rest of his/her working life. It was considered dis-loyal for someone to go off and take another job. Of course, that's all changed in today's world of downsizing, restructuring, etc.

Today, there's a notion that you can get ahead faster by jumping from place to place, with better salaries every time. I know some people who have been very successful at this… and have made a lot of money.

But I'm not sure I'd want to hire such a person. Integrity is very important to me. When I'm offering someone an exciting job opportunity, I want to believe the candidate is eager to take hold of that responsibility and stick with it.

When a candidate's employment background is spotty, I think you have to ask for an explanation. It may be, for example, that the person's entire job experience has been with start-up companies. Well, start-up companies often fail, or they are sold to—or merged with —other companies. So, it is understandable— and quite possible—that a person might be a perfectly capable employee who has been displaced a number of times.

In fact, I recently recommended such a person for a position. His explanation seemed entirely plausible to me and I was otherwise impressed with him.

Here again, if the reasons for jumping around are reasonable, the real test comes back to the basic qualities of enthusiasm, ability and wisdom—and good chemistry.

Source: Irving S. Shapiro, former CEO of E. I. du Pont de Nemours & Co., and now Of Counsel at the law firm Skadden, Arps, Slate, Meagher & Flom, One Rodney Sq., Wilmington, Delaware 19899.

How to Be a Winning Coach

Ken Blanchard, the bestselling coauthor of *The One Minute Manager* series, has coached many business leaders in his role as educator and trainer with Blanchard Training & Development, Inc.—the Escondido, California, company he cofounded with his wife Marjorie.

A football fan along with millions of other Americans, Blanchard was watching TV on

November 14, 1993, when Coach Don Shula's Miami Dolphins beat the Philadelphia Eagles —and Shula became the winningest coach of all time. His record of 325 lifetime NFL victories surpassed the previous record held by George Halas of the Chicago Bears.

Blanchard was curious about what made Don Shula such a successful coach over three decades in an ever-changing National Football League, and wondered if his secrets might help business executives perform better.

After visiting Shula's training camp and spending many hours with him, Blanchard convinced the coach to write *Everyone's a Coach* with him. As the backbone of the book, they agreed on five basic secrets of successful coaching that could be summed up with the acronym C.O.A.C.H.

The acronym provided the framework for describing some of the fundamentals of great leadership that both of these successful men subscribe to…

Conviction driven:

Shula: The biggest problem with most leaders today is that they don't stand for anything. Leadership implies movement toward something. Convictions provide that direction. If you don't stand for something, you will fall for anything.

Blanchard: All great companies and teams have visionary leaders at the top who are always pointing to the kind of organization they are going to be. That vision cannot easily come from the bottom of an organization. It begins at the top and is continually communicated from there.

People are inspired by vision. Once they understand the vision, they consciously and unconsciously begin to move toward it and even inspire others. Coach Shula sees his job as constantly communicating his vision of perfection to his team so there is no doubt about the "game plan."

But winning to Don Shula does not mean "no holds barred." His core set of beliefs and convictions sets the boundaries. His favorite saying is, "Success is not forever, and failure isn't fatal."

When you accept that failure isn't fatal, you have got the capacity to rebound.

This is a lesson that parents must teach their kids, that Little League coaches must teach their players and that business coaches must teach their work teams.

Shula believes he has avoided burnout by keeping winning and losing in perspective. He has learned from each…and then moved on to focus everybody's energy on the next game.

He knows that he needs extremely skilled players to win in the NFL, but says that a player's character has always been just as important to him—in some cases, more important. In the same way, he has always tried to earn the players' respect by leading by example and working longer and harder than anybody else. When Shula had an operation on his Achilles tendon last fall he missed his first practice in 20 years. And…usually he's the last to leave the field.

Overlearning:

Shula: Most organizations overemphasize the goal-setting process and don't pay attention to what needs to be done to accomplish goals. My ultimate goal for all of our players is performance at the highest level possible. Because I know that perfection only happens when the mechanics are automatic, I insist on overlearning. More than anything else, overlearning—constant practice, constant attention to getting the details right every time—produces hunger to be in the middle of the action. Players who develop the skill and the confidence needed to make the big play want the play to come their way.

It may be a cliché but it's true—"You play at the level of your practice." The best way is to practice hard all the time. *Coaches and players must understand all four components of overlearning:*

- Limit the number of goals.
- Make people master all of their assignments.
- Reduce players' practice errors.
- Strive for continuous improvement.

Blanchard: Shula's overlearning principle is based on high expectations. I find that people respond well to leaders, managers, coaches and parents who have high expectations and genuine confidence in them.

Shula's expectations of his players, coaches and referees keep them constantly "performing up."

Whether the players know it or not, he can sense how great they can be. He thinks coaching is getting your players to the place where they realize that they can be that good and then they actually do it.

Shula has the same attitude about officials, explains another NFL veteran, expecting them to be in the right position to make a call. If they're not, they hear from him. Because he is on the rules committee, Shula probably knows the rules better than any other coach. Also, he has officials present at preseason practices because he wants his players to know what the rules are and to live by them.

I seldom see this level of preparation in other organizational settings. I see people showing up for sales calls unprepared, knowing little about their customers. I see people chairing meetings who have given little thought to their agendas or their strategies for getting them accomplished.

Too often, it seems the American way of managing is for managers to set goals, file them, revisit them only at the end of a performance period and then wonder why things didn't go the way they wanted.

The winning way is exemplified by companies such as Disney, which trains employees so thoroughly that they automatically bend over and pick up a stray piece of paper on the ground without even knowing they are doing it.

This "autopilot" concept in business frees employees to take the initiative to act in a way that reflects the values, goals and standards of the company—and to be creative the rest of the time.

Don Shula's method of reducing practice errors echoes a five-step plan for coaching people that I've emphasized over the years:

• Tell people exactly what you want them to do.

• Show them what good performance looks like.

• Let them do it.

• Observe their performance.

• Praise progress and/or redirect them.

Emphasize trying to catch people doing something right—and complimenting them for

it. As a coach, if you let errors go unnoticed, you ensure that more of them will occur. Mistaken behavior must be corrected before it becomes entrenched.

Audible-ready:

Shula: Part of being ready is being able to shift your game plan at will. I see myself as a battlefield commander who has the guts to make the right moves to win. I want to be prepared with a plan—and then to expect the unexpected and be ready to change this plan.

If the quarterback sees the opposing team doing something unexpected, he must be able to call an audible—a command that tells our players to substitute new assignments for the ones they were prepared to perform. Audibles are not dreamed up out of nowhere. They are carefully planned strategies the players know about and have practiced.

Blanchard: This is Shula's term for adaptability. He doesn't believe in holding to a game plan that isn't working. He's always asking, *What if...?* So, if a player is injured, for example, the team isn't caught flat-footed.

"Audibles" are well-choreographed and thought out ahead of time. Businesspeople need to learn to call audibles too, because in today's world, nothing stays the same for long. A fixed game plan or fixed organization chart can be deadly today.

Consistency:

Shula: Consistency in the way you respond to people's performance is vital. Your team will quickly learn what your standards are and perform accordingly. I not only insist on practice perfection, I'm down on the field with the team to see that it takes place. You can't manage from the press box.

Even the slightest deviation from perfection needs to be noticed and corrected on the spot. Redirecting performance is strategically important—it is where we outstrip the competition. Some coaches will let the little things go. To me, it is not a matter of how many times we have done it or how late it is or how tired the players are. We will do it until we get it right.

Blanchard: I believe that 75% of performance comes from what happens after goals are set.

Performance is influenced most by consequences—that is, the response from a monitor who is on the scene.

Don Shula says, "One thing I never want to be accused of is not noticing." But he tries hard to keep his own mood out of it, letting only people's performance dictate his response. Though he may be tough on his players, they know he respects them as human beings—or they wouldn't remain on the team. In the same way, Shula himself has always gone for respect over popularity.

What we're talking about here is a special kind of consistency—responding to people's performance…not treating everyone the same. Such predictability is a gift that people will play hard for in today's world. When people know their good performance will be noticed and rewarded, it is a tremendous motivator.

Honesty-based:

Shula: While I have gained recognition for my success as a coach, I am proudest when I am recognized for my integrity. That's an intangible that can't be measured by a win-loss record. Football is a violent sport, but it's clean and it's tough. The struggle to succeed, the hard-earned nature of a win, are to me all part of the American way of life.

I have always favored rules that prevent unnecessary roughness and if I am remembered for anything as a coach, I hope it is for playing within the rules.

Blanchard: Everything Don Shula does is rooted in honesty. This is exactly what people need—and want— in a leader today.

If they can't have job security, they at least want their leaders to be straight with them. They don't want to be told there will be no more layoffs, only to find further downsizing two months later—while the boss goes away with a huge bonus. They want it the Shula way —straight.

Sources: Kenneth Blanchard, co-founder, Blanchard Training & Development, Inc., 125 State Pl., Escondido, California 92029, and Don Shula, coach of the Miami Dolphins. They are the coauthors of *Everyone's a Coach: You Can Inspire Anyone to Be a Winner,* HarperBusiness, 10 E. 53 St., New York 10022.

How an Employee is Fired Can Trigger a Lawsuit

Juries increasingly are awarding damages to people dismissed in an abusive or embarrassing way. *Translated:* While the company may escort a fired employee off the premises, do not use uniformed guards…avoid abusive criticism …do not ridicule the person—certainly not in public. *Important:* Maintain the employee's dignity and respect by minding your manners.

Source: Christopher Hedican, writing in *LaborWatch,* Berens-Tate Consulting Group, 10050 Regency Circle, Omaha, Nebraska 68114.

Legal Traps in Disciplining Employees… Can Be Avoided

Even if the company hasn't been sued by employees claiming harassment or another form of mistreatment, it's a good idea to review disciplinary procedures to make sure the company is not risking trouble down the line. *Important steps to take…*

• *Detail unacceptable behavior and the consequences of such behavior in a handbook.* An employee handbook clearly stating that harassment will not be tolerated—and that harassers are subject to disciplinary action, which could include termination—can shield the company from lawsuits by victims of harassment. In such cases, the company can use the handbook to demonstrate that it is not liable due to its explicit ban on such behavior.

Also, the handbook can defend the company against wrongful termination lawsuits by terminated harassers who deny their behavior was banned by the company.

• *Document reasons for acting.* Think in terms of being able to defend disciplinary action in court—should that become necessary. The more written evidence the company has to support its case, the better.

• *Confront problem employees in private with the evidence of unacceptable behavior.* Give them a chance to explain why they did what they did —or why they failed to take appropriate action. Not only is this fair to employees, but it can protect the company from acting on erroneous information.

• *Avoid precipitous disciplinary action.* Wait to hear and evaluate all of the facts before making a decision. If necessary, suspend the employee while investigating the facts and conducting deliberations.

• *Keep disciplinary matters confidential.* Spreading the news to coworkers—or outsiders —can result in defamation suits.

• *Follow the company's written policies.* Deviations are usually difficult to explain. If the handbook promises progressive disciplinary action before termination, for example, the company can be taken to court for failing to follow all the steps.

• *Adhere to the company's operating practices —on a consistent basis.* This means that if one employee is disciplined in a certain way for a certain behavior, the next person who does it should be similarly disciplined.

Even when there are extenuating circumstances, apparent favoritism causes tremendous resentment that sometimes results in lawsuits. An employee might claim he/she didn't really follow the rules in the company handbook because there was good reason to believe they wouldn't be evenly enforced…or that he/she did not utilize the problem-resolution procedure because harassment is tolerated.

The only way to prevent this problem is to apply discipline fairly and consistently at all times.

Source: Paul J. Siegel, an employment attorney with Jackson, Lewis, Schnitzler & Krupman, 1000 Woodbury Rd., Suite 400, Woodbury, New York 11797.

Effective Delegating… Made Simple

As management structures get flatter, the need for effective delegation unavoidably grows stronger.

But that need is not always fulfilled. Instead, many managers, fearing for the security of their jobs, keep a tight grip on their regular tasks while they take on additional work that used to be performed by people who have been let go.

Result: Managers lengthen their workdays— often at the expense of their health and families. And companies fail to achieve much of a gain in productivity because the same tasks— useful or not—keep being performed.

Delegating painlessly:

To overcome the obstacles to constructive, efficient delegating…

• *Analyze your own job.* Make a detailed list of all of your tasks and activities. For one month, keep track—day by day—of how much time you spend on each activity. Be honest. This is your own list…designed to help you. If you spend time at work reading the sports pages or playing computer games, write that down.

Leave room on the right side of your list for two sets of notes about each actual work task. "Can I delegate it?" Then, add your honest thoughts about the task, including, "Is it really necessary? Is there an easier way to do this? What would happen if nobody did this?"

• *Collect details of the jobs of subordinates.* Ask the people who work for you to track their daily activities the same way. Explain that you are most interested in their ideas on tasks that can be eliminated…and ones that can be simplified or done more efficiently.

Reward: If they find ways to eliminate or spend less time on mundane tasks, they will have time to spend on more interesting and challenging work that you can delegate to them.

What you can delegate…

• *Routine, but necessary activities.* These are the easiest to delegate. You've done them over and over, know the problems that are likely to surface and can easily explain what has to be done.

Examples: Regular information-sharing meetings…monthly reports…professional and community meetings.

• *Specialties that people in your group excel at.* Focus your own attention and work on improving the overall performance of your group —and meeting the goals of the company. Match your needs to the skills of the people available to help you.

Examples: The math-whiz clerk or assistant can double-check that figures and ratios make sense in any reports sent out of your department. The word processor can be responsible for keeping up-to-date on new systems and equipment, making recommendations when necessary.

• *Occupational hobbies.* Managers often hang on to aspects of their jobs that they should have delegated years ago just because they enjoy the work or the social interaction.

Examples: Attending trade shows…visiting customers…working the bugs out of new computer-software programs or entering data.

Often, these were the jobs that built their expertise and reputation—but they no longer represent the best use of their time and talent.

Helpful guideline: Recognize these activities for what they are. Let go of tasks that keep you from growing and doing your best work. Or, if you must, hold on to one that doesn't consume much of your time.

• *Tasks that promote the growth of others on your staff.* Use selective delegation of jobs as a way to target the development of skills in specific individuals. Be alert to opportunities to help a person develop writing skills, organizing skills, computer skills or presentation skills. And take the time to talk to members of your staff to discover what they want to do and believe they can do.

The six steps to effective delegation:

Once the decision to delegate a specific task is made, follow the basic rules of successful delegating…

• Explain the results that are to be achieved— not the methods that must be used to get those results. Stressing method over result weakens the impact of delegation by setting unnecessary limits on what the person can do.

• Write down the goals of the task…in 20 words or less. Review the stated goals regularly.

• Always delegate an entire task. This heightens interest and the sense of accomplishment.

• Provide a deadline…and try to be flexible if the person delegated to do the task thinks more time is needed. But always make the deadline specific. If you must set a deadline that you and the employee both acknowledge is tight, be sure you make clear to the person taking on the job what priority the task has. Set review times —and keep those dates firm.

• Avoid ambiguity about the assignment. Make sure the person to whom work is delegated gives you a clear statement of acceptance and commitment to complete the job.

• Avoid ambiguity among other employees. Make sure all those affected by your delegation of a task know that you have given authority to that person.

What not to delegate:

Of course, you should never delegate a task that could instead be eliminated. *And do not delegate tasks that involve:*

• *Solving a crisis.* When the heat is on, the manager must take the lead in solving a problem, eliminating a threat or meeting an urgent deadline.

• *Personnel and other confidential matters.* Evaluations, promotions and dismissals are too touchy to be delegated. And while decisions on department pay scales, bonuses and job classifications may be boring and time-consuming and seem to be perfect jobs to delegate, they rarely should be. They require a manager's judgment and authority.

• *Policy-making that sets the limits for making decisions.* But decision-making within these limits is often easily delegated.

Example: Sales reps often grant credit to specific customers within certain dollar limits that are set by the credit manager's policy guidelines.

Delegating to a team:

The key to delegating effectively to a team of people is to make sure that everyone in the group is clear about who is responsible for what and by when.

Important: At each checkpoint, monitor progress to make sure that every member of the team understands his/her task and deadline. Write down the agreements. Otherwise, you run the risk that tasks will fall through the cracks or that work will be duplicated.

Source: Frank F. Huppe, PhD, retired director of the engineering physics laboratory for the DuPont Company, and the author of *Successful Delegation,* Career Press, Hawthorne, NJ.

Motivation... Different Perspectives

In a recent study, managers and employees were separately asked to rate the importance of the same ten motivational factors.

Managers overrated pay and job security as employee motivators...and underrated the importance of interesting work, expressions of appreciation and keeping employees informed. *Here's how the managers' rankings compared with the employees' rankings...*

Managers' rankings:
1. Compensation.
2. Job security.
3. Growth opportunities.
4. Working conditions.
5. Interesting work.
6. Loyalty to employees.
7. Tactful discipline.
8. Appreciation shown by management.
9. Help with personal problems.
10. Being well-informed.

Employees' rankings:
1. Interesting work.
2. Appreciation shown by management.
3. Being well-informed.
4. Job security.
5. Compensation.
6. Growth opportunities.
7. Working conditions.
8. Loyalty to employees.
9. Tactful discipline.
10. Help with personal problems.

Source: Kenneth A. Kovach, doctor of human resources and industrial relations, George Mason University, Fairfax, Virginia.

Best and Worst Bosses

There's surprising consistency among people when they are asked to describe the worst bosses they ever had.

For years, consultants John D.W. Beck and Neil M. Yeager have been asking employees in public, private, manufacturing and service organizations of every size to identify what their worst bosses do.

Typical traits of bosses people hate:

• *Obsession with control.* These dominating bosses get stuck on details, micromanage and don't trust anyone.

• *Evasion.* Bosses who are abdicators, and who are inaccessible. Some truly trust the people who report to them and stay out of their way with the best intentions. But most are too caught up with their own work to spend time with people.

• *Arbitrariness.* This is found in bosses who tell people what to do in general terms and then leave them alone. When the project is well along, they reemerge, and criticize because things are not being done the way they wanted. (This is also called the "Seagull technique" because the manager swoops in, flaps his wings, makes a lot of noise, leaves some droppings on everyone and flies off again.)

By contrast, the best bosses start by giving a lot of direction—much like the dominators—but then they shift to giving people responsibility, like the abdicators.

Key difference: Great bosses also give employees support. They listen carefully at critical checkpoints...and help people develop their own problem-solving capabilities while diagnosing those problems.

And—superior bosses are willing to step up to the plate to make tough decisions when people clearly need them to.

Sources: John D.W. Beck, a founder of Charter Oak Consulting Group, Berlin, Connecticut, and Neil M. Yeager, organizational development consultant. They are the coauthors of *The Leader's Window: Mastering the Four Styles of Leadership to Build High-Performing Teams,* John Wiley & Sons, Inc., New York.

Beware: There's No Right Management Style

No management style is guaranteed to succeed, whatever the gurus say. *Here are two "truths" you always hear...*

• *Flawed "truth":* Build relationships with customers. IBM did this for decades—only to have customers abandon its mainframes en masse for PCs.

• *Flawed "truth":* Focus on core abilities. Xerox focused on its copier business—and missed a historic opportunity when it failed to produce the first marketable PC. It was developed by Xerox engineers but put aside because it was an unproven sideline product.

There are examples of every imaginable management approach, both successful and unsuccessful. What works depends on the details of the business. And the details are always changing—as the case of IBM illustrates.

Managers who think they've found "the key" to success run a big risk. Even if their ideas work for a while, they risk following them blindly after circumstances change and results fall off.

No one can predict the future. Continuing success requires constant testing of new ideas, readiness to admit mistakes and quick follow-through on ideas that work.

Source: Tom Peters, management consultant, and the author of *In Search of Excellence*, writing in *Office Systems*, 941 Danbury Rd., Box 150, Georgetown, CT 06829.

Cooperation in the Workplace

A very important prerequisite for long-term success today—regardless of how a company has functioned in the past—is close, constructive and consistent cooperation among employees at all levels.

But—ineffective use of teams can hurt rather than help cooperation and communication in a company. Those teams that have proven ineffective frequently were set up for the wrong purpose—to rubber-stamp a decision management had already taken...or to keep a manager from being blamed for an unpopular decision.

Or—teams may be too big, have no clear idea of their tasks or have no goals to bind and unify their efforts.

Lesson: Set up teams only when teamwork is absolutely necessary—when team members perform activities and functions that are interdependent and must collectively contribute to making decisions or solving problems. To cooperate, all team members must understand the task and the time frame for completing it.

Effective cooperation among members of a team depends on each person understanding the jobs, responsibilities, authority and accountability of all the other people engaged in solving the problem or achieving the result. This clarity is rare—and the rapid changes in many companies these days often confuse matters even more.

To avoid this trap, prepare for each team effort by carefully managing the vital components of good cooperation...

• *Clarity of responsibility.* No team effort will succeed if members of the team don't know exactly what they are supposed to do. To get this right, start by listing—in order—the major activities or decisions the team must undertake to reach its goal.

Helpful: Create a graph for each stage of the project. List the tasks to be performed on the vertical axis and the names of team members across the horizontal axis.

For each task put an R—for Responsible—under the name of the team member responsible for the activity or decision.

Put a C—for Consult—under the names of team members who must be consulted during the activity.

Put an I—for Inform—under those who should be informed after a task is completed.

Individual team members should fill out the matrix privately and then compare and discuss the results publicly to iron out differences in perceptions of responsibility.

Draw up a final responsibility matrix based on that discussion.

• *Effective communication.* The next critical ingredient for cooperation is open, constructive communication, to exchange relevant and timely information. Incentives, performance appraisals, a culture of uncompromising individualism and entrepreneurship and isolation by function are all factors that can obstruct effective communication. *To facilitate communication…*

• Be tough about eliminating routine channels and bureaucratic approvals. Set a few essential checkpoints. Make them relevant and effective. Eliminate all others.

• Keep team members physically close to one another, where they can meet face-to-face frequently. If geographic dispersion cannot be avoided, provide good telecommunications and adequate travel budgets.

• Encourage each part of the company to advertise to other parts the services it has the ability to perform and the help it can give.

Example: The head of a management information system at a regional bank prepared an information packet for each branch explaining what the central operation could do more efficiently than any branch. Names of individuals (even their nicknames), their phone numbers and the particular kind of help they could offer were listed.

• Make clear that management needs good information—even if it is negative. Communication and cooperation cannot thrive under conditions of fear and distrust.

• *Effective measurement of cooperation.* Find ways to measure the results of cooperation by results, not just by good feelings. And reward it. If the measurement tool isn't clear initially, make sure team members understand at the start of their assignment that they are responsible for finding benchmarks or goals by which to measure their results.

Examples: Evidence that customer problems have been solved consistently…that economies of scale are being achieved…that transaction costs are reduced.

Key: Measuring results is not merely another way to achieve management control. People are motivated when they recognize that there is

a real benefit—for the company and for themselves—in cooperating.

Source: Lawrence G. Hrebiniak, PhD, Wharton School, University of Pennsylvania, 2000 Steinberg-Dietrich Hall, Philadelphia 19104. Dr. Hrebiniak is the author of *The We-Force in Management: How to Build and Sustain Cooperation,* Lexington Books, 866 Third Ave., New York 10022.

Decisiveness is Key to Executive Success

When executive recruiters were asked to name the one trait that contributes most to executive success, 50% named *decisiveness.* The next most popular answer, *experience,* was given by 24%, and the third answer, *determination,* was chosen by 14%. *Key:* Many managers avoid hard decisions for fear of making a mistake. But successful executives are also decisive in recognizing and correcting their own errors.

Source: Survey of the members of the International Association of Corporate and Professional Recruiters, cited in *Executive Female,* 127 W. 24 St., New York 10011.

What All Managers Must Know About Employee Privacy

Companies that take too much interest in employees' private affairs increasingly find themselves facing legal problems.

Challenge: Even if the company is suffering because of something one of its employees is doing while off duty, extreme caution is required before taking any action.

Under the US Constitution—and many state constitutions—people have a right to privacy that protects them from unreasonable searches and seizures by government agencies.

Some states have passed laws granting similar rights to employees of private companies. And the courts have ruled that employees also have a right under common law to expect a reasonable degree of privacy in their relationships with employers both at and away from the workplace.

These laws try to balance an employee's right to privacy against management's interest in running its business.

To avoid legal problems, top management must familiarize itself with key details about the laws protecting privacy on and off the job…

• *Off-duty rights.* Not surprisingly, there is a heavier burden of proof on the employer when it seeks to influence an employee's behavior off the job than when it tries to do so during working hours.

Exception: An employer may be able to take action against an employee if it can prove that the employee's off-duty activities are harming the company.

• *Employee privacy rights at work.* During working hours, employees are expected to spend their time performing their duties. But the law says they are entitled to a reasonable degree of privacy.

General rule: Employers with legitimate business reasons to limit employee privacy can legally inform employees that their right to privacy is limited. *In these cases, however, companies must…*

•Have a detailed written policy authorizing workplace searches.

•Make sure all employees are clearly informed of the policy.

Best: The company can protect itself further by asking employees to sign a consent form indicating their acceptance of the company's search policy and the potential for having their personal effects searched.

Caution: Even if the company makes known its right to search employee lockers, it may not be legal to search a purse or lunch box stored there. Employees are entitled to bring some personal items into the workplace and must put them down somewhere, so these items should be treated with the same respect for privacy as if the employee were carrying them on his/her person.

• *Electronic privacy issues.* The federal Electronic Communications Protection Act (ECPA) prevents interception by a third party of electronic communications, including telephone calls and electronic data transmissions. However, it is not a violation when one of the parties consents to its being intercepted.

This means that an employer can monitor phone calls for business reasons if employees know about the policy.

Trap: Employees, unless informed otherwise, are entitled to assume that their boss will not listen to their private phone calls, rummage through their computer files or read their E-mail messages.

Bottom line…

If the company believes it has a need to perform such acts as searching desks or reading E-mail, make sure employees are aware of those facts when they are hired. A similar statement should also appear prominently in employee manuals. Be prepared to justify all such practices legally, with convincing explanations of why they are necessary.

While these are basic rules governing employee privacy in and out of the workplace, always consult an attorney whenever a specific question of employee privacy arises.

Source: Stuart Bompey, chair of the Labor and Employment Law Department, Orrick, Herrington & Sutcliffe, 599 Lexington Ave., New York 10022.

Feedback: How to Get It, How to Use It

No surprises! Most top managers insist on being alerted early to any developing problems.

But for business owners or managers, getting the prompt and accurate feedback they need to learn about and act on problems—in a department, a process, a new store or with a product—is often very difficult these days.

Reason: Reorganizations, reengineering and layoffs often create an atmosphere of fear within a company. When bad news breaks within a department it will be kept from top management—in an attempt to avoid any unpleasant repercussions.

Fear trap:

If fear is permitted to flourish and vital information is increasingly suppressed, management eventually will lose control of key functions—mistakes will be made, key employees will leave and customers will go elsewhere—as the lack of feedback leads to bad decisions…or no decisions.

A better way—for everyone:

The only way that top management can get the honest feedback it needs—in time—is to build and maintain a climate of trust.

Declaring an open-door policy, though, is rarely enough. A confident chief executive, willing to hear complaints and listen carefully and patiently, can sometimes create this climate with simple personal actions.

Example: The head of one company where morale sank after it barely survived a financial crisis, came to the company cafeteria early each morning at the shift change. He sat down with employees who were going home and with those just arriving and asked…

What kind of problems are we having where you work?

Is there something I can do to help you do your job better?

Are managers getting in the way of your putting in your best efforts?

Problem: Face-to-face encounters like this become harder and harder to schedule as company operations expand geographically …and more and more work is outsourced or handled by contract workers connected to headquarters only by computers and telephone lines.

Communication trap:

Memos, reports and E-mail messages addressed to senior managers often are deceptive.

The moment face-to-face contact between bosses and subordinates is replaced with another form of communication, honesty is compromised.

People simply will not put anything down on paper or on the computer screen that will make them look bad. And—some of them may actually even direct responsibility away from themselves.

Solution: Every senior manager must make time in his/her schedule to meet face to face on a regular basis with people on the front lines of company operations.

Taking the time to see what's happening *firsthand* may be the most important job a senior manager has. Give it top priority.

Key: Don't simply make presentations and speeches at these meetings—*listen…and size people up.*

And *then*, when you are alerted to a problem, stay in touch via computer and one-on-one telephone and video conferences. Promise to look into the problem further and do whatever you can to solve it.

Source: Michael LeBoeuf, PhD, a retired professor of management from the University of New Orleans, and a management consultant and professional speaker, 1328 Homestead Ave., Metairie, Louisiana 70005. LeBoeuf's book is *Fast Forward: How to Win a Lot More Business In a Lot Less Time*, Berkley Books, 200 Madison Ave., New York 10016.

8

Financial Analysis and Control in the Office

The Simple, Old Secret of Superior Cost-Cutting

Some companies, of course, are better at cutting costs than others. Less competent cost-cutters can learn from the leaders that while cost-cutting is good for everyone—there's good cost-cutting...and there's bad cost-cutting.

The good kind does more than simply make it less expensive to run the business. Effective cost-cutting moves the company toward its long-term goals. And as such, good cost-cutting must cut the fat, not the muscle.

The muscle of a company is its core business, the operations that drive profits and give the company its competitive edge. The fat is everything else.

A fresh approach:

Before embarking on a cost-cutting program, examine each of the company's activities, and ask the key question: "Is this part of the core business or is it essential in supporting the core business?"

If the answer is "no," consider targeting the activity for cost-cutting, contracting out or, even better, elimination. If the operation is part of the core business, leave it alone or consider making additional expenditures to improve it. *Examples:*

• Some airlines have tried to cut costs by paring down their reservations and baggage-handling operations. But this only hinders their ability to move passengers and freight, and that is their core business—their muscle. In-flight food service, however, is considered a noncore business by most airlines and is therefore being contracted out.

• IBM cut costs, and in the short term the effort looked impressive. But costs were cut with little thought to the company's long-term competitive edge. *Result:* Some cuts have jeopardized research and development, design and productivity, all part of the company's core—its muscle.

Once a company identifies the activities that form its core business, it can begin selecting other activities to scale back or eliminate. Base the priority on the contribution that an activity makes to the company's long-term return on investment—its personnel, plant, equipment and other tangible and intangible assets.

The calculation, of course, can only be made when the company has a strategic plan and knows how each of its operations will help it reach its long-term goals.

As a rule, cut costs first in those areas where the cut will result in the biggest increase in return on investment.

Extreme example: Don't bother cutting costs on the typing pool in a division that is going to be eliminated. The action will have no effect whatsoever on return on investment.

It's also helpful to build a consensus for change in a department that is targeted for cost-cutting. *Helpful:* Ask managers in the department how they would ideally like to see the department improved. From that ideal, the company can scale back to what it can afford.

Example: Just-In-Time manufacturing (JIT) offers big opportunities for savings. Ideally, JIT should result in the ability to operate with no inventories at all. Since that might not be easily achieved, the company can instead implement those elements of JIT that it can afford and about which its managers are uniformly enthusiastic.

Getting down to work:

Take an especially hard look at these areas for cost savings...

•*Manufacturing systems.* New manufacturing systems can now achieve huge savings by integrating production with other activities, such as purchasing, materials handling and inventories. Moreover, the costs of these systems have now dropped to the point where savings can often be realized in two or three years.

•*Outsourcing.* As the number of service companies grows, it pays to check periodically on whether the company can save money by contracting out an activity that it now performs in-house. The key candidates are obviously activities that aren't part of the company's core business.

But a noncore function doesn't always qualify for outsourcing. To make the determination, calculate how much operating divisions now pay for such services as data processing, design, maintenance, etc. Then ask each division how much it could afford to pay an outside contractor to supply the service. If it's less, target the activity for outsourcing.

In fact, don't assume that a service is needed at all. Instead, analyze the company's services to see how they are really used, an exercise often called *Activity-Based Costing*.

Example: Few companies use all of the information their data-processing department collects and disseminates.

•*Labor.* Companies often overlook one of the most effective means of holding down payrolls. When an employee leaves the company, don't assume he/she must be replaced. Instead, see if others on the job can incorporate the departing employee's tasks into their own. Often they can, with a raise in pay that's only a fraction of what the departing employee made.

Example: A Florida city employed eight groundskeepers. Two of the employees left, and the remaining six were asked if they could handle all of the work in exchange for a share in half of the former employees' salaries. *Result:* One employee said later that four of them could do the job of the former eight employees.

The example is also an illustration of something else companies often overlook—the power of financial incentives.

Labor costs can also be cut by taking a close look at each of the company's activities—who performs what and how labor is actually used.

Example: In most businesses, employees are assigned to preventive maintenance and to demand maintenance. The former, of course, is supposed to prevent the latter. What actually happens, however, is that employees are often pulled off preventive maintenance to perform demand tasks. *Result:* The need for demand maintenance increases, pushing productivity down.

Rule of thumb for beginners: Rather than embark on immediate, large-scale, cost-cutting efforts, it makes sense to test the waters by trying out a new system in one department before implementing it throughout the company.

Example: The marketing department could outsource computer services before the company decides whether to let other departments do the same.

Important: When selecting a department for cost-cutting changes, pick one that is likely to be receptive to the new methods. When success is achieved there, move on to more challenging areas.

Source: Norman Kobert, principal, N. Kobert & Associates, asset management consultants to companies that include Coca-Cola, General Electric and Exxon, Box 21396, Fort Lauderdale, Florida 33335. His book is *Cut the Fat, Not the Muscle, Cost Improvement Strategies for Long-Term Profitability*, Prentice Hall, Englewood Cliffs, New Jersey 07632.

Inventory Control Through Barter

Managing excess or obsolete inventory—efficiently and cost-effectively—will become increasingly important to all businesses in coming years. As cost pressures mount and global competition intensifies, companies with the tightest inventory operations will be the biggest winners.

Challenge of the 1990s—and beyond: Consumer needs and expectations are changing rapidly—and the trend is toward even faster change. That puts increasing pressure on companies to avoid getting stuck with excess inventory when a product suddenly goes out of favor or is repackaged.

These include stickered returns, products with approaching expiration dates, uneven inventories—all of which were once impossible to sell off. *At stake is the manufacturer's most critical asset:* The loyalty of key retail customers.

Getting rid of unwanted excess inventory can be accomplished by one of four primary methods…

•Destroy it.

•Donate it to charity for a tax write-off.

•Close out for cash.

•Barter it for media time through a barter firm.

If the product is truly worthless and can't even be given away, destroying it may be the only option.

Donating a product to charity is a good idea sometimes—if the company's unique financial situation warrants it.

Closing out for cash may create a bottom-line loss, since odd-lot and close-out retailers demand deals dramatically below regular wholesale prices.

However, bartering products—especially consumer products—almost always gives a company a much higher return. Barter can also be done in a way that meets both financial and marketing objectives.

Reason: Almost any product that is repackaged or replaced has a market somewhere—usually through the odd-lot and close-out industry, and sometimes overseas. Products such as outdated cosmetics, apparel or even toys that are no longer in favor can be bartered for advertising time or space.

Caution: When negotiating with a barter firm, seek a guarantee that your product won't be sold to regular retail customers—who routinely return unwanted products to the manufacturer at full price.

To find a barter firm, contact the company's local Chamber of Commerce or its trade association, or call the International Reciprocal Trade Association at 703-916-9020 for recommendations.

Important: Before doing business with a barter firm, check it out carefully by asking for names and phone numbers of companies the firm has helped in the past.

Try to work with barter firms that are accountable for the media they are providing. Many firms simply provide a package of media valued at a price equivalent to the amount of product being delivered.

But there is no specific commitment of media time or placement, and your company may be getting TV or radio time no one else wants.

Better: Work with a barter firm that buys the media your company needs. Make sure the firm contractually commits to agreed-on time or space.

Source: Mark Goldsmith, president, Inventory Management Systems Inc., 60 Madison Ave., New York 10010.

Collecting from Bankrupt Customers

When bankruptcy is declared by a corporate customer that owes the company money…

•Call the bankruptcy court to learn if the filing is a Chapter 7 liquidation or a Chapter 11 reorganization, from which collecting at least a portion of the debt is likely.

•Stop shipments to, and production of orders for, the customer.

•Use reclamation laws to recover goods shipped to the customer within the ten days prior to the filing.

•Get on the bankrupt company's list of creditors and make a detailed claim for the exact amount that is owed to you—don't assume the bankrupt customer will accurately report its debts to the court.

•Join the creditors' committee that will hammer out the final settlement between the bankrupt company and its creditors. It will give you insight into the process.

Source: Cindy Tursman, editor, *Business Credit*, 8815 Centre Park Dr., Columbia, Maryland 21045.

How to Use Pricing Most Effectively in Competitive Times

Cutting prices can, on occasion, be an effective way to boost market share. However, it can also be fraught with danger…

•Cash flow can temporarily drop.

•The company is at the mercy of competitors, who can slash prices even further.

Successful companies look for other ways to increase sales—especially when they are up against aggressive discounters and other lower-priced competitors. *Before tampering with prices, consider these tactics…*

•*Add value.* Adding value to a product or service is easier than most companies realize. *Examples:*

•Toro, the lawn products maker, holds "lawn party" events where potential customers are given lessons on how to care for their lawns.

•Some drugstores with high percentages of elderly customers are adding value by developing home delivery services.

•Quickway, an Iowa company that makes engine rebuilding equipment, provides a training video to show customers how to use its equipment.

Training videos are an excellent way to add value to many products, and production is cheaper now than it has ever been. But there's a trap. Unless the training is actually useful, potential customers will dismiss it as a promotional presentation.

•*Educate customers.* Some buyers, 17% to 20% of them on average, will always respond to enhanced value. Another 27% to 30% will always buy whichever line is cheapest. That leaves a huge number who must be educated to appreciate the value that a company adds to its products or services.

Horror story: Many bookstores have no chance of educating customers because their clerks don't even know how to use the standard reference—*Books in Print*.

Encouraging contrast: Home Depot, the do-it-yourself chain, has experts on staff who offer patient and ample help to customers.

Educating customers isn't limited to the retail sector.

Example: Iowa Beef Processors, the world's largest slaughtering operation, isn't the lowest-priced in its field. But it does offer high value because its meat products have less waste after they are cooked. The company has now launched a marketing campaign to educate customers about its value advantage.

• *Target the best customers.* Businesses often get so caught up in individual transactions that they forget to make a special effort to keep the 20% or so of accounts that contribute most to profits.

But these big spenders are easy to identify through the many computerized customer-tracking systems now on the market.

When companies make the effort, they usually find that their best customers have specific buying patterns. Most of their purchases, for example, may be in only one or two departments, or they may consistently buy only a few types of products.

Companies can capitalize on this valuable information by staying in contact with these customers to alert them of an event, such as an upcoming sale or the arrival of new merchandise.

Phone calls or postcards cost little, compared to profits earned from these first-tier customers. And today, there's a growing number of businesses—usually offshoots of advertising firms—that handle this type of customer contact. *Companies can also use information on their best customers to:*

• Reduce inventory levels by eliminating some low-margin, slow-selling products.

• Research the feasibility of opening a second sales channel to either the upscale or downscale customer.

In fact, if a company categorizes its best customers as As and its worst customers as Ds, its growth area will nearly always be among the B+ group.

Example: Toro markets a slightly less-expensive line of products under the Lawn-Boy brand.

This strategy not only captures customers who might be reluctant to buy the Toro label, but also raises the barrier against market entry from a lower-priced competitor.

• *Join other vendors.* Companies can also make life harder for tough competitors by strategically joining forces in the marketing area. *Examples:*

• A manufacturer can join with its distributor to put on shows and other promotional events for retailers—thereby making the product stand out against the competition.

• Two companies that sell to the same customers can join in similar promotions.

Makers of sunglasses, for instance, have joined with sporting goods shops, and drugstores have teamed up with companies that rent wheelchairs and other home health-care products.

Joining forces also enables companies to share databases. *Advantages:*

• Identifying new potential customers on the other company's database.

• Cross-marketing. There can be a big cost savings, for instance, in sending promotional material that mentions both products to a single mailing list.

• *Build loyalty.* One of the simplest, yet often overlooked, ways to boost customer loyalty also involves databases. Companies can use computerized data to track customers so they can be contacted at key points in their buying lifetime. *Examples:*

• Instead of waiting until customers bring their cars in, auto dealers can keep track of mileage and remind customers before the car is due for service.

• Retailers can alert customers who have bought winter products in the past that similar products will soon be in stock.

*Also effective…*product labels that tell customers how to contact the company.

Example: Like many other companies, Hormel now has an "800" number on its packages. Customers can use it to get product information and to let the company know what they think about its products.

Apart from this loyalty-building feedback, the company also captures important demographic information that can be used in marketing.

Good customer service also builds loyalty, but few companies know how to improve customer service.

*Most effective method…*bring customers in contact with the people in the company who serve them.

Example: John Deere invites farmers to meet with the employees who make its tractors. By talking face-to-face with customers, employees learn more than they ever could in a customer-service training program.

• *Add on, sell up and repackage.* If competitors lower prices, don't rush in to match them. Instead, consider an add-on that establishes uniqueness and raises the amount of each individual sale.

Example: A computer maker can hold its basic price steady but offer a discount on software for a specified period of time.

Selling up is a similar concept that can also increase the size of sales.

Example: Rather than tamper with the price of its basic product, an air-conditioning manufacturer can develop two or three lines with an increasing number of options.

Repackaging has a similar effect.

Example: Instead of selling razors and shavers separately, Gillette also sells them in the same package.

Source: Thomas J. Winninger, Winninger Institute for Economic Strategy, 4510 W. 77 St., Minneapolis 55435. He is also the author of *Price Wars, How to Win the Battle for Your Customers!*, St. Thomas Press, Box 24108, Edina, Minnesota 55424.

Letters of Credit

Letters of credit (LCs)—often used by exporters to facilitate payments from foreign customers when a customer resists payment in advance—aren't as safe as is commonly believed. While most exporters believe LCs are nonrecourse (so if the customer delays payment it's the bank's problem) there are, in fact, exceptions. It doesn't happen often, but there have been cases where the importer's bank withholds payment to the exporter's bank. And sometimes importers even instruct their bank to find a "discrepancy" in the documentation to justify the withheld payment. *Self-defense:* Insist on a confirmed letter of credit that guarantees the risk of the importer's bank.

Source: *International Business*, 500 Mamaroneck Ave., Suite 314, Harrison, New York 10528.

How to Delay Supplier's Price Increase

•In the supply contract, include a requirement of advance notice—a specific number of days or a particular way of giving notice—of any price increase.

•On receiving notice of an increase, negotiate its effective date—sellers often are flexible about this with current customers.

•When a sales proposal says an offered price will be good for a stated period, negotiate to extend the period.

•Accept an increase in steps over a period of time—to allow the salesperson to report an immediate increase, even though its full effect is delayed.

•Simply ask for a delay, suggesting you'll take your business elsewhere if you must.

Source: Chester Karrass, PhD, The Karrass Organization, negotiating consultants, 1633 Stanford St., Santa Monica, California 90404.

Shrewder Bill Collecting

A significant—but often overlooked—part of the customer-retention equation is in accounts receivable.

Once a transaction is in the hands of the accounts receivable department, the company's costs of goods sold have already been expended. The sales department has closed. Others have fulfilled the orders and made out the invoices.

Now...the accounts receivable department must secure payment and reinforce the customer relationship for the future.

Key: Many of the accounts they call and write to will continue to be valuable customers as long as rough treatment doesn't push them away.

On the first call—listen! State why you are calling. Then wait for a response. Listen for evidence of sincerity and willingness to pay.

The customer may need to be resold on the value of what the company sells to him/her. When an invoice is past due, but the customer voices no negative experience with the product or the company, accounts receivable people must reinforce the value of the company's product or service.

Aim: To provide reasons for the customer to pay the invoice...and ultimately to order again.

Example: A top sales manager at the American Automobile Association keeps on top of members who have failed to renew memberships. He often starts: "I notice we haven't received your renewal yet and I'd like to do what I can to keep your membership in force without paying another initiation fee. I can keep you ahead of the game by making that renewal effective today even though your membership ran out three months ago."

Don't take for granted customers who keep their accounts current. That includes customers who had payment problems and then lived up to agreements that got the account current once more. Call—or send a note—and say, "Thank you for keeping your promise by sending along that check."

Source: George R. Walther, a professional speaker, and president of Speaking from Experience, Inc., 2254 Alki Ave. SW, Seattle 98116. He is the author of *Upside Down Marketing*, McGraw-Hill, 1221 Avenue of the Americas, New York 10020.

Cash Advances Aren't Cost-Effective

Reasons: Most employees give themselves the benefit of the doubt and take advances that are larger than necessary...each advance can cost the company $25 in administrative costs ...employees holding the company's cash have no incentive to pay it back in a hurry.

To minimize advances: Limit the dollar amount of advances employees may take at one time...require one advance to be settled before the employee can take another...set a time period—such as 30 days—within which an advance must be settled. When a deadline is missed, send a "late payment" notice to the employee and to the employee's supervisor.

Source: Steven W. Alesio, executive vice president, Small Business Services, American Express Travel Related Services Company, Inc., New York, quoted in *Sales & Marketing Executive Report*, 4660 N. Ravenswood Ave., Chicago 60640.

Factoring...Affordable And Effective Financing

After several years of aggressive lending, many commercial banks are getting stingy with credit—especially for smaller business borrowers.

Reasons: Rising interest rates increase the risks of repayment...recession fears are blemishing the outlook for business profitability... and currency instability in world markets has made many banks jittery about lending—period.

One solution: Alternative financing from a

factor—a lender that buys accounts receivable from cash-hungry companies seeking credit. The factor discounts the value of those receivables, and advances the companies between 60% and 80% of the cash value of the invoices. The factor then takes over the job of collecting the receivables from the company's customers.

Proven technique:

Factoring has its roots in the days of Hammurabi 4,000 years ago.

In the US, it has long been associated with the textile and apparel industries, which have traditionally depended on factors to finance their seasonal businesses. But recently, fledgling electronics manufacturers, computer start-ups and small health-care companies have tapped into this source of financing.

Also, factoring has flourished as small banks —the traditional source of lending to small business—dramatically cut back their lending during the late 1980s and early 1990s. In the decade between 1983 and 1993, factoring volume in the US nearly doubled—from $33.1 billion to $57.5 billion.

What sort of business might use a factor?

Example: You're a small manufacturer of widgets, and you've exhausted all your credit sources. You're up to your eyebrows in debt to the bank, you've maxed out your credit cards and have second-mortgaged your home to the hilt. You have just manufactured—and shipped —a large order of widgets, but you won't get paid for 60 to 90 days. Where can you get the money to run the business until then? If you go to a single-invoice discount factor, the factor will buy that one receivable from you and you'll get the cash to continue. If the receivable is worth $100,000, the factor might give you $65,000.

Factors have suffered from a bad image and are sometimes considered to be the lenders of last resort. But for companies that have exhausted all other lines of credit, they are sometimes the lenders of only resort. Since factors are more interested in the creditworthiness of a company's customers than that of the company itself, they will often finance a business at the

start-up stage without forcing the owners to sacrifice their equity.

Example: A distributor of software for Nintendo video games turned to factoring when it began operations in 1987. Factoring permitted the company to grow very rapidly and still allowed the founding partners to retain a sizable chunk of equity in the company, something that would have been very difficult had they used a venture capital firm for financing.

The food industry is another natural for factoring. Because its business is often seasonal, there are strong parallels to the textile and apparel industries, and factors feel comfortable extending short-term credit in such an environment.

The newest arena for specialized factors is the health-care industry. Hospitals or health-care providers that furnish services to patients usually know they're going to get paid— either by an insurance company or Medicare. But they often must wait two or three months to receive payment. Enter the specialty health-care factor, which will buy those accounts receivable…providing cash today, rather than 90 days from now.

The cost factor:

Because factors assume the risk of collecting from the company's customers, and must maintain their own labor-intensive credit and collection services, this financing route is not cheap. Factors pay only 60% or 70% on the dollar for receivables—which costs the borrower much more than it would pay if it were able to get a conventional loan at 4% to 10% above the prime rate.

But the cost of getting financing from a factor may be less than meets the eye. *Reason:* A company pays only for the exact amount of money it needs to borrow, and only for the specific period the money is in use.

Example: A company takes out a typical term loan from a bank, and pays a set interest rate for a set period—for example, a one-year loan for $100,000 at 9% plus, in some cases, a required 10% to 15% compensating balance kept on deposit at the bank. The company must pay interest at 9% and leave the compensating balance on deposit for the entire year, whether or not it needs the entire $100,000 for all 365 days. With a factor, by contrast, the borrower pays interest only on the cash it uses on a daily basis. The ultimate result may be lower interest payments—even though the interest rate may be higher than on a bank loan.

Added advantage of using factors: An enhanced balance sheet. When a company sells its accounts receivable, it reduces its liabilities, thereby improving its debt-to-equity and its debt-to-asset ratios. This is often helpful in the company's attempts to get conventional bank loans, which it would otherwise not qualify for.

There are two main types of factors:

The first type of factor is the traditional old-line factor (mainly owned by a money center bank) that caters to the textile and garment industries...and has a continuing relationship with its customers. It often acts as the credit department for its borrowers. The second type of factor is the newer single-invoice discount factor, which typically finances just a single deal.

The traditional factors are huge companies that account for 95% of the volume of the factoring industry.

The single-invoice discount factors, by contrast, do a lot of little deals but account for a mere 5% of overall volume.

But these small, independent financial organizations, typically individual firms that do anywhere under $1 million in volume annually, are ideal for small businesses.

For a list of factors in your area that specialize in smaller deals, call the Commercial Finance Association at 212-594-3490. It classifies its 260 member firms into two groups—those with annual volume of $750,000 and under, and those with volume of $750,000 and above.

Source: Leonard Machlis, executive director, the Commercial Finance Association, a trade group that represents the factoring industry and the asset-based financial services industry. The members lend to businesses based on such items as accounts receivable, inventory, machinery and equipment, 225 W. 34 St., New York 10122.

How to Avoid Personal Guarantees In Bank Borrowing

Though banks almost always ask for personal guarantees, business owners should try to avoid personally guaranteeing a business loan—unless it's absolutely necessary.

Reason: Unless you are extremely careful, the action can backfire. In fact, people who are not careful can lose their entire net worth because of a loan they didn't even know existed.

How it can happen:

Case #1: A businessman personally guarantees a bank loan for a real-estate investment he makes. He dies, and there's a default on the loan. After liquidating the property, the bank has a deficiency. Since the guarantee doesn't die with the guarantor, the bank sues the man's estate.

Result: The heirs may stand to lose part of their inheritance.

Had there been no guarantee, the bank might simply have taken possession of the property. In fact, before the real-estate troubles of the late 1980s, banks usually didn't ask for personal guarantees of real-estate transactions from anyone except small investors. Today, they very often do.

Case #2: When John Doe wants to borrow $1 million for his Doe Corp., the bank asks for a personal guarantee from both him and his wife, even though she doesn't own shares in the company. Banks do this to prevent a borrower from escaping liability by diverting personal assets to the spouse. Thereafter, the business goes into bankruptcy.

Result: The bank can now go after the husband and wife. If the wife had not signed the personal guarantee, her assets would be free of any liability.

Case #3: The daughter of a widowed woman wants to borrow $250,000 from a bank to buy a business. Although she is pledging the assets of the new company to support the loan, the bank also wants her mother's personal guarantee since the daughter has no personal net worth.

The mother signs. The company is doing well and repays the loan. Then the daughter takes out a second, unsecured $1 million loan to expand the business. Soon afterward, the company gets into trouble and defaults on the loan.

Result: The bank has a $1 million claim against the mother, even though she was not aware of the second loan. Even worse, interest on the defaulted loan continues to accrue.

Reason: Personal guarantees nearly always include wording covering loans "heretofore or hereafter made, granted or extended," etc. In other words, when you guarantee the loans of a company, you also guarantee its existing and future obligations to the same bank.

To safeguard your assets...

• *Try to negotiate a loan without a guarantee ...or tell the bank that your spouse refuses to guarantee.* You can offer, for example, to pledge the company's assets—equipment, receivables, etc.—as collateral in lieu of a guarantee, rather than in addition to a guarantee. The stronger the collateral offered, the better your chances of getting the guarantee waived.

Example: When a bank asks a savvy borrower for a spouse's personal guarantee, he/she simply says it isn't available. One diplomatic excuse is that the couple is in the process of dissolving the marriage. If a bank really wants to make the loan, it will proceed without the spouse's guarantee.

From the bank's standpoint, of course, it never hurts to ask for a guarantee.

• *If you have no alternative to signing a guarantee, ask the bank to return it as soon as the loan is repaid.* Even better, send a letter drawn up by your attorney to the bank via certified mail, return receipt requested, saying that from this date forward you won't be responsible for obligations under the guarantee. *Aim:* To avoid any claims against you by the bank on future obligations of the same borrower.

Helpful: Ask an attorney familiar with this area of the law to review all documents and correspondence concerning loans and loan guarantees.

Trap: The law does not specify exactly how much time is "enough" before a guarantee becomes stale. Therefore, taking legal precautions to terminate an existing guarantee is obviously advisable.

• *Consider a limited guarantee.* If you are a 50-50 partner in a business, for example, you can limit your personal guarantee to half of the loan amount. Banks often accept a limited guarantee when company assets are also used as collateral.

• *Offer a fraud guarantee.* This is sometimes obtainable from a commercial lender, such as a factor, who would look first to the company's receivables. Here you could guarantee the loan only to the extent of bogus invoices or other fraudulent assets.

Example: A company wants to borrow $2 million from a factor, pledging its receivables as collateral. To make the loan, the factor accepts from the borrower a limited personal guarantee covering any fraudulent receivables that find their way onto the company's books.

Source: Malcolm P. Moses, Malcolm P. Moses & Associates, banking and financial consultants to businesses, and crisis and turnaround consultants, 3428 Hewlett Ave., Merrick, NY 11566.

Business Loans

With the economy expanding, it's easier for many businesses to get credit today than it has been for years. But for some companies—especially small ones—obtaining a bank loan is still tough.

Over the last six or seven years, there's been a wave of mergers in which smaller banks have been gobbled up by large regional and giant money-center banks. These big banks have no interest in lending to smaller borrowers.

Fortunately, the vacuum created by the mergers is slowly being filled by newly formed, smaller banks. Because they are young, they are hungry for business and are therefore willing to deal with companies of all sizes.

Here's what to do to increase your company's chance of success when applying for a loan…

• *Nurture your banker.* This is the single most important task. Establish a relationship with a banker—not a bank—as early as possible, preferably long before you ever need to borrow. Developing a good relationship with the individual who is going to rule on your loan application is crucial. Sit and talk with the banker about his/her family, take him/her to lunch, a ball game or a show.

We're not talking about a one-time deal here. The importance of a good relationship with a banker goes on forever, regardless of whether your company has $5 million in sales or $150 million. You never know when the company will need a loan.

• *Demonstrate strong management.* Whatever your business, lenders consider management's expertise the most important criterion. The first item in a loan application should be a description of the owner and each key manager's background, residence, education, family status, health and age. Highlight their years of experience in particular functions.

Key: The more proof of management accomplishment and technical ability, the better.

• *Furnish impeccable references.* The best references—and the only ones that really count — are from other banks that the company has borrowed from and paid back on time.

Further down on the ladder are references from top executives at large well-known companies.

Another notch down are references from customers. They provide strong testimonials for the company's products, as well as its customer service.

At the bottom are references from professionals, such as attorneys and accountants.

• *Be prepared to increase the amount of equity capital.* Banks generally want business owners to have a high enough percentage of their own money in the business to deter them from abandoning it. If your company has heavy liabilities, such as unpaid taxes and accounts payable, and there is very little equity, the bank may insist on a 1:1 ratio of debt to equity and sometimes even 1:2 or 1:3.

Of course, if the CEO has established a good relationship with the banker, the company may get a break on the equity requirement.

• *Be prepared to put up plenty of collateral.* The type of assets the company will be asked to pledge depends on the length of the loan. If your business is applying for a working-capital loan (payable within a year), "soft" assets such as receivables, inventory and marketable securities will usually qualify.

But if the business is applying for a long-term loan (payable in three to five years or more), hard assets will have to be made available to secure the loan. These are tangible items, such as buildings, land or equipment, that can be sold by the bank if the loan goes into default.

• *Show that the business has sufficient cash flow to pay back the loan.* To do this, prepare a detailed financing plan. The most important part of the plan lays out pro forma (projected) financial statements for the next five years. This provides proof that the business can generate sufficient cash to repay the loan.

A start-up company without a history on which to base projections must use market-size, market-growth and market-share projections to arrive at the sales forecast. A plan for second-stage financing should emphasize the need for additional capacity to handle increased business.

Important: When making sales projections, offer as much persuasive evidence as possible to demonstrate that the numbers are realistic.

• *Document the company's sound credit history.* If the business is operated as a sole proprietorship or a two-person corporation, the history relates to the individuals involved. If it is a multi-owner business, the history relates to the company.

Ideally, it should be demonstrated that the company has consistently paid its obligations on time, and that this has been verified by a range of different creditors.

131

•*Be prepared for the worst.* No matter how good everything else may be, if the economic trends in the bank's market are poor, the bank is unlikely to lend at all—unless the company is prepared to overcollateralize.

It may be necessary to put up collateral on a dollar-for-dollar basis. Or the loan may be contingent on putting up two dollars for each dollar of bank credit.

Source: Lawrence W. Tuller, lecturer, and vice president of Fomalhaut Press, a publishing company in Berwyn, Pennsylvania. He is the author of 18 business books, including *The Complete Book of Raising Capital*, McGraw-Hill, 1221 Avenue of the Americas, New York 10020.

Order Processing

Companies rarely pay much attention to their order-processing systems because they consider them basic, run-of-the-mill operations in which little can go wrong.

Big mistake! The order management process *is complicated*—for any business. It starts with sales planning.

It includes taking…filling…and delivering the order.

It doesn't end until the customer is satisfied and his/her check has cleared.

Results: Gains from improved order management can be enormous in terms of reduced costs…improved efficiency…greater customer satisfaction…better relationships with suppliers …and higher morale within your own business. Beware…

Warning signs that the order management process may not be working as it should…and how to make it work better…

•*Complaints from both customers and employees about unfilled or partially filled orders are increasing.* If no other warning sign gets management's attention, this one should. When the order management process is fraught with problems…customers will complain…and then take their business elsewhere.

Wrong response: Filling customer orders when received by keeping extra-large inventories, or undertaking frequent small production runs. It is no secret that both of these approaches are very expensive.

Right response: Look at the order management process from start to finish. Try not to get hung up on all the different departments the supply chain passes through. Consider the order management process as a complete chain that stretches from order planning to satisfied customer.

The more the company can integrate and automate that process from one end to the other…the more order management problems will vanish…and the business will gain in higher profits and more-satisfied customers.

•*The company still processes large numbers of orders manually.* It's amazing how much of the order-processing at many businesses still is done by hand. We recently consulted for a $13 billion company where sales reps took orders over the phone…wrote the orders out on little slips of paper…and then left the slips of paper on a desk in the scheduling department to be acted on whenever someone happened to notice them.

Any consultant, computer services company or software vendor can help design an automated order management system. Ask business contacts for referrals. Look for stories about computerized order management systems in the trade press.

Example: Many companies are adopting the R3 order management program from SAP of Germany. It works on networked personal computers. Consultants and software vendors can explain R3 to order-processing employees …and advise on what else is available in the field.

Important: Whatever system the company uses, it *must* link all parts of the order management process together. Each order entry must…

•Alert the scheduling and production people.

•Make appropriate adjustments in the inventory control system.

•Tell the shipping department when to expect the outgoing order.

Source: Peter A. Smith, senior manager, Arthur D. Little, Inc., management consultants, Acorn Park, Cambridge, Massachusetts 02140.

9

What All Businesspeople Need to Know

What All Businesspeople Need to Know: 1996...and Beyond

Edith Weiner, Weiner Edrich, Brown, Inc.

In our research, we have pinpointed eight qualities that contribute directly to an individual's success in today's fast-paced, complex work environments...

Our senses affect our productivity. For example, human beings are especially sensitive to the quality of light while they work. Most office lighting is not what's called full-spectrum light. It lacks important wavelengths of ultraviolet light, which are crucial to the stimulation of key brain chemicals.

Effective: If your office or work space lacks full-spectrum natural light, make a point of getting outdoors for a few minutes every few hours at least. The increased exposure to natural light will lift your mood, boost your energy, aid your immune system, and thereby help you be more productive on the job.

Similarly, our eyes are gateways for vital visual stimuli to our primitive (limbic) brain that can help or harm our effectiveness at work. Red (the color of blood) has, to our subconscious mind, always symbolized danger. Never wear bright red if you want to put any audience, such as a potential employer, at ease with you.

Blue is the color of calm. If you are making a conservative presentation or doing a negotiation and want to soothe people, wear blue.

If you want to convey a sense of well being and nurturing, wear green (the color of camouflage), which has always symbolized safety.

Your value to an employer is enhanced not by what you own and keep for yourself, but by what you share with others. This means that the more you establish yourself as a source of expertise, of help and support, the more valuable you make yourself to the organization.

Extremely important: Make sure that you always have time to offer help to anyone who needs it. Your reputation as an expert... as a source of knowledge and guidance... is one of the most effective sources of long-term workplace success that you can have.

Cultivate intuition about what people really need—rather than what they say they need. This is similar to the preceding point. If you can anticipate why people are asking you for specific types of information, and can then fill this need without their having to articulate the need, you further enhance your image as an insightful, efficient provider of assistance and knowledge.

Avoid excessive striving for perfection. This is especially true for women. Women are typically given jobs that require lots of detail work, because male executives have a tendency to view women as more meticulous and detail-oriented than men.

Problem: People—both male and female—who focus only on the details and not on the broad picture tend to short-circuit their careers. If you're a stickler for perfection, consider the potential drawbacks of your focus, and think about where you want your career to be five or even ten years from now. Your conclusions may require an adjustment of your focus on day-to-day work.

Empower others. Many managers say they empower people, but they really don't. If a manager gives subordinates new freedom to accomplish their work, but retains all of the important decision-making authority (like hiring and firing), he/she really isn't empowering anyone.

The key to genuine empowerment is leaving your ego at the door. Keep your eye on the *goal*, not on how people dress or what hours they prefer to work. By removing the obstacles to realizing their full potential, managers can honestly say they have empowered people.

Be very specific at all times about what you want or need. If you say to a boss, "I'd like to be reviewed again on October 15," instead of "Won't you please review my performance

again soon," you are much more likely to get the kind of one-on-one attention that can enhance your career. This kind of clear thinking also reinforces your reputation as a competent professional.

What you *really* know determines how far you go. In the 21st century, it will be less important to learn the skills of office politics than it will be to possess marketable skills and solid bodies of leading-edge, useful information.

Put another way, the 21st century will see the world taken over by the nerds. The Bill Gateses, Steven Spielbergs and Ross Perots of the world—the people who would have never made it based on social graces, but who possess vital skills, talents and knowledge, are the ones who will achieve the highest levels of economic potential in coming decades.

What you eat and how you eat can influence your workplace performance. This may sound silly, but it's not. If you have an important meeting at 10 AM, don't eat a donut or sweet roll at 9 AM. The sugar jolt can give way to a sluggish mood an hour later.

Similarly, don't overdo it with caffeine prior to an important meeting. The jitteriness caused by caffeine could impair your judgment.

Listen to your body. If it "says" it's hungry—even if it's not mealtime—consider eating light snacks and forgoing heavy regular meals. If you feel tired or sluggish at the same time each day, it may be because your body needs nourishment.

Treacherous Traps in Indoor Air Quality Can Be Avoided

Indoor air quality is becoming a major business issue of the 1990s—in every part of the country.

Lawsuits filed against building owners and managers seeking substantial damages due to poor indoor air quality are being litigated today across the country. Proposed federal legislation and regulations aimed at improving indoor air quality pose a potentially expensive new regulatory burden for building owners—and, in turn, for the companies that pay the rent.

Example: In one recent case, employees in an Environmental Protection Agency office in Washington claimed a variety of ailments due to poor air quality in the rented building they occupied, and sued the building owner—whom my firm represented—for $50 million. The jury found that the ailments were more imaginary than real—but then awarded several of the plaintiffs a total of almost $1 million. However, there are motions pending that are seeking to rescind the awards.

Air-quality problems in buildings…

Indoor air quality in commercial buildings began to deteriorate during the energy crisis of the 1970s. Building owners and managers, sometimes voluntarily and sometimes because of government regulations, sought to conserve energy by drastically reducing the amount of outside air entering their buildings.

Result: Many of today's "tight" buildings have too little circulation of fresh air to remove the many chemical compounds found in indoor air. Many of these chemicals are emitted by new furniture, office supplies, cleaning solutions and other synthetic materials. Other airborne chemicals come from tobacco smoke, perfume and cosmetics and other everyday substances.

The increased amount of all these substances in indoor air in today's buildings causes a variety of ailments reported by some office workers, and lumped together under the popular term "sick-building syndrome." The symptoms of this condition are not specific enough for medical researchers to pinpoint any specific substance as the cause. They include headache, fatigue, nausea, coughs and muscle pain. Victims typically claim that their symptoms disappear shortly after they leave the building.

To avoid air-quality problems…

The Occupational Safety and Health Administration (OSHA) is currently formulating a detailed set of regulations to govern air quality in offices and other nonindustrial workplaces. But don't wait until Washington enforces new rules. Start now to prevent future air-quality problems.

Steps to take…

• Thoroughly inspect the workplace for common indoor air pollution sources. It is often prudent to retain a professional, such as an industrial hygienist, heating, ventilation and air-conditioning engineer or indoor environmental engineer, to perform these key operations…

• Make sure exhaust from photocopiers and laser printers is properly vented. The chemicals used in these machines are a major source of indoor air pollution.

• Have furniture, carpets, wall coverings and paint professionally analyzed to determine whether they release chemical vapors into the air.

• Inspect outside air intakes to make sure they are far enough away from auto traffic, idling trucks and loading docks.

• Make sure all systems that affect air quality are operating properly.

• Perform and document regular maintenance and preventive maintenance on systems such as heating, ventilation and air conditioning (HVAC).

Examples: Change air filters at recommended intervals…regularly drain and disinfect condensate drain pans.

• Keep accurate records of maintenance activities in the event of litigation.

• Perform and document regular system operational checks to make sure everything is working properly.

Example: Check air-handling units and other HVAC equipment—daily.

• Work in cooperation with the landlord. Solving many indoor air-quality problems requires close cooperation between owner and tenant.

Example: Encourage the building management to keep all air-quality-related systems working properly and assist them in performing maintenance work and systems checks.

When it is not possible to identify the source of an indoor air-pollution problem, inform the building management immediately. Communication is vital to problem prevention.

If the problem is not resolved…

When a building owner or manager does not respond to an indoor air-quality complaint to the satisfaction of its tenants, the matter will often end up in court. Legal grounds upon which tenants have based air-quality suits in the past include…

•*Negligence.* This often can be proved if the landlord fails to operate the building in accordance with basic engineering standards.

Example: Failure to maintain the HVAC system correctly, causing a proliferation of microorganisms resulting in injury to the building occupants.

•*Breach of implied warranty of habitability.* Here, the landlord implicitly warrants that the building is fit to be occupied. The tenant claims that physical injury proves that the building is unfit.

•*Breach of contract.* Here, the lease explicitly guarantees specific environmental conditions, such as ventilation rates, temperature settings or maintenance obligations of the landlord. The tenant can claim these conditions are unfulfilled if there is clear evidence to that effect.

Source: Gregory A. Krauss, an attorney at the firm of Carr, Goodson & Lee, 1301 K St. NW, Washington, DC 20005.

High Blood Pressure/ Noise Level Connection

Hypertension has been linked to workplace noise levels. Men who worked for more than 15 years at a metal assembly plant had higher blood pressure than those who worked in a quieter plant. Almost 18% of those in the noisy plant took medication to control their hypertension, compared with 13% in the quieter plant.

Also: Hearing loss was greater among the noisy-plant workers—31.1%, compared with 20.7%.

Source: Study of 500 men, age 40 to 62, led by epidemiologist Evelyn Talbott, PhD, University of Pittsburgh, reported in *The Medical Post,* 777 Bay St., Toronto, Ontario M5W 1A7.

Create a Worker-Friendly Environment

Low-cost ways to improve work areas…

•Eliminate lifting by making sure heavy items are not stored on the floor or overhead.

•Provide foot rests (boxes will do) for employees who must stand while working. Elevating one foot relieves pressure on the spine.

•Place computers perpendicular to light sources to eliminate glare.

•Adjust all chairs for comfort and posture.

•Provide foot rests for seated employees whose legs do not reach the ground. Sitting with feet unsupported can lead to nerve and blood vessel damage in legs.

•Move all tools, parts and supplies to within arm's reach of workbenches.

•Remove all unnecessary obstacles and clutter.

Source: Roberta Carson, founder, ErgoFit, Inc., ergonomics consulting firm, Newton, Massachusetts, writing in *Occupational Hazards,* 1100 Superior Ave., Cleveland 44114.

Stephanie Winston's Best Personal Organizing Secrets

When you hear a manager claim that the dreadful mess in the office is not a hindrance to productivity, that may be the truth. But more often than not, it is bending it a bit.

True, some people can work extremely well in what appears to visitors as hopeless disarray. But these individuals are rare. Most people with disorganized lives are hurting themselves —and their employers—through reduced productivity, lateness, missed appointments or lost business.

Reassuring: In my 15 years as a personal organizing consultant, I've never met anyone who couldn't clean up his/her act. Your organizational problems can be solved and your life can become more livable with the help of some very basic, easy-to-implement techniques.

Paper management…

Since desk mess is often found at the core of disorganization and is the easiest symptom to identify, I always start there when getting managers to confront their personal chaos for the first time.

Many of my clients find that freeing up their desks—rarely an easy challenge—inspires them to tackle other organizational hot spots they had long since given up on.

Paper is the bane of our organizational existence because it is so bountiful. Every day —even in the electronic age—we are bombarded with it…surrounded by it…submerged in it. We have to do something with it, even if we just push it aside and say, "I'll think about that tomorrow."

Important: The problem with paper is usually not a problem of neatness, but rather a problem with making decisions.

Technique: Whenever you come across a letter, a bill, a bank statement, a catalog, a newspaper or a magazine clipping, ask yourself…

"What's the worst thing that could happen if this didn't exist?" If the answer is nothing, toss it then and there.

Or, "Do I think I might need it someday? If I did, could I get a duplicate?" If so, toss it.

That's the first of the four basic possibilities when a decision has to be made about a piece of paper. It is part of my TRAF system:

• *T—Toss.* "Man's best friend aside from the dog is the wastebasket." It's especially helpful to open mail over a big wastebasket.

• *R—Refer.* If it's not your job, pass it along immediately to someone else who has that responsibility…or send it to someone who might need it or be interested in it.

• *A—Act.* If it is your job, act on it personally —without delay. Examine the report, reply to the letter, etc. The easiest way is to jot a reply right on the letter and send it back.

If you can't act right away, put the piece of paper in a holding pen—a special box or drawer that you go through and deal with at the end of each week.

• *F—File.* The goal is to put the papers you decide to save in a place where you can find them again.

Effective: Create individual referral folders for the handful of people you talk to most regularly—your boss, your team colleagues, etc. —and drop things into them to discuss with those people. Then, at a convenient time say, "Jim, there are a few things I'd like to go over with you." You can use this same principle to create agendas for regular meetings. If you drop material into a *Monday Staff Meeting* file all week, by Monday you will have an instant agenda.

These folders should be especially accessible, either standing in a vertical file on your desk or placed at the front of your desk file drawer. You might use colored folders to distinguish referral folders from other files.

More filing secrets…

It's easier to work with a few fat files than a lot of skinny ones. The more files you have, the more apt you are to misfile or forget. The most common error is making files too specific. *Try following these three principles:*

• *The umbrella principle.* Use broad, umbrella headings that cover a large chunk of material and will be easy to remember.

Example: Combine *Exercise Equipment*, *Vitamins* and *Arthritis Treatments* into a single *Health & Fitness* folder.

• *The sponge principle.* Absorb isolated pieces of paper under broad headings. One or two brochures about cameras don't deserve a file of their own. Lump them into a *Hobbies* or *Interests* file—whatever works for you.

• *The personal association principle.* Choose file headings that evoke a personal association for you. Thus, a file headed *Dallas* could include your favorite hotels and restaurants there, plus names, addresses and directions as to how to get to the homes or offices of business associates and friends or relatives who live there. Be consistent about your filing system and make sure that your quirky headings are defined and listed in an index that can be consulted by anyone who needs to use your files.

Trap: Miscellaneous is another word for meaningless. Force yourself to come up with some association for the file name. It should be a noun, not an adjective—*Prospects-New* instead of *New Prospects*. One client had three pieces of paper that didn't seem to fit anywhere but all related to things she wanted to do sometime. She decided to label the folder *Aspirations.*

Keeping files lean and mean...

A lot of papers have a shelf life. For example, if you get a budget in January, chances are it will be obsolete in April. Before filing, put a note at the top, "toss April 1996." Each time you open a file, look through it quickly and weed out what's obsolete.

For a thorough file cleanout, go through six folders every day until the weeding job is done. Put the next day's six folders on the top of your desk so you won't forget tomorrow.

Helpful: A tickler file! Many busy managers who must follow up on long lists of matters find it useful to keep a tickler file. A tickler file is a set of 31 folders, with one numbered for each day of the month. Each day, you check that day's folder for any matters you need to follow up on.

Example: You request a price quote from a vendor and you think it is reasonable to have a response by February 5. You file your copy of the request in the folder labeled "5." If, by February 5, you have not heard from the vendor, you or an assistant can follow up.

Action secrets...

One of the best action-oriented organizing techniques is to set a time each day to open mail. This will force you to decide which pieces of mail to toss, pass along, act on or file.

Rolodex ideas: Rolodexes are still among the most versatile and efficient tools around for organizing your contacts and other information. I recommend using the flat-tray 3" x 5" model to avoid card fallout, which can occur with the roller type. This larger size card also gives you room to note all kinds of relevant information— a person's complete title, his/her assistant's name, birthday, spouse's name—and you can even staple the person's business card to it for handy reference.

Your Rolodex can also be used as a handy information source. For example, you can make a single *Airlines* card that lists phone numbers, your frequent-flier numbers and airline clubs you belong to. You can also make a card for each of the cities you fly to most frequently.

If your Rolodex gets overstuffed, divide the cards into three categories:
- Active contacts.
- Inactive contacts, that you can store in an index-card box for future reference or in a closed-end file folder labeled *Contacts.*
- Obsolete contacts, that you can toss.

Also, it may be helpful to try using yellow Rolodex cards to make your own *Yellow Pages.* Organize services by category.

Examples: If you collect antiques, list *Dealers, Furniture Restorers* and *Appraisers.* The Rolodex can also be a handy place to file your children's Social Security numbers, driver's license numbers, etc. Keep a card for each family member.

Time-savers...
- *Put a sign on your door.* "Hard at work 10 AM to 11 AM"..."Glad to catch up with you later" ..."Leave a message with Jane if you'd like a callback."
- *Put your desk at an angle that avoids automatic eye contact with passersby.* William McGowan, the founder of MCI, had two desks in his large office—one visible from the door, the other not. When he was at his visible desk, all visitors were welcome. But when he was working at his hidden desk, it was the red flag equivalent of "Do Not Disturb."
- *Hide out.* Take your work to an unused conference room, a vacant office or even a coffee shop down the street to avoid interruptions that ruin your concentration.
- *Meet in other people's offices.* It's much easier to excuse yourself from other people's offices than to ease them out of yours.
- *Set a time contract.* When a colleague asks to see you, say, "Sure, I've got 10 minutes at four o'clock."
- *Confer standing up.* Standing signals people not to get too comfortable. When you want to close, simply walk your visitor to the door and cordially say, "Thanks for stopping by. I really appreciate the info."

Organizing telephone use...

Telephone invasion is among the most insidious of interrupters—making already disorganized executives even more unproductive. Ask family members, colleagues and friends to call only at certain times. If you must complete a project, let your secretary screen your calls or ask a colleague to do phone duty for an hour.

To avoid phone tag, have the person who answers the phone—or the message on your answering machine—ask for the best callback time as well as the number. If a message is just FYI, be sure to say that no callback is required.

Important: Being organized does not include ignoring, forgetting or being too busy to return calls. Responsive communication is the life-blood of business.

Source: Stephanie Winston, founder and president of The Organizing Principle, time-management consultants, 230 E. 15 St., New York 10003. Her book is *Stephanie Winston's Best Organizing Tips*, Simon & Schuster, 1230 Avenue of the Americas, New York 10020.

Disaster Planning

No company can completely protect itself from disaster. Fires, earthquakes, floods and acts of terrorism are too unpredictable. But a company can make sure it recovers from a disaster with minimal loss of business.

Key to success: Determine the company's critical needs, then devise a plan to meet those needs if a disaster occurs.

Example: After the California earthquake of 1992, most of the companies that were hit hardest weren't back to normal operations for months. But, the best-prepared companies were able to resume business on an emergency basis within hours.

As a result, they were able to retain customers, minimize disruptions to the work-force and maintain cash flow.

A team and a plan:

First determine the minimum amount of office space the company will need to resume its basic operation.

List the equipment and personnel needed to resume business at a standby location. Include computers, phones, fax machines, files and other items that are essential to the day-to-day operation of the company's core business.

Important: Stick to essentials. In many companies, 80% of the business is dependent on only 20% of the equipment and personnel.

Next, select disaster-recovery teams which will be responsible for…

• Setting up the emergency operation.

• Getting the business up to speed as soon as possible.

• Caring for personnel and other company assets during the interval.

Create as few teams as possible, and include no more than four to six people on each one. Individual recovery teams typically take charge of areas such as administration and management, computers, damage assessment, communications, human resources and customer relations.

When creating the teams, choose the employees who are most knowledgeable about day-to-day operations.

Designate a command-and-control center at a temporary off-site location, where recovery teams can be headquartered as soon as possible after the disaster.

Success story: Several years ago on Thanksgiving Day, Northwest National Bank suffered a major fire at its downtown Minneapolis office. The company was well-prepared, however. It had a list of supplies it would need in case of a disaster, standby office space in nearby buildings and well-trained teams of key employees.

Within hours of the fire, the company assembled the teams at a command-and-control center and began setting up makeshift customer-service centers. On Monday, Northwest National opened for business at the standby offices.

The recovery plan should include:

• *Technology.* Few elements of a modern business are more vulnerable than the computer and phone systems, yet few are as vital to its operations. To ensure that computer and phone systems can resume work after a disaster, consider these safeguards:

• Back up all records and store them off-site.

• Select a facility where employees who use computers can go in the event their building is damaged. Arrange for transportation to the site.

• Retain computer experts to have backup communications in place, so that operators can access data during the emergency.

• Make arrangements with a telephone company to replace the switchboard and phone system either at the original site or a standby location. (Most phone companies now offer a 48-hour back-up service.)

• Contract with a computer-rental company to have back-up hardware available, or store extra hardware off-site.

• *Basic business functions.* Many companies rely on an informal reciprocal arrangement with another company to use its facilities during an emergency. In practice, however, those agreements rarely work.

Reasons: The other company may also be damaged or transportation to it may be impeded. Moreover, the other company might have had extra space when the agreement was made, but by the time a disaster actually occurs, it may have grown to the point where there's no room to accommodate anyone else. *More effective:*

• Arrange to have mobile trailers brought in that can accommodate makeshift offices similar to those used by construction companies at their work sites.

• Make an arrangement with realtors to move into a vacant building in the area and occupy it until the company's facilities are repaired.

• Contract with a hotel, motel or apartment building to use space on an emergency basis.

Essential: Update and renew these arrangements annually, to be sure that the services and facilities the company contracts for are still adequate.

Often overlooked: Customers. Several members of the recovery teams should be designated to contact customers as soon as possible after a disaster. If the recovery plan has been well thought out, team members should be able to tell customers that shipments will only be slightly delayed.

Depending on the severity of the disaster, the company may want to make price adjustments for customers who remain loyal during the recovery period.

It's also prudent to contact vendors to explain any receiving problems, and to make sure invoices are being paid on time.

• *Personnel.* Since speed is critical during the recovery period, instruct each recovery team to construct a plan, in writing, that all personnel can easily understand.

The plan should tell the essential employees where to go during the recovery period and encourage the others to stay home and wait for instructions.

It may be useful to supply key employees with cellular phones during the emergency and subsequent recovery, but don't rely heavily on them. *Reason:* Cellular service is likely to be overtaxed and only of limited use.

Better: A "calling tree," system by which instructions are relayed by having one key employee phone two others, who in turn call two more, until all essential employees receive instructions.

Newspapers and radio and television stations can also be helpful in getting messages out before phone service is back in operation. Later, it may be useful to set up an "800" number, so that nonessential employees can call for news about the recovery.

Companies should also go out of their way to help employees themselves recover from the disaster.

Examples: Day-care facilities, transportation, low-cost home repair loans.

This is more important than it might seem. *Reason:* Employees who are treated with indifference during a difficult time in their lives often start looking for other jobs when life returns to normal. The last thing a company needs during a recovery is an exodus of skilled, hard-to-replace workers.

Source: Geoffrey H. Wold, national director of information technology consulting services, McGladrey & Pullen, CPAs and consultants, 445 Minnesota St., St. Paul, Minnesota 55101.

Touching—The New Pros and Cons

While there is a growing body of law focusing attention on the risk of physical contact in the workplace today, certain "appropriate" touching can have motivational benefits.

The right touch at the right time can be one of the most effective ways for a manager to generate a feeling of warmth and respect with peers and subordinates. A soft touch can actually increase a manager's power and authority by making his/her suggestions and encouragement more persuasive. The gesture can be a supportive arm around the shoulders or a fleeting touch on the arm.

The traditional rule on touching is that it's okay downward—adult to child, doctor to patient, manager to subordinate. But touching is generally out of bounds the other way around.
Male-to-female touching don'ts:

•Never touch a woman's knee or thigh, even when sitting next to her at a conference or team meeting.

•Never put your arm around a female coworker or subordinate's shoulder. Don't hold on to her forearm. Touching her upper arm lightly—without lingering—to make a point or emphasize friendly support is generally okay. And if you pat her on the back, make very sure the pat is light and is no lower than shoulder height.

•Do not reach for a woman's hand and then hold on to it while talking to her.

Caution: For some women, any touch by a man at work is taboo. So, hold off on any such gestures until you have enough experience working with the person to make a confident judgment about whether contact would be effective or dangerous.
The female perspective:

In today's workplace, female managers have increasing freedom to use the power of touch. In dealing with a man her own age, a woman manager can both establish her authority…and soften the otherwise harsh impact of a reprimand or direct order by leaning over to a man who reports to her, patting him on the arm and making the message clear: "Hey, you've forgotten to solve that problem with John that we talked about last week."

An older woman can take a more maternal approach with a younger man. Actually, her gentle touch—coupled with the right words—

can be both a very powerful and manipulative tool.

Many men can't help responding like children, eager to please. Others, of course, will resent this approach, but might respond favorably to a firm handshake.

Source: Julius Fast, the author of *Body Language in the Workplace*, Penguin Books, 375 Hudson St., New York 10014.

Sexual Harassment Charges

Sexual harassment charges under Title VII of the 1964 Civil Rights Act can be brought only against companies—not against the illegal behavior of coworkers. *Exceptions:* Individuals can be named as defendants when the alleged harassment was undertaken in their official capacities.

Source: *Stefanski* v. *Bell Ambulance*, USDC EWis.

Workplace Violence

Workplace violence accounts for nearly 15% of on-the-job deaths—and the cost of injuries may be incalculable. Sadly, this represents a dramatic increase over the single-digit figures of the early 1980s.

Unless companies take steps to prevent violence, they will be increasingly vulnerable to it.

Violence on the job is a complex phenomenon that must be attacked on two levels—through the hiring process and by maintaining a low-stress workplace.
Careful hiring:

Effective preemployment screening won't just reduce the chance of hiring violence-prone employees. It can also protect the company from charges of negligent hiring that can be made when an employee becomes violent. Many companies have lost lawsuits because they failed to take reasonable steps to screen out violent applicants.

141

Self defense: Start with a background check into an applicant's arrest record and work history. Then check his/her military experience, credit history and driving record.

Thanks to national computerized data, it now costs less than $200 for a complete records check. Be alert to a less than honorable military discharge…a history of unpaid debts…a poor driving record. None is a sure predictor of violence, but all are signs of its potential.

Next, go beyond the data. In an interview, probe an applicant about past disciplinary actions and difficulties in dealing with supervisors. If answers aren't revealing, ask questions that challenge an applicant to tell the truth.

Example: If an applicant says he/she never had any problems in the military, ask something along these lines—"You mean you were in the military for two years and never had even one disagreement with someone?" Then ask about the most extreme disagreement.

Look for replies that show how the person responded to authority and how he/she resolved the confrontation.

Despite record-checking, it's still easy to miss a history of violence. Applicants won't tell you…there are questions you can't ask…past employers are hesitant—for legal reasons—to be forthcoming.

That means screeners should probe for signs that an applicant is antisocial, paranoid or beset with other personality problems. *Effective questions:*

• *How have coworkers taken advantage of you on the job?* An applicant with a long list of examples may be paranoid.

• *What kinds of weapons did you fight with as a youngster?* Anything above sticks and stones could reveal antisocial behavior.

• *What's the best way to discipline a pet?* People who are cruel to animals are often violent to people.

Other signs of the potential for violence: Low self-esteem and a willingness to blame others.

Especially effective: Have a team of people interview applicants. *Advantages:* Less of a chance of missing signs of potential violence and a greater chance an applicant will speak freely.

If there's doubt about an applicant, don't hire him/her. The cost of finding another applicant is trivial compared to the damages resulting from violence.

To find a professional who can train personnel for this type of screening, inquire at universities with graduate programs in industrial or organizational psychology. Many have experts on their staffs who train human resource personnel.

Reducing workplace tension:

Most workplace violence is committed by long-term employees—not recent hires. What often makes once-peaceful workers turn violent are company rules that over a period of time are enforced unfairly and inconsistently.

Example: When two employees arrive late for work, the supervisor gives one a calm, oral warning but suspends the other after screaming at him in front of his peers.

That type of discipline creates instant tension that, over time, can cause an employee to snap.

Instead, the supervisor should talk to a latecomer in private and explain why his/her actions hurt the company. After the employee has a chance to explain his/her actions, the supervisor and employee should agree on a change in behavior.

Repeated offenses should be dealt with on an increasing scale of discipline that's fair and made known to all employees. Termination should come only after other forms of discipline have been exhausted.

When terminated employees take violent revenge, they usually target companies that lack a fair discipline policy.

Also essential for reducing tension in the workplace is training supervisors to treat employees respectfully.

Warning signs that middle managers may be treating workers callously: High rates of absenteeism, lateness, employee turnover and compensation claims related to stress.

Helpful: Retain a consulting psychologist to help assess problems before they result in violence.

Example: An employee who claims she's being followed or is receiving threatening notes on her fax machine. With advice from a psychologist, the company has a better chance of determining the potential of violence and devising ways to head it off.

Industrial or organizational psychologists are also helpful after an act of violence occurs. They can advise the company on how to treat the victim, deal with the perpetrator, prevent future outbreaks and counsel employees who may be shaken by the incident.

Counseling employees is especially critical since violence often spreads unless tensions are immediately lowered.

Example: An employee punches his supervisor and is immediately suspended. Without psychological expertise, a company might ask the supervisor himself to look into the matter and recommend further action.

A trained psychologist, however, might discover the supervisor had a record of being unfair to his staff and that other employees could take the same action unless the supervisor receives quick training.

For references of psychologists, contact the graduate psychology department of a local university, or the American Psychological Association in Washington, DC, 202-336-5500.

Source: Dr. Michael Mantell, former chief psychologist for the San Diego Police Department, and assistant clinical professor of psychiatry at the School of Medicine of the University of California, San Diego. He is also an organizational consultant in private practice, 2615 Camino Del Rio South, San Diego 92108. He is the coauthor of *Ticking Bombs: Defusing Violence in the Workplace,* Irwin Publishing, 1333 Burr Ridge Pkwy., Burr Ridge, Illinois 60521.

Casual Dress

The movement to dress casually in business, which accelerated when IBM relaxed its long-standing dress code, will do wonders for productivity and overall corporate health. Casual dress has a profound impact on productivity and efficiency, due to the added comfort. It also contributes to teamwork by breaking down the barriers between peers and superiors that are typically reinforced by the symbolism of dress.

Source: Dr. Barry Lubetkin, director, Institute for Behavior Therapy.

Romance in the Office

Romance in the office is becoming more acceptable to management. With more women in the work force than ever, and men and women both working longer hours, CEOs are coming to think of romantic involvements as being inevitable. *Recent survey:* 79% of CEOs said office affairs are not the company's business if an unmarried couple is discreet and work is not affected…61% said that office romances do not harm productivity.

Source: Survey of 200 CEOs reported in *Fortune,* 1271 Avenue of the Americas, New York 10020.

When a Valued Employee Quits

When a valued employee quits, resist the temptation to make a counteroffer. Counteroffers almost never address the complexities involved in a decision to leave. And—when counteroffering does persuade an employee to stay, the stay is usually for less than one year. *Better:* When you lose a valued employee to another company, stay in touch. Make sure the ex-employee gets the company newsletter, birthday and holiday greeting cards, etc. *Payoff:* The potential future opportunity to hire the employee back—when the opportunity arises.

Source: Robert Half, founder, Robert Half International.

How to Keep Employees From Goofing Off On their PCs

Computer games are an addictive—though sometimes educational—way to kill time. And if the time being killed falls between the hours of 9 AM and 5 PM, all of those vanquished space aliens, flying missiles and bonus points can add up to a big drain on office productivity.

No one can really estimate how much time office employees waste playing computer games. Yet, numerous anecdotal accounts lead many people to suspect that the drain is substantial.

Trap: The games have an addictive quality that can easily stretch a few spare minutes into increasingly longer spans of time.

While computer games rob businesses of productivity, they also silently steal computer resources. Games consume hard disk space, processor time and network capacity, forcing companies to purchase larger, more expensive computer systems that are capable of handling their business and entertainment needs.

While the implications may not be as serious as employee theft, excessive computer game use can be just as hard to detect and eradicate. Workers often go to great lengths to hide their game addictions. Some games even offer a "boss mode" that pops a fake spreadsheet onto the PC's screen at the touch of a key.

Bottom line: For many companies, turning office fun time into work time is getting increasingly difficult. As employees gain computer skills, they become more familiar and comfortable with games. They bring in favorite disks from home and swap popular titles with their coworkers. More than one company has had a "game craze" sweep its ranks, as workers try to outdo each other on a popular new program.

Worse: Games often come bundled with office software.

Example: Microsoft Windows includes solitaire, blackjack, golf and several other digital diversions.

Ironically, while this can deter employees from bringing in their own games on potentially infected disks, it does reinforce the need for rules and regulations on game playing in the office.

Fighting back:

Though it may seem like fighting a losing battle, there are several ways a company can take control of office game playing. *Suggestions...*

• *Establish strict anti-game rules.* Let employees know that a computer game is about as welcome at their desks as a bottle of whiskey.

• *Allow only company-approved software on office computers.* This rule will justify super-

visors in purging games and other nonbusiness-related programs simply by erasing all but company-sanctioned files.

• *Put it in writing.* A company's computer game policy should be clearly outlined in its employee manual—just so there's no misunderstanding between management and employees. It's also important to describe the punishment that will result if employees are caught playing games.

• *Set up controlled game playing.* To maintain morale in the aftermath of a no-games policy, some companies place one or more "games-only" PCs in the company lounge or lunchroom. These systems, which are kept separate from the company's computer network, allow users to play on their own time in a guilt-free environment. Many businesses "retire" an older, outdated PC to recreational use.

Source: John Edwards, a computer industry analyst and freelance writer on high-tech subjects, based in Mount Laurel, New Jersey.

Productivity

Growing productivity must be the foundation of everything we do. We've been chasing it at GE for years.

We once thought we could manage it into business operations, with controls and hierarchies and vinyl books with charts.

All we did was stifle people, sit on them, slow them up and bore them to death. In the early 1980s, we fell in love with robots and automation and filled some of our factories with them, as our employees looked on sullenly and fearfully. It didn't work.

We now know where productivity—real and limitless productivity—comes from. It comes from challenged, empowered, excited, rewarded teams of people. It comes from engaging every single mind in the organization.

To get this productivity, we use a big, clumsy word we call *boundaryless* to define behavior. This behavior works in any culture, anywhere in the world, to harness every volt of productive energy—and every good idea—from every source.

Boundaryless behavior evaluates ideas based on their merit, not on the ranks of the people who come up with them.

It assumes that there isn't a customer in the world who doesn't have something valuable to share with you, so why not hand them a coffee mug and bring them into the room when you sit down to design a new product?

Boundaryless behavior recognizes that the supplier knows more about the component he makes than our engineers do, so why not let the supplier do more of the design?

Boundaryless behavior laughs at the concept of little kingdoms called finance, engineering, manufacturing and marketing sending each other specs and memos, and instead gets them all together in a room to wrestle with issues as a team.

Boundaryless behavior in our company leads a medical business based in Milwaukee…to empower a Swedish manager in Asia…to use a Japanese associate…to make diagnostic equipment with components sourced from India and China…for sale in Europe.

Boundaryless behavior is tough to embed in a culture like GE's…but we're getting there. Our early progress has grown our productivity from the pace of 2% in the early 1980s to nearly triple that today.

Source: John F. Welch, Jr., chairman and CEO, General Electric Company, speaking before The Economic Club of Detroit.

Signs an Employee Is Planning to Leave

Lack of interest in long-term issues…increased detachment…and unusual quietness. People who are trying to hide one thing—an interview, a job offer—often talk less about everything.

Source: Mark Gozonsky, editor, *Practical Supervision*, 210 Commerce Blvd., Round Rock, Texas 78664.

For More Productive Meetings

Give each meeting a title—*Fact-Finding, Brainstorming, Information Exchange*—that explains its purpose. Lock out latecomers to spread the message that promptness is mandatory. Vary seating arrangements, both to get people from different parts of the organization to mix, and to keep "buddies" from distracting each other. Distribute written materials before or after the meeting—not during it, or people will spend their time reading rather than participating. Rotate meeting leadership to encourage responsibility and preparation.

Source: Leil Lowndes, meeting consultant and seminar conductor for Fortune 500 corporations, writing in *Office Systems '94,* 941 Danbury Rd., Box 150, Georgetown, Connecticut 06829.

How to Keep Company Secrets Secret

It's easy for companies that have never lost trade secrets to become lax about the security of their sensitive information. They overlook even the simplest steps to prevent this sensitive information from slipping into the wrong hands.

But it's these measures—not sophisticated counter-espionage tactics—that are the most effective first line of defense…

•*Identify sensitive material.* High-tech businesses are usually extremely diligent about protecting their secrets. But many others rarely even recognize that there's material to protect until someone walks out the door with it.

It is both impractical and unnecessary to protect everything that would embarrass the company if it fell into enemy hands. One company, in fact, was so paranoid that it even stamped "confidential" on reprints of articles from daily papers.

Better: Concentrate on information that would cause actual harm in the marketplace if competitors knew about it.

Rule of thumb: The more vital the information is to a company's strategic business plans, the more it makes sense to protect it. *Examples:*

• Efforts to find a new marketing director with experience in Eastern Europe can tip off competitors about expansion plans.

• When a magazine shops around for different paper stock, the quotes it gets can tip off a competitor about plans to change format.

Example: Several years ago, *New York* magazine was considering the launch of a West Coast publication with a similar format. Because of a presumed leak, however, another publisher beat it to the market—using the same title and a similar format. *Result:* Costly litigation and a change in expansion plans.

• *Warn employees—discreetly.* Though it might seem that consultants and contractors in whom the company confides could be a major source of leaks, that's only the case occasionally. Far more often, the source is a former employee now in competition, a disgruntled employee getting even or a low-level employee who talks unguardedly—at trade shows, to friends in other companies or on a crowded elevator.

Even low-level personnel in such departments as accounting or marketing often know more about the company than you realize. *To enhance their discretion about sensitive information...*

Send periodic notices to low-level employees, but word the memos in a nonthreatening way. *Aim:* To get the cooperation of the staff. That can't be done with threatening memos that create an adversarial relationship. For the same reason, the memo shouldn't mention penalties the company might impose for divulging sensitive information. Penalties can be mentioned in personnel policies or employee handbooks.

Simply remind employees that their knowledge of day-to-day business operations is confidential, especially information that is not known outside the company.

Example: Knowing about a manufacturer's quality inspection routine could tip off a rival about its lead time—a very valuable piece of inside information.

The memo should caution employees against talking about information with outsiders and against leaving paperwork on their desks.

Helpful: To encourage employees to read the memo, keep it less than one page in length.

While it's not absolutely necessary to have legal advice on the wording of the memorandum, it can be a wise move to make sure it is consistent with any statements about confidentiality that appear in the employee handbook.

• Adopt a more forceful approach as an employee rises in rank and has more access to sensitive information, especially technical or marketing data. In periodic memos to senior managers and scientists, for instance, a company could actually spell out penalties for unauthorized disclosure of trade secrets.

• Label sensitive materials as "confidential and proprietary," and keep records of the employees who have access to them. Put sensitive materials away. Do not leave them out where they can be seen by unauthorized parties.

Examples: Marketing and customer lists. Both are extremely difficult to protect because most of them are derived—at least in part—from sources already available to the public.

• In the employee handbook, spell out the penalties for disclosure of confidential information. Here, advice from a lawyer is helpful. *Reason:* Some companies may simply adopt a policy of terminating workers who knowingly disclose confidential information. Others may have to go through a grievance procedure.

General rule: If possible, cite unauthorized disclosure as a serious cause for dismissal that may result in termination without warning or in a grievance procedure.

• Consider using confidentiality agreements for key employees who have access to the company's sensitive information.

Examples: An executive in charge of product development...a scientist working on a product that hasn't yet been announced.

Typically, confidentiality agreements give the company the rights to innovations that employees produce while they work for the company. They can also make employees personally liable for unauthorized disclosure and seek to bar key employees from working for competitors within a specified time or geographical area.

Legal advice is absolutely necessary, and it should come from an attorney experienced in the field. *Reason:* Laws governing confidentiality agreements are tricky and can vary dramatically from state to state. *Examples:*

•In some jurisdictions, an entire noncompetition agreement can be ruled unenforceable if a court finds it to be overly restrictive. Elsewhere, some parts of it may still be enforced.

•There is often a gray legal area concerning ownership of an invention begun by a person when he/she is employed but finished after he/she leaves the company.

•Warn terminated employees—as well as the businesses that hire them. Companies often take the first step but forget the second.

Hold an exit interview with all employees exposed to sensitive information. Explain that they—and their new employers—can be held liable for the unauthorized disclosure of trade secrets and unfair competition.

Go over the same points in a letter to the new employers—especially if they are direct competitors. Warnings of this type are usually effective because litigation can be long and costly.

If a competitor does make unauthorized use of a trade secret, the best remedy is usually a court injunction. If your company can prove that a competitor is using a trade secret, the courts will often grant an injunction for the period of time equal to the head start that the trade secret gave the competitor.

Injunctions can range from less than one year for unauthorized use of an obvious innovation to many years for using technical know-how that gives a competitor an advantage in the marketplace.

Technical, however, doesn't necessarily refer to electronics or other fields generally associated with the term.

Example: When an American company's new method for making sausage casing was copied by a foreign company, it was able to enjoin the overseas company from using the method for ten years.

Source: Mary Luria, partner, Patterson, Bellknap, Webb & Tyler, attorneys, 1133 Avenue of the Americas, New York 10036.

How to Protect the Company from Theft And Fraud...Without Hurting Morale

Employee theft and fraud—and the resulting challenge of corporate security—have become top management priorities in the 1990s for several important reasons...

•Employee attitudes toward theft and fraud have changed as a result of job uncertainty, a more competitive business climate and a general erosion of the value of loyalty to employers.

•Growing use of contract, leased and part-time workers, as well as home-based employees, has further complicated the challenge of securing company property.

•Advancements in computer technology and the explosion of related security breaches.

Challenge: While security is an urgent priority for every company today, it is increasingly difficult to achieve without becoming intrusive and counterproductive. Employee morale is threatened in the process. Even customers who expect the company to maintain tight security over its operations don't like being treated like suspected criminals when they visit.

Self-defense:

Here is our five-step program for enhancing security while maintaining a comfortable workplace environment for employees and a friendly, open atmosphere for customers...

•*Develop a detailed security policy.* Many companies shy away from the whole subject of security. That's a mistake because it's important to show pride in offering a secure business environment in today's often-dangerous world.

We urge clients to develop a security statement that parallels the company's mission statement. Involve management and employees in the process. Ask everyone to think seriously about the type of environment that fosters productivity for employees and openness for customers, but that also protects the business from theft, fraud and physical harm—such as potential violence from a disgruntled former employee.

147

Bonus: Employees are usually happy to co-operate in formulating security measures when they feel that the company is trying to protect them.

When the security policy statement has been completed, make it public. Hold employee meetings to discuss the statement—especially the reasons for having one.

While it is easy to explain the need for protecting people physically, employees often have no idea about the potential costs of theft of company secrets or of fraud against the company.

Key: Aim to make everyone understand that protecting company secrets is every bit as vital as it is for military personnel during wartime. ("Loose lips sink ships.")

Give copies of the security policy statement to employees and also send them to customers, along with a letter of explanation. Ask for feedback and suggestions for possible improvements or changes.

• *Hire carefully.* Many employee security violations could be avoided with effective hiring techniques. Never let haste get in the way of thorough reference-checking.

During the hiring process, make it clear that security is a top priority…and describe how the company handles fraud or theft of any type, including stealing information.

Example: If it is part of the company's established security policy, make it clear that perpetrators will be prosecuted, not just dismissed.

Unscrupulous individuals usually stay away from companies with such aggressive policies. They will ultimately make it clear they aren't interested in the position.

• *Review work processes.* In my security work with companies, I've learned that when there is a problem with theft, the most obvious suspects—the security people or the cleaning staff—are usually not guilty.

Culprit: It's usually a "trusted" employee who has some personal problem, or who has some unrecognized reason to want to hurt the company. Most managers are not as sensitive as they should be to changes in lifestyle or job performance that should raise questions.

Deterrence tactic: Beyond performance reviews, conduct periodic employee task reviews to find out how work is actually being done. This may or may not reveal potential problem areas, but at the very least it tells the employee that management is paying attention to what is going on.

• *Make industry comparisons.* Every business is unique, but there are many similarities within industries that can be used as guidelines for tightening security. Whenever a deviation from the industry norm occurs, find out why. Significant or persistent deviations should raise a red flag.

Example: For several years, a retail chain had shrinkage of more than 3% in one region, while a figure of 1% to 1½% was normal for the industry. The company first blamed the region of the country, saying it was more theft-prone. But careful investigation led to the discovery that within this company there was a well-organized group of night warehousemen who were regularly sending off entire truckloads of merchandise to their own fence.

• *Use covert techniques.* After fraud or theft has been detected, most companies have a tendency to demonstrate visibly that they have eliminated the problem and will not tolerate such actions by employees. This sudden get-tough approach creates a climate of suspicion and mistrust by clamping down in highly visible ways that send the message, "We don't trust you" to every employee.

Nothing is more harmful to morale, productivity and profits than upsetting innocent workers. Worse, a demoralizing atmosphere filters down and jeopardizes relationships with customers.

Moreover, highly visible measures are also self-defeating because they give perpetrators a chance to stop what they are doing and/or to cover up their acts.

Better: Use temporary covert techniques, such as hidden cameras, to obtain evidence of acts committed against the best interests of the company. The goal is not to spy on good employees, but to gain irrefutable proof with which to confront guilty individuals.

Example: After several thefts of wallets from employees taking part in its exercise program, a company installed hidden cameras outside the dressing rooms where people hung their suits before their workouts. This quickly showed that there was one person consistently present in each of the rooms where a robbery took place. He was a trusted employee who had developed a drug habit and needed quick cash.

Source: Arthur J. Bourque III, president, Surveillance Specialties, Ltd., 40 Chatham Way, Lynnfield, Massachusetts 01940. A former long-time Massachusetts state trooper, he consults and handles surveillance installations for retailers and other companies.

Protect Documents From OSHA

Companies wishing to protect confidential documents from compelled disclosure during an OSHA inspection have two avenues of recourse—*the attorney-client privilege*, which preserves confidentiality between attorney and client, and *the work product doctrine*. It protects documents prepared by an attorney in preparation for litigation. *Helpful:* Since neither avenue guarantees confidentiality, draft all documents on the assumption they may become public. Accompany any description of a potential OSHA violation with a plan for corrective action.

Source: Mark Dreux, McDermott, Will & Emery, a Washington, DC, law firm, writing in *Occupational Hazards*, 1100 Superior Ave., Cleveland 44114.

New Unionizing Troubles

The unions are using an increasing number of young, well-educated minority organizers who are prepared to assist workers in all aspects of life, not just workplace issues.

Whether your company is unionfree…facing an organizing attempt…or trying to deal with a union that is already in place, it's important to recognize that the increasing level of employee frustration and insecurity today is creating a very real threat to efficiency and workplace morale. *Latest challenges for business:*

•The National Labor Relations Board under the Clinton administration is now more support-

ive of union/employee rights than was the case under Reagan and Bush.

•There have even been recent cases of unions pushing for recognition without an election. This was a popular tactic before Reagan replaced the air traffic controllers…and it is now reemerging.

What to do:

•*Prepare now to head off union activity*. If there is a sudden push for elections you won't have much time to correct the company's image in the eyes of employees. Start by trying to understand the real frustration felt by workers. There are problems, of course, with workers who have seen many of their peers laid off in downsizing and restructuring efforts. Those efforts are still in progress in many US companies.

•*Take the initiative*. Don't wait for an outbreak of trouble. Take an aggressive stance now toward more effective and timely communications with employees.

•*Bring in outside lawyers or consultants* to train the company's employees in better communications and to help them solve real-life problems.

Example: We are now working with companies to educate employees on how to deal with issues of violence.

•*Use new tools*, such as Alternate Dispute Resolution (ADR), to remove the contention that can arise between bosses and subordinates.

•*Set up a complaint resolution system with an appeals process*. This can be done either inside the company, where there might be a provision for peer review and/or a hearing by the CEO, or outside the company, using impartial arbitration and mediation services such as the American Arbitration Association or the Federal Mediation and Conciliation Service. There also are a number of private mediation services.

Important: Make it clear whether these services have only mediation powers—or final decision powers. A landmark Supreme Court case (*Gilmer* vs. *Interstate/Johnson Corp.*, 111 SC 1647, 1991) has established that an ADR providing for binding arbitration of an employer/employee dispute was final and could even preclude the employee from bringing other court actions if the employee had previously agreed, in writing, to be bound by the decision.

Teams can be tricky:

Many companies are having success using work teams of various kinds to improve quality and productivity.

These can be particularly effective in non-union companies to reduce the incentive to organize. Even in unionized companies they are fine, as long as they avoid getting into questions of hours, wages or working conditions—legally the province of unions. In some companies, there is a union representative on every team who can convey such problems back to the union for resolution.

Recognize that there is a lot more aggravation in the workplace than ever before, and be sure that teams are perceived as parts of the same wheel. You want the employees to feel that a team is their team, not just the company's team. This may require special education to bridge various aspects of the company's labor program, such as team-building, training or suggestion awards, and explain how they relate to each other.

In all cases, be sure to assign accountability and responsibility, along with time frames for completion. Ask for feedback from employees to get reinforcement and commitment to team goals. Make use of employee surveys to find out how sentiment is running.

Understand the union:

It is official policy at the AFL-CIO today to give at least lip service to a more cooperative stance, to help US companies become more globally competitive.

In reality, much depends on the local union leaders, many of whom still espouse the adversarial thinking of the 1930s—and the 1960s. Sometimes these local officials—who want to be reelected (just like members of Congress)—must adopt a more militant stance in response to their frustrated constituency.

Defensive strategy: As with any relationship, it is useful to develop an ongoing dialogue with the union. Both parties need to be openly involved in the process for mutual advantage. This doesn't mean management must invite the union into the boardroom, but the company should make a commitment to provide enough information to the union so that it can educate and control its members.

Aim: To build respect and credibility between the two sides. Be prepared to be challenged on what you do, if it turns out to be different from what you say.

Important: The two sides don't always have to agree. You can agree to disagree, preferably without being disagreeable, handling disputes in as politely a way as possible.

Example: Making off-the-record conversations public after a negotiation is a good way to kill off any trust that has been built in the relationship.

Bottom line: Be reasonable and willing to listen, but never turn over the reins to the union Do what you have to do to run the business.

Important: Come up with a plan as to how you could continue to operate the business during a strike.

Don't turn down union demands without due consideration. Wherever possible, try to seek acceptable middle ground. But when you have to say no—out of conviction that you are doing what is right for the long-term interests of the company and its employees—stand tall and do it.

Source: Stephen J. Cabot, chairman, labor relations and employment law department, Harvey, Pennington, Herting & Renneisen, Ltd., Eleven Penn Center, 1835 Market St., Philadelphia 19103.

The Advantages of LLC Status

A Limited Liability Company (LLC) may be a better form of organization for a private business than an S corporation—or partnership.

LLC income is reported on its owners' personal tax returns, but LLC status offers more protection against personal liability in the event of bankruptcy than does a partnership. It is not subject to the restrictions on numbers and kinds of shareholders that apply to S corporations.

Endorsement: All of the Big Six accounting firms are adopting LLC status. Today, LLCs are authorized in 42 states, and authorization statutes are pending in all of the rest.

Source: Phil Laskawy, chairman, Ernst & Young, quoted in *Accounting Today*, Box 31177, Tampa, Florida 33631.

How to Be Successful at The Biggest Money-Maker Of Them All...Work

The job market remains brutal, as cutbacks continue at a record pace.

But you can advance your career...or start a new one...even in today's treacherous workplace. Here's what I recommend to get the most from your skills and experience...

• *Call your shots.* A successful career is like a game of pool. You won't run up a score unless you call the shots in advance. Set goals. Figure out what you want. Be honest enough to admit to yourself that it is what you want.

That isn't as easy as it sounds. Many people lie to themselves about what they want in a new job...or dislike about their current one. They do that to avoid the psychological pain of seeking what they're afraid they can't have. But we're at our worst when what is most important is avoiding pain.

Helpful: In the end, it's less painful moving toward something than running away.

• *Know what your skills are...and keep improving them.* The workplace is in constant change, and your training and experience don't count for as much as they used to. What you will be hired for in your next job probably won't be what you are doing now.

Know the skills you are best at...and keep working to improve them. Being able to say to a prospective employer, "This is what I can do," counts for more than, "I was a product manager at a computer company."

• *Don't expect straight lines.* There used to be clear career paths. No more. Recognize that your road to success today will be marked by countless twists and turns.

More than ever, it's dangerous to identify too closely with just one position or specialty.

Examine all possible uses of your talents instead of waiting passively in hopes of moving from assistant manager to manager.

• *Prepare to sell yourself, no matter what you do.* In the past, sales was considered a job only for someone smooth-talking and outgoing. Today, there's not a job in the world that doesn't involve the selling of your most important product...you. The marketplace is that competitive. If you're above selling yourself and your ideas, you won't get ahead.

• *Understand and use politics.* If you think you're above office politics, you'll be out in the cold. Today you need an edge. *Create your own opportunities by...*

• Knowing what you want to happen.

• Knowing who can help make it happen.

• Talking to the people who can make it happen...and convincing them you've got a good idea.

• *Don't expect fairness from others.* People will do what is beneficial for them. In today's hyper-competitive job market, we get what we are prepared to negotiate for...not what we deserve. Hard work isn't enough anymore.

• *Do what is personally hard.* Don't insist on doing only what you enjoy doing. Do what's best for your company.

If you work for a company that is sales-driven, spend time in sales. If the company is research-driven, get into research. This might not be the career path you had intended to take, but so be it. Doing what your company specializes in will make you feel challenged, and you'll be better off emotionally as well as financially.

• *Welcome scrutiny.* Employees used to be less accountable than they are today. Yet in this market, we all have to learn to welcome scrutiny. As companies focus more on the bottom line, everybody must be able to say, "This is what I do, and this is why it is worth paying for." Accountability may seem like meddling, but as employees, it makes us better.

• *Avoid the victim trap.* It's today's most popular defense...not only in the courtroom, but in the workplace: "Something was done to me first. This wasn't my fault." It's easy to claim discrimination. To remain happy in your job, you must feel in control. By becoming a victim, you give up control.

•*Live up to your own standards.* To be successful in the workplace today, you must both keep your job and maintain your identity.

Once you could be loyal to your firm, and that was that. But there aren't many 35-year jobs anymore. It's critical to decide who you are, what you value and what you want your work to provide for you.

Keep those standards in mind as you move forward. Otherwise, you won't have a career, just one job after another.

Source: Albert J. Bernstein, clinical psychologist and business consultant. He is the author of *Sacred Bull: The Inner Obstacles that Hold You Back at Work and How to Overcome Them,* John Wiley & Sons, 605 Third Ave., New York 10158.

Learn Your Burnout Symptoms

The signs are different for everyone. When yours show up, step back from your work and regain perspective before burnout actually hits. *Common signs of trouble:* Thinking that most problems are beyond your control, and are caused by forces you cannot influence—the computer, the weather, even your boss...lacking the energy or desire to have fun...becoming reactive rather than active...being unable to delegate or set priorities without second-guessing yourself.

Source: Ann McGee-Cooper, co-author, *Time Management for Unmanageable People,* Bantam Books, writing in *Working Smart,* 1101 King St., Alexandria, Virginia 22314.

Burnout... How to Prevent It

Burnout is the term used to describe the condition of emotional and physical collapse brought on by virtually unchecked escalation of pressure. Although burnout is not rampant in the business world, it is a problem that we all have to be aware of in order to protect our-

selves, our families, our business associates... and our friends.

Most emotionally well-adjusted people protect themselves against burnout intuitively by setting up defense mechanisms when the pressure gets rough...time off from work, closed doors, reduction in overall activity, etc.

Others get caught up in a self-destructive whirlpool.

Most vulnerable: People with a driving ambition for which they're willing to sacrifice a large part of their lives. Burnout victims invest their time, energy and money in tasks that are difficult, if not impossible. And they often commit themselves to a great deal of work without relief or support.

The terrible thing about burnout is that it often affects people who set out to do something wonderful or worthwhile. Little by little, they find themselves getting more stretched and desperate. The harder they try, the worse the situation becomes until they just can't try anymore.

Example #1: Jim, a business professor who offered great advice to people starting small businesses, gave workshops all over the country. But the more he traveled and the more people he helped, the more difficult his personal life became. Eventually, his marriage broke up and his two best friends drifted away—his support network disappeared. To make up for the loss, he took on more work...and eventually became exhausted. He had burned out.

Example #2: Susan opened a fantastic French restaurant. But she made the mistake of locating it in a part of town where people weren't used to going for expensive dining. It took more and more of Susan's time, effort and money to keep the restaurant afloat. When bankruptcy finally hit, so did a divorce. That was the final straw, causing Susan's emotional collapse. She sank into a long depression.

The burnout process:

Burnout usually follows a predictable sequence that can be interrupted at almost any stage. If you're aware of what the sequence is, you can take steps to prevent burnout from running its course.

Stage I: The first sign of burnout is overenthusiasm. Stage I burnout candidates tell long and nervous tales about how wonderful everything is. People who hear these monologues often wonder why this person is so intent on explaining everything.

Stage II: Physical symptoms—ulcers, rashes, back pain, neck pain, colds, flu, etc.—emerge. Stage II cases become antagonistic. They start wondering whether the people who are close to them are part of the solution or part of the problem.

Stage III: Deprivation symptoms set in. The individual starts to feel hollow because he/she is not being emotionally nourished, but this feeling is kept secret. Although the person still thinks he's doing great things, he doesn't enjoy them as much as he used to…he doesn't feel as important.

Stage IV: The sense of emptiness and of impending defeat increases. In Stage IV, desperate moves are made—scientists fake results, businesspeople borrow from the mob. They still function, but they take big risks with their careers, their finances, their relationships and their lives. They're desperate to avoid failure, even at the expense of other important aspects of their lives.

Stage V: The lies and deceptions grow. The Stage V burnout sufferer becomes cut off from people because he can't tell them what's really going on. The circle of people who are willing to help gets smaller and smaller.

Stage VI: This is the terminal phase where the person either gets fired, goes bankrupt, collapses, has a breakdown, becomes suicidal or ends up with a serious physical illness.

How to avoid burnout:

If you think you're in danger, the best way to avoid it is to open yourself to support, love and nurturing. Look for people to help you. And you've got to take care of yourself.

Recommended: Make a list of all the things you once found relaxing and rejuvenating—lying on the beach, reading mysteries from cover to cover, hiking, spending time with friends. Then figure out why you stopped doing these things and how you can get them back into your life.

Many people advise burnout victims to cut their workload immediately. *Trap:* Unless you've decided what to do with your free time, that won't help. Burnout victims are success-oriented people who need plans before they can feel good about cutting their workload.

Warning: The earlier the burnout is caught, the easier it is to treat. By Stage VI, the victim is psychologically, emotionally and financially exhausted. It will take an extensive period of nurturance and recuperation, and possibly even a career change, to recover.

Important: In an abusive environment—where self-serving or sadistic bosses rule—a hardworking, ambitious employee may go through the six stages in a matter of weeks or months if no action is taken. To avoid burnout, such an employee may have no choice other than to leave the company—or at least transfer to a different department.

Source: Martin G. Groder, MD, a psychiatrist and business consultant in Chapel Hill, North Carolina. His book, *Business Games: How to Recognize the Players and Deal With Them,* is available from Boardroom Classics, Box 11014, Des Moines.

Rules for Writing Good Résumés in Tricky Times

Most people spend less time writing and polishing their résumés than they do writing a letter of complaint to a department store. Yet a résumé may make the difference between getting a good job and losing a lifetime opportunity. *A guide for successful résumés…*

Review your résumé. Don't distribute it until you're sure there are no spelling or grammatical errors—and that all the essential facts are included.

Experience in the occupation for which you're applying is necessary. Many job applicants cite the basic facts of their previous positions, but very few include one of the most important elements—a brief description of their outstanding achievements.

Success records should be substantiated. If possible, include brief anecdotes to illustrate your achievements.

153

Update your résumé. Too often, job seekers squeeze in their current or last jobs on old résumés. Résumés should be retyped. *Remember:* Your last job will be scrutinized most carefully.

More than one version of your résumé is necessary because you probably qualify for more than one type of occupation.

Education should be part of your résumé. But if you're a college graduate, there's no need to list your high school or elementary school educations (unless they are prestigious). Indicate any special honors.

Style is important. A résumé should be neat with ample space between paragraphs. It should have wide margins and be on high-quality white or ivory paper. A résumé should be long enough to get across all the necessary facts. Most good résumés are one to two-and-a-half pages long.

Source: Robert Half, founder of Robert Half International, Inc. and Accountemps (Menlo Park, CA), employment specialists in the financial, accounting and information systems fields. His book is *Finding, Hiring and Keeping the Best Employees,* John Wiley & Sons, New York.

To Handle Problem Handshakes

Reduce your discomfort without passing the awkwardness back to the person who caused it. If you receive a bone-crushing handshake, go limp and hold your hand at a slight angle. For a limp handshake, aim for the thumb joint with your hand—this will eliminate some limpness. If you extend your hand and there is no response, just put your hand down and carry on.

Source: *Complete Business Etiquette Handbook* by Barbara Pachter, business consultant in Cherry Hill, New Jersey, Prentice Hall, Englewood Cliffs, NJ.

Job Interview Musts

- You *must* prove your capability.
- You *must* be enthusiastic.
- You *must* ask logical questions.

- You *must* highlight achievements—not just functions—at prior jobs.
- You *must* prove how past experience helped your prior companies.
- You *must* demonstrate that you have some knowledge about the company with which you are interviewing.
- You *must* get to the interview on time. *Better:* 15 minutes early.
- You *must* dress appropriately.
- You *must* have good manners but shouldn't be condescending.
- You *must* explain how you cooperate with coworkers.
- You *must* demonstrate loyalty to former employers. You *must* give your present employer adequate notice when resigning. Good employers like to hire people who are fair.
- You *must* have a comprehensive résumé, and make it a point to read it again right before every interview.
- You *must* ask for the job. No matter what your occupation is, when you're looking for a job, you're in sales.

Source: Robert Half, founder of Robert Half International and Accountemps, employment specialists in the financial, accounting and information systems fields, Menlo Park, California.

Find Out What Former Employers Are Saying About You

Reference-checking firms are being hired by ex-employees to find out what former employers say about them. If an employer criticizes an ex-employee, the reference-checking firm sends a warning letter or helps the ex-employee file a lawsuit. *Self-defense:* Verify only factual information on ex-employees—dates of employment and salary—and ask for requests in writing. Don't respond to telephone requests.

Source: *LaborWatch*, 10050 Regency Circle, Omaha, Nebraska 68114.

How to Play the 401(k) Withdrawal Game

Most people think that the only time they can take money out of a 401(k) plan is at retirement, if they become disabled or upon reaching age 59½. That is just not the case…

Special exceptions: You are allowed to take a loan or make a withdrawal from your otherwise-unavailable 401(k) money when you really need the money.

Loans:

Provided your plan permits it, you are allowed to borrow from your own 401(k). When you borrow from your 401(k), you don't have to pay taxes on the loan and you don't have to pay a penalty to the IRS.

Two types of allowable loans from your 401(k) plan…

• *Short-term loan.* You can take a short-term loan for any reason whatsoever. The loan must be repaid quarterly over a period of up to five years.

• *Long-term loan.* You can take a long-term loan for one reason—the purchase of your primary home. Your employer will require documentation in the form of a sales contract or other proof of purchase of the home.

It's easy to pay back a 401(k) loan because you pay the principal and interest through regular paycheck deductions. However, the interest paid on a loan secured by your pretax deferrals is not deductible even if it is used to purchase a home.

The interest rates are relatively low. *Advantage of these loans:* You have access to your money today while at the same time you have saved it for retirement.

Special rules: If you leave your job prior to repayment of the loan, you may be required to repay the whole unpaid balance in full. You will be treated as if you took a taxable distribution if you don't repay it. *Even worse:* You will have to pay a 10% penalty on top of the taxes.

Exception: If you leave your job because of retirement, and you still have a loan outstanding, you can make arrangements with your employer to repay the loan through deductions from your pension check. The 10% penalty may not apply.

Hardship distributions:

Another way of taking money out of your 401(k) is through a hardship distribution. A hardship withdrawal is allowed when…

• You are in a situation of significant and extreme financial need and you can't get money from another source, and…

• The distribution from the 401(k) is necessary to satisfy that financial need.

The financial need must be for one of the following reasons as set forth by the IRS:

• To purchase your primary residence.

• To prevent foreclosure on the mortgage that is on your principal residence.

• To prevent eviction from a principal residence that you rent.

• To pay significant medical expenses.

• To pay tuition and related fees for the next 12 months for you/your spouse or your children.

• To pay funeral expenses.

The amount of the hardship withdrawal cannot exceed the amount you actually need to cover the hardship.

Source: Stephen Pennacchio, benefits specialist and partner, KPMG Peat Marwick, 345 Park Ave., New York 10154.

No-Penalty Early IRA Withdrawal

Many Individual Retirement Account agreements let you have your balance paid over your lifetime in equal yearly payments. And—you can ask that payouts start at any time. The company holding your account will use IRS tables to determine your life expectancy and start sending you the money. You will pay taxes, but no penalties, on the withdrawals. *Caution:* Once started, the arrangement cannot be stopped until you reach age 59½ and have let it run for at least five years.

Source: David J. Silverman is a tax practitioner enrolled to practice before the IRS. David J. Silverman & Co., 866 UN Plaza, New York 10017. He is the author of *Battling the IRS: A Taxpayer's Guide to Responding to IRS Notices and Assessments*, available through David J. Silverman & Co.

Boost Your IRA Benefit

Boost your IRA benefit—if you qualify for an IRA tax deduction—by saving the $2,000 annual maximum plus the tax savings the contribution provides. *How it works:* In the 28% bracket, the tax on $2,000 is $560. If your IRA is deductible, invest that $560 instead of spending it. Over 20 years with after-tax earnings of 5.5%, those additional investments will grow to more than $20,000.

Source: *Kiplinger's 12 Steps to a Worry-Free Retirement*, by Los Angeles-based financial writer Daniel Kehrer. Kiplinger Books, 1729 H St. NW, Washington, DC 20006.

To Take Money Out of Your IRA

Individual Retirement Accounts (IRAs) need not be left just for retirement. There are some legitimate ways to take your IRA money or to manipulate it more effectively prior to retirement age. *What can be done right now...*

• *Withdraw without penalty before age 59½.* No matter how old you are, you can arrange to take distributions from your IRA without paying the 10% early withdrawal penalty. *How to do it:* Take money out of your IRA in the form of an annuity. An annuity is a number of substantially equal payments (at least one each year) paid out over your lifetime or life expectancy or joint lives or joint life expectancies of you and your designated benficiary. Of course, you will owe income taxes on the amounts you receive each year, just as you would at retirement.

How to manipulate a distribution: Redeposit a rollover IRA into a corporate pension plan. Distributions from a pension plan when you leave a job should be temporarily invested in a rollover IRA that is segregated from your other IRA accounts. Close this temporary rollover IRA when you start working with a new employer who has a corporate pension plan and deposit the money in the new company's pension plan.

Benefit: When you take a distribution at retirement, you may be allowed to apply the favorable five-year averaging or 10-year averaging rule to the portion that you might have otherwise lost the benefit of because you left it in the IRA.

Less favorable treatment for your IRA: IRA withdrawals at retirement are usually taxed at ordinary income tax rates, which are higher than five-year averaging or 10-year averaging.

• *Invest wisely.* Use your IRA to invest for aggressive, long-term growth *if you can afford to take a chance.* The investments that you are allowed to use for your IRA are more extensive than your choices in a company pension plan.

Even better: Tax is not due on the appreciation in value of the IRA until you take money out. Most likely when you withdraw the money at retirement you will be in a lower tax bracket.

Special advantage: You don't have to pay tax when stock is bought and sold within the IRA during the years prior to retirement. You can therefore make trades without worrying about the effect on this year's capital gains.

Caution: If your IRA is going to be the sole source of retirement income, it may be best to invest more conservatively and concentrate on preserving capital. This way your account will be safe for retirement and future growth will be more predictable.

• *Plan your distributions carefully.* The amount of the distribution from an IRA at retirement is more flexible than the distributions from a company pension plan. A typical corporate plan usually allows distributions in either a lump sum, or an annuity—or fixed installments.

Compare: You can decide on the amount you want to take out of your IRA each year as long as you take the minimum.

Minimum rules: Starting in the year you reach age 70½, a minimum amount must be withdrawn from your IRA each year. *The minimum distribution is generally calculated by:*

• *Straight life method.* Divide the amount in your IRA by your life expectancy or by the joint life expectancy of you and your designated beneficiary in the year you start taking the payments from your IRA, *or*

• *Recalculation method.* Divide the amount remaining in your IRA each year by your life expectancy or by the joint life expectancy of you and your designated beneficiary, which changes each year.

• *Avoid withholding taxes.* Don't allow your former company to give you a check in your own name when you leave the job and receive a lump- sum distribution from the company pension plan. Taxes will be withheld even if you intend to turn around and deposit it in another retirement plan or a rollover IRA.

Have the check made out to the place where you would have ultimately deposited the check anyway.

Source: Avery E. Neumark, partner and director of employee benefits and executive compensation, Weber Lipshie & Co., 1430 Broadway, New York 10018.

Company Pension Plan Mistakes Can Be Costly

Monitor your company pension plan for possible mistakes that could prove costly when you retire. First, get a summary plan description from your employer that tells how retirement benefits are calculated. It's a good idea to see the description of a prospective new employer's plan before quitting your old job and letting your old pension plan go.

Key questions: Do bonuses, overtime and commissions—or just salary—count toward retirement benefits? Are benefits at retirement based on your top-earning years...or on all years of service? How are years of service calcu-

lated if you take a pregnancy break or some other leave of absence?

Source: *Baby Boomer Retirement: 65 Simple Ways to Protect Your Future* by Don Silver, an estate-planning lawyer in Los Angeles, Adams-Hall Publishing, Box 491002-BR3, Los Angeles 90049.

Is Your Pension Plan In Serious Trouble?

Are pensions at risk—or are they safe? The media reports that the nation's retirement income programs are in both jeopardy *and* fine shape.

Reality: Most pension programs today are sound—but trouble spots exist.

Understanding pensions:

There are two basic types of plans...

• *Defined benefit.* This is the old-fashioned kind. It promises you a set income throughout retirement. The amount you'll receive varies according to how long you've worked and how much you've earned. Typically, employers make *all* of the contributions to these plans, and they appoint themselves or others as plan trustees to invest the money. If investment earnings are better than expected, the employer will contribute less money to the plan in future years. If the fund's performance is poor, the employer contributes more money.

• *Defined contribution.* With this type of plan, your benefit depends on how much money is contributed and how well it is invested. Your pension will be the amount accumulated in your account, which is usually paid as a lump sum.

There are different kinds of defined contribution plans...

• In profit-sharing and money-purchase plans, the employer usually makes the contributions.

• In 401(k) and 403(b) savings plans, employees themselves are responsible for putting money into the plans, although employers often match their employees' contributions.

In some cases, employees are covered by both defined benefit and defined contribution plans.

Pension program problems:

While most media attention has focused on defined benefit plans, there is little that individuals can do about these plans if they are underfunded. Fortunately, the government insurance program protects most benefits.

Defined contribution plans, however, are not insured and may be mismanaged. *Here's how to tell...*

Giving your plan a checkup:

You can become your *own* pension watchdog by reviewing the financial information that is given to you by your employer's plan.

Federal law requires larger company and union plans to provide an overview of the plan's finances each year. This usually takes the form of a one-page *Summary Annual Report (SAR)* that is either handed out or mailed to all plan members.

The SAR tells you how much money is in the plan and whether plan investments have performed well or poorly. It also says how much the plan trustees have paid out in administrative costs. Large losses and excessive costs can be red flags that signal problem areas.

Important: The SAR will tell you how to get a copy of the detailed financial statement the plan is required to file with the federal govern-

*Send $8.50—including postage and handling—to Pension Publications, 918 16 St. NW, Suite. 704, Washington, DC 20006-2902.

ment. This statement is called *Form 5500*. Form 5500 will disclose the types of investments (stocks, bonds, real estate and the like) your plan has made and how much money these investments gained or lost. If yours is a larger plan, you are likely to find attached to Form 5500 a detailed listing of all the investments held by the plan, along with a report by a certified public accountant and information showing the amounts paid to people providing services to the plan.

If the plan trustees have entered into unlawful transactions with company or union officials, their relatives or those with close connections to the plan, this should also appear on Form 5500.

To help employees analyze their Form 5500s, the Pension Rights Center has published a 42-page guide called *Protecting Your Pension Money.**

Strategy: If you discover any questionable transactions or other alarming information in your plan's Form 5500, contact the Department of Labor's Pension and Welfare Benefits Administration field office for your area. If you can't find the listing in the phone book, call the national office of the Department of Labor at 202-219-8840.

Source: Karen W. Ferguson, director of the Pension Rights Center, a nonprofit consumer advocacy group that protects the pension interests of workers and retirees. She is the coauthor, with Kate Blackwell, of *Pensions in Crisis: Why the System Is Failing America and How You Can Protect Your Future*, Arcade Publishing, New York 10010.

10

Marketing and Sales Management In the Office

About Marketing

To lift prices and keep customers, offer a customized version of a standard product or service…make a product a little smaller and sell it at the same price…make it a little bigger and charge an increment that offsets the size increase…offer basic services at a low price, then charge for desirable options…offer faster service at a premium price.

Source: Pete Silver, marketing consultant, Florida, quoted in *Business94*, 125 Auburn Ct., Thousand Oaks, California 91362.

How to Keep a Deal From Dying

When TCI and Bell Atlantic announced their mega-merger in February of 1995, the deal was front-page news throughout the world.

When, less than two months later, the chairmen of the two companies—TCI's John Malone and Bell Atlantic's Raymond Smith—went before the press to announce that the deal had fallen through, the headline writers had another field day.

While the TCI-Bell Atlantic example is unusual given the enormous size of the two partners, the experience of having a deal and then losing it is increasingly common. What the TCI-Bell Atlantic experience has in common with the growing number of other sudden deal deaths is the unpredictability of technical—mostly legal—obstacles.

Lesson for negotiators: There's a delicate balance between detail and generality during the early negotiation process.

Crossing too many t's and dotting too many i's at this stage risks aborting the whole deal. Conversely, glossing over differences and leaving everything until the negotiation of the final legal document can lull both parties into a false sense of agreement.

Identify deal busters early:

Solution: Identify and face up to issues that are so important that they should be resolved during the courting process—not the day of the wedding. *Common deal busters:*

• *Stock versus asset sales.* Because there are such major differences in the tax consequences between stock sales and asset sales—involving two levels of taxation—deals often come apart over this issue. A buyer might need one—and the seller might not be able to comply. This is the kind of major issue that should be addressed early.

• *Unrealistic seller conditions.* The seller says, "Of course you'll keep my top three executives." If the buyer has no intention of keeping these people, it is important to tell the seller up front.

The same is true of other issues that may be near and dear to a seller's heart, such as not closing down a plant in a certain town or stopping production of a favorite product.

Make a list:

We advise clients to list key ideas or issues that will have to be resolved during negotiations.

Helpful: Have a brainstorming session with top executives to make sure the list includes all of the main issues.

Important: Identify issues that are critical to the other side and plan how your negotiating strategy will deal with them.

Defer smaller issues:

Of course, there are some items in any negotiation that are best left aside until most details have fallen into place and the momentum of the transaction has made the deal almost inevitable.

Example: There's often a question of whether or not an escrow account will be required as part of the financing of a deal. A buyer who is paying $5 million for a business might want $500,000 in an escrow account to make sure that the facts are as represented by the seller. For his/her part, however, the seller may claim that he/she is really only getting $4.5 million in that case. If the seller complains that the buyer never raised this point, the buyer can simply say, "Oh—that was assumed. Obviously there

has to be an escrow account. But I'm willing to negotiate the amount."

Then, if the seller wants to end up with $500,000, he/she can start by asking for $750,000. The toughness of these negotiations will depend on who wants the deal the most.

Put it in writing—early:

Clients often fall into two traps...

• Not putting anything into writing until the final contract is hammered out by lawyers.

• Summing up the negotiations in a letter that is too long and overly legalistic.

Best: A letter listing the key points that have been agreed to in the early stages of negotiations. In too many situations, the parties think they have agreed to a particular solution in concept, only to find out toward the end of lengthy talks that each of them has a different understanding of what has been decided.

Key: If any problem issues emerge from the written summation, they can usually be resolved before the lawyers sit down to draft the final contract, avoiding confrontations that could shatter an otherwise satisfactory deal.

Source: Susan E. Pravda, managing partner of the Boston office of Epstein Becker & Green, PC, specializing in middle-market acquisitions and financing transactions, 75 State St., Boston 02109.

Bargain Smart for The Best Deal

Successful negotiators create a positive relationship with the other side. As for bluffing—it almost always backfires.

These are my rules for bargaining for a better deal on anything...a house...a car...even a divorce...

• *Be patient.* Impatient negotiators make unnecessary concessions and pay too much. It's easier to control the process if you're not too anxious.

Helpful: Wait to buy a car until sellers are anxious to close—between June and August, just before the new models come out. That's when dealers are under maximum pressure from their banks to get rid of old inventory.

• *Be positive.* You'll get a better deal from a friend than an enemy. A smile is a cheap concession, and the best way to lower someone's shield.

Helpful: A last-minute expression of optimism is a very effective closing tactic. Say you're negotiating to buy a house. The seller's final demand is $15,000 higher than you want to pay. Tell the seller you feel you're close to a deal, but need a few days to think it over.

You want the seller to visualize a sale and mentally start packing. When your counteroffer is less generous than expected, the seller will find it hard to walk away, even if it means a greater concession than was expected.

• *Learn before you bargain.* Information can be your most valuable asset. What about your alternatives if negotiations deadlock? What about the other side's position? Perceptions?

Get the other side involved in the process. If you make an offer they refuse, ask for a counteroffer. If they say your opening position is unreasonable, ask what is reasonable.

Strategy: Bargain so that each side must make roughly equal concessions. Say the asking price for a house is $160,000, while you want to pay $150,000. A lowball offer of $100,000 could offend the seller, making him/her inflexible. An offer of $145,000 means you can't end up at your $150,000 target unless the seller makes more concessions than you do. Offer $140,000, so equal concessions bring you to your target price.

• *Don't bluff.* Saying "This is my last and final offer," makes the other side want to find out if you mean it, by calling your bluff.

• *Know what you want.* Don't fall for the "add-on" close…"You just bought a beautiful car, Mr. Reilly. If you act quickly, I can give you a great deal on a service agreement."

• *Limit your authority.* A negotiator with limited authority is in a stronger position.

Example: A car salesperson must always go back to the sales manager. That lets him/her come back and tell you that his/her boss won't okay the deal unless you make additional concessions.

Strategy: Say you must get your spouse's okay on any deal you make. At the very least,

this will give you a chance to think it over before putting pen to paper.

Source: Leo Reilly, president, KCR Communications, management-training consultants, Los Gatos, California. He is the author of *How to Outnegotiate Anyone—Even a Car Dealer!,* Bob Adams, Inc., 260 Center St., Holbrook, Massachusetts 02343.

Sales-Rep Weaknesses

The biggest complaints about salespeople—with the percent of surveyed purchasing managers citing each trait shown:

Lack of knowledge of
  customer's operation....................................68%
Lack of interest or purpose..........................66%
Lack of follow-through 61%
Failure to make/keep appointments...........59%
Lack of preparation 59%
Lack of product knowledge.........................57%
Overaggressiveness and failure to listen.....55%
Taking the customer for granted 45%
Lack of creativity 19%
Failure to keep promises 18%
Lack of candor...11%

Source: Annual survey by *Purchasing*, 275 Washington St., Newton, Massachusetts 02158.

The Simple Secrets of Great Customer Service

Outstanding customer service is rarely the result of high-priced employee-training and performance-monitoring programs.

Before launching a costly plan to overhaul the company's customer-service operations, consider inexpensive steps that can significantly boost customer loyalty—right away…

• *Energize employees.* Pep rallies and slogans help, but nothing energizes employees more effectively than seeing senior management demonstrate enthusiasm toward customers. *Examples:*

• Bill Marriott of Marriott Corp. works the front desks from time to time. It isn't for the guests' benefit, but for his employees'. They never forget seeing the head of the company do what they do—and enjoy every minute of it.

• Fred Smith of Federal Express. His enthusiasm is infectious when he talks one-on-one with drivers about their role in serving customers.

• *Share gifts with customers.* In the rush of day-to-day business, small favors might seem trivial. To customers, however, they can be the key factor in a decision to develop a long-term relationship with a company.

On the low end of the scale, the gift can be a compliment an employee gives to a customer. Or, it can be a piece of fine china given for placing a big order.

Somewhere in the middle are gifts such as the brochure AT&T gives its business customers on better ways to use its phones. Even if customers don't read the brochure, the gesture itself tells them that AT&T values their business.

Important: To encourage employees to go the extra mile for customers, do more than just reward them with higher salaries and promotions. Lavish conspicuous recognition on those who go out of their way for customers.

Hold a celebration and recount their actions for other workers to hear. The event not only rewards one employee, but it also inspires others to do the same.

• *Keep pace with changes in buying trends.* The expectations and experiences of customers are constantly changing. Companies that don't keep up with them have little chance of developing long-term relationships.

The most effective way: Instead of simply asking customers how they like the company's service, ask them, "What can the company do to provide the best service in the business?" Or, "What would have made your last buying experience the best one you ever had?"

Answers will keep you up-to-date on what customers expect of the company.

Elicit feedback from customers as often as possible—with "800" number hot lines...questionnaires mailed with invoices...focus groups.

Listen especially carefully to disgruntled customers. Ironically, those who complain

spend more as a group than those who don't. *Reason:* Noncomplainers often start buying elsewhere. To make sure feedback affects customer policies...

• Reward and recognize employees who take action on feedback.

• Instruct middle managers to consult often with employees on the front lines, those who hear customer feedback first-hand.

• Invite front-line employees to interdepartmental meetings to discuss ways of making the company more responsive to customers.

• Let customers know that the company has taken action on their comments. Failure to do this will dilute subsequent efforts to elicit feedback.

Example: Marriott guests who fill out suggestion cards receive a letter signed by Bill Marriott. Even though these people realize the signature is computer-generated, they appreciate the gesture.

• *Be honest with customers.* It almost seems that customers have built-in lie detectors, and they reward companies that stick to the truth. To encourage employee honesty...

• Tell employees they'll never be penalized for delivering bad news as long as it's true.

• Treat employees as you'd want them to treat customers—honestly. Many companies would be surprised to learn how fast honesty with employees is transferred to their dealings with customers.

When a customer is dissatisfied, do what it takes to correct the problem—including a full refund if necessary.

Example: The Hampton Inn hotel chain refunds the entire price of a room if a guest is dissatisfied for any reason, even after he/she has spent the entire night. *Rationale:* What the company loses to a few rip-off artists is more than made up by the fact that it has one of the highest occupancy rates in the business.

• Think from the customer's point of view. Most customer problems arise from flaws in basic operations—ordering, delivery, invoicing, etc. Minor flaws, however, may never become apparent because customers do not complain about them. They simply never make repeat sales. To uncover these flaws...

• Ask key customers to walk you through the buying process—as they experience it.

• Hold periodic focus groups with samplings of customers.

• Hire people to shop or order as customers would. Sometimes called "spotters," these employees are useful when they later share what they learned with employees who are on the front line with customers.

• Involve customers and employees in re-designing systems.

Example: The tracking software that Federal Express now puts in the hands of customers.

Source: Chip R. Bell, a customer-service consultant whose clients include Blockbuster Video, GE, Microsoft and MCI. He is the manager of Performance Research Associates, Inc., 25 Highland Park, Dallas 75205. His book is *Customers as Partners: Building Relationships that Last,* Berrett-Koehler Publishers, 155 Montgomery St., San Francisco 94104.

The Probe…a Very Powerful Selling Tool

The gentle art of probing is one of the most valuable skills a sales rep can master…

Frontal probes for information—such as, "Are you the decision maker for the company for these products?"—run right into the prospect's thickest armor.

Frontal probes can generally be answered with a single word. They sound like attacks—or, at the very least, like challenges.

Flanking probes are much more effective and subtle. *Example:* "How are decisions like this made inside your firm, Mr. Rogers?"

This kind of question forces a prospect to think and reach inside for the answer—often revealing needs the sales rep can then fulfill with a product or service. Flanking probes work well because the prospect…

• *Can give information non-defensively.* By answering openly, the prospect carries the burden of the presentation. The sales rep has more time to listen and think.

• *Must think to develop a reasonable answer,* which reduces the chance of an automatic response such as, "We don't need it now."

Flanking probes start with…

• *How.* How is the new computer impacting your operations?

• *Who.* Who will be the person in charge now?

• *What.* What kind of fitness goals are you pursuing now?

• *Why.* Why is it better for you to handle it this way?

• *When.* When do you think would be the best time to get started on that?

• *Where.* Where do you think the market is going?

Source: Jerry Vass, a sales trainer for 40 years for major corporations, Atlanta, and the author of *Soft Selling in a Hard World,* Running Press, 125 S. 22 St., Philadelphia 19103.

About Sales Leads

The best time to ask a customer for a referral is after delivery of a product or service. At that point the customer has a feeling of satisfaction about receiving something, and is likely to be in a frame of mind to give you something in return. Another good time to ask for a referral is after being turned down on a sales call—you have nothing to lose, and the customer may feel he/she owes you something. It is not a good idea to ask for a referral when closing a sale—you'll be asking for too much at once.

Source: Warren Greshes, motivational speaker, New York, quoted in *Sales & Marketing Executive Report,* 4660 N. Ravenswood Ave., Chicago 60640.

"Backdoor" Opportunity

Revive a dormant account through an independent sales agent. A customer who has had a problem with a supplier may duck calls from its salespeople after he/she stops placing orders, leaving the supplier in the dark about what went wrong. *Effective:* Find an independent sales agent who sells unrelated products to the customer, and who is on good terms with him/her. Retain the agent to approach the customer. At the least, the agent can use his contacts to find out what went wrong with the account—at best, the agent may find a way to revive it.

Source: Bert Holtje, editor, *Agency Sales*, Box 3467, Laguna Hills, California 92654.

Very Dumb Direct-Marketing Mistakes

These errors can hamper the success of a direct-marketing campaign…

• *Using old customer lists.* No company can sell to customers it doesn't reach. A six-month-old list is too old.

• *Inadequate testing.* The way to make a sales package effective is to test it on customers and make the necessary changes.

• *Lack of records.* Don't get caught up in fulfilling orders and neglect to keep records. Without complete records, it is impossible to duplicate success.

• *Treating all customers the same.* Target specialized packages at different market segments.

Source: Mark S. Bacon, author, *Do-It-Yourself Direct Marketing,* John Wiley & Sons, quoted in *Sales & Marketing Executive Report,* 4660 N. Ravenswood Ave., Chicago 60640.

Successful Sales Closings… The Basics

Golden rule of selling for the 1990s: Close when your customer wants to buy, not when you want to sell.

Closing may be the moment of truth, but don't let it terrify you. If you've probed effectively so that you know your client's needs and have led the prospect to the point of buying, your close is a done deal. The only thing that can stop you is—you. Here are some helpful pointers to get beyond that. They may sound basic, but sales reps often benefit from the reminder…

Understand buying signals:

• *The slow head nod.* It often means that the customer is communicating that he/she is ready to buy, but might not be willing to say "yes" at the moment.

But because you've got the prospect motivated, try a trial close, such as "How does this sound to you?"

If the customer still seems tentative, keep going. If he/she is smiling while nodding, that is an additional sign of readiness to buy.

Caution: Fast nodding is not a buying signal, but a sign of impatience.

• *Pupil dilation.* When people are excited, their pupils dilate. Remember the last time you gave a wonderful birthday present to your spouse or child, and his/her eyes widened?

When you establish eye contact with a prospect and feel that rapport is good, notice the eyes. If they seem dilated it is a signal for you to try to close.

• *Gestures that show interest.* When a person is pondering something, he/she will often use gestures, such as scratching a part of the head or rubbing the chin. If a customer appears lost in thought, stop talking because it means he/she is seriously considering whether or not to buy. Wait for the customer to regain eye contact and then try a trial close, such as "How does this sound to you?"

• *Voice signals.* A customer can display interest by a change in voice, too. If you point out something about your service and the customer, with a rising voice asks, "Really?"—you've caught interest. The customer might be receptive to a trial close at that point.

• *Buyer possessiveness.* If the customer is eager to hold on to your sales materials or asks for other copies, it is a strong signal that the person is motivated to buy. But if he/she returns a paper after a brief glance or pushes it aside, it means you have more selling to do.

Important: Make sure that the close is made by you, the rep. You can't wait for clients to close themselves.

This is the point at which fear often trips up salespeople. Not wanting to seem too pushy, they don't really get the point across. They either remain vague…or hope the prospect will take the next step and place the order. While the decision is the client's, as the rep, you are the one who must get the client to that point.

Think of it as the last time you will be able to lead your client—to the most important decision of all.

Important: "No" doesn't necessarily end an attempted sale. In fact, it can be a valuable sign, pointing to an objection that can be addressed for a successful close.

Example: A client of mine, a loan officer for a Kansas bank, was trying to sell financial services to an executive, who said, "No, I want to think about it first." The loan officer said, "I appreciate your cautiousness, but what exactly do you want to think about? Perhaps I can be helpful."

"Well," said the executive, "to be honest, I'm really not the one who makes these decisions. But I will take it up with my boss, the executive vice president."

This signaled to the loan officer that he was barking up the wrong tree and could have spent months pursuing the wrong prospect. He asked, "Can you give me his name so I can follow up?" The prospect obliged and with the resulting sale, the loan officer made his entire year's quota.

Master different closing techniques:

Some closes work better with certain types of people, while others are more effective when combined with different techniques. The important thing is to be familiar with many different techniques so that you can use them when the time is right. *Examples:*

• *The Assumptive Close.* The most powerful, and my favorite. The rep assumes that the client will buy even though he/she hasn't specifically said "yes." And the rep doesn't give the client the chance. The rep acts in a way that implies—without actually using these words—"We've already agreed that you'll buy this product. I'm going to take care of all the details so that you don't have to make the effort of saying 'yes.' Just don't say 'no.' "

For example, a fund-raiser for public broadcasting would say, after questioning my programming preference, "I'd like to put you down for $100 a year." Without skipping a beat, he/she would ask me to confirm my address and thank me for my generosity. He/she wouldn't give me a chance to say "no."

Key: In this close, the rep lays out the scenario and proposes a course of action based on a strong sense that the client wants to buy, but just doesn't know how to say it.

• *The Alternate or Choice Close.* Another one of my favorites, because here the rep focuses on one or two minor choices after assuming the client is sold. The rep asks, "Would this be credit card or cash?" "Do you want a super VGA color monitor or is VGA okay?" "We can print 500 copies, but for a few dollars more, we can print 1,000. Which would you prefer?" This close works because people like simple choices. The rep makes saying "yes" easier by limiting the choices the customer must make.

Key: With the alternate close there is the implied assumption that it is not a question of whether the client will buy, but rather what will be bought.

By focusing on the details, you don't leave room for an outright "no" and if you don't get a "yes," you can go back and handle any objection that comes up.

• *The "I Recommend" Close.* With this one you, the rep, emphasize your role as problem-solver. If you've earned the customer's trust and have fully provided for his/her needs, all you have to say is, "I recommend such and such," and your customer will respond. This technique is analogous to a patient's trust in a doctor and unquestioning acceptance of prescriptions and therapies.

Key: To make this close effective, you must be especially good at listening to—and probing for—your customers' needs. If customers sense that you really understand their needs, they will follow your recommended course of action.

• *The Benefits Close.* The rep simply lists the benefits of a product with the understanding that the customer agrees with the benefits. If there are no objections, the rep assumes that the customer agrees to buy, and the order is written up.

Variation: Compare the pros and cons of buying a particular product. This is useful if many objections have been raised.

Key: Acknowledge any negative feelings that may still be on the customer's mind, but then lead him/her away from negatives by focusing on what is positive about the product or service.

• *The Ultimatum or Last-Chance Close.* This works well when going back and forth with a prospect who just doesn't want to commit, or with a telephone prospect you've called four or five times, each time getting a vague promise that he/she will think about it. It is not worth your while to keep pursuing such a person. Give him/her one last chance. "OK, this is my last call. We've talked a number of times and I guess you really feel you can't invest right now." Or, "Since you haven't bought anything from us, I'd like to know whether I can take you off our files." When so informed, many prospective clients suddenly feel like buying.

Key: Presenting customers with an ultimatum gives them the little extra push they needed all along.

• *The Recurrent "Yes" Close.* If you can get the customer to answer "yes" to a number of questions, you can use the momentum to lead into a close.

Example: A sporting-goods salesperson got me to switch from a fiberglass tennis racket to a graphite version by prompting me to agree to certain qualities that a good racket should have, such as the ability to get both velocity and top spin. Hence, the graphite racket.

Key: The customer is made to realize that he/she can't disagree with his/her own logic in selecting specific, necessary product qualities.

Source: Kerry L. Johnson, motivational speaker, International Productivity Systems, Box 3665, Tustin, California 92681. Johnson is the author of several books, including *Sales Magic—Revolutionary New Techniques that Will Double Your Sales Volume in 21 Days,* William Morrow, New York.

Interruption Technique For Non-Stop Talkers

Salespeople are trained to let prospective customers do most of the talking during the "interest phase." But if a customer rambles for too long, ask a question that will get the discussion back on track. *Key:* When the customer takes a breath, say the person's name. This will stop the monologue, and be received in a positive way. Acknowledge what the person has been saying, followed by the question. *Example:* "Joe…I see this point is really important to you. Something else I'd like to ask you is…"

Source: Brian Jeffrey, an Ottawa-based sales trainer and consultant, and publisher, *SalesTalk,* 1451 Donald Munro Dr., Carp, Ontario K0A 1L0 Canada.

Better Telephoning

When calling someone, never ask "Did I catch you at a bad time?" For busy people, it's always a bad time. And if the other party doesn't want to talk to you, you give them an excuse not to. They can say it's a bad time whether it is or not. If your call is important enough to make, get right into it.

Source: Harry Newton, publisher, *Teleconnect,* 12 W. 21 St., New York 10010.

11

Office Equipment

Never Assume a Voice-Mail Message Was Delivered

The voice-mail system may have crashed after you sent the message…the message may have been accidentally deleted or gotten lost amid a crowd of other messages…the recipient may have written down the message, erased it from voice mail and then lost it…the intended recipient may have been out of the office, and failed to call in.

Source: Harry Newton, publisher, *Teleconnect,* 12 W. 21 St., New York 10010.

Reduce Long-Distance Costs

Reduce long-distance costs—without changing carriers. Small companies can cut long-dis-

tance costs by up to 25% by subcontracting with a reseller of their carrier's services. *Example:* General Electric and Hertz offer contracts for AT&T services.

How it works: Under deregulation, high-volume users of long-distance services that qualify for the lowest rates are permitted to resell those services. The reselling companies make a commission, while their customers get higher discounts than they could qualify for on their own. *To find a corporation that resells phone services:* Contact a telephone consultant in your area.

Source: Shirley Reif, controller, Crest Foods Co., Inc., dry-food manufacturers, Ashton, IL, quoted in *The Cost Controller,* 525 Cayuga St., Storm Lake, IA 50588.

The Myth Behind High-Speed Modems

New high-speed modems that transmit at 28,800 bits per second (bps) are not twice as fast as the now-standard 14,400 bps modems. Most phone lines can't carry data fast enough to utilize the high-speed modems' full capabilities. In practice, 28,800 bps modems run about 60% faster than 14,400 bps modems—a significant speed-up, but not as much as many buyers expect.

Source: Harry Newton, publisher, *Teleconnect*, 12 W. 21 St., New York 10010.

How to Buy Office Furniture Better

Office furniture is an investment that amazing numbers of businesses make with virtually no research or analysis. Not until it's too late do these companies realize—to their regret—that office furniture is a major factor in overall productivity, employee morale and public image. Guidelines to help the company make prudent and cost-effective office-furniture buys...

• *Systems furniture.* The largest single segment of today's $8 billion office furniture market is systems furniture. Systems are based on a set of elements combining work surfaces, partitions, pedestals, panel-hung components and free-standing desks, tables and filing and storage units. These modules can be mixed and matched in many different ways.

This provides a great degree of flexibility, enabling the company to change office layout over the years as it reorganizes in response to changing business conditions.

Systems are made by many manufacturers. When considering a furniture purchase, begin by contacting a number of different dealers and manufacturers to see their products. Ask for price lists, as well as brochures, to decide which lines fit your budget. *Top manufacturers:*

• *Allsteel, Inc.*, Allsteel Dr., Aurora, Illinois 60507, 708-859-2600.

• *Haworth, Inc.*, One Haworth Center, Holland, Michigan 49423, 800-344-2600.

• *Herman Miller*, 855 E. Main Ave., Box 302, Zeeland, Michigan 49464, 800-851-1196.

• *Steelcase, Inc.*, Box 1967, Grand Rapids, Michigan 49501, 800-227-2960.

Once you have a general idea of what is available in the marketplace, go back to the office and carefully research the company's specific needs.

How to assess needs:

Review the activities of your company and how they affect the furniture needs of each group of employees. *Useful questions:*

• Must the new furniture fit into the existing office layout?

• How often does the company reorganize work units? The more often furniture will be moved around, the sturdier it must be.

• What equipment must the office layout incorporate?

Examples: The number of power cables... phone lines...data lines.

• How much filing and storage is necessary ...and what must be stored?

• What activities must be done at each desk?

Examples: Using a computer...telephone work...mail sorting.

• Is visual and/or sound privacy needed by some employees?

• Do any employees have disabilities that require additional equipment?

Helpful: If the company does not have an in-house designer and no one has the time to learn about office furniture, consider hiring a consultant.

A space-planning consultant will help design the new furniture layout, determine the exact specifications for the furniture you need and select a supplier.

To find one: Contact the local Chamber of Commerce, ask companies in the area for references and/or check the *Yellow Pages*.

Caution: Many furniture dealers provide design services. But the advice you receive may be more objective if you hire an independent space planner.

Research the product:

When the company's needs have been determined, look through the manufacturers' brochures to see which lines seem most suitable. Before making a decision, take the following steps:

•Consult the people in your company who will be using the furniture. Show them the specs to determine whether the furniture satisfies their needs.

Example: After one company had new furniture installed, it was discovered that the drawers in the new storage units were too small to accommodate the large binders of statistical information used by many of the employees.

•Ask for references from other companies who have several years' experience using the line you are considering. Ask these references how well the furniture is wearing...if they have had any problems...how good the service is.

•Assess the quality of the furniture by examining it at an office where it has been installed. Take along some of the employees who will be using the new furniture to see how comfortable and functional they find it.

Possibility: To assess durability, visit the factory where the furniture is made and form an impression of the quality of the materials and the workmanship.

•Do some research on the manufacturer's financial status to gain confidence that the company will still be in business and able to supply parts for as long as your company expects to own the furniture.

How to choose a dealer:

Over the life of the new office furniture, your company will have more contact with the dealer than with the manufacturer.

After deciding which line of furniture to buy, choose the dealer that is right for you by...

•Considering a wide variety of dealers who offer products from your chosen manufacturer.

•Contacting all of the references each dealer provides. Ask the references about their satisfaction with the dealer...the quality of installation...the service.

•Checking out the dealer's financial background and stability through Dun & Bradstreet.

•Visiting several sites where the dealer has installed products.

•Finding out how the dealer operates.

Examples: Can the dealer handle large-volume purchases? Is delivery subcontracted out? Are installations and repairs done by in-house staff or subcontracted out?

Effective: Before placing a large order with a dealer, try a small test order. See if your expectations for quality, dependability of service and delivery time are met.

Negotiating strategies:

As with most products, the bigger the order, the better the discount you can expect.

A recent survey found that for office-furniture orders under $5,000, discounts were typically between 25% and 40%, while orders over $5 million received discounts of over 50%.

Delivery problem: Purchasers must often wait much longer for their new furniture than expected. Dealers typically promise delivery within two to ten weeks, but the furniture often arrives late.

Some manufacturers offer "quick-ship" programs that deliver in-stock items in less than two weeks. But this usually applies only to a limited number of standard items.

Solutions: Order furniture well in advance of when it is actually needed...make the dealer specify delivery time in writing.

Cheaper alternative—used furniture:

It is often possible to save 50% to 70% of the cost of new furniture by buying refurbished furniture.

While there are companies that sell only refurbished furniture, there are also divisions of major office-furniture manufacturers, such as Steelcase and Herman Miller, that also refurbish used furniture and resell it.

Depending on the condition of the old pieces, refurbishing can involve anything from simple cleaning to substantial rebuilding.

Added advantage: Delivery time for refurbished furniture is generally two to three weeks. Refurbishers often have a large range of products, although it may take some time to find the best ones.

Source: Lynda Perini, associate editor, Buyers Laboratory, Inc., an independent office-products testing laboratory, 20 Railroad Ave., Hackensack, NJ 07601.

Advertising on The Internet

Until recently, advertising agencies made a living by negotiating favorable advertising rates with the media, marking up those rates and then charging their clients those marked-up rates. The agency was not paid according to how effective its ads were or how much business they generated. The compensation was based on volume rather than results.

But now—in the dawning of the era of electronic media, advertising is taking on a whole new character. Advertisers must revolutionize their thinking to make their promotional dollars work in this exciting new business environment.

Cyberspace:

What's there?

Before we can go into detail about advertising in cyberspace, it is important to mention some of the terrain's unique features...

•Everything is completely countable. Like an amusement park, it is easy to figure out how many people come through and which rides are the most popular. However, unlike an amusement park, in the electronic-information world it is possible to figure out how long each person spends in the park, how long it takes an individual to decide what to ride next, when a person decides to eat lunch and where he/she sits down to rest his/her feet.

•It is next door to wherever you are right now. *Interesting statistic:* Fifty percent of all Americans live within a tankful of gas of America's new gambling Valhalla—Atlantic City. And that, no doubt, accounts for the "why" of Atlantic City. In cyberspace, however, Orlando, Las Vegas and Paris, Texas, are all just a "point and click" away from each other.

•The infrastructure is very inexpensive. You've heard the word that computers are commodity products. Sufficient bandwidth, the capacity to carry everything back and forth, is already installed as telephone lines or cable. All the hype about building the information superhighway is just that—hype. That's because it's already here.

•Anything goes. There are no ground rules for advertising on the information superhighway because no one has any idea what will work and what won't. After perhaps a decade of using the computer to present information, we only have a faint inkling about what is successful, and even less insight about why. Therefore, the work that demands the most imagination and discipline still lies ahead of us.

Cyberspace and...media/sponsors/content/audience:

When Gutenberg invented the printing press and Marconi invented radio, it took a generation or more to build up a critical mass of experience to guide people who wanted to put the medium to work. Even today, the world of print media continues to evolve.

So—from today's perspective, it would be impossible to describe the specific methodology of advertising on the Internet. However, there are some general principles to at least consider before making a bet one way or another, especially when it is your company's money...

•Determine whether you are on the buy side or the sell side. *Consider this:* You run a successful national business magazine. You see other magazines and media properties signing up with large online information aggregators such as America Online, CompuServe or Prodigy. You make a call and learn that the cost of putting the editorial content of your magazine online is minimal. You think this might be a pretty good way to build magazine subscriptions, which is, traditionally, a very expensive and inefficient process.

Trap: If you sign up with one of these services, the service will have become more valuable at your cost.

Better: Ask to be paid a share of the increased income generated by having your company online.

•Sponsors will no longer pay for the physical space their advertisements occupy. In cyberspace, the actual costs of this space—disk space and bandwidth—is completely trivial. Instead, sponsors will pay for the value they receive. *They will pay for...*

•Only the number of people who actually see their advertisement. This will create a whole new meaning for the advertising measure of cost per million or cost-per-thousand.

•The names of the people who see their ads. There certainly won't be an invasion of the audience's privacy. But sponsors and media have always been able to motivate members of the audience to offer their names.

•Only the direct value they receive. The sponsor will sell goods and services through the media and pay the media a commission on the amount sold.

•Advertising agencies will have to refocus their business—away from the media-buying model to one where they are charging only for creative services. However, agencies will be required to assume more risk—in exchange for being eligible for much greater reward.

Key: The ability to accurately measure the effectiveness of an individual advertisement will enable clients to reward the agency based on the precise sales generated by that ad.

•Sponsorship will be a big deal in electronic advertising. Sponsors have already assumed this role. *For example...*

•During the past winter Olympics, Sun Microsystems sponsored the complete results to thousands of people on a daily basis. In fact, this was so successful, they sponsored the results of the World Cup soccer tournament.

•In November of 1994, Digital Equipment Corp. sponsored the election results for the state of California, and provided candidates the opportunity to stump in cyberspace.

•Pepsi sponsored Woodstock '94 in cyberspace.

Bottom line: Every day, thousands of people turn on their computers, tune in their own personal cyberspace channel and drop out of the consumer media patterns of yesterday.

Where to begin:

The following steps will help the company decide whether advertising on the Internet makes sense...

•*Explore.* Get your own Internet access and jump in to the deep end of the pool. Until you become an educated consumer, it is impossible to decide whether you have something to say to the world, much less how to say it.

To get started, contact the Internet specialists at any of the major online services, such as Prodigy, CompuServe and America Online. They all have experts who are able to help companies get started in the business of marketing on the Internet.

Alternative: Find local advertising agencies that have developed specialties in Internet marketing. They can be found through trade associations or via references from companies that are already using the Internet to sell their products or services.

•*Decide.* At the very least, the Internet is a tremendous resource for research, and this alone justifies the investment in access. But, realistically, given the low cost of putting the Internet to work as a marketing communications medium, it is hard to resist trying it out. *Options:*

•*E-mail.* Because of the way Internet technology was created, no one knows how many people are on the Internet. *But one thing is certain:* Everyone has an E-mail account. Therefore, the simplest and most far-reaching marketing technique is to build what are called "mailbots." Think of them as the cyberspace equivalent of "fax-on-demand" service. People will write to an address and then automatically receive information in return. These can start out simple and become tremendously complex, depending on the need. And, of course, it is a tremendous way to build a mailing list.

•*Mailing lists.* On a completely voluntary basis—and this is a key point—people can subscribe to a mailing list. The voluntary part is important because to simply send out unsolicited mail willy-nilly is considered a breach of "netiquette" that will cause irreparable damage to a company's image in cyberspace.

•*Newsgroups.* Given enough appeal, it might pay to create a newsgroup or bulletin board on the Internet that focuses on topics related to your company or products. This is a fantastic way to hold a public dialogue with customers and prospects, as long as a company can live with both the good and bad feedback. And, given the fact that there are more than 10,000 newsgroups, the odds are good that there are at least one or two already established that are relevant to your business. However, keep in mind that fewer people have access to newsgroups than they do mail.

• *Gopher*. It is an odd name for a service that presents information in a simple, menu-driven format. The type of information that can be stored and presented this way includes anything that can be saved to a computer disk—brochures, overhead presentations, photographs. But even fewer people have access to Gopher than they do newsgroups.

• *The Worldwide Web*. This is a forum for presenting information in a way that's dramatically different from any of the other ways described above. First, the Worldwide Web lets people create pages of information that include different type sizes and illustrations, much like very rudimentary newsletter pages. The second difference is that the Worldwide Web lets people link together different pieces of information in a way known as "hypertext."

The best way to describe what hypertext does is by referring to the chain reference of an encyclopedia where, at the end of an article, there are references to other articles of related interest.

Source: Brian Johnson, director of Internet Services, Alexander Communications, 25 Lake St., White Plains, NY 10603. He is also a freelance correspondent covering information technology for the CBS News program, *Up to the Minute.*

E-Mail Libel

Electronic-mail messages placed on computer bulletin boards are deemed published, so they may be deemed libelous. And a company may incur liability for messages sent through its computer system by employees.

Safety: Kodak does not allow employees to post Internet messages using the Kodak return address. Other firms add a "not speaking for the company" disclaimer to each message. But these are only partial defenses—harassing or libelous messages sent through the company's computers may still create liability.

Best: Inform employees of the risk, then set and enforce standards for E-mail use.

Source: Robert L. Mirguet, information security manager, Eastman Kodak Co., Rochester, New York, quoted in *Computerworld*, 375 Cochituate Rd., Framingham, Massachusetts 01701.

Smart PC Shopping Strategies

With new desktop PC standards and specifications appearing at a dizzying pace, how can the company be sure that the computer it buys today will be able to run tomorrow's software?

No computer lasts forever, but finding a system that will serve the company well over the next five or six years is an attainable goal.

Key: The trick to buying PCs that will meet the company's needs both today and tomorrow lies in some basic and easy-to-follow guidelines...

• *Choose the right processor.* The PC's "heart" is now easily upgradeable. While older PCs were locked in to their original processor, newer 486 and Pentium computers can readily accommodate more powerful chips as they become available.

Important: Considering the rapid pace of processor evolution, it makes no sense to buy a machine equipped with processors less powerful than a Pentium chip. If money is a problem, consider buying a PC that uses a Pentium-upgradeable 486 processor—and upgrade later, when additional cash is available.

• *Invest in memory-expansion slots.* The more of these the machine has, the more modems, printers and other peripherals can be added on internally. But you'll have to give up desk space to accommodate the larger "footprint" of a PC with five or more slots.

Generally, "low-profile" desktop systems offer fewer slots than full-size desktop PCs.

Helpful: Consider buying a "mini-tower" system. These units sit on the floor and leave your desk clear of computer hardware, except for a keyboard, monitor and mouse or trackball.

• *Buy additional drive bays.* These PC features allow for the eventual addition of an extra floppy, hard-disk or tape-backup drive, as well as a CD-ROM unit (if the system wasn't pre-equipped with one).

• *Buy adequate hard-disk capacity.* The rule of thumb among experienced computer users is that you'll always need 10MB more storage capacity than your current hard-disk provides. These days, with operating systems like Windows and OS/2 gobbling up dozens of megabytes of space, and even modest applications requiring 5MB to 10MB of capacity, your best bet is to buy a PC with a 500MB—or larger—hard disk.

• *Don't buy just any old monitor.* PC monitors come in two basic types—interlaced and noninterlaced. A noninterlaced monitor is easier on the eyes.

Also pay close attention to a monitor's "dot pitch"—the spacing between the screen's color phosphors. Dot pitch typically ranges from 0.21 to 0.39 of an inch. The smaller the pitch, the sharper the image and the less eyestrain.

Monitors come in various sizes, with the most popular being 14, 15 and 17 inches. If the company's operations involve desktop-publishing work, the 17-inch screen is important. Otherwise, save $200 or $300 by opting for a 14- or 15-inch display.

• *Consider adding a CD-ROM drive.* All PC CD-ROM drives offer the same storage capacity. The biggest difference between models is the speed at which they retrieve and move data into the PC. Most current CD-ROM drives are labeled as "double-speed" units, but several companies have started offering "triple-speed" and even "quadruple-speed" units. A triple-speed drive offers the best trade-off between price and performance.

• *Boost computing speed with added memory.* While most newer Windows programs require at least 8MB of RAM, many manufacturers try to trim costs by packing only 4MB of RAM into their systems. For maximum efficiency, and to keep pace with the growing demands of PC software, consider equipping new PCs with 16MB of RAM.

• *Shop at volume outlets.* Computer superstores, such as CompUSA and Computer City, generally offer better technical support and more knowledgeable salespeople than consumer electronics chains. They can also configure a system to meet your specific needs.

Most also have separate departments dedicated to business computing.

Warehouse outlets, such as Sam's Club and Price Club, target home-computer shoppers with "bargain" systems that usually incorporate older or discontinued technology.

Mail-order computer shopping is an approach best left to computer users who can order and install a system without much outside help.

Source: John Edwards, a computer industry analyst and freelance writer on high-tech subjects, based in Mount Laurel, NJ.

Internet Harassment Is on the Rise

Never give out your name, phone number, etc., in an online computer forum. *Problem:* Creeps pretend to be friendly and gain trust. Harassment and pranks may follow. *Self-defense:* Use a pseudonym...supervise children and explain dangers...meet a new computer acquaintance in a public place. If harassed, don't respond. Ask the service to block messages, and contact the police.

Source: Frank Clark is a detective with the economic- and computer-crimes unit of the Fresno, California, Police Department.

Internet Cost Trap

The electronic superhighway is rapidly becoming a costly drain on productivity and financial resources.

Employees are spending more and more hours aimlessly searching the Internet for business information because they lack the necessary know-how and training to efficiently focus their efforts.

To take advantage of this vast information opportunity and avoid major problems, companies should formally train those employees who must use electronic-information sources for research in how to use these vast resources efficiently and economically.

Source: Leonard Fuld, business-intelligence consultant, Cambridge, Massachusetts.

The Great Information Superhighway Can Work Wonders for Your Company, Too

It's the new catchphrase you can't escape: "The information superhighway." While online communications are getting plenty of media coverage, few managers have any experience with the world of bits, bauds and modems.

And...fewer still have received any tangible business benefits from cyberspace technology.

For most companies, the greatest value of online communications is, of course, the ability to instantaneously access business news wires, government and business information databases, industry publications and a wide range of other information resources.

However, finding and retrieving information in the electronic jungle is akin to hacking through a rain forest with a pocketknife. If you're thinking of hitching a ride on the "info-bahn," here is key information you should have...

The basics: There are three major commercial online services—America Online (800-827-6364), CompuServe (800-848-8199) and Prodigy (800-776-3449).

To access these networks, all you need is a computer and a modem. Communications

software is usually supplied at no additional cost with the modem and/or service.

The Internet—perhaps the most publicized part of the information superhighway—isn't a commercial information service, but a network of separate computers operated by companies, universities, government agencies and other organizations. The Internet is a vast, unregulated place in which business information gems are "hidden" among piles of digital junk. All of the major online services provide "gateways" to various portions of the Internet.

Important: The best way to find business information on the Internet is with the help of an "Internet Yellow Pages," such as *The Internet Directory* by Eric Braun (1994, Fawcett Columbine) and *NetGuide* by Peter Rutten, Albert F. Bayers III and Kelly Maloni (1994, Random House Electronic Publishing).

Paying your "toll" on the information superhighway can be a headache.

Online-service pricing makes cable-TV subscription rates seem simple and understandable.

Generally, you can expect to pay $8 to $15 per month for electronic mail and access to several basic features. There may be an extra charge for access to most business database services. The typical individual user can expect monthly charges of between $30 and $100—although prices can quickly spiral much higher if the user decides to conduct lengthy and detailed information searches. Access to the Internet is usually provided on a cost-per-minute basis and is billed by credit card through the online service.

Richest information gold mines:

• *Business news.* All three major online services offer continuously updated business and financial news, including reports from the Associated Press, Dow Jones, United Press International, Reuters and other wire services. Additionally, CompuServe members can take advantage of several magazine and newsletter services that offer users access to articles—in a variety of fields—dating back several years.

• *Mailing lists.* The Internet contains thousands of mailing-list services that will send subscribers regular updates on topics ranging from microelectronics research in Israel to total quality management theory.

Usually sponsored by major universities and corporations, these mailing lists are typically free except for the amount the online service charges for connect time and electronic mail.

• *Business databases.* Access to vast amounts of "archival" data is CompuServe's strong point. Users can retrieve company profiles, credit reports and other types of information from such diverse sources as Standard & Poor's, Citibank, Dun & Bradstreet and TRW. Many business publications maintain a "presence" on Compu-Serve.

Prodigy offers *Dun & Bradstreet Solutions*, which provides detailed information on a range of companies. The data can be used to find new business leads, target businesses for direct mail or research competitors and customers.

America Online's business database resources are on the skimpy side. But the service is growing quickly and the situation is likely to change in the near future.

All three major online services provide stock quotes on a time-delayed basis, in addition to online trading capabilities.

• *Networking opportunities.* All of the services, plus the Internet, enable users to communicate with other users through electronic mail and various types of online bulletin boards.

Example: On Prodigy, the "Your Business Bulletin Board" allows users to discuss business management, marketing, accounting, taxes, insurance and numerous other topics with fellow users.

Caution: While online bulletin boards are great places to brainstorm ideas with fellow business pros, it's important to be on guard, since you never know for sure who's giving you advice.

• *Demographics reports.* CompuServe offers services that provide demographics reports on all Standard Industrial Classification (SIC) categories. CompuServe subscribers can access ZIP-code neighborhood reports, state and county reports and various types of government-sponsored research.

• *Travel information.* Subscribers to all three services can view national and international airline schedules and make reservations through American Airlines' Eaasy Sabre Network. Users can also book hotel reservations and reserve rental cars while online.

Bottom line: For detailed information on online communications, check your local bookstore or library for a newcomer's guide. Two good titles are *Cruising Online* by Lawrence J. Magid (1994, Random House Electronic Publishing) and *Get Online* by Lamont Wood (1993, John Wiley & Sons).

Source: John Edwards, a computer-industry analyst and freelance writer on high-tech subjects, based in Mount Laurel, New Jersey.

Keeping It Confidential

Secure E-mail and other confidential computer messages with encryption software such as AT&T's *SecretAgent* software. It employs state-of-the-art public-key encryption technology. *How it works:* Each user has two "keys," a public key and a private key. The public key is made openly available and anyone can use it to send a coded message to the user. But only the user's private key can decode the message. The code is practically unbreakable with existing technology by any party lacking the private key. *Ease of use:* The program works with Windows, and automatically encodes every message using the public key of the recipient. It can be used with laptops, PCs and workstations.

Source: Mark Bentley, information-systems analyst, Techmatics, naval engineers, Fairfax, Virginia, quoted in *Security Management*, 1655 N. Fort Myer Dr., Arlington, Virginia 22209.

Replacing Passwords

For better computer security, replace passwords with "passphrases" that may include punctuation, numbers and upper and lower case letters. *Risk:* Typical passwords of eight or fewer characters can be easily broken by hackers who use programs that quickly run through all possible combinations. But each character added to the passphrase increases the number of combinations to test exponentially, greatly reducing the chance it will be broken.

Source: Winn Schwartau, technology adviser to the National Computer Security Association, writing in *Security Management*, 1655 N. Fort Myer Dr., Arlington, Virginia 22209.

Foolproof PC Security Essentials

Internet invaders, computer viruses and snooping employees are all out to get the company's valuable data. But PCs can be turned into digital fortresses by following these pain-free steps:

•Use antivirus software on any computer that connects with or gets disks from another computer. *Windows* and *Windows 95* provide built-in antivirus programs. Run this software on a weekly basis to make sure PCs are safe and sound.

Important: To guard against new viruses, buy an antivirus product from a company that sends its customers regular updates.

•Use backups. Make frequent backups of vital data and store in a fireproof, theftproof location—preferably in another office or, better yet, in a separate building.

•Encrypt data. If someone does steal data, an encryption program will keep the thief from deciphering the information. One of the best programs is PGP 2.7.1, a product that's so powerful it is prohibited from foreign export under a federal munitions law.

Besides protecting hard and floppy disk data, encryption is a powerful tool for safeguarding information that's sent over in-house networks or public phone lines.

•Install password systems. The software prevents the unauthorized use of a PC and its resources by requiring its user to supply an ID and password.

Important: Avoid words that a hacker could successfully guess—such as the name of your company or a loved one.

Effective: Random letters make the best passwords, but can be difficult to remember. Instead, add extra protection by sticking a random number or punctuation mark in the middle of a password—such as "ICE6HOLIDAY" or "GROVER*JULY."

•Terminate idle connections. You would never leave your car running unattended. Likewise, you should never allow computers to be left unattended while they are connected to other PCs or to an on-line service or the Internet. An unguarded modem link is like an open door to a computer's data.

•Beef up physical security. To guard against "wandering disk syndrome," install a key-locked security device on all PC floppy disk drives.

A drive lock isn't foolproof, since the device can be pried open. The unit will, however, deter individuals who don't want to leave physical evidence of their crime.

Bottom line: Be determined and consistent in the company's security efforts. A halfhearted computer protection initiative makes about as much sense as closing a door halfway.

Source: John Edwards, a computer industry analyst and writer on high-tech subjects, based in Mount Laurel, New Jersey.

12

Winning Formulas

Winning Formulas: 1996…and Beyond

Edith Weiner, Weiner Edrich, Brown, Inc.

There are six truths about winning in the coming millenium—whether you're in business, just starting a career or planning future life changes…

- For every trend there is a countertrend. This applies especially to business. When it seems the competition is all going in a single direction, the really sharp business strategist spots an overlooked opportunity in an area far removed from where everyone else is headed.

Examples: The upscale market was suddenly very attractive in the 1980s because of the growing numbers of high income households. Most marketers flocked to satisfy this segment, but Wal-Mart and K-Mart were there to save money for those at the lower ends of the market. Today, many of the high-end companies are suffering because too many marketers are trying to capitalize on the upscale trend, and now those who went in the opposite direction are expanding and capturing the entire population.

The trend today is toward everyone being accessible all the time through portable electronic communications. Those marketers (e.g. retreats, excursions) that allow people to be inaccessible will gain in popularity. Most marketers did not recognize the handicap, but they are becoming a significant market with the passage of the Americans with Disabilities Act and new technologies that allow them to work more effectively. They are an ignored but fabulous countertrend market.

The astute person will learn to spot the fact that every trend actually sows the seeds of its own countertrend(s). For example, decades of secularism gave rise to the countertrend of religion and spirituality which is now very strong alongside secularism. And within the countertrend (religion and spirituality) there are two countertrends, each becoming stronger *because* of the other—fundamentalism and New Ageism. These are creating huge business opportunities from book sales to seminars.

• Compromise is often the unwinning approach to problem-solving. In business and personal life, we tend to take the easy way out in solving problems by settling for the compromise. The problem is that this often means settling for less. The winning option is almost always one that meets all the requirements of all parties.

Example: A couple setting out to choose a color to repaint their house needs to find a solution to the problem in which the husband favors the earthy colors, like green, while his wife is in love with cheerful colors, like yellow. The "easy" compromise would be to settle on chartreuse—a blend of green and yellow. But knowing that no sane person would do this, the two spend an entire weekend sifting through color samples in paint stores until they finally agree on an earthy *and* cheerful peach color they both like.

Another example: Your son asks you for $25 a week and you have already agreed that his allowance should be $15 a week. The compromise would be to give him $20, but that exceeds the level that you feel is acceptable and doesn't meet what he apparently needs for spending money. *Common denominator:* Give him $15 for allowance and find some way he can earn the other $10 each week, either from you or someone else.

The result is a long-lasting mutually satisfactory solution. It requires extra effort to find the real common denominator, but it's always better than taking the easy compromise.

• It is increasingly important to recognize and counteract your educated incapacity. *What it means:* People, by the time they've been working for 15 or 20 years, become so expert in a field that they lose sight of how that field is changing or how they must adapt to stay on top in their field.

Ironically, this is more often a weakness in smart people than it is in not-so-smart individuals. *Reason:* Most smart people have a hard time forgetting what they've learned so well. They become so knowledgeable about their area of expertise that they simply can't imagine excelling in any other way.

Helpful: Jot down the names of the ten people you most admire. Then scan the list, comparing each one with the next. If the entire list seems to be made up of people more or less the same, it's a clear sign that your outlook is also narrow. Try to acquaint yourself with different types of people…make an extra effort to experience new routines, new approaches to challenges, new reading material, etc.

Aim: To unlearn the constrained way of living your life…and to expose yourself to variety, stimulating alternatives and change.

• Good communication is critical to winning in coming years. Knowledge is clearly an important component of success today. But if you know all there is to know about a hot topic but can't explain it, you're not going to be a winner.

Today, and increasingly in the future, good communication equates with outstanding verbal skills, writing skills and computing skills. If you're weak in any or all of these, get to work.

• Networking is key. In coming years, who you know will be just as important as what you know. Of course, having marketable skills and knowledge about your industry is indispensible. But—if you possess wonderful management skills or computer skills or writing skills, etc., you're less likely to make the most profitable use of them if you don't have contacts who can help you find the best places to apply those skills.

Effective: Develop a program of making three new substantive contacts each month.

Key: These should be people you develop long-term relationships with…not superficial acquaintances. They should be people in your professional field or social circle whom you can call once every two months or so to see how they're doing.

Aim: To have a wide network of meaningful contacts at all times, so that when you really need help you won't be at a loss to find it.

• Become very comfortable with change. The pace of change—in technology…work environments…market trends, etc.—will continue to accelerate in the coming years. Individuals who are invigorated by change rather than intimidated by it will be the big winners.

Key: Being able to focus on the positive aspects of change—the opportunities and fresh energy that result from change.

Secrets of Happiness And Inner Peace

When I wrote *Your Erroneous Zones* nearly 20 years ago, the purpose of the book was to show people how to achieve true happiness. Back then, I said that happiness was only possible if you took charge of your inner feelings and exchanged negative thoughts for positive thoughts.

Today, most of my original thinking on the subject is still valid. But over the years, as our society and the world have changed, I've added another concept that is equally important—*the ability to get in touch with your higher self.*

Erroneous zones revisited:

Erroneous zones are the self-defeating behavior patterns that rob us of our happiness. For example, constantly seeking approval and giving in to guilt. We cling to our erroneous zones because maintaining deeply learned habits feels safe and secure. This behavior stands in the way of our personal growth.

You can overcome this self-defeating behavior by concentrating on the present rather than dwelling on the past or worrying about the future. The present is the only moment during which you can experience happiness—or misery—and the only moment over which you have any control.

Also important is understanding that feelings are reactions over which you *have* control. You choose your thoughts, and you are the sum total of these choices. I still urge people to take charge of their emotions by choosing the thoughts to which they react.

But today I emphasize how vital it is to distinguish from where these thoughts originate—the ego or the higher self.

Listening to your higher self:

The *ego* is the part of ourselves that keeps telling us that more is better—more money, more power, etc. Such self-absorption can create a lot of inner turmoil.

The *higher self* promotes the feeling of peace. The higher self wants you to enjoy rather than strive endlessly...to relate honestly with others ...to feel connected by love, rather than separated by fear. By listening to your higher self, you will have more power...you will be free to choose intelligently...and be able to see more confidently.

Four steps to higher self:

• *Shut down your inner dialogue.* It has been estimated that we think 60,000 thoughts each day. The trouble is that most of them are pretty much the same thoughts we had yesterday.

Examples: Taxes, laundry, shopping, conversations, upcoming meetings.

Just below this constant stream of chatter in your brain is a space of calm and quiet. You don't have to go into a cave and meditate to connect with this quiet space. You can do it anywhere.

Strategy: Take a moment of silence—a break from the barrage of analyzing your thoughts. *Ideal:* A ten-minute walk. The key is to become aware of the thoughts as they pass through your mind, and the space between the thoughts. Your pulse will slow, your blood pressure will drop. You'll feel relaxed and in charge of your emotions.

• *Banish your doubts.* To eliminate doubt, recognize the difference between what you *believe* and what you *know.*

Beliefs: These opinions are handed to you by other people—usually your parents, your teachers, etc. It's important to realize that whatever your objective in life, beliefs won't get you there. A belief is a guess, and there is doubt associated with a guess because it comes from outside you.

Knowledge: This is the opposite of doubt. What you *know* comes from within...that is, it comes from your direct experience.

In a relationship, for example, doubt may lead you to dwell on what you don't like or what irritates you about the person with whom you're involved.

But if your inner mind is filled with the *knowledge* of who your partner is—if you can fully accept that what you love are the parts that make him/her unique—your doubt will disappear.

• *Cultivate the witness in you.* There are two people living within you...

• One who thinks, moves and acts.

• An innermost self that just observes. This allows you to study yourself objectively.

Strategy: Learn to step outside yourself by using visualization. Instead of being completely absorbed in everything that is happening to you, try to cultivate the part of you that stands a little apart.

The process of being an *observer* of yourself cuts through the nonsense of even the most tense and heated meetings. You will find that you are able to laugh inwardly at the absurdity of it all.

Surprisingly, it is a position of great power. You will be able to see what has to be done, what the opposition to your goals will be and that other people are getting worked up. You will be able to talk less and listen more.

I never learned anything while talking. If you become peaceful and sure of yourself, you'll convey that to those around you.

• *Tame your ego.* Anything that offends you is the result of your ego clashing with what you've heard or experienced. By taming your ego, you will experience that higher self that deserves love. With nothing to prove, you won't need approval and you'll feel special when you know that all human beings are special. *Strategies...*

• Work at not being offended and allow other people to be who they actually are. Strive for tolerance rather than dominance, and you'll go in peace rather than turmoil. Practice the highest level of heightened awareness—being independent of the good opinion of other people.

• Use "I" as infrequently as possible. Instead, keep your conversation focused on the other person.

• Forfeit your need to always be right. When you have the choice between being right or being kind, always choose to be kind. Letting go of your need to judge and dominate can incredibly transform relationships.

Source: Wayne Dyer, PhD, a psychotherapist in Fort Lauderdale whose book *Your Erroneous Zones* (HarperCollins, Ten E. 53 St., New York 10022) has sold more than six million copies. He is the author of nine books, including *Everyday Wisdom,* Hay House, 1154 E. Dominguez St., Carson, California 90746.

Spare Moments Can Be Very Valuable to You

We all have more time on our hands than we think we do. The key is to make use of the small intervals that we typically overlook—time between meetings...in waiting rooms...or standing on line at the store.

What you can do in five minutes:

• Read your mail.

• Set up your monthly appointment calendar.

• Start the guest list for an upcoming client reception.

What you can do in 10 minutes:

• Think of ways to solve a particular problem at work.

• Write a letter or memo.

• Scan a newsletter.

• Give yourself a brain break. Sometimes the best use of time is just to look out the window and do nothing at all.

What you can do in 30 minutes:

• Skim a report, and mark the parts that need future study.

• Read journals, newspapers and magazines that you haven't gotten to.

• Take a few bites out of a complex project.

Example: If you have a speech to write for an upcoming conference, use this time to jot down some preliminary thoughts on the subject.

Other time-savers:

Start your morning the night before. You'll get out the door faster—and with less hassle—if you minimize the number of decisions you have to make under pressure.

Strategy: Review your schedule for the following day and make notes. Before you go to bed, put coffee in the coffee-maker...set out a nonperishable breakfast, such as a bowl of dry cereal...choose the clothes you'll wear the next day...and pack your briefcase, and place it by the front door.

Source: Stephanie Winston, president of The Organizing Principle, a time-management consulting firm, 230 E. 15 St., New York 10003. Her book is *Stephanie Winston's Best Organizing Tips,* Simon & Schuster.

Mastering the Fine Art of Conflict Resolution

During the course of our personal relationships and business dealings, at least some conflict is inescapable because differences inevitably emerge…but not all conflict is bad.

Conflict need not be adversarial—where one side wins and the other loses. It should be regarded as just one part of a broader relationship in which two partners seek to use their diversity in a mutually beneficial way.

Arriving at that mutually rewarding outcome is not easy…but it is far more rewarding than being locked in hostility. It requires adopting a new outlook on conflict and practicing specific skills that are used in the following techniques of conflict resolution…

1. *Create an effective atmosphere.* Begin by making it clear that the aim of conflict resolution is to change the relationship of *I vs. You* to *We*, a mutually rewarding outcome.

Even if only one party starts out with that perception, the conflict can be resolved successfully. As the process continues, the other party will be drawn in when it sees how its needs can be met. It is essential to begin the process with an opening statement to make the objective clear.

Example: "I know we both feel strongly about this issue. I just want you to know that I am not looking at this situation as a battle between us, but as a chance for us to work together to resolve this particular conflict and improve our relationship."

Helpful: Meet at a time when both partners can devote full attention to the process… choose a setting where both parties feel comfortable.

Example: If company management is negotiating with dissatisfied workers, don't meet in the plush executive boardroom—it looks like an attempt at intimidation.

2. *Clarify perceptions.* Each conflict partner tries to understand his/her own needs as well as the other partner's needs and perceptions of the conflict.

While they do not need to force a common perception of the conflict, both sides need to clarify what they think the conflict is about. Then they can determine if there really is a conflict and work together to understand how important that conflict is to the relationship and what needs to be done to make each side feel better.

If they perceive the conflict differently, each side can do something to help the other deal with its perception. And there will still be some shared needs in the relationship that they can work on together.

For perspective: Look beyond the immediate conflict and define the other side by more than just its current negative behavior. Think about the positive potential of a partnership.

3. *Focus on individual and shared needs.* The conflict partners discuss their individual needs and how the conflict affects their common needs. These common needs can serve as building blocks to replacing conflict with cooperation.

Important: Needs—things critical to your well-being—are not the same as desires—things you would like to have.

4. *Build shared positive power.* Parties involved in a conflict try to use negative power—the ability to gain an advantage over the other side. Conflict resolution aims for positive power—the ability to work with the other person.

When power over is replaced by power with—and conflict partners recognize that they need each other—it drives conflict resolution.

Example: Frank, a college professor, is great at research but terrible at paperwork. One day, he received a note from Beverly, an administrative assistant who works in the dean's office, telling him that his grant would be terminated unless he submitted his overdue budget promptly.

Frank went to see Beverly. Instead of trying to pull rank (a negative power tactic), he admitted he could not finish the budget in time and asked if she could help him. When she said she was already swamped, Frank offered to persuade the dean to pay her overtime to straighten out his budget. This mutually beneficial arrangement was an example of positive power.

5. *Look to the future...learn from the past.* Conflict partners often attack each other about past problems. Learning where the relationship went wrong in the past and discussing how it could have been handled better makes the past a tool—instead of a weapon—to derive lessons for a better future relationship.

Example: "I am sure we both could have done some things better in the past. How do you think we could have handled this disagreement better?"

6. *Generate options.* The conflict partners brainstorm creative new ideas to meet their needs. Then they cut that list down and find the key options that...

• Meet one or more shared needs.

• Meet one party's needs and are compatible with the other party's needs.

• Require active participation by at least one party to be implemented.

• Have the potential to improve the future relationship.

• Are acceptable to both parties.

7. *Develop doables.* These are modest but practical suggestions that build trust and serve as stepping stones toward wider agreement.

Example: When working as a community organizer in an inner-city neighborhood, I found that the different factions could not agree on any major community project. We identified one modest doable—installing lights on the ten most dangerous streets. It was a valuable first step because it required all of the groups to cooperate to get City Hall to agree, thus helping to build the mutual trust needed for more ambitious community-development projects.

8. *Make mutually beneficial agreements.* After proceeding through the earlier stages and taking small steps together, you and your conflict partner have reached the goal. You can now develop mutually beneficial agreements to resolve specific conflicts because of your improved relationship.

Each partner is aware of the other's needs as well as his/her own and is willing to negotiate flexibly by searching for agreement rather than making rigid demands. You have turned conflict from a problem into an opportunity.

Source: Dudley Weeks, PhD, professor of conflict resolution at American University School of International Service, Washington, DC. He has worked with conflicting parties in more than 60 countries. He is the author of *The Eight Essential Steps to Conflict Resolution: Preserving Relationships at Work, at Home and in the Community*, Jeremy P. Tarcher/Putnam, 5858 Wilshire Blvd., Los Angeles 90036.

Better Decision-Making

Questions to ask yourself before making up your mind about anything important...

• Is the information I've gathered timely, accurate and complete?

• What is my objective in making this decision?

• What will happen if the objective is not achieved?

• Once the decision is made, how will it be executed?

• What can go wrong during the execution of the decision?

• What future decisions will be necessary as a result of this first decision?

Source: *Hit the Ground Running: Communicate Your Way to Business Success* by Cynthia Kreuger, communications consultant in Wheaton, Illinois, Brighton Publications, Box 120706, St. Paul 55112.

The Greatest Time Wasters

Most people who have trouble managing time at work face similar disruptions. *The biggest time wasters and how to avoid them...*
Interruptions:

There are two ways to minimize drop-ins and telephone calls:

• *Create privacy.* Every day, schedule an hour for priority tasks. Set up your environment so that you can't be reached during that time. Transfer all your calls to voice mail or the receptionist…duck into an empty office or conference room…leave the premises and work in a public library or park…put a sign on your door that says "Working—please call or stop by later."

Some executives have worked out other creative ways to ensure privacy.

•*Minimize interruptions.*

On the phone: After a friendly greeting, start with "What can I do for you?" rather than "How are you?" Also—practice polite conversation-enders such as "Let me recap those points… Thanks for the information…I'll talk to you soon."

In person: Hold spontaneous meetings in other people's offices rather than in your own —it's easier to excuse yourself from someone else's office than to kick somebody out of yours. And if someone drops into your office, stand up and walk them out the door as if you were leaving.

Procrastination:

Most procrastination occurs because a task seems overwhelming.

Solution: Break big tasks into smaller parcels. *Ways to do it:*

•*Chunking.* Identify the components of a job. Tackle them one at a time.

Example: For a transportation report, elements might include research history of monorails, draw up outline, draft introduction, etc.

•*Set aside time.* Allocate a time period that you devote to the project. One entrepreneur spent every Sunday morning from 6 AM to 8 AM —her only "free time"—preparing her business plan.

Meetings:

Unnecessary or rambling meetings are probably the worst time wasters. *To keep meetings from eating up valuable time…*

•*Eliminate any unnecessary meetings from your schedule.* Hold meetings by conference call, if possible…don't attend meetings at which your presence isn't mandatory…when you do attend and if it is not offensive to others, stay only as long as the discussion is relevant to you.

•*Set an action agenda.* When you're in charge of a formal meeting, have a list of meeting objectives and topics typed and distributed in advance. Note which papers and other information participants should bring.

•*Set time limits.* Start at the announced time, even if not everyone is present. Colleagues will recognize you're serious about punctuality. Five minutes before the meeting is scheduled to close, review decisions and assignments.

Helpful: Meetings held shortly before lunch or at the end of the workday provide built-in time limits.

Source: Stephanie Winston, president of The Organizing Principle, a time-management consulting firm, 230 E. 15 St., NY. She is the author of *The Organized Executive—New Ways to Manage Time, Paper, People and the Electronic Office,* Warner Books, 1271 Avenue of the Americas, New York.

How to Get Control of Your Time and Your Life

Those who achieve the most in this world are not those with the highest IQs…not those with the greatest natural skills…not those who work hardest…but those who make the best use of their time.

Interestingly, the search to find better ways to use your time each day is not a recent phenomenon.

Americans were grappling with the issue two decades ago, when Alan Lakein, a leading expert on personal time management, wrote *How to Get Control of Your Time and Your Life.*

The book is still a rich resource when looking for ways to create and to make better use of time…and to decide what you really want to do with your time.

Choosing how to use time:

The key to taking control of your time is to make conscious decisions. Mr. Lakein explains that all too often, we tend to make decisions by default. We let outside forces decide for us, continue long-outmoded routines and limit our options by waiting until the last minute.

Too often, we don't do what we really want because we don't think through our priorities. Lack of planning leads to wasted effort and regret.

Take the time to determine your long-term goals…and schedule your activities to make time for those that move you toward your goals.

Mr. Lakein suggests setting aside 15 minutes to answer three questions:

• *What are my lifetime goals?* First write down as many answers as you can think of in just two minutes. Then give yourself another two minutes for additional thoughts and corrections.

You'll probably have a lot of generalities… success, happiness, love. They don't give very much practical guidance. So continue the process by spending two minutes answering and two minutes more refining your answers to:

• *How would I like to spend the next three years?* Then spend another four minutes writing what is really important to you and what your current life may be missing.

• *If I knew now I would be struck dead by lightning in six months, how would I live until then?* The answer to this question may be very different from what you're doing now. If it is, you probably need to make serious changes in your life.

But even if there isn't a major contradiction, you're almost certain to find that your list contains more items than you can do in the time you have available. Your next task is to set priorities.

Setting priorities:

When you take control of your time by considering your priorities, you will also do better at performing routine activities. The key is to consider everything you have to do…and decide how important it is to you.

Divide your activities into three priority grades—A for the most important, C for the least and B for those in the middle. Rank the As, Bs and Cs in their own groups as well. Try to do all the As before the Bs…the Bs before the Cs.

If you can't get to some or even any of the Cs, don't worry—because they don't matter.

Example: Every day we are bombarded by mail. We don't have to give up prime time to read it all thoroughly. Just take a few minutes to scan it rapidly and decide what priority to give each piece.

Some must be answered promptly—put them in your A pile. Some are totally irrelevant —not even C. And some may be important in

the future. Put them in your B pile, and if you get through all your A projects, take care of them. After a few weeks, they will move into categories A or C…if you don't hear any more about some, just dump them.

Use this A/B/C grading system for all your activities. Every day, set out a list of what you have to do with the As on top. Take care of them before starting on anything less urgent… even though the Bs and Cs may be quicker, easier and more enjoyable.

Concentrate on your priorities:

If one of your A priorities in life will take a great deal of time and effort, try to set aside a significant block of time for it each week.

Even if you don't have enough slack in your schedule to spare more than a few minutes for an A priority, don't give in to the temptation to put it off. Make sure to spend at least a little time on it…or be honest with yourself and take it off your A list.

If you procrastinate, you will probably never get around to it. But if you persist, even a few minutes a day, you will be surprised and encouraged to find out how much you have accomplished after only a few weeks.

You will be encouraged to continue…perhaps even to make more time by changing your other priorities.

Always stay in control of your time:

To plan effectively you need to consider both what you want to get done and how you function best. You must know your most effective working hours—morning, afternoon or night— and when the most productive use of your time is to buckle down to work.

At other times your body will signal you are better off doing something else…required reading, telephone calls or routine chores.

After spending considerable time on a taxing project, you need to allow time for relaxation, perhaps via some physical activity. And when you need to come up with creative ideas, make sure to allow time for sleep, refreshing both your mind and body.

The secret to making the most of your time is to constantly ask yourself the question: *What is the best use of my time right now?*

In short, while nobody can stop the clock, Mr. Lakein teaches us that a little effort can help us pass the hours, days and years more wisely.

Source: Jeffrey Marsh, PhD, president, Marsh Communications, a consulting firm, Baltimore. He learned much about time management from Alan Lakein's book, *How to Get Control of Your Time and Your Life,* Signet, New York.

How to Give a Better Speech

Listen with your eyes when speaking to an audience. Audience members will give you clues about whether they understand and agree with what you say. Learn to look at individual audience members, not over their heads. Watch for frowns, puzzlement, approval, confusion and other reactions. Include as many people as possible in your viewing. Look around the audience at random and pick people out. *Caution:* Do not seek one-to-one eye contact as you might in face-to-face talks. Speeches are not staring contests.

Source: *Speak and Get Results: A Complete Guide to Speeches and Presentations that Work in Any Business Situation* by Sandy Linver, president of a communications-consulting company in Atlanta and San Francisco, Fireside Books, New York.

How Men and Women Can Communicate Much Better

Many couples are frustrated in their relationships even though they love each other.

Although they both want to live happily together, they continually get into quarrels they are unable to resolve.

Arguments frequently erupt because men and women inhabit emotional worlds so different that they seem to come from different planets. Good intentions alone are not enough to overcome those differences. But when partners learn to respect and understand each other's emotional needs and modify their behavior appropriately, they can avoid quarrels and allow their love to blossom.

Who's who:

Men define themselves through their ability to achieve results by their own efforts. As long as something is working, they will leave it alone, and when a problem arises, they will try to solve it by themselves. They'll only ask others for advice as a last resort. So when a man is offered unsolicited advice, he regards it as an insulting suggestion that he doesn't know what to do or can't do it on his own.

Women define themselves through their feelings and the quality of their relationships. They would sooner share their personal feelings than achieve a concrete goal or solve a problem. They always want to improve things and regard it as a sign of love to offer help and assistance to someone else without being asked.

Result: When a woman thinks of a way to improve a man, she is eager to tell him about it. But he translates her concern as a message that she thinks he is broken and wants to fix him. He rejects her caring efforts because he regards them as an attempt to humiliate him.

Stress:

Men under stress go off by themselves to think through their problems or to forget about them temporarily by absorbing themselves in something completely different. In either case, they cannot pay full attention to their relationship with their partners at that time.

After a while, they feel more relaxed and are ready to come back and focus more on the relationship.

Women react to stress by sharing their problems and talking about their feelings.

Result: Misunderstanding. Women expect their husbands to open up and talk about all their problems—but they go off into their own world instead, leaving their wives feeling hurt and ignored.

Meanwhile, when wives start to talk at length about problems they perceive, their husbands think they are talking because they want advice on how to solve the problem. Instead of just lending a sympathetic ear, husbands try to offer a quick, concrete solution and cut the conversation short. That approach leaves women feeling frustrated and misunderstood.

Disagreement vs. argument:

It is natural that couples do not agree on every subject all the time. But differences do not have to lead to arguments or fights. Men and women can learn to communicate in a loving and respectful way that lets them discuss differences in an honest and open way.

Most arguments begin not because of what you are saying, but how you are saying it. If you understand your partner's emotional needs, you will be able to talk to him/her in a way that delivers a reassuring message and prevents arguments from erupting.

Messages men want from women:

Men want to be accepted the way they are. If a man feels his wife is trying to improve him, he will think—"She feels upset over the smallest things I do or don't do. I feel criticized and rejected."

Men want to be admired. If a man feels his wife is putting him down, he will think: "She is always telling me what to do. I feel I am being treated like a child."

Men want to be encouraged. If his wife tells him her complaints, he will think: "She is always blaming me for her unhappiness. I don't feel motivated to be her knight in shining armor."

Men want to be trusted. If his wife keeps worrying about everything that may possibly go wrong, he thinks to himself: "She doesn't trust me."

Hint to wives: When your husband does something that upsets you, address the specific behavior rather than complaining in general terms.

Example: If your husband forgets to pick up a carton of milk, don't ask, "When will you ever remember?" Just say: "I would appreciate it if you will pick up some milk." He will realize his mistake himself and take care of it.

Messages women want from men:

Women want to be validated. If her husband minimizes the importance of her feelings, she thinks: "He thinks I am unimportant."

Women want to be respected. If her husband forgets to do what she asked him, she thinks: "He puts everything else ahead of me and I have to nag him to get what I want."

Women want to be understood. When her husband is annoyed because she is upset, she thinks: "He expects me to be perfect and doesn't love me for myself."

Women want to be appreciated. When her husband is impatient at her questions when a decision has to be made, she thinks: "He regards me as a burden."

Hint to husbands: When you say something to your wife and she responds with a long speech that shows you have hurt her feelings, take a deep breath and just listen.

When she pauses, say: "You are right. Sometimes I really am insensitive. Let's start this conversation over again in a better way."

If she still feels upset and doesn't want to start over, don't make her feel wrong for feeling that way. If you validate her right to feel the way she does, she will be more accepting and approving of you.

Source: John Gray, PhD, who conducts seminars on relationships. He is the author of *Men Are from Mars, Women Are from Venus: A Practical Guide for Improving Communications and Getting What You Want in Your Relationships,* HarperCollins, Ten E. 53 St., New York 10022.

Make a Gratitude List

Make a *gratitude list* of things in your life for which you are grateful and appreciative. *These may include:* Health…family…special talents …relationships, etc. Making the list will help improve your emotional well-being, clear your vision and, as a consequence, begin to improve the quality of your entire life. *Realize:* No matter how pressured and impoverished your life might *seem* to be, there is probably much, much more in your life that is good and pleasurable than you have given yourself to believe.

Source: *Earn What You Deserve: How to Stop Underearning & Start Thriving* by Jerrold Mundis, New York–based writer and former underearner, Bantam Books, 1540 Broadway, New York 10036.

Secrets of Much Better Relationships

Many of the conflicts between men and women arise from age-old differences. Pretending that these differences don't exist builds misunderstanding, frustration and distrust.

But when we accept that the sexes are coming from "different directions," with different goals, we can begin to understand each other better.

Dr. Diane Ackerman tells about these differences—and how they affect our relationships…

What are the basic conflicts that produce differences between men and women? Many of them stem from competing biological agendas that have been passed along from earliest time.

Men have always been driven to impregnate as many women as possible in order to ensure the existence of future generations.

Women have always been acutely aware of their childbearing responsibilities. A woman's investment in reproduction has always been far more demanding. Pregnancy makes her physically vulnerable, and once she gives birth, she makes great sacrifices to ensure the survival of her child and herself.

She also expects one man to stick by her, helping at least until the baby is born and safely on his/her feet.

To apply this to contemporary life, men are naturally inclined to avoid being tied down, whereas women are more likely to think about relationships in terms of always, forever and commitment.

It's partly a testament to the power of love that men and women, despite their differences, are able to stay together at all.

Haven't some of these attitudes changed as society has changed? Relative to human history, contemporary civilization has happened in the blink of an eye. Men and women today may be wearing suits and carrying briefcases, but we still respond to the same instincts and concerns that have been developed over time.

Though our instincts haven't changed much, our expectations have. As society has changed, men and women have come to expect more from their relationships than ever before.

For instance, we expect our marriages to be happy. But during most of human history—and even today in many parts of the world—people did not marry for love. They married to forge family alliances, raise their social status and combine wealth or real estate. Marrying for love would have been considered selfish or irrelevant.

While marital happiness is not an unrealistic expectation today, it is a relatively recent one in the Western world.

Another big difference today is the fact that most people bring more personal history to relationships. Most people enter into romantic unions having had previous ones. In some cases, they have learned painful lessons and carry with them a great deal of psychological "baggage."

Result: In self-defense, many of us subconsciously have built barriers to intimacy, shielding ourselves from any future emotional damage.

To make matters even more complicated, we are constantly bombarded with images of perfect relationships in movies, on TV and in advertisements. It seems that everyone is having better romances than we are. Therefore, we're measuring our success against almost impossible criteria.

Fortunately, we're not forced to feel this way. Biology doesn't have to be destiny, and human nature isn't static. Despite the great array of instincts, cravings and traits that we have inherited from previous generations, we still have free will, control and choice. We are constantly developing new patterns of behavior in relationships.

How can we use this adaptability to improve our modern-day relationships? When we understand our differences, we're better able to sort out puzzling or tough situations. Too often, we assume the other person is displaying bad character when in fact he/she is simply communicating in a masculine or feminine way.

Example: A man and a woman are in a car. He's driving. The couple is lost, but the man refuses to ask for directions. The woman gets exasperated. She says, "Why won't you ever ask for directions?" He snaps, "Stop nagging me."

To some extent, what's happening in this example is instinctive. Based on biological urgings and social systems over the centuries, men have evolved a concern—bordering on obsession—with losing face. Women have developed a concern—that also borders on obsession—with losing attachments.

Once we understand that the same situation or behavior often means something very different to a man or a woman, we can move through the conflict and begin to negotiate. We can get along better and enjoy each other more.

How can we begin to break negative, instinctive patterns? First, we need to recognize that working at a relationship does not mean demanding that the other person change. It also doesn't mean believing that if you love somebody enough, everything will resolve itself without any effort by either party.

Working at a relationship involves two statesmanlike qualities—compromise and negotiation—which imply a willingness to be flexible. It's important to discuss conflicting desires and needs—so that you can explore ways to balance your partner's needs with your own.

Key strategy: Be willing to give up some of your less important desires occasionally—and try to reach decisions with which you both can live.

Play—not just work—is also an important part of strengthening a relationship. We need to share fun as well as work and goals. We need to take ourselves less seriously and be good-humored about the differences—maybe even rejoice in them.

Important: Romances are more likely to succeed when people are friends first. This contradicts the myth most of us grew up with—that someone special will gallop into our lives and make everything perfect.

People fall head-over-heels in love all the time. But, in the long run, that is not enough. The relationships that last are those in which the partners have gotten to know each other before deciding they will be passionately attached forever.

It's also useful to recognize that a shift in feelings from excitement to comfort is part of a natural, chemical process. It doesn't mean that there's anything wrong with you, your partner or the relationship.

Instead of bemoaning the fact that you don't feel as precipitously in love as when you first met—laugh about the chemistry…talk to each other…and find new ways to stir up excitement. Some couples set off on exotic vacations. Others might choose to read books together. Anything different that keeps you from taking each other for granted is helpful.

Is it possible to work too hard at a relationship? Probably, although there is no rule that holds for all couples. Some people need to constantly dissect and reinvent their relationships, while for others, this analytical focus might be too much of a strain.

Some couples find it more comfortable to schedule discussion time on a weekly—or even monthly—basis…others prefer not to talk about these issues at all until a crisis comes up. It's a matter of finding the rhythm or style that works best for you and your partner.

Whatever the style of your particular relationship, the key is to deal with conflict—when it occurs—in a nonthreatening, nonblaming way. Focus on describing your needs and what would make you happy rather than on what you consider your partner's defects.

Source: Diane Ackerman, PhD, award-winning poet, essayist and naturalist. She is currently working on a five-part PBS series based on her book, *A Natural History of the Senses*, Random House, New York.

Self-Hypnosis Can Help

Self-hypnosis can help you focus on concerns and find ways to handle them. *Example:* If you're afraid of public speaking, and see yourself making a mess of a presentation, self-hypnosis can make it easier to visualize a positive reaction to speaking. You can then act that out. *To learn self-hypnosis:* Talk with a hypnotherapist. He/she can help you make a tape of your own voice to help you focus. Using the tape keeps attention from wandering and creates the concentration at the heart of hypnosis. In time, you can teach yourself to stay in hypnosis without the tape.

Source: *Essentials of Hypnosis* by Michael D. Yapko, PhD, clinical psychologist and director, Milton H. Erickson Institute, San Diego, Brunner/Mazel Publishers, 19 Union Square W., New York 10003.

Larry King's Secrets of Good Conversation

Making conversation with someone you've just met doesn't have to be awkward or difficult. Whether you're in a professional or social setting, the key is to ask engaging questions... pay attention to what the other person is saying...and respond to what's being said to keep the conversation going.

Over the course of my 37-year career as an interviewer, I've had the chance to observe many great conversationalists. I've also developed my own techniques to keep conversations going.

The basics:

• *Break the ice with a warm topic.* Open with a cliché—and don't worry that it might sound dull. Clichés are terrific conversation starters because they are subjects to which everyone can relate.

You can't go wrong if you pick topics like the weather, movies or any subject that interests most people. Other good universal topics include sports, pets and children.

Example: Dolly Parton was a guest on my TV show recently, and I knew she was a little nervous. She has homes in both California and Nashville, so shortly before we went on the air, I asked her about the difference in weather between the two places.

That question launched us into a fascinating discussion about the effect of weather on quality of life and why different people prefer different parts of the country. That one simple question established an immediate conversational bond and helped us move smoothly on to other topics.

• *If you're shy, say so.* Nothing beats honesty when you're trying to break the ice. If you're feeling awkward, use it to advance the conversation. Telling someone you've just met that you're shy is disarming and creates empathy.

Example I: I experienced the power of this principle in 1957 when I began as a radio disc jockey. I told my listeners, "This is my first day, and I'm nervous. If anything goes wrong, please forgive me." Being honest allowed me to be more comfortable. I knew that if I started a record in the wrong place or played the wrong commercial, my listeners would probably understand.

Example II: In a social setting, there's nothing wrong with admitting to someone you've just met that big parties are overwhelming. Letting the other person know you're human creates a strong connection.

If you're nervous when interviewing for a job, remember that the other person is probably uneasy, too. No one is completely comfortable when meeting someone for the first time.

• *Pick up the pace by asking open-ended questions.* These types of questions prompt discussion because they can't be answered with a simple "yes" or "no." Since answers will be longer, you'll have an opportunity to notice other things that are being said to keep the conversation going. My favorite open-ended questions:

• *Why?* If someone tells you he/she is in sales, ask, "Why did you choose that?" People love to expound on choices they've made.

• *What do you think?* Ask people what their impressions are of any big event in the news.

• *What if...?* Hypothetical questions perk up people because they ask for opinions—and people love to share their points of view. The what-if technique works especially well when speaking to several people. It's a fun way to get many people to open up and talk about what's really important to them.

• *Show sincere interest.* When someone else is speaking, most people spend that time planning what they themselves are going to say next. This is not only impolite, it can cause you to miss important information.

Listening is just as important to good conversation as talking—maybe even more important. I never met a good conversationalist who wasn't also a good listener…and I've never learned much while I was talking.

Solution: Instead of rehearsing your next clever line while the other person is speaking, focus on your genuine response to what he is saying. Challenge yourself to come up with questions about the points the person has raised.

Listening is also a way to show respect for others.

Strategy: Let the other person know that you are paying attention to what he is saying by making eye contact frequently. This is harder to do than most people realize. When there are people moving all about, it's easy to let your eyes drift around the room. But doing that gives the impression that you're looking for someone more interesting to talk to—or that what is being said isn't holding your interest.

On the other hand, staring relentlessly into someone's eyes will also make him uncomfortable. It's fine to take your eyes off the person briefly when it's your turn to talk.

•*Develop a broad outlook.* All the best talkers from Oprah Winfrey to Los Angeles Dodgers manager Tommy Lasorda—have this characteristic in common. They don't just talk about themselves. In fact, they rarely use the word "I" in conversation. They know a little bit about a lot of subjects, and they're curious about everything. *Strategies:*

•Make a point of expanding your awareness beyond just your personal concerns.

•Get to know people of many different ages and backgrounds. Find out what they think, and carefully consider their questions.

•Read a variety of opinions about a wide range of issues. Challenge yourself to think about things in new ways.

You'll become more interesting to others—and you'll find them more interesting as well.

•*Don't judge others in advance.* Whenever I start an interview, I suspend judgment about the person across from me. Coming to conclusions about people before you've even spoken to them—either because of what you've heard or the way they look—shuts down your curiosity and prevents you from learning something new.

Conversation is always surprising, but you have to put aside your expectations in order to be surprised.

Example: When I was preparing to interview G. Gordon Liddy in 1981, I was sure that I wouldn't like him based on everything I had read about him. Before we met, however, I reminded myself to suspend judgment, and I prepared to be as open-minded with him as I would be with any guest. As it turned out, I actually liked him. I don't agree with anything he stands for, but he's funny, off-the-wall and very interesting. I wouldn't have been able to appreciate this about him had I not forced myself to be open.

•*End a conversation gracefully.* Breaking away from a conversation is often more difficult than starting one. After bonding with someone, most people hesitate to interrupt when they need to move on because they feel it will hurt the other person's feelings.

The fact is that there will come a point in any conversation when you have to end it—either to see other people or simply because you have run out of things to say.

Making such a move doesn't have to be hard. You just need a great excuse. *Examples:*

•"The food is so delicious, I'm going back for seconds."

•"I've got to say 'hello' to the host."

The key to leaving a great impression when ending a conversation is to make the excuse in a polite, friendly and unapologetic way…and then leave.

Source: Larry King, the country's best-known interviewer of celebrities. The host of CNN-TV's nightly *Larry King Live,* he also writes a weekly newspaper column and is the author of several books, including *How to Talk to Anyone, Anytime, Anywhere: The Secrets of Good Conversation,* Crown Publishers, Inc., New York.

Procrastination Symptoms

Over-organizing a project by meticulously straightening out your desk, reviewing unrelated mail and so on...waiting for the right time to get started...being easily distracted... underestimating the time needed to do a project...often being too tired to start or finish... trivializing a task by saying it is not worth doing ...spending more time hoping for good times than taking steps to create them...having vague rather than specific goals...lacking action plans to achieve your goals.

Source: *Getting It Done* by Andrew J. DuBrin, PhD, professor of management, Rochester Institute of Technology College of Business, Rochester, New York, Peterson's Books, 202 Carnegie Center, Princeton, New Jersey 08543.

How to Win Any Argument

Many people would be happy if they never had to argue at all. Unfortunately, this is a crowded and disputatious world, and there undoubtedly do come times when we are all forced to argue or debate in meetings with colleagues or one-on-one with peers.

•*Decide your purpose.* The main reason why we argue is to win a point—to state the case for or against something so convincingly that we prevail. Other reasons people argue are to work off aggressions...to clear the air...or to clarify an issue or problem. Even if your only goal is to win an argument, there are various refinements of an argument's purpose that need to be determined:

•Winning at once vs. winning in the long run.

•Winning as a matter of cold logic vs. winning the audience.

Decide your goal in advance. This will help you plan your argument's strategy.

•*Size up the opposition.* An important factor to be considered at the outset of any argument is the precise nature of the opponent—his/her general attitude, strengths and weaknesses, and current mood. This is equally true whether the opponent is your brother-in-law, your employer or a rival.

Don't assume that just because you like your opponent, your opponent will like you. Pay attention to his general attitude toward the subject—and his attitude toward you personally.

Toward the subject: Is he passionately concerned? Rather indifferent?

Toward you: Is he an old and implacable foe? A friend who merely needs guidance? A thoroughly professional adversary?

If your opponent's weakness is inferior factual information, you can take advantage of that flaw because it is a weakness that he simply has no business having.

One danger you must guard against is overwhelming your opponent so spectacularly that the people you're hoping to sway will be sympathetic toward him. Another danger is creating ill will with your opponent and damaging your relationship.

•*Marshal relevant facts.* If you are going to argue, be prepared. The mistake most people make is to rush into an argument without being sufficiently sure of the factual support for the position they are taking.

The competent arguer analyzes the structure of his case and knows all of the factual data available to support him. It will automatically tell him what the weak points of his own case are.

A competent arguer is entitled to feel a certain serenity before the argument even begins. The argument he plans to make is one he fully understands, and he is prepared for his opponent's conduct.

•*Invoke a principle.* To win an argument, you must either demonstrate that your position follows from relevant facts—or demonstrate that your proposition follows from relevant principles.

A principle is based on a general experience that has been enshrined in some permanent form.

191

- Honesty is the best policy.
- Thou shalt not kill.
- Defend freedom at all costs.

Strategy: If your opponent invokes a principle, you can attack it by citing extreme instances, which often reveal intrinsic flaws in principles—or at least demonstrate significant limitations on their applicability.

- *Ask questions.* A question may be asked during an argument for the purpose of gaining more information…

 - "What do you mean by 'aggressive'?"

 Or to narrow a loose contention…

 - "Are you saying it would be wrong…or merely that it would be indiscreet?"

But questions can also be asked during an argument to force some answer—usually one that is not beneficial to the person being questioned.

Questions can also force a hostile opponent to publicly air facts that you already know. They can compel him to corroborate negative information that you are fortunate enough to possess, such as the fact that he once took the position opposite the one he is now taking.

Strategy: Just about any point can be put in the form of a question—such as, "Isn't it true that…?" As a result, you will be cast in the role of someone innocently seeking enlightenment.

Questions should be shaped to compel a desirable response or at the very least to avoid an undesirable one.

- *Make eye contact.* Displays of emotion, such as humor, pity and anger, can be used to maximize the effect of a point.

Strategy: One of the most effective physical advantages you have is eye contact. Looking directly into the other person's eyes suggests openness, innocence, simplicity or that you have nothing to hide.

It can also challenge the other person to be completely honest…or it can be used to simply hold his attention.

Conversely, an unwillingness to look another person in the eye is usually a serious disadvantage. It connotes deviousness, guilt and, at the very least, uncertainty.

- *Be courteous.* Courtesy is essential and can be demonstrated by your tone of voice, words and body language. It's important because it makes you seem rational, gentle and in control.

Courtesy requires that you listen to your opponent for a reasonable time—and keep interruptions to a minimum. The necessary assumption in almost every argument is that, however wrong he may be, your opponent's points are worth examination.

Important: If you believe your opponent is frivolous, stupid or evil, then you shouldn't be arguing with him at all.

- *Employ understatement.* Both overstatement and understatement have exactly the same purpose—to stress your point. Overstatement accomplishes this by exaggerating it. Understatement achieves the same effect but more subtly. It diminishes the point and leaves it to the people you're trying to win over to correct the imbalance by enlarging the point to its legitimate proportions.

Example: Abraham Lincoln's speeches avoided overstatement. It was as if Lincoln sensed that the problems he addressed were too profound and too precariously balanced to permit the slightest exaggeration. That's why his words are so powerful.

By contrast, overstatement might lead an audience to feel manipulated and sympathetic toward the other side.

Example: "If we don't adopt my plan, our business will be set back 30 years."

In such a case, the audience tends to unconsciously overcorrect for the overstated point, valuing your argument less than when you started. What's more, the audience may conclude that the arguer is deceiving them right across the board.

- *Admit blunders, then move on.* When you make a mistake, admit it as promptly and in as few words as possible. Then back away, and change the subject.

Important: Do not try to defend a mistake or ignore it. An unadmitted mistake is like a wounded man on the battlefield—it requires constant attention and is in imminent peril of being lost at any time. Besides, a competent arguer will exploit your mistake to the hilt, to your inevitable and deserved discomfort.

Source: William A. Rusher, distinguished fellow of Claremont Institute, syndicated columnist, publisher of *National Review* for 31 years and former television commentator for PBS's *The Advocates* and *Face Off,* the debate segment of ABC's *Good Morning, America.* He is the author of six books, including *How to Win Arguments,* University Press of America, Lanham, MD.

Better Living

Beat obstacles to your true goals by recognizing them as forces you can overcome. *Values absorbed from others* may tell you what car to drive, where to live and how it is appropriate to act at a certain age. But your life is your own—it doesn't matter what others think. *Being walled in* is the feeling of being controlled by circumstances, past mistakes, obligations or perceived limitations. But if you accept yourself and live for your values, others will accept you, too. *Fear of change* is a type of fear of failure. But it is worth trying to do something truly meaningful to you—no matter what other people think.

Source: *The 10 Natural Laws of Successful Time and Life Management: Proven Strategies for Increased Productivity and Inner Peace* by Hyrum Smith, CEO, Franklin Quest Co., Salt Lake City, Warner Books, 1271 Avenue of the Americas, New York 10020.

Body Language— How to Use It to Get What You Want

Our first impressions of others are almost always formed within the first two to four minutes of meeting them. During this time, we are concentrating less on what is being said and more on the other person's facial expressions, gazes, gestures, posture, stance and proximity.

Most body language occurs unconsciously. But if you are aware of what messages your body is sending, you will have a greater advantage in any personal interaction. *How to leave a stronger first impression…*

The eyebrow flash:

Within seconds of making eye contact with another person, both your and his/her eyebrows will lift briefly. This visual handshake is done unconsciously.

To use it to your advantage: If possible, initiate the eyebrow flash. *Reason:* You draw the attention of the person you are greeting, who will unconsciously recognize your approval and openness—and will be inclined to respond similarly.

Exceptions: If your intent is to signal hostility or domination, withhold your response. Likewise, a person who is angry with you may not reciprocate your eyebrow flash.

If you do not receive an eyebrow flash in return, don't assume that it is a negative sign—the person may be shy, anxious or nearsighted.

Direction of gaze:

After a rapid scan of the person's face, briefly break the gaze with a quick downward glance. You are signaling a wish to continue the encounter, with no intent to dominate the other person.

Trap: Breaking eye contact sideways conveys distraction or lack of interest and will generate discomfort in the other person.

Looking up will also throw the other person off balance and may cause him to look up as well so as to see what you are looking at.

Length of the gaze:

In the initial stage of a meeting, never hold eye contact for more than three seconds—break the gaze briefly. Holding eye contact for too long signals either disapproval and hostility…or a wish for greater intimacy—depending on circumstances and other signals. Your companion will feel disconcerted, without understanding why.

But don't avoid making eye contact…you may be seen as devious or dishonest.

Exception: If your intent is to dominate someone, use a prolonged gaze…or refuse to *return* prolonged eye contact…and break your gaze to the side, not downward, to appear uninterested.

The smile:

An inappropriate smile conveys as bad an impression as not smiling at all. When meeting people with whom you are not very close but whom you wish to impress favorably, use a relaxed smile with lips closed or parted only slightly.

At the same time, use a warm, steady gaze and allow your eyes to crinkle at the corners. To increase favor or cooperation, tilt your head sideways while smiling and making eye contact.

Avoid: A broad, open-mouthed smile that exposes your upper teeth. This smile is often faked and usually inspires distrust.

Stance:

To generate receptivity, pay attention to your placement. Women are more comfortable conversing face-to-face, while men prefer a side-on position that moves to a more frontal one.

Best: Never position yourself *opposite* an unfamiliar male...or *next* to an unknown female. Don't remain standing when others are sitting unless you intend to signal dominance. Most people feel dominated when they are seated while others are standing.

Proximity:

The distance you stand or sit from another person sends powerful silent signals. We feel aroused or uncomfortable when someone invades our personal space, even if we are not conscious of the reason. "Comfort zones" vary with culture and gender, so it's easy to send an unintentional discomfiting signal.

Example I: A man who stands too close to a woman may be considered obnoxious or intrusive. A woman who moves in close to a man may be thought to signal sexual desire.

Example II: Western men working in Saudi Arabia feel uncomfortable with their hosts, who prefer to work at a distance of 18 to 36 inches. Americans and Europeans prefer 30 to 48 inches. Even though everyone's intent is friendly, the Arabs may perceive Western colleagues as remote and unfriendly, whereas the Westerners feel intimidated as their hosts keep moving in closer.

Best: Learn to feel comfortable with a variety of distances...respect other people's signals regarding *their* preferred proximities...and never invade another person's space unless you wish to increase his anxiety.

Be aware that controlling distance can work positively or negatively for you. Closing distance may signal dominance in a business discussion but can elicit greater intimacy as a conversation grows more personal.

Source: David Lewis, BSc (Hons.), PhD, FINSTD (Fellow Institute of Directors), chartered psychologist and chairman of the David Lewis Consultancy, a firm that conducts international research and training in the use of nonverbal communication, Kent, England. He is the author of *The Secret Language of Success: Using Body Language to Get What You Want*, Carroll & Graf, New York.

Know It All

Do you know why the sky is blue, or why you often wake up just before the alarm goes off? Are you sure your hair and nails keep growing after death?

• The sky is blue because sunlight is partially scattered as it bounces off particles of air in the atmosphere. The blue part of that prism effect scatters more easily than the rest, making the sky seem exclusively blue even though all of the colors of the prism are present.

• Before the alarm goes off in the morning, your body temperature, which is lowest at night, begins to rise to the daytime levels that make you more alert. Slight sounds can now wake you. One of these is the faint click many alarm clocks make a few minutes before going off...which you hear without realizing it.

• Hair and nails do not continue growing after death. But they do look as if they do. As the skin dries out it shrinks away from both hair and nails, exposing more of each, so that it seems they are growing.

Source: Ed Zott, the author of *Know It All: The Fun Stuff You Never Learned in School*, Random House, Inc., New York.

How to Live to Be 100... And Enjoy It

For my book, *100 Ways to Live to 100*, we asked centenarians to divulge the secrets of their longevity. Their answers were simple...

• Few drank much alcohol or smoked.

• When serious illness struck, they paid attention to the underlying physical condition and took swift steps to correct it.

• They kept fit through farm work, yard work or active sports.

• They always had something pleasurable to do.

• They loved and appreciated the gift of life.

To prolong our own lives, we would do well to follow their example and to take care of ourselves in other very specific ways.

Safety:

Accidents are the fifth leading cause of death in the US and they cause 9,100,000 disabling injuries each year. To avoid them...

• *Play it safe at home.* Tack or tape down throw rugs (or get rid of them). In the bathroom, use handrails and nonslip mats. Repair worn stair runners. Install three-way light switches. Treat firearms responsibly. Don't use kerosene space heaters...they cause fires. Put up a smoke detector on each floor, and change the batteries twice a year.

• *Play it safe on the road...and at sea.* Drive a heavy car with air bags. Wear a seat belt. Don't drink alcohol before driving, swimming or boating...a classic drowning scenario.

• *Play it safe in the environment.* Live in a healthy place, far away from nuclear-power plants, smog, toxic-waste dumps and highways.

Don't leave everything in the hands of the professionals. How you can participate in promoting your own longevity:

• *Choose excellent doctors.* The staffs of major teaching hospitals (medical centers affiliated with medical schools) tend to be highly regarded.

• *Choose helpful doctors.* Your doctor should communicate well...spend the time you need ...openly discuss treatment costs and alternatives...treat you pleasantly and respectfully... diagnose accurately...charge reasonably...instill trust...advocate for you with your health insurer...believe in preventive medicine.

• Practice preventive medicine yourself. All men should perform testicular self-examinations each month.

Men older than 40 should have yearly prostate-cancer screenings and rectal and colon exams.

Women should perform breast self-examinations monthly and have a baseline mammogram at age 35, then every two to three years until age 50 and annually thereafter. Breast cancer is the most common cancer among American women, but the disease is usually curable if detected early.

An annual Pap smear can identify cervical cancer early, when it's most easily treated.

• *Keep your immunizations up to date.* Get a tetanus/diphtheria booster every ten years and a flu shot every fall.

• *Watch your medicines.* Drug-related mistakes are frequent and sometimes life-threatening, especially in older people. Prescription and over-the-counter drugs account for a third of all fatal poisonings.

Buy all medications at the same pharmacy and give all your doctors a list of what others have prescribed for you. When a doctor recommends starting a drug, ask about its benefits, negative side effects, interactions with other drugs you take and how long you'll have to take it. Double-check with your pharmacist.

• *Play it safe in the hospital.* Choose the least-invasive techniques available: Lasers, ultrasound, laparoscopy. Don't stay overnight if you can help it. More than half of surgical procedures can be done on an outpatient basis. Every year about two million people contract infections in the hospital...and 100,000 of them die.

Diet:

Here's where you're really in control. To promote nutrition and health:

•*Eat less fat.* Arteries clogged with fat contribute to cancers of the breast, colon and ovary and to heart disease—America's greatest killer. Women's heart risk catches up with men's after menopause, as the protective effects of estrogen disappear. Fat intake should constitute no more than 30% of your total daily calories…preferably less. The greatest sources of saturated fat, the most dangerous kind, are from meat and dairy products.

•*Use less salt.* By retaining fluids, salt raises blood pressure, a significant risk factor in heart disease, stroke and kidney disease. *Most in danger:* Anyone who is overweight or has a family history of diabetes, cardiovascular problems or kidney disorders.

•*Drink more water.* The goal is eight to ten eight-ounce glasses a day…whether a glass or a sip at a time. Water helps keep bowel movements regular, removes toxins from the kidneys, carries nutrients and oxygen in the blood throughout the body, moistens the lungs to ease breathing, lubricates joints and muscles and helps metabolize fat.

•*Eat more fiber.* Like water, it encourages regular bowel movements…and has many other benefits. *Two types…*

•*Insoluble fiber* helps prevent colon cancer—bran cereals, whole grains, dried beans and peas.

•*Soluble fiber* lowers cholesterol and triglyceride levels in the blood (related to heart disease) and makes you feel full, so you'll eat less—carrots, corn, dried beans, lentils, oat bran, prunes.

Strive for six to 11 servings of bread, cereal, rice, pasta and grains, three to five servings of fresh vegetables and two to four servings of fresh fruit daily (one serving = ½ cup).

•*Wash fruits and vegetables well.* They may have been sprayed with pesticides. Or buy or raise organically grown produce.

Habits:

How you spend every day affects how many days you'll have to spend. *Important:*

•*Don't smoke.* Smoking has been related to a vast array of serious illnesses. Banish cigarette smoke from your home. Passive smoke increases a nonsmoker's risk of lung cancer by 30%.

•*Stay active.* Do something physical every day—dance, swim, take a walk, garden, clean house, make love.

Moderate exercise aids weight loss, lowers cholesterol and blood pressure, prevents diabetes, fights osteoporosis, reduces stress and enhances a positive spirit.

Strengthen your heart with 15 to 60 minutes of aerobic exercise three to five times a week. Check with your physician before starting a fitness program.

To strengthen muscles, lift weights or use a Nautilus-type machine.

"All my friends are dead because they didn't exercise," said a 102-year-old woman who attends dance class daily.

•*Keep planning and enjoying.* Want to buy a new car at 70? Go ahead! Don't doom yourself by deciding prematurely that it's too late.

•*Positive outlook.* One 90-year-old woman considers her mirror a window into the future. She says it indicates what's coming next rather than reflecting a change from the past.

•*Continue to improve.* It's never too late to break a bad habit. You'll benefit whenever you stop smoking or start exercising.

•*Reduce stress.* This is one of the most valuable life-lengthening steps you can take. People who live lives of tremendous anxiety and hostile anger are more prone to heart attacks, which typically strike men in their 50s. Look around—how many ogres are still around at 80?

Stress contributes to illness, and illness causes death. Embrace calmness, acceptance and tolerance in any way that works for you…meditation, deep breathing, psychotherapy.

If you don't feel alert and rested when you wake up, get more sleep. Switch to a less frenzied job, perhaps transferring within your firm. At lunchtime, instead of sitting around griping with colleagues, take a walk.

Heredity:

Many of the 100-year-olds interviewed for my book were fortunate to have come from long-lived families. Not everyone is so lucky.

While we can't control our own genetic make-up, we can learn to use it to protect ourselves. Here's how:

• Ask family members how older relatives died. Review marriage and death certificates. Photo albums can also jog memories.

• Advise your doctor about any serious diseases, conditions or trends you uncover.

• Obtain medical care right away if you develop any signs of those problems.

Source: Charles B. Inlander, president, People's Medical Society, Allentown, Pennsylvania. He is the co-author of *100 Ways to Live to 100: The First Complete Guide to Living a Long and Productive Life,* Wings Books, Avenel, NJ.

Encouraging Words

Write down words of encouragement on small pieces of paper and put the papers in your wallet, purse or clothing. *Example:* "Today could be the day you do the impossible." When you rediscover your words, you will get a wonderful boost.

Source: *The Little Book of Big Motivation* by Eric Jensen, business consultant, Del Mar, California, Fawcett Columbine Books, 201 E. 50 St., New York 10022.

How to Get Out of Embarrassing Situations

When you make a mistake in a social setting, it is usually awkward for everyone there. The damage can be controlled if you know how to gracefully wriggle out of sticky situations. How to handle highly embarrassing moments…

• *Someone gives you a holiday gift—but you don't have one in return.* Be effusive in your thanks, and talk about how thoughtful the gift is. Do not apologize for your lack of a gift. It will only draw attention to the awkwardness of the situation.

As soon as you can, write a thank-you note stressing how surprised you were and how much you are enjoying the gift.

Important: Don't rush to buy the person a gift. It looks phony, and you'll have to buy that person a gift next year. Give presents only to those close to you. If it is from a business associate, you can refuse it by referring to company policy. However, be gracious.

• *You suddenly must introduce someone whose name you've forgotten.* If it is someone you've just met, an easy way around the problem is to gently touch the person's arm and say, "Forgive me, I didn't catch your name." Avoid saying, "Sorry, I've forgotten you name." It is less embarrassing not to have heard the name than to have forgotten it. If it is a person you've met before, put your hand to your forehead and say, "I'm an absolute idiot. Today, I can't even remember my own name."

Everybody forgets names. The person who gets most upset is the person who forgot the name, not the person whose name has been forgotten.

Key: Get beyond the mistake quickly.

Source: Letitia Baldrige, renowned expert on manners who in the early 1960s was Jacqueline Kennedy's White House chief of staff. She is the author of 14 books, including *Letitia Baldrige's New Complete Guide to Executive Manners,* Simon & Schuster, 1230 Avenue of the Americas, New York 10020.

How to Do What You Really Want to Do… At Any Age

Contrary to popular opinion, it's never too late to do what you want. The biggest barrier is not age, but fear. As one woman who went back to college in her 80s said, "I'm going to be 88 in five years no matter what I do—so I might as well do what I want to!"

Getting ready—first steps:

Few of us embrace change with open arms …but we can gear ourselves up to make the most of it by taking some important preparatory steps:

• *Grieve if you need to.* Almost any change creates at least some feelings of loss.

•Retirement may mean giving up status and contact with colleagues.

•The freedom when your grown children leave home is offset by the loss of their company—and a shift in what you have to offer as a parent.

Though optimism can be an excellent coping mechanism, don't force yourself to "think positive" if what you really need to do is admit that you feel bad. Acknowledge the loss and shed whatever tears you need to, so that you can move on.

•*Be willing to be a beginner.* One of the defining characteristics of change is that we don't know what's coming next or how to handle it when it happens. Instead of getting upset by this fact, *get curious.*

Let go of your preconceptions, especially those about your capabilities and limitations.

It's not your job to know exactly what to do. Let uncertainty keep you open to a variety of exciting possibilities.

•*Spend time with yourself.* Build into your life—every day, if possible—some kind of uninterrupted time to reflect, to acknowledge frustrations, to celebrate victories—and dream. You'll need this emotional compass to steer by as you advance toward your goals.

•*Recognize the gifts of age.* Far from holding you back, age can propel you toward what you want. No matter what you've done with your life, you can't reach midlife without accumulating a great deal of knowledge, experience and understanding of the world. This information and wisdom puts you well ahead of younger people who may have ambition but lack perspective.

Self-discovery exercises:

Some people have no problem getting in touch with their dreams—they easily remember their youthful fantasies of raising horses or learning to sail or practicing the clarinet.

Others may have had to spend so many years doing what was expected of them that they aren't sure anymore what they'd love to be doing. If this sounds like you, try some of the following exercises:

•*What did you like to do at age five, 10, 15, etc.?* Jot down the activities you remember enjoying most at various stages of your life, using five-year intervals to focus your thoughts.

Write whatever pops into your mind, even if it seems silly or illogical...from singing in a choir...to riding a bicycle...to hunting for pinecones.

Return to this exercise over a period of several days—new ideas will keep occurring to you.

Don't worry if your list doesn't immediately suggest a grandiose new life direction. Over time, you'll begin to spot patterns that suggest avenues for you to explore.

•*What do you like to do now?* Again, nothing is too trivial to put on your list—you can learn a lot about yourself from even the most ordinary things.

If one of your indulgences is a particular TV game show, ask, "What do I love best about this show?" Is it that you enjoy solving puzzles? Picturing yourself in a new house? Driving down the street in a luxury car and having all your neighbors smile and greet you?

Each of these elements—intellectual challenge, a new addition to the house, a better relationship with your neighbors—is something you might be able to create more of in your life right now, once you recognize the need.

•*Write the life story of your imaginary twin.* Imagine that you have a twin who got to do all the things you were afraid to or didn't have permission to do...or who had time to do everything you were too busy for. What would that twin have done, and where would he/she be today? Which of those activities could you try now?

Find your touchstone:

Sometimes, these exercises alone are enough to trigger a vision for the future.

More often, though, you need to lay out all your answers and analyze them, looking for patterns.

I call this process finding your touchstone.

For each exercise, try to get beneath the surface of your answers. Ask, "What is it about that appeals to me the most? What aspects of this can't I live without?" You'll find common threads among your answers—the essential elements that make up your touchstone.

Example: Someone who enjoys taking long walks and noticing the changing of seasons realizes that what she really craves is a life far away from the urban hustle. Her dream might be satisfied by a cabin in the mountains. Another person with the same love for leisurely, seasonal walks might have no desire to leave the city—her touchstone is a fascination with the weather itself, and her secret dream could be to take some college classes in meteorology.

Figure out how to get there:

I don't believe people have to be self-motivated to make their dreams real. What they do need is support from other people.

When we're doing what's expected of us, support is easy to come by. But when we strike out in new directions, the people who know us are more likely than not to discourage us—after all, they're afraid of change, too!

Of course, it's possible to pursue a dream on your own, but most of us need encouragement and assistance to keep us from giving up. *Where to get this support:*

• *Build a network.* Networking can be formal, such as joining organizations that interest you. It can also be informal—going to lectures you read about in the paper or simply making a point of meeting many different kinds of people and finding out what they're up to.

Networking has several important purposes. The people you come in contact with may be able to give you good advice or suggest resources.

On a more basic level, meeting people who share your interests assures you that you're not crazy for wanting what you want—in fact, these folks can serve as role models for success.

Example: A woman who came to see me for career counseling turned out to be fascinated by gorillas, but she didn't take that interest seriously as a career goal—there were hardly any jobs out there that involved gorillas, she said,

and besides, she wasn't a zoologist—who'd hire her? I suggested she simply take her interest one step further and find a group of people who also loved gorillas. She went to a slide presentation on the subject and met two women who were raising baby gorillas in captivity as part of an animal protection program. My client volunteered to assist them, and when the gorillas were returned to the zoo, she accompanied them to help ease the transition. The zoo director saw her playing with the animals, and she was so obviously suited to the work that he hired her as a zookeeper. She's happier than she ever imagined—and all this resulted from a slide show!

• *Get a telephone buddy.* Agree to call each other regularly—say, once a week—to share ideas and progress, deal with setbacks and give each other pep talks.

• *Join or start a Success Team.** This is a group of six to eight people who meet regularly to help each other identify their dreams and make them come true. In the 20 years since I developed this model, I've seen Success Teams make an incredible difference in many, many lives.

There's something very powerful about hearing a group of people say, "What a great idea! I have a friend (or cousin or accountant) who knows something about that—why don't you talk to her? What else do you need?"

Invite people you know to start a team with you…or put up a notice in a bookstore. Then agree to meet once a week to brainstorm, encourage each other, trouble-shoot and share resources, leads and ideas.

Feed your soul:

Whether you're ready for a big change in your life or not, start now to do what you love —at least for part of every day. Life is made up of the things you do today, and you owe it to yourself and to this planet to live at least an hour a day from your spirit.

This might be as simple as taking a walk, gardening, drawing, going for a swim, reading

*For a list of Success Teams in your area, send a stamped, self-addressed envelope to: Wishcraft and Success Teams, Box 20052, Park West Station, New York 10025.

Shakespeare or sitting quietly and listening to the birds, but be sure to allow yourself time for whatever feeds your soul.

Source: Barbara Sher, a New York City-based therapist and career counselor. She is the coauthor of many books on personal fulfillment including *I Could Do Anything If I Only Knew What It Was: How to Discover What You Really Want and How to Get It*, Delacorte Press, 1540 Broadway, New York 10036.

"Exercise" Your Brain

In much the same way physical exercise builds muscle mass, developing mental substance and stamina through resistance training builds character and allows us to learn how to better overcome obstacles. It's getting through the little steps that's most important.

Source: *Diamond in the Rough* by Barry J. Farber, president, Farber Training Systems, Florham Park, New Jersey, Berkley Books.

Rejection Opportunity

Being turned away by someone with whom you've been in a relationship should be viewed as positive—a chance to move forward with your life.

While the rejection may sting, such a positive attitude will prevent you from obsessing over the one that got away. Instead, you'll spend your time more productively…and find others who will appreciate you for the great person you are.

Source: *How to Attract Anyone, Anytime, Anyplace: The Smart Guide to Flirting* by Susan Rabin, MA, relationship therapist, New York, Plume.

Motivational Energy

Negative thinkers may succeed where optimists fail, by using their anxiety as motivational energy. By worrying over potential problems, *defensive pessimists* arm themselves with contingency plans to deal with obstacles. Optimists—who tend not to consider possible problems—may find themselves less prepared when problems do arise.

Source: Julie K. Norem, PhD, department of psychology, Wellesley College, Wellesley, Massachusetts.

13

Your Family— Your Home

Family Harmony... Siblings Can Get Along Wonderfully

Though it's impossible for siblings to be loving playmates all the time, you can keep rivalry from getting out of hand and help your kids learn creative problem-solving techniques. *Strategies:*

•*Have realistic expectations.* Some parents have idealistic goals, such as, "I want my kids to be best friends and love each other all the time."

This is a perfectly understandable wish. In fact, one of the motives for having a second child is so the first child has someone to keep him/her company and guarantee him/her a friend for life.

But sharing isn't something that comes naturally to kids. Sharing toys and household space is hard enough. Sharing someone you love and depend on—a parent—is much harder.

It's realistic to expect siblings to play happily together and love each other some of the time.

But we cannot legislate other people's feelings. Siblings typically have very strong positive and negative feelings toward each other, and we need to expect and accept this.

•*Don't be too quick to intervene.* One reason siblings fight is that it forces parents to pay attention to them. Many skirmishes resolve themselves much more quickly if you refuse to get involved. In many cases, parental attention only encourages more fighting.

•*Make it clear that siblings don't have to like each other—but they may not hurt each other.* If a fight has progressed so far that either child is extremely angry or unable to calm down, call time-out and separate the kids.

But when neither child is in danger of being harmed, it's better to let them work out their solutions rather than impose your own. Kids are more likely to abide by agreements they've designed themselves, and that will enable them to get along with other people.

Example: When my sons, Eric and Todd, were younger, they often disagreed about whose turn it was to do the dinner dishes. As a result, the dishes often didn't get done. Instead of trying to figure out whose turn it was, I finally said, "The dishes need to be washed. They don't have any names on them. As long as they're done by 7:00 PM, I don't care which one of you washes them."

The two of them worked out a deal. Since Eric would do anything to avoid a chore and Todd loved to accumulate possessions, they agreed that Todd would wash dishes in exchange for one of Eric's toys. It was an unconventional solution, but both boys were satisfied with it—and the dishes were washed.

• *Avoid taking sides.* It is tempting to assume that one child is innocent and that the other is guilty. Often, it's the older sibling who gets blamed, via parental statements such as, "You're bigger, and you should know better...What kind of example are you setting for your little brother?"

In many cases, though, there is no "bad guy" —both kids have contributed to the conflict.

Trap: Taking sides is likely to start a new fight. The child who was scolded will feel victimized and obliged to even the score as soon as you leave the room.

"Who started it?" is another red-flag phrase. Not only is the question inflammatory, it's pointless. Have you really ever heard the guilty one admit that he was to blame? Instead of trying to place blame, make a strong, brief, impersonal statement, such as:

• "I will not allow one child I love to hurt another child I love."

• "There will be no hitting."

• "You have a choice—you can work out a peaceful solution to decide which program to watch, or I'll turn off the TV and nobody will get to watch. Let me know what you have worked out."

Exception: If one child is repeatedly being taken advantage of or consistently winds up with hurt feelings, it's appropriate to empower the victim—privately. Help him analyze the problem, and come up with more effective responses.

Example: "Every time your sister calls you a baby, you start to cry. Do you think you're a baby? Does crying make you feel better or worse? What else could you do when she calls you names? Could you make a joke? Walk away? What do you think you'll try next time?"

• *Don't try to achieve absolute fairness.* Some parents make an effort to treat every child the same, but playing that game will leave you exhausted and unsuccessful.

Kids are very good at keeping score. No matter how much you try to be fair, they'll find a reason to disagree.

Besides, kids aren't the same and shouldn't be treated as such. Each one is at a different level of development and has different needs and capabilities. *Examples:*

• A five-year-old isn't ready for a five-speed bike simply because her eight-year-old sister has one.

• On the five-year-old's birthday, her older sister doesn't need presents—that's the birthday child's special day.

Acknowledge a child's frustration at not being entitled to a privilege that a sibling receives. Remind the resentful sibling of his own privileges. Don't be bullied into giving every child the same privileges.

• *Pay attention to the good times.* It's common for parents to complain, "My kids are always fighting"—when in fact, their children often get along fine. Unfortunately, the conflicts are more noticeable than the pleasant moments.

I suggest that parents notice and enjoy the moments when their kids are being loving, empathic or helpful—such as when the four-year-old offers a toy to his older sister...or the two-year-old tries to make the baby laugh.

These moments remind you why you had more than one child.

• *Take the long view.* In most families, siblings who didn't get along in childhood manage to reach some sort of understanding by the time they become adults. Even siblings who were enemies as children come to realize that no matter what their differences, they share important commonalities—history, inside jokes, a point of view. For most of us, the sibling relationship is the longest-lasting one of our lives and one that we learn to value deeply.

Source: Nancy Samalin, founder and director of Parent Guidance Workshops, New York. She is the author of *Love and Anger: The Parental Dilemma*, Penguin Books, New York. Ms. Samalin's parenting strategies are also available in an audiotape series, *Good Parents, Great Kids.*

Get Your Kids to Really Listen to You

Lower your voice so they have to focus on what you're saying…tell them what you want in a hard-to-ignore written note…call a time-out when you're angry and discuss things later when everyone has cooled off…spend a few quiet minutes before bedtime sharing private thoughts and worries.

Source: *The Single-Parent Family* by Marge Kennedy, former editor of *Sesame Street Magazine,* and Janet Spencer King, founding editor and editor-in-chief of *Working Parents*, Crown Publishers, 201 E. 50 St., New York 10022.

Career vs. Family— How to Win the Balancing Game

For nearly everyone in the American workforce today, it is harder than ever to comfortably balance a satisfying family life with a successful career. *Reasons:*

• The downsizing of companies has left managers burdened with more work than ever, but less job security.

• The proliferation of two-income families puts enormous strain on both parents, who must share the responsibilities of child rearing while working longer hours than ever before.

A rewarding balance of home and career is possible, however. The solution isn't to make one or two dramatic changes in your life, but to begin doing several small things differently…

The triage approach:

Some businesspeople enjoy spending more time at work than at home because they feel they have greater control over their lives at the office. They say that when problems arise at home, there are too many variables that they can't control.

As a result, these career people avoid domestic confrontations. They hide behind alibis and use the office as an escape from family problems. But in fact, when domestic problems do exist, you have a far better chance of solving them if you're at home than if you're at work.

Effective: The triage method. When problems emerge at home, don't think you have to solve all of them at once. Instead, sit down with your spouse and decide which ones need your immediate attention and which ones can wait.

Example: If your spouse has an absolutely unbreakable appointment in the morning, you can agree to be a little late in order to take the children to school—a task your spouse normally would have done.

Benefit: The triage approach forces you to tackle issues head-on. In the process, you become more open with your spouse, and problem solving becomes less onerous. The more you use it, the less you'll rely on excuses.

Key: Always try to reach agreement on the important issues, even if it means putting off decisions on some of the others. Children learn how to manipulate divided parents. *Bonus:* Reaching an agreement lets the kids see a unified and cohesive household, which in turn teaches them the elements of cooperation.

Critical occasions:

No one can be on call either at home or at the office every time he/she is needed. But there are certain critical times when you should absolutely be present, unless there's a job emergency.

Examples: The memorable, formative events, such as an open house at a child's school…the appearance of a child in a play or recital… birthdays and anniversaries. These critical children's events cannot be run through for a second showing.

But don't be afraid to say that a late business meeting will prevent you from going to other events, such as a friend's appearance in a school play.

When you are present on the important occasions, absences on others won't seem so inexcusable.

Other critical time: Before school and after school—when kids often need to talk with a parent about their personal problems or their achievements during the day.

If you—or your spouse—aren't there, small problems have the potential to mushroom into crises.

Solution to consider: One parent arranges to be present when children leave for school… the other when the children return.

If neither parent can be home in the afternoon, make sure both are available by phone. School-age children often can get problems off their chests by having a brief conversation with Mom or Dad at the office. Venting is sometimes all that is necessary to prevent a minor problem from becoming a catastrophe.

Also, when it's impossible for either spouse to be in the house in the afternoon, one or both should arrange to be home for the evening meal or the children's bedtime.

Enthusiasm for work:

Few things alienate family members more than not understanding what a working member does. Without that understanding, they will not appreciate your difficult balancing act, and demands on your time may become unreasonable.

The last thing you want to hear is a family member who says, "You care more about your work than you care about me."

Solution: Explain to your children, and certainly to your spouse, exactly what you do at the office and how important it is to the family's livelihood. Also describe the pressures you are under.

To enhance that understanding, take the children to the office once in a while or ask them for their advice on some of the minor problems you face at work. This is not merely a rhetorical exercise. Often, a fresh approach is helpful.

Payoff: Family members will be more understanding when your work schedule forces you to miss an event, even a critical one.

Caution: Don't relive your workday over the dinner table. Just hit the highlights you believe others may enjoy hearing about.

New technology:

Beepers, computer modems, cellular phones and other new products make it easier today to keep in touch with family members.

Examples: If you cannot fulfill a promise to be home when your daughter returns from school, phone her beforehand. Or send a fax that can be waiting for her at home.

And—if an emergency prevents you from attending an important Little League game, ask another family member to videotape the game for you. Then plan a "party" to show the tape of your child's game.

Technology also helps when you are away on business. Phone home at least twice a day, and talk to as many family members as you can —not just about perfunctory matters but about any important subjects they want to discuss.

Beepers can help working families stay in touch, but they have a drawback—children may grow to think of them as a leash, not a convenience. At an early age, however, beepers can help kids who are left alone feel more secure.

Source: Mortimer R. Feinberg, PhD, chairman of BFS Psychological Associates, a company that conducts psychological tests, counsels executives, helps develop more effective teams and assists companies in selecting managers, 666 Fifth Ave., New York 10103.

Teach Your Dog to "Drop It"

This is one of the most useful commands a puppy can learn—it can prevent your best pair of shoes or a living room armchair from being chewed. *Helpful:* Wait until the puppy picks up something in his mouth...lean over and put your hand on either side of its jaw, where the hinges are...apply gentle but firm pressure to the jaw while saying, "Drop it"...remove the object from the puppy's mouth with the other hand...after removing the object, praise and pet him. *Important:* Be firm—especially if the puppy doesn't cooperate, pulls away or growls.

Source: *Teach Your Dog to Behave: Simple Solutions to Over 300 Common Dog Behavior Problems from A to Z* by New York dog trainer Bashkim Dibra, E.P. Dutton, 375 Hudson St., NY 10014.

Veterinary-Visit Caution

If possible, wrap your pet in a large, clean towel, and carry him when at the vet's office to avoid contact with other animals that may have infectious diseases. Parvovirus, distemper and gastrointestinal infections can easily be picked up from other pets being treated for those conditions.

Source: *Never Say No! The Complete Program for a Happier and More Cooperative Dog* by Roger Mugford, PhD, founder, Animal Behavior Center, Chertsey Surrey, England, Perigee Books, New York.

Pet Introductions... Kitten vs. Puppy

It is easier to introduce a kitten to a dog household than a puppy to a cat household. Cats are more territorial and take longer to adjust. When introducing a puppy to an adult cat, protect the puppy—not the cat. A puppy's curiosity is likely to provoke even a mild-tempered cat. And do not let cats and dogs share food from the same bowl. They have very different nutritional needs.

Source: Dan Carey, DVM, veterinarian, The Iams Company, pet-food manufacturers, Dayton, OH.

House Cats Can Transmit The Human Plague

Cats can pick up the disease from infected fleas or rodents and pass it on when they bite, scratch, lick or even breathe on humans. Most reported cases of cat-to-human transmission in the United States since 1977 have occurred in 13 southwestern states, but people living in the western US are also at risk. The plague is unlikely to spread eastward because infected rodents and fleas live only in semiarid climates.

Warning signs: Fever, chills, headache, nausea and swollen lymph glands. See a doctor right away if you experience this combination of symptoms.

Source: Kenneth L. Gage, PhD, acting plague section chief, division of vector-borne infectious diseases, Centers for Disease Control and Prevention, Atlanta.

Quality Family Time

Schedule family "quiet time" each day—a period when the whole household is quiet. Eliminating TV, radio or loud activity can help reduce stress and conflict. *Helpful:* Plan a quiet activity that the whole family can enjoy together. *Examples:* Reading...meditation... prayer...exercise...yoga...massage.

Source: *A Better World for Our Children: Rebuilding American Family Values* by child development expert Benjamin Spock, MD, National Press Books, Bethesda, MD.

How to Help Your Kids Think Like Entrepreneurs

When I was seven years old, I owned six lemonade stands in a joint venture with my father. *Before I turned eight, I bought him out.*

Around our house in Pearson, Georgia— back in the 1920s and 1930s—we never used the word *entrepreneur.* I don't even think anyone knew what the word meant back then. To my family, work and money meant survival, and *everyone* was expected to be smart and clever about business.

Though times have changed, it is still important for children to learn how to think for themselves and be their own bosses. Jobs at even the largest and most profitable companies are no longer for life, and the odds are high that your kids will have to work for themselves sometime during their careers.

Doing all you can to stimulate that can-do, business-minded spirit will help your children to be stronger and more successful—even if they never have to draw on the experience.

Here are the strategies that my father used with me and that I used with my own five children—three of whom now run their own companies:

• *It's never too early to begin.* In place of a weekly allowance, give your children money for completed household chores. You can start this process as early as age five. Their ages will dictate how many chores are appropriate and how much you should pay them.

Example: Encourage your preteens to create little businesses by making it clear that doing more work around the house can earn them more cash.

If your kids complain that their friends' parents just *give* their kids money, explain that their friends will probably wind up working for someone else. While this argument won't persuade most five-year-olds, it is really meant to set an independent tone.

Your child, on the other hand, is learning responsibility and may end up hiring other people. Using money as payment for activities will teach children the importance of work and completing chores correctly.

Important: Paying your kids to do chores does not mean that you should ignore birthdays and holidays. Give generously on these special occasions. People get gifts because they are loved—and not every acquisition has to be earned.

• *Praise your children's entrepreneurial efforts.* When my children were growing up in the 1960s, I bragged about them all the time when I was in their presence. I told friends, neighbors and relatives how hard they worked. If one of them bought a new bike with earned money, everybody heard about it.

I also told my kids privately how proud I was and how I admired their initiative. Your children have to hear you say it. It gives them confidence, self-esteem and a sense of accomplishment.

To keep from spoiling them with praise, however, you can blend compliments with doses of reality.

Example: If your children suggest any offbeat ideas—ones that you know won't fly—praise their creativity but show them why a trip back to the drawing board is probably necessary.

• *Teach them financial independence.* Children as young as age 4½ should have total control over the money they earn. Of course, this does not mean they should be permitted to use their money to buy items that you have forbidden, such as candy.

But in most cases, let them spend the money they have earned the way they want to. Let them make mistakes. If they squander it on snacks, then they won't have it for bigger things they might want.

Important: Don't bail out your kids.

• *Encourage capitalism.* All kids want something material, whether it's a new toy or game when they're young…or a special sweater or bike when they're older.

My 4½-year-old son just started earning 10 cents a day by getting my morning paper. That's no small task, since it's a four-minute walk from his room.

If you have teenagers, point out that they can get the items they desire by creating a business that serves the community, such as painting or hedge trimming.

Strategies: Ask your children for *their* ideas about profit-making services that they would like to provide. Help them understand exactly why one idea might be better than another.*

Talk often about business at the dinner table or in the car. Let your kids know that business can be exciting and fulfilling, as well as profitable. Tell stories about entrepreneurs you admire and why you respect them.

• *Establish a joint venture with your children.* This strategy will sound brutal to some parents, but it's a great way to help get a child's business off the ground and to teach real-world lessons.

Strategy: If your children are using your lawn mower and gasoline to tend other people's lawns, don't let them reap all the profits. Split the money—or take a cut. After all, you're providing the capital—in this case, the mower and the gas.

The more formal your children's business structure, the better. Hold regularly scheduled "board" meetings to discuss the business and divide the profits.

A good time to have these meetings is immediately after dinner, when you won't have to compete with many distractions. Hold the meetings in an office-like setting.

Example: The dining room is better than the living room or the children's room.

You wouldn't believe what a powerful effect these meetings will have on most kids.

Example: When my father and I started our lemonade business, he provided the lemons, sugar and mixing equipment. One of my greatest thrills was giving him his share of the proceeds each month. When I handed him the money, I felt nine feet tall. It was like saying, "Look, Dad, here's a tangible sign of what I achieved in the last month."

There was another benefit as well. I knew that my father, who owned cotton gins, had frequent business meetings with his associates. And here he was having a formal business meeting with me, a seven-year-old. That made me feel great.

*Business Kids, a company that helps children become entrepreneurs, sells a package of booklets and audio cassettes to show them how to start businesses and put together business plans. One Alhambra Plaza, Coral Gables, FL 33134.

Important: You and your spouse can sit on the board of directors, but remember that your children are the CEOs. Encourage them to bring agendas and oversee the meetings. When your kids make suggestions that you know won't fly, discuss them gently until they understand the flaws.

• *Open bank accounts in your children's names.* Do this early—soon after birth—and consider giving children checking accounts as early as age six. Depending on their maturity, you can do this as soon as they become proficient with adding and subtracting.

Reason: When a six-year-old writes a check —even if you have to cosign it—he feels serious, grown-up and important. It's a solemn occasion, in the best sense of the word. If the check-writing privilege is abused, your child's account will dry up—another lesson learned.

• *Charge interest if you lend your children money.* There's nothing wrong with giving a child an advance on next month's earnings, but do it in a real-world way. I charged my kids interest—the prime lending rate at the time plus one or two percentage points.

Important: Even if the total interest charge is 17 cents, don't let the payment slide. Losing that 17 cents is a terrific way for a child to learn about the cost of capital and the penalty for buying now and paying later.

• *Attitude is more important than profits.* One of the biggest mistakes parents make is taking some of these ideas too far. By encouraging entrepreneurship, you don't want to turn your children into money-crazed workaholics.

To keep this from happening, tell your children how entrepreneurship is consistent with your family's values…that entrepreneurs serve their communities…that the good ones sell good products or services at fair prices…and that total integrity is good for your soul and business.

Important: To keep your kids from becoming too materialistic, mix entrepreneurial lessons with spiritual lessons. Talk about families that are less fortunate. Suggest that your children might want to give some of their earnings to charity.

Finally, you can communicate what my father told me: "Running your own business isn't about power and money. It's about freedom, fun, creativity and new challenges."

Source: Wilson L. Harrell, president of Harrell Consulting Inc., which helps entrepreneurs get started, 7380 Pine Valley Rd., Cumming, GA 30131. The founder of more than 100 companies, he is the author of *For Entrepreneurs Only*, Career Press, 180 Fifth Ave., Hawthorne, NJ 07507.

Giving Money to Kids Is Getting Trickier

Parents who want to build a college fund for a child often assume the best strategy is to put money into a custodial account in that child's name.

Custodial accounts are easy to create under the Uniform Gifts to Minors Act (UGMA) or the Uniform Transfers to Minors Act (UTMA), depending on your state. You don't need a lawyer. The bank or mutual fund that will hold the account can arrange it while you wait.

But custodial accounts can cause big problems if you don't know all the pitfalls. *Here's what to watch out for...*

•*Once you give it away it's gone.* The instant you put money into a custodial account, it becomes your child's money...irrevocably. You can't take it back without the child's permission. The law might not catch you—but your child could sue to recover the money.

Example: You need more cash for the down payment to buy a new house, so you borrow the money from a child's custodial account.

Better: If you think you might ever want the money back, don't use an UGMA. Keep the money in your own name and pay it out on the child's behalf as needed.

• *You lose control over how the money is spent.* You can direct how money in a custodial account will be spent only as long as your child is a minor. You cannot place limits on what your child can do with money in an UGMA or

UTMA when he/she reaches majority...which can be 18, 20 or 21, depending on the state.

At that age, your child could spend the money on anything...including a new car, a trip to Europe or even drugs. The only power you have to direct the spending is moral suasion.

Suggestion: If you fear the child may not be ready to handle the money even when he/she reaches majority...use a child's or minor's trust rather than an UGMA or UTMA. In this type of trust, you determine at what age your child will receive the money.

Example: When I set up a child's trust, I usually give the child the income from the trust at age 18 and then one-third of the principal at age 25, one-third at 30 and one-third at 35.

Also, I give the trustee the ability to withhold money if the child suffers any type of "disability." I define that very broadly to include drug and emotional problems. No UGMA statute builds in the safeguards and contingencies of such a trust.

•*It can mess up college financing plans.* Putting money into a custodial account to help pay college bills can hurt your chances of getting financial aid.

Even higher-income families can sometimes qualify for aid, depending on family circumstances. Having assets in your child's name works against that. When a college assesses family need for aid, they assume that assets in your child's name can help pay school bills. UGMA assets are considered the child's assets for the test.

Example: The college will assume that 5.65% of your assets are available for school expenses. It will assume that 35% of your child's assets are available for college.

Suggestion: If there is any possibility you will apply for financial aid, keep the money in your name...not the child's. But the rules vary. In some situations, you might be better off with the money in a trust.

•*It can nullify estate planning.* Many parents and grandparents use UGMAs to get money out of their estate for estate planning purposes. Then they make themselves custodians of the account, unaware that if you are custodian of an account and you die, the money goes back into your estate.

Suggestion: If you have a large estate and want the money out of the estate, name a trustworthy relative—not yourself—as custodian of the trust.

• *It won't shield you from creditors.* Some parents believe that using a UGMA account can protect assets if they file for bankruptcy. But transferring money to your child's name to protect it from creditors can be considered a fraudulent conveyance that the courts can set aside.

Suggestion: If you fear bankruptcy, set up a foreign situs (Latin for "situated") trust offshore, in a place like the Cayman Islands. That puts the assets beyond the reach of creditors…and beyond the reach of the US legal system. But do it before the claims against you arise.

If you don't have time to do that, don't make a transfer at all.

Source: Martin M. Shenkman, CPA, and estate planning attorney, 1086 Teaneck Rd., Teaneck, New Jersey 07666. He is the author of the *Complete Book of Trusts*, John Wiley & Sons, Inc., New York.

Colicky Baby Relief

Colicky babies who lift their knees to their stomachs after eating may be suffering from gastric disturbances caused by cow's milk. *If you're breast-feeding:* Eliminate cow's milk products from your diet. *If you're bottle-feeding:* Talk with your doctor about returning to breast-feeding, if possible…switch to a soy-based formula…try burping the baby more frequently.

Source: *Great Expectations: An Illustrated Guide to Your Pregnancy, Your Birth, Your Baby* by Antonia Van Der Meer, New York health writer, Delta Books, 1540 Broadway, New York.

Children/Fat Link

Children need fat and cholesterol for proper growth and brain development. Children under age two need fat and cholesterol every day—even if they look chubby. Breast-fed babies get what they need from breast milk, which draws 50% of its calories from fat. Preschool children should gradually move from a high-fat infant diet to a lower-fat diet appropriate for an older child.

Source: James A. Taylor, MD, director of the Pediatric Center, University of Washington, Seattle.

To Childproof Your Home

Each year, household injuries kill an estimated 2,400 American children under the age of five. Most home owners are savvy enough to keep firearms, plastic bags and other obvious hazards out of a child's reach. But that isn't enough.

The best way to safeguard your home is with a painstaking, room-by-room inspection.

What to do: Periodically, walk through every room in your house. Examine things from the perspective of an infant or toddler. Watch out for pot handles protruding over the edge of the stove, sharp edges on furniture, etc. Place loose change, marbles, hard candies and other small items that might cause choking out of reach.

Important: Start at the same end of the house (or on the same floor) each time, so you establish a routine.

Commonly overlooked hazards:

• *Bathtub.* To prevent a fall, drowning, scalding, etc., all children under the age of five should be supervised as they bathe. *Also:* Equip tubs with nonskid decals. Don't rely on plastic "suction seats" that let kids sit up in the water. They can tip over.

• *Coffee table.* Don't use a coffee table until kids are at least two years old. Tots can cut themselves by hitting their heads on a table's sharp edges.

• *Crib.* Use a crib made after 1980—earlier models may lack certain safety features, such as closely spaced slats and a tight-fitting mattress. Make sure there are no loose joints—children have been injured and even killed by collapsing cribs. If the crib's corner posts protrude over the top railing, saw them off and sand them down so that children's clothing can't get caught. Place a rug on the floor in case the child tumbles out.

• *Diaper pail.* The diaper pail should have a secure top. *Reason:* The plastic bag inside the pail can suffocate—and the disinfectant can be poisonous.

• *Household cleaners.* Never keep cleaners, solvents, drain openers, etc., in unlocked cabinets under sinks. Store them on high shelves, or lock the cabinets.

Caution: Paint thinner, turpentine, furniture polish and other toxic substances should be stored in their original, childproof containers. Drano crystals are particularly deadly. Dishwasher detergent is highly caustic.

• *Electrical cords.* Make sure toaster and coffeepot cords don't dangle from countertops, where tiny hands can reach. If you use a percolator, Crock-Pot, etc., be sure to detach cords from both the appliance and the electrical outlet. Plugged-in, dangling cords can give kids nasty electrical burns.

• *Electrical outlets.* To reduce the risk of electrocution, equip kitchens and bathrooms with circuit-interrupting outlets. They automatically turn off the current if a hair-dryer or other plugged-in appliance comes in contact with water.

Note: Your home already has circuit interrupters if you see two buttons and the words "test" and "reset" on the outlet's faceplate.

• *Tablecloth.* Don't use tablecloths. Kids can tug on them, overturning hot soup, heavy dishes, etc.

• *Television/VCR.* TV sets should be housed in shelving that's firmly attached to the wall. Don't use a TV stand or freestanding bookshelf —kids can reach up and pull the set down on top of them.

Keep your VCR on a high shelf to keep little hands from getting caught in the mechanism.

• *Toilet bowl.* To prevent toddlers from falling in the bowl and drowning, equip all toilets with safety locks. Toilet locks and other safety gadgets are available from Perfectly Safe, 7245 Whipple Ave. NW, North Canton, Ohio 44720 (800-837-5437) and The Safety Zone, Hanover, Pennsylvania 17333 (800-999-3030). Call for free catalogs.

• *Toiletries.* Keep all cosmetics and prescription and over-the-counter drugs out of reach.

• *Toy box.* Check toy boxes for jagged edges. If there is a hinged lid, remove it. Hinged lids can slam down suddenly, injuring children.

Source: Mark Widome, MD, professor of pediatrics, Pennsylvania State University College of Medicine, Hershey. He is the former chairman of the Committee on Injury and Poison Prevention, American Academy of Pediatrics, 141 NW Point Blvd., Elk Grove Village, Illinois 60009.

Better Baby-Sitting Checklist

When parents go out for an evening, they often call a neighborhood teen to babysit. Here's how to make sure that the baby-sitter will properly supervise your child—and react well in a crisis.

Questions to ask:

• *Ask the candidate to provide references from two current or former employers.*

• *Ask the candidate how he/she would handle an emergency.* What would he do for a fever…choking…head injury…heavy bleeding? Make sure the answers he gives are appropriate to the situation. Ask about any special training he might have—including classes for CPR certification or first aid.

• *Ask what method of discipline would be used with your child.* Evaluate the candidate's answers in terms of how well they fit your family. Is his method the same as yours?

Cite specific problems: Two children fighting over the same toy…or a child who won't go to bed on time. Would the candidate use reason? Time-outs? Stern words?

•*Ask the candidate how a temper tantrum would be handled.* Would he ignore your child? Try to distract the child? Look for a sitter who understands that tantrums are normal.

Important: Make sure the candidate's answer demonstrates he is patient.

Before you go out:

•*Leave the phone number at which you can be reached.* In an emergency, have the sitter call you.

Important: Leave a second emergency number—your neighbor's or a nearby relative's—to be used if he can't reach you.

•*Leave a list of all important emergency phone numbers.* Create a list of these names, numbers and addresses…

•*Your child's pediatrician.* The sitter will probably reach an answering service. Remind him to identify himself as your child's sitter, then leave information with the service so that the doctor can return the call.

•*The hospital at which the pediatrician practices.* This is important in case the doctor wants the child rushed to the emergency room. Leave emergency money in an envelope in case the sitter has to take a cab.

•*Fire, police, ambulance and a poison-control center.*

These phone numbers should be listed in large, black lettering on a sheet of white paper. Also include instructions on when to use the phone numbers. Post the list on the refrigerator or in some other obvious place.

•*Explain basic security issues.* Review the use of keys, alarms and intercoms. Let the sitter try them before you leave. Indicate where the flashlights and candles are stored in case of power failure.

Instruct the sitter not to open the door to strangers. If you expect anyone, such as a delivery person, let the sitter know who to expect, what time the person will arrive, and what he is supposed to do. Otherwise, through the door, the sitter should tell the stranger to come back another time.

•*Review child-development issues.* Ask yourself, "What kind of mischief can my child get into?" Is he just learning to crawl, putting everything in his mouth? Give some related strategies, such as keeping the carpet clean of small objects that can be choking hazards.

•*List any foods to be avoided,* such as nuts, chocolate, and/or hot dogs if they can cause choking or trigger allergies.

Source: Joy Wayne, director of Nannies Plus, a nanny-placement service in New Jersey.

How to Get Through To Your Teens

Teenagers tune out when adults use the word *responsibility* because it triggers panic and resentment. That prompts teens to ignore—or not take seriously—the message you're trying to get across.

Better: Instead of the word *responsibility*, use the word *resourcefulness*. It captures everything you want to say about responsibility but also encourages teens to deal effectively and imaginatively with problems.

Example I: Instead of telling your daughter she is responsible for earning money to help pay for a bike, urge her to be resourceful about earning the money herself.

Example II: If your son says he isn't doing well in history because he's bored, urge him to be resourceful and find sources of information that are interesting.

Important: Also avoid phrases such as "Change your attitude"…"When I was your age"…"You should." All will produce the same negative results as the word responsibility.

Source: Adam Robinson, education consultant, 154 Reade St., New York 10013, and the author of *What Smart Students Know: Maximum Grades, Optimum Learning, Minimum Time,* Crown Publishers, Inc., 201 E. 50 St., New York 10022.

When Adult Children Come Home

When a child moves back home after graduating from college, he/she should not expect to receive the benefits of childhood with none of the responsibilities of adulthood. Ask him to outline his future plans…let you know how he intends to pitch in around the house…contribute rent money. *Usually fair:* 12% to 15% of his take-home pay. If he does not have a job, substitute additional household work for rent until he is earning regular income.

Source: *The Amy Vanderbilt Complete Book of Etiquette* by Nancy Tuckerman, etiquette expert, and Nancy Dunnan, financial writer, Doubleday, New York.

When You Can't Make The Mortgage Payment

If you're having trouble paying your mortgage, take stock of your financial situation and then immediately get in touch with your mortgage loan officer. Schedule a personal meeting. Most lenders prefer to reschedule payments and avoid foreclosure—it's an expensive, time-consuming process that would force the lender to sell your home in an uncertain market.

Source: *The Mortgage Book* by John Dorfman, *The Wall Street Journal* writer and author of seven books on investing and personal finance, New York, Consumer Reports Books, Yonkers, NY.

Burglaries/Break-Ins

What is the most effective way to prevent break-ins and burglaries? The single best thing you can do is to install standard dead-bolt locks on all doors—and use them when in or out.

Can't burglars simply pick the locks you install? Yes. A determined professional can beat almost any home security setup. But there are very few professionals. You cut your vulnerability by making things difficult for the ordinary burglar.

Even a locked weak door actually has a fair chance of discouraging a break-in by amateur thieves, especially if it has a simple rubber doorstop wedged under it.

What about installing an alarm system? Of course this is a good idea. And if you do plan to install a system, ask your insurance company if doing so earns a discount.

There are other simple things you can do such as trimming your shrubbery. By keeping your doors and windows open to view and your grounds neat and clean, you reduce the house's appeal to criminals. No one knows why neat grounds also protect, but they do. So does having a dog.

What should I do when I go away on vacation? Leave a light on somewhere in the house, and have a TV or radio turned on low. For just a few dollars you can get timers to turn on lights and appliances at different times.

Also, make sure your mail is picked up every day if your box can be seen by outsiders. The best arrangement is a mail slot right into the house.

Do not leave a message on an answering machine revealing that you are away. Instead, say something like, "Hello, if you leave your name and number, we'll get back to you." Always say "we," even if you live alone. "We" is discouraging.

What should be done if a break-in occurs while someone is at home? In advance, you should secure your bedroom by installing locks on its door to use in an emergency.

If you hear an intruder, try to get out of the house and go to a neighbor for help. If you cannot get out safely, go to the bedroom, lock the door, force a chair under the doorknob and jam any kind of wedge under the door. This will make even a hollow core door virtually impenetrable. Phone the police.

Source: Criminology expert J.L. Simmons, PhD, author of *67 Ways to Protect Seniors from Crime*, Henry Holt & Co., New York.

How to Choose a Safe Home Safe

Burglars hate safes. They take too long to crack…and a good one is too heavy and secure to move. But some safes are safer than others. Here's what you need to ask before you buy one…and the different types to consider.

•*Will your valuables fit inside?* At home, put all your valuables in a box. If there's room left inside, fold all the sides down around your valuables. Remove your valuables, and take the empty box along with you to slip inside different safes.

•*Will your valuables survive a fire?* A tag on the safe will indicate whether temperatures inside will remain below 451 degrees—the point at which paper burns.

Types of safes:

No matter which safe you decide to buy, a combination lock is better than one that requires a key. Consider safes with labels from Underwriters Laboratories, Inc. (UL), an independent product-testing lab.

•*Wall safe.* One great advantage to a wall safe is that it can be easily hidden behind a painting or other wall hanging.

Drawback: Most walls in newer homes are thin, so these safes are small and may not hold all valuables. They can hold jewelry, coins and papers, but not much else.

A good wall safe has sides made of half-inch solid steel with a one-inch-thick door. The combination lock should have a device that freezes the bolt mechanism in the locked position if someone tries to drill a hole through the lock. In addition, you can make the safe harder to pry out of a wall by using larger screws when you install it.

Best location: Away from the master bedroom, which is where thieves look first. The safest location is the basement.

•*Floor safe.* Safes that stand on the floor and are bolted into either the floor joists or a wall are ideal for a large amount of possessions. They can hold all of your jewelry, important papers and small objects. A floor safe can be bolted into a cement floor.

Important: Bolting a safe into the floor makes it very difficult to remove if you ever want to redecorate or relocate.

•*Gun safe.* These safes are the size of a large wardrobe and are very heavy. They are designed to keep guns out of children's hands and prevent guns from being stolen. They can also hold other valuables.

Gun safes have more sophisticated locking mechanisms and thicker doors. They're not disguised. These safes can weigh up to 1,000 pounds, so the basement may be best able to support them.

Some gun safes have quick-open locks, which are designed to allow you to access a loaded weapon quickly. These quick-open safes can hold one or several guns, but they are not intended to hold other valuables.

Source: David Alan Wacker, former police officer and now president of Smart Systems, a home-security company in Denver. He is the author of *The Complete Guide to Home Security*, Betterway Books, Cincinnati.

Nontoxic Pest Control

Keep your home clean…cool…and dry. Pests thrive in damp, warm and dirty environments.

•*Never leave food out.* Store it in airtight containers. Wipe up crumbs and spills immediately. Keep garbage pails tightly covered.

•*Seal off all points of entry.* Caulk cracks in woodwork, or stuff them with steel wool. Weather-strip doors. Place screening over heating vents.

•*Set a roach trap.* Wrap a clean jar with masking tape. Rub a one-inch band of petroleum jelly inside the rim. Fill the jar half full of beer. Set it in the corner of any roach-infested room overnight. In the morning, empty the bugs into a bucket of hot, soapy water. Don't leave the trap out during the day—it may attract flies.

•*Be sure to buy pest-free food.* Avoid packages with scrape marks or holes. Don't buy from open bins.

•*Throw out any bug-infested food.* Place it in a sealable plastic bag in a covered garbage pail. Keep the pail in the sunlight.

•*Prepare clothes carefully before storing them for the season.* Hang them in the sun for eight hours, then brush with a clothes brush. Store in sealable plastic bags or zippered wardrobe bags. Fine fabrics should be wrapped in a pillowcase, covered with newspaper and taped shut.

•*Treat cats and dogs with lemon-water (not flea powder).* Cut four lemons in eighths, cover with water, bring to a boil and simmer for 45 minutes. Let cool, strain and store in a glass container. Two or three times a week, rub the solution on your pet, brushing the mixture down to the skin. Towel-dry, then comb.

•*Eliminate standing water outside your home.* Mosquitoes breed in water as shallow as one-quarter inch.

•*Plant basil and/or burn citronella candles in your yard.* Eat garlicky foods, too. Garlic repels mosquitoes.

•*Plug ant nests with petroleum jelly—then patching compound.* If you spot an ant trail indoors, sponge it down with dishwasher detergent.

Source: Bernice Lifton, the author of *Bug Busters: Poison-Free Pest Control for Your House & Garden*, Avery Publishing Group, 120 Old Broadway, Garden City Park, New York 11040.

Accident-Proof Your Home

•*Light stairways.* If you don't already have them, consider installing light switches at the top and bottom of stairways, so you can turn the light on and off from either place. *If that's not possible:* Plug night-lights into the nearest outlets.

•*Never run an electrical cord or telephone wire under a rug.* Over time, they fray and can cause a fire.

•*Place smoke detectors where they'll do the most good.* Inside the room of any family member who sleeps with the door closed… away from air vents, where fresh air can keep smoke from activating the unit…away from the corner where the walls and ceiling meet and air circulation is poor.

•*Open containers of flammable liquids outside.* When liquids such as gasoline evaporate, flammable vapors collect in the container. When the container is opened, these vapors are released and can be ignited by a nearby heat source, such as the pilot light on your stove or sparks from an electric motor.

•*Keep plenty of oversized ashtrays on hand* if you, your spouse or your friends smoke. A large ashtray is more difficult to miss with a lit cigarette. And…never balance an ashtray on the arm of a chair or couch, where it can more easily spill and drop still-smoldering cigarette butts onto carpets, furniture or clothing.

•*Examine over-the-counter medicines carefully.* Beyond looking to see that the tamper-proof packaging is in place, check the medicine itself. Look for capsules that appear different from the rest.

Source: Ken Lawrence, the author of *Accident-Proof Your Life*, Thomas Nelson Publishers, Box 141000, Nashville 37214.

14

Smart Tax Moves

Strategic Recordkeeping To Help You Lower Your Taxes

Keeping good financial records is easy…and there are many financial and psychological rewards to doing so. One of the biggest payoffs is the tax savings. *Reasons…*

•You won't overlook any deductions or income when you file your taxes.

•You won't have to pay an accountant to reconstruct records for you.

•Your records will back up your claims in case the IRS ever audits you. Without evidence for your deductions, you would probably have to pay what the IRS says you owe.

Buy a file box and folders…or clear a drawer in your desk or filing cabinet and get started. What you need to keep and for how long…

Personal residence:

While most people keep their original purchase documents and mortgage records, they neglect to set up a folder for home-improvement receipts. These costs include anything that is built-in and adds to the house's value.

Examples: Central air cleaner, alarm system, attic fan, built-in barbecue, built-in bookcases, closets, doorbell, greenhouse, wall-to-wall carpeting, hot tub.

Important: The costs of these improvements are added to the house's purchase price when determining your cost basis for tax purposes. If you are a do-it-yourselfer, materials and supplies count but your labor does not.

If you lose these receipts and forget about several small improvements, when you sell your home you could wind up paying tax on a larger capital gain than you actually owe.

Routine maintenance such as painting the house or making plumbing repairs does not count. Keep records regarding these routine repairs only as long as their warranties are in effect. After that, they can be thrown out.

Example: A better roof counts, but replacing a leaky roof with one of the same kind does not.

Under the tax code, you generally do not have to pay a capital-gains tax on a principal residence as long as you buy another one of equal or greater value within two years of the sale. That means a family that has moved several times may have a fat filing folder, as the cost basis of one house is transferred to the next one and the next one. You need to keep records on all your previous residences until you don't have a gain to roll over.

If you have failed to keep these records, re-create a history—look at your old checks...go to contractors and ask them for duplicate bills.

The sooner you do this, the better. People can usually remember $5,000 or $7,000 outlays, but several $100 or $200 items over a period of years are a lot tougher to recall—and they add up.

Home offices:

People who deduct home offices—which, according to the IRS, must be their principal places of business and used regularly and exclusively for business—must keep more detailed records until they sell their homes. Depreciation on the portion of the house used as an office reduces your current year's taxes. In addition, you are entitled to deduct a pro-portionate share of utilities, repairs and insurance. Therefore, you need to keep records of these expenses until you sell the home.

Trap: Be aware that the cost basis of your house goes down for the part that you depreciate. When you sell the house, you cannot roll over the gain on that portion of the house.

Stocks and bonds:

Keep the transaction slips that your broker sends you each time you buy securities for as long as you own them. When you sell, match the purchase slip with the sales slip, so that you can report capital gains and losses on your return. Keep the records with the tax return for at least three years.

Mutual funds:

You need to keep all those documents that a fund manager sends you each month—or each quarter—showing your dividend reinvestments, fund trades or redemptions.

Reason I: When you sell shares—especially if you are going to sell bits and pieces at a time

—you have a choice about which ones to sell. That matters in terms of trying to keep down taxable capital gains or even taking a capital loss of up to $3,000 against ordinary income.

Reason II: Since you pay taxes each year on dividends and capital-gains distributions, you want a record of them even if they are rein-vested. Otherwise, you might pay taxes twice, if you merely subtract the purchase price from the eventual sale price.

Important: In addition to keeping the state-ments, have a summary sheet listing each trans-action in the front of the folder. Then you can see at a glance which shares you should sell.

Individual retirement accounts:

It is important to keep detailed records on IRAs, separating the records pertaining to those that are deductible and those that aren't de-ductible, depending on your level of income.

Indeed, keep careful records on all tax-de-ferred retirement accounts. If you borrow from such an account, keep records to show that the money was put back in on time.

Rental real estate:

Keep closing statements if you bought or sold property that you rented out. Also, keep checks, invoices and documentation for all the deductible items listed on Schedule E of your tax return, including repairs, advertising, utili-ties, gardening and other help.

Automobile records:

Keep records on the unreimbursed use of your car for business. You can deduct 30 cents per mile. If your car requires high-maintenance care, it might pay to deduct actual costs, includ-ing washing, waxing, repairs and maintenance, registration, licensing and garage rent.

For most people, however, it is easier to take a mileage deduction. If you use the car for charitable work, such as delivering food for a charity, you can deduct 12 cents per mile.

If you are eligible to deduct your medical expenses, you can also deduct the costs of driving to and from your doctor's office.

Keep these records with the returns for three years after filing.

Charitable records:

Starting with tax year 1994, a canceled check does not prove a deduction for a charitable contribution of cash or property of $250 or more at one time. You need a receipt from the organization.

If you attend a charity's dinner or event that costs more than $75, you need a written record from the charity specifying how much you donated and the cost of the dinner.

Keep the records with the return for three years after filing. For gifts of less than $250, a canceled check is sufficient.

Casualty or theft loss:

Videotape your home and its contents—a lot of insurance companies will do free videotapes for you. Keep a copy of the tape in your safe-deposit box or with your lawyer or accountant …and another copy at home.

In case of theft, you will want a police report and appraisal, and the videotape will help document the loss.

Casualty losses are deductible only to the extent that the lesser of cost or market value, after any insurance recovery, exceeds 10% of Adjusted Gross Income plus $100.

Warning: Casualty losses are practically a red flag for an audit. Still, if you suffer a severe loss, claim it and prove your case with the records of the loss and insurance proceeds.

Interest:

Interest on home-mortgage and home-equity loans on your principal residence and one other residence is generally deductible. And, if you borrow money to invest or for business, that interest is also deductible.

But if you take out a margin loan through your broker to pay for a vacation, a car or any other consumer goods, that is consumer interest, which is not deductible.

All of this makes it important to keep close records when you borrow money. If you take an interest deduction, you may need to justify it.

Past tax returns:

Normally you need to keep tax returns and the supporting documentation for deductions and income for between three and four years. The IRS has three years to audit a return after it has been filed. However, the limit can extend to six years if income has been substantially understated.

If you have any carryforwards (deductions, losses or credits you can't take in the current year but which the tax law allows you to take

in future tax years—for example, passive losses that cannot be taken until you have passive income), then keep the return and records as long as necessary to claim the losses.

In the case of more complicated situations, such as trusts, estates, S corporations and partnerships, it is prudent to keep the records for at least six years.

Some people keep their tax returns—though not all of the supporting documents—forever because these forms often are their only comprehensive records of family finances.

Source: Carol R. Caruthers, national director of personal financial services for Price Waterhouse. She is a partner in the firm's St. Louis office at One Boatman's Plaza, St. Louis 63103.

Filing Separately to Save Your House

Even though *married filing jointly* generally results in a lower tax calculation than *married filing separately,* there may be good reason to incur a greater tax liability. More and more taxpayers are finding that they owe the IRS more money than they will ever be able to pay. A house owned by a nonworking spouse could be spared from an IRS tax lien for unpaid income taxes if a separate return, rather than a joint return, is filed. *Caution:* Transferring property to a nonworking spouse after the tax liability has been created will usually not protect against an IRS claim.

Source: Ms. X is a former IRS agent still well connected.

How to Cut Your Taxes By Planning Ahead

A nip here and a tuck there before year-end can pare what you must pay next April…or bring you a bigger refund to spend in 1995.

Here's how to trim your taxes…and help avoid unpleasant surprises from the tough new rules that came into play in 1994. And the same techniques can help save taxes in 1995 and beyond…

•*Maximize retirement savings.* Money in qualified retirement plans, including IRAs, 401(k)s and Keogh accounts, compounds tax-free until you begin withdrawing it after age 59½. That makes a big difference, compared with regular savings accounts that are reduced each year by the tax bite.

Check with your company benefits office to be sure you are putting all you can into your 401(k) plan. If you have self-employment income, set up a Keogh account before the end of the year. You don't have to put money into the account until you actually file your return for this year…sometime in 1995.

•*Tune up your investment portfolio.* If you are sitting on paper losses in stocks, bonds or mutual funds, there's still time to trade your clunkers for tax savings. Capital losses reduce capital gains dollar for dollar. Once you've offset gains, up to $3,000 of capital losses can go to offset ordinary income. Losses beyond $3,000 can be carried forward to future years.

If you think a depressed issue will eventually bounce back…sell it and replace it with a similar but not identical security. You get the tax loss while sticking to your investment plan.

Warning: If you buy the same issue back within 30 days, you run afoul of the "wash-sale rule," meaning that for tax purposes no sale has taken place.

You can lock in gains on investments while deferring taxes by "selling short against the box." You sell short shares identical to those you hold…taking your profit on the shares you sell. Then you use your own shares to close out the short position after the first of the year.

•*Manage your mutual funds.* Most mutual funds have built up capital gains from years past. If they sell and realize those gains, you owe the tax on all past gains, even if you bought your shares the day before yesterday.

Helpful: Never buy fund shares until capital gains have been declared.

•Call the 800-number of any fund you are interested in to find out if and when there are likely to be capital gains.

•Call the 800 number of any fund you own right now to find out the prospect for year-end capital-gains distributions…to give yourself time to take offsetting losses before December 31.

•*Give to charity…not the IRS.* Avoid capital-gains taxes by fulfilling any pledges you've made to charities with appreciated property, such as stocks or bonds that you have owned more than a year. You avoid paying income taxes on the appreciation and you get to deduct the fair market value of the asset as a charitable contribution.

Personal property, ranging from old clothing or furniture to valuable art works, is also generally deductible at fair market value. Be sure you have records or appraisals to show how you arrived at the valuation.

Important: Under tough new rules that took effect for 1994, you must be able to show a receipt from the charity for each donation of $250 or more. Do not send receipts with your return. Keep them on file for at least six years in case the IRS asks to see them.

Another new rule affects few people, but could have a big impact on those it does hit. People with private foundations have only until year-end to donate appreciated property and deduct it at market value. Starting in 1995 you can deduct only what the donated property cost you.

•*Deduct your dues.* After denying deductions for many club dues a year ago, the IRS recently restored part of the deduction under temporary regulations. Dues to professional groups like the American Medical Association or the American Institute of Certified Public Accountants are deductible. So are dues to groups like the Lions, the Elks or Chamber of Commerce if you can show a business purpose was served by your membership.

•*Deduct business meals and gifts.* The deduction for business meals has been cut to 50% of the meal's cost from 80%. But business gifts costing up to $25 are fully deductible. More gifts and fewer lunches this holiday season can shave taxes.

•*Get the most from mortgage points.* The IRS recently announced that seller-paid points are deductible by the buyer of a principal residence, effective back to 1990. Anyone affected may file an amended return to claim the deduction for past years.

Refinancing a mortgage may qualify you for a deduction. You qualify if you went to a different lender and paid off unamortized points from a previous loan.

• *Give tax-wise family gifts.* Gifts of up to $10,000 a person ($20,000 per couple) to any number of recipients incur no gift- or estate-tax consequences. Parents and grandparents in the higher tax brackets often give securities to children 14 and older to pay college costs. The income tax on the interest and dividends earned by the gift will be at the child's presumably lower rate.

Important: The $10,000-gift rule is widely seen as a tax break favoring the wealthy and could vanish in new Congressional efforts to cut the budget deficit next year. To be safe, do your giving this year instead of putting it off until 1996.

• *Withholding and estimated taxes.* Taxpayers must pay at least 90% of the current year's tax liabilities through withholding from wages or by making quarterly estimated tax payments.

Taxpayers who had adjusted gross incomes (AGI) below $150,000 in 1994 may pay an amount equal to 100% of their 1994 tax liability. Those above $150,000 can pay 110% of their 1994 bill.

Underwithholding can subject you to penalties. But withholding is treated as though it occurred evenly throughout the year. If you face such a penalty, step up withholding at the end of the year.

• *Make the most of business deductions.* If you own a business, even a small sideline business like consulting or freelance work, you can deduct up to $17,500 of equipment immediately each year without having to depreciate it over several years.

The deduction can't exceed income. But if your business did well this year, you can both upgrade your equipment and cut your taxes.

Helpful: If you need extra help around the business, hire your children.

Children can have earned income of up to $3,900 tax-free. If they put $2,000 into an IRA, the amount rises to $5,900. You deduct the wages you pay them...shifting income from your bracket to theirs...while keeping it in the family.

Important: It must be bona fide work paid at the same rate you would pay an outsider.

• *Bunch your deductions.* Medical expenses can be claimed only to the extent unreimbursed outlays exceed 7½% of AGI. Miscellaneous itemized deductions can be taken only to the extent they exceed 2% of AGI. Hence few people qualify for either deduction.

Check actual and anticipated spending. Could you qualify for a deduction if you bunched spending into this year...or delayed spending until 1996? You may not qualify for either deduction every year, but bunching spending might win a deduction every second or third year.

Source: Sidney Kess, certified public accountant and tax attorney, 630 Fifth Ave., New York 10111. He is a frequent lecturer on taxation to CPAs and attorneys and also is the author of *Financial and Estate Planning Reporter*, CCH Incorporated, Chicago.

Deductions Without Records

Deductions without records were allowed after a business's office was destroyed in a severe storm. The Tax Court upheld the business's deductions over the IRS's objection that they were unsubstantiated. *Key facts:* The company's records had been lost due to factors beyond its control, the owner's testimony concerning the deductions was completely credible and the deductions were reasonable in kind and amount in light of the nature of the business and the damage it had sustained.

Source: *Marvin Eugene Huff*, TC Memo 1994-451.

Real-Estate Loopholes

There are many tax breaks in owning real estate. A major benefit is that the increase in value is not taxed until the property is sold. And even then tax on the gain may be deferred—

even excluded. *How to make the most of your real-estate tax breaks...*

Personal real estate:

• *Loophole:* Tax deferral. When you sell your primary residence and reinvest the proceeds into a new, more expensive house, you can delay paying the tax on any gain until you sell the new house.

• *Loophole:* Step up in basis. If you own real estate at your death, the gain that has built up over the years is not taxed at all. The tax cost (basis) of the property is stepped up to its value on the date of your death. When your heirs sell the property they avoid paying tax on this gain.

• *Loophole:* Tax exclusion. If you are 55 or older when you sell your home, you can elect to permanently exclude from tax up to $125,000 of your gain.

• *Loophole:* Itemized deductions. Real-estate taxes on all your residences and vacation homes are deductible. Mortgage interest on loans secured by your principal residence and one second residence is deductible on up to $1 million of "acquisition indebtedness." This is debt incurred in acquiring, constructing, or substantially improving a residence.

Exception: Acquisition indebtedness that was incurred prior to October 14, 1987, is not subject to the $1 million limitation. *Bonus:* Interest on up to $100,000 of home equity interest is also deductible.

Points paid to secure a mortgage to buy or improve your principal residence are deductible in full in the year of payment. However, points paid to refinance an existing mortgage must be written off a bit each year over the life of the loan. Points paid on a loan to purchase or improve your second home do not qualify for deduction.

• *Loophole:* Tax-free rental income. If a residence or vacation home is rented out for fewer than 15 days during the taxable year, the rental income is not taxable. You don't have to report it on your tax return.

Commercial/investment:

• *Loophole:* Tax deferral. You can defer tax on a gain by swapping one piece of commercial or investment real estate for another of a similar nature. You don't pay tax on the gain until you sell the second piece of property.

To execute a swap, have the person who wants your property buy the property you want and then swap the properties. This can be done simultaneously. Swaps, technically called like-kind exchanges, are authorized by section 1031 of the Tax Code.

• *Loophole:* Charitable deductions. You can donate an easement on your property to charity and get a deduction for the fair market value of the easement.

Example I: If you live in a historic district, you might donate an easement of the facade of your home to a charitable organization. You would get a deduction for the value of the facade. In reality, though, you haven't given anything away since you aren't permitted to alter facades in historic districts.

Example II: You could give a township an easement to allow a fire break through your property, or to make part of your property into a parking lot for commuters.

• *Loophole:* Contiguous land. Owning undeveloped land does not give you any deductions. However, if the land is contiguous to your residence you can claim that it is part of your home and deduct real-estate taxes and mortgage interest.

If the land is simply held for investment, and not contiguous, you can add your expenses for taxes and interest to the tax cost of the property. This will reduce your tax when you ultimately sell the land.

• *Loophole:* Depreciation. Depreciation deductions shelter part of the cash flow from investment real estate. You can increase the cash flow by having a low mortgage on the property, thereby giving you a higher after-tax return.

• *Loophole:* Rental losses. An exception to the passive loss rules applies to real estate rental activities in which you are an active participant. Active involvement would include making management decisions such as approving new tenants or making capital expenditures.

Each tax year you can deduct up to $25,000 of your losses against your salary and other income. This $25,000 deduction is reduced by 50% of the amount by which your Adjusted Gross Income (AGI) exceeds $100,000. You get no deduction when your AGI is $150,000 or more.

Bigger losses:

Real estate losses are deductible against salary and other income for certain qualifying real-estate professionals.

A person qualifies for the deduction if…

•More than half of his/her personal services are performed in real-estate trades or businesses.

•He/she spends more than 750 hours a year on such activities.

•He/she materially participates in such activities.

Suppose a husband is a real-estate developer who spends only 500 hours in the real estate business. The husband has substantial losses from real estate in addition to a substantial salary. There is a way to make those real-estate losses deductible.

•*Loophole:* Put your spouse to work in a real-estate business. A husband and wife filing a joint return meet the eligibility requirement for deductible losses if, during the tax year, one spouse performs more than 750 hours in a real-estate trade or business. So, if one spouse puts in 750 hours selling real estate, say, no matter how much that spouse earns, the other spouse's real-estate losses would be deductible against the couple's salary and other income.

Caution: The spouse with losses would have to put in 500 hours in the activities he/she was engaged in and otherwise qualify as a material participant in real-estate activities.

Source: Edward Mendlowitz, partner, Mendlowitz Weitsen, CPAs, Two Pennsylvania Plaza, New York 10121.

Tax Trap: Independent Contractors

Avoid owing back employment taxes on independent contractors who may be recategorized by the IRS as employees.

How: Back taxes won't be due if…

•The company has treated its workers as contractors for all purposes, not just to avoid taxes.

•All 1099s and other tax filings due for contractors have been filed.

•There is a standard industry practice of treating workers as contractors, or some other "reasonable grounds" that justifies such treatment.

Defense: A company that makes regular use of contractors can protect against a future tax bill by documenting that it meets these conditions now.

Source: *Joey Bentley,* E.D. Tenn., No. 3:94-CV-446.

Overlooked Tax Break for Employees with Children

Employees with annual income under $24,396 who have dependent children may increase take-home pay by up to $105 per month, by having the Earned Income Credit (EIC) added to their paychecks. Only 1% of eligible employees do so. Most don't claim the credit until they file their tax returns—and many overlook it altogether. Inform employees that they can use this tax break by filing IRS Form W-5, *Earned Income Credit Advance Payment Certificate,* with the company.

How Self-Employeds and Moonlighters Can Avoid Trouble with the IRS

Self-employeds and moonlighters are entitled to special tax breaks. They are also subject to special IRS scrutiny. Avoid trouble with the IRS by following these simple rules when deducting items that could trigger an audit.

•*Travel and entertainment.* The IRS may challenge travel and entertainment deductions by saying that they were really nondeductible personal expenses.

Don't let the IRS take this deduction away from you when the expenditure was made for your freelance business or while you were moonlighting at a second job. You are entitled to deduct meals, travel and entertainment, including sporting or cultural events for yourself and your clients.

How to nail down these expenses: The IRS will want written documentation of the expenses. Save all relevant receipts and discipline yourself to carry a diary at all times. Diligently record all business-related expenses in the diary on a daily basis. Include all pertinent information, such as where you went, who you met, the business purpose of the meeting, the cost of meals and mileage put on the car.

The IRS has cut the deduction for business meals and entertainment from 80% of the expenses you incur to only 50%. So it's more important than ever to get the most out of this deduction by documenting every expense.

•*Business trips.* You can deduct all costs of a trip including airfare, hotel rooms and meals when the main purpose of the trip is for your self-employed business.

•*Schedule C advantage.* Moonlighting and self-employment income and expenses are reported on Schedule C. Any expense taken on Schedule C is more valuable than the same exact expense reported as a miscellaneous itemized deduction on Schedule A.

Reason: Miscellaneous itemized deductions are subject to severe limits. When taken on Schedule A, the deduction is available only to the extent that your miscellaneous expenses exceed 2% of your Adjusted Gross Income (AGI).

Schedule C expenses, on the other hand, are worth much more. They are subtracted from your gross freelance income dollar for dollar, without a percentage limit.

Trouble avoider: Don't flag your return by reporting all miscellaneous expenses, including personal expenses, on Schedule C. Take only legitimate business expenses that you can prove. Show your personal miscellaneous expenses on Schedule A.

•*Mileage advantage.* Moonlighters can deduct the cost of traveling to a second job. When you work at two places in one day, you can deduct the expense of getting from one job to the next.

When you use your car: You can take either the standard mileage rate of 30 cents for each business mile, plus tolls and parking, or your actual expenses.

You can deduct the cost of round-trip business-related travel between your home office and business customers or clients. (Your home office must qualify for the home-office deduction.) Avoid trouble with the IRS by keeping written records to separate business mileage from personal mileage on your car, since personal travel is not deductible.

•*Home office.* The IRS has attempted to restrict deductions for home offices, but it's still a perfectly legitimate deduction if you meet the requirements. IRS guidelines must be strictly adhered to in order to nail down your home-office deductions.

If you do qualify—you can deduct the proportionate part of the expenses of operating your home, such as utilities, fix-up expenses, painting, repairs and depreciation.

•Your home office must be the focal point of your business, the place where you actually perform most of your work.

•You can't use the space designated as your home office for any other purpose. If your children use the room to watch television at night, for example, it will be disqualified as a home office. The home office does not have to be an entire room, however. It can be a specific space in a room that otherwise fulfills the home-office requirements.

•You must use the home office regularly as a place of business. An occasional meeting or telephone call in the home office is not enough to qualify for the deduction.

Amount of your deduction: Use any reasonable method to figure out the percentage of space taken up by the home office. Apply the percentage to the total of each deductible home-office expense.

Source: Pete J. Medina, is a principal and tax consultant on practice and procedure before the IRS, Ernst & Young, LLP, 787 Seventh Ave., New York 10019.

Tax-Filing Traps

Certain legal income tax deductions are known to tax professionals as *red flags*. They attract the IRS's attention and are likely to trigger an audit.

Reason: Through long experience, the IRS has found that many of these deductions are abused. As a result, IRS agents are more likely to say "Show me" when these red flags appear on a return.

If you plan to take any of these deductions or have any of these red flags, be sure you have the paperwork to back them up…

•*Home-office deduction.* This is one of the IRS's favorite targets. In fact, the IRS has gone to court repeatedly, winning support for its tough stand in rejecting taxpayers' deductions.

To take depreciation on a portion of your home—or deduct a portion of your rent—for the space you use as a home office, you must be able to show that the room is used regularly and exclusively for business…and that it is the *principal place of your business.* People who take work home at night are not eligible for this deduction.

•*Travel and entertainment expenses.* Many entrepreneurs and even employees find it necessary to entertain prospective customers to win business.

The IRS knows that a lot of these people tuck personal bills in with their business receipts.

For 1995 returns, fewer expenses can be written off—only 50% of the cost of meals, down from 80% in recent years.

To make sure your legitimate tax deductions stand up, keep carefully organized and documented receipts and a diary stating the business purpose of all entertainment.

•*Losses on property you rented to others.* Because of complex tax rules introduced by the Tax Reform Act of 1986, the IRS may demand proof that you have actively participated in a rental activity—selecting tenants and supervising property-management employees, for example.

Satisfy that requirement and you can offset up to $25,000 of a rental loss against income from other sources, such as salary. If you did not actively participate, you generally get to offset the loss only against passive income, say, from a limited partnership investment.

•*Interest deduction.* Although home-mortgage interest is generally 100% deductible and investment interest is deductible to the extent it is matched by investment income, personal interest—interest paid on personal debts such as credit cards and car loans—is not deductible.

The IRS, however, suspects that taxpayers fudge sometimes.

Examples: Someone who incurred margin debt on a brokerage account to buy a car might list it as investment interest…or someone with a sideline business who properly files Schedule C to report the income might try to deduct interest on a personal debt as a business expense.

If you take this deduction, be sure you have the paperwork to back up legitimate deductions.

•*Miscellaneous itemized deductions and casualty losses.* Items such as professional or union dues, unreimbursed business expenses, safe-deposit-box rentals or job-hunting expenses are miscellaneous itemized deductions on Schedule A. They can be taken only if they exceed 2% of your Adjusted Gross Income (AGI).

The IRS tends to eagle-eye deductions in schedule categories that do not have minimums. *These categories include:*

•Schedule C—personal business.
•Schedule E—rental income.
•Schedule F— farm income.

The IRS looks carefully at these forms because many of the deductions may actually belong on Schedule A.

Casualty losses are deductible only if they exceed 10% of AGI, and there is no deduction for the first $100 of each casualty. Except in disaster areas, claiming a casualty loss is almost like putting a label on the return that says, "Audit me."

•*Avoiding self-employment taxes.* Both employees and employers must pay Social Security and Medicare taxes.

Self-employed individuals essentially have to pay both sides of these two taxes. The income—even a few thousand dollars of sideline consulting income, for example—is reported on Schedule C and Schedule SE for the self-employment tax of up to 15.3%.

If maximum Social Security tax has been withheld on salaried income, that will not be owed on Schedule SE—but Medicare tax will be owed.

Sometimes taxpayers list the income on the front of the IRS Form 1040 under "Other Income" (Line 21) and do not file Schedule SE. Line 21 is for such things as prizes or jury pay, not for earned income.

• *Hobby losses.* Taxpayers often have hobbies—photography, painting or stamp collecting, for example—that they find so enjoyable, they try to turn them into businesses.

Generally, a business needs to turn a profit in three out of five years to pass muster with the IRS. However, if you have a money-losing business—such as writing articles and books—and have records to prove that it is a business, with some effort you may be able to prevail.

• *High income.* Although fewer than 1% of taxpayers are audited, if your income is above $50,000, you are four times as likely to be audited as someone whose income is between $10,000 and $25,000 and who takes the standard deduction.

Your best defense is a carefully prepared return with all calculations double-checked and neat…and detailed records in your files in case you are called to substantiate any deductions.

Source: Julian Block, a former criminal investigator, special agent and attorney for the IRS who is now a tax attorney, Three Washington Square, Larchmont, New York 10538. He is the author of several books, including *It's Not What You Make—It's What You Keep,* which can be ordered directly from the author. He also answers tax questions on the Prodigy computer network, EXPT16B.

Preventing the IRS from Seizing Your House

What do you do when the IRS has notified you that they will seize your house next week? Before the IRS takes such drastic action a taxpayer must usually create an aggravating situation. The taxpayer has either failed to provide financial information or has failed to make any good faith payments at all. *Best approach:* File for a *taxpayer assistance order* (IRS Form 911)

with the Problem Resolution Office at your local IRS district office. This usually has the effect of adjourning all enforced collection action for at least 30 days. During that period you have the opportunity to raise money to make a down payment or otherwise arrange for an installment payment plan. If all your efforts fail, you can file a petition with the bankruptcy court to seek relief and stay the IRS seizure of your house.

Source: Ms. X is a former IRS agent still well connected.

The Best Ways to Avoid a Tax Audit

• Follow preparation instructions to the letter. Answer all questions. Attach all schedules. Sign and date the return.

• Check for mistakes. Recalculate every figure. Trace every schedule total and compare it with the figure used. Reread the description on every line—putting the right figure on the wrong line may cause problems.

• Explain unusual items. A schedule with appropriate explanations will usually avoid an audit. Explain differences reported on 1099s and W-2s. Explain large deductions. When in doubt, overinform the IRS.

• File on time or get an extension. File the extended return when due, even if you don't owe additional tax. File on time even if you don't have the money to pay the tax.

• Mail your return by certified mail, return-receipt requested, so you can prove it was filed on time if timeliness becomes an issue.

Source: Irving Blackman, partner, Blackman Kallick Bartelstein, 300 S. Riverside Plaza, Chicago 60606.

IRS Auditors Attack Exaggerated Deductions

Most auditors do not waste much time reviewing tax deductions that are reasonable. Taxpayers who tend to exaggerate their deductions receive much closer attention. A deduction that is commonly overstated is entertainment expenses. Some taxpayers take the position that every time they take anyone out for lunch or dinner it is deductible on the grounds that everyone is a potential customer or client. Another exaggerated deduction some taxpayers try to get away with is claiming their vacation homes as their out-of-town offices.

Source: Ms. X is a former IRS agent still well connected.

Audit Self-Defense

During a tax audit, resist the urge to talk and explain. People under stress tend to talk too much. *Trap:* They blurt out revealing information. IRS auditors are trained to exploit this by creating periods of silence during which they wait for you to say something. *Self-defense:* Wait for the auditor to ask a specific question, and provide exactly the information requested —and no more. Never volunteer anything. *The five best answers to an auditor's questions:* "Yes" ..."No"..."I don't recall"..."I'll have to check"... "Specifically—what item do you want to see?"

Source: *Stand Up to the IRS: How to Handle Audits, Tax Bills and Tax Court* by Frederick W. Daily, tax attorney in San Francisco, Nolo Press, Berkeley, CA.

When the Auditor Meets the Taxpayer

At the first interview the IRS auditor wants to gain a quick and complete understanding of the taxpayer being audited. This information is filed away in the auditor's mind, and is later used by him to evaluate the financial information he will begin to review. The worst thing you can do is to disclose too much personal information, especially information that is not relevant to the information reported on your tax return. Common auditor questions include wanting to know if you've ever been married (if filing singly)...the reasons you needed to consult with a psychologist (if medical deduc-

tions for a psychologist are claimed)...whether you have inherited any money recently.

Strategy: Don't tell the auditor you refuse to answer personal questions. The auditor will suspect you're hiding something. Rather, shift the conversation to personal questions, such as, "Where do you like to vacation?" or "Where do you live?"

How to Get the IRS to Settle for Less Tax Than You Owe

If you owe more in taxes than you can afford to pay, you may benefit from the IRS's new "kinder and gentler" approach towards tax collections.

The IRS is much more willing now than it has been in past years to accept...

• Installment payments on tax bills that taxpayers can't afford to pay right away, and

• Compromise settlements of tax debts that taxpayers won't ever be able to pay.

The IRS's real goal is not to show kindness to taxpayers, but to speed up tax collections by settling for smaller amounts more quickly, rather than having uncollected amounts pile up during litigation. But you can benefit from the IRS's new approach just the same. Here's how...
Basics:

First, be sure to file your tax return on time even if you can't afford to pay the tax due. If you don't file, you'll incur a late-filing penalty of 0.5% a month, up to a total of 25% of your unpaid tax bill...a late payment penalty of 5% per month, up to 25% of the unpaid tax bill...plus interest.

These amounts will be added to the tax bill you will have to negotiate with the IRS and this will make any agreement you reach that much more costly.

Trap: The IRS collects interest on amounts collected through installment payments. So it's possible to wind up paying several years' worth of interest on late-filing penalties that easily could have been avoided. After figuring the tax you owe, consider these options:

• *Simplified installment agreement.* If the amount you owe is less than $10,000, you can simply file IRS Form 9465 with your tax return to indicate that you currently can't afford to pay the tax due, while proposing to pay it off in full through installment payments made over a set period of time.

If the IRS accepts your proposed installment schedule, it will simply bill you as installments come due, and you'll have no further trouble.

If the IRS rejects your proposal, it will give you the chance to amend it to make it acceptable.

Guideline: Shorter-term agreements have a better chance of being approved. Propose to pay off the tax bill within 18 months or less, and the IRS will likely agree.

• *Negotiated installment agreement.* If the tax you owe exceeds $10,000, to obtain an installment agreement you must file your tax return showing the amount you owe, pay what you can and indicate that you wish to enter into an installment agreement. The IRS will ask you to prepare Form 1127 and a Form 433 financial-disclosure statement on which you list your assets, income, liabilities and living expenses.

Using this information, you meet with an IRS agent and negotiate the terms of an installment agreement under which you will pay off the tax you owe in full. The IRS will expect you to pay as much as you can afford—and may well ask you to cut "luxury" items, vacations and the like from your personal budget and apply the money saved to your taxes.

Your final monthly payment will be a negotiated amount. But the IRS generally is reasonable when negotiating installment agreements since it has little to gain by litigating a tax bill that the taxpayer has offered to pay off in full.

• *Offer in compromise.* If you are facing a tax bill so large that you won't ever be able to pay it off, you can seek to reduce the dollar amount of your liability through a compromise settlement.

You make an offer in compromise by filing IRS Form 656 and a Form 433 financial-disclosure statement.

The IRS will use the disclosure statement to compare your assets and liabilities, and com-

pute your net worth. This is the amount it will seek to collect from you. If you offer to pay the IRS an amount that's less than your net worth, the IRS will decline your offer because it knows it can collect your net worth through property seizures.

Thus, to have your offer accepted, you must offer the IRS a little more than your net worth. In a typical case, the taxpayer will finance such a payment by borrowing from family members, taking out a second mortgage on property or some similar action.

Note: Your net worth does include retirement accounts from which you have the power to withdraw funds, such as IRAs, 401(k) accounts and Keogh plans.

Follow-up:

After reaching an installment agreement with the Internal Revenue Service, you have the obligation to make all payments on time and remain current on all other tax obligations, or the agreement will be abrogated and the full tax you owe will come due immediately. Similarly, during the five-year period after an offer in compromise is agreed to, you are required to stay current on all tax obligations or your full tax liability may be reinstated.

Trap: When negotiating an offer in compromise, taxpayers sometimes overlook the fact that they will owe gains tax on assets that are sold to raise cash to pay the IRS, and income tax on funds withdrawn from IRAs or other retirement accounts for the same purpose.

Danger: After paying their entire net worth to the IRS, they may not be able to pay the taxes incurred as a result of their cash-raising efforts. And if they can't pay those taxes, the entire original tax bill may be reinstated—leaving them worse off than before.

Critical: When figuring how much you can afford to pay through an offer in compromise, be sure to figure in gains taxes and other expenses incurred in raising cash, or you may not be left with enough to live on.

Last defense:

If you can't reach a compromise, an agreement on a tax bill you can't afford, your last defense may be bankruptcy.

Surprise: In some cases, bankruptcy may be a better option than a compromise agreement.

How it works: Bankruptcy generally will not reduce the dollar amount of the tax you owe, since taxes incurred within the last three years cannot be discharged in bankruptcy.

However, you may receive better terms for paying off the tax bill, since payment terms will be set by the judge, not the IRS. And a judge may be more sympathetic to your situation.

Thus, while a bankruptcy judge will order you to pay off your entire tax bill, he/she may give you more time to do so than you'd have gotten from the IRS.

Bankruptcy can also be relatively advantageous if…

• The IRS wishes you to make a distress sale of assets to raise cash to finance a compromise agreement. You may get more value for your assets through bankruptcy proceedings.

• The IRS threatens your home or household assets. This may happen in cases where a person owing a large tax bill also owns a luxury home—the IRS may wish to take the home's value and have the taxpayer move to more modest quarters. But a home and household possessions generally are safe from creditor claims in bankruptcy court.

Source: Robert E. Mirsberger, former IRS district director for Manhattan, now of Ernst & Young, LLP, 787 Seventh Ave., New York 10019.

Tax-Free Income… Eight Different Ways

Believe it or not, many types of income are free from tax. *Here are the top eight…*

• *Municipal bond income.* Interest earned on municipal bonds is free of federal income tax. State tax may be imposed when you purchase bonds in a state other than where they were issued. Be aware that the interest on certain municipal bonds may impact the calculation of Alternative Minimum Tax (AMT).

Example: A person who lives in New Jersey and purchases a New York City bond will have to pay New Jersey state income tax on the New York City bond income.

• *Gifts and inheritances.* Generally, you do not have to pay any federal tax on gifts or inheritances that you receive. The tax, if any, is paid by the donor or estate. However, if the gift or inheritance is income-producing and you receive dividends, interest, or other income as the owner, tax will be due on the income.

• *Whole life insurance.* The interest income earned in a life insurance investment is tax-free until you cash in the policy.

• *Return of capital.* Shareholders of a corporation sometimes receive a payment categorized as a return of capital rather than as a dividend or capital gains distribution. These payments are not taxable because they are a return of your investment in the company. They are not derived from the current earnings of the company. Your Form 1099-DIV will indicate what part of any distribution received during the year is a return of capital.

• *Life insurance proceeds.* When an insured person dies, the recipient of the life insurance proceeds does not have to pay tax on the lump-sum amount payable at the insured's death. If more than the lump-sum amount is received for any reason, such as when installment payments are made, then the aggregate amount received above the lump sum is taxable. A portion of each installment payment would be tax-free, and a portion would be taxable.

• *Income from the sale of your home.* Tax on the profit from the sale of your home can be deferred when you invest the proceeds in a home that is more expensive than the home you sold.

Extra advantage for taxpayers age 55 or older: $125,000 of profit from the sale of your home is tax-free even if you don't reinvest the proceeds in a new home. This is a one-time exclusion that is available when you sell a home that has been your principal residence for at least three of the five years prior to the date of sale. The exclusion is only available once per couple. If your spouse ever took this exclusion, even if it was before you were married, you lose it.

• *Scholarships and fellowships.* If your child receives a scholarship, this money does not have to be included in income. For the payment to be tax-free, the recipient must be a degree candidate and the amount must be for tuition and fees and required books, supplies, and equipment. Any part of the scholarship that is for room and board is taxed.

• *Disaster proceeds.* Reimbursements received to compensate you for insurance and other reimbursements for a casualty such as fire, flood, earthquake, or other disaster are not taxed to the extent of your cost of the property damaged or destroyed. Reimbursements must be accounted for when you are figuring out the amount of your casualty loss deduction for tax purposes. Any amounts reimbursed are subtracted from your tax deduction.

Source: Richard J. Shapiro, partner, Goldstein Golub Kessler, 1185 Avenue of the Americas, New York 10036.

The Most Common Mistakes Taxpayers Make... And How to Avoid Them

In our search for ever-more exotic ways to shelter income and offset capital gains, many of us overlook—or fail to maximize—the basic tax-saving strategies. The most common mistakes—and the solutions that can help you cut your taxes next year...

Mistake: Not deferring your retirement savings. Congress allows everyone to save for retirement in a variety of ways—including Individual Retirement Accounts (IRAs), Keogh accounts for the self-employed, employer-sponsored 401(k) plans, 403(b) annuities for nonprofit organizations and tax-deferred annuities.

The beauty of these investments is that you pay no taxes on the interest earned until you gradually withdraw the sum between the ages of 59½ and 70½.

Much of these investments can be pretax contributions—an ideal situation in which the money is not taxed before it is diverted into the account.

In addition, pretax money that is diverted into a retirement account, such as a 401(k), compounds much faster than money saved in a taxable account.

Example: If at age 40 you invested just $2,000 at 8% in a tax-deferred account, it would grow to $22,761 by the time you reached 70½, when withdrawals must begin. That leaves you with about $14,000 after taxes. *Comparison:* A taxable investment would grow to only about $10,000 after taxes.

Because of the complexity of the tax laws and the variations in individual plans, many people make critical planning errors. *Strategies:*

• *Take full advantage of the plan.* Only 61% of those eligible participate in a 401(k)...and of those people who do participate, many do not contribute the maximum allowed each year—up to $9,240. They hesitate because they fear they might need the money in the near future and do not want to incur the 10% tax penalty that is assessed for premature withdrawals.

What these people do not realize is that most plans allow loans. When you borrow from your 401(k), you pay back the money to yourself. You must, however, put together a payback schedule with your benefits department. The money will be taken directly out of your paycheck.

• *Don't withdraw too much from an IRA.* In general, the maximum that you can withdraw annually is $150,000. If you exceed this amount, you will have to pay a 15% excise tax for excess distributions.

• *Don't request that a former employer send you your vested retirement savings.* When you switch jobs, ask your previous employer to deposit your retirement savings directly into the IRA of your choice. If the distribution check is made out to you, your former employer will deduct 20% for taxes.

In addition, any sum of money you withdraw from a qualified retirement plan before you reach age 59½ is subject to a 10% excise tax.

Helpful: Set up a rollover IRA rather than having the money deposited into an existing IRA. A rollover IRA will make your tax paperwork easier when it's time to withdraw the money.

Mistake: Misunderstanding the "kiddie tax." Most people have a vague notion of the kiddie tax. Many parents think it means they will be liable for extra taxes if their children earn money or own investments. Actually, there are great tax-saving opportunities to putting investments in children's names.

For your 1995 tax return, for a child under age 14, the first $650 of investment earnings is tax-free and the second $650 is taxed at the child's rate, which in most cases is 15%. So putting some investment money in a child's name is a great way to help save for college expenses. Investment income that exceeds this amount is taxed at the parents' maximum rate.

For children age 14 and older, all earned and unearned income is taxable at the child's rate. Parents can still claim the children as dependents if the parents provide more than half of the children's support. In addition, each parent may give up to $10,000 to each child per year with no gift- or estate-tax consequences. It doesn't matter how old the children are.

Mistake: Using a simple will for estate planning. Estate taxes are even higher than income taxes. They range from 37% to 55%, and in many cases they begin when estates are valued at more than $600,000. This is a threshold that is easy to reach when you factor in a middle-class home and retirement savings.

Important: No estate taxes are due on assets left by one spouse to another. Most basic wills leave everything to a surviving spouse. Estate taxes kick in, however, when the second spouse dies and assets are left to the couple's children.

Solution: For estates in which assets exceed $600,000, each spouse should consider adding a credit shelter trust to his/her will. Each of their assets are placed in the trust for the benefit of the surviving spouse. Upon the second spouse's death, the assets pass estate tax-free from the trust to the children or other beneficiaries. In this way, a couple can shelter up to $1.2 million from estate taxes—instead of $600,000—for a tax savings of up to $330,000.

Mistake: Not realizing that certain mutual-fund moves are taxable events. As most people know, over time, stock mutual funds generally produce greater returns than CDs, savings accounts or Treasury bonds.

Mutual funds also provide shareholders with several convenient services. These include check-writing privileges and the ability to switch from one fund to another in the same fund family by phoning in the order.

Problem: What most people don't realize is that writing a check against your shares or switching an investment is considered a sale. There may be tax consequences, even if the money is reinvested in another fund.

Solution: Keep money that you know you will need for critical payments in the upcoming year, such as insurance premiums or tuition payments, in a money-market fund and use it to write checks. There will be no tax consequences. In addition, do not switch funds often and do so only when it is absolutely necessary.

Mistake: Letting the fear of taxes govern your investment strategies. Some people's entire portfolios are made up of tax-advantaged investments with little attention paid to whether this strategy actually makes sense in their case.

Today, many people rush to municipal bonds and tax-deferred annuities, even though those may not be the most appropriate choices for their personal situations—or at least not for their entire portfolios.

Solution: Be aware of tax consequences—but don't let them rule how you invest your money. Put together a diversified investment portfolio with good asset allocation. Consider factors such as long-term growth prospects and liquidity needs.

Source: William J. Goldberg, Southwest partner in charge of personal financial planning for KPMG Peat Marwick LLP, 700 Louisiana St., Houston 77210.

Top Filing Mistakes... According to the IRS

Error: Miscalculating medical and dental expenses. The deduction is based on Adjusted Gross Income (AGI). Figure your AGI on your

1040 before calculating your medical expense deduction.

Error: Taking the wrong amount of earned income credit. Use the worksheet in the 1040 instruction booklet to avoid mistakes.

Error: Entering the wrong amount of tax from the tax tables. Be sure to use the table that applies to your filing status (married filing jointly, single, etc.).

Error: Confusing Social Security tax and federal income tax. Form W-2 shows both. Be sure to use the right figure for income tax withheld.

Error: Making a mistake in calculating the child- and dependent-care credit. Use Form 2441 and be sure to double check your math.

Error: Incorrect refund of balance due. Verify your math. Compare the tax you owe with the amount you have paid through withholding and estimated tax payments.

Error: Failing to claim the earned income credit. Refer to the instructions in the tax package if your income is low and you have a child.

Error: Making a mistake in figuring the taxable amount of your Social Security benefits. Use the Social Security benefits worksheet in the instruction booklet.

Source: IRS Publication 910.

The IRS Loses Too... New Opportunities for You

Use these best taxpayer victories over the IRS to help you plan your tax-cutting strategies this year.

Winners all:

• *Get IRS inside information before trial.* Before suing the IRS for a refund, Thomas E. Worrell, Jr., sought depositions from several IRS agents who had worked on his case, seeking to learn the meaning of various IRS codes and notations that appeared in his case file and in IRS reports.

The IRS argued that information obtained from the agents would be privileged and inadmissible at trial.

Court: The inadmissibility of the agents' statements at trial is not an obstacle to pretrial discovery. The depositions were allowed.

Source: *Thomas E. Worrell, Jr.,* S.D. Fla. No. 92-8034-CIV-GONZALEZ.

• *Free $500,000 deduction.* A person who owned a tract of land created a conservation easement that limited the way the land could be developed and claimed a $500,000 charity deduction for the easement. The IRS argued that he never intended to develop the land. The IRS also said that the land's market value hadn't been reduced by the easement, so no deduction should be allowed.

Court: Before-and-after valuation was insufficient. The easement sharply limited the ability to earn income from the land through development and exploitation of hunting and fishing rights. A $500,000 valuation for the easement was reasonable, and a corresponding deduction allowed.

Source: *Charles R. Schwab,* TC Memo 1994-232.

• *Yacht tax shelter upheld.* Two people bought a yacht, financing 90% of its cost and chartering it back to the same company from which they bought it. The two people then deducted six years of losses that resulted from the depreciation deductions and interest on their loan. The IRS disallowed their deductions, saying they had no profit motive.

Tax Court: Ruling for the owners. They had kept businesslike books and records and consulted with experts in the chartering business. They also could hope to gain through appreciation in the yacht's value. All this indicated that they had a profit motive, so their deductions were allowed.

Source: *William Hellings,* TC Memo 1994-24.

• *Right to silence.* Your Fifth Amendment right not to give evidence against yourself applies if you think you are the target of an IRS criminal investigation—even if no charges have been made against you.

Case: Eugene J. Peters refused to give his records to the IRS after it brought criminal charges against persons with whom he'd had dealings. He had seen IRS agents peering into his house through his living-room window… and IRS agents had warned him he "had better" have his tax papers in order.

Court: Peters had reasonable grounds to fear that the IRS was preparing a criminal case against him, therefore he did not have to produce his records.

Source: *Eugene J. Peters*, C.D. Calif., No. CV94-0622-JGD.

• *Fees paid to secure taxable income are deductible.* Therefore, an individual could actually deduct the portion of an attorney's fee that is allocated to the negotiations over the amount of interest that was to be added to a payment received in settlement of a lawsuit. This is true even when the settlement itself was determined tax-free and the base portion of the attorney's fee was not deductible.

Essential: An itemized bill from the lawyer.

Source: *James V. Crews*, TC Memo 1994-64.

• *Sideline farm tax shelter.* A full-time airline pilot who bought a farm could deduct $180,000 in farming losses over three years, even though he had only $11,700 of farm income over the same period. The Tax Court rejected the IRS's argument that his farming had no profit motive.

Key facts: The pilot changed farming methods in an effort to cut losses, adopted new technology, consulted with experts and spent time working the farm, showing he was more than a weekend farmer. All this indicated he had a profit motive, so his losses were deductible.

Source: *David E. Buckner*, TC Memo 1994-376.

• *Misplaced-records excuse.* Late-filing penalties were lifted when a taxpayer showed that she had given her records to a professional return preparer on time and he had misplaced them (putting them in the trunk of a car that his grandson drove to California).

Court: This was a reasonable excuse for not filing until the preparer recovered the records.

Source: *Elizabeth A. Gravett*, TC Memo 1994-156.

• *Expert advice saves penalty.* A person who improperly took large deductions escaped having penalties added to his tax bill by showing that he had relied on the advice of a tax lawyer and an accountant who had reviewed the deductions and concluded they were proper. The

individual had filed his return in good faith, so penalties would not be added.

Source: *George S. Mauerman*, CA-10, No. 93-9009.

• *Bank records are confidential.* If a bank releases your financial records to the IRS without receiving a subpoena first, you can sue the bank for damages plus the legal fees and expenses incurred in bringing your suit.

Case: A bank gave a couple's financial records to the IRS in response to an IRS agent's informal request. The couple sued the bank and recovered more than $83,000 in damages and expenses.

Source: *Peggy J. Neece*, CA-10, No. 93-5127.

• *Sloppiness isn't fraud.* A taxpayer delivered "a sack" of records to his accountant each year when it was time to prepare his tax return, and his taxes were regularly underpaid due to the poor paperwork. The IRS treated the consistent underreporting as fraud and assessed taxes and penalties going back several years.

Tax Court: Negligence isn't fraud. The individual had demonstrated no organized plan to evade taxes—so there was no fraud. The IRS could not assess back taxes for years protected by the statute of limitations.

Source: *Gong Yok Tsun Chin*, TC Memo 1994-54.

• *New demolition deduction.* Losses resulting from the demolition of a building are not deductible. But when a real-estate investor discovered structural defects in a building that required its demolition, the Tax Court said the resulting loss was deductible.

Reason: The loss didn't result from the demolition but from the discovery of the defects, which reduced the building's market value to zero before it was demolished. The loss was realized and deductible at that point. The subsequent demolition was incidental.

Source: *Charles H. DeCou*, 103 TC 6.

• *Unsigned joint return is valid.* The IRS rejected a couple's joint return because the husband signed his wife's name on it instead of having her sign it herself. The IRS then tried to collect tax at higher separate-return tax rates.

Court: The husband had signed his wife's name to the return with her permission, since she had been out of town tending a sick relative when the return was prepared. Because the wife had intended to file a joint return, the return was valid even though she hadn't signed it.

Source: *Frank G. Boyle*, TC Memo 1994-294.

• *Refund claim after settlement.* A new refund request can be made even after reaching a "final" settlement of a year's disputed tax bill with the IRS, provided the new claim is unrelated to the prior dispute and settlement agreement. Thus, a taxpayer could file a new refund claim even after signing a final settlement agreement that specifically stated the taxpayer would file "no claim or refund...for the year" in the future.

Source: *Tyco Laboratories, Inc.*, D. N.H., No. 93-362-M.

• *Late refunds allowed.* A woman suffered from senility during the last years of her life. Her son, a stockbroker, managed her finances but did not file tax returns for her. After she died, her estate filed late returns asking for refunds going back several years. But the IRS said the statute of limitations had expired and argued that since the son had been fully capable of filing returns for his mother, the estate deserved no special consideration.

Court: The son had no obligation to file his mother's returns, so his financial expertise was irrelevant. The limitations period was set aside due to the woman's incapacity. The refunds were allowed.

Source: *First Interstate Bank of Nevada*, D. Nev., No. CV-S-94-0034-PMP (RLH).

• *Extension saved.* An individual filed an extension for filing his tax return, estimating that he owed no more taxes for the year and making no payment with it. When it turned out that he still owed more than $90,000 in taxes, the IRS revoked the extension and imposed late-filing penalties.

Court: The individual's accountant had underestimated the tax still due because full records for the year weren't yet available—which was why the extension had been requested. The extension had been filed in good faith, so it was valid.

Source: *Paul E. Harper*, E.D. Okla., No. CIV-94-073-S.

• *Property seizure revoked.* The IRS seized Norman E. Anderson's property to pay off a back tax bill. When it tried to auction the property, it received no acceptable bids. The IRS declined to bid itself and postponed the sale for four months.

Court: The Tax Code requires that seized property be sold within 40 days of the time the IRS gives public notice that it is to be sold. Because the IRS didn't sell the property and didn't buy it itself, it must return the property to Anderson.

Source: *Norman E. Anderson,* CA-9, No. 93-16114.

Owing More Money than You'll Ever Be Able to Pay

Someone you know filed his/her 1993 personal tax return and owes more money than he'll ever be able to pay. To make matters worse, he hasn't paid any estimated tax in 1994 and knows that he will fall even farther behind. Solution: Tell him to consider filing an offer in compromise to wipe out most of his unpaid tax liabilities. Tell him not to file the offer in compromise until early 1995, after his 1994 tax return has been filed. The IRS will not accept an offer in compromise from a taxpayer who continues to incur unpaid tax liabilities. Make sure that the correct amount of estimated tax is paid in 1995. The money that would otherwise have been used to reduce 1993 or 1994 unpaid tax liabilities should be used toward 1995 estimated taxes.

Source: Ms. X is a former IRS agent still well connected.

How to Cut Your Property-Tax Assessment

Many home owners unnecessarily pay too much in property taxes. But by learning how the property-tax system works, you may be able to lower your property-tax bill yourself, without paying big legal fees. A reduction in a tax assessment can produce thousands of dollars in tax savings. Here's what you need to know...

The time to start examining your property-tax assessment is right away.

Local tax jurisdictions typically allow only a short "window" of time—such as 15 to 30 days—in which to formally file a property-tax appeal. You should prepare your case for a tax reduction before that "window" arrives.

Typical Calendar

Months 1 to 5	Prepare case.
Months 5 to 8	Seek informal hearing with assessor about your assessment and possibly get an adjustment without a formal appeal.
Month 8	Proposed tax notice arrives.
Month 9	Appeal deadline.
Month 10	Tax rates that apply to assessments are set.
Month 11	Final tax bill arrives.

The "tax calendar" varies for different jurisdictions, so the first thing to do is learn the dates and deadlines that apply in your jurisdiction for challenging assessments and filing appeals. Your jurisdiction's property-tax year may begin on any month of the year.

Procedures for contesting an assessment vary in each jurisdiction, so contact your local assessor's office for details.

Once you are familiar with the deadline you must meet, you can take steps to prepare your case for a tax reduction.

How property taxes work:

Your property taxes are determined by a two-step process.

First, local authorities assess the value of all properties within the jurisdiction.

Second, they impose a tax rate on the total assessed value that is sufficient to collect enough revenue to meet the needs of local government.

It's important to realize that your house's assessed value for property-tax purposes is not the same as its market value.

•The market value of your home is the price you could expect to obtain for it on the open market.

An appraisal of your home obtained from a bank, realtor or insurance company will tell you its market value.

•The assessment on your home is a tax value as determined by a government official. Usually it is a percentage of your home's market value. Thus, a home with a $100,000 market value may have an assessed value of $85,000.

State guidelines impose this percentage on the local tax assessor. If the state mandates an assessment-to-market-value ratio of 85%, the house with a market value of $100,000 should be assessed at $85,000.

Note: When local authorities announce that there will be "no tax-rate increase" or "no increase in tax assessments" in the current year, it does not mean that there will be no tax increase in the current year.

That's because when tax rates remain the same, the government can collect more tax by raising assessments...and when assessments remain the same, it can collect more tax by raising rates.

Knowing how the system works, you can take steps to cut your assessment and your tax bill.

Cutting the tax bill:

•*Find assessment errors.* The government can't assess every house every year—so it conducts mass assessments.

The assessment is the average assessment that the local authorities think is appropriate for homes like yours in your area. Thus, the first way to reduce an assessment is to point out particular factors that differentiate your house from other houses in a way that reduces your home's relative value. *Examples...*

•*Physical deterioration.* Faults in your home such as a cracked foundation, leaky roof, old wiring or plumbing—defects that reduce your home's value.

•*External deterioration.* This can include a generally declining neighborhood, an increase in the local crime rate, the location of "undesirable" facilities—prison, airport, highway—near your home.

•*Functional obsolescence.* Your home may have a poor layout or other design problems—three bedrooms and only one bathroom instead of two, a lack of windows, out-of-date kitchen facilities.

Be prepared to document these problems when meeting with an appraiser.

• *Determine market value.* The generally weak real estate market prices can also provide justification for a reduced appraisal.

The most direct way to document your home's market value is to find comparable sales. Look for homes similar to yours that have been sold in your neighborhood or nearby in recent months.

How to do it: First, visit the assessor and ask for a copy of your property record card. This will contain the description of your house that's used for assessment purposes. Then seek out sales of homes with similar descriptions.

• *Visit a broker and ask for a list of previous year's sales*—1994 sales for example. Check with your Value Adjustment Board (part of the Clerk of the Court's Office) to see if you can use 1995 sales.

Many realtors now have fast access to up-to-the-moment information through computer databases. You can say you want a search of low-price sales because you are preparing to sell your home quickly—or be open about preparing your tax case and make an alternate arrangement with the broker.

• *Look up the information yourself* in records kept at the local assessor's office, courthouse, library or on your county computerized tax roll.

Tactic: Watch local newspapers to learn of sales of homes similar to yours, then look up a detailed description of the sold properties in the appraiser's office and save them for next year.

Important: You must have hard evidence of what comparable homes have sold for. Match property descriptions with actual sales prices as recorded in public documents.

A second way to document the value of your home is to produce independent appraisals of its value that have been recently obtained. If you recently refinanced your home, the lender probably required an independent appraisal of the home's value. You can present this to the local assessor as evidence of value.

• *Technical errors.* When you obtain the property record card that describes your home

from the assessor, examine it for errors. Mistakes in the recorded square footage or number of rooms may inflate your assessment, as may other errors. Also…

• *Check appraisal norms.* Federal National Mortgage Association appraisal norms say that no house can be financed for more than 115% of the highest sale price received for a home in the area in the past year.

Catch: Assessors' computers are programmed to automatically assess homes by square footage, even if this produces a value above the 115% figure. If you have a large-square-footage house with an assessed value over the 115% amount, you may be entitled to a reduction.

Your keys to property-tax reduction: (1) Finding sales of houses near and like your house that are lower than your tax assessed value. (2) Repairs.

Source: Henry Willen Sanchez, ASA, a Florida state-certified general real-estate appraiser and a special master property-tax judge in three Florida counties. He has heard more than 1,000 cases and has written *Save Thousands on Your Property Taxes,* available through Willen Sanchez Associates Inc., Hialeah, FL.

Remarriage/Home Trap

If you're 55 or older and planning to remarry, and both you and your spouse-to-be each own a home, you should sell the homes before you marry. *Reason:* A married couple is only entitled to one $125,000 exclusion from tax on home-sale profits. But if you sell your homes before you marry, you'll both get the exclusion.

Source: Laurence I. Foster is a tax partner in the personal financial-planning practice of KPMG Peat Marwick, LLP, 345 Park Ave., New York 10154.

Accountant-Client Privilege Doesn't Exist Against the IRS

The IRS can compel your accountant to produce "confidential" work papers. *Tactic:* Hire an accountant through your attorney to obtain attorney-client privilege for accounting papers. The privilege extends to an accountant's work in preparation for litigation, or to help an attorney defend a client.

Source: *Jack Bell*, N.D. Ca., No. C-94-20342-RMW.

Tax-Planning Strategies—1996

The start of a new year is the best time to find ways to cut your tax bill. Consider these tax-saving strategies that you can use all year.

Savings ideas:

•*Invest for capital gains.* Long-term capital gains are taxed at a favorable maximum rate of only 28%—compared with tax rates of up to 39.6% that are imposed on ordinary income.

Moreover, the new leadership in Congress has promised to reduce the tax rate imposed on long-term gains—it could go as low as 14% —by providing a 50% exemption for long-term gains.

The details of any tax code changes to be enacted can't be known now—but any further preference granted to gain-producing investments will make them even more attractive compared with investments that produce current income.

With this in mind, consider shifting some of your portfolio out of income-producing investments and into growth stocks.

•*Make the most of retirement accounts.* If you have an IRA, Keogh plan, employer-sponsored 401(k) account, or other tax-favored retirement savings account, plan to make maximum contributions to it during 1995—and make your contributions as early in the year as possible.

Your contribution will reap the double tax benefit of a deduction for the amount put in the plan, and tax deferral for investment earnings that accrue within the plan—which lets them compound on a pretax basis.

Opportunity: By making your contribution to an IRA or Keogh early in the year—instead of at the last minute, just before you file your tax return—you get an extra year's worth of tax-deferred investment earnings in the account plus further annual compound earnings on this amount every year until you retire and withdraw the money.

•*Supplement retirement savings.* Recent tax law changes provide that qualified retirement benefits can be based on no more than $150,000 of compensation. That limits the benefits available to high-paid executives and business owners.

If your qualified retirement benefits will be "capped" by the new rule, consider supplementing them with nonqualified savings devices such as *Supplemental Executive Retirement Plans* (SERPs), stock options, and stock appreciation rights.

If you are an employee, ask your employer about these possibilities. If you own your own business, explore them yourself with your professional advisers.

•*Consider tax-exempt income.* Judge an income-producing investment by the amount of income it provides after taxes.

If you are in a high tax bracket, a low-yielding, tax-exempt investment may be worth more than a higher-yielding taxable one.

Example: For a person in the 40% tax bracket (federal and local combined) a tax-exempt yield of 5% equals a taxable yield of 8.33%.

Work through the numbers for the investments in your portfolio and adjust them accordingly.

•*Make gifts to children.* This is another tactic often used at year-end that can be more beneficial when exercised early in the year.

Key: When you give assets to children, you remove them from your taxable estate—and also may shift income earned on the assets into a child's lower tax bracket. The earlier in the year that you make a gift, the more your family will benefit from such income shifting.

•*Use your annual gift-tax exclusion* to make tax-free gifts of up to $10,000 each to as many different recipients as you wish—the limit is $20,000 when gifts are made jointly with a spouse. You can make even larger gifts tax-free by using some of your unified tax credit of $192,800, which protects up to $600,000 of your assets from estate tax. Use of the credit now can make sense if you expect the transferred property to rise in value over the years, so that it would be subject to a much larger future estate-tax liability if passed by bequest.

•*Contribute to your 401(k) plan.* Its terms may require you to increase your contribution rate early in the year to make the maximum permitted annual contribution.

Payoff: By making early contributions to your retirement accounts every year, you may significantly increase the amount of money you will have to live on when you reach retirement age.

Note: If you are not eligible to open a deductible IRA because you are covered by a company retirement plan, consider supplementing your retirement savings with contributions to a nondeductible IRA. While you get no deduction for your contribution, you will receive tax-deferred investment earnings within the account.

•*Borrow from a retirement account.* Some retirement programs—often 401(k) plans and Keogh plans—let plan participants borrow against their accounts to finance expenses such as children's college costs.

Limit: You can borrow only 50% of your account balance, or $50,000, whichever is less. And the loan must be repaid within five years.

Amounts borrowed out of a plan are tax-free, and since you borrow from yourself, you avoid the difficulties of dealings with banks and loan officers.

College aid: Retirement account savings are not considered available to pay tuition under the tuition assistance formulas used by most college financial aid offices. So saving a large amount in a retirement plan may not reduce your child's eligibility for tuition assistance in the same manner that having a similar amount of savings in a normal investment account might.

Be sure to check with your retirement plan's trustee in order to see if borrowing is permitted, and on what terms.

•*Prepare retirement plan withdrawals.* If you are nearing retirement age, begin planning how you will take money out of your retirement accounts.

Trap: A 15% excise tax applies to "excessive" plan withdrawals—those exceeding $150,000. If you have a large amount saved up in qualified retirement accounts, and put off making withdrawals until the last moment—at age 70½—you may be forced to take out an amount that exceeds the $150,000 limit and be forced to pay excise tax as well as the income tax.

If you've saved a large amount in qualified retirement plans, consult with an expert about withdrawal strategies well before withdrawals are required to begin.

•*Play the kiddie tax.* Investment income earned by children under age 14 is taxed at parental tax rates.

However, up to $1,300 of income is exempt from the kiddie tax in 1995—so assets producing that much taxable income can be placed in a child's name without incurring the tax.

Even larger amounts can be invested in a child's name without incurring the tax if the money is invested to earn tax-exempt income or capital appreciation, rather than taxable income.

Possible investments: Growth stocks, tax-free bonds, Series EE savings bonds.

After the child reaches age 14, these assets can be cashed in with any gain that results being taxed at the child's own rate.

•*Roll over a retirement plan distribution into an IRA.* If you leave an employer, consider taking a lump-sum distribution of your accrued retirement benefits and rolling it over into an IRA. It is important to be aware that if you don't elect a direct transfer to the institution, you will be subject to a 20% withholding. A rollover will defer tax on the distribution, and if you put the money in an IRA you'll have more control over it—managing investments and distributions—than you would if you left the money in the employer's plan or transferred it to the plan of a subsequent employer.

• *Beware the Alternative Minimum Tax (AMT).* The AMT is a special tax calculation designed to prevent individuals with large amounts of economic income from eliminating their tax bills through the use of large deductions and exclusions.

The AMT is most likely to apply to persons with large deductions for state and local taxes, large miscellaneous itemized deductions, and large long-term capital gains. If the AMT does apply to you, normal tax-planning strategies may not produce the results you desire. Alternative Minimum Tax rules are very complicated, so if you think you might be subject to the tax, consult with an expert early in the year.

Source: Joseph P. Toce, Jr., partner, Stamford, Connecticut, Keith E. Oates, senior tax manager, and Marjorie A. Beutel, tax manager, Arthur Andersen, LLP, 1345 Avenue of the Americas, New York 10105.

Deferred Pay Trap— And Opportunity

The Clinton Tax Act extended the 2.9% Medicare portion of Social Security taxes—1.45% each owed by employer and employee—to *all* wages. This change was effective in 1994. In prior years only the first $135,000 of wages were taxed.

Trap: Bonuses and deferred compensation amounts are subject to this tax *when earned,* even if they aren't paid until a later year. And employers must withhold this tax from current salary—reducing the current net income of employees receiving deferred pay. Don't overlook this new obligation to collect withholding on deferred pay.

Refund opportunity: In 1994, when the 2.9% tax was extended to all income, many companies assumed the tax was owed when income *was paid.*

Result: They withheld and paid taxes on bonuses and deferred pay incurred *before* 1994.

This was an error. When compensation in excess of $135,000 was earned before 1994

and deferred until 1994 or later, the 2.9% FICA tax does *not* apply. Companies and employees in those situations can request refunds.

Source: Mark Wertlieb, partner, KPMG Peat Marwick, 345 Park Ave., New York 10154.

Big New Tax Savings from Your Old Tax Returns

It may pay to review your old tax returns. If you find a deduction or other tax-saving strategy that was overlooked during the past three years—even longer with regard to bad debt—you can file an amended tax return (IRS Form 1040X) to obtain tax refunds.

If you *underreported* tax owed in a prior year—possibly because of a mathematical error, improper deductions or omissions of income—that could result in a back tax bill and penalties, filing an amended tax return can correct the mistake and help you avert tax penalties that might be imposed if the IRS discovers the underreporting first.

Here's what to look for in your old tax returns…

Retroactive breaks:

Recent tax-law changes create *retroactive* tax breaks that some taxpayers can use to obtain refunds from past years' tax returns.

• *Seller-paid points.* The IRS ruled that the buyer of a principal residence can deduct mortgage "points"—loan finance fees—paid on a home loan, even when the seller pays the points for the buyer.

Rationale: The seller's payment of the points is reflected in the purchase price of the home, so the buyer is the "real" payor.

When announcing this position, the IRS specifically stated that home buyers purchasing a home after December 31, 1990, who benefited from seller-paid points can file amended returns to claim the points deduction back to 1991.

• The Clinton Tax Act retroactively extended certain tax breaks that had expired on June 30, 1992…

•The 25% deduction for health-insurance premiums that is available for self-employed individuals. This tax break was extended until December 31, 1993.

•The income exclusion for up to $5,250 of certain employer-provided education assistance. This was extended until January 1, 1995.

•The exemption from the Alternative Minimum Tax (AMT) for gifts of appreciated personal property to charity. This is still in place.

Examine your 1992 and 1993 tax returns. If you were eligible for any of these retroactive tax breaks but did not claim them, file amended returns now.

Errors on income forms:

Errors often occur with regard to the 1099 forms that are filed by banks, brokers, etc., to report payments of income made to individuals.

Such forms may report incorrect amounts… they may arrive too late to be included in your return…or they could be overlooked when you tally up income amounts on your return.

IRS computers match these forms with tax returns, and any discrepancies are likely to bring extra attention to your tax return—so be sure the numbers on the forms and your returns agree.

What to do: If you failed to report income shown on a late-arriving or temporarily misplaced 1099 form, you can file an amended tax return that includes it.

If you copied the numbers from an incorrect 1099 form onto your tax return and later discovered the error, you can ask the issuer for a corrected 1099 form and file an amended tax return.

Best: All 1099 forms are supposed to be mailed to taxpayers by January 31. As soon as they arrive, check that the numbers reported on them are correct—and that you have received all the 1099 forms you are expecting. If you find any errors, act quickly to have them corrected before April 15.

Bad debts and worthless securities:

You can claim a loss deduction for bad debts and securities that become worthless—but the deduction must be claimed for the year in which the debt goes bad or the security becomes worthless.

Special rule: You can use amended tax returns to claim deductions for bad debts and worthless securities up to *seven* years back, instead of only three.

Whether or not a debt or security is completely worthless may be unclear. Often—as in cases involving litigation—the date on which a debt or security became worthless is determined only after the fact, perhaps after the normal three-year statute of limitations on tax returns has run out. Thus, the Tax Code allows extra time to claim such deductions.

Opportunity: Review your portfolio before year-end, especially if you have received investments through inheritances or gifts. You may find loss deductions that were previously overlooked.

Casualty losses:

If you suffered a casualty loss during an event that results in your area being declared a federal disaster area, you get a special tax break—you have the choice of deducting your loss either in the year it occurs or in the prior year.

Example: If you suffered such a loss during 1995, you can wait and deduct it on the return that you will file for 1995…or file an amended return to deduct the loss on the return you filed for 1994.

By filing an amended return to claim the deduction for the prior year, you can speed up your refund, since you don't have to wait for the current year's return to be filed and processed.

The choice of years also may give you a *larger* deduction, since casualty losses are deductible only to the extent that they exceed 10% of your Adjusted Gross Income (AGI). You increase the amount of your deduction by taking it in the year when your AGI is lowest.

House sales:

If you sell your home, file IRS Form 2119 (Sale of Your Home) to defer gain on the sale and then fail to buy a replacement residence within the two-year replacement period, your gain is taxable in the year during which the sale occurred. You will have to file an amended return to report the gain in the year the house was sold.

Key: Deferral of gain is mandatory when a taxpayer is eligible for deferral—and in most cases, home sellers will want to defer gain. But a home seller who had large net investment losses during the year of the sale may want to recognize gain—because the losses can be used to offset the gain and shelter it permanently from tax.

Thus, a home seller may intentionally fail to qualify for tax deferral by failing to buy a replacement residence before the deadline, then file an amended return to report the gain in the past year.

Filing:

File an amended tax return by using IRS Form 1040X. You can get a copy by calling the IRS at 1-800-TAX-FORM.

Form 1040X is a one-page form on which you simply note the changes to be made to your original tax return. You do not need to attach a copy of your entire original return, but it's a good idea to attach copies of the particular pages or schedules that are being corrected.

The deadline for filing an amended tax return is three years after the date on which your original return was filed, or two years after the date on which you paid the tax, whichever is later. If you filed early, you have three years after the due date of the return. (To claim deductions for bad debts and worthless securities, you have seven years.)

Audit risk:

Amended returns are reviewed carefully by the IRS, so filing an amended return may expose you to extra audit risk.

In the case of routine error corrections, the risk is slight—but a Form 1040X that dramatically cuts your tax bill for the year is likely to undergo more serious scrutiny.

On the other hand, filing an amended return does *not* give the IRS extra time to audit your original return.

Thus, some advisers recommend that an amended return can be filed *without* increasing audit risk to the original return if it is filed *just before* the return's three-year statute-of-limitations period runs out.

Source: Robert A. Pedersen, partner in charge of personal financial planning for the southwest Dallas area, KPMG Peat Marwick, 200 Crescent Court, Suite 300, Dallas 75201.

Liquid Assets Are "Sitting Ducks" for the IRS

If you are expecting a big tax bill, liquidate cash-value life insurance, bank Certificates of Deposit, IRA and Keogh accounts, stock and bond investments and savings accounts *before* the IRS can seize them. Then disperse the funds by paying off legitimate debts to family members and other "friendly" creditors, prepaying personal and business expenses and making gifts to family members. If you have over $100,000, deposit it in a legal tax haven such as the Cayman Islands or Isle of Man, where the money will be out of the reach of the IRS.

Source: *How to Settle with the IRS for Pennies on the Dollar* by Arnold Goldstein of Goldstein & Randall, attorneys, Boston, Garrett Publishing, 384 S. Military Trail, Deerfield Beach, Florida 33442.

How to Get More By Giving "It" Away

Two things will happen at the stroke of midnight on December 31. The old year will end …and so will your last chance to give to charity and have it count as a deduction on your 1995 tax return.

Important: Tax rates are higher now…up to 39.6%…so deductions count for more. And time is running short to plan charitable giving to offset those higher tax rates.

Most people realize that charitable donations are deductible from income. Drop a $10 bill into the church collection basket, and you can take $10 off your taxable income. That's Charitable Giving 101.

More advanced techniques like giving appreciated securities or careful use of trusts can enhance the value of your deductions.

Here's what you must know to get the most from your giving…

• *Beware of the paperwork burden*. The IRS now requires that taxpayers get substantiation from organizations they give to for contributions of $250 or more.

Your canceled check is no longer sufficient evidence. There must be something in writing from the charity…listing how much you gave …and whether you got anything in return.

Example: You bought $250 tickets to a dinner-dance sponsored by a charity, of which the charity received $100 while $150 went to the hotel where the event was held. In that case your deduction would be $100.

• *Make the most of appreciated securities.* If you're giving a sizable amount, you'll gain the most if you can give securities with substantial unrealized gains.

The charity can sell the securities to meet its needs. You can deduct the fair market value of the securities on your tax return…with no capital-gains tax on the appreciation.

Even if you want to keep a stock in your portfolio, you can give away the shares you own…and immediately buy the same stock at today's price. You don't owe tax on the gain… and you now own the stock with a cost basis of today's higher price.

Or suppose you have too much of one issue …your employer's stock, for example. Using a portion of your holdings to give to your church or college will help your tax picture…and help you diversify your portfolio.

• *Know about the Fidelity Charitable Gift Fund.* Fidelity Investments, the mutual-fund company, sponsors a very viable plan for charitable giving that I mention to many clients.

It accepts donations of appreciated stock, with a minimum gift of $10,000. Fidelity sells the stock and invests the proceeds. You decide what charity gets the money…and when.

Example: You usually give $2,000 a year to your college. This year you give $10,000 in appreciated stock to the Fidelity Fund. You get the entire $10,000 deduction this year…while paying no capital-gains tax on the appreciation.

You then direct the trust to make annual gifts of $2,000 for five years to the college. (For illustration purposes, we have ignored earnings when the money is in Fidelity.)

Result: Nothing has changed as far as your giving to the college is concerned. You got a

big deduction when you needed it and avoided capital-gains tax on your stock.

• *Know how to give away property.* If you are giving a valuable gift…say art work or an antique worth $5,000 or more…and you want to take a deduction at fair market value, you must have it appraised by a qualified appraiser. Then attach a copy of the appraisal to your tax return.

Important: Before giving such an item, be sure the charity will use it in its tax-exempt purpose. If the charity sells it immediately, you can deduct only your cost.

More common for most people are donations of used clothing and furniture…to church rummage sales or the Salvation Army. Such donations are deductible. But retain an itemized list showing what you paid for each item…and the value you are assigning for tax purposes.

Example: You bought a suit at Saks Fifth Avenue several years ago for $350. Now, 20 pounds later, you decide to donate it to the hospital thrift shop. If the thrift shop features a rack of suits for $35, then $35 would be a reasonable deduction.

• *Don't let deductions get away.* If you drive your car while doing volunteer work for a charity, you can deduct 12 cents a mile. If you buy craft supplies for the Boy Scouts…that too is deductible.

Important: Your time is not deductible, no matter how highly trained a professional you may be. Similarly, if you donate your own art work, the value is limited to what you paid for the canvas and paint, even if your paintings hang in the Metropolitan Museum.

• *Make use of charitable remainder trusts.* Many middle-class individuals assume that trusts are for the wealthy. In fact, they can be most beneficial for many families and are not esoteric at all.

The most common use of a trust is to donate appreciated securities or real estate.

Example: Say you retire with a fair amount of your company's stock. You would like to diversify your portfolio…or move some of it into bonds that would pay interest each year. But if you sell the stock you will face a federal capital-gains tax of 28%…plus state taxes that may bring the overall tax rate above 30%.

By donating the stock to a trust, you and your wife get a tax deduction now…and avoid capital-gains tax…while continuing to earn the income from the trust for the rest of your life. Not until you and your wife die does the stock go to the charity.

Important: You do need to work with a competent accountant and attorney to be sure your trust is tailored for your situation. You don't want any guesswork.

• *Selecting a charity.* For most people, selecting a charity poses no problem. Most want to help their own church, temple or college or a well-known organization like the Red Cross.

If, however, you feel a tug at the heartstrings for every solicitation you receive in the mail, be wary. There are scams with names very close to those of real charities, and there are organizations that are legitimate and yet spend a great deal on overhead instead of on good deeds.

One way to check them out is through the Council of Better Business Bureaus' Philanthropic Advisory Service. It publishes *Give But Give Wisely*…a book that evaluates numerous charities ($2 plus a stamped, self-addressed envelope to PAS Council of Better Business Bureaus, 4200 Wilson Blvd., Suite 800, Arlington, Virginia 22203).

• *Limits on giving.* Should you feel especially charitable…remember that annual deductions are limited to 50% of adjusted gross income for cash and 30% for property. However, charitable deductions too big to be used this year can be carried forward and deducted for up to five years.

Source: William G. Brennan, an independent financial consultant who is both a certified public accountant and a certified financial planner, 1455 Pennsylvania Ave. NW, Suite 250, Washington, DC 20004.

If You Can't Pay Your Taxes

If you can't pay the tax shown on your tax return, ask to pay off the balance through monthly installments. *How:* Fill out IRS Form 9465 (Installment Agreement Request), and staple it to the front of your tax return. This allows you to obtain an extended payment period of up to 36 months. The IRS is required to respond to your request within 30 days. If you owe less than $10,000, you shouldn't have a problem obtaining a payment extension—although the IRS will add interest and penalties to your monthly payments. If you owe more than $10,000, you will have to file a financial-disclosure statement and negotiate the details of your payment schedule with the IRS.

Source: *Stand Up to the IRS: How to Handle Audits, Tax Bills and Tax Court*, by Frederick W. Daily, tax attorney in San Francisco, Nolo Press, Berkeley, California.

Lost Records

The worst impression you can make when meeting with a revenue agent for the first time is to explain that your records have been lost or destroyed and you have nothing to show. *Better strategy:* Make every reasonable effort to reconstruct the records needed to document the expenses you deducted on your tax return. Contact your bank for photocopies of canceled checks. If possible, obtain an affidavit or a duplicate receipt from the person you paid. For instance, medical expenses can be reconstructed by contacting the doctors visited during the year of the audit or your medical insurance company.

Source: Ms. X is a former IRS agent still well connected.

Before Lending Money

When lending money to a family member or close friend, put the loan terms in writing. If the terms aren't spelled out, misunderstandings can easily lead to disagreements and ill will. *Example:* A lender who says, "Pay me back when you can" may mean "as soon as possible," but the borrower interprets this to mean "when it's convenient." *Also:* Loan documentation will help you claim a bad-debt deduction should the borrower default. *Requirement:* A legitimate loan must carry a market interest rate. Refer to the Applicable Federal Rate for loans of various terms that is published monthly by the IRS. You can minimize the interest rate by making a short-term loan that is renewable.

Source: Lew Altfest, president, L.J. Altfest & Co., financial planners, New York City.

Using a CPA Saves Penalties

A woman trusted the preparation of her tax return to a CPA who understated her income and overstated her deductions. The IRS imposed penalties. *Court:* The penalties were set aside. The woman's trust in her accountant may have been "misplaced and unfortunate," but it was not unreasonable given his credentials. She had not been negligent.

Source: *Dona E. Conway,* TC Memo 1994-405.

IRS Etiquette

If you get an IRS notice in the mail, make sure that you understand what it means...

• Never ignore a notice from the IRS, even one that is unjustified. Answer it promptly, before the time limit given in the notice. If you ignore the notice, interest and penalties will pile up. It will become harder to straighten out and the IRS collection division will demand payment.

• Never pay without checking the figures first. The IRS may have made a mistake.

• Don't try to straighten out mistakes in person at your local IRS office. Write to the address indicated on the notice.

• Include a copy of the notice with your response.

• Keep copies of your letters.

• Put your Social Security number on every letter to the IRS.

• See your tax adviser if you have any questions about the notice.

• Send your tax adviser copies of all correspondence with the IRS.

Source: Pete J. Medina, tax consultant on practice and procedure before the IRS, Ernst & Young, LLP, CPAs, 787 Seventh Ave., New York 10019.

Big Opportunities for Itemized Deductions Loopholes

Itemized deductions used to offer tremendous benefits. But Congress has cut them back sharply. It now takes more planning than ever before to take full advantage of your itemized deductions. *Loopholes...*

• *The standard deduction* is the basic deduction amount that everybody is allowed. For 1994 tax returns, the standard deduction amounts are $6,350 for couples and $3,800 for singles.

Loophole: Bunch two years' worth of deductions in one year to get above the standard deduction amount. Take itemized deductions in one year and the standard deduction the next. This will increase the amount of deductions you can write off.

Example: Suppose your itemized deductions average $5,000 a year. If you do nothing, you're stuck taking the standard deduction amount of $6,350 on a joint return. But suppose you were to pull $2,000 worth of deductions from next year into this year. That would allow you to take $7,000 worth of itemized deductions in the current year. The following year you would take the standard deduction amount. *Tax impact:* Your total deductions for the two years would be $13,350 ($7,000 + $6,350). If you took the standard deduction in both years, your total deductions would only be $12,700 ($6,350 + $6,350), or $650 less than if you had bunched.

Deductions that you may be able to accelerate for bunching include state and local taxes and real-estate taxes.

• Percentage limitations. Certain deductions are subject to percentage of Adjusted Gross Income (AGI) limitations.

Medical expenses, for example, are deductible only if they exceed 7½% of AGI. Other deductions subject to limitation are casualty losses and miscellaneous itemized deductions. With a little planning, a married couple with both people working can maximize their deductions when one spouse has high expenses that are subject to limitation.

Loophole: File separate returns. This will reduce the income that is the basis of the percentage limitation and increase the amount of deductions that can be taken.

• *Children's investment income.* Parents of children younger than 14 who have less than $5,000 of investment income have a choice to make when reporting that income. Income can be reported on the child's own return, or on the parents'.

Loophole: Don't report the income on your return if you have itemized deductions that are subject to percentage-of-Adjusted Gross Income limitations. Reporting the child's income on your return will only increase your AGI and reduce the amount of deductions you can take.

• *Medical expenses* must exceed 7½% AGI before they become deductible.

Loophole: The medical expenses you pay for your dependents are deductible on your return. Suppose you're supporting your dependent mother and pay her medical expenses. You can deduct them on your return.

Loophole: A child of divorced parents is considered the dependent of both parents for the purposes of deducting medical expenses.

You can also deduct the medical expenses of a person whom you could have claimed as a dependent had that person not received more than $2,450 of income. So, you can deduct the medical expenses of a parent you are supporting even though your parent has $10,000 of income and you can't claim a dependency exemption for him/her.

Loophole: The medical portion of nursing home payments is deductible. If you are supporting a parent in a nursing home and make a lump-sum payment for his/her care, you can deduct that portion of the payment that is attributable to the medical care of that parent. It is deductible in full in the year of payment.

• *Taxes.* State and local income taxes and real-estate taxes are deductible. That is a loophole in itself.

Trap: Big deductions of state and local taxes can trigger the Alternative Minimum Tax (AMT). You get no deduction for them in an AMT year.

Caution: Accelerate or postpone state and local taxes out of a year when you're subject to the AMT.

Loophole: Certain state withholding taxes are deductible.

Example: New Jersey's unemployment insurance, which is a mandatory employee withholding item, is deductible as a tax payment.

• *Interest* on money borrowed to buy or build a primary residence and one second home is deductible on up to $1 million of debt.

Loophole: If you have more than two homes, you are able to designate on a year-by-year basis which two homes you are going to take the interest deduction for, depending on where you have the higher interest expense.

Loophole: Interest on home equity borrowing, up to $100,000, is also deductible.

• *Charity.* The limit on cash contributions is 50% of AGI per year.

Loophole: Amounts over the limit can be carried forward for five years. Gifts of appreciated property are deductible based on the fair market value of the gift, providing they meet certain requirements. *Limit:* Gifts of appreciated property are limited to 30% of AGI. The excess can be carried forward for five years.

Loophole: Gifts that exceed the limit should be split. Make a partial gift now and the balance in six years.

• *Casualty losses.* Personal casualty losses in total must exceed 10% of AGI, plus $100 per casualty, to be deductible.

Loophole: If the loss is a business loss, it is not subject to limitation.

Example: If you have an uninsured auto loss while it was used for business purposes, that is a business casualty loss and not subject to the 10% of AGI limitation.

•*Miscellaneous itemized expenses* are deductible to the extent they exceed 2% of AGI. If you are given an expense account by your employer, you must include the expense account in your income and your deductions are subject to the 2% limit.

Loophole: If you account to your employer for the exact expenditures and are reimbursed, you don't have to include the reimbursement in income or take deductions, so you don't have to worry about the 2% limitation.

Among the expenses that are included in the category of miscellaneous itemized deductions are…

•Investment expenses.

•Unreimbursed employee expenses.

•Business expenses.

•The portion of a divorce lawyer's bill that relates to tax matters.

•Union dues and professional association fees.

•Business gifts up to $25 per year per recipient.

•Job-hunting expenses.

•Fifty percent of employee business entertainment expenses.

Loophole: If you have large, miscellaneous expenditures in any one year, explain them in detail when you file your return. Attach copies of receipts to your return. This could help you avoid an audit.

Source: Edward Mendlowitz, partner, Mendlowitz Weitsen, CPAs, Two Pennsylvania Plaza, New York 10121.

 # New Marriages Need Tax Planning Too

If you and your prospective spouse each own your own home, some tax planning before marriage can save big dollars later. *Options…*

•You can each sell your present home and within two years buy a new home together that costs at least as much as the combined sale prices of the homes you each sold. All gains on the sales will be deferred and rolled over into your new home.

•If you intend to live in one of the homes after your marriage—and plan to sell a home with a low basis—have the owner of the low-basis home buy the home with the higher basis so the gain will be deferred. If the high-basis home is worth much more, consider the purchase of a partial interest.

•If you (or your intended) are older than 55, you might want to take advantage of the special $125,000 exclusion of gains on a home sale. But planning before your marriage is very important. *Each* of you can use the exclusion on your own home before you are married—but once you are married—you get only one exclusion. And if either spouse used the exclusion before, it can't be used again.

Source: David S. Rhine, CPA, is a partner with BDO Seidman, LLP, 330 Madison Ave., New York 10017.

Offshore Income Loopholes

American citizens and residents are required to report their worldwide income on US tax returns. However, there are situations where that income does not have to be taxed twice.

Working abroad:

One exception to the rule that US citizens must pay US tax on income earned anywhere in the world applies to citizens who are working abroad.

Individuals who qualify may exclude from US taxation up to $70,000 of wages, salary, professional fees, or moving expenses from foreign sources.

Two tests: You must be a bona fide resident of a foreign country for the full tax year…or be physically present in the foreign country for at least 330 days of any 12 consecutive months.

Loophole: Even if you aren't a bona fide resident, you may qualify for the exclusion by meeting the "physical presence" test.

Whether you're a bona fide resident of a foreign country depends on your *intention* about the length and nature of your stay. If you go to a foreign country with a definite purpose for a temporary period and return to the US after you accomplish it, you're *not* a bona fide resident of that country. But if accomplishing the purpose requires an extended, indefinite stay—and you make your home in the foreign country—you might be considered a bona fide resident.

To figure the minimum 330 full days of the physical presence test, add all separate periods you were present in a foreign country during the 12-month period. The 330 full days do not need to be consecutive.

Social Security:

Loophole: When you work abroad, Social Security tax is *not* deducted from your earnings. You are not required to pay it.

Self-employment tax, on the other hand, is treated differently—depending on the tax treaty the US has with the country you're working in.

Example: The treaty with Australia does not provide for an exemption for self-employment tax. So, even though your earnings in Australia may be exempt from US income tax, you'll have to pay self-employment tax on those earnings.

Foreign tax credit:

Most income that is earned in a foreign jurisdiction is taxed by that country. You're also required to pay US tax on most foreign-earned income.

Loophole: You get a credit on your US tax return for taxes paid to a foreign country.

The credit is limited to the lesser of the foreign taxes paid or the US tax on that income.

Example: Suppose you earned $100,000 in a foreign country. US tax on that income is $35,000, but you paid $45,000 in foreign taxes. Your US foreign tax credit is therefore limited to $35,000.

Loophole: The US has treaties with many foreign countries limiting the tax rate that the foreign country will assess on foreign-earned interest and dividend income. The tax is withheld at the source—that is, by the company paying the dividend or interest.

Example: You get a dividend from a Dutch company and the company withholds 15% tax. You have no responsibility now to file a tax return with the Netherlands. And you can take a credit on your US return for the 15% tax that was withheld in the Netherlands.

Foreign bank accounts:

Two questions on Schedule B of Form 1040 ask whether the taxpayer has—or is—a signatory on any foreign bank accounts. Answering the question in the affirmative won't result in any *additional* tax. (You do have to pay tax on the interest your account earns. If you lie, and are caught, however, you will be subjected to penalties. If you leave the questions unanswered, you could get a letter of inquiry from the IRS.

Foreign trusts:

Many people establish trusts in foreign countries to shelter or hide income or for privacy reasons. It's much harder to sue someone who has a foreign trust. When the trust is irrevocable, the income earned by the trust will be fully taxed by the US. Even if the trust is irrevocable, the income may also be taxed depending on its nature and what rights the beneficiary has.

Preparing your tax return:

All tax credits, including the foreign tax credit, are figured on IRS Form 1116. See instructions to IRS Form 2555 for complete details of the tax exclusion for foreign-earned income.

Loophole: Expenses attributable to foreign-earned income are allocated between taxable and excludable income. You can deduct the expenses attributable to taxable income.

Loophole: If you account to your employer for your expenses and you are reimbursed for them, the reimbursement is not included on your W-2 form and you don't have to report the expenses on your return.

Source: Edward Mendlowitz, partner, Mendlowitz Weitsen, CPAs, Two Pennsylvania Plaza, New York 10121. He is the author of *New Tax Traps, New Opportunities,* Boardroom Special Reports, 55 Railroad Ave., Greenwich, Connecticut 06830.

Best Ways to Shelter Income from Taxes

Don't miss any tax sheltering items. You can shelter much of your income from needless taxes simply if you know where the tax shelters are.

• *Invest in tax-exempt rather than taxable investments.* The yield on a tax-exempt investment may be lower on its face than a taxable investment is. Don't be deceived. The tax-exempt investment will probably end up giving you more money.

Reason: Tax-exempt investments are free of federal tax. The investment is worth more.

Better: Some tax-free investments are actually triple tax-free because they are exempt from state and local tax as well as federal tax. When you live in the state or city that issued the bond, it will be free of state and local taxes.

How to decide between taxable and tax-free investments: Analyze both the taxable and tax-free investments, after taxes, to see which one actually has a higher yield.

• *Reduce the overall family tax bill.* Transfer income-producing property to either your parents or your children who are in a lower tax bracket.

Special rule for children under age 14: Children can have up to $1,200 of income taxed at their lower rate.

Compare: Your tax rate could be as high as 39.6%. Children age 14 or older can have an unlimited amount of income taxed at their own rates.

• *Don't borrow unless you can deduct the interest.* Car loans or credit card loans should be avoided when purchasing personal assets because the interest is not deductible.

Self-defense: Take out a home equity loan on which the interest is deductible. Use the proceeds from the home equity loan to make purchases and to pay off existing debt.

By using this strategy the non-deductible interest payments will be converted to deductible interest expense. You can deduct interest on home equity loans of up to as much as $100,000.

• *Document your charitable contributions.* Canceled checks for gifts of more than $250 to a charity are no longer sufficient proof of the contributions for the IRS. You are now required to get actual documentation from the charity itself in some other form such as a letter from the charity acknowledging the gift and its worth.

• *Don't lose your deduction.* Follow up with the charities that you donate money to and obtain the proper documentation of your charitable contribution.

• *Rather than cash, give gifts of appreciated securities to charities.* If you have held a security for more than one year, the charitable deduction is generally equal to the fair market value of the security. You will avoid paying long-term capital gains tax on the gain.

• *Take advantage of your company's 401(k) plan.* Contribute the highest amount allowable to your company's plan.

Maximum limit for 1995: You can contribute 25% of your salary up to $9,240. Contributions to 401(k)s are great tax shelters because they are subtracted from your taxable income. Many companies will match all or part of your contribution.

More advantages: The tax on both the principal that you've contributed and the earnings is tax-deferred until you withdraw the money at retirement.

• *Contribute to your own retirement plan.* Self-employeds can contribute to a SEP or Keogh plan as long as they are set up properly. The contributions are subtracted from your taxable income and the earnings in the plan are tax-deferred. A substantial amount of your income can be sheltered if the plan is set up correctly. Your broker or accountant can help you figure out your maximum deduction and set up the plan for you.

• *Analyze miscellaneous deductions.* You are only permitted to deduct miscellaneous deductions to the extent that they are greater than 2% of your Adjusted Gross Income (AGI).

Special strategy: If you expect your income bracket to be lower this year than it will be next year, maximize your miscellaneous deductions. This way you will be able to meet the 2% limit in at least one out of the two years.

How: Make your payments this year even though the bills could wait until next year. Employees can pay dues to professional societies and associations, pay malpractice insurance premiums, renew subscriptions to professional journals and magazines, purchase tools and supplies needed for their work, pay union dues and expenses, and purchase work clothes and uniforms. Your tax adviser may be aware of other payments you should make this year.

•*Reverse tax-planning.* Project your tax for the rest of the year to see if you are subject to the Alternative Minimum Tax (AMT). This is a special type of tax that is imposed instead of the regular tax when you have certain types of deductions or credits. This tax is lower than the regular income tax.

Special tax-sheltering strategy: Reverse the usual tax strategies if you are subject to the Alternative Minimum Tax. *How to accomplish this:* Accelerate income wherever possible into the AMT year. Defer your deductions to the non-AMT year because they will be more valuable when deducted in a year that you will be subject to the regular income tax.

Source: Barry Salzberg, partner in charge, personal tax and financial planning group, Deloitte & Touche, LLP, Two World Financial Center, New York 10281.

Business Trips for Two

Double hotel rooms cost little more than singles do, and many airlines offer double fares that cost little more than singles. And if you extend your stay over a Saturday night you may reduce airfare costs further. *Tax break:* If you take a business trip with a companion, you are *not* limited to deducting half of the trip costs. You can deduct the *full* amount you would spend traveling alone, even if traveling with a companion adds little to your total cost.

Source: Laurence Foster, partner, KPMG Peat Marwick, New York, quoted in *Tax Hotline,* 55 Railroad Ave., Greenwich, CT 06830.

Buying-a-Business Loopholes

Buying a business today presents a considerable number of hidden tax-saving opportunities…
Allocation loopholes:
Loophole: Write off assets purchased. When a business is bought, the purchase price is allocated among the various assets. How the purchase price is allocated to the various assets of

the business determines the deduction. The allocation is based on the fair market value of the assets at the time of purchase. This is the figure used to calculate the tax deductions—and the gain or loss when the assets are later disposed of.

List the assets in the purchase contract and assign specific amounts to each. *There are four categories of tax treatment…*

•*Depreciable.* Certain business assets can be depreciated over a useful life that is determined by IRS tables. *Examples:*
 •Cars and trucks—five years.
 •Office furniture and fixtures—seven years.
 •Buildings—39 years.

•*Amortizable.* Most intangible assets—see list below—can be amortized over 15 years, that is, written off a bit each year.

•Deductible. Some assets are deductible. Included:
 •Inventory as it is sold.
 •Prepaid expenses, such as the assumption of the insurance policies of the business.

•*Nondeductible.* Certain assets, such as land, bank accounts, and accounts receivable are not deductible at all. The purchase price becomes the tax cost of the asset when it goes on the company's books.

Also not deductible…the price paid for the corporate stock of the company being acquired plus any costs associated with buying the stock, such as brokerage fees.
Interest:

Interest on debt used to acquire any business is fully deductible by the business.

If the buyer personally borrows the money to buy the business, and uses the money to buy stock in the company, the interest expenses are deductible on the buyer's personal 1040 as investment income.

Imputed interest: If no interest is stated in the contract to buy the business, interest will be imputed—calculated according to IRS tables.

Loophole: The interest payments are deductible in full in the year they are paid. This is not necessarily when the assets being acquired are deducted. *Impact:* The buyer may be able to write off interest payments before fully writing off the assets.

Amortization loophole:

Most intangible assets that are acquired when a business changes hands can be amortized over 15 years. *Examples:*

- Goodwill.
- Going concern value.
- Work force in place, business books and records, operating systems, or information databases.
- Patents, copyrights, formulas, processes, designs, patterns, know-how, formats, or similar items.
- Customer-based intangibles…a customer following, market share, customer advance payments, or a deposit base (for a bank).
- Supplier-based intangibles, such as contractual arrangements or allocations of items in short supply.
- Licenses, permits, and government rights.
- Franchises, trademarks, and trade names.
- Covenants not to compete.

Assets vs stock:

It's better to buy the individual assets of a company than its stock. The premium paid over the value of the assets when stock is acquired in a company is not deductible. It's added to the tax cost (basis) of the stock acquired. If the buyer acquires the individual assets, the excess paid is considered goodwill and is amortizable.

Loophole: Buy the individual assets of the company and write off the excess value over 15 years.

When a person sells the assets of the company, the corporation will be required to pick up the profit on the sale of the assets. In addition, the seller will have to pick up as capital gains any proceeds he/she receives on liquidating the company. Of course, this situation results in a double tax.

Loophole: The seller should try to sell the corporate stock, not the individual assets.

Nonamortizable allocation:

There are other items that are neither amortizable nor deductible when the purchase of a business is completed. *Examples:*

- Purchase of land.
- Interest under existing leases of tangible property.
- Sports franchises.
- Certain residential mortgage servicing rights.
- Interests in partnerships.

Source: Edward Mendlowitz, partner, Mendlowitz Weitsen, CPAs, Two Pennsylvania Plaza, New York 10121.

IRS to Finance Business Operations

It is increasingly common for business owners who are unable to borrow money from a bank to use the IRS to finance their business operations. Payroll taxes, which are withheld from employee salaries, are simply not remitted to the government, but rather, are used to pay other bills. Since these companies typically keep very low balances in their checking accounts, the IRS knows that placing a levy on the account will produce only a small amount of money. *IRS tactic:* Attempt to learn the names and addresses of companies that owe the delinquent taxpayer money. Then the IRS levies on the accounts receivable by notifying those companies that they should make their check payable to the IRS instead of the delinquent taxpayer.

Source: Ms. X, a former IRS agent still well connected.

15

Insurance Information

What You Don't Know About Insurance Can Hurt You...Badly

Consider two houses...side by side...both destroyed in a disaster. One home owner gets an $18,000 check from his insurance company to rent temporary housing. The other gets just $500 a month...and must haggle each month to get even that.

Sound unlikely? As an insurance company disaster supervisor, I saw this happen after the 1989 San Francisco earthquake. People who were savvy about their insurance received bigger settlements than those who trusted their insurers to look out for them.

What you don't know about your homeowner's policy could permanently reduce your standard of living after a calamity. It could even cost you your home.

My rules for insurance self-protection...

•*Don't rely on fluffy language.* Regardless of how a policy is advertised, read the fine print of a homeowner's policy before you buy. Don't depend solely on your insurance agent. To wrap up the sale quickly, he/she has an incentive to sell you something basic and cheap.

•*Read your policy now.* If you aren't sure what your policy covers...if something isn't absolutely clear...have your insurer or agent explain it and confirm the conversation in writing.

•Don't expect the insurer to put you first if disaster strikes. If the company had known you were going to have a loss, it would never have written a policy on you.

How to buy the protection you need...

•*Buy coverage to restore your home exactly as it was before the disaster.* This is the "face value" of the policy. Coverage for other possessions, such as furnishings and landscaping, are usually expressed as a percentage of the replacement cost.

The cost of restoration has nothing to do with the price you paid for the home.

Key question: What would it cost to exactly reproduce this dwelling on this property?

Answer: Only an expert contractor can tell you. Invest $150 or so to get an estimate.

• *Tailor the insurance to your own home.* Insurance companies like to base their payments on the cost of modern, tract-house-style construction. Your home—especially if it is older—could have more costly features, like lathe-and-plaster instead of sheetrock walls.

Strategy: Buy a policy that provides "Guaranteed Replacement Cost" (GRC) coverage. This will pay the cost to replace your dwelling regardless of the "face value." *Helpful:* Some policies that claim to be "Guaranteed Replacement Cost" have a limit usually expressed as a percentage of the face value. Even if the policy has GRC on the dwelling, the other coverages that are expressed as a percentage are usually a percentage of the face amount, not the actual replacement cost.

• *Don't neglect "code and ordinance or law" coverage.* After Hurricane Andrew, many homes had to be elevated 13 feet—or they couldn't be rebuilt. After the San Francisco quake, new homes in the area had to have much stronger foundations.

Home owners without this additional protection had to pay those extra costs themselves. The cost of code protection is about 10% of the annual premium.

• *Know what replacement cost means.* While your coverage may say "full replacement cost," you must complete the replacement to collect.

If you can't—because you can't afford to elevate the home or build that new foundation—you might collect only the "actual cash value" of the lost home, which might be one-third less.

• *Your possessions.* Make sure your furnishings and possessions are covered for replacement cost, not current value. A used sofa is worth half its replacement cost, at best...but you won't replace it with used merchandise.

Most policies cover the contents of a home only up to 50% or so of the face amount. If your possessions are worth more than that... pay around $1.50 per each $1,000 of coverage per year.

• *Your valuables.* If you have artwork, collections, antiques or other valuable personal property, study the "limits of coverage" section of your policy to see how much of the value of lost or destroyed valuables the insurer will pay.

Consider a "floater" to provide supplemental coverage. It will cost about $0.25 to $2.50 for each $100 of coverage.

• *Know about "other structures."* Structures separated from your dwelling are covered separately in your homeowner's policy...usually for 10% of the "face value" amount. But what about attached decks and patios? Are they considered other structures, or are they included in the face amount?

Any structure that is "attached" to the dwelling should be included in the face value, but be sure to clear this up at the time of purchase.

• *Take inflation into account.* Construction costs rise every year. So do the costs of replacing your furniture, snow blower, kitchen appliances, etc. Make sure the policies covering contents—as well as the dwelling itself—are protected with a rider that raises coverage periodically to reflect rising costs.

• *Buy all the liability coverage you need.* Standard policies provide some protection in the event your neighbor trips over your sprinkler and breaks his leg. But consider "umbrella" coverage, which unifies liability under all your policies...cars and boats as well as the house.

Umbrella policies often cover hazards that homeowner's insurance does not, such as a claim of slander when your neighbor doesn't like what you said about him/her. You would pay about $100 a year for $1 million of umbrella coverage.

• *Protect yourself in case of disaster.* Make sure the policy will pay all expenses necessary to maintain your standard of living for as long as necessary while your home is being restored.

Important: Avoid coverage of "actual incurred costs." That will skimp on paying for temporary quarters...and force you to argue with your insurer over every receipt.

• *Don't be penny-wise/pound-foolish.* The best coverage doesn't necessarily cost more. In fact, insurance companies price their best policies very competitively because "better" customers are good prospects for the companies' other products.

• *Don't just buy a policy and forget it.* Every few years review your coverage to make sure it still meets your needs. And then shop around to make sure you're still getting the best price.

Helpful: Start with your current agent. He may be willing to improve your coverage—and trim the price—if he fears losing his annual commission.

Source: Ina De Long, president of United Policyholders, a nonprofit group devoted to consumer education on insurance. Box 2071, Merced, California 95344.

Late-Discovered Damage

Insurance covers damage to property even if the damage isn't discovered until after the insurance lapses. *Case:* A wood processing company obtained comprehensive liability coverage from a number of insurers during the years 1942 to 1986. Then it was discovered that the company's property had been polluted by leaching chemicals. The insurers argued that they weren't liable because the harm to the property wasn't discovered until after their policies had lapsed. *Court:* The language of the policies clearly stated that they covered damage that occurred during the policy periods. The fact that the damage wasn't discovered until later didn't matter. The insurers are liable.

Source: *St. Paul Fire v. McCormick & Baxter*, Court of Appeals of Oregon, 3/19/94.

Insurance for the Uninsurable

If your health prevents you from buying life insurance, you can still obtain insurance protection for your family. *How:* Select a "surrogate insured." This person usually is a member of your family—an aunt, uncle or sibling—who is insurable. You create a trust for your children or other beneficiaries, and give the trust the money to buy an insurance policy on the surrogate insured. Eventually, the policy proceeds will pass to the trust's beneficiaries free of estate tax—providing a substitute for the insurance benefit you couldn't obtain on your own life.

Source: *Die Rich and Tax Free* by Barry Kaye, CLU, financial adviser, Los Angeles, Forman Publishing, 2080 Westridge Rd., Los Angeles 90049.

Long-Term-Care Insurance...Essentials

To offset the future expense of a nursing home or of home health care, many people who are in their 50s and 60s should consider long-term-care insurance.

But while long-term-care insurance policies have specific benefits, they are not for everyone. Here's what you need to know before you buy.

Long-term-care insurance basics:

Long-term-care insurance emerged about 10 years ago to help people pay for extended health care themselves without wiping out their assets. This type of insurance also protects the assets of family members at a time when they may have other financial obligations.

Residence at a private nursing home is expensive. Today it can cost as much as $74,000 a year. An insurance policy's annual premium depends on your age and health at the time you apply for the policy, the benefit amount selected, the benefit period, the elimination period (the time that must elapse before a policy begins paying benefits) and any inflation option.

Examples: A basic policy may provide for a $100-a-day benefit for three years with an automatic inflation option. It could also include a 100-day elimination period. If purchased at age

251

55, this basic policy would cost about $800 a year...at age 60, $1,100 a year...and at age 70, $1,800 a year.

By contrast, a top-of-the-line policy can provide a $250-a-day lifetime benefit with a 5% compound inflation rider and a 20-day elimination period. At age 55, the annual premium would be $2,900...at age 60, $3,970...and at age 70, $7,090.

Who needs it?

The ideal candidates for long-term-care insurance are healthy and between the ages of 55 and 75 with assets of $500,000 to $2.5 million —not including the value of their homes.

These people usually want to preserve their assets for their heirs rather than use them to pay nursing home or home health care bills. In addition, this group can usually afford to pay the premiums now.

But others should consider long-term-care insurance for different reasons...

•40- to 65-year-olds. This group may want to protect their children from having to take care of them when they are older.

•65- to 99-year-olds may want to be able to continue living in their own homes...and understandably they may be reluctant to transfer their assets to their children in order to qualify for Medicaid.

What the right policy provides:

•Guaranteed renewability. As long as you pay the insurance premiums, the policy cannot be canceled. The premium can be increased only for the entire group, not on an individual basis.

•Nursing home and home health care. The policy should include both options...and your personal physician should decide when and what level of care you need.

•Payment triggered by the policyholder's inability to perform at least two of five basic activities of daily living—bathing, feeding, administering medications, toileting and transferring from a chair to a bed.

•Coverage throughout the US. You want a policy that provides protection no matter where you live. Some will even provide coverage in other countries.

•Coverage in the event you develop Alzheimer's disease.

Before buying a policy:

•Consider the term of the policy. If you are under age 60, lifetime coverage is preferable. If you're over age 80, opt for two or four years. Those people between the ages of 60 and 80 should buy what they can afford.

Important: A single person may opt to take out lifetime coverage because he/she doesn't have a spouse to handle some of the burden.

•Consider the policy's elimination period. The longer the elimination period, the lower the premium.

Strategy: Consider the trade-off between price and peace of mind. For most people, a 100-day elimination period may make the most sense because, if they are eligible, Medicare may pay some of the expenses for the first 100 days.

Source: Howard Klein and Dale Kramer, long-term health insurance experts. Mr. Klein is chairman of Klein, McGorry & Klein Ltd., an insurance consultant and broker, 21 E. 40 St., New York 10016. Ms. Kramer is a consultant for the firm.

Before You Sign On the Dotted Line

For extra health or life insurance, buying supplemental coverage through your employer's group policy often is not a good deal. *Reason:* Group plans must supply coverage to all employees regardless of their health and other risk factors—so group plan premiums often are higher than you can obtain elsewhere in the market. Insurance is like other consumer products—you find the best deal by shopping around.

Source: Thomas Ford, Ford and Associates, financial advisers, Mountain View, California.

How to Buy the Right Disability Policy

When people ask me whether they really need to buy long-term-disability insurance, I ask them— "Could you pay your bills if you were out of work for an extended period of time due to illness or injury?" Some think for a moment and realize that they could not. Others reply, "My company's long-term-disability policy would cover me."

Reality: Most company short- or long-term-disability plans do not provide enough coverage.

They also do not include the same level of consumer safeguards that individually purchased policies do...nor do they provide the same financial benefits, since they are considered taxable income by the IRS.

The fact is that disability insurance is more important in many cases than life insurance, since you are more likely to be injured or disabled than you are to die.

Here's what you need to know when considering long-term-disability coverage...

The basics:

Disability insurance replaces a portion of your income if you become sick or injured and are unable to perform the substantial or material duties of your job.

Important: Each policy includes its own definition of a qualifying sickness or injury. Generally any illness must have begun after your policy was issued in order for you to qualify for benefits.

Whenever you buy long-term-disability insurance, your goal is self-protection. To accomplish this goal, you need a policy that offers you the largest amount of coverage and the most flexible options for reimbursement in the event that you ever need to apply for benefits. Rates for such coverage vary, depending on your age and sex.

Example: A 40-year-old male should expect to pay $500 a year for a good basic policy in order to receive a benefit of $1,000 a month. A 40-year-old female would average $600 a year.

Company traps:

Employer long-term-disability plans are regulated under the Employee Retirement Income Security Act (ERISA) guidelines. As a result, you lose your individual rights. If you become disabled due to an illness or injury—and your company's insurer unfairly denies or delays your benefits, even after appeal—here is what is likely to happen...

•You will have to sue the insurer in federal court, where your case would likely be decided in 15 months by a federal judge—not by a jury. If the court can find any basis to uphold the insurer's denial of your benefits, you lose.

•Under ERISA, you are not permitted to sue for emotional distress or punitive or other damages. These restrictions limit your ability to hire a lawyer on a contingency basis—meaning that you'll have to pay for all legal services out of your own pocket, no matter what the judgment.

•Whatever benefits you receive will be considered taxable income.

•During the first year of your illness or injury, your group benefits are reduced by any amounts you receive or are eligible to receive, even if you don't apply for them from state disability...workers' compensation...or Social Security disability benefits. As a result, your group plan could wind up paying you as little as $50 per month after any waiting period.

Why individual policies make sense:

If you're disabled, your monthly payment from most insurers cannot be taxed or reduced by any other benefits you receive—even those that come from an employer's long-term-disability plan.

Individually owned policies are not regulated by ERISA and, therefore, offer greater consumer safeguards if claims are being unfairly denied or delayed and you must take legal action. *You can sue the insurer for...*

•Denied or delayed benefits plus emotional distress.

•Damages suffered as a result of the delay, such as a repossessed car or home, and punitive damages, where the insurer has acted with malice, oppression or fraud.

• Your attorney fees.

The case would be decided by a jury from the county in which you live.

Shopping for a policy:

• If possible, rely on a licensed and appointed insurance agent—not a broker. Agents give you the highest level of consumer safeguards.

Reason: Insurers are responsible for their agents' errors in taking down application information.

When you buy individual long-term-disability insurance through brokers, however, you're not protected from their errors because brokers work for you.

Important: Verify the agent's credentials by requiring license documentation issued by your state department of insurance. Then call or write your state insurance department. Give your agent's license number, and request a complete list of all the insurance companies that have appointed him/her. Look for an agent who is appointed by at least several disability insurance companies to give you a good range of policy options and benefits.

Great policy essentials:

Here are what I consider to be the best disability insurance policy features, in order of their importance to consumers. *Choose as many as you can afford...*

• *Own-occupation coverage* guarantees benefit payments if you are unable to perform the substantial and material duties of your own profession.

Example: If a heart surgeon with an own-occupation policy develops a heart condition and can no longer operate on cardiac patients but could work as a general practitioner, he would be considered disabled.

General-occupation coverage is cheaper, but it won't pay up if you can perform any other job for which you are suited by education, training and experience.

Example: If the same heart surgeon could teach in a medical school, he would not be considered disabled or entitled to his benefits.

• Waiver of premium rider forces the insurer to waive the premium for your coverage while you are totally disabled.

• Waiting period of no more than 60 to 90 days for benefits to begin after you become disabled. Some policies make you wait as long as one year.

• Lifetime benefits provide payments for as long as you are disabled.

Problem: While desirable, they are expensive and add 20% to the cost of a policy. In addition, it is increasingly difficult to find an insurer that will provide them.

Second best: Benefits that will pay until age 65.

Avoid policies that limit benefit payouts to between two and five years. The longer your benefits last, the longer you will be protected.

• *Cost-of-living adjustment* guarantees that your benefits will get adjusted annually to keep up with inflation. This option costs more, but it's worth it.

• *Noncancelable–guaranteed renewable.* As long as you pay your premiums on time, you are guaranteed that the contractual language of your long-term-disability coverage will not change and that your premiums will not increase—even if your insurer stops selling policies in your state.

• *Coverage for a psychiatric condition.* Limitations are undesirable. *Better:* A policy that pays for at least 24 months, should a psychiatric condition disable you.

Bottom line:

Don't try to save money on premiums by accepting a partial or residual benefit option. Some policies will pay part of your benefits if you can perform one but not all of the duties of your job.

Example: A surgeon who can consult with patients in the office but due to illness or injury cannot operate.

Some buy this option because it increases their chances of receiving some benefit.

Problem: Such policies can be used by an insurer to avoid paying the full disability benefits for which you paid. If you have such an option, the insurer can often find one or more duties that you can perform. That means you will receive only a prorated part of your benefits rather than the full amount.

Better: Purchase a straight total-disability policy without any residual option or rider. It will pay your full benefits if you are unable to perform the substantial and material duties of your occupation.

Source: Frank Darras, an attorney who specializes in disability insurance. He is a name partner with Shernoff, Bidart & Darras, a law firm that represents consumers trying to reverse bad-faith actions by their insurance companies, 600 S. Indian Hill Blvd., Claremont, California 91711.

Beware of "Free" Group Life Insurance

If you are in a high federal income tax bracket and your employer provides group life insurance as a benefit, you may be paying more in taxes on the policy than you would pay in premiums if you bought your own coverage. *Reason:* The IRS overvalues group term insurance. *Example:* A healthy, nonsmoking 50-year-old male executive who earns $275,000 a year would be taxed $1,400 on a $500,000 policy he could buy for $1,240 a year. The disparity increases with the age of the taxpayer. *Self-defense:* Withdraw from the group policy in favor of an individual term policy.

Source: Kenneth Brier, tax lawyer, Sherburne, Powers & Needham, Boston, quoted in *Forbes*, 60 Fifth Ave., New York 10011.

Life Insurance Formula

To determine how much coverage you need —assume surviving dependents need 80% of your current income. Divide that number by the interest you would expect to earn over time on a lump-sum insurance payout. *Example:* If you earn $50,000 a year, you need to provide 80% of that, or $40,000 a year. If your principal

would earn an average of 5% a year, divide $40,000 by 0.05. *Result:* $800,000 in insurance is needed to avoid eating into principal.

Source: Diane Pearl, partner, Moneywise, a St. Louis-based financial education and training company, and the coauthor of *99 Great Answers to Everyone's Investment Questions*, Career Press, Hawthorne, NJ.

Life Insurance Trade-In Trap

Beware when an insurance agent encourages you to trade in one cash-value life insurance policy for another—even if it was indeed a mistake to buy the policy you now own. *Reason:* When a policy is dropped during the first few years that you own it, you forfeit the large up-front fees and commissions that you paid to buy it. Years five through 10 are when most policies begin paying good returns, so that's a poor time to drop them as well. *Best:* In most cases, if you need more coverage than is provided by a cash-value policy, simply supplement it by buying extra term insurance or another cash-value policy.

Source: Glenn Daily, insurance consultant, New York.

Auto-Insurance Danger

Clear up your credit report before applying for a new policy. *Reason:* A growing number of auto insurers are using credit reports to determine the riskiness of applicants. A bad credit report can result in higher premiums. *Strategy:* Call TRW (800-682-7654), Equifax (800-685-1111) and Trans Union (800-851-2674) for your credit reports. Examine them for problems—and mistakes.

Source: Gerri Detweiler is a consumer credit consultant in Woodbridge, Virginia, and the author of *The Ultimate Credit Handbook*.

Teenager Insurance Moneysaver

Cut the cost of insuring teenagers by adding them to your own auto policy instead of insuring them separately...telling your agent when the teenager attends a school at least 100 miles from home (to lower your premium while he/she is not using the car)...shopping around —rates for teenage drivers, as for others, vary widely...checking for special discounts. *Example:* Some companies give discounts of up to 25% for high school or college students who maintain a B average or better.

Source: *How to Get Your Money's Worth in Home and Auto Insurance* by Barbara Taylor, former vice president of consumer affairs, Insurance Information Institute, New York, McGraw-Hill, 1221 Avenue of the Americas, New York 10020.

How to Cut Your Car Insurance Costs

Every year, thousands of drivers spend more than they need to on auto insurance premiums. By shopping around for the cheapest—and best—insurance company and by taking a hard look at your policy, you can trim your premiums by as much as two-thirds.

Example: The average cost of car insurance is about $750 a year. By shopping around, you can easily cut that amount by a few hundred dollars. If you have a young driver in the family and live in a major city, the savings can amount to several thousand dollars.

Here's how to reduce the cost of your car insurance...

• *Buy the right car.* The more expensive the car, the more expensive it is to insure. This is particularly so for sports cars, such as Corvettes and Porsches, which tend to get stolen more frequently.

Example: It can cost three to four times as much to insure a Porsche as to insure a Buick.

Furthermore, these expensive cars can be incredibly costly to repair compared with other cars.

If you're satisfied with your current insurer and are in the market for a new car, call your company before you buy and ask what the insurance costs are for several different models. At least that way there will be no surprises.

• *Take as large a deductible as is prudent for you.* Pay for fender benders and other small claims yourself rather than seek coverage for them. By paying for these damages yourself, you can save a bundle on premiums and use your coverage only for the purpose it was intended—large claims.

Example: By raising your deductible from $100 to $500, you can save 10% to 15% on your total premium...and by raising your deductible from $100 to $1,000, you can save 25% to 30%.

Analysis: If you still believe that a low deductible makes sense, ask yourself whether you would submit a claim for $200. Chances are you wouldn't. It's so small that you would probably pay for the damage yourself rather than risk higher premiums in the future. If that's the case, then why are you paying for coverage that you're not going to use?

• *Consider dropping collision coverage on older cars.* Collision covers the cost of repairing your car if you are in an accident—regardless of which driver is at fault.

Collision coverage can cost $300 to $400 or more—depending on the type and age of your car. For older cars, the cost of collision coverage can be a lot more than the cost of repairing the car.

Strategy: Drop collision if the premium is equal to 10% or more of the value of your car. To check the value of your car, look in the *National Automobile Dealer's Association Official Used Car Guide*, also called the *Blue Book*.

• *Don't drop comprehensive coverage.* Unless the coverage is very expensive, comprehensive covers damage to your car from all other types of incidents, such as fire, theft and storms. Typically, the cost of this coverage is modest— about $50. The chance of a total loss due to theft is greater than the chance of a total loss due to a collision.

• *Consider dropping coverage for medical payments—if you already have good comprehensive health insurance.* Medical-payments coverage pays for medical expenses resulting from an auto accident—regardless of who is at fault. It's redundant if you have medical insurance.

• *Consider dropping coverage for expenses such as towing, labor and car rental.* While the annual cost of these provisions isn't great—perhaps $15 to $25—these charges can add up, particularly if you insure more than one car… and they are usually poor values.

• *Make use of all the discounts for which you qualify.* Many insurance companies give discounts for a variety of reasons. *Examples:*

• Insuring more than one car with the same company (15% off).

• Having your homeowners' policy with the same company (15% off).

• Having a young driver take a driver-training course (10% to 15% off).

• If the young drivers in your family have good grades (10% off, although some states have disallowed this discount as discriminatory).

Call your insurer to ask about other discounts it may offer.

Important: Never lose sight of the total cost of coverage. A company that offers you 10 different types of discounts can still charge more for the same amount of coverage than a company that offers you no discounts.

• *Consider dropping your insurance company for one that is a "direct writer."* These insurance companies sell coverage directly to the public, not through insurance agents.

Opportunities: Your premium could be about 10% lower than rates charged by the major companies because you won't have to pay an insurance agent's commission.

You won't have to sacrifice service if you use a direct writer. Surveys show that direct writers often provide better service than companies that depend on a network of agents for sales.

Two large direct writers with good reputations: Amica, 800-242-6422…GEICO, 800-841-3000.

Important: In the case of a mutual company—an insurer that is owned by its policyholders—call the company and ask about its dividend history. What percentage of its premiums has it returned to policyholders in the past? Only with that information can you accurately compare policy costs.

Example: The premiums charged by Amica may seem high compared with the premiums charged by Allstate. But Amica has regularly paid annual dividends of about 20% to policyholders.

These dividend checks—usually distributed on the anniversary of the date you started coverage—reduce the true cost of insuring your car.

Source: Robert Hunter, head of the insurance group at the Consumer Federation of America (CFA) in Washington, DC, a consumer advocate organization, 1424 16 St. NW, Suite 604, Washington, DC 20036. He is the former president of the National Insurance Consumer Organization (NICO), a consumer advocacy group that merged with the CFA, and author of *NICO's Buyer's Guide to Insurance,* available from CFA.

Better Life-Insurance Policy Buying

A new way to pay for long-term health care is *single premium insurance.* You make a single, up-front premium payment to buy a life insurance policy with a specified death benefit. If nursing care needs arise during your life, the policy pays a monthly benefit equal to 2% of the death benefit…or 1% of the death benefit for home care. These amounts are offset against the ultimate death benefit.

Major advantage: If you don't need the health benefit, you retain the policy as a financial asset that goes up in value, earning investment returns on a tax-deferred basis.

Source: Alan Nadolna is president of Associates in Financial Planning, 100 S. Wacker Dr., Suite 1650, Chicago 60606.

Insurance Premium Moneysaver

Consolidate insurers to cut premium costs. It rarely makes sense to obtain home, vacation home, auto, boat and other forms of property and casualty insurance from different insurers. By consolidating your policies through a single insurer, you may cut 10% to 15% off your premium bill. You'll also simplify your paperwork and reduce the risk that a premium will go unpaid—and a policy lapse—by accident.

Source: Ray Martin, vice president of client relations, Ayco Corp., Albany, New York, a financial counseling firm that is a subsidiary of American Express.

Life Insurance "Churning"

Life insurance "churning" is on the rise as tricky agents hustle commissions by urging people to switch policies…or to buy additional coverage at "special low prices."

What they don't tell you: Surrender fees are high…and the premiums for low-cost coverage may come out of your existing policy's cash value. *Solution:* Carefully evaluate any proposal to replace or add to an existing policy.

Source: Glenn Daily is an independent, fee-only insurance consultant, 234 E. 84 St., New York 10028.

Insurance Cost-Cutters

Central alarms that ring at a police or fire station in an emergency can earn insurance discounts of 15%. Smoke detectors, fire alarms and deadbolt locks can earn discounts of up to 5%. Increase your deductible to as much as you can afford to lower your premium. You probably won't make a small claim anyhow for fear of raising your rates.

Look into renovation credits. Many insurers provide these for significant upgrades of wiring, plumbing, roofing and so forth. Obtain home and auto insurance from a single insurer —for discounts of up to 10%.

Source: David L. Scott, PhD, professor of accounting and finance, Valdosta State University, Valdosta, Georgia, and the author of *The Guide to Buying Insurance*, The Globe Pequot Press, 6 Business Park Rd., Old Saybrook, Connecticut 06475.

Paying Off Future Estate Tax Bills

Buy insurance to pay off future estate tax bills. The sooner you do it, the less you will pay and the more you'll save for your heirs. *Trap:* If you don't buy insurance to pay estate taxes, your estate will have to finance the tax bill by paying cash, liquidating assets or borrowing and then repaying the lender. All three options will leave your heirs much poorer. But by using life insurance to pay future estate taxes, you may greatly cut their real cost.

Example: If you and your spouse are each age 60, a single-premium, second-to-die insurance policy costing $1 million will buy a $10 million benefit—and cut the cost of a $10 million estate tax bill by 90%.

Source: *Die Rich and Tax Free* by Barry Kaye, CLU, financial adviser, Los Angeles, Forman Publishing, 2080 Westridge Rd., Los Angeles 90049.

16

Driving with Ease

Safer Winter Driving

The type of car tire is the most important factor for safe handling in bad winter weather. *Best tire for snow:* Blizzak, made by Bridgestone (800-543-7522). This tire has air pockets that grip slick surfaces far better than any other tire. Unless otherwise recommended by the car manufacturer, snow tires are only needed on drive-axle wheels. Driving a front- or four-wheel-drive car is also important for good handling—but be careful. People with all-wheel-drive cars tend to take more risks, overestimate their cars' abilities and end up in dangerous driving situations. *Surprising:* The weight of a car is not so important—heavier cars do not always drive better on ice than lighter cars. If you drive in difficult conditions and have a high risk of damage to your car, buying an inexpensive car without a lot of extras will minimize your financial losses.

Source: David Solomon, editor, *Nutz & Boltz,*® Box 123, Butler, Maryland 21023.

Snow Tire Alert

Only two snow tires are needed on your car. They should be on the drive axle—the front for front-wheel-drive cars...the rear for rear-wheel-drive cars. The only vehicles needing four snow tires are four-wheel drives, unless the manufacturer recommends otherwise.

Source: David Solomon, editor, *Nutz & Boltz,*® Box 123, Butler, Maryland 21023.

Tire Blow-Out Strategy

If your car tire blows out while you are driving—don't hit the brake. Contrary to most people's instincts, it is best to keep your foot on the gas—and hold the steering wheel firm. Once you gain control of the car, ease off the gas... but still don't apply the brake. Let the car come to a natural stop. Braking can set your car into a spin—especially since most blow-outs are on the right front tire, and most newer cars have front-wheel drive. *Bad news:* There may not be any way to tell if your tire will blow out. Blowouts can or may occur from a weakening in the tire, usually caused by clipping the tire edge along the curb. *Vital:* Pay attention to the road to prevent such clipping…and be ready to perform emergency steering maneuvers to prevent accidents.

Source: David Solomon, editor of *Nutz & Boltz,*® Box 123, Butler, Maryland 21023.

Better Daytime Visibility

Daytime running lamps are standard on some 1995 General Motors vehicles and will be available across the board by 1997. The system turns on headlights—at less than low-beam intensity—whenever the engine is on. *Objective:* To make the car more visible to other drivers during the day. Daytime running lamps are already required in Canada, Finland, Norway and Sweden—and are credited with significant drops in accident rates.

Picking a Crashworthy Car

When it comes to passenger safety, bigger is almost always better. Of the 12 vehicles with the lowest driver death rates, eight are large passenger vans or luxury sedans. Small pickup trucks and small two-door cars tend to be the least safe.

Best: 1988–1992 passenger vehicles with lowest driver death rates during 1989–1993:

Vehicle	Type	Death rate (100=average)
Volvo 240 (4-door)	midsize car	0
Plymouth Voyager	large passenger van	18
Volvo 740/760 (4-door)	midsize luxury car	18
Mercedes-Benz 190 D/E	midsize luxury car	27
Acura Legend (4-door)	large luxury car	36
Buick Riviera	midsize luxury car	36
Dodge Caravan	large passenger van	36
Ford Aerostar	large passenger van	36
Jaguar XJ6	large luxury car	36
Lexus LS400	large luxury car	36
Lincoln Town Car	large luxury car	36
Mazda MPV	large passenger van	36

Worst: 1988–1992 passenger vehicles with highest driver death rates during 1989–1993:

Vehicle	Type	Death rate (100=average)
Chevrolet Corvette	small sports car	327
Pontiac LeMans (2-door)	small car	300
Isuzu Amigo	small utility vehicle	291
Ford Mustang	midsize sports car	264
Ford Festiva (2-door)	small car	236
Nissan Pickup 4x4	small pickup truck	218
Ford Escort (2-door)	small car	209
Geo Metro	small car	209
Chevrolet Pickup S10	small pickup truck	200
Dodge W50 Ram 4x4	small pickup truck	200
Nissan Pickup	small pickup truck	200

Source: Insurance Institute for Highway Safety, 1005 N. Glebe Rd., Suite 800, Arlington, Virginia 22201.

Cellular Phones and On-the-Road Emergencies

Although cellular phones are being marketed as potential lifesavers in emergencies, cellular calls cannot be traced by a 911 dispatcher.

Result: If the call is cut off or the caller does not know where he/she is, emergency help may be delayed.

Also: Because of the way cellular sites are arranged, dialing 911 on a cellular phone may not put the caller through to the nearest dispatch station. Consequently, time might be wasted transferring the call or getting emergency crews to a location farther away.

Solution: A wireless telephone with enhanced 911 may be a better choice. Or try to use a regular phone.

Source: S. Robert Miller, 911 Director for New Jersey, Office of Emergency Telecommunications Services, West Trenton.

Beware of Car-Phone Number Bandits

Foil car-phone number bandits by turning off the unit when driving near airports, bridges and tunnels. *Problem:* Thieves pirate phone numbers with electronic scanners in areas where traffic moves slowly. The owner is not responsible for false charges, but working out the bill can be a hassle. See if your company will add a free line-protection feature.

Source: Neil Sachnoff is president of TeleCom Clinic, a telecommunications research firm, 355 South End Ave., New York 10280.

Worst Place to Park Your Car

Avoid parking your car next to two-door cars. Their doors have a longer arc when opened than the doors of four-door cars…so there is more chance of your car's door or side being hit and dented.

Source: David Solomon, editor, *Nutz & Boltz,*® Box 123, Butler, Maryland 21023.

Sure Signs of Car Troubles

Transmission fluid color should be clear pinkish-red or clear, depending on the type your car uses. If it looks white and milky, there may be a radiator leak allowing coolant to mix with the fluid. If it looks dark reddish brown and has a burning smell, it should be replaced immediately because it has lost its lubrication ability. If metal particles are visible in the fluid, serious transmission damage may have occurred. Have the car checked by a trustworthy dealer or mechanic.

Source: David Solomon, editor, *Nutz & Boltz,*® Box 123, Butler, Maryland 21023.

Car-Repair Self-Defense

Make sure the garage accepts credit cards… and get a detailed written estimate before work

begins. One of the top consumer complaints at the Better Business Bureau involves shoddy auto repairs and unauthorized charges. By using a credit card, you can withhold payment if there is a problem while the credit card company investigates. *Best:* Ask in advance that your bill state that you will not pay anything over the written estimated price.

Source: Barbara Berger Opotowsky, president, Better Business Bureau of Metropolitan New York, 275 Park Ave. S., New York 10010.

Car Dealers' Dirty Little Tricks

Beware of improper charges when buying a car. *Scam I:* The dealer orders cars without some standard equipment—such as carpeting—and then claims you'll have to pay extra for it. *Self-defense:* Get a manufacturer's brochure detailing the list of standard equipment. Review it to make sure you are charged properly. *Scam II:* The dealer tries to get you to pay for his/her cost of doing business. *Examples:* Dealer prep charges—all domestic and some import manufacturers include prepping in the price of a car …advertising fees, which are often paid mostly by the manufacturer. *Self-defense:* Refuse to pay them, and be prepared to walk out of the dealership if the charges are not removed.

Source: *Money Secrets the Pros Don't Want You to Know* by financial journalist Stephanie Gallagher, Amacom, 135 W. 50 St., New York 10020.

New Car Buying Strategies

When buying a new car, your first offer to the salesperson should be the dealer cost—don't start out negotiating any markup. Fair markup for cars costing up to $15,000 is between $300 and $500. For more expensive cars, markup could be between $500 and $2,000 above dealer cost, depending on the car. *Note:* Foreign dealers tend to negotiate for higher markups than domestic dealers. *Good news for domestic luxury car buyers:* You may not have to pay any markup at all. *Reason:* Car dealers often sell these models at cost, since they also receive payment (known as *dealer incentive*) from car manufacturers for every sale. *To find out dealer cost for a car:* IntelliChoice (800-227-2665)—the only car-pricing service that includes real-world repair record data instead of reader-survey repair data. *Price:* $14.95 for a report on a single model line, including costs of optional features…$19.95 for a comparison report of two models that interest you.

Source: David Solomon, editor, *Nutz & Boltz,®* Box 123, Butler, Maryland 21023.

Mistakes to Avoid When Buying a Used Car

When shopping for a car today, many people choose a used vehicle instead of a new one. *Reasons:*

• The average cost of a new car is $19,500—up 70% from the $11,500 price 10 years ago. During this period, however, household incomes increased only about 40%.

• The growth of leasing has increased the supply of high-quality two- and three-year-old vehicles in dealers' showrooms. That—combined with today's emphasis on frugality and value—has considerably narrowed the status gap between new and used cars.

The most common mistakes people make when buying used cars…

Mistake: Assuming that you'll always get a better deal buying from an owner. A two-, three- or four-year-old vehicle may still have some warranty protection, but this is transferable only if you buy from a dealer. To find out if the car has this protection, call the regional office of the manufacturer or contact its financing arm, such as Ford Motor Credit, GMAC, etc.

Buy from an owner only if his/her price is 15% or more below the price a dealer is charging for a similar model.

Remember: If you buy from an owner, you'll have no recourse if you're dissatisfied. In a private transaction, whatever goes wrong is your headache. With a dealer, you can always complain to the state authorities.

Note: The more adept you are at fixing cars, the more incentive you have to seek a deal from an owner.

Mistake: Not driving a vehicle before buying it. More than 60% of used-car buyers never take a test drive. Many believe that doing so constitutes an agreement to buy—but they are wrong. They also worry that if they drive the vehicle, the dealer or owner will start pressuring them.

Strategy: Take a test drive—or walk away from the deal. Try every knob, button and option while driving the car. Listen for odd noises. If there are any problems—and you still like the vehicle—include in the contract that the problems must be fixed before you put down any money.

Mistake: Buying a company-owned car. Of the 3.5 million two- and three-year-old vehicles that come back to dealers every year, only 1.5 million were owned by individuals. The rest were owned by companies. Avoid these company cars whenever possible. They take much more abuse because they're driven more and maintained less.

Reason: Drivers of company cars simply have less economic incentive than owners to take good care of their vehicles.

How to tell: First, ask the salesperson if the car was company-owned. He may give you a straight answer…sometimes, he just won't know. Then check the mileage. Leased cars average 15,000 to 16,000 miles per year. Company cars average 20,000 miles per year.

Mistake: Relying heavily on used-car price guides. Most are notoriously out-of-date.

Better: Review the classified ads in your Sunday newspaper for several weeks to get an idea of the prices of the models in which you are interested.

Mistake: Not examining details carefully. Tires are usually one of the most expensive parts of a used car that you'll have to replace. This expense can be avoided if you carefully examine the tires and have the dealer replace faulty ones before you sign a contract. Looking the tires over or kicking them is not enough.

What to do: Rub your hand on top of each tire in both directions. Well-balanced tires should feel smooth. Then put a penny into the tire tread. Insert Lincoln's head first, and run the penny around the tire. If you can see the top of his head at any point, the tires are worn and you will have to replace them.

Check the stitching on the seats to see if they have been repaired improperly. If the stitching is stretched, it is likely to tear soon.

Source: Art Spinella, vice president of CNW Marketing/Research, a fee-based company that provides auto buying and leasing data to corporate clients, Box 744, Bandon, Oregon 97411.

Options that Pay Off for Resale

Options that pay off when you resell a car: Air-conditioning, power steering, larger engines, antilock brakes, traction control, security and safety options. *Ones that do not pay off:* Heated seats, multidriver memory seats, dashboard trip computers, digital dashboard, exterior wood-grain paneling. *Marginal choices:* Super-premium sound systems, custom wheels, built-in cellular phones.

Source: Jan Ocean, editor, *National Automobile Dealers Association Official Used-Car Guide: Retail Consumer Edition,* 8400 Westpark Dr., McLean, Virginia 22102.

Traps to Avoid When Leasing a Car

Leasing a car makes sense if you want to drive a new or expensive model but don't have the money or desire to own the car outright. Leasing is an *especially* good deal if you do not plan to keep the car for more than five years… do not drive more than 15,000 miles per year …*and* are careful not to damage the car's exterior or interior.

But while leasing a car is generally less expensive than buying it, most people end up paying more than they should.

Biggest traps:

Trap: Being fooled by the dealership's ads. To attract customers, most ads stress low monthly payments in large type. In smaller lettering, you may find that you have to make a down payment of several thousand dollars to get that low rate.

Ads that stress low monthly payments also play down the fact that the lease may run for longer than you think—30 months, for example, rather than the customary 24 months, so you may wind up paying additional interest charges.

Important: Read the entire ad before going to the dealership. In the case of TV or radio ads, call the 800 number that is now legally required to be announced in the ad to learn about all of the lease's details.

Trap: Not being aware of *all* the leasing fees. For example, all leases charge *acquisition fees,* which you may be asked to pay up front.

You can also expect to be charged a *disposition fee* of $300 or more. This fee covers the dealer's cost of shipping the car to a used-car dealer or selling it at an auction.

Important: If you are a regular customer, these fees are negotiable and, in some cases, waived.

Trap: Not discussing the dealer's "wear-and-tear" policy before you sign the papers. There's no industry definition or standard for "wear and tear" on a leased car. But a misunderstanding at the beginning can be costly when the lease expires. Dents in the frame, dog hair or food stains on the seats and a broken power seat all add up.

Strategy: When negotiating a lease, spend an extra 15 minutes with the dealer going over his/her definition of "wear and tear." If he is vague, ask him to join you for a look at cars parked along the sidewalk…or to walk around a used-car lot. Point out specific types of damage, and ask what the costs might be. Then have the dealer put these costs in writing.

The key is to think about other, less-obvious questions to ask the dealer.

Examples: Cigarette burns on the upholstery always cost you money. But what about the smell of cigarette smoke in the car? Or tiny chips in the windshield that were caused by small stones?

Trap: Not negotiating the cost of the car. Most people are unaware that they should negotiate the total cost of the car before discussing their intent to lease. In fact, only about 9% of people looking to lease bother to haggle—compared with 75% of those who plan to buy.

Haggling is a smart move because lease payments are based on the car's total price. *Steps to take…*

• *Research the dealer's cost of the car.* You can find the dealer's cost in a new-car price guide, available on most newsstands.

• *Call several competing dealerships to find the lowest price.*

• *Try to negotiate a lower price.* Indicate that you want the lowest monthly payment without adding any money to the down payment. Ask the dealer to check leases from various finance sources, including banks and auto companies to find out who has the lowest rates.

Only then should you discuss the monthly lease payments and other terms of the contract.

Trap: Not using the finance company owned by the automaker. There's nothing bad about obtaining financing for your lease from a national or local bank. All else equal, it's just easier to deal directly with the auto-maker's own financial group, such as Ford Motor Credit, GMAC, etc.

Car companies make their money producing cars, not lending money. Therefore, they're less concerned about squeezing every dime out of you for excess wear and tear or whether you drive 1,000 miles over the limit set in your lease contract.

Problem: If you finance a lease through a bank and you plan to move out of state, you'll need the bank's permission to continue the lease.

Trap: Not buying a gap-insurance policy. Monthly lease payments do not cover the total cost of the car. You're just borrowing the car and paying rent on it. If the car is stolen or totaled while you're leasing it, you are liable for the car's cost.

For this you need *gap insurance*, which covers the difference between what the car is worth and what you still owe on the lease. Some lessors include gap insurance in the cost of your lease. Most auto insurers, however, do not. Be sure to ask the dealer about it before signing the papers.

Trap: Not buying extra miles when you first sign the lease. The number of miles you *expect* to drive and what you *actually* will drive over three to five years probably will be different. About 35% to 40% of people who lease cars take 12,000-miles-per-year deals—and most of these people exceed the limit, resulting in higher mileage costs.

Example: One excess mile costs 10 cents to 15 cents if you don't buy it up front. Buy in advance, however, and the per-mile cost is only 8 cents to 9 cents.

Strategy: Purchase an excess-mileage package when you lease. If you don't use the miles, the fee is usually refundable.

Trap: Not taking care of the repairs yourself. Have any excess wear and tear repaired yourself. An independent mechanic will charge you considerably less than the dealership's mechanic.

Helpful: If you're leasing a front-wheel drive car, be sure to rotate the tires every 10,000 to 15,000 miles, switching the front tires for the back tires so that they wear more evenly. This can save you a tire charge.

Also: Never take a lease for longer than 42 months. *Better:* One for 36 months or less. Otherwise you may end up making costly repairs that are not covered by the warranty.

Trap: Accepting a dealer's offer to terminate the lease early. The offer is fine if it suits your needs at the time. Just be aware that the dealer probably has a motive. In most cases, such an offer means that your car is a hot seller and the dealer can make money reselling—or releasing—it to another customer.

Important: If the dealer can sell the car at a profit, so can you. Turn down the deal—and when the lease runs out in a year or two, consider buying the car. Then sell it and pocket the difference. In all likelihood, the car will still be popular.

Source: Art Spinella, vice president of CNW Marketing/ Research, a fee-based company that provides auto buying and leasing data to corporate clients, Box 744, Bandon, Oregon 97411.

17

Retirement and Estate Planning

The Mistakes in Retirement Planning Can Be Avoided

When it comes to retirement planning, what are the mistakes people make? The most common one is to wait too long to plan for retirement. Sometimes a couple in their early 60s comes in and wants to know how things will look when they retire at 65. All I can do is look at their financial assets and their current spending…and project what their situation will be when they retire. It doesn't leave much time to accumulate assets.

What puts blinders on such people? A company pension plan? A feeling they have a house and enough to live on? No. Usually it's fear that they do not have enough…so they refuse to look at the facts.

When people do wait that long to start retirement planning, how can you help? I tell them to cut back on current spending—and save more —fast. Most people don't budget because they

hate counting every penny. If you're going to crash-save for retirement, you have to do it.

Aside from saving more, what else can late-starters do? Change where they plan to live when they retire. Moving to a less expensive part of the country is one of the best ways to get by on less in retirement.

Caution: Make your move for sound reasons …not merely because it's somewhere you spent a few pleasant vacation weeks. If you don't know anybody who lives in that community before you move, that could be a big mistake. Too often what happens is that retired people sell their homes…buy in the new place…discover they don't like it…but can't afford to move back home.

What's the smart way to make such a retirement move? Test out a community. Rent out your current home for a year…and rent where you think you might like to move. *Then* decide.

Caution: Don't base your move on where your children live. We've known couples who move closer to a married child—only to find the child transferred to another part of the country.

265

There's also the risk that a relationship with children that's great long-distance may not be so great when you live close to one another.

What other big retirement mistake is being made? Taking money out of an IRA too soon. Many people start taking money out at age 59½ because that's the first time they can withdraw from an IRA without facing a 10% penalty.

Unless your IRA is your major source of retirement income, you don't have to start withdrawing from retirement accounts until the year after you turn 70½. The longer you compound that money without paying current taxes on it, the better off you will be. During those 12 years, you could double your money.

What about planning to live on Social Security and a company pension? Don't count too much on either Social Security or your pension. More and more of Social Security will be taxed in the future and may not be indexed to inflation. And most company pensions are fixed. The monthly pension check may be worth only half as much in real dollars within 10 years after retirement. Think seriously about saving some of that pension income during your early retirement years because you may need that money later on.

What's the most common mistake you see in investing retirement money? Too many people invest entirely, or primarily, in fixed-income securities once they retire. That was fine when people retired at 65 and died at 70. Now they retire at 60 or earlier and live to 90-plus.

People used to figure their expenses would go down when they retired. But the reality for people who have to live on retirement income for 10, 20 or 30 years is that their expenses will go *up*.

Therefore, you want to invest to produce a rising stream of income during retirement. Think of *total return*…with your capital and your income stream continuing to build while you're retired.

What about long-term care insurance, to pay for a nursing home, as part of retirement planning? Until this year, many older people hoped a national health bill would take care of that. *Now we have to ask:* What bill? And long-term care isn't part of anybody's proposed health bill.

If you have over $1 million in assets, you can probably use your own assets if you need long-term care at home or in a nursing home. If your assets are $100,000 or less, you'll probably qualify for Medicaid to handle those expenses.

If you fall somewhere in between…people in their early 50s can now buy good long-term care insurance for about $900 a year that will pay $100 a day plus up to 5% a year inflation adjustment…for 20 years. These policies are much improved over those first offered years ago.

Source: Alexandra Armstrong, chairman, Armstrong, Welch & MacIntyre, Inc., financial advisers, 1155 Connecticut Ave. NW, Suite 250, Washington, DC 20036. She is the coauthor of *On Your Own: A Widow's Passage to Emotional and Financial Well-Being*, Dearborn Financial, Chicago.

Retiring to a Foreign Country

Retiring to a foreign country does not let you avoid paying US taxes. Unlike most other countries, the US taxes its citizens—not just residents—regardless of where they live. *Exception:* US citizens can earn up to $70,000 annually tax-free while residing overseas and receive a tax-free housing allowance. This exclusion applies only to wages, salaries and self-employment income, not to investments, annuities and pensions. *Problem:* The IRS has admitted that there's no effective way to enforce tax laws on expatriates and that it has no way of tracking down Americans living abroad who do not file returns. *Bottom line:* Unless you're willing to repudiate your US citizenship moving abroad does nothing to avoid US taxes—unless you're willing to break the tax law.

Source: *Bob Carlson's Retirement Watch*, 1420 Spring Hill Rd., Suite 490, McLean, Virginia 22102.

How Working Affects Social Security

People who work while collecting Social Security benefits face the possibility of a partial reduction of their Social Security check.

There is a limit to the amount you can earn from wages or self-employment income while still collecting your full benefit.

Exception: People who are age 70 are exempt and won't face this reduction no matter how much they earn from age 70 onward.

The limits: The amount that you may earn before your Social Security check is reduced changes every year and depends on your age.

1995 limits for people under age 65: You can earn up to $8,160 and still receive your full Social Security check. For every $2 that you earn over $8,160, your check will be reduced by $1.

1995 limits for people age 65 to 69: You can earn up to $11,280 and still receive your full Social Security check. For every $3 you earn over $11,280 your Social Security check will be reduced by $1.

Special first-year rule:

There is a special monthly rule that applies during the first year that you receive Social Security. During 1995, if you are under age 65 and earn less than $680 in any month ($940 for those age 65 to 69), you will receive your full benefit for that month.

It is up to you to report your earnings to Social Security by April 15 of the year following the year you earned over these limits.

Write an informal letter to the Social Security office with the appropriate information or fill out an Annual Report of Earnings Form, available at any Social Security office.

Penalty for failure to report this income: As high as one month's check for the first violation, two months' checks for the second.

Income that counts towards your earnings: Bonuses, commissions, fees, vacation pay, pay in lieu of vacation, cash tips of $20 or more a month, severance pay. Also, some noncash compensation, such as meals or living quarters, can count under certain circumstances.

Income that doesn't count towards the earnings limits...
- Investment income.
- Interest income.
- Veterans' benefits.
- Annuities.
- Capital gains.
- Gifts or inheritances.
- Rental income, in most cases.
- Income from trust funds.
- Jury duty pay.

Source: Herbert Loring, program specialist, Social Security Administration, 26 Federal Plaza, New York 10278.

Social Security Traps

Guarantee smooth and fast processing of your Social Security retirement application by avoiding these mistakes...

• *Mistake:* Walking into the Social Security office unannounced. Save time and aggravation by calling 800-772-1213 and scheduling an appointment with your local Social Security office.

You will avoid a potentially long wait at the office.

Even better: You may be able to complete your application by telephone. You will be given directions for mailing supporting documentation.

• *Mistake:* Not bringing proof of your income from the last year you worked. The Social Security office has records of most of the income you have earned over your lifetime.

Exception: Your most recent (and perhaps your highest) income records.

Example: When applying for benefits during 1995, bring your 1994 W-2 or self-employment tax return. This way your 1994 income will be added to your account immediately instead of when Social Security gets around to it.

• *Mistake:* Not bringing your birth certificate. Your claim may be delayed if you show up at the Social Security office without a certified copy of your birth certificate.

Get a certified copy from the proper authority in advance and bring it with you on the day you apply for Social Security.

It will be returned to you.

• *Mistake:* Not bringing family information and documents. If you are married—bring your spouse's Social Security number and birth certificate, if your spouse is at least 62 years old. Your spouse may get benefits on your record.

Your divorced spouse may also be entitled to benefits. Inform Social Security that you were previously married and the Social Security office will handle the claim from there. You will be asked for your ex-spouse's Social Security number and last known address, if available.

Source: Alex W. Bussey, New York assistant regional commissioner for field operations, Social Security Administration, New York.

Best and Worst Tax Spots for Retirees

Best tax spots for retirees: Anchorage and Juneau, Alaska...Fairhope and Gulf Shores, Alabama...Dover and Wilmington, Delaware...Naples, Florida...Honolulu and Kahului, Hawaii. All have low taxes based both on income and the value of one's home. *Worst tax spots:* Milwaukee...Pittsburgh...Lincoln, Nebraska...New Haven, Connecticut...Cedar Rapids and Des Moines, Iowa...Topeka, Kansas...Detroit and Lansing, Michigan.

Source: Alan Fox, publisher, *Where to Retire* magazine, which compiled a report ranking total state and local tax burdens in 149 cities around the US. 1502 Augusta #415, Houston 77057.

The Ten Biggest Tax Traps In Retirement...and How to Avoid Them

IRS penalties for not handling your retirement nest egg properly can be substantial. Some of the biggest tax traps are the easiest to avoid, if you know what to do.

1. *Taking distributions too late.* You must begin taking distributions from your retirement plan by April 1 of the year after the calendar year in which you turn age 70½. If you don't, the IRS will take 50% of the amount you should have taken as a penalty.

Don't fall into this trap: Prevent the IRS from getting any part of your hard-earned retirement money by taking the proper distribution at the proper time.

Amount you are supposed to take: An annual distribution calculated to deplete your entire retirement account over your life expectancy or the life expectancy of a beneficiary you designate.

2. *Taking distributions too early.* If you take money out of your retirement plan before you reach age 59½ you may be subject to an additional 10% tax on the distribution. Consult your tax adviser for details. This is on top of the regular tax you'll have to pay from being forced to include the distribution in your taxable income.

Avoid this tax trap: Leave your money in the plan even if you are desperate for money and have to look for an alternative source. In some cases employees can borrow from retirement plans when the money is needed for a specific reason, such as medical care.

3. *Taking a distribution by mistake.* When you leave a company you may be given the option to receive the balance of your retirement account.

Warning: If the plan provides an option for you to take the distribution, do tax-planning with the distribution. You might transfer the distribution into an IRA, put it into your new employer's plan if allowed, or keep it in the former employer's plan. This full distribution will be taxed if you keep it, and the IRS may impose a 10% penalty.

Tax trap avoider: If you receive a distribution, roll it into the plan at your new job or into your own Individual Retirement Account.

4. *Failing to contribute to a retirement plan.* If you are employed by someone else or you are self-employed, retirement plans defer tax in two ways...

•The amount that you contribute is subtracted from your taxable income for the year for which the contribution is made. The contribution isn't taxed until withdrawal at retirement.

•Tax on the earnings in your account are deferred until withdrawal.

Avoid this tax trap: Make the maximum contribution to every type of retirement plan that you are eligible for. Don't miss out on the double benefit.

5. *Not realizing that you can extend the time to make your contribution.* You have until your

tax return is due on April 15 to make your IRA contributions for the prior tax year.

Even longer: If you are an individual or a small company, the due date for your Keogh or SEP plan contribution is extended for as long as you have extended the time to file your tax return. This may give you up to the extended due date of your return to complete your contribution for the prior tax year.

Even better: You will have had the use of the money up until this extended due date while you were waiting to make the contribution.

6. Not making your maximum contribution. Every type of self-employed retirement plan has a formula to calculate the maximum allowable contribution. The formulas can be complex and tedious.

Avoid this tax trap: Take the time to understand the rules and make the proper calculations. Or, retain an accountant to do it for you.

7. *Taking a loan that is not allowed.* Self-employed business owners, S-corporation shareholders and certain partners are not allowed to borrow against their retirement plans. Loans between the plan and its other participants must meet certain specific rules before a loan is allowed.

Tax trap avoider: If you are in a plan that allows you to take a loan, make sure you adhere to its requirements to avoid any additional taxes.

8. *Not contributing on behalf of your employees.* Self-employed business owners often make the mistake of contributing to a plan that covers themselves only. They don't realize that they are also required to make contributions for all eligible employees each year.

Additional rule: The plan must be in writing and it must be set up by the last day of the calendar year for which you are making the contribution. You need not make the actual contribution until the due date of your return, plus extensions.

Eligible employees: Full-time employees who have reached age 21 and have worked for you for at least one year. Amount: The contribution formula for employees is the same formula that you use for yourself.

Example: If you contribute 10% of your salary then you must contribute 10% of your employees' salary on their behalf.

Penalty: If these employee contributions have not been made, the Internal Revenue Service will declare the plan "discriminatory" and it could be disqualified as a tax deduction. Your contributions won't be deductible and the amounts would then be taxed as current income.

9. *Investing in prohibited transactions.* Self-employeds must be extremely careful when deciding where to invest their retirement plans.

Prohibited investments: A plan that involves a sale, exchange, or lease of property between the owner and the plan, may constitute a prohibited transaction. Consult your tax adviser before undertaking such a transaction.

10. *Not contributing the maximum amount to your 401(k) plan.* You are allowed to contribute 25% of your salary up to $9,240 during 1995. The contribution to the plan is tax-deductible. The income from your 401(k) is tax-deferred.

Special bonus: Your employer may have a program where it matches all, or a portion, of the amount you contribute. Get into your company's plan as soon as you are eligible.

Source: Avery E. Neumark, partner, employee benefits and executive compensation, Weber, Lipshie & Co., 1430 Broadway, New York 10018.

Common Estate Planning Mistake

Many people, after executing a living trust, neglect to take the next step of transferring legal title of their assets to the trust. The result is that the living trust is a worthless stack of paper. The rule is simple: Assets held in your name at the time of your death will be included in your probate estate and will be subject to estate tax.

Source: Irving L. Blackman is a partner in the accounting firm Blackman Kallick Bartelstein, 300 S. Riverside Plaza, Chicago 60606.

Living Wills... Who Should Have One...

Suppose you became comatose after a stroke, serious accident or surgery. Without a living will or other health-care directive, you could spend months or even years being kept alive by a mechanical ventilator.

In this dire situation, you might prefer to be allowed to die...or maybe you'd like to live no matter what and fear that someone would pull the plug. Either way, consider putting your wishes into a living will now.

In most jurisdictions, you can create a proxy directive or health-care proxy, which designates someone to make health-care decisions for you if you become incapacitated...and another health-care document called a medical directive or living will, which makes specific stipulations regarding your wishes concerning your care if you are incapable of expressing them.

A simple mistake in preparing these documents could nullify your wishes. Sloppy or incomplete preparation of your living will, for example, could prevent the document from being legally binding, especially if the directions are challenged in court...and a videotape or hastily scribbled note does not suffice. *Other mistakes to avoid:*

•*Mistake:* Failing to comply with state law. Each state has its own medical decision-making legislation. To obtain a free set of sample forms for your state, contact Choice in Dying, 200 Varick St., 10th Floor, New York 10014, 212-366-5540. The group also answers questions about patients' rights.

•*Mistake:* Being stricken in the "wrong" state. You can't be sure exactly where you'll be "hit by a bus," but certain precautions will help protect your wishes no matter where you become sick or injured. If you work or vacation regularly in states other than your home state, prepare additional health-care decision-making documents that adhere to those states' require-ments. Of course, it's unreasonable to make 50 different documents. Deciding how many living wills to prepare is a judgment call.

•*Mistake:* Choosing the wrong proxy. Your papers should designate one or more people, ranked in order of authority, to make medical decisions for you if you become incapacitated. Be sure to notify everyone on your list...and make sure they fully understand your wishes. Some states allow only one designated proxy to serve at a time, but alternates can be named. Avoid choosing people whose moral, ethical or religious outlooks might preclude them from doing what you ask of them.

•*Mistake:* Choosing the wrong witnesses. When choosing people to witness the signing of your health-care document, look for adults over age 18...and make sure they can be contacted quickly in case they are needed. *Caution:* Health-care providers and anyone who might conceivably stand to benefit financially from your death should not be used as witnesses. Otherwise, the document might not be valid.

•*Mistake:* Having too few witnesses. Obtain the signatures of three witnesses, even if your state requires only one or two. The seal of a notary public makes the document appear more official, although it is seldom required.

•*Mistake:* Misplacing the living will. Your living will should be accessible immediately when needed. File a copy with other important personal papers at home. Be sure to tell family members, your doctor, lawyer, etc., where to find it. Also, insert a card in your wallet describing this location. Do not store your living will in a safety deposit box or at work—these locations are not easily accessible. And consult the law in your state. In Minnesota, driver's licenses indicate whether the holder has a living will.

Source: Sanford J. Schlesinger, JD, a partner in the law firm of Kaye, Scholer, Fierman, Hays & Handler, New York. He is the coauthor of *Planning for the Elderly or Incapacitated Client,* Commerce Clearinghouse, Chicago.

18

Healthier Exercising/ Healthier Eating

Weight Training Is Not Just for Kids

Between the ages of 30 and 70, up to 30% of one's muscle cells are converted gradually to fat. But this deterioration can be prevented—and even reversed—with a smart weight-training program.

Recent findings: Weight training is just as important to older people's physical fitness as aerobic exercise and stretching.

We rely on healthy muscles for our mobility —and ultimately our independence. The stronger we are, the more we can do for ourselves, whether that includes carrying groceries or lifting a grandchild.

A well-rounded weight/strength training program will also...

• Increase energy and the ability to enjoy sports.

• Aid in weight loss or maintenance while toning the body—without giving women a "muscle-bound" look.

• Prevent falls and injuries.

• Improve posture.

• Build bone mass and decrease the effects and risk of osteoporosis.

• Enhance self-esteem and confidence.

How to start:

Check with your doctor before beginning any exercise program. Maintain a low-fat diet, and drink plenty of water throughout the training period.

• *Don't stop exercising.* Remember, weight training is an essential supplement to your aerobic and flexibility exercises, not a replacement.

• *Don't do it yourself.* Incorrect form can lead to serious injury, especially as you get older.

Find an experienced partner, personal trainer, exercise physiologist, or weight-training class. These classes are increasingly available at health clubs, Y's and senior citizen centers. At the very least, use a detailed weight-training book or video for guidance.

• *Train regularly.* To be effective, you must train at least twice a week. Always take at least one day to rest—but no more than three days —between sessions.

 • *Warm up before each session…*

 •Five minutes of rhythmic aerobic activity —fast walking, marching in place, stationary cycling, etc.

 •Five to ten minutes of stretches for the torso, thighs (front and back), calves, chest, shoulders and back. Stretch to the point at which you feel mild tension and hold each stretch for ten to 15 seconds.

 •Cool down after each workout by repeating each of the warm-up stretches for 30 seconds—a must to avoid soreness.

 •*Don't touch weights for the first week.* Use body-weight resistance, and focus on proper form and body alignment. Then start with free weights (dumbbells, barbells, soup cans) or weight machines.

 •*Listen to your body and go at your own speed.* If you've had a hard aerobic workout, rest and do your weight training the next day. If you've had a gentle aerobic workout and don't feel tired, weight training would be fine. Weight training is a very individual type of exercise.

The sessions:

 •For each exercise, start with two sets of between eight and 12 repetitions each, giving yourself a 60- to 90-second rest between sets.

 •Push your muscles to the point of maximum lift. Begin with weights that are so heavy you can barely do the last repetition while maintaining good form. You should feel physical stress but not exhaustion. It's better to lift lighter weights than to lift heavier weights and hurt yourself.

 •Lift slowly, counting to four or five, and lower the weights, also counting to four or five. If you find yourself ending an exercise without feeling tired, you may move up to a maximum of three sets of 12 to 15 repetitions per set, increasing one variable at a time. After you adjust to the maximum number of repetitions, gradually increase the amount of weight—the most important variable in building muscle mass. There is no set timetable for stepping up—it may take you four weeks or three months.

 •Proper weight training works on all major muscle groups, not just the weaker ones. The American College of Sports Medicine recommends a minimum of eight to ten strength-building exercises. Here are several basic ones. This is not meant to replace firsthand instructions.

Upper body:

 •*Triceps extension.* These are for the muscles in the back of your arms. Before picking up the weights, bring both arms straight over your head. Keep your arms as close to your ears as possible. Bend elbows, bring palms behind you and try to touch the back of your shoulders, keeping your palms flat. Now do it with dumbbells.

 •*Biceps curl.* Before you pick up the weights, in a seated position, with arms out in front of you and palms upward, make a fist and tighten your upper arm muscles. Slowly bend your elbows and bring your hands toward your face. Now add weights.

 •*Dumbbell bench press.* Lie on the floor or weight bench on your back, with your arms out to the side. Slowly lift the dumbbells or barbell up until you've straightened your arms. Slowly lower to the starting position. This exercise works the shoulders, arms and chest.

Lower body:

 •*Squat.* Stand with good posture, with your feet shoulder-width apart and toes straight ahead. Slowly bend your knees until your thighs are just above parallel to the floor. Keep your heels on the floor and your back in its natural alignment. Push up to starting position. When you have this mastered, add dumbbells or a barbell. This exercise works your quadriceps (the fronts of your legs, your buttocks and your hips).

 •*Leg extension.* Sit on the edge of a chair, feet flat on the floor. Raise one leg at a time until it is parallel to the floor, with weights on your ankles. This exercise also works the quadriceps.

 •*Leg curl.* Stand behind a chair. Using ankle weights, bend your knee until your lower leg is behind you and parallel to the floor. This also works the hamstrings.

Stomach:

• *Roll-up.* Lying on the floor or a bed, bend your knees and put your feet flat on the floor, with your arms at your side or supporting your head. Gently lift your head and shoulders off the floor. As you roll up about halfway, tighten your stomach muscles. Do not attempt to sit up completely.

• *Pelvic tilt.* Lie on the floor with knees bent, feet flat on the floor. Tilt hips, arch your lower back, flatten your lower back into the floor, and pull in your stomach muscles. Repeat several times.

Source: Jo Murphy, national fitness expert, yoga instructor and producer of the *More Alive* fitness video for older adults. She is the author of *Keys to Fitness Over 50*, Barron's Educational Series, 250 Wireless Blvd., Hauppauge, New York 11788.

Home Exercise Machines— Do's and Don'ts

• *Treadmill.* Don't grip or lean on handrails …do keep arms moving while walking…don't lean too far forward while walking up an incline…do maintain good posture.

• *Stairmaster.* Don't lean all your weight on the handrails…do rest your hands on top of the machine for stability…don't let pedals hit the top or bottom of the machine's range…don't take "baby steps," using only a small portion of your own natural range of motion.

• *Stationary bicycle.* Don't hyperextend your legs on the downstroke…do adjust the seat so you maintain a slight bend at the knee.

• *Rowing machine.* Don't pull by lifting with your back…do use your legs to push your body away from your feet.

• *Cross-country ski machine.* Don't let your feet slide in front of the stomach pad…do lift your heels on the backstroke…do always keep knees slightly bent.

Source: Chris Vincent, MA, fitness consultant at the Athletic Club Illinois Center, Chicago.

Inside Health Clubs… What You Should Know

More than ten million Americans work out in health clubs and spas across the country. They pay substantial amounts for the privilege—but things don't always turn out as planned. Club members face three common dangers—club insolvency, staff incompetence and personal injuries. *To protect yourself:*

• *Check with consumer watchdog groups.* Call your state or local consumer protection agency and the Better Business Bureau. Ask whether any negative reports have been filed against the club you have in mind. At least 36 states have enacted legislation designed specifically to protect the interests of health club members.

For more information, contact the International Health, Racquet & Sports Club Association.* This trade group investigates complaints against clubs to ensure that they meet minimum standards.

Caution: Never join a health club before it opens, no matter how sterling its prospects. Look for a club with at least three years of continuous operation—or a new branch of an established chain.

• *Conduct a thorough inspection of the club.* Go at peak time—for example, at lunch or after work. If the place is wall-to-wall with people, it probably lacks equipment or instructors. If it's empty, something else is wrong.

What else to look for: The pool, bathrooms, locker rooms and weight rooms all should be clean and well-maintained. Equipment should be in good repair. Faulty or worn equipment can cause injuries.

As you walk around the club, ask members what they like most about it—and what they like least.

• Make sure the club is bonded. Some states require health clubs to post a minimum bond of $500,000 to protect members against losing their money if the club goes out of business.

*263 Summer St., Boston 02210. Send a self-addressed, stamped, business-sized envelope. Free.

That's hardly enough for a large club, but it suggests some financial security on the part of the owner. Request evidence of bonding from the club or consumer protection agency.

• *Insist upon qualified instructors.* Though many fine trainers lack formal credentials, competent ones often will be certified by professional groups such as…

• *Aerobics and Fitness Association of America.* 800-445-5950.

• *American College of Sports Medicine.* 317-637-9200.

• *American Council on Exercise.* 800-825-3636.

• *Resist hard-sell tactics.* An eager salesperson may offer you a special membership contract that expires "at midnight tonight." Don't take the bait—no matter how interested you are in the club. Instead, request a one-day trial membership.

Cost: No more than a few dollars—perhaps free. If possible, try a sample session with a personal trainer.

• *Negotiate your membership fee.* Annual fees range from several hundred dollars for a family all the way up to $3,500 for an individual. Some clubs tack on a nonrefundable initiation fee of several hundred dollars. But no matter what the initial quote, membership fees and conditions are almost always negotiable.

• *Insist on a short-term contract.* Sad but true —90% of health club members stop going after three months. To avoid paying for workouts you never use, arrange to pay on a monthly basis— or sign up for a 90-day trial membership.

Important: Don't sign on the spot. Take the contract home and review it with a friend or family member.

• *Read the fine print.* A typical health club contract is two pages. Each portion must be scrutinized not only for what it includes, but also for what it *omits.* Make sure you will have full access to all facilities that interest you— swimming pool, squash courts, etc. Avoid contracts that limit the hours you can use the club —unless those hours fit your schedule. If the

contract does not include an "escape" clause, insert one. It should stipulate that you will get a prorated refund if you move or become disabled before the term is up.

Caution: Watch out for the club's escape clause—a waiver of liability in case you are injured. If a club tries to escape liability for injuries caused by its own negligence, then that clause should be crossed off and initialed before signing.

Finally, make sure the contract covers everything you've discussed with club employees. *Never* rely on verbal agreements.

If you have second thoughts after joining a health club, ask for a full refund. Most states mandate a three-day "cooling-off" period, during which consumers can back out of contracts and major purchases.

Source: Stephen L. Isaacs, JD, professor of public health at Columbia University and a practicing attorney, 685 Third Ave., 26th Floor, New York 10017. He is the coauthor of *The Consumer's Legal Guide to Today's Health Care: Your Medical Rights and How to Assert Them,* Houghton Mifflin, 215 Park Ave. S., New York 10003.

How to Tighten Your Midsection

As we age, our bodies store excess fat around our abdomens. Once this happens, it isn't easy to flatten your stomach, but you can if you follow these guidelines…

• *Exercise alone is not enough.* Physical activity burns calories, but more slowly than you might think.

Fact: You would have to run 35 miles to burn off one pound of fat.

To trim your abdomen, you must first restrict the number of calories that you eat each day.

Example: You might have two-thirds cup of bran flakes with two tablespoons of raisins and one cup of skim milk, and a half-cup of orange juice for breakfast…two slices of whole wheat bread with three ounces of turkey or chicken, two teaspoons of reduced-calorie mayonnaise, lettuce and tomato and one large apple for lunch…one nonfat sugar-free yogurt for an afternoon snack…and one cup of spaghetti with one-half cup of meatless spaghetti sauce, a spinach salad with two tablespoons of fat-free dressing and one slice of Italian bread for dinner. This adds up to 1,220 calories.

If you add aerobic exercise—say, five three-mile walks or four 45-minute aerobic dance classes per week—you'll shed one to two pounds per week. That's a healthy rate for losing weight and keeping it off.

• *Eat early in the day.* Most obese people consume the bulk of their calories after 6 PM.

Problem: The later in the day you eat, the more efficiently your body stores calories as fat. To lose weight effectively, consume 75% of your calories before 1 PM. Eat a light dinner before 7 PM, and avoid evening snacks.

Example of a light dinner: A vegetarian meal of one medium-sized baked potato topped with some plain nonfat yogurt, a romaine lettuce salad with raw vegetables and two tablespoons of reduced-calorie dressing and a small pear. This totals 395 calories.

• *Eat smaller quantities of food throughout the day.* This will help you stabilize your insulin at a lower level. The less insulin—a hormone produced by the pancreas to control the metabolism of sugar in the body—produced, the less fat stored in your cells and the more fat that is free to be burned by other tissues.

• *Exercise late in the day.* Exercise anytime during the day has considerable merit. Yet, to control body weight and stress, exercising at the end of the day is most effective. A predinner workout will suppress your appetite. Your heart rate stays elevated for two to three hours, so you will digest that dinner much more effectively.

• *Tone your abdominal muscles.* You don't need elaborate exercise equipment. *Focus on three classic exercises:*

• *Sit-up.* Keep knees bent and arms across your chest or to your sides—don't clasp your hands behind your neck, where an abrupt movement could fracture a cervical vertebra.

Progress to between 35 and 50 sit-ups per session, one to three times a day.

For lower abdominal muscles, the crunch type of sit-up can be used. Lie flat on the floor, knees bent, and rotate your shoulders off of the floor a few inches with your hands across your chest or to your sides. Once you reach a 45-degree angle, gradually rotate your shoulders back to the floor. This crunch type of sit-up helps to build strength in the lower abdomen better than the classic sit-up.

• *Leg lift.* For side muscles, do leg lifts on both the right and left sides. Turn so your body is perpendicular to the floor and raise your heel to a 45- to 50-degree angle. Repeat this exercise 25 to 30 times. Both legs should be incorporated into the exercise.

• *Push-up.* If you can't do the standard kind, leave knees on the floor. Advance to 25 push-ups per session, one to three times a day.

Caution: To prevent pulled muscles, stretch before doing any exercise. Hamstring and quadriceps muscles are the most frequently injured as a result of inadequate stretching. The Achilles tendon also needs to be stretched prior to exercise. This becomes even more important as you age.

Source: Kenneth Cooper, MD, founder of the Cooper Aerobics Center, 12200 Preston Rd., Dallas 75230. He is the author of *The Aerobics Program for Total Well-Being*, Bantam Books, New York, and *The Antioxidant Revolution*, Thomas Nelson Publishers, Nashville.

Eight Exercises that Strengthen…Gently

Once you reach age 60, consistency—not intensity—should be your exercise goal. Start slow…progress at your own pace…and work up to 20 repetitions of each per day. You don't need any special equipment.

• *Rocker warm-up:* Simple exercise designed to get you ready for the rest of the program. On hands and knees, rock backward until your buttocks touch—or almost touch—your heels. Rock forward to the original position.

• *Modified push-ups:* Similar to traditional push-ups, only your knees stay on the floor. Lie face down...place palms on the floor, one under each shoulder...raise your upper torso without letting knees leave the floor...lower yourself to the floor.

• *Stretch up/pull down:* For your arms, shoulders, neck and back. Lie on your back with your arms at your sides, palms down... keeping them straight, raise your arms up over your head until the back of your hands touch the floor behind your head...return arms to their original position.

• *Fist-clenched pushes and pulls:* Stretches chest muscles. While lying on your back make two fists...cross your arms up over your chest with your right hand above your left...return to starting position...repeat, with your left hand above your right.

• *Push to the sky:* Gently stretches your back. Lie on your back, kick your left leg straight up as far as it will go with the knee still straight... keep toes pointed...return to starting position. Repeat with right leg.

• *Sidekicks:* Lie on your right side with your right hand under your head and your left palm on the floor for balance...lift or kick your left leg straight up as far as you can. Repeat with your right leg.

• *Side walks:* Trim the buttocks. Lie on your right side...keeping your right leg still, swing your leg forward and backward, as if you were walking. *Important:* Do not lift your left foot more than three inches off the floor. Repeat while lying on your left side and walking with your right leg.

• *Knee crosses:* Good for those prone to backaches. Lying on your back, bend your right knee until your heel is almost to your buttock ...cross your left knee over your right knee and press down...spread your arms on the floor for balance...keeping your right foot flat on the floor, swing your knees as far left and then right as they'll go. Repeat with your right knee over your left knee.

Source: Morton Edell, president, Vitality Corporation of America, 1001 N. Washington Blvd., Suite 206, Sarasota, Florida 34234. He is the coauthor, with Norman M. Wall, MD, FACP, of *Aerobic-Isometric Exercises for Men and Women Over 60*, available through Vitality Corporation.

Exercise Prolongs Life

Previously, the only life-extending benefits of exercise were inferred from studies that linked exercise with a reduction in the risk of heart attack.

A study that lasted more than 20 years has found that men who were initially unfit were 44% less likely to die if they improved their fitness. Men who were already fit and remained so were 67% less likely to die than those who remained unfit.

Source: Study of 9,777 men ages 20 to 82 by Harold W. Kohl III, PhD, an epidemiologist at the Cooper Institute for Aerobics Research, Dallas, published in *The Journal of the American Medical Association*, 515 N. State St., Chicago 60610.

Exercise and Bad Moods

Exercise can hurt your mood if you have a competitive, Type A personality. Type A people who compare their performances with those of others tend to be more depressed and anxious after exercise than other exercisers. It is not the exercise that causes the bad moods, but the idea of competition. *Self-defense:* Concentrate on exercising *for yourself*—not comparing yourself with other people.

Source: Kevin Masters, PhD, clinical assistant professor of psychology, University of Utah Health Sciences Center, Salt Lake City 84108.

Beware of Band Exercisers

Band exercisers are inexpensive kits of fat rubber bands for isometric exercises. Stretching and pulling on the bands firms and tones muscles. But the bands can snap out of a user's hand and into the face, neck or groin—possibly causing serious injury. It is not always easy to tell when a band may go out of control and in what direction it may go.

Source: Edward Jackowski, founder, Exude, the nation's largest personal-training service, based in New York and the author of *Hold It! You're Exercising Wrong*, Simon & Schuster, 1230 Avenue of the Americas, New York 10020.

Exercise Injury Prevention

Replace worn athletic shoes every 500 miles …build endurance gradually…warm up with a short walk or jog before you exercise—then stretch after exercising…after sports, be sure to cool down and stretch again…cross-train by doing different activities on different days, to spread strength among muscle groups…listen to your body—if you start to feel pain, stop before you overdo things and suffer an injury.

Source: Herbert Haupt, MD, orthopedic surgeon in private practice in St. Louis and member of American Orthopedic Academy of Sports Medicine, Chicago.

Sit-Ups: Fewer May Be Better

Some people feel if 20 sit-ups a day are good, 100 or 200 sit-ups must be better. *Reality:* After a while, the body starts doing the exercises with muscles other than the abdominal ones that sit-ups should strengthen. *Best:* Concentrate on contracting abdominal muscles as much as possible when doing each sit-up by doing each one slowly and holding the position. Stop when you have trouble doing sit-ups this way. The quality of sit-ups matters more than the quantity.

Source: R. James Barnard, PhD, professor of physiological science, University of California, department of physiological science, Life Science Bldg. 405, Hilgard Ave., Los Angeles 90024.

Covert Bailey Answers The Big Questions About Exercise

I know I need to exercise more, but I'm intimidated by the scene at the health club. Any suggestions?

Challenge a friend or family member to a game of tennis, basketball or racquetball. Participating in a high-energy sport is often less intimidating and more effective at boosting fitness than aerobics classes.

Sports tend to be better than classes or machines at taking your mind off the exertion needed for exercise to be beneficial. A level of exertion that might be unbearable on a treadmill or in an aerobics class can occur almost without notice on a basketball court.

• *Once I start exercising, will I need to change the way I eat?*

As long as you're already eating a high-fiber, low-fat diet, there's no need to make any changes. At one time, nutritionists believed that people who exercised regularly needed extra protein in their diets—to repair sore muscles.

We now know that the average diet provides all the protein needed to build and maintain muscle. There's absolutely no need to take protein supplements or boost your consumption of meat or other proteins—even if you're a dedicated bodybuilder.

• *What's the best food to eat immediately after exercise?*

Although it's a good idea to limit your intake of fat and sugar most of the time, sugar is the best thing to eat during the two-hour period after long, strenuous exercise.

Reason: Sugar is better than complex carbohydrates (beans, pasta, rice, etc.) at replenishing glycogen, the starchy substance that serves as the body's energy supply. Gatorade, fruit, hard candies or jelly beans are good choices for a post-exercise pick-me-up.

• *Is it true that exercise weakens the immune system?*

Yes—but that's true only for long-distance runners and other serious exercisers. In a recent study, 13% of marathoners fell ill soon after a race, compared with only 2% of long-distance runners who followed the same training program but did not run the marathon. Runners who cover more than 60 miles a week are twice as likely to get sick as those who cover less than 20 miles a week.

Self-defense: If you exercise every day, alternate "easy" and "hard" days. Avoid exercise at least once a week.

• *How hard should I exert myself during my workouts?*

Exercise at a comfortable pace—that at which you must breathe deeply but without panting...and at which you can talk haltingly but not fluently. To increase your speed and endurance, consider mixing in brief intervals of intense exercise.

You may have heard that it's best to work out at 70% to 85% of your maximum heart rate. However, the familiar formula—220 minus age equals your maximum heart rate—is unreliable. Thirty percent to 40% of the population have maximum heart rates faster or slower than predicted by the formula.

• *Does it make any difference whether I exercise in the morning or at night?*

No. All that matters is that you pick the time that best fits your lifestyle.

Source: Covert Bailey, MS, star of the PBS television program *Smart Exercise* and the author of four books on fitness and nutrition, including *Smart Exercise,* Houghton Mifflin, 215 Park Ave. S., New York 10003.

The Best Home Weight-Training Machines

Working out at home with a weight-training machine has become a lot more appealing. New units are solidly built, designed to fit into small spaces...and many look good enough to display anywhere in the house.

My favorite at-home weight-training machines in different price ranges...

• *Lifeline Off the Wall Gym 2000.* This wall-mounted unit is ideal for someone who wants to exercise but has little or no floor space for a traditional weight-training machine. Users need only four square feet to work out. Instead of stacks of iron weights, heavy-duty rubberized tubing provides resistance and builds strength.

How it works: A seven-foot-long, 1½-inch-wide, U-shaped track is bolted flat against the wall. Two brackets can slide along the track and can be easily locked into various positions. The user grabs the two heavy-duty rubber tubes that are attached to the brackets and extends them to correctly exercise different parts of the body.
Lifeline International, Inc., 800-553-6633.

• *Parabody 350.* With this modestly priced, high-quality machine, users can do 25 strength-building exercises without ever having to get up to change the cables that operate the iron weights.

Features: Lower-body workout station is ergonomically designed to effectively exercise your legs...the weights start at only five pounds—a plus for beginners since the first weight on most machines is ten pounds.

Floor space: 3' x 5'.
Parabody, Inc., 800-328-9714.

• *Hoist 880.* This machine is versatile and can be used in the corner of a room. Unlike others, which require users to move to different workout stations, exercises are done in one position.

Features: Unique bench-press bars simulate lifting free weights. This system helps develop balance and coordination as well as strength.

Floor space: 3' x 4½'.
Hoist Fitness Systems, Inc., 800-548-5438.

• *Pacific Fitness Malibu.* With three workout stations, this machine is ideal for people who want to exercise with comfort. The seat tilts to provide proper muscle isolation and has contoured upholstery for back support. The user can adjust the weight-lifting bar, depending on his size and level of flexibility.

Floor space: 6' x 7'. Includes optional weight-stack enclosures and other accessories.
Pacific Fitness Corp., 800-722-3482.

• *Vectra On-Line 1800.* This technologically advanced unit has sculpted cylinders that hide its cables, giving it a sleek, high-tech look.

Features: This clever design eliminates all unnecessary adjustments and accommodates users of any ability. Seven-position adjustable bench includes decline, and it can be moved away from the unit for a variety of dumbbell workouts.

Floor space: 7' x 10'.

Vectra Fitness, Inc., 800-283-2872.

Source: Patrick Netter, independent home fitness equipment expert and consultant, 11693 San Vicente Blvd., Suite 111, Los Angeles 90049.

Reaction Time/ Exercise Connection

Reaction time in situations like having to quickly move a foot from a car's gas pedal to the brake can be improved by toning muscles. Strengthening muscles increases the blood flow and develops functional nerve fibers, which then speed the brain's messages to their destination more quickly.

Source: Roberta Rikli, PhD, professor of kinesiology and health promotion and codirector of the Lifespan Wellness Clinic at California State University, Fullerton.

Exposing Widely Accepted Nutrition Myths

As the dramatic links between good nutrition and good health have become increasingly evident with each passing year, so too has the outpouring of nutrition advice from a variety of sources.

Sometimes it's hard to separate the good advice from the hype. *Here are the biggest nutrition myths and realities...*

• *Myth:* Small, gradual dietary changes are easier to make than big changes.

Reality: When you make small, gradual changes in your eating habits and lifestyle, you have the worst of both worlds. You experience a sense of deprivation from not being able to eat the foods you enjoy, but you don't make big enough changes to see much benefit.

Example: If you're trying to lower your cholesterol level or blood pressure through diet, small changes such as eating less red meat won't have much impact. You'll also end up feeling frustrated.

Solution: It is actually easier to follow a low-fat, vegetarian diet in combination with stress-management techniques and moderate exercise. You'll feel much better very quickly.

For many people, dietary and lifestyle changes are worth making, not out of fear of dying but to increase the joy of living.

• *Myth:* You need nutritional supplements or weight-loss shakes to lose weight. Instead of looking for a magic bullet to help you lose weight fast, simply change the kinds of foods you eat and reduce your intake of fat.

You'll naturally lose weight without dieting, deprivation, austerity or hunger. A low-fat diet not only helps you lose weight, it also fights heart disease and many forms of cancer.

• *Myth:* Commercial weight-loss centers are the best places to go to lose weight.

Reality: The National Institutes of Health came out with a report three years ago that surveyed all of the major commercial weight-loss programs and found that none of them worked very effectively.

The study showed that within one year, two-thirds of those who had lost weight through one of these programs had gained back all of the weight. Within five years, 97% had gained back all of the weight.

Solution: My research indicates that if you change the types of food you eat, you don't really need to be as concerned about the amounts of food you eat. Commercial weight-loss plans focus on the amounts of food.

If you follow a diet composed predominantly of fruits, vegetables, grains, beans and nonfat dairy products and minimize fat and sugar intake, you'll lose weight naturally.

You'll be able to eat until you're satisfied because these foods will fill you up before you consume too many calories.

• *Myth:* Olive oil is good for you.

Reality: No oil is good for you. All oils are 100% fat. From a weight-loss standpoint, fat is fat. It doesn't matter if it's polyunsaturated, monounsaturated or saturated.

Olive oil is 14% saturated fat. From a cardio-vascular standpoint, the more saturated fat you eat, the higher your cholesterol level will be.

Solution: Eliminating all oils from your diet is the easiest way to reduce your intake of fat. If you did nothing more than eliminate all oils from your diet, you would likely lose weight and reduce your cholesterol.

Strategy: When cooking, use nonstick pans or nonfat sprays instead of butter or oil to prevent sticking. When sautéing, substitute citrus juice or broth for oil or butter.

• *Myth:* Health food stores have the healthiest foods. The words "health food" on packaging don't necessarily mean that what is inside the can or box is healthful. You can find low-fat foods in supermarkets—and high-fat foods in health food stores.

Example: Candy and energy bars sold in health food stores tend to be very high in fat and cholesterol.

Solution: It doesn't matter if you shop in a health food store or a supermarket. The key is to buy products that are low in fat and sugar. Be sure to read the nutrition label on the packages.

• *Myth:* "Smart" drinks—trendy potions containing herbs, amino acids, vitamins and minerals—can make you more alert, improve your memory and health, and extend your life.

Reality: No definitive scientific studies have been conducted on these trendy drinks. *Problems...*

• Many of these drinks cause some side effects, such as sleepiness or overstimulation of mental and physical functions. The result is shakiness or an inability to concentrate.

• Vitamins and minerals have many benefits, but they have never been shown to improve memory or intelligence in humans.

• Some amino acids, such as glutamate, can cause headaches.

Solution: Most people who follow low-fat, vegetarian diets, especially when combined

with exercise and stress-management techniques, find that they have more energy and think more clearly. Most people feel sluggish after a big meal with meat. Conversely, reducing fat will help you think more clearly and feel more energetic.

Source: Dean Ornish, MD, president and director of the nonprofit Preventive Medicine Research Institute, 900 Bridgeway, Suite 1, Sausalito, California 94965. He is the author of several best-selling books, including *Eat More, Weigh Less*, HarperCollins, New York.

Best Heart-Healthy Nutrient

Vitamin E works better than the other two natural antioxidants—vitamin C and beta-carotene—at clearing arteries of fatty plaque. Taken together, vitamins E and C and beta-carotene inhibited oxidation of LDL (bad) cholesterol—the process that initiates plaque formation—by 50%. But vitamin E taken alone had the same effect.

Source: Ishwarlal "Kenny" Jailal, MD, associate professor of pathology and internal medicine and a senior investigator in the Center for Human Nutrition, University of Texas Southwestern Medical Center, Dallas. His study of 36 men with and without heart disease, 25 to 65 years of age, was published in *Circulation,* St. Luke's Episcopal Hospital, Texas Heart Institute, MC 1-267, 6720 Bertner St., Houston 77030.

Food and Mood

Folk wisdom has long held that our moods are influenced by the food we eat. That belief is gaining support from scientific research.

Food-mood strategies can't cure clinical depression or other serious psychological disorders. These problems call for professional help. But they can be used to boost alertness at work...increase your sense of relaxation at home...and make it easier for you to tolerate life's ups and downs.

Mood-altering foods aren't unusual or hard to find. You don't have to follow a long, complex regimen before seeing results. They are ordinary, everyday foods...and in some cases, their effects are felt within as little as 30 minutes.

How food acts on our moods:

Recent research suggests that food affects mood by altering the brain's production of chemical messengers called *neurotransmitters*...

The neurotransmitters *dopamine* and *norepinephrine* have an energizing effect. When your brain is producing these chemicals, you're alert, highly motivated and have fast reaction times.

The main building block of these "alertness chemicals" is the amino acid *tyrosine*. Eating protein—which contains lots of tyrosine—raises tyrosine levels in the brain. This, in turn, boosts synthesis of dopamine and norepinephrine. *Result:* Greater mental energy.

The neurotransmitter *serotonin* has a calming effect. Its presence in the brain boosts concentration, relieves feelings of anxiety and—at night or if you're sleep-deprived—makes you feel drowsy.

To make serotonin, your brain needs a supply of the amino acid *tryptophan*. Like tyrosine, tryptophan is found in proteins. But eating more protein won't increase levels of tryptophan inside your brain. In fact, a high-protein diet depletes the brain's tryptophan supply.

Reason: Tryptophan must "compete" with tyrosine and other, more plentiful amino acids to enter the brain. It tends to be "crowded out" by them when you eat protein.

To increase the brain's supply of tryptophan, eat carbohydrates—without protein. Doing so triggers the release of insulin, which shunts some of the amino acids from the blood to other organs. Tryptophan, however, is left behind in the blood. With less competition from other amino acids, it can easily enter the brain.

Basic food-mood prescription:

Because tyrosine and tryptophan can be dangerous when taken in pill form, it's best to use food to affect levels of these neurotransmitters.

Caution: The following principles are no substitute for eating a healthful, well-balanced diet. If you have diabetes, hypoglycemia or another diet-related condition, consult a doctor before changing your eating habits.

•For greater alertness, motivation and mental energy...eat protein. Just three to four ounces (less than half the size of a typical restaurant entrée) is enough to get tyrosine to the brain so it can be used to make dopamine and norepinephrine.

Best sources of protein: Fish, shellfish, skinless chicken, veal, lean beef and egg whites. Because these foods are essentially pure protein—with little or no fat or carbohydrates—they work especially quickly.

Other good sources: Low-fat dairy products, dried legumes, tofu and other soy products. These contain carbohydrates but are low in fat.

Avoid: Fatty foods, such as pork, lamb, fatty cuts of beef, most hard cheeses and other whole-milk products. High-fat foods divert blood from the brain to the digestive tract. They take a very long time to digest.

•To calm down, relax and focus...eat carbohydrates. As little as one to one-and-one-half ounces is all most people need. Overweight people and women during the two or three days just prior to menstruation may need up to two-and-one-half ounces.

Eating the carbohydrate without protein is crucial. *Reason:* Protein will boost levels of amino acids that compete with tyrosine for entry to the brain. Instead of feeling calmer, you'll feel hyped-up. (If alertness is your goal, eating carbohydrates along with protein usually does not interfere with tyrosine's energizing effect.)

Best sources of carbohydrates: Gumdrops, licorice, marshmallows, jam and other sweets ...grain-based foods such as bread, crackers, pasta, rice, popcorn and pretzels...and starchy vegetables such as potatoes.

Fruits and nonstarchy vegetables are not good materials for the brain's serotonin factory. A healthful diet includes plenty of both, but these are not the foods to eat when you need to feel calm or focused.

Food-mood strategies and weight-loss diets:

Dieters often wonder whether these food-mood strategies lead to overeating—and to weight gain. In fact, these strategies are more likely to promote healthful eating...

Reason #1: Very small portions are needed to produce results.

Reason #2: The recommendations call for little or no fat. Not only is fat bad for you, but it also interferes with the food-mood effect.

Mealtime power:

For consistent results, use the food-mood principles to time your intake of proteins and carbohydrates...

• *Breakfast.* It should contain protein but little or no fat. *Possibilities:* An orange, eight ounces of low-fat yogurt and a low-fat bran muffin...or cranberry juice and hot cereal with skim milk.

• *Morning snack.* A snack is OK for those who find it hard to eat even a light meal first thing in the morning...and those who eat breakfast so early that they feel hungry by mid-morning. It will keep these individuals from coming to lunch so hungry that they overeat and feel sluggish all afternoon. *Good choice:* A small can of grapefruit juice, two rice cakes and one slice of skim-milk mozzarella.

• *Lunch.* It should be high in protein to keep you alert...and low in fat and calories, so you won't have to expend your energy digesting a heavy meal.

Don't begin lunch with a carbohydrate. If you have a roll or pasta before the entrée arrives, for example, you'll be sending trypto-phan to the brain. That will dull your mental edge. Instead: Start your meal with a salad, juice or consommé.

• *Afternoon snack.* Few people need a snack after an energy-boosting lunch—unless they're carbohydrate cravers. For reasons we don't understand, these people start to feel irritable and scattered at midday. A handful of crackers or jelly beans will help them feel calmer and more focused.

• *Dinner.* Make sure it's high in carbohydrates if you want to relax. If you need to keep your energy up for classes or volunteer work, your dinner should be high in protein.

• *Bedtime snack.* If you have trouble unwinding at bedtime, eat one-and-one-half ounces of carbohydrates 30 minutes before retiring. (That's the equivalent of five or six graham crackers.) Make sure the snack is low in fat and protein.

Warm milk at bedtime is a bad idea. *Reason:* Milk contains quite a bit of protein, which most people find energizing.

Stress relief:

If you feel frazzled and need to calm down, have a small carbohydrate snack. *For fastest results:* Have a cup of cocoa with melted marshmallows. You should feel better within 20 minutes.

If you need sustenance during an all-day stressful situation—waiting to hear the results of a medical test, for example—nibble high-carbohydrate, low-fat foods. Avoid full meals. Follow this strategy for no more than a day or two at a time.

Power-eating at conferences:

To avoid the exhaustion that plagues many conference-goers, bring your own light break-fast—or skip breakfast altogether. Avoid heavy coffee shop meals. Easy choices include a mini-box of fruit juice plus eight ounces of yogurt, or a single-serving box of cereal with low-fat milk and a banana.

If a buffet breakfast is part of the program, skip the hot table, where the high-fat foods are clustered. Instead, stick with fruit, cereals and low-fat muffins. During the coffee break, have coffee or tea, but skip the pastries.

At lunch, don't touch your roll until after you've eaten the protein part of the meal. If the entrée is a large serving, eat only half.

Pack a carbohydrate snack (such as graham crackers or fat-free cookies) in case you need to revive yourself during mid-afternoon presentations. Have it with a cup of coffee.

At dinner, emphasize protein if you need to be "on," carbohydrates if you're ready to un-wind—just as you would at home. Wind down with a few crackers or candies at bedtime.

Source: Judith J. Wurtman, PhD, research scientist, department of brain and cognitive science, Massachusetts Institute of Technology, Cambridge. She is the author of *Managing Your Mind & Mood Through Food,* Harper-Collins, New York.

Eat Less and Enjoy Your Food More

Playing slow, soothing music while you eat will curb your appetite. Studies have shown this helps people eat less—and enjoy their food more.

Source: Maria Simonson, PhD, ScD, director of the Health, Weight and Stress Clinic at the Johns Hopkins Medical Institutions, Baltimore.

Macrobiotics… The Ultimate Anticancer, Antiheart Disease Diet

It's well known that a vegetarian or near-vegetarian diet reduces the risk of heart disease and certain cancers. Even more healthful is a macrobiotic diet—a mostly vegetarian, natural foods diet that's little known in the United States.

A macrobiotic diet is even more effective at lowering the risk of heart disease. And it contains more of the natural antioxidants thought to prevent cancer of the breast, uterus, prostate and colon.

Some recent research suggests that a macrobiotic diet may also play a role in treating heart disease, cancer and Crohn's disease.

A macrobiotic diet (literally "big life") is one that emphasizes…

• *Natural, locally grown and minimally processed vegetables.* These should be eaten in season and organically grown if possible. Margarine and other highly processed foods are forbidden.

• *Whole grains.* Brown rice is usually the main staple.

• *Beans.* The emphasis is on soybeans and soybean products, including tofu, miso soup and soy sauce. Japanese foods are emphasized simply because the diet originated in Japan—not because there's any dogma specifying these foods. Recently, students of macrobiotics in the US helped rediscover quinoa and other native North American grains, as well as tempeh, a meatlike soybean product originally from Indonesia.

• *Sea vegetables, such as nori and kombu.* These vegetables should be eaten at least several times a week.

Eggs, dairy foods and meats are discouraged. The only animal foods not discouraged are fish and shellfish.

Most US public health authorities now recommend a diet containing no more than 30% of calories from fat…no more than 10% of calories from saturated fat…a maximum of 300 milligrams (mg) of cholesterol a day…and 20 to 30 grams (g) of fiber a day.

Most Americans have a hard time meeting these goals. However, a macrobiotic diet is even more stringent. *It contains…*

• Total fat…20% or less of calories.

• Saturated fat…3% to 5% of calories.

• Dietary cholesterol…30 mg or less per day.

• Fiber…25 to 30 g per day.

The macrobiotic philosophy:

Macrobiotics is more than a set of foods. It's also a philosophy of eating. *Key principle:* Eating low on the evolutionary scale. That means lots of fruits, vegetables and grains…and no beef, pork or other mammal meat—with rare exceptions.

Macrobiotics also involves a respect for tradition and local culinary customs. *Theory:* Locally grown foods are in greater harmony with your body than foods grown elsewhere and shipped in. If you live in Florida, for example, citrus fruits would probably be a staple of a macrobiotic diet. In Alaska, the staple might be seal meat.

Finally, macrobiotics involves balancing the diet according to the concepts of *yin* and *yang*. These opposite, but complementary, forces exist within the foods we eat and within all other aspects of our lives. Yang is contractive, solid, active and hot.

Yin is expansive, liquid or gaseous, passive and cold. Foods are classified as more yin… or yang. Whole grains are the most balanced. Animal foods are more yang…vegetables, more yin.

A diet high in salt content, with lots of red meat, would be extremely yang. An extremely yin diet would include lots of sugar and artificial chemicals. A macrobiotic diet provides just the right balance of yin and yang.

The benefits of macrobiotics:

Americans who eat macrobiotically have an extremely favorable cardiovascular risk profile —even better than that of people who eat a lacto-ovo vegetarian diet, which includes dairy products and eggs.

People who eat a macrobiotic diet weigh less, have lower blood pressure and have serum cholesterol levels 30% below Americans of the same sex and age who eat a traditional "meat-and-potatoes" diet.

They also have a favorable ratio of antioxidants to LDL (bad) cholesterol. Recent research suggests that oxidation of LDL cholesterol in the bloodstream injures coronary arteries, leading to the accumulation of fatty plaque.

Macrobiotic foods are abundant in natural antioxidants that help prevent oxidation of LDL cholesterol.

A macrobiotic diet also helps protect against cancer. Plant forms of estrogen found in soybeans, for instance, help reduce the amount of circulating estrogens in a woman's body... reducing her risk of breast cancer.

To the rescue: A macrobiotic diet may be an important adjunct to cancer treatment. In one recent study, people with advanced prostate or pancreatic cancer who adopted a macrobiotic diet lived longer than similar cancer patients who did not start eating macrobiotically.

How my family eats:

My family follows a fairly strict macrobiotic diet. I recommend such a diet both to those who want to reduce their risk of heart disease and cancer...and to those already stricken with these diseases.

Sample meals:

Breakfast:
Miso with wakame and daikon
Radish-boiled tofu with ginger-parsley sauce
Bancha tea or grain "coffee" (caffeine-free)

Lunch:
Vegetable-fried whole wheat spaghetti
Bancha tea
Dinner:
Brown rice and barley
Boiled string beans and almonds
Chick pea soup
Hiziki (seaweed) salad with tofu dressing
Baked butternut squash and onions
Strawberry couscous cake

Eating out:

Since you must be strict about avoiding sugar and refined grains, it can be difficult to eat macrobiotically in restaurants. But you can come close by sticking to Indian, Thai, Chinese or other ethnic or vegetarian restaurants.

For more information, visit your local health food store. Or contact the Kushi Institute, Box 7, Becket, Massachusetts 01223. 413-623-5741. Or the George Ohsawa Macrobiotics Foundation, 1511 Robinson St., Oroville, California 95965. 916-533-7702.

Source: Lawrence H. Kushi, ScD, associate professor of epidemiology, School of Public Health, University of Minnesota, Minneapolis. Dr. Kushi's parents, Aveline and Michio Kushi, were instrumental in bringing the macrobiotic philosophy and diet to the US, beginning in the 1960s.

The Role of Alcohol In a Healthy Diet

Alcohol is truly a puzzle. In moderation, it can prevent disease. But when abused, it can cause a host of serious health problems—and it can even hasten death.

Should you drink? If so, how much? *Here's everything you need to know to determine the role that alcohol should play in your life...*

Disease prevention:

A vast amount of evidence—including data from 31 long-term studies—shows that people who have one to two drinks a day reduce their risk of heart attack by 25% to 40%.

In addition, having one to three drinks a day reduces your risk of ischemic stroke, the kind caused by a clot in an artery.

These benefits are believed to stem from alcohol's ability to raise HDL (good) cholesterol. HDL helps remove harmful cholesterol from the blood before it is deposited on artery walls.

Alcohol may also reduce the stickiness of platelets, cells in the bloodstream that form clots. Less stickiness means a reduced chance of clotting.

Our studies have also found that healthy women who have a drink a day are far less susceptible to gallstones and diabetes. And we're now finishing up a study showing that one to two drinks daily cuts men's risk of diabetes by 20% to 30%.

Despite these findings, I hesitate to tell abstainers to start drinking.

Reason: It's estimated that one out of every ten individuals who starts drinking will develop a drinking problem.

If you already drink and you have risk factors for heart disease or a family history of heart disease, however, you may want to consider alcohol as part of a healthy lifestyle.

Similarly, one or two drinks with dinner may be appropriate for individuals without obvious risks who are nonetheless concerned about heart disease.

Caution: Drinking should not take the place of exercising, watching your weight, quitting a smoking habit or eating a healthful diet.

Which beverage is best?

Researchers disagree as to whether the type of alcohol consumed makes a difference. To date, few of the 31 studies have broken down data by type of beverage.

A study at Kaiser Permanente Medical Care Program in California found that wine was more protective than other alcoholic beverages.

At Harvard, we found that distilled spirits (vodka, scotch and other "hard" liquor) were more protective in men—but that wine was more effective in women. However, more men in our study consumed spirits and more women consumed wine, so it's hard to come to a firm conclusion.

Red vs. white wine: The hypothesis is that red wine contains antioxidants found only in small quantities in white wine and not at all in beer or spirits. But the experimental evidence for any difference in the protective effects of red and white wine is very weak.

If any specific beverage is more beneficial than the others, the additional benefit is probably quite small compared to the benefit from alcohol in general.

Health risks:

Most studies find an increased risk of colon cancer in people who consume two to three drinks a day. But we've also found that diets high in the nutrient folic acid protect against colon cancer.

Implication: If you're eating the recommended five servings of fruit and vegetables a day, moderate drinking may not increase your risk of colon cancer.

Far more troubling than alcohol's link to colon cancer is its link to breast cancer in women. A recent review of 30 to 40 studies found that women who consume one to two drinks daily have a risk of breast cancer 25% higher than women who drink less than that.

Considering that breast cancer strikes one in eight women, a 25% increased risk is very significant. And it applies to both premenopausal and postmenopausal women.

When deciding whether or not to drink, women must weigh all their risk factors. Any woman with a family history of breast cancer …who experienced puberty before age 11… who hasn't had children or who hasn't breast-fed her children faces a higher risk of breast cancer.

These women may want to consider very seriously how much to drink. Any woman who does decide to drink should probably limit herself to seven drinks a week—or less.

For women at average risk who are nevertheless concerned about breast cancer, it's probably a good idea not to consume more than a drink a day. At that level, alcohol may still reduce the risk of heart disease.

Because they have less of the enzyme that breaks down alcohol, women will have a higher blood alcohol level than men of the same weight who drink the same amount. As a general rule, women should drink a little bit less than men anyway.

Pregnancy: Experts still aren't sure what—if any—level of alcohol consumption is safe during pregnancy. Pregnant women who have six or more drinks a day are more likely to have a baby with fetal alcohol syndrome. However, there is little or no evidence that a few drinks per week alters fetal development.

Ultimately, the decision to drink while pregnant is a personal choice. Each woman should discuss the matter with her obstetrician.

The bottom line:

Moderate drinkers live longer than teetotalers. According to a recent American Cancer Society study of 275,000 men, those who consumed one to two drinks a day had a 10% to 15% lower risk of dying from all diseases combined than did nondrinkers.

A Kaiser Permanente study found that one drink a day cut women's death rate by 10%.

Almost all studies suggest that the benefits of alcohol apply only to low to moderate intake. All available evidence shows that long-term, heavy drinking is harmful to health.

Five or more drinks a day increases five- to ten-fold your risk of cirrhosis of the liver and cancers of the liver, mouth, throat and digestive tract.

That amount also doubles or triples your risk of ischemic stroke...and raises your risk of hemorrhagic stroke, in which blood seeps from a hole in a blood vessel wall inside the brain.

There's also the risk of driving while intoxicated. Regardless of your gender or body size, your ability to drive and make quick decisions behind the wheel is impaired after only a few drinks.

Finally, if you start at one to two drinks a day and find you can't control your drinking, you must seek help. It's important to focus on a healthful lifestyle—not just on alcohol.

Source: Eric Rimm, ScD, assistant professor of epidemiology and nutrition, Harvard School of Public Health, Boston. An expert on the health effects of alcohol on chronic disease, Dr. Rimm is the author of several studies on the topic.

Cancer-Fighters

Vitamin C isn't the only cancer-inhibiting substance found in fruits and vegetables. Produce also contains p-coumaric and chlorogenic acids, both of which fight cancer by blocking formation of powerful carcinogens called *N-nitroso* compounds. While these cancer-fighting acids are found in many different fruits and vegetables, the common garden tomato seems to have the highest concentrations.

Source: Joseph Hotchkiss, PhD, professor of food science, Cornell University, Ithaca, New York. His study of N-nitroso compound formation in 16 men was published in the *Journal of Agricultural and Food Chemistry,* Box 3337, Columbus, Ohio 43210.

Milk May Impair Fertility in Women

In parts of the world where milk consumption is highest, women suffer the sharpest age-related falloff in fertility. *Possible culprit:* Galactose, a sugar found in milk and other dairy products. It appears to be toxic to human egg cells. Additional research is needed to determine if women should reduce their milk consumption.

Source: Daniel W. Cramer, MD, ScD, associate professor of obstetrics and gynecology, Brigham and Women's Hospital, Harvard Medical School, Boston. His comparison of fertility rates and milk consumption in 36 countries was published in the *American Journal of Epidemiology,* 2007 E. Monument St., Baltimore 21205.

One More Reason to Eat Green Leafy Vegetables

Green leafy vegetables seem to help prevent age-related macular degeneration, the leading cause of blindness among elderly people. People who eat the most of certain types of carotenoids—found in spinach and other dark, leafy greens—had a 43% lower risk of developing the eye disorder than those who ate the least.

Source: Johanna M. Seddon, MD, associate professor of ophthalmology, Harvard Medical School and Harvard School of Public Health, and director, epidemiology unit, Massachusetts Eye and Ear Infirmary, all in Boston.

What You Should Know About Vitamins...the Case *For* Supplements

Few subjects stir up as much controversy among health experts as the value of vitamin supplements in our diets. Some doctors believe that taking vitamins and minerals does virtually nothing for you. I believe that vitamins play an important role.

Reason: The Recommended Dietary Allowances (RDAs) set by the government are the amounts of vitamins and minerals needed to prevent obvious deficiencies.

But in order for the body to function at its best—not merely to be deficiency-free—you need to take in optimal amounts of nutrients that are far larger than the RDAs.

Why don't some mainstream practitioners recognize this? They don't understand nutrition—and they believe that the government knows what it is doing in terms of establishing nutrition guidelines.

Myth I: You can get all your nutrients from food.

Reality: The majority of people don't eat a healthy, balanced diet.

Instead, we tend to eat a diet that's high in fat, including hydrogenated and saturated fats that damage the body. We also eat many refined products, which are devoid of many nutrients.

Even if you fill up on fresh produce, the farming methods in this country tend to strip fruits and vegetables of important vitamins and minerals. *Result:* You may not be getting all your nutrients from *healthy* foods—even if you eat what the government says you should eat.

Myth II: Vitamin supplements give you nothing more than expensive urine.

Reality: While it's true that any excess of water-soluble vitamins and minerals is eventually excreted in the urine, these nutrients still have positive value as they travel through your system—you are not just excreting them.

Supplements for maximum health:

To maintain optimal health, I recommend the following daily supplements:

•A multivitamin/mineral capsule, which is easier to absorb than a tablet. Health food store supplements tend to be of higher quality and are a better source of trace minerals than supermarket supplements, which are mostly synthetic.

What to look for in a multivitamin: B vitamins—50 milligrams (mg) to 100 mg each...a wide variety of trace minerals.

Important: Your multivitamin should not contain iron. Excess iron, especially in men and postmenopausal women, can increase the risk of heart disease. If you suffer from an iron deficiency, talk to your doctor about taking a separate iron supplement.

•Antioxidants—200 to 400 International Units (IU) of vitamin E and 1,000 to 3,000 mg of vitamin C.

Beta carotene, a third antioxidant, is found in sufficient amounts—usually 5,000 to 25,000 IU per day—in the multivitamin/mineral capsule, so there's no need to take a separate pill.

For some of my older patients, whose bodies don't absorb nutrients as well as they once did, I prescribe even higher dosages—400 to 800 IU of vitamin E...2,000 to 3,000 mg of vitamin C ...and 25,000 IU of beta carotene. Encapsulated vitamins, available in health food stores, are best. They are more easily absorbed than tablets, especially if you are over age 60.

Many trace minerals are deficient in foods because of our current farming methods. *Helpful antioxidant mineral supplements:* Zinc (30 mg/day)...selenium (200 *micro*grams/day). *Also recommended:* Magnesium (300 to 400 mg/day)...chromium (200 *micro*grams/day). Chelated minerals are bound to amino acids or organic molecules and are much more easily assimilated than other mineral supplements.

Studies have shown that 2,000 to 3,000 mg of vitamin C each day has an optimal effect on the immune system, helping to prevent colds and sore throats short-term...and to ward off heart disease and cancers long-term.

There have also been more than 100 studies showing that vitamin E helps prevent heart disease. Given that the results of one recent Finnish study negating the value of antioxidants was flawed, I still recommend them to my patients. That study involved people who had been smokers for 20 to 30 years taking such low doses of vitamin E that its conclusions were valueless.

•Essential fatty acids (Omega 3 and 6 oils, such as fish oils, flaxseed oil, evening primrose oil) are beneficial since they are depleted or rancid in the Western diet. *Recommended:* One tablespoon flaxseed oil per day...or 3,000 mg fish oil per day.

Supplements—everything in balance:

While I generally recommend nutritional supplements, people have to be smart about them. The biggest problem I see is imbalance —taking a lot of one nutrient and not enough of another...without understanding the relationship between the two.

Example: There's a link between magnesium and calcium and between copper and zinc. If you take too much of one in each pair, you may deplete your body's supply of the other.

Also, a few vitamins can be toxic when taken in excess, such as the fat-soluble vitamin A, which in excessive amounts (more than 50,000 IU taken chronically over several months) may cause liver problems, dermatitis and other ailments.

Eating right:

Just because you take supplements doesn't mean you should neglect your diet, which should be a key source of nutrients.

•Eat plenty of yellow, orange and green leafy vegetables—four to six servings per day —for their antioxidant value.

•Eat grains, especially whole grains—available at health food stores and supermarkets— which are sources of B vitamins and trace minerals. Sources of grains include brown rice, whole wheat, quinoa, buckwheat, oats, spelt and millet. Serve larger portions of grains and smaller portions of meats and other animal products.

•Avoid refined foods as much as you can. Refined foods are processed by grinding, milling, bleaching, cooking, etc., which removes or destroys fiber, color, vitamins, oil and minerals. I recommend organically grown foods. They're a better source of nutrients, particularly trace minerals, than other produce. Organically grown foods use fertilizers made from organic materials, which replete the soil with more nutrients than other fertilizers. Therefore, organic produce has more trace minerals.

Important: Organic foods are grown without pesticides. New evidence shows that pesticides are toxic to humans. In order to detoxify and excrete them, the liver is forced to utilize many nutrients, specifically trace minerals and antioxidants, further depleting the nutrient status.

•Whenever possible, buy fresh foods. Don't let them stand around. They lose nutrients in your refrigerator.

Also, nutrients are lost when vegetables are cooked in water and the water is then discarded. Cook vegetables in minimal amounts of water. Then freeze the liquid and use it as a base for soups.

Better: Steaming, microwaving or lightly stir-frying vegetables in olive oil.

•Juicing is another way to increase your nutrient intake. It helps make the nutrients in fruits and vegetables more easily accessible to the body. Drink the juice fresh so you don't lose the nutrients.

•Don't overlook red meat, which supplies vitamin B_{12} and folic acid. You don't have to eat meat every day, but once or twice a week is acceptable.

An optimal diet varies from person to person due to individual metabolisms. If you are not sure what the best diet is for you, get help from a knowledgeable doctor or nutritionist.

Source: Robban Sica-Cohen, MD, director of the Center for the Healing Arts in Orange, Connecticut. She specializes in environmental and nutritional medicine.

Vitamin C Dosage

Vitamin C taken twice a day keeps blood levels of the powerful antioxidant higher for a longer period of time than a single daily dose. If you would like to get 1,000 mg a day, consider taking a 500-mg dose once every 12 hours, rather than a single 1,000-mg dose every 24 hours. By taking vitamin C twice daily, one ensures that there is sufficient vitamin C in the body and that a small excess is always being excreted. If one takes 1,000 mg of vitamin C once a day, much more vitamin C will be excreted during the first 12-hour period. *Result:* There will be no excess during the second 12 hours, so the protective effect against free radicals may only occur half the day.

Source: Roc Ordman, PhD, professor of biochemistry, Beloit College, Beloit, Wisconsin. His study of students who took varying amounts of vitamin C at different times was reported in *Age*, American Aging Association, 2129 Providence Ave., Chester, Pennsylvania 19013.

What You Should Know About Vitamins...the Case *Against* Supplements

The value of vitamin and mineral supplements is highly overrated. I never prescribe them unless patients need them to make up for a deficiency in their diets...or to treat specific conditions.

I also don't believe in over-the-counter vitamin supplements. They help some people, harm others and have no effect on most.

Last year, the Centers for Disease Control and Prevention published a major study comparing Americans who take supplements with those who don't.

Result: Longevity and overall health were identical.

And the US Department of Agriculture (USDA) published this statement on its list of seven dietary guidelines: *For the average American, there is no need for supplements.*

Many people feel compelled to take vitamin supplements because they eat poorly balanced diets and believe they aren't getting all their nutrients from food.

Reality: Most Americans don't have poor diets. That's a lie created by the supplement industry to sell its products.

The average American diet is loaded with vitamins and minerals and provides all the nutrients that the average person needs. Even the much-maligned fast-food hamburger, for example, provides a full day's requirement of every vitamin and mineral. The problem with that hamburger—and most everything else Americans eat—is that it is too high in fat and calories.

The biggest nutritional danger Americans face isn't vitamin deficiency—it is being overweight. One-third of Americans are overweight. That leads to heart attack, cancer, diabetes and other life-threatening diseases.

Don't knock the RDAs:

I was a part of the committee that authored the *10th Recommended Dietary Allowances (RDAs)* in 1985. I believe that the RDAs are more than adequate in establishing necessary nutrients. Our 10th RDAs were published in 1989 by the National Academy of Sciences. Anyone who eats a diet that conforms to the RDAs does not need to take vitamin pills.

How were the RDAs established?

•First, the committee determined the floor—the level of vitamin and mineral intake below which a deficiency develops.

•Next, we determined the ceiling above which toxicity or adverse reactions occur.

•Then we asked ourselves: *How big a body store of nutrients do we want the average American to have?*

We set the RDAs sufficiently above the floor to allow the body to store up three to six months' worth of vitamins without exceeding the ceiling.

Example: The current RDA for vitamin C is 60 milligrams—you need ten milligrams a day to protect against deficiency. The extra 50 milligrams builds up over five months to provide the body with a five-month surplus.

If you were to stop your vitamin C intake today—given your existing body storage—it would take you five months to develop a vitamin C deficiency.

That's nearly impossible to do, since the typical American diet averages 72 milligrams daily of vitamin C, the amount in one-half cup of orange juice. Even with 60 milligrams of vitamin C a day, you're getting more than you need.

The antioxidant hype:

Vitamin C, along with vitamin E and beta carotene, is touted as an antioxidant that destroys harmful free radicals in the body and protects against heart disease and cancer. Sometimes, vitamin C is a pro-oxidant—it creates free radicals and promotes disease.

Example: If you happen to be in the 12% of the population that has a high level of iron in the body and if you also have high cholesterol, absorbing just 100 milligrams daily of vitamin C doubles your chance of heart attack.

In short, the antioxidant hype is just that—*hype.* None of the "antioxidant" vitamins are pure antioxidants. They all are *redox agents*—sometimes antioxidant, sometimes pro-oxidant. Any claim that taking a vitamin C pill is just like taking vitamin C in your orange juice is false. The vitamin C in juice is biochemically balanced, partly in the reduced form and partly in the oxidized form. The vitamin C in pills is in the potentially harmful reduced form. Reduced vitamin C can promote free radicals.

Too much vitamin E can also be dangerous. In large quantities, vitamin E acts like an anticoagulant drug—which means it will prevent blood from clotting. That's good for preventing heart attacks. But it also means that when blood can't clot, you could die from a hemorrhagic stroke.

The whole idea that people need vitamin E supplements is a scam. Only once has there ever been a case of vitamin E deficiency, and that was 40 years ago, when a researcher deliberately induced a deficiency in a group of hospital patients by completely removing vitamin E from their diets. Even then it took five months before any adverse reaction was seen.

Beware of supplements:

There are only four times in life when vitamin supplements may be appropriate…

• In early childhood—up to age four—when the body is first developing.

• At the onset of puberty—because there's such an enormous growth spurt that the body's nutrient stores, especially its store of iron, may be inadequate.

• For women of childbearing age—10% of women will have an iron deficiency due to menstruation.

• During pregnancy—because the fetus drains the mother of vitamin B_6, folic acid, iron and calcium.

Otherwise, you should always follow the three basic rules of good nutrition—moderation…variety…and balance.

Each day, be sure to get your three to five daily servings of vegetables and two to four servings of fruit, and eat between 15 and 35 grams of fiber (the best sources are grains, fruits and vegetables) to promote regularity and protect against diseases such as colon cancer.

Source: Victor Herbert, MD, JD, professor of medicine and director of the nutrition program at the Mount Sinai School of Medicine in New York and the Veterans Affairs Medical Center in the Bronx, New York. He is the coauthor, with Stephen J. Barrett, MD, of *The Vitamin Pushers: How the "Health Food" Industry Is Selling America a Bill of Goods*, Prometheus Books, 59 John Glenn Dr., Buffalo, New York 14228.

Seafood Self-Defense

• Never eat raw oysters, clams or mussels. They can contain microbes that cause hepatitis or gastroenteritis. Even in a trusted restaurant, it can be risky to visit the "raw bar."

• Avoid bluefish, lake trout and freshwater fish caught in inland lakes. They can contain polychlorinated biphenyls (PCBs).

• Eat swordfish and fresh tuna no more than once a week. More often, and you risk mercury poisoning.

• Limit consumption of canned tuna to no more than two medium-size cans (or six tuna salad sandwiches) a week.

•In tropical areas, avoid locally caught barracuda, grouper, amberjack and snapper. They can harbor a dangerous parasite known as ciguatera. Also avoid fresh tuna, bluefish and mahi mahi, which also can harbor parasites.

Fish least likely to contain harmful chemicals: Cod, flounder, haddock, Pacific halibut, ocean perch, pollock, sole, catfish, salmon (except those caught in the Great Lakes) and cooked shellfish.

Source: Caroline Smith DeWaal, JD, director of food safety, Center for Science in the Public Interest, 1875 Connecticut Ave. NW, Suite 300, Washington, DC 20009.

How to Make Sense of The New Food Labels

Check food labels for the Percent Daily Values of fat, saturated fat and cholesterol. These three values are found on the right-hand side of the new "Nutrition Facts" label and have a direct bearing on your health and diet.

•*Fat*. The Food and Drug Administration (FDA) recommends that total daily fat intake be no more than 65 grams—based on a 2,000-calories-per-day diet. Total fat includes saturated, polyunsaturated and monounsaturated fat. Only saturated fat and trans fat, found in partially hydrogenated oils, raise cholesterol.

Strategy: Because the average person eats as many as 15 to 20 different types of foods per day, most people are better off choosing foods with low levels of fat. Ideally, each serving you eat should contain 5% or less of the Daily Value for fat (that is three grams).

•*Saturated fat*. Saturated fat is included in the total fat count and is broken out separately. It can raise blood cholesterol levels and increase the risk of heart disease. Consume no more than 20 grams a day.

Strategy: Choose foods that have only 5% of the Daily Value per serving.

•*Cholesterol*. Foods labeled "low cholesterol" are preferred. They contain no more than 20 milligrams of cholesterol per individual serving...or approximately 60 milligrams in

a 10-ounce main dish or meal (main dishes are allowed 20 mg per 3½ ounces of food).

Common food-label traps:

•*Serving sizes can be misleading*. Serving sizes are set by the FDA, but these standards are often smaller than the amounts most people eat.

Result: You may be eating more fat, sodium and calories than you realize.

Strategy: Check the serving size listed at the top of the food label, and adjust your intake or adjust your fat and calorie calculations. *Also helpful:* Limit the fat content of other foods you eat that day.

•*Low-fat claims on frozen entrees can be misleading*. The FDA says that when any food manufacturer makes a "low-fat" claim on its food label, the food must contain no more than three grams of fat per serving.

Frozen entrees and dinners, however, are allowed three grams of fat for each 3½ ounces. Most entrees weigh at least nine ounces, which means that even if they contain as much as eight grams of fat, they can still make a "low-fat" claim.

Strategy: Ignore low-fat claims on frozen foods and entrees. Instead, read the nutrition label, and look for entrees that contain no more than about three grams of fat (again, about 5% of the Daily Value for fat) per serving.

•*Avoid partially hydrogenated oil*. If it is listed as an ingredient, the food also contains trans fat, which raises blood cholesterol levels just as saturated fat raises cholesterol.

Formula: Total trans fat values can be estimated if the "monounsaturated," "polyunsaturated" and "saturated" fat grams are listed on the label. Add them up and subtract them from the total fat value.

Note: If a food's packaging says "low fat" on its label, it probably doesn't contain much trans fat.

Source: Bonnie Liebman, MS, director of nutrition at the Center for Science in the Public Interest, a nonprofit, consumer advocacy organization that works to improve the nation's health and publishes *Nutrition Action Healthletter*, 1875 Connecticut Ave. NW, Suite 300, Washington, DC 20009.

Foods that Can Improve Your Health

A growing body of scientific research shows that many natural foods contain vital nutrients that can help you stay well or regain your health. Greatest benefit is usually obtained when these foods are eaten in a close-to-natural state…raw or only lightly cooked…because our digestive tracts are designed to absorb nutrients from uncooked food.

Be cautious about eating manmade, imitation foods because processing removes vital nutrients and adds many substances that can trigger food sensitivities and allergies.

Here are two of the diseases and unhealthy conditions that can be treated effectively or, better still, prevented, by good nutrition…

• *Arthritis.* Traditional medicine can give little help…other than pain-killing drugs…to the 35 million Americans who suffer from rheumatoid arthritis and osteoarthritis.

More than 1,000 years ago American Indians learned the juice of the yucca plant could relieve arthritic pain. Modern research shows that *saponin* (the scientific name for yucca juice) protects friendly intestinal bacteria that compete with harmful microorganisms and prevent them from causing allergic reactions associated with arthritis. Yucca is available from health food stores.

Other ways that arthritis is relieved: Reduced consumption of fat, increased intake of folic acid, protein, zinc, vitamins C and D, pantothenic acid.

• *High cholesterol.* Drugs used to reduce cholesterol in the blood have a variety of dangerous side effects, but natural ways can be both safe and pleasant.

Eating the suggested amounts of the following foods can help reduce cholesterol significantly…

• Two or three apples a day.

• A serving of barley in hot or cold cereal or in baked goods several times a week.

• One cup of navy or pinto beans a day.

• Three medium carrots daily.

• Half or a whole green plantain daily.

• Three cups of yogurt a day.

Source: Maureen Salaman, an international nutrition and health lecturer. She is the author of *Foods that Heal,* distributed by Bay to Bay Distribution, Mountain View, CA.

Dietary Fat Update

Several studies show that *mono*unsaturated oils—such as olive and canola oils—are no better for the heart than polyunsaturated oils, such as corn, soybean and sunflower oils. For years, it was believed that monounsaturated oils were superior at reducing blood cholesterol. *Bottom line:* The type of oil won't make much difference if you decrease your total fat intake. Reduce *saturated* fat by decreasing meat and high-fat dairy products in your diet. Replace them with fruits, vegetables and grains, but don't increase your intake of other fats.

Source: Alice Lichtenstein, DSc, associate professor of nutrition, Human Nutrition Research Center on Aging, Tufts University, Boston.

How to Talk Yourself Out of Overeating

Our reasons for overeating have little to do with food itself. Rather, they stem from the way our minds have been programmed to respond to food.

During the first 18 years of our lives, we receive thousands of messages about food from our parents, our friends, the media and advertising. These messages are stored away in our minds—without any distinction between those messages that are true and those that are false …those that are helpful and those that are harmful.

Example: Being taught during childhood that eating sweets will make us feel better when we're anxious or sad.

Result: When we're adults, we reach for these desserts whenever we're under pressure or when things don't go our way.

How self-talk can help:

Using *self-talk,* you can *reprogram* your way of thinking and reverse a lifetime of automatic eating behavior.

Self-talk is based on neurological and behavioral research that shows the human brain is programmed very much like a computer. If you want your computer to do something new, you buy a new software disk for that function.

Here is a six-week plan for talking yourself into a weight-loss program...

Week one:

Monitor your behavior. During the first week, write down everything you catch yourself saying or thinking about food, dieting or your weight. Use one 3" x 5" index card for each statement. *Examples...*

- *This diet won't work—none of them do.*

- *Everything I eat goes right to my waist.*

- *This one piece of chocolate won't hurt.*

Don't try to analyze these comments. Simply capture in writing your thoughts about food. The exercise will help you build awareness of what you are thinking—an important first step in the self-talk program.

Weigh yourself this week and every week thereafter.

Important: Only weigh yourself once each week and at the same time of the day. People who weigh themselves every day become obsessed with their weight rather than with changing their negative life-long habits.

Week two:

Edit your cards. Consciously edit those Week One messages from your vocabulary.

The strategy here is to eliminate the comments while you are in the process of thinking or acting upon them in order to gain greater control over your mental programs.

Example: Instead of saying, "Eating a piece of candy just this once won't hurt" or "I'll start my diet on Monday" as you reach for that midnight snack, catch yourself mid-sentence and stop. Replace the message with a healthier one.

This procedure may make you feel somewhat uncomfortable. Thoughts about food do not go away that easily, and you might wonder how this exercise could possibly help.

Remind yourself that the point of this exercise is to help you recognize your old habits and gradually change your way of thinking.

Also during Week Two, begin some form of physical exercise. Choose a moderate workout plan that you intend to continue five to ten years from now.

Week three:

Reprogram your mind, and set goals. On the flip side of each 3" x 5" card from Week One, write a healthier version of the message.

Example: On the back of "This one piece of chocolate won't hurt," write, "I decided to take care of myself today" or "I only eat healthy, nutritious foods."

Don't be discouraged if you stray. Self-talk takes practice before it becomes second nature. In effect, you're learning a new language. The clearer your messages and the more often you repeat them, the sooner change will occur.

At the end of this week, set a weight-loss goal that you want to achieve by month's end (the last day of the month). Also set one- and five-year goals.

After having actively practiced self-talk all this week, you will start to believe that your goals are attainable. Be sure to weigh yourself, and stick with your exercise plan.

Week four:

Avoid "food talk." By Week Four, you've made yourself aware of your old programs, learned to turn them around and created new ones.

Now that you're aware of them, it's time to stop the behavior—such as talking obsessively about food to yourself and others.

Example: Stop planning dinner while you're eating lunch. If the topic of food or your weight comes up, change the subject.

Goal: Block out the topic of food, making a choice to make it less important.

Week five:

Act like a thin person. Now that you've begun to change your mindset about food, reinforce the belief that you can be someone who is naturally thin. By naturally thin, I mean someone who is in control of his/her eating, not someone who was born thin.

This is a good time to begin doing some activities you would not ordinarily do until you have lost weight. Walking more, for example, or engaging in a sport, even if it is just for a few minutes.

Key: Try to behave like people whose lives do not revolve around food or weight problems.

Example: Stroll through the section of a department store that sells clothes in the size you would like to wear. Imagine yourself buying those smaller-sized items, and get used to the way it feels to shop there.

It's like test-driving an expensive car you covet and telling yourself, "Someday I'll own this car."

Week six:

Live the changes every day. Focus on what has been happening to you and all the changes you've made. *Examples…*

• Your portions and types of food are different from what you used to eat.

• You don't finish everything that is put on your plate.

• You don't make excuses about food.

• You don't avoid yourself in a mirror. You may even smile when you see your reflection.

• Other areas of your life may change as well. Your relationships improve…you're more organized…things at work are better.

During Week Six, reward yourself for all your accomplishments. Give yourself something—a new CD, a book or something that you can look at from time to time. The gift will remind you that you've accomplished something important and will help you continue the program.

The more control you take over your life through self-talk, the greater the likelihood your fear of food—and your weight problem —will go away for good.

Source: Shad Helmstetter, PhD, founder of Self-Talk Information Services, which develops Self-Talk training programs for corporate and individual clients, 5930 E. Pima, #144, Tucson 85712. He is the author of seven books, including *Self-Talk for Weight Loss* and a starter set of *Self-Talk for Weight Loss* cassette tapes. Both are available through his company.

How to Take Weight Off And Keep It Off

Each year, Americans spend $33 billion on commercial diet programs—and much of that vast sum is essentially wasted.

Reason: The premise on which these programs are based—cut calories, and you'll lose weight—is at least 20 years out of date. In study after study, it's been thoroughly discredited.

Weight loss just isn't that simple. As we all know, the hard part isn't losing weight, but keeping it off. Unless you're willing to eat frozen dinners and drink low-cal shakes for the rest of your life, that is almost impossible on most of the commercial weight-loss programs.

Not surprising, then, that many dieters shuffle unsuccessfully from one diet plan to the next—losing weight on one program, putting it back on, and then moving on to another plan.

In fact, counselors working for the leading commercial diet plans freely admit that perhaps nine of ten people who try one commercial diet program wind up trying two or three…or more.

Weight-loss principles:

How do you take weight off and keep it off —once and for all? *There are three fundamental principles for effective and lasting weight loss…*

Principle #1: Take control of your life and your weight. Turning responsibility for what you eat and what you do over to anyone else is deadly. You need to design a program for yourself. You also need to open up your life to self-inspection.

Often, eating is a survival skill. It's a way of coping with frustrations and disappointments. Life can be very difficult. Eating can get you through it.

Overeating becomes a way to maintain emotional health—although, of course, physical health is jeopardized as a result.

To overcome this self-destructive approach to food, you must learn to separate food itself from its emotional symbolism. You may need the help of a psychologist specializing in weight problems.

For referrals to a psychologist in your area, contact the National Association of Anorexia Nervosa and Associated Disorders, Box 7, Highland Park, Illinois 60035. 708-831-3438.

Principle #2: Accept your body. Focus not upon how your body looks, but on what it enables you to do. And don't compare yourself with the ideal body put forth in sexy movies or magazine ads. After all, body shape is determined largely by heredity. We tend to look like our mothers and fathers—and that persists even if we're successful at losing weight.

Principle #3: Make food a pleasure. Avoid thinking of food as a moral issue. "Good" foods are those you think you should be eating— fruits, vegetables, beans, pasta, etc. "Bad" foods taste good but are fattening—cakes, candy, sugary soft drinks, etc.

Substituting good foods for bad sounds like a good idea, but odds are it's just setting you up for failure. *Problem:* Even if you could steer clear of "bad" foods for several months, you'd give in to temptation—possibly by going on an eating binge.

Better way: If you like cheesecake, allow yourself the freedom to eat it on occasion. By removing this cheesecake "taboo," you reduce your obsession with it.

Dieting vs. your set-point:

The only way to ensure lasting weight loss is to lower your set-point. That's the weight your body "thinks" it should weigh.

When people overeat, they generally gain weight only temporarily, returning to their usual weight, or "set-point" when they resume their previous eating habits.

Similarly, when you go on a low-calorie diet, your body wants to keep you from starving. As a result, your metabolism slows to maintain your set-point. *Result:* Weight loss occurs very slowly. When you resume your normal eating patterns, your weight quickly rises to its former level.

To lower your set-point, you must reduce your intake of dietary fat and increase your lean muscle mass. In other words, lighten up your eating habits and get enough exercise to build muscle.

The importance of exercise:

The more you exercise, the more muscle you build. And because muscle cells burn dietary fat more efficiently than fat cells do, gaining muscle mass speeds your metabolism. *Payoff:* A thin person can eat much more fat than a fat person without gaining weight.

If you've been inactive for a long time, begin by exercising just five or ten minutes a day. Gradually build until you're exercising at least 20 minutes a day, three to four days a week.

Source: Kathleen Thompson, the coauthor of *Feeding on Dreams: Why America's Diet Industry Doesn't Work & What Will Work for You,* Macmillan, New York.

How Herbs Can Keep You Healthy

I never stop being amazed by the remarkable healing power of herbs. As a dedicated physician, I've been recommending them to my patients for more than 25 years. Unfortunately, herbal medicine isn't taught in US medical schools, and few physicians have taken the initiative to learn about herbs.

Herbs have several advantages over conventional drugs. They're inexpensive, potent and —if you take care not to overdose—far less likely to cause allergic reactions or other side effects. (Potentially dangerous herbs, including sassafras and chaparral, have been taken off the market.) Herbs are readily available without a prescription at health-food stores—although it's best to check with your doctor before using herbs.

Here are the herbal remedies I find most useful...

• *Aloe vera* is wonderful for soothing minor burns and preventing subsequent infection. Although it's available in gel form, research suggests that fresh aloe vera leaves are more potent in their anesthetic and antibacterial properties. I urge my friends, family and patients to keep an aloe vera plant in the kitchen and use its leaves to dab on minor burns.

• *Chamomile tea* contains oils that have anti-spasmodic and anti-inflammatory effects. It's good for indigestion, anxiety, insomnia and exhaustion. Babies given chamomile tea in their bottle fall asleep faster.

• *Comfrey* contains allantoin, a compound that speeds healing by promoting growth of muscle and connective tissue. It helps prevent bruising and swelling associated with muscle sprains and strains. Applied to the skin as a paste...not to be taken by mouth.

• *Echinacea*—sometimes blended with the natural antibiotic goldenseal—stimulates the body's production of the virus-fighting compound interferon and boosts the number and activity of white cells. That makes it a perfect all-around remedy for colds or flu. It's also good for urinary tract infections. Often taken as drops mixed in a glass of water.

• *Garlic* lowers cholesterol, boosts the immune system and kills disease-causing germs. People who eat lots of garlic get fewer colds. *Important:* Deodorized garlic preparations—used by individuals worried about bad breath—are somewhat less potent than fresh garlic. Parsley helps eliminate bad breath.

• *Ginger tea* relieves nausea caused by motion sickness, morning sickness, influenza or radiation therapy. In tincture form, ginger is also effective against flatulence and indigestion. It may also be useful for lowering serum cholesterol, although at this point the data are preliminary.

• *Milk thistle* is widely used in Japan to treat liver problems, including hepatitis A, B and C. It contains compounds that promote the flow of bile and stimulate production of new liver cells. Taken in capsule form.

• *Nettle* contains the compounds choline, acetylcholine and histamine. It reduces inflammation, helping to relieve runny nose, watery eyes and other allergy symptoms. It also stimulates the immune system. Studies at the National College of Naturopathic Medicine in Portland, Oregon, demonstrated that two milk thistle capsules a day reduced symptoms of hay fever. Taken as capsules or brewed as a tea.

• *Saw palmetto* contains liposterol, a compound that inhibits action of the male hormone dihydrotestosterone. It's an extremely potent remedy for prostate problems, including frequent urination, groin pain, prostatitis (prostate inflammation) and benign prostatic hypertrophy (prostate enlargement).

• *St. John's Wort* contains an antibacterial oil. It's good for treating stubborn colds or coughs—and possibly flu and other viral infections. Taken as capsules or drops.

Source: Sandra McLanahan, MD, director of the stress-management training program at Dr. Dean Ornish's Preventive Medicine Research Institute in Sausalito, California, and executive medical director of the Integral Health Center and Spa, Buckingham, Virginia.

19

The Shrewd Shopper

Government Auctions...
Great Opportunities

Government auctions are not what they used to be. In the late 1980s and early 1990s, many different federal agencies were flush with confiscated assets—such as real estate, luxury cars and furnishings—and they sold them off to the public.

Today it's harder to find great bargains at government auctions, but they're still out there —if you know where to look.

Key: The best auctions are those that are not heavily promoted and, therefore, have fewer bidders competing.

The hottest auctions now and what to do when attending...

Department of Defense:

Like anyone who has gone on a supermarket shopping spree, the Pentagon often buys more goods than it can use and winds up selling off its surplus.

Much of the surplus is offered in bulk—such as dozens of tires or pairs of boots—and bought by dealers who resell the goods at flea markets.

Amid the piles of merchandise, however, are often individual items, such as stereos, VCRs, used cars and Rolex watches. Since dealers survive on profit margins, which are best generated through bulk purchases, they are not likely to compete with you for these items when the bidding starts.

Defense auctions are usually held at the more than 177 military bases around the US and at another 20 or more locations worldwide. They are generally held every month, but frequency varies with each base, depending on the availability of surplus merchandise. The condition of goods that are sold ranges from scrap to new.

City, county and state auctions:

Every sector of the bureaucracy—from the local police department to the division of motor vehicles, utility companies and state purchasing departments—now auctions off surplus or confiscated merchandise.

Goods range from cars and bicycles to boats and computers. Jewelry and real estate also wind up on the block.

The frequency of these auctions varies with the size of the city or community. For information, call each local branch of the government.

Avoid: Any state or local auction that is publicized in large print or media ads. These will likely be too crowded, and novices routinely overbid, pushing prices up beyond what the items are really worth.

Before you bid:

• *Examine the goods in advance.* The secret is to preview goods that will go on the block. Amateurs neglect the importance of this step, but professionals take great care to inspect auction goods.

• *Write down a set price before attending the auction, and stick to it.* Public auctions are designed to get people excited—and carried away. When they do, prices rise rapidly.

• *Make plans in advance to transport the merchandise from the auction site.* Auctions do little more than let you see the merchandise in advance and then let you bid on the goods. Getting the items home is your problem.

• *Find out what forms of payment the agency accepts.* Though more government auctions accept credit cards, many insist on cash or cashier's checks and will not accept personal checks.

• *Bring your driver's license—and a friend who drives—to car auctions.* You will have to drive away the car you buy.

Guerrilla bidding strategies:

• *Offer a ridiculously low bid at the outset.* This should make other bidders question the value of the merchandise and avoid competing.

Example: One fisherman bid $15 and bought a $55,000 fishing trawler. Other bidders were so busy laughing and remarking to each other that he won.

• *Open by shouting out a higher price than the initial one asked by the auctioneer.* This will unsettle the auctioneer and demonstrate to other bidders that you really want this item.

• *Catch the auctioneer offguard by bidding one-half or one-quarter of what he/she is asking.* This tactic is acceptable but mildly disruptive

and may anger the auctioneer. It will also slow down the bidding by cutting the auctioneer's asking price by half.

Or increase your bids by only $1 or $5 increments—even if the auctioneer is jumping in higher increments.

Be prepared. The auctioneer may ignore or needle you in return, causing you some embarrassment. But he may give in to you, in an effort to generate bidding activity.

Source: Financial author and professional investor George Chelekis, who has attended hundreds of government auctions and purchased everything from cars and rugs to collectibles and army tents. He is the author of *The Official Government Auction Guide,* Crown Publishers, New York.

The Right Way to Examine Diamonds

Diamonds should be examined on a white surface—not the black velvet that jewelers usually use to show them. A white background makes it easier to see the stone's color. Diamonds are best observed under controlled, consistent lighting conditions from the profile-faced-down position on a white background. *Also important:* Examine diamonds by themselves, not in settings. Settings of white gold, yellow gold or platinum can alter the appearance of the true color of the diamonds...and the prongs in a setting can easily hide small inclusions.

Source: Jerry Ehrenwald, GG, ASA, International Gemological Institute, New York.

Spotting a Flawed Diamond

Viewing strategies:

• Examine a diamond against a white background. Slight tints and visible flaws will stand out more easily. If a white background is not available, use the back of a business card ...or ask for a blank piece of white paper.

•View colored gems in three kinds of light…

…under an incandescent (lamp) light.

…in daylight, if possible.

…under fluorescent lights.

The gem's true color may look entirely different in each situation. Examining it under different lighting conditions will give you an idea of what the stone will look like in any light and prevent you from being disappointed after you buy it.

Source: Antoinette Matlins, a professional gemologist and consumer advocate. She is the coauthor of *Jewelry & Gems: The Buying Guide*, Gemstone Press, Woodstock, VT.

Wonderful New Ways to Cut Costs

The penny in one of Benjamin Franklin's most famous sayings has gone up in value. Today, a penny saved is worth more than a penny earned. *Reason:* You pay about 30% in taxes on the pennies you earn. Those you save are all yours—with interest.

Here are some ways to save your pennies that will add up to big bucks…

• *Share tasks, tools and time.* Organize exchanges and bargaining co-ops with friends and neighbors.

Examples: You buy the electric drill, they buy the leaf-blower. You agree to baby-sit in exchange for help with chores. When contracting for services—lawn care, carpet cleaning, window washing, driveway resurfacing—coordinate with neighbors and negotiate a group discount.

• *Stop buying specialty cleaning products and use vinegar.* Replace your $2 to $3 window cleaner, bathroom cleaner, carpet cleaner, drain opener, insect spray and weed killer with a 60 cent bottle of vinegar.

•Clean windows with a mixture of half warm water and half vinegar. When you are done, dry the windows with crumpled newspapers.

•Wash kitchen surfaces with half vinegar, half water to deter ants.

•Use a cup of vinegar per gallon of water on carpet spots, then blot dry.

•Use vinegar to remove bathtub rings and rinse with water.

•Clear drains with a handful of baking soda, followed by a half cup of vinegar, cover, then flush with cold water.

•Spray weeds with a quarter cup of vinegar to one cup water.

•Kill sidewalk or driveway weeds by pouring undiluted vinegar in cracks.

•Add a teaspoon of vinegar per quart to pets' drinking water to help keep away fleas and ticks.

• *Buy store brands.* Supermarkets make a higher profit on their own products, so they are motivated to keep customers happy. Most store brands are of comparable, or even superior quality to name brands. Switching from name brands to store brands can save 30% or more every time you shop.

• *Shop seasonally—year-round.*

•Buy winter holiday supplies (ribbons, ornaments, cards) and toys in January.

•Buy winter clothing, including parkas, rain gear, sweaters, leggings, boots, hats and gloves, as well as leather goods, in February.

•Purchase appliances in March and April.

•Get indoor furnishings in May and June.

•Shop for bathing suits, jewelry and major appliances in July.

•Look for summer clothes, lawn furniture and sporting goods in August.

•Buy lawn and garden equipment in September, which is also the time to put in a pool.

•Purchase school supplies in October.

•Scan the classified ads in November and December for deals from people trying to raise cash before the holidays.

• *Buy furniture wholesale.*

• *Give up "prestige" credit cards.* Most "gold" credit cards charge higher annual fees, so unless yours offers special services that you need, drop it. Avoid "affinity cards" that are supposed to donate a portion of your charges to charity. In most cases, the organization receives little and you pay more for the card. *Better:* Shop for the best credit card deal, send your donation directly and take the tax deduction. Don't forget to ask merchants, especially small ones, for a 5% to 10% discount when you pay cash.

• *Choose healthy food—it's often cheaper.* Buy plain frozen vegetables (when you can't buy fresh). They are cheaper than those with butter or sauces and better for you. Likewise, skim milk is cheaper than whole. Buy legumes for low-cost, low-fat, high-fiber meat substitutes.

Avoid costly weight-loss products such as liquid meals. *Better:* Eat an apple before meals or as a snack instead. The pectin absorbs water in the stomach and makes you feel full, curbing your appetite while providing nutritious fiber. *Also great:* Bake a potato and top with skim mozzarella or yogurt and chives. Potatoes are cheap, nutrient-rich and low in calories.

Source: Dean King, the author of *The Penny Pincher's Almanac, Handbook for Modern Frugality,* Simon & Schuster, New York. Mr. King and his wife, Jessica, are currently working on a cost-cutting guide for at-home entrepreneurs.

Exploitive Casket Charges Can Be Avoided

There is no evidence that any type of casket preserves a body better than a wooden one, but funeral directors can push expensive caskets making such a claim. Shop around. Caskets constitute 40% to 60% of the cost of a funeral. *Buying knowledge:* The 1993 survey by the National Funeral Directors Association revealed these average prices for different types of caskets—wood/$194...steel/$90... bronze/$6,000.

Source: Lee Norrgard, senior investigative analyst, American Association of Retired Persons, 601 E St. NW, Washington, DC 20049.

Dumpster Diving

For radical tightwads in search of a hobby:

Try dumpster diving, particularly behind businesses and older city apartment buildings in affluent neighborhoods, where pickings can be of excellent quality. Carry a duffel bag, flashlight and stick for poking through trash. Wear gloves, heavy shoes and sturdy clothing. Early evenings are best.

Note: Dumpster diving is legal in most towns. (Check with local police beforehand). However, dumpster diving is illegal if the dumpster is located on clearly marked private land, behind a fence or if it is locked. Don't take anything that is outside the dumpster. Don't create litter.

Source: Amy Dacyczyn, the author of *The Tightwad Gazette* and *The Tightwad Gazette II,* published by Villard Books, New York. Subscriptions to *The Tightwad Gazette*— RR1, Box 3570, Leeds, Maine 04263.

Watch the Pennies and The Dollars Take Care Of Themselves

Many of the easiest ways to save money are simply a matter of asking questions and planning ahead. *Here are some of the best...*

• Buy a luxury retirement home at a bargain price by dealing with the Resolution Trust Corporation (RTC). In the aftermath of the savings and loan crisis of the 1980s, the RTC has many resort properties for sale at as much as 50% off the original price. For a list of properties in the location you desire call 800-782-3006. Call the contact person in the listing you receive for more information about the property.

• Don't use a realtor when inspecting a development with model homes. Instead, ask the developer to reduce the purchase price by the portion of the 6% fee that would be paid to the real estate agent or to add the equivalent amount in interior upgrades.

• Before moving, get a binding estimate from the moving company. The actual cost of moving exceeds almost 25% of nonbinding estimates. A binding estimate costs more, but the price is guaranteed.

• Keep life insurance proceeds out of your taxable estate and the taxable estate of your spouse by creating an irrevocable trust that owns the policy. The trust can be devised so your spouse gets money from the trust if he/she needs it. On your spouse's death the assets remaining in the trust go to your children or other beneficiaries. Seek advice from your attorney.

• Buy low-cost, store-brand film from retail chains such as Target and Kmart. Their 35mm film is made by 3M Company and other high-quality manufacturers. *Cost:* 25% less than Kodak or Fuji.

• Buy disposable cameras before leaving home. The same item at a resort or tourist area will be overpriced.

• Call the specific hotel rather than the chain's 800 number to ask about promotional rates.

Example: I found three national-chain hotels that offered weekend specials during the Boston Marathon, but their national headquarters had no information on the bargain packages.

• Save 10% to 50% on condo rentals. Condo International lists weekly—and some nightly—rentals of one- to four-bedroom units at 3,300 resorts. 800-293-2582.

• Save on hotel rates. The Hotel Reservations Network buys up unreserved economy, first-class and deluxe hotel rooms in 20 major US cities, London and Paris and sells them to consumers at discounted rates. There is no fee or service charge. 800-964-6835.

• For low car-rental rates, pick up the local newspaper's Sunday travel section. The best discounts are short-term promotions that aren't in the rental company's computer system. You must quote a code from the ad to qualify for the discount.

• Look into two-tier electricity pricing. In most parts of the country, electricity costs less at night. Run the dishwasher, do the laundry and clean your oven in the evening, rather than during the day, after the rates go down.

• Divorced women can collect on their ex-husband's Social Security at age 62 even if the ex-husband has not stopped working, provided the marriage lasted at least ten years and the divorce has been final for at least two years.

• Cancel your collision coverage for any portion of the year you keep the car in a garage.

Example: You spend the winter in Florida and leave your car up north.

• Consider a corporate credit card. The Ford Citibank credit card allows you to accumulate up to $3,500 in credits over five years towards the purchase of a Ford car. 800-374-7777.

The GM card allows you to accumulate $3,500 over seven years. 800-846-2273.

The GE Rewards card issues savings coupons worth up to $1,000 a year, plus 2% of your charges back in rewards coupons towards purchases from participating companies. 800-437-3927.

• Get discounts on home owner's and car insurance if you have turned 50 or you are retired.

• Shop for discounts on car insurance if you drive less than 7,500 miles a year…if you have completed a defensive driving course…if your car is equipped with antitheft devices or air bags. (The discounts can pay for the options within three years.)

• Use a no-fee credit card. The credit card business has become highly competitive. Banks will often drop their annual fees if you threaten to leave the bank for a competitor bank. Banks will also waive or reduce annual fees if you have a good credit history. *Key:* You must ask.

• Buy refills. Choose products that offer refillable containers—laundry detergents, shampoos, fruit juices—even pens. It helps the environment and saves money.

• Cash in series EE savings bonds if you've been holding them since the late 1940s or early 1950s. Reason: They stop paying interest after 40 years.

Source: Lucy H. Hedrick, a Greenwich, Connecticut time management consultant, and the author of *365 Ways to Save Money,* Hearst Books, New York.

Dollar-Stretching Strategies

Groceries:

• Shop the bottom and top shelves. The middle, eye-level shelves are reserved for higher-priced items.

•Don't buy more meat or produce than you need—it spoils. Just because there are six pork chops or tomatoes in a package doesn't mean you must buy six when you only want three. Ask the butcher or produce clerk to package the amount you need.

•Ask if your supermarket will accept other stores' coupons and advertised specials. Many stores do this, but don't advertise it.

•Don't buy health and beauty products at the supermarket. It's usually cheaper to go to a discount drugstore.

•Be careful at warehouse stores. Many items are lower-priced than at the supermarket, though you must buy large quantities.

Examples: Sugar, flour, milk, eggs, coffee.

But many staples usually cost the same or a few cents more than at the supermarket—peanut butter, jelly, spaghetti sauce, pasta, potatoes, meats.

General shopping:

•When making major purchases, bargain. The more you buy, the more leverage you have.

Example: When remodeling the kitchen, agree to buy all appliances from one dealer for a negotiated discount.

•When paying cash, always ask for a 5% discount. Stores must pay extra when you use a credit card, and may be willing to give you a break if you offer to pay cash.

•Ask about upcoming sales. Large chains' sales are planned well in advance. If one is starting soon, many stores will give you the sale price early, or will refund the difference between the regular and the sale price if you bring in your receipt when the sale starts.

•Ask for extras. If you can't get a break on the price, ask if the owner will "throw in" accessories.

Traveling:

•Write to the Chamber of Commerce for the area you plan to visit. Ask if they have any discount coupons for area attractions or restaurants.

•Stop at the tourist information center. *Special target:* Look for brochures that include discount coupons.

•Ask for a discount if you take an upstairs motel or hotel room. Ground floor rooms are preferred, usually cost more and fill up faster. If you're assigned an upper-story room, ask for a discount for agreeing to take it.

•Ask for free upgrades on rental cars and motel rooms. Sometimes economy class is well booked—with upgraded rooms or cars to spare.

•Cook meals in the motel room, picnic or buy meals at a supermarket deli. Travel with a small hot plate, electric skillet, coffeepot, utensils and paper plates. Eat out as a treat, not at every meal. We save hundreds of dollars per trip by avoiding restaurants, and use the savings to do things.

On the homefront:

•Make inexpensive curtains from twin sheets on sale. They are already hemmed and cheaper.

•Don't buy special skirt or trouser hangers. Use clothespins on a regular hanger.

Source: Ron and Melodie Moore, publishers of *Skinflint News,* 1460 Noell Blvd., Palm Harbor, Florida 34683. Their book is *Smart Cents: Creative Tips & Quips for Living the Skinflint Way,* available through *Skinflint News.*

20

Protecting Yourself

How Not to Be a Victim in Today's Crime-Ridden World

Crime may be rampant today, but there are many practical steps to reduce the chance that you'll ever be a victim. And you can take them without becoming paranoid or living in a fortress.

On the street:

When victims of assault are asked what they wish they'd done differently, they almost always answer I wish I hadn't been caught off guard.

And they're right. Since about 85% of the people confronted on the street end up injured, vigilance is the best protection you have.

In the real world, of course, you can't walk down every street anticipating an assault.

What you can do, however, is to better the odds by making yourself less of a target—and by creating an environment that makes it difficult, not easy, for a criminal. *How to do it...*

• Adopt an assured, confident attitude. That might sound simplistic at first, but it isn't. Professional criminals learn to single out the insecure and to prey on them.

Confident people walk purposefully at a steady, moderate pace. They occasionally look around, but never nervously—or in a way that leads others to think they're lost.

• *Take away the mugger's advantage of time.* By walking with someone else, you send a message to the would-be assailant that it might take more time than anticipated to rob you than he/she is willing to spend. Walking with a dog has the same effect.

Choose a breed of dog that doesn't just look mean but one that criminals know is good protection. *My choices:* Golden retrievers, Labrador retrievers and German shepherds.

The toughest question: If an assailant confronts you, do you run...fight back...or comply? All experts have their own ideas, but in reality there's no perfect answer.

Safest procedure: Don't run or fight back unless all your instincts tell you that your life is in certain peril.

Example: A gun-wielding mugger says he's going to kill and begins herding you into a secluded alley.

Except for imminent peril, it's usually best to comply with a mugger's request. If he is unarmed, however, you may be able to face him down by talking tough, something that street thugs occasionally respect.

Tell him forcefully to leave you alone. Or say you have a friend on the way—or even that you're suffering from a fatal disease. Be aware, however, that it's all a calculated risk. Some assailants may be more violent to victims who talk tough.

In the home:

The biggest mistake in protecting the home is to invest in a system that protects property more efficiently than life.

Example: An elaborate alarm system that alerts police, but not before burglars discover you alone in the house with nowhere to hide.

Best system: Multiple alarms that alert people in the house, police and a security company. If you buy an alarm system, don't forget to turn it on, a mistake that many home owners make before they're robbed.

• *Don't plant concealing shrubbery.* That means large shrubs that give burglars cover for entering a window or door. Alternatively, plant prickly shrubbery, such as holly. (Apart from being a deterrent, it can pick up bits of identifying clothing or blood.)

• *Consider buying a dog among the breeds that criminals fear.*

• *Consider a registered weapon.* Guns in the home aren't recommended, but they may make sense if you cannot move quickly, know how to use a gun and live in a high-crime area.

Best weapon: If you choose a gun, make it a shotgun. Criminals are terrified of them for good reason—even a wild shot from a nearsighted home owner can do terminal damage. If you prefer a pistol, use a simple nonautomatic .38 that's easy for even a groggy person to fire.

Alternatives: A golf club, a length of lead pipe, a pool cue.

• *Set up a safe room.* If you can't escape when your alarm system is breached, a safe room is your best protection. The room, which can be as small as a closet, should be equipped with a solid door that doesn't leak light, an inside lock, a phone with the ringer set on low, internal lighting and a second escape door, if possible. Stock the room with food, water, medications, blankets and a weapon if you want one. If you can't make it out of the house, run to the safe room and call the police.

Alternative: In the event that burglars are able to enter your bedroom, pretend to be asleep. It's about your only hope if the alarm system has failed and you don't have a safe room or a weapon.

Source: Richard A. Fike, a self-defense teacher and the author of *Staying Alive, Your Crime Prevention Guide,* Acropolis South, Sarasota, FL. Mr. Fike is the director of the Madison Combined Martial Arts Association, international headquarters of Sanchi-Ryu Karate, Box 441, Madison, Ohio. He conducts self-defense seminars throughout the country.

Women and Assault

Screaming can often thwart an attack if other people are nearby. *Best:* Specifically worded appeals. *Example:* "Help me! I don't know this man!" *Less helpful:* Wordless screams. When a man and a woman are engaged in an altercation, most onlookers assume it is a domestic dispute and rarely step in.

Source: *The Danger Zone: How You Can Protect Yourself from Rape, Robbery, and Assault* by crime-prevention police officer Patricia Harman, Hazelden Publishing, 15251 Pleasant Valley Rd., Center City, Minnesota 55012.

The Ultimate Guide to Avoiding Violent Crime

The first rule of avoiding violent crime on the street or in the home is to understand this—it can happen to you. These days, no neighborhood is immune.

You can improve your odds that the bad guy won't pick you. How? Make yourself a tough target.

Just as the lion chooses the weakest antelope to pick off from the pack, the bad guy chooses the easiest victim—the weak one, the one who isn't paying attention, the one least likely to resist.

But there's a trick to this game. It's not how tough you really are—it's how tough you look.

Psychologists use the term, "displaying the weapons of aggression." Dogs bare their teeth, cats show their claws and you should show the bad guys you have something to fight back with, too.

Pepper sprays and personal alarms:

Another weapon of aggression you should consider is pepper spray. It's easy to use. Pressing the button sprays a stream of oleoresin capsicum more than 1,000 times more powerful than Tabasco sauce. Unlike tear gas, pepper spray deters even crazed drug users and vicious animals. That's why mail carriers use it.

If you're afraid you wouldn't be able to use pepper spray on someone, consider a personal alarm. Pull out the pin, and it emits a piercing alarm until you reinsert the pin. They're better than whistles, because whistles stop making noise the moment you stop blowing.

People often ask me whether it's a good idea to own a gun. It's always a personal choice, but I don't recommend it. A gun in the home is far more likely to be fired by accident, during a domestic dispute or in a suicide, than used to protect the family from an intruder. Any situation that reaches the point where you need to use a gun has already gone too far. Prevention is much better.

Avoiding sexual assault:

To keep a date from turning into date rape, a woman should resist unwanted sexual advances strongly and clearly, or she runs the risk of being misunderstood.

If a man kisses you against your will, bite down on his lower lip...or grab his scrotum and wring it like a towel.

Teach your children that it's okay to say no to adults—especially in the area of forced affec-tion. Never insist that a child must allow Grandpa to kiss him/her—give him/her the choice. Otherwise, you'll be giving him/her the message that it's okay for adults to force themselves on him/her.

When kids go somewhere together, remind them never to leave one another behind. If they have to run, the faster one should always wait for the slower one.

Bank machine self-defense:

Automatic teller machines (ATMs), are certainly convenient, but they can leave you exposed to muggers.

To minimize risk: Use a drive-through ATM whenever possible. If anyone approaches, drive away. Failing that, stick to an ATM in an enclosed kiosk—one that requires a magnetic card for entry and which is equipped with a security camera. ATM kiosks inside a building or store are safer than stand-alone kiosks.

Avoid ATMs located directly on the street—especially if it's a deserted street at night. If the ATM is next to an alley, where someone can pop out with no warning, that's even worse.

If you must use a street ATM, do so during the day or with a friend—in an area with people around.

On the street:

Don't make things easy on muggers by wearing headphones and listening to loud music. Headphones prevent you from hearing someone coming up behind you—making you an easy target.

Don't flash jewelry on the street, subway or bus either—even if it's fake.

Women: Carry your purse in front of you, not bouncing on your hip.

Men: Keep your wallet in your front pants pocket or in the vest pocket inside your coat. Using the back pants pocket only invites pickpockets.

If you're approached by a suspicious-looking character, cross the street or walk in the middle of the street to maintain your distance. Don't worry about appearing overly cautious.

Helpful: Wrap two $1 bills inside a $5 bill and put them in a money clip. If a robber demands your money, toss the clip in one direction, say "That's all I've got," and run as fast as you can in the other direction.

In your home:

There's no doubt about it—good locks and bright lighting are your best bet against a break-in. Keep shrubs pruned so that they don't hide your windows from neighbors' view.

The best alarm systems are those monitored by the company that sells them. Typically, these alarm systems call the police or fire department when a signal goes off.

You're provided with code numbers to use in case you set it off accidentally...and a "hostage code" to secretly alert police that you're being held.

At the first sound of an intruder, dial 911. If you own a cellular phone, keep the recharger near your bed. That way, if an intruder cuts your phone lines, you can still call 911.

Thwarting carjackers:

A car phone is a great investment in safety. You can use it to dial 911 in any emergency. And just the sight of it is often enough to deter would-be attackers.

Some motorists are now equipping their cars with electronic homing devices that automatically alert the police if their car is stolen—and lead them to it. These devices are effective—but expensive for many people.

Every car is already equipped with the best possible anti-carjacking device—the door locks. Use them even when you're inside the car. It's hard for a carjacker to be successful if he cannot get inside your car.

If someone does get in—get out. No car is worth dying for.

If someone orders you into a car—his or yours—don't do it. Odds are you'll never come back. *Instead:* Run for it. Statistics show that 95% of people who run from an armed kidnapper survive. Most kidnappers won't shoot. The few who do usually miss.

Source: J.J. Bittenbinder, a retired detective with the Chicago Police and a frequent lecturer on personal safety. For a free copy of Det. Bittenbinder's booklet *Tough Target: Guide to Staying Safe,* call Speakers International at 800-345-8255.

How to Keep Your Wealth Safe from a Lawsuit

In today's litigious society anyone can be sued. And once sued...anyone can get hit with a judgment that strips away assets.

But with foresight and nimble footwork, you can shield your assets from predators, including the IRS, former spouses, creditors and legal opportunists.

Step 1: If you think you're at risk of being sued, consult an attorney who specializes in asset protection.

Each state's laws are different...and what is legal and advisable depends on individual facts and circumstances. But here are a half dozen successful judgment-proofing techniques to discuss with your attorney...

• *Go abroad.* The surest protection is to move your assets out of reach of US courts. Look for banks or financial institutions in countries that offer a combination of secrecy...low or no taxes for foreigners...and financial and political stability.

Execute a *durable power of attorney* to make sure someone you trust completely has access to these assets if you become incapacitated.

• *Buy collectibles.* Valuables like antiques, jewelry, gold bullion and stamp and coin collections are more difficult for creditors to attach than assets in financial institutions. One reason is that there need be no public record of them.

• *Buy insurance and annuities.* Every state offers significant protection of insurance policies from creditors. Often protection extends to annuities. Therefore, moving money from bank and brokerage accounts into insurance and annuities will often lawsuit-proof those assets.

Even when states offer total insurance protection, the exemption does not extend to claims from the IRS. But you may be able to protect your holdings from the IRS by having an irrevocable life insurance trust own the insurance policies.

• *Set up a family limited partnership.* A limited partnership is a legal entity to which you can transfer assets. A husband and wife can serve as general partners and control the assets. The assets can be controlled by trusts to provide an additional layer of protection.

• *Use irrevocable trusts.* Irrevocable trusts offer asset protection because the trust owns the assets—not you. Among the types of trusts your attorney may recommend are charitable remainder trusts, spendthrift trusts, insurance trusts and foreign-based trusts.

• *Know your state exemptions.* Every state specifically exempts certain assets from creditors. For example, Texas and Florida give 100% homestead protection, meaning that a home of any value is safe.

The IRS can take assets protected by state law. That is why going offshore or using more complex arrangements is the best protection from the IRS. The harder it is for the IRS to go after your assets, the less likely it will try.

Source: Dr. Arnold S. Goldstein, president, The Garrett Group, consultants to small businesses, 384 Military Trail, Deerfield Beach, Florida 33442. He is a lawyer and the author of *Asset Protection Secrets.*

Check-Forgery Self-Defense

Today's sophisticated color copying machines may be used by a wrongdoer to duplicate blank company checks with a great degree of accuracy. *Defense:* Have checks printed on special "void pantograph" paper. Such checks have an invisible "VOID" imprinted on their face that will become visible on any photocopy of the check.

Source: Michael Mancini, product manager, Standard Register, quoted in *Update*, 20 Railroad Ave., Hackensack, New Jersey 07601.

Terrorist Self-Defense

Survival lesson: Terrorism can be motivated by virtually anything. That means it can strike almost anywhere. Active self-defense is no longer an option—it is a necessity.

Assessing risk:

The first line of defense against terrorism is the gathering and analyzing of intelligence.

Key questions: Just how substantial is the company's risk of terrorism based on your industry? Line of business? The company's location? *To find out…*

• Periodically interview local law enforcement specialists.

• Regularly read all relevant trade publications.

• Stay in close touch with your trade association, local business management group and Chamber of Commerce. They are all potential sources of useful information about risks to businesses in the area and in the industry.

While protecting the business is certainly a top priority, overdoing it can be expensive. It also can hurt employee morale and drive customers away. *To help in accurately measuring your company's risk, use these comparisons…*

• *Low risk:* For a small printing plant in an isolated area—the risk is virtually nil.

• *Medium risk:* For an electronics business in Silicon Valley, the risk goes up. Your business could become a terrorist target…or it could suffer damage from an attack on another company.

• *High risk:* Any business related to the US oil industry is now a likely target given President Clinton's embargo on Iranian oil. Iran has a history of sponsoring anti-US terrorism. The risk is now high to US interests in general…and to oil facilities in particular.

Action plan:

Helpful: If management concludes that the company is a potential target, enlist an outside security specialist to review your conclusions and—more importantly—to help in formulating a program of enhanced security measures.

With the help of the security specialist, determine how visible the company wants to make its increased security precautions.

Specific approach: If you want potential attackers to know the company's facility is protected it is important to take high-visibility steps, such as installing video cameras and alarm systems…hiring uniformed guards…and putting up barriers that will keep traffic away.

Security steps should be more subtle if the company is dealing with the public and doesn't want to scare customers away. Then, additional security guards might be in plain clothes. You might use trees and other landscaping as barriers instead of obvious installations.

The following security steps can be used by any company. Your company should tailor them to fit its specific needs, based on its size, how much it wants to spend and its level of risk...

• *Relocate.* The decision to relocate is a complicated and potentially costly one. Companies in downtown areas must weigh the security benefits of relocating against the many, many repercussions of a move, such as employee turnover...tax considerations...distribution costs.

• *Screen employees.* This is a touchy issue that can lead to legal problems. There's a fine line between screening employees and invading their privacy.

• *Physically reengineer the premises.* Redesigning an existing facility to prevent damage from bomb blasts is extremely difficult and expensive. It is not to be considered unless there is a serious, documented threat to the business.

• *Keep intruders out.* Various devices can be used to channel vehicles and pedestrians to specific entrances, which are then secured.

Adopt additional screening procedures as necessary: Passwords...use of fingerprints or voiceprints...a sniffer to detect explosive compounds.

• *Bolster parking garage security.* The risk is two-fold...users of the garage could become victims of a crime and the building could be car-bombed.

Effective: Assign parking spaces and make sure only authorized cars use them. Use video monitors to survey the garage.

Security plans often overlook the exit from the parking garage. Be sure it doesn't offer unguarded access to the building.

• *Use security guards.* For maximum security, use a mix of uniformed and plainclothes guards. Outside contractors can provide trained guards. But—if you use company employees you have control over how well they are trained.

Important: Plainclothesmen should be trained and dressed so they appear to be employees—not security guards.

• *Use monitoring devices.* Video monitoring —at key locations throughout the facility— helps security people do a better job because it enables them to be in more than one place at a time.

Monitors can be almost invisible if you want to downplay your security measures...highly visible if you want to advertise that you have taken steps to protect the business.

• *Screen mail.* All companies should alert employees to the risk of packaged bombs, and train them in how to handle suspicious packages.

Source: Clark Staten, executive director of the Emergency Response & Research Institute, security consultants and counter-terrorist analysts, Chicago.

Questionable Package... Here's What to Do

Call the police. Do not cut tape, strings or wrapping from any suspicious package that arrives in the mail room or that arrives anywhere in any company that may be a terrorist target. *Warning signs:* No return address...oil stains on the package...an odor of shoe polish or almonds...springiness in the top, bottom or sides.

Source: US Department of Justice Marshals Service.

21

Funtime

Hidden Treasures In Your Attic

An attic, your bureau drawers, flea markets and garage sales are great places to find buried treasures. Long-forgotten cans of tennis balls, fishing flies and even board games may have great value in today's market for collectible pop culture.

Whether you're interested in starting a collection or trying to sell what you own, you must know what you're doing in order to profit.

Junk that is hot now:

Not everything that has dust on it is valuable. Set aside only those items that are in great condition. Then research the market for each item by checking price guides or discussing them with experts in the field.

Nostalgia plays a big role in collecting. Buyers often look for items that remind them of their youth. *Examples:*

•Memorabilia—from movies, TV and comic books or from specific pop-culture icons and TV shows, such as the Beatles, Disney characters, *The Lone Ranger* and *Star Trek.* Collectors are always hungry for new material in these fields.

Hot pop-culture items include old Lionel electric train sets (some now sell for more than $1,000)...vintage Barbie and GI Joe dolls (which may now be worth $200 to $400 each) ...*Soakies,* plastic bubble bath containers from the 1960s (a Huckleberry Hound model could be worth as much as $100)...and any decades-old giveaway from fast-food outlets and gas stations.

Check your local library or bookstore for additional information on buying and selling memorabilia.

•*Old baseball mitts.* Pre-World War II gloves labeled with the name of a hall-of-famer are especially prized. Unlabeled models are valuable if they're in good condition. Look for unusual mitt designs.

Example: A Babe Ruth Home Run Special, circa 1927, recently sold for $2,475. When it was first manufactured by Spalding, it sold for between $6 and $8.

For information: The Glove Collector, 14057 Rolling Hills Lane, Dallas 75240. 214-699-1808.

• *Cans of tennis balls.* The old key-wind cans that contained white tennis balls are selling for between $15 and $300.

Examples: Wilson cans—either full or empty —from the late 1920s and the Pennsylvania brand from the 1930s sell for $300 each.

For information: Past Times, Antique Advertising Association of America, Box 1121, Morton Grove, Illinois 60053. 708-446-0904.

When starting a collection…

• Don't expect to make a killing without a lot of work. The hunt for hot collectibles can be very exciting. But it is almost always a mistake to think that collectibles will pay for your children's college educations or your retirement. Even if you collect entire sets of things, the most you can hope for is a profit of a few thousand dollars.

• Collect items that are salable. Whether you're collecting for fun or for profit, it doesn't hurt to buy those items that are popular with collectors. Then, if you ever need to sell, it won't be difficult. *Strategies…*

• Check the bookstore to see which areas of collecting are covered by new titles. This is a sure sign of interest in a particular category and an indication of a hot market.

• Visit antique shows and flea markets. Look for items that are especially popular with dealers and collectors. It will give you an indication of how easy—or hard—it will be to sell what you own. See what kinds of items are being displayed and which ones command the highest prices. Ask dealers why they are charging particular prices. Their answers will likely help you assess the value of your items.

Note: A fad typically lasts 25 years—building steam during the first 12 years or so.

• Only buy items that are in great condition. *This is a sound strategy for two reasons:*

• Your collection will be more presentable for resale and likely to command the most interest, thus making it even easier to sell.

• Mint-condition items always appreciate faster than those that are marred or tarnished.

Important: The original boxes—particularly those with interesting graphics can double the price of the items.

• Avoid categories that are overhyped. As soon as you see an entire category being promoted in the media for its investment value— beware.

Source: Ralph and Terry Kovel, editors of the monthly newsletters *Kovels on Antiques and Collectibles* and *Kovels' Sports Collectibles,* Box 22900, Beachwood, Ohio 44122. They are also the authors of *Kovels' Antiques and Collectibles Price List 1995* and *Kovels' Guide to Selling, Buying and Fixing Your Antiques and Collectibles*, Crown Trade Paperbacks, 201 E. 50 St., New York 10022.

Where the Best Beaches Are

Twelve of the top 20 beaches in the US are in Florida. *Best beach of all:* Grayton Beach in northwest Florida. Factors in the ratings include water quality, temperature and visual beauty.

Source: Annual rating by coastal geologist Stephen Leatherman, PhD, University of Maryland, College Park.

Guerrilla Gambling

Last year, Americans spent $330 *billion* at casinos…and they left a lot of it behind at the gaming tables.

Casinos win most of the time because they hold a big edge over the average player. They have virtually unlimited bankrolls to reduce players' chances of winning repeatedly over several hours. They also use a variety of psychological strategies to lure customers into careless play—free beverages, loud slot machine jackpots, etc.

How can average players improve their odds of winning? By using guerrilla-gambling strategies that take advantage of casinos when their advantages are minimized, if not eliminated.
Blackjack:

Before sitting down to play, observe the games that use either single decks of cards or two decks combined. Look for ideal opportunities to jump in and play a few hands. You must know "basic" strategy or have a "basic strategy card" (sold in casino stores) to inform you of the correct hit and stand decisions. *Favorite strategies...*

• *Bombing for blackjack.* Stand at the table, and watch the first hand dealt from a new deck. If aces appear, move on to another blackjack table. If no aces appear, enter the game with a bet of two times the minimum.

Reason: Since a higher-than-normal ratio of aces remains in the deck, there is a high probability that someone will wind up with blackjack—an ace and a picture card or a 10. If the dealer gets blackjack, you lose your bet. But if *you* get blackjack, you are paid at three-to-two—a net advantage.

Example: If you bet $100 and are dealt blackjack, you win $250—$150 plus your original wager.

Note: Blackjack bombers should play no more than two consecutive hands at a single-deck table or three hands at a double-deck table. After that, the favorable odds often disappear.

• *Three-round martingale.* In a game that uses four or more decks combined, use what's called a "limited martingale." This strategy involves increasing your wager after a loss.

Begin by betting the minimum allowed at your table, which could range from $1 to $25 or more.

If you win, collect your chips and approach another blackjack table. If you lose, stay for another hand and double the bet.

If you lose the second hand, bet four times the minimum for the next hand. If you lose that hand as well, quit and look for another game.

If you win the second bet, also leave the table.

The odds are quite good that you will come out ahead, since you need to win only one of the three hands. Do not stay for more hands. This is a very dangerous strategy if pursued for too long a period.

Roulette:

In theory, roulette is unbeatable since it's purely a game of chance. But certain roulette *wheels* can be beaten.

Example: The ball may land on certain numbers because of flaws in the wheel's balance or the wood separating the grooves...or the dealer may release the ball in a way that makes certain numbers come up more often.

In guerrilla roulette, you exploit these short-term biases to win.

• *Big-number roulette.* Observe 10 spins of a roulette wheel before placing a bet. Then bet any of the numbers that have won twice. These are your *big numbers*. For the next 37 spins, continue to bet only the number or numbers that have hit the most times.

Example: Over the first 10 spins, you see 12 and 33 each hit twice. On the 23rd spin, you bet both numbers—and see 33 hit a third time. It now becomes your *big number,* and you bet 33 exclusively on the next spin.

Check your stake after 38 spins. This amount of spins is long enough to allow number repetitions but short enough to protect your bankroll if your numbers don't hit. Continue to play another 38 spins only if you could lose every one of them and still walk away with a net profit.

• Sector slicing. Ask the casino for a diagram of the wheel—most are only too happy to supply this—to record the hits. Then log the results of 10 spins, and see if there is a hot sector.

Examples: Four or more hits within six or seven adjacent numbers on the wheel...or six or more hits within nine or 10 adjacent numbers. Then bet on every number in that sector—even those that haven't yet hit—and play for 38 spins.

Caution: Be alert to see old sectors crumble and new ones emerge. If a large sector—nine or more adjacent numbers—fails to produce a profit within 10 spins, either look for a new sector or move to a different wheel.

Slot machines:

The loosest, best-paying machines are not scattered randomly throughout a casino. Guerrilla slots players use a strategy to maximize their return. They play...

• *The highest-denomination machines they can afford.* The highest paybacks are on machines that require five-dollar tokens or higher. Nickel machines return the lowest percentages.

• *Maximum coins per pull.* In most cases, your odds improve by investing the maximum that a given machine allows—usually three or five coins—on each play.

• *In areas where "loose" machines are most likely to be found.* Not all slot machines are created equal. A "tight" machine will pay out only 83% of the money poured into it. A "loose" machine may give players back as much as 99%. Most loose machines are placed outside the casino's coffee shop…near the change booths…in slot aisles or crosswalks…on elevated carousels…at highly visible locations from other slot aisles. That's because when someone wins, the commotion will attract others to play.

Source: Frank Scoblete, publisher of *Chance and Circumstance,* a newsletter of insider information on all aspects of gaming and wagering, Paone Press, Box 610, Lynbrook, New York 11563. He is also the author of *Guerrilla Gambling* and *Break the One-Armed Bandits* both available from Paone Press.

Favorite Historic Inns

• *The Keeper's House.* The 48-foot tower, built in 1907, was used to guide vessels into a once-bustling fishing village on the Isle au Haut in Maine. It was converted into a six-room inn in 1985. To get there, guests take a 45-minute boat ride from Stonington, Maine, where they park their cars. You can spend your days hiking, fishing, biking or just watching the seals and porpoises swim in the waters below. The inn provides guests with picnic lunches. *Nightly rates:* $267.50*/double occupancy. Breakfast, lunch and dinner are provided. Open May 1 through October 31.

Box 26, Lighthouse Point, Isle au Haut, Maine 04645. 207-367-2261.

• *The Inn at Weathersfield* was built in 1795 by a Revolutionary War veteran. Before the Civil War, it was a station along the Underground Railroad. The original four-room farmhouse has been expanded several times over the years, and the inn's 12 rooms are furnished with Early American antiques. Guests can go

*All prices are subject to change.

sleigh riding, cross-country skiing and snowmobiling. *Nightly rates:* $149 to $220*. Breakfast and dinner included. Open all year.

Rte. 106, Box 165, Weathersfield, Vermont 05151. 800-477-4828.

• *L'Auberge Provencale.* Built in 1753 from fieldstones gathered in the area, the inn's interior woodwork was done by Hessian soldiers during the Revolutionary War. The 10 guest rooms have modern conveniences—air-conditioning and individual bathrooms. The interior is decorated in the Revolutionary period style. Guests can enjoy live theater, antiquing and the beautiful vineyards and countryside. *Nightly rates:* $145 to $185*. Breakfast is provided… dinner is available. Open all year, except every other January.

Box 119, White Post, Virginia 22663. 800-638-1702.

• *Guest House Cottages* are on 45-mile-long Whidbey Island in Puget Sound near Seattle. Accessible by a car ferry, the inn dates back to the 1920s. Each of the seven cottages has a different design, from a "gingerbread" house to a carriage house. Each cottage has a Jacuzzi tub. Two towns are just 15 minutes away. Guests can also enjoy hiking, cycling, fishing and whale watching. *Nightly rates:* $135 to $285.* Breakfast is provided. Open all year.

3366 S. Hwy. 525, Greenbank, Washington 98253. 360-678-3115.

• *The Inn at Mitchell House* was built in 1743. It is set on 10 acres overlooking a pond. The six guest rooms and several parlors are preserved in their original splendor. The Eastern Neck Island National Wildlife Refuge is 10 minutes away, and Annapolis Naval Academy is one hour away. Nearby Chestertown dates back to the 18th century. *Also available:* Boating, hunting, swimming, fishing, hiking, horseback riding. *Nightly rates:* $75 to $100*. Breakfast is provided…dinner is available on Fridays and Saturdays. Open all year.

8796 Maryland Pkwy., Chestertown, Maryland 21620. 410-778-6500.

• *Rose Inn* is an Italianate mansion built in 1851. Today it is owned by Sherry Rosemann, a noted interior designer specializing in mid-19th-century architecture and furniture. Set on 20 landscaped acres, Rose Inn is only 10 minutes from Cornell University in upstate New York. *Also available:* Cross-country skiing, sailing, fishing, antiquing. *Nightly rates:* $100 to $250.* Breakfast is provided…dinner is available for $50 per person. Open all year.

Rte. 34 N., Box 6576, Ithaca, New York 14851. 607-533-7905.

• *The Scofield House* was built in 1900 by a wealthy businessman. Today it reflects its original lavish design. Interiors include inlaid floors with intricate borders patterned in cherry, birch, maple, walnut, and red and white oak. The guest rooms—six of them—are equally impressive with fluffy comforters and rose wallpapers. *Nightly rates:* $69 to $180*. Breakfast is provided. Open all year.

908 Michigan St., Box 761, Sturgeon Bay (Door County), Wisconsin 54235. 414-743-7727.

Source: Tim and Deborah Sakach, who are among the leading authorities on historic inns, American Historic Inns Inc., Box 336, Dana Point, California 92629. They are the authors of *Bed & Breakfasts and Country Inns,* available through their company.

How to Have a Special Birthday

White House birthday cards are sent free upon request to people age 80 or over. Cards are also sent for births and 50th wedding anniversaries. Condolence and get-well wishes may also be requested. Send requests four to six weeks prior to the occasion. *For more information:* White House Greetings Office, Rm. 39, 1600 Pennsylvania Ave. NW, Washington, DC 20500.

Stamp Collecting Is More Fun than Ever

• *The US Post Office is now the collector's best friend.* In an effort to increase revenues, the post office has mounted a $25 million ad campaign to get people interested in stamp collecting. Recent issues—like the set of classic Broadway musicals—are both creative and handsomely designed.

• *Collectors have changed their approach for the better—and the cheaper.* We used to collect stamps by country. Our goal was a complete set for a given nation—which was either impossible or extremely expensive, especially for pre-1930 stamps. Most collectors wound up frustrated.

Today we collect by topic. Collections can focus on a profession (medicine, architecture), a famous individual (Columbus, Franklin) or any of dozens of miscellaneous categories (flowers, sports, horses).

Typical flaws: Heavy postal marks…imperfect centering…faded color…missing perforations …less-than-neat placement on an envelope… marks on an uncirculated stamp's original gum (from using an adhesive "hinge" to attach the stamp to an album).

In my experience, these stamps can be just as enjoyable as those stamps that are in mint, uncirculated condition.

For those starting a new collection, it's still possible to buy a bag containing 1,000 circulated stamps for $5. Every now and then a rarity sneaks through.

Recent case: A young boy found a stamp with a waterfall printed upside down. *The error's value:* More than $10,000.

• *Envelopes are now part of the collection.* Twenty years ago, a dealer would invariably pay less for any stamp still attached to its envelope. Collectors would routinely cut out the stamp and soak it off.

Today, however, an original envelope—particularly those mailed before 1940—can significantly enhance a stamp's monetary and historic value.

• *More sources of information and support than ever before.* Scott's Stamp Catalogue is as much the basic tool as it was 30 years ago. *Linn's Stamp News*, a weekly publication that includes a full listing of stamp shows and mail-order offerings, remains the hobby's bible. The American Philatelic Society publishes a monthly journal, as do a number of collector subgroups (the American First-Day Cover Society, the American Topical Association) and associations which narrow the field even further. There are networks for collectors of stamps with biblical subjects…or Vatican City or cats.

Source: Edward Mendlowitz, a CPA and partner in Mendlowitz Weitsen, 646 Highway 18, East Brunswick, New Jersey 08816, and an avid stamp collector for more than 40 years.

Vinyl Records Are Back

Sales of analog vinyl disks—and the equipment to play them—are surging. Some consumers and audio professionals say vinyl provides a sound that is inherently better than the sound of digital CDs because of the way CDs are made and the way CD equipment reproduces sound. *Result:* Vinyl has returned as a boutique market, with some companies reissuing classic and hard-to-find recordings and others manufacturing turntables, cartridges and tonearms.

Source: Michael Fremer, editor, *The Tracking Angle,* an audio newsletter, quoted in *Forbes ASAP,* 60 Fifth Ave., New York 10011.

Reach Out and Touch Someone Via Personal Ads

For people over 50 years old who have lost a longtime partner, whether through death or divorce, one of the best and safest ways to make connections is through personal ads.

If you have already investigated all your friends' suggestions, and decided that the organization route is not for you, then an alternative option is to take out a personal ad.

Twenty or 30 years ago—probably the last time you were interested in dating—turning to the personals was regarded as the last resort of the hopeless. In today's very different, faster-moving and more dangerous society, the level of acceptance of personals is much higher. *Their advantages include…*

• *Efficiency:* With one ad, you can contact many more people than you can meet in months of normal social activity.

• *Safety:* You do not have to supply other people with your full name, address or telephone number until you are confident you want to meet.

• *Convenience:* You are able to sift through the responses at your own pace, free of time pressure and fear of embarrassment.

• *Mutual interest:* When two people are brought together by a personal ad, each one knows the other is interested in finding a long-term partner. This eliminates much of the fumbling, insecurity and embarrassment that occurs when people meet randomly.

Step one:

Decide what kind of person you are seeking, and write an ad tailored to attract the right prospects. Place it in a publication he/she is likely to read.

The ad: Since you are already a mature individual, you know a lot about yourself and your likes and dislikes. You have experience with relationships and have a clear idea of what you are looking for and what you can offer the other person.

Your objective: Write an ad that describes succinctly who you are and what kind of partner you are looking for. Strive to make it interesting enough to attract other people's attention…but not so individualistic or offbeat that they will be afraid to respond.

Where to place your ad: There are three possibilities…

• *Local general-interest newspaper or magazine.* Your ad will find a lot of close-by readers …but many of them will not have much more than geography in common with you.

• *National publication.* This will give your ad a wider circulation and attract responses from more people of the type you seek…but you may have to travel long distances when the time comes to meet them in person.

• *Specialized publication geared to people who share some of your interests.* These may be magazines or newsletters put out by organizations for people with those interests.

If you are strongly involved in a particular activity, this may be your best chance of finding a kindred soul.

Step two:

Filter out the responses to your ad to select those you feel have the potential to mesh well with your personality. Then begin to make telephone contact.

Important: If your ad does not draw any promising replies, go back to the drawing board. Rewrite your ad and/or consider advertising elsewhere. Don't be embarrassed, because the people who read the second ad will not connect it with the first…or know it is your second attempt.

First phone contact: During the first phone call, you need only use your first name. Within about 10 minutes, you should realize if you are not interested and bow out gracefully.

Step three:

If one or two conversations have proved mutually satisfying, the time is right for a face-to-face meeting. Most people meet for the first time for a fairly brief period—usually brunch or lunch—in a public place. That way, each can feel secure that he/she has gotten a correct impression of the other's intentions.

Step four:

Where you go from here is up to you. Good luck!

Source: Martin G. Groder, MD, a psychiatrist and business consultant in Chapel Hill, North Carolina.

Good Golf Resorts For Bad Golfers

• *The Golf Clinic*, Pebble Beach, California, has refreshingly friendly and patient instructors. The Monterey coastline provides spectacular scenery. The three-day/four-night package includes one day each at Pebble Beach, Poppy Hills and Spyglass Hill courses.

Cost: $2,895, double occupancy. Includes breakfast and lunch, but not airfare. 800-321-9401.

• *Sea Pines* on Hilton Head Island, South Carolina, is the home of the *Academy of Beginners Golf.* It offers instructions from golfing regulations to putting and chipping. One of its courses, Harbour Town, is a favorite among

PGA Tour players. Includes four days of instructions—two hours per day. Monday through Friday. Call ahead for available days.

Cost: $200. Airfare and resort accommodations are not included. 800-732-7463.

• *Walt Disney World Resort* in Orlando, Florida, has five great courses with rolling terrain that makes them more interesting than the typical flatlands at most other Florida resorts. There is also a nine-hole course for players who like to walk instead of ride in carts.

Cost: $556 for the two-night "Golf Getaway" for two adults and two children, not including airfare. Baby-sitting services and planned children's activities are available. 407-827-7200.

Source: Robin McMillan is editor-in-chief of Times Mirror Magazine's Sports Publishing Group in New York. He is the author of *365 One-Minute Golf Lessons: Quick & Easy Stroke-Saving Tips*, HarperCollins, 10 E. 53 St., New York 10022.

Today's Trash... Tomorrow's Hot Collectibles

If you need an incentive to clean out that hall closet—consider what you might find. You could turn up a pennant that cost $5 when the Philadelphia Phillies won the World Series in 1980—but fetches $55 at sports memorabilia shows today.

Maybe you're kicking yourself because the baseball cards and Barbie dolls of your childhood got dumped before you knew how valuable they would become.

Don't throw out your kid's McDonald's Happy Meal toys. Put them safely away somewhere—fast-food giveaways are rapidly becoming hot collectibles.

The new rules:

It used to be that something had to be old to have collector value. That's still true for genuine antiques, of course. But these days collectors will pay hundreds of dollars for items less than two decades old.

Reason: Many people got burned in the art boom of the 1980s. They spent a lot of money

Funtime

for things that shot up in value—and then lost it all when the market crashed.

Cheap collectibles may be perfect for the more cautious 1990s. In a tight economy it doesn't cost much to get into as a hobby and the possibilities are endless.

Opportunity: Not everything in your closet today will be worth big bucks in a few years. But chances are that you do have some things stashed away that will be worth money.

Picks for the future:

Here are our guidelines for sorting through what you own—and finding items that collectors someday will pay big for. Generally, only consider things that can meet these five standards…

• *Possible to find*, but not so plentiful that it turns up at every rummage sale.

• *Well-known enough* that it will attract a number of collectors.

• *Priced low enough* that it will be affordable even to novice collectors.

• *Useful, historic* or visually or emotionally appealing.

• *In the best possible condition.*

Our best bets for fairly common household items likely to increase in value—whose prices in some cases already are gaining…

• *1980s high-tech.* There is a lot of interest today in old handheld electronic games, teapots and actual usable high-tech items from the 1980s. *Also:* Things like first-of-a-kind phones, answering machines and computers.

• *Almost anything with a "smiley" face on it.* Those smiley faces showed up everywhere in the early 1970s—on cups, T-shirts, mugs. We're just waiting for the first mug collectors to show up. We figure they'll pay $20 for them.

• *Kid stuff.* Good bet—children's dishes—done in plastic with cartoony drawings on the cup, saucer and plate. Some of the better designers of the 1980s also did doll dishes (the little, bitsy size), that already are showing signs of popularity. Disney items of any kind are going to stay good.

Source: Ralph and Terry Kovel, editors of *Kovels on Antiques and Collectibles*, Box 420347, Palm Beach, Florida. They are also the authors of *Kovels' Antiques & Collectibles Price List 1995*, Crown Publishing, New York.

Great Backyard Games

• *Back-to-back* is always a lot of fun and a lot of laughs.

Supplies for each team: All you need is a beach ball or large, sturdy balloon.

How to play: This relay is done in teams of two. Each pair balances a beach ball or balloon between their bodies without using their hands from the starting point to the finish line. If the ball is dropped, the game leader can help by placing the ball between the partners' bodies again. The ball can be balanced in a variety of ways—back to back, head to head, stomach to stomach, etc. The first team to finish wins.

• *"Board" of Directors* is a relay race played with two or more even-numbered teams. Played with partners.

Supplies for each team: A sheet of cardboard or corrugated paper—about 12 inches by 12 inches—and a tennis ball or an orange.

How to play: At the signal *go*, the first pair on each team picks up their board with the ball on it. They try to walk to a specified spot and back without dropping the ball. If the ball falls, one player picks it up, puts it back on the board and proceeds from there. If there are more than two players on a team, the first pair passes the board and ball to their partners. The first team to have all its members complete the task wins.

• *Sugarless-Gum Bag* is a great game for kids of all ages.

Supplies: One grocery bag, individually wrapped sticks of sugarless gum and one pair of new, heavy gardening gloves per team.

How to play: Two or more teams line up. The first person on each team runs to a designated spot, puts on the gloves and tries to get a piece of gum out of the bag. The person unwraps it, with the gloves on, and places it in his mouth before running back to tag the next player. The first team to finish wins.

Source: Dinah Krenitski, president of DynaGames, 38 Mary Dr., Towaco, New Jersey 07082. She is producer of *DynaGames*, a 28-minute videotape demonstrating 12 games for children that use materials that cost next to nothing and can be played almost anywhere. Vision Video, 2030 Wentz Church Rd., Worcester, Pennsylvania 19490.

316

22

A Smart Education

College Drinking... The Sobering Facts

Binge drinking at college is very common. Nearly 50% of more than 17,500 college students surveyed said they were binge drinkers—consumers of five or more drinks in a row. Frequent binge drinkers were more likely to be injured, sexually harassed or otherwise assaulted.

Source: Henry Wechsler, PhD, department of health and social behavior, Harvard School of Public Health, Boston. His study of students at 140 four-year US colleges was published in *The Journal of the American Medical Association*, 515 N. State St., Chicago 60610.

Music Lessons Boost Intelligence

Fifteen minutes a week of keyboard instruction plus group singing will boost kids' intelligence—especially the spatial reasoning skills needed for high-level math and science. *Theory:* Music lessons strengthen the connections between brain cells. In a study of 33 preschoolers, those given music lessons had a 46% increase in their spatial IQs, compared with a 6% increase in children not given lessons.

Sources: Frances Rauscher, PhD, research psychologist, and Gordon Shaw, PhD, professor of physics, University of California, Irvine. Their eight-month study was presented at a meeting of the American Psychological Association, 750 First St. NE, Washington, DC.

Savings and College Financial Aid

Some people fear that if they save to finance college, they will be penalized—with more financial aid going to someone who did not save at all. *Reality:* Financial aid formulas weigh income more heavily than assets. If you have good income but no savings, you will still be expected to make a substantial contribution to college costs. *Also:* A significant amount of aid is in the form of loans—which have to be repaid. The more cash you save before college, the less debt you and your children will have afterward.

Source: Kalman A. Chany, president of Campus Consultants, Inc., a fee-based firm that assists families in maximizing financial aid eligibility, and the author of *The Princeton Review Student Access Guide to Paying for College*, Random House, New York.

Score Higher on the SAT

Students should mark answers carefully. Check every fifth question to make sure the question number corresponds to the number on the answer sheet. *In the math section:* Calculate the answer first, then mark the answer. Don't waste time considering other choices. *In the verbal section:* Read all the possible answers first before choosing the one you feel is best.

Source: Bart Astor, editor, *College Planning Quarterly,* Box 844, South Orange, New Jersey 07079.

Cheaper College Housing

Cut the cost of college housing by buying an apartment or small house for your child to live in. Hire your child as building manager for free rent and rent the extra bedrooms to other students.

Payoffs: Your mortgage payments give you equity in an asset of value while payments for a dorm or apartment would be lost forever.

Rental income may offset the cost of the property or provide a profit. By treating the property as an income-producing asset, you can deduct related expenses—insurance, maintenance, depreciation and the fee paid to your child to manage the property. You may also be able to deduct trips made to inspect the property—and visit your child at the same time.

Source: Jonathan Pond, president, Financial Planning Information, Inc., 9 Galen St., Watertown, Massachusetts 02172, and the author of *The New Century Family Money Book*, Dell, New York.

How to Win the Tricky Saving-for-College Game

College costs are rising every year, causing parents and grandparents to grow ever more concerned about how to put enough money aside for their children's education.

Many families set up trusts or savings accounts in children's names to hold college funds—often hoping to cut the family tax bill as well. *But families using these strategies face costly traps…*

•Recently enacted increases in the tax rates paid by trusts reduce the tax savings they provide—after paying administrative costs, many trusts now may be providing no savings at all.

•Inappropriately designed savings arrangements may reduce the amount of financial aid a child qualifies to receive—increasing the cost to the family for the child's education.

Here's what you need to know about college savings now…

Common methods:

The simplest and most commonly used method of saving for a child's education is to set up a savings or investment account in a child's name under the Uniform Gifts to Minors Act (UGMA). These accounts are actively marketed by banks and brokerage firms.

How they work: You set up a UGMA account for your child with a bank or broker and act as the account trustee, controlling investments. Account income is taxed to the child.

•If the child is older than age 13, the first $22,750 of income is taxed at the 15% rate. That income would be taxed at a higher rate if taxed to you. The benefit of the 15% bracket is that it lowers the family's tax bill overall.

•If the child is younger than 14, the "kiddie tax" applies, so account income is taxed at your tax rate.

Self-defense: You can minimize taxes by investing in tax-exempt bonds or appreciating stocks, cashing them in for income-producing assets after the child reaches age 14.

But UGMA accounts have major drawbacks that sometimes are not fully explained by those who market them.

Beware: Upon reaching the age of legal majority—18 in most states—the child receives full legal ownership of the UGMA funds. And the child can use the funds in any way that he/she wishes. A child who then decides to spend the money on something other than school has the full legal right to do so.

Beware: When a college financial aid office determines how much aid a student is qualified to receive, the first thing it looks at is the child's own wealth. If you've shifted a large amount of assets into a child's name, the amount of tuition aid the child receives may be dramatically reduced, a loss that may far outweigh taxes saved through the UGMA account.

2503(c) trusts:

Because of the drawbacks of UGMA accounts, many families have set up more restrictive 2503(c) trusts over which parents can exert more control. *The major advantages…*

•Such trusts are not subject to the "kiddie tax" so even children younger than 14 can benefit from lower tax rates.

•Children have less chance to withdraw funds from such a trust. A child must be given the opportunity to withdraw funds at the age of 21—but withdrawals may be restricted to a limited "window" of time, such as 30 or 60 days. Funds not withdrawn within that period can remain subject to trust terms indefinitely.

…but these trusts have drawbacks too:

•The 1993 Tax Act applies higher top tax rates to all trusts, including 2503(c) trusts, at lower income amounts.

Result: The tax-saving potential of these trusts has been greatly reduced. They are likely to save only a few hundred dollars annually.

•Tax returns and other paperwork must be filed for each trust each year—the cost of which may offset tax savings.

•The problem remains that the child has the legal right to withdraw all funds at age 21 and spend the funds in a manner that may not correspond with your wishes.

Conclusion: For college-saving purposes, a 2503(c) trust may not provide the benefit you desire. If you set up such a trust before the tax rates were increased, review it now.

Doing it right:

It is still possible to save for a child's college education while cutting the family's tax bill and maximizing eligibility for college aid. *Here's how:*

•*Maximize use of retirement accounts.* Most college financial aid formulas either do not count your retirement account funds as being available to pay tuition or include only a small portion. Thus, by saving money in an Individual Retirement Account, Keogh plan, Simplified Employee Pension (SEP) plan, or 401(k) account—instead of a normal, taxable savings or investment account—you may increase the amount of college financial aid a child qualifies to receive.

In addition, you will receive the tax benefits of a contribution deduction and tax deferral on investment earnings that compound within the retirement account.

Opportunity: Many 401(k) plans and Keogh plans let plan participants borrow against their accounts on a tax-free basis. Thus, these accounts can serve as a tax-favored source of college funds.

When you save for college through a 401(k) or Keogh with borrowing rights, you get much larger tax benefits than from a UGMA account or 2503(c) trust, and keep full control over the college funds.

•*Save in your own name.* After maximizing retirement plan contributions, keep any additional college savings invested in your own name. If you wish to cut taxes on investment earnings, put the money in tax-favored investments such as appreciating stocks, tax-exempt bonds, or variable annuities.

By keeping money in your own name, you keep full control over it and avoid reducing a child's eligibility for aid that would result if the child held assets in his/her name.

Grandparents also should avoid making well-intentioned gifts to children that reduce their eligibility for financial aid by increasing their wealth.

Better: Set aside funds to help a grandchild pay for college but keep the money in your own name. When the child enrolls in school make a direct payment to the school for the child's tuition. A special provision of the Tax Code exempts such payments from gift tax.

• *"Crummey" trust.* This is a trust used to cut future estate taxes while shifting funds to a child in a way that prevents the child from obtaining premature control over them.

How: A parent or grandparent with sufficient assets to be subject to estate tax—$600,000 for an individual or $1.2 million for a married couple—makes yearly gifts to a trust set up for a child. Use the annual $10,000 gift tax exclusion ($20,000 when the gift is made by a married couple).

The trust allows the child to withdraw each gift within a "window" of 30 to 60 days after the gift is made. Funds not withdrawn remain subject to the trust's terms for an extended period —such as until the child reaches age 35.

Self-defense: Tell the child that if he/she prematurely withdraws a gift, he won't get another. You prevent the child from taking premature control of trust assets. Only the current year is at risk.

The trustee of a Crummey trust may be given sole authority to determine how trust funds will be spent on behalf of a child. Because a child who doesn't control trust assets may be deemed not to own them, a Crummey trust may avoid reducing a child's eligibility for financial aid even if the trustee does spend money on school costs—although the details of state law and specific aid formulas will have an impact here.

But the family is sure to benefit by reducing future estate tax bills.

What to do: Examine college financial aid formulas as well as your tax situation when forming college savings strategies.

If you are currently using a trust arrangement that was set up before the recent tax rate hikes were enacted, or are planning to set up a new trust, be sure that you get advice of a tax expert.

Source: David S. Rhine, partner BDO Seidman, 330 Madison Ave. New York 10017.

College Financing Mistake

Putting college savings in a child's name is a mistake. Reason: Standard college tuition aid formulas consider 35% of a child's total assets to be available to pay tuition…compared with only 6% of a parent's total assets. So putting assets in a child's name can reduce—or eliminate—his/her eligibility for tuition aid. Better: Keep tuition savings in your own name. If you've already put money in a child's name, consider transferring it back to yourself or to another trusted family member—through a gift —before applying for tuition aid. Annual gifts of up to $10,000 each to as many separate recipients as desired can be made free of gift tax.

Source: David Jaffe, founder of the New York consulting firm College Pursuit and Associates and the author of *The New College Financial Aid System: Making It Work for You*, Council Oak Books, Tulsa.

Grandparents Can Help With College Costs

Grandparents who want to help out with college costs can get a special tax break. When payments are made directly to the university for the child's education, the amounts are not subject to gift tax.

Source: David S. Rhine, tax partner, BDO Seidman, 330 Madison Ave., New York 10017.

23

Personally Speaking

Personally Speaking: 1996…and Beyond
Edith Weiner, Weiner Edrich, Brown, Inc.

Your personal life—encompassing family relationships, mental and emotional health, and your relationship with your community—is for everyone (except perhaps hard core workaholics) more important to overall wellbeing than success at work.

And many of the norms surrounding personal and social life are changing dramatically…

More and more people in their 20s and 30s are living at home with their parents. Recent estimates suggest that one-third of men in their 20s now live with their parents. And, one byproduct of the divorce boom of the past 20 years is that more people in their 30s are moving back in with their parents.

This is changing the nature of American home life. Parents have less privacy and their grown children have less, too. This puts new emphasis on the importance of family—a trend that also has potentially significant implications for marketers.

Grandparents are playing increasingly significant roles in the child-rearing and financial affairs of their children. The parents of the Baby Boomers, now in their 60s and 70s, lived their greatest wealth-building years during the boom time immediately following World War II.

Result: These older Americans have enormous nest eggs. Because their children are notorious spendthrifts, often caught with no savings at times of great need, the grandparents' generation is increasingly called on for financial assistance.

The older generation is therefore a huge market for financial planning services.

Menopause is becoming a major social issue. The huge population of female Baby Boomers is poised to move into its late 40s and early 50s in the next decade.

Implication: A major sector of the American workforce—the female working population entering mid-life—is nearing the important biological period marked by menopause. The dramatic hormonal changes and myriad physiological symptoms caused by menopause may change behavior and relationships in the workplace in coming years.

The same can be said of men. Male menopause (a gradual diminishing of male hormone over many years)—while less physically and emotionally distressing—does cause many men to mellow and become less aggressive in both their home life and work life.

Time is getting tighter and time management is becoming increasingly important. The by-now typical two-income American family is a portrait of hyperactivity and stress. Running from home to the day care center, to the office, to a late dinner at home and non-stop errand-running and children's activities on the weekends has put an enormous strain on the American middle class.

The only way for people to get a grip on their lives and prevent stress from overwhelming them is to plan their time better. Make lists! Whatever it is, write it down! Much of our mental stress comes from trying to *remember* all we need to do. If everything is written down, there's less chance of this happening.

The same applies in the office. There are wonderful computer programs to help super-busy business people organize their time. And again, there's nothing as effective as the trusty *To-do List!*

There is a lot more depression in American society today. Or, at least, depression is more widely recognized today. And depression can be a major impediment to individual effectiveness. Depressed people have a hard time learning. And difficulty in learning in today's culture is a major handicap. If depression is a problem for you, consult your doctor. There are wonderful pharmacological antidotes for depression.

Overcome Premature Ejaculation

Premature ejaculation can now be overcome with clomipramine (Anafranil)—a drug long

used to treat depression and obsessive-compulsive disorder. A dose of 50 milligrams (mg) increased time before ejaculation from an average of 81 to 409 seconds. At 25 mg, ejaculation was delayed to an average of 202 seconds. *Side effects:* Dry mouth and constipation.

Source: Stanley Althof, PhD, psychologist in sexual disorders, Case Western Reserve University, Cleveland. His study of 15 monogamous couples 21 to 65 years of age was presented at a meeting of the American Urological Association, 1120 N. Charles St., Baltimore 21202.

The New Female Condom Explained

It's just as effective as the diaphragm or cervical cap at preventing pregnancy. Along with the conventional condom, it's the only form of birth control capable of preventing sexually transmitted diseases. A thin plastic "baggie" inserted into the vagina prior to intercourse, the female condom looks a little odd. But its loose fit and ability to transmit heat afford better sensitivity than the conventional condom—for both partners. And there's no danger of the condom slipping off if the man loses his erection. *More:* Some people are allergic to the latex used in most conventional condoms. The female condom is nonallergenic.

Source: James Trussell, MD, director, office of population research, Princeton University, Princeton, New Jersey.

Male Infertility and Blood Pressure Drug Trap

Blood pressure drugs are an often-overlooked cause of male infertility. The drugs—calcium channel blockers—keep sperm from maturing properly. But because the drugs do not alter sperm count, appearance or swimming ability, the actual cause of a patient's fertility problems may go undiagnosed. *Self-defense:* Men taking channel blockers who want to have children should consider stopping their medication or using an alternative drug, with their doctor's permission. *Turnabout:* With further research and development, calcium channel blockers could become an effective male contraceptive.

Source: Susan Benoff, PhD, laboratory director, North Shore University Hospital, Manhasset, New York.

Flatulence...
Everything You Always
Wanted to Know

Flatulence—also known as passing gas, farting, breaking wind—is a fact of life...although one that we rarely talk about after adolescence.

At one time, passing gas was socially acceptable—even fashionable. Now, of course, Americans tend to regard flatulence as an embarrassment. But that doesn't mean we're not curious. Flatulence expert Dr. Terry Bolin explains the medical aspects of intestinal gas...

• *What is intestinal gas made of?* Intestinal gas contains nitrogen—from air inadvertently swallowed at mealtime—as well as hydrogen, carbon dioxide, methane and other gases generated by the fermentation of undigested food in the intestinal tract. Fermentation is the process by which intestinal bacteria break down undigested food.

• *How many times a day does a normal person experience flatulence?* In a recent survey, 120 healthy men and women monitored their flatulence for three days. On average, the men passed gas 12 times daily, the women seven times. But frequency varied widely, from three all the way to 40 times a day.

In general, the more air you swallow while chewing, the more gas you'll have. But the single biggest factor in determining flatulence levels is diet.

• *Which foods produce the most gas?* Any food that is rich in fiber promotes gas—fruits, vegetables, beans, whole-grain cereals. Of course, high-fiber diets are considered healthful because they prevent constipation and reduce the risk of certain cancers. Better to tolerate

more flatulence than to raise your risk of serious health problems.

It should be reassuring to know that flatulence is generally a sign of a healthful diet.

Certain sugars, including fructose (found in fruit juices and soft drinks) and sorbitol (the sweetener used in "sugarless" gum), are fermented in the large intestine to produce gas. So consumption of these foods also contributes to flatulence.

"Lactose-intolerant" individuals are especially prone to gas if they eat dairy products. *Reason:* Their bodies lack lactase, the enzyme needed to digest milk sugar (lactose). Most non-whites and many whites of Mediterranean ancestry are lactose-intolerant.

• *Does psychological stress play a role in flatulence?* Absolutely. Stress can cause flatulence in three ways. First, it causes people to swallow more air. Second, it causes food to pass too rapidly through the digestive system...so more of it remains undigested (and available for fermentation) when it reaches the large intestine. Finally, stress-induced chemical changes in the intestine can cause proliferation of hydrogen-producing bacteria—which generate a great deal of gas.

• *Why does some intestinal gas smell so bad?* Ninety-nine percent of intestinal gas is odorless. The remaining 1% consists of strong-smelling sulfur compounds—created when you eat meats, garlic, onions, cabbage, broccoli and certain exotic spices such as asafoetida (a pungent herb akin to fennel) and dried shrimp paste.

Dried fruits, many wines and certain other foods contain sulfur-containing preservatives. These foods tend to give rise to particularly smelly gas.

Men tend to have stronger-smelling flatulence than women—although the reasons for this are unclear.

• *What can I do to have less gas?* One obvious way to have less gas is to cut down on fiber-rich foods. But because of the health benefits of such a diet, that's not a good idea.

If you're lactose-intolerant, eliminating dairy from your diet will reduce flatulence. *Alternative:* Use Lactaid drops or tablets and/or reduced-lactose milk products.

• *Are anti-gas preparations effective?* If you're troubled by excessive flatulence, evidence suggests that over-the-counter remedies containing charcoal or simethicone will help reduce symptoms of bloating and abdominal cramps.

• *What about cooking techniques?* Cooking can make a big difference. Soaking beans overnight and discarding the water reduces levels of gas-causing compounds.

Broccoli, cabbage, cauliflower, turnips and brussels sprouts should be cooked as briefly as possible—to reduce the formation of potent gas-producing sulfur compounds.

There's a Mediterranean folk custom of adding mustard seed when cooking cabbage and legumes, to reduce gas. It can't hurt, although there's no solid evidence that it helps, either.

• *Is it harmful to "hold flatulence in"?* No. Doing so may be uncomfortable, but it's not harmful. If gas is held in the large intestine long enough, much of it will simply be reabsorbed into the body.

• *Is flatulence ever a sign of disease?* Particularly malodorous flatulence is occasionally the result of bleeding in the digestive tract...or of pancreatic disorders that interrupt the digestion of proteins. But in most cases, how much gas you have and how it smells is simply a reflection of your diet.

However, any sudden change in bowel habits—including a change in flatulence levels or odor—should be brought to your doctor's attention.

Source: Terry Bolin, MD, associate professor of medicine at the University of New South Wales, Kensington, New South Wales, Australia. He is the coauthor of *Wind Breaks*, Bantam Books, New York.

Prostate Cancer Explained

Prostate cancer is the second-leading cause of cancer death in men (after lung cancer). It kills an estimated 38,000 men a year.

Experts disagree on how to fight the disease. Should men take the blood test to detect pros-

tate cancer? And how should they treat the cancer if it's detected? Gerald Chodak, MD, clears up the confusion...

What causes prostate cancer? We don't yet know the precise causes, but we have identified several factors that put men at increased risk...

• Being African-American.

• Having a father, grandfather or uncle who had the disease.

• Eating a diet high in fat, especially animal fat.

• Possibly infrequent sexual activity.

Exposure to sunlight seems to help prevent prostate cancer, although the reason for this protective effect is unknown. But it's possible to get prostate cancer even in the absence of these risk factors. Any man can get prostate cancer.

What's the best way to detect prostate cancer? In the past few years, doctors have begun to rely on the prostate-specific antigen (PSA) test. This test measures the blood level of PSA, a protein released in microscopic amounts by the prostate gland. The digital rectal exam is also an important diagnostic tool.

But I've heard that the PSA test isn't always accurate. That's true. A high PSA reading may be a sign of cancer. But high readings sometimes occur in men who are cancer-free—causing needless alarm and the expense of additional tests.

Even if prostate cancer is accurately detected, it may grow so slowly that the man dies of an unrelated ailment long before the cancer has a chance to harm him.

What's your view of the PSA test? I tell my patients that if their desire to minimize their risk of prostate cancer outweighs their concern about being subjected to possibly unnecessary, possibly harmful medical care, then they should get tested. You can discuss the matter with your own doctor, but ultimately it's your decision.

What role does a man's age play in determining whether he should be tested? For men younger than 50, there's not much to be gained by getting tested. *Reason:* Prostate cancer is very rare in men that young. If you have a family history of the disease or if you're African-American, however, you might benefit from getting the test before age 50. That's something to discuss with your doctor.

If you are older than 70, or if other ailments have cut your life expectancy to 10 years or less, odds are you won't benefit much from the test, either. Even if you did have prostate cancer, you'd probably die of another cause. There would be no reason to treat the cancer.

Men between the ages of 50 and 70 are most likely to benefit from PSA testing. Men at the lower end of that age range are especially likely to benefit.

What do the test results mean? The traditional view has been that any PSA level over 4.0 suggests trouble. But recent evidence suggests that numbers well below 4.0 might be risky for younger men…while higher numbers might be normal in elderly men.

New standard: For a 40-year-old man, a PSA above 2.5 is now considered abnormal. But among 60-year-olds, a reading as high as 6.5 might be normal.

What if cancer is found? The decision about treatment is about trade-offs. The older the patient and the shorter his life expectancy, the smaller a chance of benefitting from aggressive treatment. But at any age, some of the treated men will probably benefit. The question is whether the benefit is worth the risk.

For younger men who are otherwise healthy, the benefits of treatment outweigh the risks. If the cancer were to remain untreated, your risk of dying of prostate cancer in the next 20 years would be about 60%.

What's the best treatment for prostate cancer? Complete surgical removal of the prostate (a procedure called radical prostatectomy) offers the best chance for a cure. But surgery has drawbacks. Recent studies of Medicare patients have shown that up to 70% of men experience impotence following surgery. Of course, many older men are already impotent due to other diseases.

Good news: It's often possible to remove the prostate without injuring the nerves to the penis. Ask your surgeon if you're a candidate for nerve-sparing surgery.

About 18% of men will experience at least minor incontinence after surgery. But only 2%

to 4% say that post-surgical incontinence is a serious problem.

What about radiation therapy? Radiation is roughly comparable to surgery in terms of its ability to prolong life. And radiation controls the cancer while avoiding some of the complications of surgery.

Problem: For at least two years following the treatment, it's hard to tell whether radiation therapy has worked. In cases where radiation therapy does not work, it becomes very difficult to find a cure. And when incontinence and impotence occur following radiation, they're often harder to treat than the same problems caused by surgery.

Bottom line: Either surgery or radiation is a reasonable alternative, depending on your own preferences.

I read that it's possible to treat prostate cancer with radioactive "seeds." Is that effective? Studies of radioactive pellets have been inconclusive. Some suggest that the pellets are effective, others suggest that they're not. For this reason, I don't recommend them. We'll have to wait several years before we know the results of current tests.

Source: Gerald W. Chodak, MD, professor of surgery at the University of Chicago Hospitals, and director of the prostate and urology center at the Louis A. Weiss Memorial Hospital in Chicago.

Sperm Count Decline On the Rise

The decline in sperm counts, which has been reported in the media following several studies worldwide, is real. *Possible factor:* Increased exposure to estrogen and estrogen-like substances, which inhibit testosterone production. Until about 15 years ago, estrogen-like substances were given to beef cattle. Estrogen in urine of women on birth control pills could be contaminating the water supply. Estrogenic substances are by-products of gasoline combustion. Soy-based foods contain weak estrogens. Exposure to toxic chemicals, such as pesticides, may also be a factor. *Lifestyle factors may in-*

clude: Having children later—sperm count declines with age…sitting too much, which causes testicles to get too warm…regular use of steam rooms and saunas…obesity…use of cigarettes, alcohol or marijuana…varicose veins in the scrotum (varicoceles). *Important:* There is little evidence that fertility is declining. Increased awareness of infertility may, though, make it seem so.

Source: Marc Goldstein, MD, professor of urology and director, Center for Male Reproductive Medicine & Microsurgery, New York Hospital–Cornell Medical Center, New York.

Recurrent Vaginal Infection Self-Defense

Your partner should be examined by a doctor. *Reason:* Although men don't usually suffer symptoms of yeast infections, they can harbor the fungus that causes the infection under the foreskin of the penis and reinfect their partners.

Source: Michael Spence, MD, director of Community Health, Medical College of Pennsylvania and Hahnemann University, Philadelphia.

More Facts About Sex

Men and women want sex for different reasons at different points in their lives. In order to establish his own identity, a young boy separates emotionally from his mother—thus, his early relationships keep women distant. The maturing process enables men to have more loving and connected sex. Young girls are always connected with mother, and therefore, the maturing process for a woman is to learn more "separate," freer sexuality. *As teenagers:*

Boys have sex for pure pleasure, while girls often are motivated by affection. *Ages 21 to 35:* Men still yearn for physical pleasure, while love remains the prime motivation for women. *After age 35:* Women are now free to seek sexual pleasure, while men are more open to the love and intimacy that comes with sex.

Source: Dagmar O'Connor, PhD, psychologist and sex therapist in private practice in New York. She is the author of *How to Make Love to the Same Person for the Rest of Your Life and Still Love It,* a book and video set from Dag Media Corporation, 57 W. 58 St., New York 10019.

Birth Control Pill Myth

In a recent study of 166,755 women, those who used oral contraceptives were at no greater risk of premature death than those who'd never taken the Pill. And risk of death did not increase in relation to the length of time they were on the Pill.

Source: G.A. Colditz, MD, associate professor of medicine, Brigham and Women's Hospital and Harvard Medical School, both in Boston.

Breast Implants

Silicone breast implants can cause a range of painful and debilitating ailments, despite two highly publicized studies that contended otherwise. One of the studies was funded by former manufacturers of implants. The other, funded by a branch of the American Society of Plastic and Reconstructive Surgeons, looked at connective tissue illnesses such as scleroderma and rheumatoid arthritis—not the problems said to be caused by implants.

Source: Norman D. Anderson, MD, associate professor of medicine and surgery, Johns Hopkins University, Baltimore, and former scientific adviser to the FDA.

24

The Entrepreneur

Interesting Job Opportunities Overseas

Working overseas lets you travel, lead a life-style you won't find at home and, in most cases, pay lower taxes. Working overseas is great early in life—or as the setting for a second career.

More advantages: Low-cost health care and housing that some firms give to overseas employees.

If you're hired overseas by an American company, you may not be paid as much as those transferred from home. But you'll often wind up with more attractive perks.

Example: A six-week paid vacation in many European countries.

The cautious approach:

Today, finding a job overseas is easier than ever, thanks to a burgeoning number of international companies that want to hire Americans. Unfortunately, however, those who want to work abroad often fail to land a job because they:

• Don't target specific companies where their skills are needed.

• Fall prey to agencies and advertisers that purport to sell access to foreign jobs.

Example: Some agencies charge big fees for nothing more than a copy of the want-ad pages from overseas newspapers.

Rule of thumb: Don't pay an up-front fee without knowing precisely what you're getting. That rarely includes a job offer unless the agency is actually in the business of recruiting Americans for overseas positions.

A wide search:

Just as you would look for a position in the US, start an overseas job search by targeting companies that need your skills.

Overseas employers are especially eager to hire Americans with experience in telecommunications, financial services, health care, engineering, computers and consumer marketing.

Teachers are very much in demand by international and nonprofit organizations.

Fluency in the local language is always a plus, but it's usually not an absolute requirement, especially if you have a skill that an employer needs. Many companies pay for language instruction once they hire you.

Growth areas:

•The Pacific Rim, including Hong Kong, Singapore and Taiwan.

•South America.

•Western Europe, provided the European Community's unification plans result in the anticipated business growth.

•Mexico and Canada, as a result of the recent free trade agreement between them and the United States.

In the next few years, the greatest job opportunities for Americans are expected to open up in Russia, China and the former East Bloc countries.

Prospective employers:

•Scan periodicals that list job openings abroad.

•Visit countries where you hope to work one day.

Source: Edward W. Knappman, the coeditor of *American Jobs Abroad,* a book that lists more than 900 businesses, international organizations and nonprofit corporations that hire Americans for overseas jobs, Gale Research, Inc., Detroit.

Greeting Cards Open Doors

A copy machine salesman doubled his commissions when he began to send humorous greeting cards to request appointments. The hand-addressed cards always made it past secretaries, and many prospects wanted to meet him just to compliment his creativity. Three years ago, he began to publish his own line of business greeting cards, including thank-you, sales promotion and birthday cards, that he markets to large sales forces and trade show contacts. *Result:* The products virtually sell themselves, since recipients of the cards experience firsthand how well they work.

Source: Randy Rosler, president, IntroKnocks, New York, quoted in *Crain's Small Business,* 220 E. 42 St., New York 10017.

How to Buy a Franchise

There are two ways to become your own boss. You can either start your own business… or you can buy a "piece" of someone else's.

The second strategy is called franchising. There are about 650,000 owner-operated franchise units in the US, ranging from fast-food restaurants to educational services. Franchises make up 35% of the nation's total retail sales.

While buying a franchise may require less experience and knowledge than starting your own business, it still demands the same drive and commitment…and there are just as many opportunities to make mistakes.

Finding a healthy franchise:

Some franchises are much better than others …and some are much worse. Most people who become franchise owners think only of the money-making possibilities—not of the dangers and pitfalls.

Helpful: Before becoming a franchise owner, read the *Uniform Franchise Offering Circular (UFOC).* The franchise company is legally obligated to give you the UFOC at least 10 business days before you sign the franchise contract. Surprisingly, most franchise buyers never read this document carefully or even consult a lawyer.

Franchise contracts have specific territory rights…quality controls…performance obligations…and tough termination clauses.

Review the UFOC with a franchise attorney to identify the negotiable areas. Ask your accountant to gauge the company's financial strength to make sure it has the resources to help you succeed.

The UFOC provides 20 categories of information about the company and its executives. The categories include background of management…information on lawsuits or bankruptcies…and details on any deals, such as discounts on franchise fees and financial interests in suppliers.

Contract red flags: Numerous recent lawsuits …very few written obligations for the company …many obligations for the franchise buyer… no franchise fee refunds…no franchisee rights to end the contract.

Talk to between five and 10 of the company's current franchise owners to find out if the company is dedicated to helping them succeed. Franchise owners' names are listed on the back of the UFOC.

Healthy signs: Current franchise owners say they're meeting or exceeding revenue and profit projections…have numerous two-way communications…have an active Franchisee Advisory Council (FAC) with decision-making power…receive help promptly when they ask for it…and receive new marketing programs and products frequently.

Bad signs: Franchise owners complain about sales and profits…tell horror stories about lack of support from the company…know of other owners who have failed…express negative attitudes toward the franchisor. If you find more than one or two out of 10 or 20 franchise owners have had bad experiences, be careful about your choice.

Check the UFOC for the annual turnover rate. Only about 5% of franchise owners fail outright, but many leave the business for a variety of reasons. An annual turnover rate of 3% or less is outstanding…between 3% and 5% is satisfactory…more than 5% signals trouble.

Making the deal:

Most people choose to handle the research and dealing involved in buying a franchise themselves, out of ignorance.

Better: Have an experienced accountant review the franchisor's financial reports, which must be placed at the back of the UFOC. If the reports are outdated, call the company for interim reports.

Good news: There are no secrets to the numbers. Any good CPA can figure them out.

A franchise lawyer—not a regular attorney—should review the fine print of your franchise agreement. To find a qualified franchise attorney in your area, consult Franchise Update's *Directory of Franchise Attorneys, 1996 Edition* (Box 20547, San Jose 95160-0547, 800-289-4232).

Have your lawyer negotiate any onerous provisions of the franchise agreement. Be prepared to find that, because the franchise contract applies to many people, you have little leeway on major issues, such as franchise fees and quality standards—but you have room on other issues.

Examples: You can try to eliminate some ancillary fees, like additional training costs…you may be able to defer royalty fees until you reach a certain sales level…you may be able to defer some advertising fees until a certain number of franchises open in your area…and you might water down default or termination clauses.

Most agreements allow franchise companies to terminate a contract with just 30 days' notice for a variety of franchisee transgressions, such as nonpayment of royalties or failure to meet quality standards. Most franchisees can't cancel an agreement unless the company commits a gross violation, such as filing for bankruptcy or being found guilty of a felony.

What it takes to succeed:

Owning a franchise is not like being an employee. At the start, the work is a lot more demanding. To make the business take off, you may have to be willing to put in six 10- or 12-hour days per week for several years. After that, you can expect to work fairly normal hours.

Many corporate refugees aren't aware that they—and not someone from the franchisor—have to pick up the slack if anything goes wrong.

Examples: If the bathrooms have to be cleaned and there's no one there to do it, it's your job. If an important employee calls in sick or makes a last-minute decision to go to the prom, you may have to work from 8 AM to midnight.

You also have to be willing to follow the franchise company's guidelines, even if you disagree with its latest marketing efforts. Extremely opinionated or stubborn people may not enjoy being franchisees. Even a successful franchise may not turn a quick profit, so don't expect a windfall overnight. Ideally, you should have enough cash in the bank to carry you for six to 12 months if the early stages are rough. Budget for unexpected costs.

Examples: You may have hefty legal fees to get a zoning variance. Giving away coupons to attract business in your first few months may also reduce your initial revenues.

Source: Robert L. Perry, president of Enterprise Unlimited, a franchise-relations consulting firm, 5111 Berwyn Rd., Suite 204, College Park, Maryland 20740. He is the author of *The 50 Best Low-Investment, High-Profit Franchises.* Prentice Hall, Rte. 9W, Englewood Cliffs, New Jersey 07632.

Secrets of Safer Franchise Buying

Running your own business is far different than working for an employer. Yet half the roughly 600,000 franchises in the US are now owned and operated by corporate refugees. The perils are obvious…

Mistake: Buying a franchise touted as a "safe" investment. According to one recent study, 40% of all franchises fail in the first five years.

The safest franchises are those offered by established companies with a well-known and respected trademark that have sound marketing and business plans and offer franchisees good training and support.

Mistake: Expecting to be your own boss. Looking to satisfy an entrepreneurial urge? Franchising is probably not for you.

The franchise agreement, a legal contract between a franchisor and franchisee, typically gives the company control over the business. It covers everything from how the store looks and the hours it will be open, to how many pickles go on each hamburger.

Have a lawyer who knows franchising read the fine print of this key document before you invest.

Mistake: Underestimating start-up costs. They can range from less than $10,000 to $1 million or more.

At the low end are home-operated businesses, such as selling cosmetics or cleaning supplies. The most expensive franchises—and best opportunities to make money—are hotels, soft-drink bottling plants and beer and wine distributorships.

Royalty payments can be as low as 1% to as much as 60% of gross annual sales.

As a general rule, you will need enough capital to get through two years without collecting a salary yourself.

Source: Robert L. Purvin, Jr., author of *The Franchise Fraud: How to Protect Yourself Before and After You Invest,* John Wiley & Sons, Inc., 605 Third Ave., New York 10158. Purvin is chairman of the American Association of Franchisees and Dealers, San Diego, and vice chairman of the American Bar Association Franchise Law Committee, Chicago.

Start Your Own Business… With Just a Computer… And Less than $3,000

One way to generate extra income without taking too much risk is to start a home-based business in the evenings or on the weekends. Computer and software prices have declined steadily during the past few years, making it possible to start your own business for less than $3,000.

If you already have a personal computer, your initial cost may be only a few hundred dollars to buy the appropriate software. In fact, the highest costs associated with starting a home business are those for materials, phone calls and travel.

Your new business will probably not pay for itself immediately. It typically takes a new business between three months and one year to begin generating income.

Strategy: Keep your full-time job, and develop your business as a sideline. Plan to spend at least eight hours a week on your new venture. You'll need this time to get familiar with your software, build a customer base and execute assignments.

Getting customers:

One benefit of starting small is that it may not be necessary to sell your services through direct mail or cold calling. *Here are a few alternative marketing strategies…*

• *Sampling.* Displaying your work allows potential customers to see the quality before they use your service.

Example: A desktop publishing expert specialized in designing dissertations for students at a nearby college. She prepared flyers that asked, "Do you want your dissertation to look like this—or like this?" Two samples accompanied the ad—a professional-looking one that she had done and a shoddy one.

• *Use gatekeepers.* These people work with key contacts or corporate clients in the markets you would like to reach. Identify the gatekeepers, and contact them. Create a datebook or database of the key contacts you should call once a month.

Examples: An individual who set up a service to help people keep track of their medical claims used doctors as gatekeepers. A résumé writer contacted job-placement centers and career counselors.

Getting started:

• *Purchase a brand-name computer.* This may cost less than $1,000. Get an ink-jet printer, which sells for about $300.

Today's equipment may be easy to use, but making it all work together can be frustrating.

Solution: Employ a computer consultant—possibly recommended by the store at which you made the purchase—to help with the initial setup of your hardware and software. *Cost:* $60 to $80 an hour.

Note: If you live in an older home, make sure the electrical system is adequate. Also, invest in a "surge protector," which shields equipment from power surges during storms or when power is restored after an outage. *Cost:* $60 to $80.

• *Make sure your equipment is covered under your homeowner's insurance policy.* If not, get a separate endorsement for business equipment that covers the property.

Best home-based businesses:

• *Mailing-list service.* Compile and maintain mailing-list databases for clients, using their invoices or customer receipts. *Two other mailing-list alternatives...*

• Sell specialized mailing lists that you develop yourself from publicly available information. Sell them to companies that are looking for sales leads for direct-marketing or mail-order businesses.

• Design a direct-mail campaign for a company using its list, a rented list or your own list. Manage the printing, sorting, addressing and mailing.

Full-time income potential: $40,000 to $100,000 per year.

Equipment: A computer with at least a 200-megabyte hard drive, a high-quality dot matrix or laser printer that can handle mailing lists, a software package, such as *Arclist* or *Accumail.*

Group 1 Software, 4200 Parliament Place, Lanham, Maryland 20706, 800-368-5806.

• *Medical-claims assistance.* Similar to a tax-return preparer, you gather information and complete and file medical claims. Then you follow up on them. Some also provide advisory services.

Full-time income potential: $20,000 to $60,000 per year.

Equipment: A software program called *Medsure.*

Time Solutions, 45 Kellers Farm Rd., Easton, Connecticut 06612, 800-552-3302.

• *Newsletter publication.* Publish your own *special-interest* newsletter for $300 to $1,000 per annual subscription...or a consumer newsletter for $30 to $125 per subscription.

You can also write and produce newsletters for companies or associations to communicate with employees, members or clients. The going rate is $200 to $500 a page to write, typeset and manage printing and distribution.

Alternative: Create a "template" newsletter that you can use for many different clients, customized slightly for each.

Example: Monthly newsletters for doctors or dentists with their names on the mastheads. *Going rate:* $300 to $500 to create the newsletter plus a per-name fee of 35 cents to $1 for each mailing.

Equipment: A desktop publishing package such as *Microsoft Publisher,* One Microsoft Way, Redmond, Washington 98052, 800-426-9400. Or a more sophisticated package, with more complex features and capabilities, such as *QuarkXPress,* Box 480787, Denver 80248, 800-995-4343.

• *Résumé-writing service.* You interview clients to select the content of their résumés, write biographical descriptions and design effective résumés.

Full-time income potential: $40,000 per year, based on full-time work at $75 per résumé.

Equipment: You can use any good word-processing program, such as *Microsoft Professional Office* 4.3, One Microsoft Way, Redmond, Washington 98052, 800-426-9400.

• *Technical writing.* Every new technological product must be explained to the people who sell, service and use it. These companies sometimes have difficulty making their product manuals clear and usable.

Key: You must be able to communicate technical information well.

The four markets for this service are:
- Trade magazines.
- Manufacturing and service companies.
- Technical books and instructional material publishers.
- User manuals and instruction booklet publishers.

Full-time income potential: $30,000 to $60,000 per year, assuming that you bill half your time at $30 to $60 an hour.

Equipment: Word-processing program with desktop publishing and layout capabilities.

Source: Paul and Sarah Edwards, hosts of the Business Network radio show *Working from Home.* They are the authors of *The Best Home Businesses for the '90s* and *Making Money with Your Computer at Home,* Jeremy P. Tarcher, New York.

How to Start Your Own Business with Little Money...or No Money

If you follow a few simple rules, starting your own business is not very costly. And it has some terrific advantages...

- *Extra income.* $500 a day isn't unreasonable. *Reason:* When you work for an employer, that company usually takes in at least $2 to $3 for every $1 it pays you in salary. When you work for yourself, the profits are yours.

Moreover, by starting small—perhaps in your home—you can hold overhead to a minimum.

- *Use your skills at something you truly enjoy.* Sadly, few regular jobs offer this advantage. When you go into business for yourself, always pick a field you like. You'll immediately be motivated—and the long hours won't be a burden.

- *Control over your time.* While starting a business is *very* demanding, you have more control over the hours you work. If you want to take off on Thursday instead of Sunday, for example, you don't need your boss's approval. Many businesses also offer you the opportunity to travel and to expense the cost for tax purposes.

Best businesses:

Like any other enterprise, the best business to start is one that offers a product or service that you can produce cheaply for consumers who are eager to buy it. Finding that niche takes a lot of preliminary work, but there are more niches than you might imagine. *Examples:*

- *Exporting.* It's especially attractive today because American products have a cachet overseas and because many once-poor nations now have burgeoning economies.

Exporting is usually easier and more profitable than importing because it requires you to find only one overseas distributor to buy your products. When you import, you usually bear the entire burden of sales.

Once you have experience at exporting, you can consider opportunities in importing.

- *Brokering.* What might sound like an esoteric niche is actually a straightforward business —bringing lenders together with other businesses. Nearly every company, from IBM to your local newsstand, needs cash at some point in its lifetime. Lenders have the money, but they don't always have time to look at all the potential borrowers in the business community. A financial broker charges a fee for helping them do that. Some business experience is needed, but you don't need a background in finance.

- *Mail order.* You might think that the world can't sustain another mail-order company, but that's not the case. There's always room for a company with a product people want. And there's no predicting what products might be wanted.

Good bets today: Specialty foods, pet products, instruction courses and home needs—all of which require little capital to start up.

Aside from these three big opportunities, there are thousands of other business niches that creative entrepreneurs have started with almost no cash.

Examples: Boarding pets, selling patterns for making stuffed animals, publishing political newsletters, locksmithing and making specialty home furniture.

Solving the cash problem:

The best sources of funding are your own savings or a loan from a family member or friend. If these aren't available, consider taking in a partner who can put up capital in return for a share of the profits. (A partner may also be necessary if you need someone else's know-how for the business.)

High-potential business ideas, especially in the technology area, can attract professional investors, known as venture capitalists. You can find them through several directories located in public libraries. It also pays to contact local and state governments. Many have venture capital programs, some of which aren't widely publicized.

If you're willing to put up your own home or other asset as collateral, consider a loan from the Small Business Administration.

How to save on start-up costs: Rather than immediately buying expensive equipment, consider leasing it or, in the case of manufacturing, farm out jobs to other companies. It may cost slightly more, but there's no point in investing in costly equipment until you have a steady stream of orders. To make that happen, put money you might have invested in equipment into marketing and promotion—the activities that bring in orders.

Other needs:

• *Place of business and equipment.* Don't splurge on an office. The object is to hold down overhead until you work up a healthy cash flow. A basement or den in your home is often a perfect site for the phone line, desk and office equipment you'll need. Remember, Apple Computers started in a garage.

• *Professional services.* It usually isn't necessary to pay big retainer fees to lawyers and accountants. Instead, use recommendations to find reliable professionals whom you can call on as needed.

• *An account that enables you to accept credit card purchases—called a merchant account.* This isn't absolutely necessary, but it makes it easier to sell certain types of products.

Problem: Most large banks won't open merchant accounts for small businesses.

Solutions: Contact an Independent Sales Organization (ISO) that acts as an intermediary between banks and small businesses. Most banks and chambers of commerce can tell you how to find an ISO. They are also frequently listed in the business pages of the telephone book.

Some small regional banks also set up merchant accounts for home-grown businesses, as do a few credit unions.

• *Marketing plan.* The biggest mistake is trying to force on the market something *you* think is a great idea. Always let the market lead you. Test out ideas on a small scale before committing yourself to them in a big way, financially.

How to do it: Test direct mailings, or put a few modest ads in niche publications that cater to the market you're aiming at. Responses to inexpensive classified ads can often tell you if your product is marketable. If it is, then consider other sale methods, such as regional distributors, display ads in national publications or a major direct mail campaign.

To keep up with consumer trends, study the ads in *Popular Science, Modern Franchising, Popular Mechanics* and similar publications. Also helpful are the auction and business opportunities columns in local papers, *The Wall Street Journal,* big-city newspapers and the new-product columns in magazines that interest you. All of these publications are available in most libraries.

Low-cost ways to promote your business: The local press and the new-product columns in magazines that cover the field you're in. Niche publications—hobbies, sports, automotive, etc.—thrive on telling their readers about new products and services. And there's no cost. Also consider writing articles for these publications and subtly mention your product.

The local press is often hungry for business and feature articles about interesting products, so it pays to cultivate one or two people on the editorial staffs. Keep in mind that some types of businesses are easier to promote than others.

Examples: A new accounting service probably won't generate much media interest. A new sled will.

Underpricing can also be a fatal blunder. Neophytes believe that sales increase as the price goes down. But just as often, the opposite is true. On some items, a moderately high price brings in customers who associate the price with good value.

Source: Tyler G. Hicks, the author of *How to Start Your Own Business on a Shoestring,* Prima Publishing, 3875 Atherton Rd., Rocklin, California 95765. He is a consultant to businesses and publisher of the newsletter *International Wealth and Success,* 24 Canterbury Rd., Rockville Centre, New York 11570.

How to Become a Successful Weekend Entrepreneur

End of the month and short of cash? Again? Don't hold your head in your hands, bemoan your fate and curse your boss. Get a *SAM*—a *source of additional money*—by becoming a weekend entrepreneur.

If you can steal a few hours over the weekend, you can launch a part-time, home-based business that can put $100 or more a week into your pocket. How to choose your *SAM*:

Some successful weekend entrepreneurs spot trends and climb quickly on the bandwagon. Other entrepreneurs recognize and meet needs that make other people's lives easier.

Thinking it through:

Here are four questions to help you get your *SAM* organized and launched...

• *How much spare time can you devote to a SAM?* A *SAM* is not supposed to require a 40-hour workweek. But a consistent number of hours each week should be devoted to your *SAM*, whether those hours are for promoting your business, sending out bills or rolling your sleeves up and sewing quilts at home or hauling furniture across town for a local store.

• *Are you aware of the insurance needs—licensing requirements and tax laws, etc., regarding your SAM?* You don't want any surprises six months down the road from your insurance agent, the town or the IRS.

SAMs that work:

SAM opportunities are everywhere! The key to determining the one for you is to establish a weekend business that takes advantage of your interests, abilities, knowledge or skills. Here's a list of *SAM* ideas that have paid off for other weekend entrepreneurs:

• *Car detailer.* Try real estate brokers first (their cars have to be immaculate). March right into the office, introduce yourself, drop off flyers and offer to do the first car free. Hit medical complexes and wealthy neighborhoods next. Charge a minimum of $40 per car.

• *Pet meals on wheels.* Deliver cumbersome 20 pound bags of dry pet food and heavy cases of canned goods to pet owners' doors. Blanket a neighborhood with flyers, contact veterinarians and dog groomers to let them know you're in business. Don't charge a delivery fee, just mark up the pet food after negotiating a close-to-wholesale price from local distribution centers or retailers.

• *Recycling pickup service.* Save your neighbors the trouble of hand-feeding cans and bottles into recycling machines at the supermarket or loading their cars with recyclable material that must go to the dump. In exchange for keeping any cash refund, also volunteer to recycle items that don't have a cash value, like newspapers in some states, and you'll get an occasional tip, as well.

• *Special-occasion sign rentals.* If you're handy with a saw and have an artistic flair, create 20 or 30 ready-to-rent "yard cards" for high-profile celebrations. Signs in the shape of bunny rabbits, teddy bears and carousel horses are great for kids' parties and a humorous "Grim Reaper" sign planted on a front lawn for a 40th birthday party will bring you $25 a day, $35 for three days or $50 for a whole week. You make the signs, install them and pick them up.

• *House portraits and custom stationery.* People love to use portraits of their homes to create distinctive stationery or to send as holiday greeting cards or simply to frame beautifully and hang in the house. If you're good with a camera or a sketch pad, show your portfolio to homeowners in an upscale neighborhood, and offer to photograph, sketch or paint their homes. Try charging from $85 for a pen-and-ink sketch to $150 for a color photograph, and adjust your prices depending upon response.

Source: Jennifer Basye, the author of *How to Become a Successful Weekend Entrepreneur,* Prima Publishing, Rocklin, CA.

Where Entrepreneurs Get Their Ideas

A study of 3,000 business start-ups looked at where their founders got the idea for the business. *Results:*

• *Prior employment*—74%. The business copied or refined an idea of a prior employer.

• *Serendipity*—20%. The business owner got the idea from reading or conversation, or "just thought of it."

• *The computer revolution*— 4%. The business owner spotted a way in which to exploit new technology.

• *Organized search*—2%. The business owner conducted a systematic search for a business opportunity.

Source: Study by the National Federation of Independent Business, quoted in *The Newsletter of Corporate Renewal*, 230 N. Michigan Ave., Chicago 60601.

How to Get Ahead In Business...Today

Getting ahead in any business takes more than just talent and hard work. It also takes courage.

Being courageous doesn't mean being ruthless, reckless or obnoxious. It is being able to think critically about problems, overcome fear and act on your convictions.

Both men and women believe that simply following orders leads to their career advancement. To do well and get ahead at work, you have to do that—and much more.

You have to anticipate problems and fix them before they actually emerge... you have to be creative about developing new ideas and strategies...and you have to feel strongly enough about yourself and your work that you will not be afraid to present those ideas and strategies to your superiors.
The essentials:

• *Know which rules to break.* People who rise through the ranks of a company or start their own businesses do not succeed by doing what they were told. True, rule-breakers stir up controversy and make other people uncomfortable. But many come to be seen—and admired —as innovators and creative thinkers.

Of course, you should never throw ethics or courtesy out the window. The challenge is to know which rules to break and how to break them.

Caution: Most rules are based on practical experience, and they provide valuable structure. The rules you can consider breaking are those that have outlived their usefulness—or that exist only to preserve the status quo.

Breaking the rules can mean coming up with a proposal for something outrageous that has never been tried before...or simply approaching your current responsibilities in a different way.

• *Bold actions aren't enough to ensure success.* You need a clearly stated vision to back up your actions. Regularly step back from thinking about your day-to-day responsibilities and focus on the big picture. Think about your overall goals—for your particular area of responsibility, your department and your career.

Come up with *mission statement*—preferably no more than one sentence—and think about the steps that can get you there. Then make sure that everything you do is related in some way to that vision. Your mission statement doesn't have to be overly poetic or extraordinarily far-reaching, but it should be focused and related to the overall vision of your company.

Strategy: Ask yourself what has been the plan for your department up until now—the goals toward which everyone has been working? What has been done well, and what has been done badly? Acknowledge the strengths as you create new job-related goals.

• *Don't waste time on things that aren't essential.* It's true that many successful executives put in long days. But work for work's sake is a waste of your time. Spending long hours on the nitty gritty can keep you from developing truly creative solutions to your company's problems. To concentrate your effort on what's really important...

• *Manage your interruptions.* You don't want to cut off staff input, which is an essential source of information. But you must strike a balance by setting boundaries. Otherwise, interruptions will become more frequent and eventually eat up your day. The result is that little essential work will be accomplished.

• *Delegate.* Pass along any task that doesn't specifically require your expertise. In the beginning, these tasks may not get done exactly as they would if you handled them yourself. But if you monitor the tasks and the person handling them by carefully reviewing the work when it's complete, you will free yourself to work on more important issues. Eventually, the tasks you delegate will be executed exactly to your standards—or you can delegate the work to someone else.

• *Simplify complex tasks.* Busy people handle a great deal of work and responsibility. Their desks are junctions where critical paperwork lands. They also attend a great many meetings.

Find ways to speed up the work you handle. To avoid being bogged down, route paperwork as soon as you look it over.

Example I: Instead of letting papers and projects sit, scribble on the upper right-hand corner the next action you want to take—such as file, phone or follow up. This will keep you from wasting time when you pick up the paper again and need to remember what you wanted done.

Example II: Instead of taking voluminous notes at meetings—which will only be difficult to read and analyze later on—quickly summarize the key points in a notebook or computer immediately afterward.

• *Be decisive.* Matters that dramatically alter the course of how you and your department do business require lengthy weighing of pros and cons. But most day-to-day decisions don't. The longer you wait to make up your mind on small issues, the more time and energy are eaten up.

• *Be conscious of conflict.* Taking risks is possible only if your new approach or ideas are accepted, encouraged and even improved along the way.

If there is great resistance due to misunderstandings, miscommunication or personality conflicts between you and others, your radical approaches may be undercut—even if they are terrific.

Solution: Stay in frequent, informal contact at all levels—and in many different departments. Not only does this contact help you to be informed, but if problems arise about you or your staff, you'll know about them early on.

Strategy: When trouble becomes apparent, don't just wait for it to go away—take action immediately. Deal with the issue that is raised. If it has to do with you, consider the source, the messenger and the message. Does the criticism make sense? What is the motivation for the criticism?

Whatever the answer, try to solve the problem yourself by meeting with the person, one-on-one. Be firm but diplomatic. A problem-solving approach is usually much more effective than a confrontational one. Losing your temper signals a loss of control, and that won't help your case—or your reputation.

Start the conversation with the "confusion" technique. Introduce the issue by saying, *I'm confused. I've noticed that....Can you clear this up for me?*

If the pattern continues, take notes documenting each situation or confrontation. When a solid paper trail has been established, involve your superiors.

• *Don't be afraid to take smart risks.* Teaching yourself to take chances at work actually involves a few steps:

• *Look hard before you leap.* Don't rush headlong into a new project just because it's new. There is always great resistance from others to anything "new." First, you have to do your research and answer all questions that might come up challenging your idea's validity.

• *Overcome your fear of taking the plunge.* Once you have done all the background work, you must be willing to go forward. If you freeze, all of your hard work researching the new idea will be wasted.

The more homework you do, the more confidence you will have in your own instincts.

Solution: To overcome risk-anxiety, replace words that are intimidating with ones that are more positive.

If the final result isn't what you had hoped for, treat the information you receive as feedback rather than as a personal challenge. Then modify your plan and try again. Risk-taking gets easier with practice.

Source: Kate White, editor-in-chief of *Redbook* and former editor-in-chief of *McCall's, Working Woman* and *Child.* She is author of *Why Good Girls Don't Get Ahead...But Gutsy Girls Do.* Warner Books, 1271 Avenue of the Americas, New York 10020.

Index

X

Z